D1050525

Thailand's Islands & Beaches

Andrew Burke, Celeste Brash,
Austin Bush, Brandon Presser

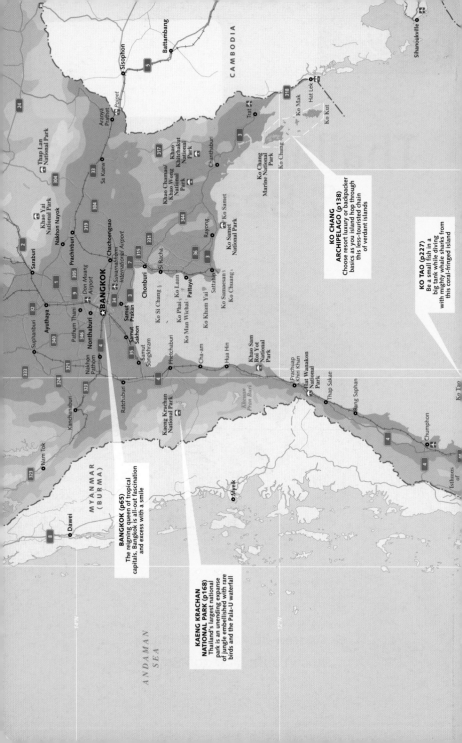

BANGKOK (p65)
The reigning queen of tropical capitals, Bangkok is all-out fascination and excess with a smile

KAENG KRACHAN NATIONAL PARK (p168)
Thailand's largest national park is an unending expanse of jungle embellished with rare birds and the Pala-U waterfall

KO CHANG ARCHIPELAGO (p138)
Choose resort luxury or backpacker basics as you island hop through this less-touristed chain of verdant islands

KO TAO (p227)
Be a small fish in a big tank while diving with mighty whale sharks from this coral-fringed island

KO PHA-NGAN (p211)
Steaming jungle, all-around beaches and a beach-bum, laid-back vibe, except at Hat Rin where the beach parties come loud and often

SIMILAN (p279) & SURIN ISLANDS (p274)
Go Cousteau on a live-aboard dive or snorkelling safari around these fantasy coral islands

AO PHANG-NGA (p281)
Kayak around this scenic bay filled with limestone towers such as 'James Bond Island'

RAILAY (p338)
A stunning beach and limestone cliffs rising out of the sea make this about the best rock-climbing spot on earth

KO PHI-PHI (p343)
The 'paradise on earth' is quite a crowd-puller, but escape is still possible

TRANG BEACHES (p362)
A bleach-blonde coast of undeveloped beaches and islands; perfect for escaping the masses

KO TARUTAO MARINE NATIONAL PARK (p374)
Remote islands and uninhabited beaches where you can live out your *Survivor* fantasies

LEGEND
Freeway
Primary Road
Secondary Road
Tertiary Road
Unsealed Road

ELEVATION
1000m
500m
200m
100m
0

Gulf of Thailand

ANDAMAN SEA

MALAYSIA

On The Road

ANDREW BURKE Coordinating Author
People say Banglamphu is not the 'real Thailand', but for me the little alternative bars on Th Phra Athit and Th Samsen are both very real and very Thai. Modern Thai. I love the energy, the creativity and the atmosphere on what is Bangkok's most progressive edge.

BRANDON PRESSER
There I was posing for this picture at Sail Rock, arguably the Gulf Coast's best dive site, when 30 seconds later I had my first encounter with an elusive, school-bus-sized whale shark. I was lucky enough to swim with the gentle creature for 45 minutes.

AUSTIN BUSH
Chinatown is Bangkok's most hectic neighbourhood, and in my opinion, the most ripe for exploration. Tiny alleys can lead to crumbling hundred-year-old homes, a previously unknown food vendor, or if you're lucky, a rare performance of *ngéw*, a type of Chinese drama.

CELESTE BRASH
On a calm day with just enough sunshine, nothing beats travel by long-tail boat. This was my primary mode of transport for my research in the Trang islands – it's more expensive but saves time and is a perfect way to soak up both culture and scenery.

For full author biographies see p441

Thailand's Islands & Beaches Highlights

On these pages, travellers and Lonely Planet staff share their top experiences on Thailand's islands and beaches. Do you agree with their choices, or have we missed your favourites? Go to lonelyplanet.com/thailand and tell us *your* highlights.

BERNARD NAPTHINE

1 SONGKRAN: NEW YEAR IN APRIL

Mobs of wet, smiling children take control of the streets to drench passing vehicles and pedestrians with water. Roaming pick-up trucks carry kids armed with water guns and buckets looking to soak anyone who has miraculously managed to stay dry. Trying to walk down the street is like trying to walk on water – you're going to end up wet.

Michael Rossi, Sydney, Australia, traveller

MASSAGE OR MASOCHISM?

Nothing beats lying on a Thai beach with fresh pineapple juice and book in hand. Nothing, that is, apart from a beachside massage (surely?). I was at Hat Thian Beach on Ko Pha-Ngan and feeling full of adventure, so I stepped onto the beach-side platform for a traditional Thai massage. More extreme workout than relaxing massage, I found myself bent over 'mama' as she grabbed my shoulders, placed her feet in my back and rolled me into a backwards arch. Boy, I felt good afterwards.

Katie Lynch, Lonely Planet staff

SIMILAN ISLANDS

Best reached from Phuket via a live-aboard, these lovely islands (p279) harbour prolific marine life, gorgeous soft corals and even the occasional whale shark. Undersea boulders provide both a sense of scale as well as a home for all sorts of critters.

SirVerity, traveller

SHRINE OF THE SERENE LIGHT, PHUKET

4

Hidden down a narrow alleyway in downtown Phuket is the tiny Shrine of the Serene Light (p302). Surrounded by buildings, this little oasis is free from traffic noise and large throngs of tourists. A great place to find some peace and serenity.

Renée Barker, Brisbane, Australia, traveller

INGO JEZIERSKI/ALAMY

5

KO SAMUI

Where lazy is accepted, and bored is unheard of, Ko Samui (p191) is an escape of indulgence. I will never bore of the ocean over my feet at dinner, nor the flowing cocktails from sunrise to sunset.

Lisa Downs, Sydney, Australia, traveller

ANDREW LUBRAN

6

KO TAO

Learning from its big brother Ko Pha-Ngan (epicentre of Thailand's full moon debauch), 'Turtle Island' (p227) knows a thing or two about nightlife. Most spend their days in the blue waters chasing fish; evenings are spent drinking like them.

Alexander L Cross, Stillwater, USA, traveller

RICHARD I'ANSON/LONELY PLANET IMAGES

CHATUCHAK WEEKEND MARKET, BANGKOK

Countless stalls line the dozens of dimly lit aisles where everything from reels of bright fabrics to exotic animals are sold (p108). Cries of *'sà·wàt·dee kâ'* echo while noodles fry and incense burns – an exhilarating day. Are your haggling skills top notch?

Nick Boulos, London, UK, traveller

7

NOT FOR THE SQUEAMISH: VEGETARIAN FESTIVAL, PHUKET

8

If you're lucky enough to be in Phuket in September/October, take a deep breath because it's time for the annual Vegetarian Festival (p302). Buddhist mediums expressing the presence of deities flood the streets while inserting sharp objects through their faces. Though in their trance they may feel no pain, for many onlookers, it's excruciating to watch.

Christine Murray, San Francisco, USA, traveller

Contents

Regional Map Contents

Destination Thailand's Islands & Beaches

Images of sweeping white-sand beaches, palm trees, colourful fish and dramatic karst formations rising from the sea are the essence of our idea of a tropical paradise. But this is reality in Thailand's islands and beaches – and a bit more. That southern Thailand can cater to almost any taste adds to the allure. The footprints in the sand could be yours and yours alone. Or you can stomp the ground with thousands of others at a heaving full moon party. Stay in a beachside hut or a resort with its own spa, go scuba diving or snorkelling, take out a kayak or climb those karst formations – or just lay in a hammock. Enjoy Thailand's islands and beaches whichever way you choose.

Enjoy, yes, but keep in mind that the wave of faràng seeking a slice of paradise has had a variety of impacts on the local population. Tourism brings plenty of money and for that most Thais are thankful. It is also accompanied by rapid improvements to roads, schools and health centres. But tourists, and those who cater to their tastes, have also brought some less-desirable changes; most notably a sharp increase in drugs and prostitution.

The political volatility of the country is likely to be one of the talking points from a local point of view. The election of the People's Power Party, essentially the renamed party of ousted prime minister Thaksin Shinawatra, suggests the continuation of Thaksin's approach to tackling Thailand's problems. New prime minister Samak Sundaravej is an old hardliner who has stumbled into the top job after an almost miraculous rehabilitation from the obscurity of a TV cooking show. Thaksin's return from exile saw newspapers gleefully featuring cartoons depicting Samak as Thaksin's puppet. Thaksin insists he will not return to politics, yet commentators believe he will remain a major influence in Thai politics.

For many in the south, Samak represents a continuation of the inflexible approach to the Islamic separatist movement. Talks with Thai Muslims to try to find a solution seem as far off as ever. Instead the insurgency looks likely to bubble on, with government officials, teachers and Buddhist monks being murdered and the army taking retribution on young Muslim men, in turn driving them deeper into the arms of the Islamic militants. Another example of a hardline policy is Samak's declaration of a second War on Drugs, which was cheered by many in the drug-fuelled southern islands. The UN Commission on Human Rights isn't so pleased; it hopes thousands are not summarily executed this time around.

Essentially, though, the locals of southern Thailand have many of the same concerns as you: jobs, money, safety, health and education for their kids. The uncertainty following the coup saw economic growth slump in 2007 as investors sat on their cash. But the rapid recovery from the devastating 2004 tsunami has seen tourism reach all-time highs, mitigating the impact. What you are most likely to hear about from taxi drivers and locals on the beaches, though, is the rising price of food. As rice prices climb so fast that rice is actually being 'rustled' from paddies at night, everyone will be affected.

The unrest in Thailand's deep south should not deter tourism in other parts of the peninsular, but travellers should monitor the situation through Thailand's English-language media at www.bangkokpost .com, and seek feedback from other travellers on the Thorn Tree bulletin board at lonelyplanet.com. For more on the south, see p28 and p255.

FAST FACTS

Population: 64,632,000

Religion: Buddhist 94.6%, Muslim 4.6%

GDP per capita: US$9100

Minimum daily wage: 185B

Inflation: 5.6%

Number of attempted coups d'etat since 1932: 19

Coastline: 3219km

Number of yellow shirts worn on Mondays: about 15 million

Number of 7-Elevens: almost 4000, and rising

Getting Started

Thailand is a traveller's paradise and it's easy and cheap to eat, sleep and get around. If you have your heart set on staying at a particular place you should book it. But, if you're a bit flexible, outside the busiest periods of the high season you can pretty much just turn up and make all your decisions as you go. No immunisations are required (p420), visas are easy to obtain (p401), and seats on discount flights (p409) or on comfortable long-distance buses (p411) and trains (p417) keep most of Thailand within easy reach for not much money. Food (p44) and accommodation (p380) are plentiful and the beauty of Thailand is such that, even on a shoestring, you can see everything and still have money left over for a shopping binge before you head home.

WHEN TO GO

If the weather sounds too confusing, see the Climate Charts, p386, or check out Travelfish's excellent interactive weather map (www.travelfish.org /weather_fish.php) with stats on average rainfall and the number of rainy days per month for many southern provinces.

The best time to visit coastal Thailand is during the tourist high season between November and April. Accommodation prices are at their highest but almost everything in the country is open, the weather is mainly dry and temperatures are reasonable. During this time the mid-December to late January period is busiest (and priciest). Local festivals (p19) also cause spikes throughout the year, notably for a week either side of Songkran (Thai New Year; 13–15 April). At either end of the high season, resorts, tours and ferry routes will be just opening up or closing down. The rest of the year (May to October) is the low season and prices for accommodation plummet. However, many resorts and islands shut down completely and ferry routes don't run due to stormy seas and dwindling demand. Water visibility for diving also drops dramatically.

Between May and October the southwest monsoon drenches the country and during this time you can expect some rain every day, although often not that much. While this period is known as the rainy season, southern Thailand also receives rain from the northwest monsoon from November to January, so it can never be said to be truly 'dry' in the south. If you want to maximise your chances of sunny days, visit between December and March and prioritise the gulf coast over the Andaman coast, which gets more of the northwest monsoon and is generally wetter year-round.

Temperatures from November to March hover between 22°C and 30°C throughout Thailand, then rise from March to May when they almost always peak above 30°C. The south is usually a few degrees cooler during the monsoon, which can make the weather more bearable if the humidity isn't too bad.

COSTS

HOW MUCH?

Restaurant dinner 80-1000B

Entry to a national park 200B or 400B

Three-day dive trip 8000-15,000B

Boat trip between Surat Thani and Ko Samui 150B

2nd-class air-con sleeper train from Bangkok to Surat Thani 768B

Thailand is cheap by Western standards and it's possible to get by on as little as US$25 a day and still live reasonably comfortably. If you stay only in budget guesthouses, eat at street stalls or local restaurants and travel by train or government buses, you can get by on less, but even the smallest appetite for beer will soon stretch your budget. Guesthouse accommodation ranges from US$10 to US$30 a day on most beaches.

For a little more pampering (air-conditioned bungalows, flights in and out, romantic dinners, boat tours and motorbike rental on the islands), raise your daily budget to about US$50. Style costs more but it's possible to get a quality room for between about US$50 and US$100, depending on the season. The upper midrange and associated lifestyle (think mud masks, diving, cocktails) is expanding fast, and you're looking at US$100 a day minimum. At the top end, the sky (actually, maybe it's the outer atmosphere) is the limit. Luxury resorts start at about US$150 and attached restaurants, bars and spa facilities

---

DON'T LEAVE HOME WITHOUT...

- Checking the visa situation (p401) – travellers of most nationalities can get an entry permit on arrival, but make sure you're one of them.
- Checking travel advisory warnings.
- A copy of your travel insurance policy details (p394).
- Earplugs (so you can hear yourself think on noisy long-tail boats).
- Long-sleeved and leg-covering clothes for showy dinners, visiting temples and staying warm on air-con buses.
- A mix of credit cards, travellers cheques and cash (p395).
- Unpacking all the useless things that make your bag weigh a tonne; lighten your load physically and mentally.
- Your sense of humour: you're on holiday, enjoy it.

---

are also expensive; though you can always pop out for a 40B green curry. To all these prices add about 20% to 30% in Bangkok.

Children can usually stay free in their parents' room. Discounts for children are available at museums and on internal flights, trains and some tours and activities.

TRAVEL LITERATURE

Most English-language books about Thailand, be they fiction or nonfiction, focus on Bangkok, but a few do take trips to the south.

The Beach, Alex Garland's account of a backpacker's discovery of a beach Eden that is spoiled somewhat by drug lords and sharks, is a highly appropriate Thai beach read. Emily Barr's *Backpack* is the chick-lit equivalent. It follows a young British woman's attempt to rediscover herself, against a backdrop of holiday romances and backpacker murders.

John Burdett's cop dramas are also great beach reads. In *Bangkok 8* and *Bangkok Tattoo,* hard-boiled Sonchai, a Bangkok police investigator, cracks open several page-turning whodunits.

Rattawut Lapcharoensap crawls into the head of Thai characters you might meet along the way – a guesthouse clerk, a coming-of-age Bangkok teen and a village girl – in his short-story collection *Sightseeing.*

Jasmine Nights, by Thai champion-of-the-arts SP Somtow, uses the fictional 1960s friendship between a 12-year-old Thai boy and an African-American boy to closely examine Thai culture.

On the nonfiction shelf *Very Thai: Everyday Pop Culture,* by Philip Cornwel-Smith, colourfully explains all manner of Thai oddities, from why taxis have dashboard shrines to why Thais put salt in their fruit drinks. *Travelers' Tales Thailand: True Stories* features travel essays by Charles Nicholls, Pico Iyer and others, with some savvy travel tips sprinkled throughout the text.

INTERNET RESOURCES

The Web is awash with websites about Thailand and Thai culture. Useful sites include:

2Bangkok.com (www.2bangkok.com) English translations from the Thai press, ongoing monitoring of the situation in the south and other 'almost like being there' news.

Lonely Planet (www.lonelyplanet.com) General information, long reviews of hotels and resorts with a booking function and, of course, the Thorn Tree travellers forum.

Thai Visa (www.thaivisa.com) An expat message board dealing with Thai current events and FAQs.

Tourism Thailand (www.tourismthailand.org) Official website of the Tourist Authority of Thailand.

Travelfish (www.travelfish.org) The best independent travel site for backpackers coming to Thailand.

TOP PICKS

Best Adventure Experiences

When you're ready to climb out of the hammock there's plenty on offer. For more adventure activities, see Diving & Other Activities (p289).

- **Rock climbing** – The awesome limestone walls at Railay (p338).
- **Diving** – Coral? Wrecks? Whale sharks? Take your pick of some of Asia's best diving (see the boxed text, p290).
- **Hiking** – Stride into one of the world's oldest rainforests at Khao Sok National Park (p244).

- **Sea kayaking** – Paddle through the limestone cliffs, hidden lagoons and peach-coloured beaches of Ang Thong Marine National Park's 42 islands (p240).
- **Snorkelling** – The Gulf of Thailand and Andaman Sea are like one vast snorkelling possibility, but it's hard to beat the reefs around Ko Phi-Phi (p345).

Fabulous Resort Hotels

Thailand's best resort hotels come in all shapes, sizes...and price ranges. See also the boxed texts: p288 for our favourite resorts in Phuket, p199 for top-end and midrange resorts on Ko Samui, p347 for Ko Phi-Phi's accommodation gems, and p176 for Hua Hin's best.

- **Jungle retreat** – Anantara (p205) on Ko Samui, and Golden Buddha Beach Resort (p275) on Ko Phra Thong.
- **Arty chic** – Library (p201) and Zazen (p204) on Ko Samui, Putahracsa (p176) in Hua Hin and Indigo Pearl (p323) on Phuket.
- **Modern luxury** – Zeavola (p349) on Ko Phi-Phi, Evason Phuket Resort (p306), Amanpuri

Resort (p320) on Phuket, and Sila Evason Hideaway (p203) on Ko Samui.
- **Private beach** – Four Seasons (p205) on Ko Samui, Chedi (p320) on Phuket and Birds & Bees Resort (p125) in Pattaya.
- **High style, low price** – Ko Kood (p158) on Ko Kut, Jungle Club (p199) on Ko Samui, and Sri Lanta (p355) on Ko Lanta.

Great Films

Get into the mood for exotic Thailand with these flicks. For more on Thailand's home-grown cinema, see p40.

- *Krung Thep Antara* (Bangkok Dangerous, 1999) – The Pang brothers' stylish, award-winning story of a deaf hitman who has a crisis of confidence after unexpectedly finding love. A Nicolas Cage remake was released in 2008.
- *OK Baytong* (2003) – A monk enters the modern world to care for his orphaned niece; set in southern Thailand, the story touches on the violence between Thais and Muslims.
- *Ploy* (2007) – Psycho-drama about a Thai couple who return to Bangkok after years

in America and face a relationship acid-test when a young woman moves into their room.
- *The Beach* (2000) – A big and beautiful Hollywood spectacle based on the Alex Garland novel and often credited for turning Thailand's beach scene from backpacker to flashpacker.
- *The Man with the Golden Gun* (1973) – James Bond thwarts Scaramanga's plot for world domination via a long-tail boat chase and a showdown in the villain's idyllic island lair, filmed at Ao Phang-Nga.

Itineraries
COASTAL ROUTES

FIRST-TIMER ISLAND HOPPING
Two to Three Weeks

Spend some time in **Bangkok** (p65), before bussing south to **Chumphon** (p185), the jumping-off points for diving or snorkelling in **Ko Tao** (p227) and full-mooning in **Ko Pha-Ngan** (p211). These islands are supremely chilled with a dash (you say when) of hedonism thrown in. Ko Pha-Ngan is one of the most diverse islands in the Gulf: 20-somethings go for trance-crazed **Hat Rin** (p215), 30s-and-beyond burrow further north, maybe peeping into the party for old-time's sake, and families dig the toddler-friendly bays.

When you tire of your hammock head via Surat Thani to the beautiful Andaman coast, decorated with the iconic limestone sea cliffs that have made Thailand's beaches famous. From **Krabi** (p326) squeeze into a minivan to explore the surrounding beaches or go to **Railay** (p338) to climb the world-famous seaside karst cliffs. For more beaches, check out **Ko Lanta** (p350) before returning to Krabi via **Ko Phi-Phi** (p343) to see what all the fuss is about.

Balance out the prostrate position with some jungle trekking in **Khao Sok National Park** (p244) or **Khao Sam Roi Yot National Park** (p180), closer to Bangkok. Then back to Bangkok for a wrap up of souvenir shopping and city pampering.

Join the classic beach-hunters' trail by dipping your toes into both the Gulf and the Andaman seas and leap-frogging across the peninsula (1400km round trip).

HAMMOCK TOUR EXTRAORDINAIRE   One Month

A month, you say? There are thousands of perfectly good itineraries to think up but, well, why not consider a hammock tour extraordinaire. Not just any old beach trip, this is enough time to really get to know southern Thailand's islands, beaches, jungle parks and cuisine – you'll eat a lot of *kà·nŏm jeen* (a southern noodle dish). On your way south from **Bangkok** (p65) stop in at **Cha-am** (p169) for a taste of beach culture Thai style (nary a *faràng* to be seen). Continue south via Chumphon out to the odd-couple island twins of **Ko Tao** (p227) and **Ko Pha-Ngan** (p211).

With a bit of experience under your (dive) belt it's time to leave the pack behind for some real travelling along the beaches between **Surat Thani** (p241) and **Nakhon Si Thammarat** (p246), where you can spend a day soaking up the Jatukham buzz (p248). Continue to **Hat Yai** (p253), the gateway to the 'deep south', and then west to the sleepy Muslim town of **Satun** (p369), the jumping-off point to the wildly beautiful natural islands of **Ko Tarutao Marine National Park** (p374).

Turning north, head up to **Trang** (p359) and pop over to the beaches of Hat Chao Mai National Park, including delightful **Ko Kradan** (p366) or the wild mangroves of **Ko Libong** (p367), home to endangered dugongs and exotic birds. Hopscotch through a series of beach resorts: quickly morphing **Ko Lanta** (p350), backwater **Ko Jum** (p358) and **Ko Phi-Phi** (p343), which can be crowded but is also stunningly beautiful. Don't forget the beaches around **Krabi** (p326) for real sand credibility. Then high-tail it to **Phuket** (p300), Thailand's most powerful tourist tractor beam, and push on north to more idyllic **Hat Khao Lak** (p276). From here, sail on out on a live-aboard dive or snorkelling safari into the **Similan Islands** (p279) or the **Surin Islands** (p274).

Take your time exploring the beauty of a broad range of Thailand's beaches, islands and national parks – above and below the water (1800km round trip).

EAST COAST POP-IN   Seven to 10 days...maybe more

Thailand's southern islands might draw the big crowds, but if you're pushed for time (or heading into Cambodia) this route along the eastern gulf coast is both easier to get to and relatively less touristed. From **Bangkok** (p65) head directly to **Ban Phe** (p128), the transfer point for trips to rustic **Ko Samet National Park** (p129), where Bangkokians kick off their flip-flops.

Continue along the mainland to **Trat** (p136) and take the boat into the Ko Chang Archipelago, where you can choose your level of comfort and how remote you want to be from almost 50 islands. Jungle-topped **Ko Chang** (p140) is the largest and most-developed island, with diversions ranging from **elephant trekking** (p143) and guided **hikes** (p143) of the rugged interior to diving into the underworld. To get further off the beaten beach, jump on a boat to more secluded **Ko Mak** (p159) or jungle-clad **Ko Kut** (p157), or further... You're entering the Thailand of *The Beach*, remote islands that are harder to get to and have fewer facilities. For now, anyway. If these charming isles aren't remote enough, then you'll definitely have to start thinking up excuses for not making it back to work on time. Having changed your ticket and informed your loved ones that your impending disappearance is entirely intentional, take a boat over to **Ko Kham** or **Ko Rayang** (p162) for some stunning coral, or to the national park at **Ko Rang** (p163) for a genuine *Survivor* experience, sans pesky host, cameramen and tribal councils.

If and when you're heading back to Bangkok, consider a stop in (brace yourself) **Pattaya** (p119), where the sleazy, cheesy side is giving way to some more appealing aspects – temples, a zoo and live shows that don't involve ping pong balls.

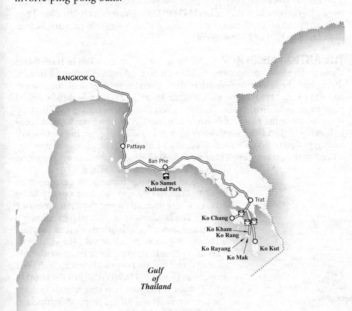

Pressed for time or tied to the capital? You can deposit your beach towel on silky sand within a half-day's journey of Bangkok, or go a couple of hours further to the relatively untouched Ko Chang Archipelago (500-600km round trip).

TAILORED TRIPS

HONEYMOON DREAMING
One to Two Weeks

Wedding = stress. Honeymoon = romantic. With just a week, touchdown for a night in a boutique hotel in **Bangkok** (p96) then fly direct to **Ko Samui** (p191) or **Phuket** (p286) to minimise your travelling time. These islands have long, voluptuous beaches and amenities developed for package tourists, but they also have quiet corners for down-to-earth relaxing.

Skip Samui's rowdier beaches for less beautiful but more romantic **Hat Bo Phut** (p204). Drop into a **spa resort** (p197) for a well-earned chance to be rubbed and revitalised while just laying back and thinking of...anything except seating plans. Suitably destressed, join a tour to the wilderness of nearby **Ang Thong Marine National Park** (p240).

Phuket is Thailand's most famous island but there's more to it than gaudy resorts. Stay at a romantic, out-of-the-way beach, such as **Hat Mai Khao** (p322). Once settled, soak up some culture in **Phuket Town** (p300), a spice trade–era port with mixed Chinese, Indian and Portuguese influences – and some fine restaurants. For a little more action dive or snorkel in the Andaman Sea (p288) or explore the beaches of **Sirinat National Park** (p322).

With two weeks, you can split your affections between two islands. Motor from Phuket over to stunning **Ko Phi-Phi** (p343). Too much civilisation? Then embrace your inner Tarzan and Jane and go 'native' on the napping islands of **Ko Lanta** (p350) or **Ko Jum** (p358).

THE ANTI-HAMMOCK
Two to Three Weeks

If you prefer climbing limestone rock faces than climbing out of your hammock, diving into the unknown realm than diving into the infinity pool, then you've come to the right part of the world. While **Ko Tao** (p227) is undoubtedly a good place to get your dive licence, Thailand's best diving, snorkelling and climbing is spread along the remarkable Andaman coast. Fly south from **Bangkok** (p65) to **Trang** (p359) and kick on to lesser-known but stunning beaches and islands such as **Ko Ngai** (p363). This area is a favourite hangout for endangered dugongs among many others. Take a boat up to **Ko Phi-Phi** (p343) for a change of scene, both above and below the surface.

Time to trade your flippers for carabiners so head to **Krabi** (p326) and around to pretty **Railay** (p338), where you can ascend the karst limestone walls in Thailand's most-renowned rock-climbing region and sneak in a little hammock time (it is fun, after all). But we're not done yet. The cliffs conquered, it's time to strap on the tanks or snorkelling gear again for the *coup de grace*. Meet up with your live-aboard yacht in **Phuket** (p288) or **Hat Khao Lak** (p277) – yes, invite your new dive friends to share the cost – and set sail for the tropical archipelago of the **Similan Islands** (p279). With enough time and money, finish the trip in the **Surin Islands** (p274), where you might meet some of Jacques Cousteau's old manta mates at Richelieu Rock.

Events Calendar

Exact dates for most festivals vary from year to year. Some, particularly the Muslim festivals, follow the lunar calendar, while others are changed by organisers or local authorities. Some smaller festivals are covered in the regional chapters. The website of **Tourism Authority of Thailand** (www .tourismthailand.org) has dates for some festivals; for more on Buddhist festivals see www.buddhanet. net/thai_cal.htm. For dates of some Muslim festivals, see p392; for public holidays, see p393.

JANUARY

NEW YEAR'S DAY   30 Dec-1 Jan
This is the first of Thailand's three New Year's celebrations and features Western-style revelry.

FEBRUARY–MARCH

PHRA NAKHON KHIRI FAIR   early Feb
Notable temple festival in Phetchaburi with classical dance and dramatic performances and a beauty contest for local widows; see p168.

CHINESE NEW YEAR   Jan-Feb
On the first day of Chinese Lunar Year the Chinese celebrate *drùd jeen* with lion dances and fireworks, most spectacularly in Bangkok and Phuket.

**MAGHA PUJA
(MAH·KÁ BOO·CHAH)**   Feb-Mar
The full moon of the third lunar month is celebrated countrywide to commemorate the Buddha's spontaneous, unannounced preaching to 1250 enlightened monks. It culminates in a candle-lit walk around the main chapel at every wát.

APRIL

CHAKRI DAY   6 Apr
Across the country, celebrations are held for the founding of the Chakri royal dynasty.

SONGKRAN   13-15 Apr
Buddha images are 'bathed' and a lot of water is tossed about in a nationwide water fight to celebrate the Thai New Year. Tourists are not exempt, so dress to be soaked!

MAY–JUNE

SAILBOAT REGATTA   early May
Hat Chao Mai (p363), near Trang, holds an annual regatta for traditional wooden sailboats, accompanied by music and theatre.

**VISAKHA PUJA
(WÍ·SĂH·KÀ BOO·CHAH)**   May-Jun
The full moon of the sixth lunar month commemorates the Buddha's birth, enlightenment and *parinibbana* (passing away). Activities are centred around the wát, with candle-lit processions, chanting and sermons.

HUA HIN JAZZ FESTIVAL   Jun
This is Thailand's best jazz festival; see http://jazz festivalhuahin.com.

JULY

**ASALHA PUJA
(AH·SĂHN·HÀ BOO·CHAH)**   Jul-Aug
Full moon of the eighth lunar month commemorates the sermon preached by the Buddha upon attaining enlightenment.

KHAO PHANSA (KÔW PAN·SĂH)   Jul-Aug
The day after Asalha Puja is the beginning of Buddhist 'lent', when young men enter the monkhood for the rainy season and monks station themselves in a single monastery for three months.

**BANGKOK INTERNATIONAL
FILM FESTIVAL**   late Jul
One of two Bangkok film festivals. The dates vary, but it was held in late July in 2007; see www .bangkokfilm.org.

AUGUST

PHUKET GAY PRIDE   Aug-Sep
A multiday event that's been running for years. The dates change a lot. See p316 and www .phuketpride.org.

SEPTEMBER–OCTOBER

VEGETARIAN FESTIVAL   Sep-Oct
For nine days at the start of the ninth lunar month, devout Chinese Buddhists give up meat and engage in stomach-turning acts of self-mutilation. Mainly celebrated in Phuket, though Krabi and Phang-Nga celebrate on a smaller scale. See p302.

OK PHANSA   Oct-Nov
The end of Buddhist lent on the full moon of the 11th lunar month sets off a national party. It celebrates the Buddha's three-month retreat to heaven to talk to his mother.

NOVEMBER

LOI KRATHONG   Nov-Dec
During the full moon, Thais launch hand-made lotus-shaped baskets and boats bearing a candle and flowers into rivers, lakes and canals to thank the water goddess for life.

DECEMBER

KING'S BIRTHDAY   5 Dec
Across the country, formal processions and cultural displays take place. Bangkok's festival centres around the Grand Palace.

BANGKOK JAZZ FESTIVAL   Dec
Three-nights of jazz are held in Dusit Park, Bangkok featuring international and Thai performers; see www.bangkokjazzfestival.com.

CONCERT IN THE PARK   Dec-Feb
The Bangkok symphony plays at Lumphini Park every Sunday (5.30pm to 7.30pm) between mid-December and mid-February; see www.bangkok symphony.net.

History

EARLY CULTURES

Little evidence remains of the cultures that existed in Thailand before the middle of the 1st millennium AD, partly due to the destructive effects of the tropical climate and encroaching jungle. What is known about these civilisations comes from a handful of archaeological sites in the northeast and far south of the country, most notably Ban Chiang in Udon Thani Province and the area around Krabi in the south. These early peoples buried their dead with complex rituals and left mysterious cave paintings throughout the south and northeast of Thailand, including the caves of Tharnbok Korannee National Park (p332) near Krabi.

EMERGING EMPIRES

From the 3rd century BC Indian traders began visiting the Gulf of Thailand, introducing the peoples of the region to Hinduism, which rapidly became the principal faith in the area. By 230 BC, when Chinese traders began visiting these shores, large parts of Thailand had been incorporated into the kingdom of Funan, the first state in Southeast Asia. The name Funan means 'king of the mountain', a reference to Mt Meru, the home of the Hindu gods. Funan established its main port at Oc Eo at the mouth of the Mekong River in Vietnam, and traded as far afield as India and possibly even Europe. At its peak, the state included large parts of Thailand, Laos, Cambodia and Vietnam and had active trade with the agrarian communities along the Malay Peninsula as far south as modern-day Pattani and Yala. A factory producing trade beads for the Funan empire was recently discovered at Khlong Thom near Krabi.

During the first few centuries AD, and possibly even much earlier, it is thought that present-day Thailand began to be populated by Tai peoples moving south from China (see the boxed text, p22).

After the peak of the Funan Kingdom, around AD 600, a new star was rising in Southeast Asia, the kingdom of the Khmer, from modern-day Cambodia. This Hindu kingdom became famous for its extravagant sculpture and temple building; Khmer styles of art and design – as featured on the magnificent Hindu temples at Angkor Wat in Cambodia – had a profound effect on the art, language and religion of the Thais. Many Thai men became mercenaries for the Khmer armies and are clearly depicted in the bas-relief carvings in the Angkor compound.

During this period, much of central Thailand was still dominated by the dark-skinned indigenous peoples of the Malay Peninsula, known today as Negritos. A few small pockets of tribal Negrito people still survive in the

Evidence of hunter-gatherer peoples from up to 180,000 years ago has been found in caves in northern Thailand.

Khmer influence on early Thai society was so strong, that even as late as the 15th century, public documents tended to be written both in Thai and Khmer.

TIMELINE

3rd Century BC	1-300 AD	2nd-13th Century
Hinduism is thought to have arrived in Southeast Asia from India, and will remain the dominant religion in the region for the next thousand years.	Increasingly displaced by the spreading Han in China, the Tai people begin to arrive in the fertile river valleys of mainland Southeast Asia.	Based in present-day Sumatra, the Srivijaya kingdom comes to dominate much of Indonesia and the Malay Peninsula, eventually extending as far as Madagascar.

THE TAIS THAT BIND

The Tai, an ethno-linguistic group that includes modern-day Thais, the Lao, the Shan and other smaller groups, range in area from Hainan Island in China to Assam in northeastern India. Although it was long assumed that modern-day Thais originally separated from Tai groups in southern China in the first few centuries AD and moved south, remains found in northeastern Thailand suggest Tais have been living in present-day Thailand much longer than previously thought. The evidence, some of it dating back to 2500 BC, suggests that the people living there were among the earliest farming societies in the world, as well as some of the first metalworkers. The Tai may have even introduced the concept of tone to the languages of China and Southeast Asia, and today China, not Southeast Asia, is home to the greatest diversity of Tai ethnic groups.

central forests of southern Thailand. Increasingly, the fertile river basins of central Thailand became inhabited by groups of Tai-speaking people moving south who formed various independent city-states known as *meu·ang*. These people, the forerunners of modern Thais, would eventually refer to their territory as Syam or Sayam, later transliterated to 'Siam' by the English trader James Lancaster in 1592.

As the power of the Khmer grew, another culture began to have an influence on Thailand – the Mon people of current-day Myanmar (Burma), who had been converted to Buddhism by the missionaries of the Indian king, Asoka. The Mon dominated western and upper-southwestern Thailand from the 3rd to 6th centuries, spreading Buddhism and building Thailand's first Buddhist stupa at Nakhon Pathom, west of Bangkok. The conversion of Nakhon Pathom, then capital of the Dvaravati kingdom, was recorded in the 5th century in the Mahavamsa (the sacred chronicle of Sri Lankan Buddhism). The Mon were later driven back into Myanmar by the Khmer and subsequent Thai kingdoms, but vestiges of Mon culture can still be seen on Ko Kret in north Bangkok.

Thailand is 543 years ahead of the West, at least according to their calendar, which measures the beginning of the modern era from the birth of Buddha instead of Christ.

KINGDOMS OF THE MALAY PENINSULA

Two distinct spheres of power existed within the region by the 12th century: the Khmer kingdom and minor Thai city-states dominated central Southeast Asia, while the Srivijaya kingdom of Sumatra and smaller entities dominated the Indonesian archipelago and Malay Peninsula, including parts of modern-day Thailand.

Thai script is based on southern Indian writing systems adopted and adapted by the Mon and Khmer; the first examples date back to the 13th century.

Of the series of city-states that grew to prominence along the Malay Peninsula, Tambralinga established its capital on the site of present-day Nakhon Si Thammarat. Tambralinga eventually became part of the Srivijaya kingdom, a confederation of maritime states that ruled southern Thailand and Malaysia from the 7th to 13th centuries. The Srivijaya became hugely wealthy from tolls extracted from traffic through the Strait of Malacca.

5th Century	7th-11th Century	1238
Introduced by the Mon people, Theravada Buddhism gains a foothold in present-day Thailand. The religion initially mixes with eventually replaces Hinduism as the dominant religion in the region.	The Angkor kingdom extends its control from present-day Cambodia into northeastern and central Thailand, dominating the culture of much of mainland Southeast Asia for more than 500 years.	Phor Khun Si Intharathit forms the first Thai kingdom at Sukhothai, which also sees the emergence of art, architecture and design that today are regarded as classically 'Thai'.

Remains of the Srivijaya culture can be seen around Chaiya, near modern-day Surat Thani, and Nakhon Si Thammarat, which has relics from Srivijaya times in its museum. Many art forms of the Srivijaya kingdom, such as Thai *năng dà·lung* (shadow play) and *lákon* (classical dance-drama), were developed in Nakhon Si Thammarat and incorporated into modern Thai culture. Also in Nakhon Si Thammarat is the ancient monastery of Wat Phra Mahathat, reputedly founded at the height of the Srivijaya kingdom. (For more information on the historic attractions of Nakhon Si Thammarat, see p246.)

Although Buddhism is thought to have been introduced to the Chaopraya Basin by the Mon as early as the 5th century, it was not until the 13th century that trade between Sri Lanka and various Thai kingdoms resulted in the spread of Theravada Buddhism. The southern port city of Trang was a gateway for much of this exchange, which also saw the introduction of influential ideas in science, law, medicine and literature.

During the Ayuthaya period, the upper classes flaunted their wealth by brandishing elaborate silver betel nut boxes.

THE FIRST THAI KINGDOM & THE RISE OF ISLAM

During the 13th century, several Tai principalities in the Mekong Valley united and wrested control of central Thailand from the Khmer, making their new capital at Sukhothai (Rising of Happiness). Many Thais consider Sukhothai to have been the first true Thai kingdom. Under King Phor Khun Si Intharathit, Sukhothai declared its independence from the Khmer empire in 1238 and expanded its sphere of influence, taking over many parts of the Srivijaya kingdom in the south.

In its prime, the Sukhothai kingdom extended as far as Nakhon Si Thammarat in the south, to the upper Mekong River Valley in Laos and to Bago (Pegu) in southern Myanmar, an area larger than present-day Thailand.

Roughly in this same period, Islam was introduced to southern Thailand via Malaysia during the reign of Sultan Iskandar, reaching Pattani by 1387 and spreading as far north as Songkhla. The Malay dialect of Yawi became the main language of the deep south and Islam came to replace Buddhism through that region. Even many of the semi-nomadic *chow lair* (sea gypsies) who migrated up and down the coast were eventually converted. Although no great monuments from this time survive today, the culture of the deep south is still predominantly Malay, and Yawi is still widely spoken.

Another early Malay kingdom was Pattani, which evolved in the 15th century into a prosperous trading port on the gulf-coast side of the peninsula. Ancient Pattani included parts of modern-day Malaysia as well as the Thai provinces of Pattani, Yala, Narathiwat, Songkhla and Satun. After the decline of the Srivijaya kingdom in the 14th century and the rise of the Thai kingdoms, Pattani struggled with its northern neighbour for more than 100 years until it was successfully invaded in the late 18th century by Rama I.

Inscriptions written in Thai, Khmer, Chinese and Arabic have been found inside temples in Ayuthaya, showing just how cosmopolitan this early Thai kingdom was.

13th Century	1350	1511
Islam begins to gain a foothold in mainland Southeast Asia, having been introduced by Muslim traders from India up to 500 years previously.	Under the leadership of U Thong, also known as Ramathibodi I, Ayuthaya usurps power from Sukhothai and begins building a regional empire that will last 400 years.	The Portuguese are the first European visitors to Ayuthaya, eventually establishing a consulate and forming a cultural and economic relationship that will last 150 years.

THE RISE & FALL OF AYUTHAYA

The Thai kings of Ayuthaya extended their influence deep into Khmer territory, conquering Angkor in 1431. To this day, some Thais still regard Angkor as part of Thailand, a cause of frequent diplomatic rows between Thailand and Cambodia. Ayuthaya became one of the greatest and wealthiest cities in Asia, far larger and more powerful than most European capitals at that time, attracting trade and visitors from across the world. The kingdom sustained an unbroken monarchical succession through 34 reigns, from King U Thong (1350–69) to King Ekathat (1758–67).

By the early 16th century Ayuthaya was receiving European visitors, and a Portuguese embassy was established in 1511. The Portuguese were followed by the Dutch in 1604, the English in 1612, the Danes in 1621 and the French in 1662. In the mid-16th century, Ayuthaya and the independent kingdom of Lanna came under the control of the Burmese, but the Thais took back control of both by the end of the century.

The Burmese besieged Ayuthaya again in 1765 and conquered it two years later. The Burmese were determined to eliminate the rival capital, and proceeded to destroy not only the town itself, but all remnants of its cultural and intellectual life as well. Thai resentment ran high, and Phaya Taksin, a charismatic half-Chinese, half-Thai general, declared himself king of the Thais in 1769, ruling from a new capital at Thonburi on the banks of the Chao Phraya River, opposite present-day central Bangkok. Over time, Taksin's inner circle began to fear his power and claims of divinity, and the king was executed in the custom reserved for royalty: he was beaten to death with sandalwood clubs while enveloped in a velvet sack so that no royal blood would touch the ground.

BANGKOK RULE

Bangkok first appeared as a power in 1782, under another general, Chao Phaya Chakri – crowned as Phraphutthayotfa Chulalok. He moved the royal capital directly across the river to Bangkok and assumed a new hereditary title system, taking the name 'Rama I' for himself. The Chakri dynasty continues as the ruling family of Thailand to this day.

Rama I was successful in centralising power and employing the military to expand the borders of his kingdom, which eventually extended east into modern-day Laos and Cambodia, north into Chiang Mai (which, since the 16th century had been part of Myanmar) and as far south as the modern-day Malaysian states of Kedah and Terengganu.

Rama IV, commonly known as King Mongkut (r 1851–68), was one of the more interesting and innovative of the early Chakri kings. After being passed over as heir to the throne for 27 years – during which time he was a Buddhist monk and became adept in Sanskrit, Pali, Latin and English, and studied Western sciences – the new king expertly courted ties with European nations.

Thailand's first printed periodical was the *Bangkok Recorder*, a monthly newspaper founded in 1844 by American missionary Dr Dan Beach Bradley.

The relationship between King Mongkut and Anna Leonowens was given the full Hollywood treatment in *The King & I* (1956).

Male literacy rates in parts of Thailand during the 1890s were higher than those of Europe or America.

1765	1769	1782
The Burmese sack Ayuthaya, essentially rendering the city to rubble and making it necessary to relocate the capital. The city is virtually abandoned until the early 20th century.	Under the leadership of Taksin the Great, Siam expands its territory into the Malay Peninsula, northern Thailand and present-day Laos. By 1778 Cambodia would also be under the loose control of Siam.	Phraphutthayotfa Chulalok, now known as King Rama I, reestablishes the Siamese court across the river from Thonburi, resulting in both the current Thai capital and the beginning of the Chakri dynasty.

ALL THE KINGS' WOMEN

Until polygamy was outlawed by Rama VI, it was expected of Thai monarchs to maintain a harem consisting of numerous 'major' and 'minor' wives, and the children of these relationships. This led to some truly 'extended' families: Rama I had 42 children by 28 mothers; Rama II, 73 children by 40 mothers; Rama III, 51 children by 37 mothers (he would eventually accumulate a total of 242 wives and consorts); Rama IV, 82 children by 35 mothers; and Rama V, 77 children by 40 mothers. In the case of Rama V, his seven 'major' wives were all half-sisters or first cousins, a conscious effort to maintain the purity of the bloodline of the Chakri dynasty. Other consorts or 'minor' wives were often the daughters of families wishing to gain greater ties with the royal family.

In contrast to the precedence set by his predecessors, Rama VI had one wife and one child, a girl born only a few hours before his death. As a result, his brother, Prajadhipok, Rama VII, was appointed as his successor. Rama VII also had only one wife and failed to produce any heirs. After abdicating in 1935, he did not exercise his right to appoint a successor, and once again, lines were drawn back to Rama V, and the grandson of one of his remaining 'major' wives, nine-year-old Ananda Mahidol, was chosen to be the next king.

Mongkut became famous in Europe due to the largely fictitious memoirs of his English governess, Anna Leonowens. The stories spawned a Rogers and Hammerstein play and several movies; the most recent, *Anna & the King*, was banned in Thailand for some glaring historical inaccuracies.

The real Mongkut was notable for his savvy dealings with European powers. He instructed his followers: 'Whatever they have invented or done which we should know of and do, we can imitate and learn from them, but do not wholeheartedly believe in them.' Mongkut died of malaria in 1868 and was replaced by his son, King Chulalongkorn (Rama V, 1868–1910), who continued his father's steps toward modernisation and openness to the West. King 'Chula' abolished prostration before the king as well as slavery and *corvée* (state labour).

Like his father, Chula was regarded as a skilful diplomat and is credited for successfully playing European powers off against one another to avoid colonisation. However, in exchange for this independence, Thailand was forced to cede much of the territory originally gained by Rama I, and present-day Laos and Cambodia were ceded to French Indochina between 1893 and 1907. In 1902 the former Pattani kingdom was ceded to the British, who were then in control of Malaysia, but reverted back to Thailand five years later. Many from this region continue to consider it to be occupied by the Thai government (see p28).

Of all the historic kings, Rama V enjoys a cult-like devotion. He gladly embraced the new technology of photography and pictures of him in European dress, ordinary Thai farmer garb or military pomp decorate homes and businesses today.

> At its peak in the late 1930s, Thailand's Opium Monopoly accounted for nearly 20% of the country's national budget.

> During the first three decades of the 20th century more than half of Bangkok's population was Chinese.

1851–1910	1893	1909
The modernisation of Thailand occurs during the reigns of Rama IV and Rama V, which saw the introduction of Western culture and technology, reform of the role of the monarchy, and increased infrastructure.	After a minor territory dispute, France sends gunboats to threaten Bangkok, forcing Siam to give up most of its territory east of the Mekong River. Siam takes on much of its modern boundaries.	The Anglo-Siamese Treaty allows Siam to keep Yala, Pattani, Narathiwat and Songkhla, while relinquishing control of Kedah, Kelantan, Perlis, and Terengganu to Britain.

REVOLUTION

Four Reigns, a novel by Kukrit Pramoj, describes the changes in Thai society from absolute monarchy to the modern era as seen through the eyes of a fictitious noblewoman.

In the early 20th century, the Thai military began to take an active interest in governing the kingdom, staging an unsuccessful coup in 1912. Thai students educated in France staged another bloodless coup in 1932, which led to the end of absolute monarchy in Siam. Thailand adopted a constitutional monarchy along British lines, with a mixed military-civilian group in power. King Rama VII abdicated in 1935 and retired to Britain. The king's nine-year-old nephew Ananda Mahidol was crowned King Rama VIII, but power really remained with Phibul Songkhram, one of the military masterminds of the 1932 coup. Under the influence of Phibul's government, the country's name was officially changed in 1939 from Siam to Thailand.

Ananda Mahidol ascended the throne in 1935, but was shot dead in his bedroom under mysterious circumstances in 1946 and to this day his death remains a taboo subject in Thailand. In the same year, his brother, Bhumibol Adulyadej (pronounced *Poomípon Àdunyádèt*), was appointed the ninth king of the Chakri dynasty. He continues to reign today, and you'll see his image everywhere, including at the cinema before the movie starts (see the boxed text, p30).

WWII & THE COUP ERA

During WWII, much of southern Thailand's railway system was disassembled and relocated by the Japanese in order to build the 'Death Railway' into Burma.

Thailand's rulers collaborated with the Japanese during WWII, allowing troops access to the Gulf of Thailand, which helped in the annexation of the Malay Peninsula. In the process, the Japanese troops occupied a portion of Thailand, and Phibul went so far as to declare war on the USA and Great Britain in 1942. His ambassador in Washington, Seni Pramoj, refused to deliver the declaration, and Phibul later resigned under pressure from growing underground resistance to his rule.

After V-J Day (marking the Allied victory over Japan in WWII) in 1945, Seni Pramoj became prime minister. Thus began a political chess game in which one leader after another was displaced by popular uprisings, elections and military coups. First to go was Seni, who was unseated in a general election in 1946. A democratic civilian government took over under the leadership of Pridi Phanomyong, a law professor who had been instrumental in the 1932 revolution. Thailand reverted to its old name of 'Siam' for about a year, until Phibul returned to power and suspended the constitution, reinstating 'Thailand' as the country's official name. Phibul's political rivals and dissidents were sent to the prison island of Ko Tarutao (p376), off the coast of Satun. Under Phibul the government took an extreme anticommunist stance and became a loyal supporter of French and US foreign policy in Southeast Asia. This had profound implications for Thailand's role during the Vietnam War.

Phibul lost his post again in 1951 to another general, Sarit Thanarat, though he retained the title of prime minister until 1957 when Sarit finally

1914	1917	1932
Official opening of Don Muang, Thailand's first international airport; the airport will remain the country's main domestic and international airport until the opening of Suvarnabhumi in 2006.	In a move meant to gain favour with France and Britain and assert its sovereignty, Siam joins the allied side in a mostly token role in Europe during WWI.	A bloodless coup transforms Siam from an absolute to a constitutional monarchy. The disposed king, Rama VII, by most accounts a willing accessory, continues to remain on the throne until resigning three years later.

had him exiled. That same year, Sarit was voted out in the elections and went abroad for 'medical treatment', returning in 1958 and seizing control in another coup. He promptly abolished the constitution, dissolved the parliament and banned all political parties, maintaining effective power until he died of cirrhosis in 1963.

Meanwhile, in the south of the country, long-held Muslim resentments against the ruling Buddhist government began to boil over (see the boxed text, p28).

From 1964 to 1973, Thailand was governed by the army officers Thanom Kittikachorn and Praphat Charusathien, who negotiated a package of economic deals with the USA in exchange for allowing the US to develop military bases in Thailand to support the war in Vietnam. Thailand found itself flooded with American GIs, who pumped US dollars into the Thai economy and created a culture of financial dependency on foreign investment that continues to be a problem in Thailand. Another effect of the American presence was the massive expansion of the sex industry. Although prostitution and extramarital affairs were culturally accepted, Thailand's relationship with US troops as an R&R destination developed its lasting reputation as a destination for sex tourism.

Despite the effects of the USA presence, most Thais were more worried about military rule. Reacting to political repression, 10,000 students publicly demanded reinstatement of the constitution in June 1973. In October that year, the military brutally suppressed a large demonstration at Thammasat University in Bangkok, killing 77 and wounding over 800. King Bhumibol stepped in, forcing Thanom and Praphat to leave Thailand. Oxford-educated Kukrit Pramoj took charge of a 14-party coalition, creating a leftist government that introduced a national minimum wage, repealed anticommunist laws and ordered the departure of US forces from Thailand.

Constitutional government lasted until October 1976 when students demonstrated again, this time protesting against Thanom's return to Thailand as a monk. Thammasat University again became a battlefield as the Border Patrol Police, along with right-wing, paramilitary civilian groups, assaulted a group of 2000 students holding a sit-in. Hundreds of students were killed and injured; more than a thousand were arrested.

The breakdown of order gave the military the perfect excuse to step in and reinstall a right-wing military government, this time with Thanin Kraivichien as prime minister. After this, many Thai students and intellectuals joined the People's Liberation Army of Thailand (PLAT) – a group of armed communist insurgents, based in the hills of northern and southern Thailand. However, with the dramatic evidence of USA opposition to communism in Asia still fresh in people's minds, the most they were able to achieve was the replacement of Thanin with the more moderate General Kriangsak Chomanand in 1977.

The dominance of the central Thai dialect as the country's standard language didn't occur until centralisation of the education system under the reign of King Rama V.

Global Terrorism Analysis (www.jamestown.org /terrorism) publishes online articles about the southern Thai insurgency as well as other international hot spots.

The History of the Malay Kingdom of Patani, by Ibrahim Syukri, is a nationalistic history of the southern provinces from the Muslim perspective.

1939	**1946**	**1946**
Military dictator and 1932 coup leader Phibul Songkhram renames Siam as Thailand, a nationalistic gesture meant to imply the unity of all Tai people.	King Bhumibol, Thailand's current king, is crowned after the death of his brother. This ushers in a period of revived interest in the monarchy, an institution that had been waning since the reign of Rama V.	Pridi Phanomyong, an architect of the 1932 coup, becomes Thailand's first democratically elected prime minister. After a military coup the following year, Pridi flees Thailand, returning only briefly once in his life.

CONFLICT IN THE SOUTH

Long before being incorporated into Thailand in 1902, the three border provinces of Pattani, Narathiwat and Yala previously formed a Malay kingdom known as Pattani. The majority of inhabitants of these provinces continue to be ethic Malay Muslims, and speak a Malay dialect called Yawi. During the 1930s, the Phibul government tried to impose Thai language and culture on the region, and proceeded to shut down religious schools and Islamic courts. This led to growing dissatisfaction with the central government, which eventually manifested itself as a desire for more autonomy, and in some cases, separatism. In 1948, in what is regarded as the beginning of the modern insurgency, Haji Sulong Tomina, a prominent religious leader, proposed that the people of the border provinces should be led by a locally born governor. He was charged with treason, prompting an uprising in the southernmost provinces that led to the death of hundreds. In 1954 Haji Sulong mysteriously disappeared, ostensibly executed by the authorities.

Throughout the latter 20th century, despite an official government policy of religious tolerance, the people of the region continued to be largely left out of state affairs, and their religious beliefs and language were viewed with scepticism by officials in Bangkok. In 1968 the Pattani United Liberation Organization (PULO) was created with the goal of creating a separate Muslim state. Unrest flared again in the 1970s and 1980s, but the issues raised by PULO were largely resolved by negotiation.

The most recent phase of the insurgency began in earnest in 2004 when a raid on an army depot in Narathiwat led to the death of four soldiers and the theft of hundreds of weapons. A brutal form of marshal law was immediately imposed on the three border provinces. In April of that year, after simultaneous attacks on several police outposts, 32 suspected militants hiding out in Pattani's Krue Sae Mosque were killed by the Thai military after a tense standoff. In October of the same year in the town of Tak Bai, Narathiwat, 78 Muslim protesters suffocated to death after being arrested and carelessly packed into military vehicles. In both cases the Thaksin government showed little remorse, claiming in the case of the Tak Bai incident, that the deaths were due to the fact that the protesters were already weak from fasting during the month of Ramadan.

Since the 2006 military coup, led by the Thai army's first Muslim commander, Sonthi Boonyaratglin, there has been only a slight lull in the virtually daily murders and bombings, which have moved as far north as Hat Yai, in Songkhla Province. Despite the scale of the rebellion, the identity of the insurgents and their goals are still largely unknown, although they are thought they have possible links to extremist groups such as Jemaah Islamiyah. Despite having resulted in over 2700 deaths since 2004, the conflict has received scant international attention.

The military subsequently appointed Prem Tinsulanonda in 1980, who set about dismantling the PLAT insurgency, banning the Communist Party of Thailand, launching military offensives against PLAT and granting amnesty to members who surrendered. Simultaneously, Prem created political and economic stability, removing the primary motivation for the armed uprisings. There was just one coup attempt in the 1980s and that was resolved peacefully through the intervention of King Bhumibol. Communism briefly reared its head one more time, in the form of the Communist Party of Malaysia, which established a guerrilla base in the tunnels of Khao Nam Khang National Park, but the organisation was dissolved in 1989.

In 1988 Prem was replaced in elections by Chatichai Choonhavan, who created a government dominated by business executives and who set about transforming Thailand into an 'Asian Tiger' economy. Thailand seemed to be entering a new era during which the country's economic boom coincided with increasing democratisation. Yet, by the end of the 1980s, some high-ranking military officers had become increasingly dissatisfied, complaining that Thailand was being governed by a plutocracy.

A History of Thailand, by Chris Baker and Pasuk Phongpaichit, is a good source of information regarding the significant events of Thailand's modern era.

MONEY POLITICS & THE POLITICS OF MONEY

Thailand had three peaceful years before the army seized power again in February 1991, handing power to the newly formed National Peace-Keeping Council (NPKC), led by General Suchinda Kraprayoon. It was Thailand's 18th coup attempt and one of 10 successful coups since 1932. Once again, the Thai constitution was abolished and parliament was dissolved.

The NPKC appointed a civilian leader, Anand Panyarachun, as prime minister, to dispel public fears that the junta was planning a return to 100% military rule. However, a new draft of the constitution effectively ensured that the real power would remain with the military, no matter who was in charge of parliament. The new charter also included a provisional clause allowing for a 'four-year transitional period' to full democracy.

It is thought that Thai boxing may have its origins in unarmed warfare during the Ayuthaya period.

General elections were held in March 1992 and a five-party coalition government came to power under Narong Wongwan, but the military promptly exercised its constitutional prerogative following a series of seemingly trumped-up allegations about Narong's involvement in the drugs trade and handed power back to General Suchinda.

In May 1992 Bangkok was once again rocked by demonstrations, this time led by charismatic Bangkok governor, Chamlong Srimuang. After street confrontations between protesters and the military near Bangkok's Democracy Monument resulted in nearly 50 deaths and hundreds of injuries, Chamlong and Suchinda were publicly scolded by King Bhumibol, and Suchinda resigned after less than six weeks as prime minister. The military-backed government also agreed to institute a constitutional amendment – Thailand's 15th – requiring that Thailand's prime minister come from the ranks of elected parliamentarians. Anand Panyarachun was reinstated as interim prime minister for a four-month term.

For one of the more readable 20th-century histories of Thailand, David Wyatt's *Thailand: A Short History* is still the definitive guide.

The September 1992 elections squeezed in veteran Democrat Party leader Chuan Leekpai with a five-seat majority. A food vendor's son and native of Trang Province, the new prime minister was well regarded for his honesty and high morals, but didn't really achieve a lot that the Thai people could take home with them. By the end of 1993, the opposition was calling for

1970s	**1973**	**1975**
The beginning of a period of insurgency in Thailand's southernmost provinces. The unrest continued until the 1990s when the government agreed to provide more representation and funding.	Large-scale student protests in Bangkok lead to violent military suppression. The 1971 coup leader Thanom Kittikachorn is ordered into exile by King Bhumibol.	After 14 years of using the country as an operating base for the Vietnam War, US troops depart Thailand. The US presence has a large and lasting impact on Thai culture and economy.

THE KING

If you see a yellow Rolls Royce flashing by along city avenues, accompanied by a police escort, you've probably just caught a glimpse of Thailand's longest-reigning monarch – and the longest-reigning living monarch in the world – King Bhumibol Adulyadej. Also known in English as Rama IX (the ninth king of the Chakri dynasty), Bhumibol was born in the USA in 1927, while his father Prince Mahidol was studying medicine at Harvard University.

Fluent in English, French, German and Thai, His Majesty ascended the throne in 1946 following the death of his brother Rama VIII (King Ananda Mahidol), who reigned for 11 years before being shot in mysterious circumstances.

An ardent jazz composer and saxophonist when he was younger, King Bhumibol has hosted jam sessions with the likes of jazz greats Woody Herman and Benny Goodman. His compositions are often played on Thai radio.

His Majesty administers royal duties from Chitralada Palace (Map pp72–3) in the city's Dusit precinct, north of Ko Ratanakosin. As protector of both nation and religion, King Bhumibol traditionally presides over several important Buddhist and Brahmanist ceremonies during the year. Among the more colourful are the seasonal robe-changing of the emerald Buddha in Wat Phra Kaew and the annual Royal Ploughing Ceremony, during which ceremonial rice is sown to ensure a robust economy for the coming year, at Sanam Luang.

The king and Queen Sirikit have four children: Princess Ubol Ratana (born 1951), Crown Prince Maha Vajiralongkorn (1952), Princess Mahachakri Sirindhorn (1955) and Princess Chulabhorn (1957).

After over 60 years in power, and having reached his 80th birthday, the King is preparing for his succession. For the last few years the Crown Prince has performed most of the royal ceremonies the King would normally perform, such as presiding over the Royal Ploughing Ceremony, changing the attire on the Emerald Buddha and handing out academic degrees at university commencements.

Though Thailand's political system is officially classified as a constitutional monarchy, the constitution stipulates that the king be 'enthroned in a position of revered worship' and must not be exposed 'to any sort of accusation or action'. With or without legal writ, the vast majority of Thai citizens regard King Bhumibol as a sort of demigod, partly in deference to tradition but also because of his impressive efforts to promote public works.

parliamentary dissolution and King Bhumibol stepped in and appointed a new cabinet for Chuan in December 1994.

Chuan did not complete his four-year term, and was replaced by 63-year-old billionaire Banharn Silapa-archa, whom the Thai press called a 'walking ATM'. Barnharn wasn't very popular with the Thai media, who immediately attacked his tendency to fill senior government positions with cronies known to be heavily involved in money politics. In September 1996 the Barnharn government collapsed amid a spate of corruption scandals and a crisis of confidence. However, the Thai economy continued to grow and Thailand

1976	1980	1985
Former coup leader Thanom returns to Thailand as a monk. Protests at Thammasat University are brutally put down by the military, leading to the deaths of 46 students.	Prime Minister Prem Tinsulanonda successfully negotiates peace with the country's communist insurgents by following a dual policy of urging cadres to defect and offering amnesty.	Chamlong Srimuang is elected mayor of Bangkok. Three years later, after forming his own largely Buddhist-based political party, the Palang Dharma Party, he is elected mayor again.

appeared to be on the verge of joining its neighbours South Korea, Taiwan, Hong Kong and Singapore as an Asian Tiger economy.

Barnharn was replaced that November by former deputy prime minister and army commander, Chavalit Yongchaiyudh, of the New Aspiration Party, in an election marked by violence and accusations of vote-buying. Like his predecessor – and most other political leaders in Asia and around the world for that matter – Chavalit failed to see that the Asian economic bubble was about to burst. In mid-1997, the Thai currency fell into a deflationary tailspin, losing 40% of its value, and the economy crashed to a virtual halt.

On 27 September 1997, the Thai parliament voted in a new constitution, Thailand's 16th since 1932 and the first to be decreed by a civilian government. Known as *rát·tam·má·noon ˈbràchahchon* (people's constitution) it put new mechanisms in place to monitor the conduct of elected officials and political candidates and to protect civil rights, achieving many of the aims of the prodemocracy movement. Unfortunately this wasn't enough to save the Chavalit government, which was judged on its failure to deal effectively with the economic disaster. Chavalit was forced to resign in November 1997.

An election brought Chuan Leekpai back into office, just as many banks and finance companies went into total collapse. The International Monetary Fund (IMF) stepped in with US$17.2 billion in loans, with the stipulation that the Thai government follow the IMF's prescriptions for recapitalisation and restructuring. The IMF medicine seemed to work, though it must be said, this benefited American and European global investors more than ordinary Thais. After shrinking 10% in 1998, the Thai economy grew nearly 5% in both 1999 and 2000. The weak baht helped make Thai products more attractive overseas and Thailand's exports grew by nearly 13%. These encouraging developments allowed Thailand to take an 'early out' from the IMF's loan package in 2000.

THE THAKSIN ERA

Economic survival wasn't enough to save Chuan, who was replaced in January 2001 by Thaksin Shinawatra, a billionaire telecommunications tycoon from Chiang Mai. Thaksin was able to capitalise on rural discontent by promising a suspension of farmers' debt payments and a million baht in development funds for each and every village in Thailand, and overwhelmingly defeated Chuan in the general elections. Thaksin was generally able to deliver on his populist promises and won another sweeping victory in 2005.

In 2003 a Thaksin-supported war on drugs led to the deaths of more than 2700 alleged drug dealers. Although the campaign was popular among Thais, some of the deaths were thought to be the result of extra-judicial score settling, and Thaksin was criticised by the UN Commission on Human Rights.

However, soon after his second victory, the Thaksin era began to be filled with political high drama. First there were the troubles in southern

> For an epic modern take on Thai history, seek out *The Legend of Suriyothai* (2003), the most expensive film ever made in Thailand.

> In 2005 the government of Thaksin Shinawatra became the first elected civilian administration to complete a four-year term.

> Thailand's King Bhumibol Adulyadej, who marked the 60th anniversary of his accession to the throne in 2006, is the world's longest-reigning monarch.

1992	1997	July 1997
Street protests led by Chamlong Srimuang against 1991 coup leader Suchinda Kraprayun leads to violent confrontations. Both Chamlong and Suchinda are publicly scolded by the king, leading to Suchinda's resignation.	A civilian government introduces Thailand's first constitution drafted by an elected assembly. The document emphasises human rights, advances political reform, and empowers and protects citizens.	Thailand devalues its currency, the baht, heralding the Asian economic crisis; massive unemployment and personal debt, and a significant crash of the Thai stock market.

COBRA SWAMP

If you arrived in Bangkok by air, bear in mind that the sleek glass and steel terminal you most likely pulled into was nearly 40 years in the making. Suvarnabhumi (pronounced sù·wan·ná·poom), Sanskrit for 'Golden Land', could hardly be a more apt name for Thailand's new airport, particularly for the politicians and investors involved.

Originally begun in 1973, the location chosen for Thailand's new international airport was an unremarkable marshy area with the slightly less illustrious working title of Nong Ngu Hao, Thai for 'Cobra Swamp'. Despite the seemingly disadvantageous setting, over the years the flat marshland was eagerly bought and sold by politicians and developers hoping to make a quick profit.

It wasn't until the self-styled administration of Thaksin Shinawatra that work on the airport began in earnest. Thaksin harboured desires to make Bangkok a 'transportation hub' to rival Hong Kong and Singapore, and went on a virtual spending spree, commissioning construction of the world's tallest flight control tower, as well as the world's largest terminal building.

Not surprisingly, the construction of Suvarnabhumi was rife with allegations of corruption, including the use of faulty building materials and substandard, insufficient runways. Undoubtedly the most embarrassing single scandal associated with the airport was the suspect purchase of 20 CTX security scanners from a US company.

On 29 September 2005, Thaksin presided over a much-criticised 'soft' opening ceremony. The event was essentially little more than a face-saving measure considering that the airport was still far from operational. Suvarnabhumi eventually began flights a year later, on September 28, 2006. In an ironic twist of fate, Thaksin, the main catalyst behind the project, was in exile in England, having been ousted in a military coup the week before, the junta citing corruption and shoddy construction of the airport among their justifications for the takeover.

Despite being the largest airport in Southeast Asia, and among the largest in the world, in March 2007, many domestic flights were relocated back to the old Don Muang Airport, with officials citing overcrowding of runways and safety concerns as reasons for the move. With little foresight, a train link to the distant airport was only begun after its opening, and is not expected to be operating until early 2009.

Thailand (see p28), public discontent with Thaksin's desire to privatise certain state agencies, and even allegations of Thaksin's perceived ambitions to take on roles associated with the monarchy when Thaksin presided over the ceremonies during a merit-making ritual at Wat Phra Kaew, a role traditionally reserved for the monarch. The final nail in Thaksin's coffin occurred when members of his family sold their family-owned Shin Corporation shares to the Singaporean government for a tax-free profit of 73 billion baht (US$1.88 billion), thanks to newly introduced telecommunications legislation that exempted individuals from capital gains tax. Thaksin responded to the growing displeasure by dissolving parliament and calling for re-elections in a month's time, promising to step down if his party did not win a majority.

2001	January 2004	December 2004
Thaksin Shinawatra, Thailand's richest man, is elected prime minister on a populist platform.	The modern phase of southern Thailand's Muslim insurgency begins when militants raid an army base in Narathiwat, killing four guards and stealing hundreds of weapons.	An earthquake-triggered tsunami on Boxing Day damages much of Thailand's Andaman Sea coast, causing deaths of more than 5000 and the destruction of much of the tourist industry.

In the lead up to the 2006 re-elections, Thaksin announced massive populist measures aimed directly at the rural poor. With just a month to organise and campaign, the opposition realised the task was monumental and chose to boycott the election. When the ballots were tallied, Thaksin proclaimed victory. However, just one day later, after a private council with the king, Thaksin announced that for the sake of national unity he would not accept the position of prime minister.

The 2006 coup leader, General Sonthi Boonyaratglin, was the first Muslim to head the Buddhist kingdom's army.

On the evening of 19 September 2006, while Thaksin was attending a UN conference in New York, the Thai military led by General Sonthi Boonyaratglin took power in a bloodless coup. Calling themselves the Council for Democratic Reform under the Constitutional Monarch, the junta cited the Thai Rak Thai (TRT) government's alleged *lèse majesté*, corruption, interference with state agencies and creation of social divisions as justification for the coup. The public initially overwhelmingly supported the coup, and scenes of tourists and Thai families posing in front of tanks remain the defining images of the event. Thaksin quickly flew to London, where he lived in exile and busied himself by buying the Manchester City football club.

In January 2007, an Assets Examination Committee put together by the junta found Thaksin guilty of concealing assets to avoid paying taxes. Two months later, Thaksin's wife and brother-in-law were also charged with conspiracy to evade taxes. In late May, a court established by the military government found TRT guilty of breaking election laws. The court dissolved the party and banned its executive members from public service for five years.

One of the only sources of information during the 2006 coup, www.2Bangkok.com, features background and perspective on local news with summaries of the Thai-language press updated on a daily basis.

In a nationwide referendum held on 19 August, the Thai people approved a military-drafted constitution. Although the document includes a number of undemocratic provisions, including one that mandates a Senate not entirely comprised of elected politicians, its passage was largely regarded as a message that the Thai people want to see elections and progress.

Under the new constitution, long-awaited elections were finally held on 23 December. The newly formed People Power Party, of which Thaksin has an advisory role, won a significant number of seats in parliament, but failed to win an outright majority. After forming a loose coalition with several other parties, parliament choose veteran politician and close Thaksin ally Samak Sundaravej as prime minister. Samak has expressed his desire to clear Thaksin of all charges. This, and Thaksin's return to Thailand in March 2008, have ushered in another period of uncertainty in Thai politics.

Thailand has had 19 coups since 1932, of which 10 resulted in a change of government.

September 2006	August 2007	December 2007
A bloodless coup sees the Thai military take power from prime minister Thaksin Shinawatra while he is at a UN meeting in New York.	In a nationwide referendum, voters agree to approve a military-drafted constitution, Thailand's 17th, despite being regarded by many Thais and international observers as deeply flawed.	A general election sees the Thaksin-allied People's Power Party gain a significant number of seats in parliament. A coalition, led by veteran politician, Samak Sundaravej, is formed.

The Culture

REGIONAL IDENTITY

Religion, royalty and tradition are the defining characteristics of Thai society. That Thailand is the only country in Southeast Asia never colonised by a foreign power has led to a profound sense of pride in these elements. However, the country is not completely homogenous, and in the south, another strong cultural identity prevails that is more in tune with the Islamic culture of nearby Malaysia.

Before modern political boundaries divided the Malay peninsula into two countries, the city-states, sultanates and villages were part of an Indonesian-based Srivijaya empire, sharing intermingled customs and language, all vying for local control over shipping routes. Many southern Thai towns and geographic names bear the hallmark of the Bahasa language, and some village traditions would be instantly recognized by a Sumatran but not by a northern Thai. Chinese culture is also prominent in southern Thailand, as seen in the numerous temples and clan houses, and it is this intermingling of domestic and 'foreign' culture that defines the south.

Culture Shock Thailand, by Robert and Nanthapa Cooper, is a humorous and helpful introduction to confusing Thai ways.

Saving Face & Having Fun

An important Thai concept across all religions is the idea of 'saving face', that is, avoiding confrontation and trying not to embarrass yourself or other people. For this reason, Thais shy away from negative topics in everyday conversation and generally won't interfere with others unless someone complains or asks for their help. This is one of the sources of the Thai smile – it's the best possible face to put on in almost any situation. Arguing over prices or getting angry while haggling causes everyone involved to lose face and should be avoided. The only time you'll see Thais failing to show due respect is when it may be a source of *sàn·ùk* (fun). The Thais love to joke and *sàn·ùk* plays an important part of saving face.

When speaking with or about royalty, a special vocabulary called rāh·chá·sàp is used by Thais.

LIFESTYLE

The ordinary life of a southern Thai can be divided into two categories: country and city.

Those in rural areas are typically employed with rubber farming or fishing, though rice and livestock farming are also evident. Rubber farmers live in small, typically inland settlements identified by straight rows of trees and pale sheets of drying latex. Surviving fishing villages are typically as close to the sea as possible, so that their inhabitants can watch the tides and their boats. Traditional Muslim villages are built directly over the water in a series of connected stilt houses. Because the Andaman Sea had a history of tranquil behaviour, there was no fear of the ocean's wrath, a preconception painfully destroyed by the 2004 tsunami.

Instead of a handshake, the traditional Thai greeting is the wâi – a prayer-like gesture with the palms placed together.

Within the cities, life looks a lot like the rest of the country (busy and modern), but the presence of Chinese and Indian merchants marks the uniqueness of southern Thai cities. The commercial centres are also the market towns, where the brightly coloured fishing boats ease into the harbour, unloading the catch and filling the marina with the aroma of fish.

Family Values

The importance of the family unit in Thai society is immediately apparent to a visitor in the many family-owned and operated businesses. It is still common to see three generations employed in a family-run guesthouse, or sharing the same house. The elderly are involved in day-to-day life, selling sweets to neighbourhood kids, renting motorcycles to tourists and many other ways. Although tourism has significantly altered the islanders' traditional way of life, the presence of jobs helps to keep many ambitious children from seeking employment on the mainland.

DOS & DON'TS

The Thais are generally very understanding and hospitable, but there are some taboos you should be aware of.

Temple Etiquette

- Always dress neatly and conservatively when visiting temples. No shorts or sleeveless tops for men or women.
- Take your shoes off when you enter any building that contains a Buddha image.
- Women should not touch a monk or a monk's belongings. To avoid an accidental brush, don't sit next to a monk on a public bus and let them pass first on a crowded street.
- Sit with your feet pointed away from any Buddha images: the feet are regarded as the lowest part of the body and pointing your feet towards someone is highly disrespectful.

Everyday Etiquette

- Avoid disparaging remarks about the king, queen or anyone in the royal family.
- Treat objects with a picture or image of the king, including coins and banknotes, with respect.
- Stand with respect for the royal anthem, which is played in movie theatres before the show, and for the national anthem, often played through loudspeakers at 8am and 6pm.
- The rules of returning a *wâi* are quite involved; in general return a *wâi* to an adult but not to children or servers.
- A smile and *'sà·wàt·dee kráp'* (male) or *'sà·wàt·dee kâ'* (female) is the standard all-purpose greeting and is acceptable for all ages.
- Don't show anger or lose your temper; it causes a 'loss of face' for everyone present. Even talking loudly is seen as rude by cultured Thais, whatever the situation.
- The head is regarded as the highest part of the body, so never touch Thais on the head or ruffle their hair. For the same reason, you should never sit on pillows meant for sleeping or put a hat on the floor.
- The feet are considered the lowest part of the body. You should never step over someone, even if they are lying on the floor – squeeze around them or ask them to move instead.
- When handing things to people, use your right hand and place your left hand on your elbow, a sign of good manners.
- Mind your appearance. Thais are very fastidious in their appearance and are sometimes displeased by foreigners' unkempt looks. Clean it up if you've got to pay a visit to a government office.
- If invited to a home, bring a small gift, either food or drinks, but not flowers, which are typically reserved for merit-making.

Beach Etiquette

- Avoid public nudity on the beaches. Thais are traditionally very modest and all but the most flamboyant Bangkok Thais will swim fully clothed.
- Men should wear shirts away from the beach unless they want Thai people to think that they are real lowlifes.

STOPPING CHILD-SEX TOURISM IN THAILAND

Sadly, Thailand has become a destination for a significant number of foreigners seeking to sexually exploit local children. A range of socioeconomic factors renders many children vulnerable to such abuse, and some depraved individuals seem intent to prey upon this vulnerability.

The sexual abuse and exploitation of children has serious, lifelong and even life-threatening consequences. Child-sex tourism is a crime and a violation of the rights of a child. Strong laws exist in Thailand to prosecute offenders. Many countries also have extraterritorial legislation that allows nationals to be prosecuted in their own country for such crimes.

Responsible travellers can help to stop the scourge of child-sex tourism by reporting suspicious behaviour. Don't ignore it! Your actions may be critical in helping to protect children from future abuse and exploitation.

In Thailand, travellers can report on a dedicated hotline number: ☎ 1300. If you know the nationality of the individual, you can report them directly to their embassy.

ECPAT (End Child Prostitution & Trafficking; ☎ in Bangkok 0 2215 3388; www.ecpat.net) is a global network focusing on these issues with more than 70 affiliate organisations around the world. Its head office is located in Bangkok. ECPAT is actively working to combat child-sex tourism in Thailand and around the world.

Child Wise (www.childwise.net) is the Australian member of ECPAT. Child Wise has been involved in providing training to the tourism industry in Thailand to counter child-sex tourism.

Even the Thai pronouns reflect a strong sense of family. Thais will refer to people in their own generation as an older (*pêe*) or younger (*nórng*) sibling, regardless of bloodline. Sometimes Thais will translate this tribal custom into English, referring to non-family members as 'sister' or 'brother', inadvertently amazing foreigners with the vastness of Thai families.

ECONOMY

Due to tourism, fishing, shrimp farming and rubber, the south is Thailand's wealthiest region. Most rubber tappers are born into it, inheriting the profession of their fathers and mothers. Shrimp and fish farming, on the other hand, are relatively new industries, introduced as an economic development program for rural communities losing ground to commercial fishing operations. The venture proved profitable and Thailand is one of the leading exporters of farm-raised shrimp. However, fish farms have been largely unregulated until recently, leading to a host of environmental problems, such as water pollution and the destruction of mangrove forests.

Every Thai person has a nickname, which range from Thai words such as Nóy ('small') or Nŏo ('mouse'), to English words such as 'Chief' or 'Ice'.

Tourism has undoubtedly had the most tangible impact on the economy of the area, transforming many small villages into bilingual enterprises. Women who would otherwise sell products at the market have studied Thai traditional massage, and walk up and down the beach beseeching customers. Other do-it-yourself franchises, so prolific in Thai communities, have been tailored to tourists: shopfronts along the beach thoroughfares sell sunscreen and postcards instead of rice whisky and grilled fish, itinerant vendors hawk sarongs and henna tattoos instead of feather dusters and straw brooms, while fishermen sometimes abandon their nets for bigger catches – tourists on snorkelling trips.

Pah·săa·va tăi, the southern dialect of the Thai language, is known for its rapid cadence and inclination to omit entire syllables and words.

Across Thailand, the size of the middle class is growing with successive decades, bridging the gap between rich and poor. Thailand doesn't suffer from poverty of sustenance; even the most destitute Thai citizens can have shelter and food. Rather, the lower rung of Thai society suffers from poverty of material: money isn't available for extensive education, material goods or health care. This is most obvious from an economic perspective: the average Thai income stands at around US$2000 a year, but many in rural provinces earn as little as US$570 a year.

POPULATION

Over one third of all Thais live in urban areas and Bangkok is, without doubt, the largest city in the kingdom, with nearly eight million inhabitants – more than 10% of the total population. The four next-most-populated cities are located in the northeast and the northern part of the country. Most of the other towns in Thailand have populations well below 100,000.

About 75% of the citizenry are ethnic Thais, predominantly Buddhist, and are divided into a number of cultural subgroups with their own dialects. People of Chinese ancestry make up 14% of the population and fill the shopkeeper niche in southern Thai society. The second-largest ethnic minority group living in Thailand are Muslims of Malay origin (4%), most of whom reside in the southern provinces of Songkhla, Yala, Pattani and Narathiwat. The remaining 10.5% of the population is made up of smaller non-Thai-speaking groups such as the Vietnamese, Khmer, Mon and Moken (chow lair, often spelt as chao leh; see boxed text, below), and small numbers of Europeans and other non-Asians in Bangkok, Phuket and Chiang Mai.

One in 10 Thai citizens lives and works in Bangkok.

Check out www.thai-blogs.com to peek into the lives of various Thais and expats and link to sites translating Thai music or offering free Thai cooking video downloads.

RELIGION
Buddhism

Approximately 95% of Thais follow Theravada Buddhism, also known as Hinayana or 'Lesser Vehicle' Buddhism to distinguish it from the Mahayana or 'Great Vehicle' school of Buddhism. The primary difference between the faiths is that Theravada Buddhists believe every individual is responsible for their own enlightenment, while Mahayana Buddhists believe society can work together to achieve enlightenment for all.

The ultimate end of all forms of Buddhism is to reach nibbana (from Sanskrit, nirvana), which literally means the 'blowing out' or extinction of all desire and thus of all dukkha (suffering). Having achieved nibbana, an individual is freed from the cycle of rebirths and enters the spiritual plane. In reality, most Thai Buddhists aim for rebirth in a 'better' existence in the next life, rather than striving to attain nibbana. To work towards this goal, Buddhists carry out meritorious actions (tam bun) such as feeding monks, giving donations to temples and performing regular worship at the local wát (temple). The Buddhist theory of karma is well expressed in the Thai proverb tam dee, dâi dee; tam chôo·a, dâi chôo·a (do good and receive good; do evil and receive evil).

There is no specific day of worship in Thai Buddhism; instead the faithful go to temple on certain religious holidays, when it is convenient or to commemorate a special family event. Most temple visits occur on wan prá

Every Thai Buddhist male over the age of 20 is expected to become a monk. This ordination can last as long as several months, or as brief as a few days.

CHOW LAIR

Southern Thailand is home to one of Thailand's smallest ethnic groups, the chow lair, literally, 'people of the sea.' Also known as Moken (môr gaang), or sea gypsies, the chow lair are an ethnic group of Malay origin who span the Andaman coast from Borneo to Myanmar. The remaining traditional bands of chow lair are hunter-gatherers, living primarily off the sea. They are recognized as one of the few groups of humans that primarily live at sea, although many are turning to shanty-like settlements on various islands. Perhaps as a result of generations of this marine lifestyle, many chow lair can hold their breath for long periods of time and also have an uncanny ability to see underwater. Life at sea has also helped them in other ways; during the 2004 tsunami, virtually no chow lair were killed, as folk tales handed down from generation to generation alerted them to the dangers of the quickly receding tide, and they were able to escape to higher ground. For details on the threat to the chow lair culture, see p353.

(excellent days), which occur every full and new moon. Other activities include offering food to the temple *sangha* (community of monks, nuns and lay residents), meditating, listening to monks chanting *suttas* and attending talks on *dhamma* (right behaviour).

After his death, the Buddha's body was supposedly dealt up into 84,000 relics, many of which are claimed to be entombed in various religious structures throughout Thailand.

MONKS & NUNS

There are about 32,000 monasteries in Thailand and 200,000 monks, many of them ordained for life. Traditionally, every Thai male is expected to spend time as a monk, usually between finishing school and marrying or starting a career. Even his Majesty King Bhumibol served as a novice at Wat Bowonniwet (Map pp74–5) in Banglamphu, Bangkok. Traditionally boys would devote a year or more to monastic life, but these days most people enter the *sangha* (monastery) for two weeks to three months during *pan·săh* (Buddhist lent), which coincides with the rainy season.

Women can become *mâa chee* (eight-precept nuns) but this is held in slightly lower regard than the status of male monks, as most Thais believe that a woman can only achieve *nibbana* if she is reincarnated as a man. Both monks and nuns shave their heads and wear robes – orange for men, white for women – giving up most of their personal belongings and living on charity. Thais donate generously to the local *wát*, so monks often live quite comfortable lives.

Thais follow the lunar calendar, with the traditional New Year falling in mid-April.

An increasing number of foreigners are coming to Thailand to be ordained as Buddhist monks or nuns. If you want to find out more, see p386 or visit the websites **Access to Insight** (www.accesstoinsight.org) and **Buddha Net** (www.buddhanet.net).

MULTICULTURAL THAILAND

Buddhism typically enjoys a worldwide reputation for being peaceful and accommodating, which makes the current tensions (see p28) in the Muslim majority regions of southern Thailand (Narathiwat, Pattani and Yala provinces) perplexing. Why do the cultural and religious beliefs of the Muslim Thais clash with the Buddhist administration?

Firstly, Islam mandates concrete rules for living a good life; a Muslim's day is strictly governed by sacred rituals, from the performance of daily prayers to the preparation of meals and the education of children. But the laws outlined in the Quran aren't represented in the policy-making decisions of the national government, and several well-intentioned economic development schemes have deeply offended Muslim Thais. The government-run lottery, for example, is used to fund need-based scholarships, but gambling is viewed as sinful by Muslims, and clerics have instructed the faithful to reject these much-needed financial opportunities for their children. Interest-based loans for struggling villages also run counter to Islamic beliefs.

Another stumbling block for cross-cultural understanding is the private *pondok* (or *madrasah*) schools, where Muslim children receive religious education. A *pondok* is a village boarding school where male children live a studious and religiously contemplative life before returning to the village with religious leadership skills. The *pondok* custom is viewed as vital to the Islamic way of life but is lacking modern application, and increasingly, many are suspected of imparting a militant Muslim education. In the 1970s the Thai government forced the schools to start teaching secular subjects, a move viewed as distracting and destructive to the Islamic faith.

In recent years, the education ministry has been more sensitive to the importance of the *pondok* tradition while trying to educate its citizens, mainly in Thai language and other subjects that might help relieve the economic hardships of the region. This has been coupled with more conciliatory central government policies, as well as increased representation and funding, but continued scepticism of each other's traditions ensures that the conflict between Buddhists and Muslims is likely to continue.

For more on the conflict, see p28.

As long as you dress appropriately and observe the correct etiquette (p35) you will be welcome at most monasteries. However, take care not to disturb monks while they are eating or meditating – nothing breaks the concentration quite like tourists snapping photographs!

Islam

Thailand is home to 1.6 million Muslims (around 4% of Thailand's population), concentrated in the south of the country. Most Thai Muslims are of Malay origin and generally follow a moderate version of the Sunni sect mixed with pre-Islamic animism.

A decade-long revival movement has cultivated more devote Islamic practices and suspicions of outside influences. Under this more strenuous interpretation of Islam, many folk practices have been squeezed out of daily devotions and local people see the mainly Buddhist government and education system as intolerant of their way of life (see the boxed text, opposite). Schools and infrastructure in the Muslim-majority south are typically underfunded and frustration with the Bangkok government is sometimes defined as a religious rather than political struggle.

There are mosques throughout southern Thailand but few are architecturally interesting and most are closed to women. If you do visit a mosque, remember to cover your head and remove your shoes.

Many Muslims from the southernmost regions of Thailand speak Yawi, a dialect of Malay, as their native language.

Other Religions

Half a percent of the population – primarily hill tribes converted by missionaries and Vietnamese immigrants – is Christian, while the remaining half percent is made up of Confucians, Taoists, Mahayana Buddhists and Hindus. Chinese temples and joss houses are a common sight in the south and in Bangkok's Chinatown, and Bangkok is also home to a large, colourful Hindu temple.

ARTS

Much of Thailand's creative energy has traditionally gone into the production of religious and ceremonial art. Painting, sculpture, music and theatre still play a huge role in the ceremonial life of Thais and religious art is very much a living art form.

Elaborate wooden bird cages holding cooing doves can be found along the streets of many towns in southern Thailand. Even dove singing contests are held.

Literature

The most pervasive and influential work of classical Thai literature is the Ramakian, based on the Hindu holy book, the Ramayana, which was brought to Southeast Asia by Indian traders and introduced to Thailand by the Khmer about 900 years ago. Although the main theme remains the same, the Thais embroidered the Ramayana by providing much more biographical detail on arch-villain Ravana (*Thótsàkan* in the Ramakian) and his wife Montho. The monkey-god, Hanuman, is also transformed into something of a playboy.

The epic poem, *Phra Aphaimani*, was composed by poet Sunthorn Phu (1786–1855) and is set on the island of Ko Samet. *Phra Aphaimani* is Thailand's most famous classical literary work, and tells a typically epic story of an exiled prince.

Modern Thai literature is usually written in Thai, so it isn't very accessible to non-Thais. Modern authors you may find translated include Seni Saowaphong, whose most famous title *Pisat, Evil Spirits* deals with conflicts between the old and new generations. Former prime minister, Kukrit Pramoj, is another respected author – his collection of short stories, *Lai Chiwit* (*Many Lives*), and the Rama V–based era novel *Si Phandin* (*Four Reigns*) have been translated into English.

There is no universally accepted method of transliterating from Thai to English, so some words and place names are spelled a variety of ways.

Celebrated contemporary writer Pira Sudham was born into a poor family in northeastern Thailand. *Monsoon Country,* one of several titles Sudham wrote in English, brilliantly captures the region's struggles against nature and nurture.

Chart Korbjitti is a two-time winner of the Southeast Asian Writers Award (SEA Write): in 1982 for *The Judgement,* the drama of a young village man wrongly accused of a crime; and in 1994 for a 'mixed-media' novel, *Time.*

SP Somtow has been described as 'Thailand's JD Salinger'. *Jasmine Nights,* Somtow's upbeat coming-of-age novel, fuses traditional ideas with modern Thai pop culture. *Jasmine Nights* won acclaim throughout the world.

Writer Sri Daoruang adapted the Ramayana into modern Bangkok in *Married to the Demon King.* Short stories by modern Thai women writers appear in the collection *A Lioness in Bloom,* translated by Susan Kepner.

The leading post-modern writer is Prabda Yoon, whose short story 'Probability' won the 2002 SEA Write award. Although his works have yet to be translated, he wrote the screenplay for *Last Life in the Universe* and other Pen-ek Ratanaruang–directed films.

Depending on the speaker's relationship with his listener, personal pronouns can take many forms in the Thai language.

Cinema

Thailand has a lively homespun movie industry, producing some very competent films in various genres. The most expensive film ever made in the country, not to mention the highest grossing, was director Prince Chatrichalerm Yukol's epic *Legend of Suriyothai* (2003), which tells the story of a 16th-century warrior princess. But what has propelled Thai viewers to forsake Hollywood imports are generally action flicks such as *Ong Bak: Thai Warrior* and the follow-up *Tom Yum Goong,* directed by Prachya Pinkaew.

Thailand has cropped up in various foreign film festivals over the years, with several critically acclaimed art house movies. Pen-Ek Ratanaruang's clever and haunting movies, such as *Last Life in the Universe* and *6ixty9ine* have created a buzz on the film-festival circuit. Apichatpong Weerasethakul leads the avant-garde pack with his Cannes-awarded *Tropical Malady* and *Sud Sanaeha.*

The Thai government is now actively touting Thailand as a location for foreign film-makers. The most famous film to be made here in recent years was *The Beach* (2000). Based on the Alex Garland novel, it was filmed at Maya Bay on Ko Phi-Phi, Phuket, and several jungle locations near Krabi and Khao Yai National Park. The film caused controversy for allegedly damaging the environment in Maya Bay, which was also a location for the 1995 pirate stinker *Cutthroat Island.* Other famous films made here include the James Bond romp *The Man with the Golden Gun* (1974), which was filmed in Ao Nang Bay, *Good Morning Vietnam* (1987), *The Killing Fields* (1984) and *The Deer Hunter* (1978).

Thailand's third sex, the *gà·teu·i* (often spelt *kàthoey;* transgender men), get a starring role in *Iron Ladies,* a movie about the true story of an all-transvestite volleyball team that became the national men's champions.

Music

Traditional Thai music may sound a little strange to visitors, as the eight note Thai octave is broken in different places to the European octave. Thai scales were first transcribed by Thai-German composer Phra Chen Duriyanga (Peter Feit), who also composed Thailand's national anthem in 1932.

The classical Thai orchestra is called the *bèe·pâht* and can include anything from five to 20 musicians. The most popular stringed instrument is the *ja·kêh,* a slender guitar-like instrument played horizontally on the ground, which probably evolved from the Indian *vina.* Woodwind instruments include the *khlùi,* a simple wooden flute, and the *bèe,* a recorder-like instrument with a reed mouthpiece, based on the Indian *shennai.* You'll hear the *bèe* being played if you go to a Thai boxing match. Other popular instruments include the *saw,* a three-stringed fretless instrument,

In 1913 King Rama VI introduced the concept of surnames to Thailand, granting many himself.

MADE IN THAILAND

You've undoubtedly seen his lanky frame on billboards, enthusiastically sporting his band's forked-finger salute to promote their eponymous energy drink. You may also have caught him on TV, singing a rallying anthem to sell Chang beer. And you've likely heard taxi drivers make passing references to his hit song, 'Made in Thailand'. All these sightings probably have you thinking, Who is this guy?

The guy is Yuengyong Ophakun, better known as Aed Carabao, lead singer of Carabao, a Thai band many consider the Rolling Stones of Thailand.

The name Carabao comes from the Tagalog word for buffalo, and implies diligence and patience. Not unlike the Ramones, the founding members of Carabao, Aed and Khiao (Kirati Promsakha Na Sakon Nakhorn), adopted the word as a surrogate surname after forming the band as students in the Philippines in the early 1980s. Their style of music was inspired by Thai protest music, Filipino music, as well as a healthy dose of Western-style rock and roll. Since their first album, *Chut Khîi Mao* ('Drunkard's Album'), and in the 24 that have followed, Carabao's lyrics have remained political and occasionally controversial. *Ganchaa* (marijuana), a song from their second album, was promptly banned from Thai radio – the first of many. In 2001 Carabao dedicated an album in support of Shan rebels in Myanmar, a source of consternation for the Thai government. When not generating controversy they are almost constantly performing, and have also played in most Southeast Asian countries, as well as Europe and the USA. Your best chance of seeing them is in Bangkok or a major tourist centre.

similar to the Japanese *shamisen*, and the *rá·nâht èhk*, a bamboo-keyed xylophone played with wooden hammers.

Perhaps the most familiar Thai instrument is the *kĭm* or hammer dulcimer, responsible for the plinking, plunking music you'll hear in Thai restaurants across the world. The dulcimer resembles a flat harp played with two light bamboo sticks and has an eerie echoing sound. Another unusual Thai instrument is the *kórng wong yài*, a semicircle of tuned gongs arranged in a wooden rack. The double-headed *đà·pohn* drum sets the tempo for the whole ensemble.

See www.seasite.niu .edu/thai/music for snatches of Thai tunes, from classical music to pop.

The contemporary Thai music scene is strong and diverse. The most popular genre is undoubtedly *lôok tûng*, a style analogous to country and western in the USA that tends to appeal most to working-class Thais. The 1970s ushered in a new style dubbed *pleng pêu·a chee·wít* (literally 'music for life'), inspired by the politically conscious folk rock of the USA and Europe. Today there are hundreds of youth-oriented Thai bands, from chirpy boy and girl bands to metal rockers, making music that is easy to sing along with and maddeningly hard to get out of your head. The three biggest modern Thai music icons include rock staple Carabao (see the boxed text, above), pop star Thongchai 'Bird' MacIntyre, and *lôok tûng* queen, Pumpuang Duangchan, who died tragically in 1995.

In the 1990s an alternative pop scene – known as *pleng tâi din* (underground music) – grew in Bangkok. Modern Dog, a Britpop-inspired band, is generally credited with bringing independent Thai music into the mainstream, and their success paved the way for more mainstream alternative acts such as Apartment for Khun Pa, Futon, Chou Chou and Calories Blah Blah. Thai headbangers designed to fill stadiums include perennial favourite Loso, as well as Big Ass, Potato and Bodyslam.

See www.thaistudents .com for Thai pop downloads, language tips and culture chat.

Architecture

Most traditional Thai architecture is religious in nature. Thai temples, like Thai Buddhism, gladly mixes and matches different foreign influences from the corn-shaped stupa inherited from the Khmer empire to the bell-shaped

Nine is largely considered a lucky number in Thailand because it sounds similar to the Thai word for progress.

stupa of Sri Lanka. Despite the foreign flourishes, all Thai temples' roof lines mimic the shape of the *naga* (mythical serpent) that protected the Buddha during meditation and is viewed as a symbol of life. Green and gold tiles represent scales while the soaring eaves are the head of the creature.

Traditional teak-wood homes can be seen throughout northern Thailand, but are also present in the capital. The capital's finest teak building is Vimanmek Mansion (Map pp72–3), said to be the largest golden-teak building in the world. Teak houses are typically raised on stilts to minimise the damage caused by flooding and provide a space for storage and livestock. The whole structure is held together with wooden pegs and topped by sweeping eaves that rise to distinctive gables at either end of the house. Houses are traditionally roofed with glazed tiles or wooden shingles.

In the south, houses have traditionally been simpler, relying heavily on bamboo poles and woven bamboo fibre. You might also see Malay-style houses, which use high masonry foundations rather than wooden stilts.

Architecture over the last 100 years has been influenced by cultures from all over the world. In the south, you can still see plenty of Sino-Portuguese *hôrng tăa·ou* (shophouses) – plastered Chinese-style masonry houses with shops below and living quarters above. Classic examples of this style can be found in Phuket's main city (p300). Since WWII the main trend in Thai architecture has been one of function over form, inspired by the European Bauhaus movement. As a result, there are lots of plain buildings that look like egg cartons turned on their sides.

Thais believe it is unlucky to get a haircut on Wednesday, and it is on this day that barbers take their holiday.

Thai architects began experimenting during the building boom of the mid-1980s, resulting in creative designs such as Sumet Jumsai's famous robot-shaped Bank of Asia on Th Sathon Tai in Bangkok, or the Elephant Building off Th Phaholyothin in northern Bangkok.

Painting

Except for the prehistoric and historic cave paintings found in the south of the country, not much ancient formal painting exists in Thailand, partly due to the devastating Burmese invasion of 1767. The vast majority of what exists is religious in nature, and typically takes the form of temple

---

TEMPLE MURALS

Because of the relative wealth of Bangkok, as well as its role as the country's artistic and cultural centre, the artists commissioned to illustrate the walls of the city's various temples were among the most talented around, and Bangkok's temple paintings are generally regarded as the finest in the country. Some particularly exceptional works include:

- **Wat Bowonniwet** (Map pp74–5) Painted during the reign of Rama II (r 1809–24), the murals in the panels of the *bòht* (chapel) of this temple show Thai depictions of Western life during the early 19th century.
- **Wat Chong Nonsi** (Map pp70–1) Bangkok's earliest surviving temple paintings are faded and missing in parts, and depict everyday Thai life, including bawdy illustrations of a sexual manner.
- **Phra Thii Nang Phutthaisawan** (Buddhaisawan Chapel; Map pp74–5) These murals, finished during the reign of Rama III (r 1824–51), depict the conception, birth and early life of the Buddha – common topics among Thai temple murals.
- **Wat Suthat** (Map pp74–5) Almost as impressive in their vast scale as much as their quality, these murals are among the most awe-inspiring in the country.
- **Wat Suwannaram** (Map pp70–1) These paintings inside a late Ayuthaya-era temple in Thonburi contain skilled and vivid depictions of battle scenes and foreigners.

paintings illustrating the various lives of the Buddha. Several Bangkok wát have accomplished 17th- and 18th-century paintings; see the boxed text, p42.

Since the 1980s boom years Thai secular sculpture and painting have enjoyed increased international recognition, with a handful of Impressionism-inspired artists among the initial few to have reached this vaunted status. Succeeding this was the 'Fireball' school of artists such as Manit Sriwanichpoom, who specialise in politically motivated, mixed-media art installations. And in recent years Thai artists have again moved away from both traditional influences and political commentary and towards contemporary art. For information about visiting Bangkok's galleries and art museums, see p87.

Theatre & Dance

Traditional Thai theatre consists of four main dramatic forms: *kŏhn* is a formal masked dance-drama traditionally reserved for royalty, depicting scenes from the Ramakian; *lá·kon* are dance-dramas performed for common people; *lí·gair* are partly improvised, often bawdy, folk plays featuring dancing, comedy, melodrama and music; and *hùn lŏo·ang (lá·kon lék)* is traditional puppet theatre enacting religious legends or folk tales.

Most of these forms can be enjoyed in Bangkok, both at dinner shows for tourists and at formal theatrical performances. There are also some distinctively southern theatrical styles, predating the arrival of Islam on the Malay Peninsula. The most famous is *má·noh·rah,* the oldest surviving Thai dance-drama, which tells the story of Prince Suthon, who sets off to rescue the kidnapped Mánohraa, a *gin·ná·ree* (woman-bird) princess. As in *lí·gair,* performers add extemporaneous comic rhymed commentary. Trang also has a distinctive form of *lí·gair,* with a storyline depicting Indian merchants taking their Thai wives back to India for a visit.

Another ancient theatrical style in the south is shadow-puppet theatre, which also occurs in Indonesia and Malaysia, in which two-dimensional figures carved from buffalo hide are manipulated against an illuminated cloth screen. The capital of shadow puppetry today is Nakhon Si Thammarat, which has regular performances at its festivals. There are two distinctive shadow-play traditions. *Năng dà·lung* uses delicate puppets manipulated by a single puppet master to tell stories from the Ramakian, while *năng yài* (literally, 'big hide'), uses much larger puppets with several operators, but is sadly a dying art. Both kinds of puppets are popular souvenirs for tourists.

Much of Thai culture and art, particularly literature and dance and a significant amount of language, originally came from India along with Buddhism.

Food & Drink

Eating is one of the highlights of any trip to Thailand, and it doesn't take long to see that the locals are equally enthusiastic about their national cuisine. Thais appear to spend a significant part of their lives snacking and eating, and rightfully so: the spectrum of things to eat in even an average sized Thai city is mind-boggling, and a visit to Thailand's southern provinces will expand your culinary horizons even further (see the boxed text, p47). Such an abundance of eats would result in waistline problems elsewhere, but Thai food, with its fresh ingredients and emphasis on bold tastes, fills diners with flavour rather than bulk.

The closest thing to being Thai without surrendering your passport is to jump headfirst into this jungle of flavour. To guide you, we've put together a primer of the essential ingredients and dishes you're bound to run into along the way.

> Cookbook writer Kasma Loha-Unchit features recipes and other culinary events on her website www.thaifoodand travel.com.

STAPLES & SPECIALITIES
Rice
Thailand has been a leader in rice exports since the 1960s and the quality of Thai rice, according to many discerning Asians, is considered the best there is. Thailand's *kôw hŏrm má·lí* (jasmine rice) is so coveted that there is a steady underground business in smuggling bags of the fragrant grain to neighbouring countries.

Rice is so central to Thai food culture that the most common term for 'eat' is *gin kôw* (consume rice) and one of the most common greetings is *'Gin kôw láa·ou rĕu yang?'* (Have you eaten rice yet?). All dishes eaten with rice – whether curries, stir-fries or soups – are simply classified as *gàp kôw* (with rice).

> Written and photographed by the author of this chapter, RealThai (www .austinbushphotography .com) is one of the few blogs that details food and dining in Thailand.

Two dishes that use rice as a principal ingredient are *kôw pàt* (fried rice), which is found all over the country, and *kôw mòk gài* (chicken biryani), typically a Muslim–Malay dish. A sure sign that the staff at your guesthouse are from the northeastern part of the country is if you spot them eating *kôw nĕe·o* (sticky rice), usually eaten with the hands and accompanied by fried chicken and *sôm·đam* (spicy green-papaya salad).

Noodles
You'll find four basic kinds of noodle in Thailand. Given the Thai fixation with rice, the overwhelming popularity of *gŏo·ay dĕe·o* (rice noodles) is hardly surprising. They're made from pure rice flour mixed with water to form a paste, which is then steamed to form wide, flat sheets. These are then sliced into noodles of varying sizes.

> You eat rice dishes with a spoon and a fork, treating the spoon like the fork and the fork like a knife. Noodle soups and *pàt tai* are the only dishes eaten with chopsticks.

The king of Thai noodledom, *gŏo·ay dĕe·o* comes as part of many dishes. The simplest, *gŏo·ay dĕe·o nám*, is noodles served in a bowl of meat stock along with bits of meat (usually pork), bean sprouts and *pàk chee* (coriander leaf) as garnish. When you order a bowl of noodle soup from a vendor, you'll need to call your noodle size – *sên lék* (flat, thin rice noodles), *sên yài* (flat, wide rice noodles) or *bà·mèe* (egg noodles) – and the meat of your choice. You then flavour the bowl with the four seasonings that appear on the table – a dash of sugar, dried chillies, fish sauce and vinegar. Foreigners think that curries define the national food consciousness, but the humble noodle dish is more emblematic: Thais eat *gŏo·ay dĕe·o* for breakfast and lunch, and as a predinner snack and hangover cure.

Chilli-heads must give *gŏo·ay dĕe·o pàt kêe mow* (drunkard's fried noodles) a try. A favourite lunch or late-night snack, this spicy stir-fry consists of wide rice noodles, fresh basil leaves, chicken or pork, and a healthy dose of chillies.

For foreigners, the most well-known *gŏo·ay dĕe·o* dish is *gŏo·ay dĕe·o pàt tai* (*pàt tai* for short), a plate of thin rice noodles stir-fried with dried or fresh shrimp, bean sprouts, fried tofu, egg and seasonings. On the edge of the plate the cook usually places little piles of ground peanuts and ground dried chilli, along with lime halves and a few stalks of Chinese chives for self-seasoning.

A speciality of southern Thailand, *kà·nŏm jeen* is stark white noodles produced by pushing rice-flour paste through a sieve into boiling water. The noodles are topped with spicy fish curry and loaded up with an assortment of pickled and fresh vegetables.

Finally there's *wún·sên*, an almost clear noodle made from mung-bean starch and water. *Wún·sên* (jelly thread) is used for only a few dishes in Thailand: *yam wún·sên*, a hot and tangy salad made with lime juice, fresh sliced *prík kêe nŏo* (mouse-dropping peppers), fresh shrimp, ground pork and various seasonings; and *'bòo òp wún·sên*, which is bean thread noodles baked in a lidded clay pot with crab and seasonings.

> Despite their importance in modern Thai food, chillies are a relatively new addition to the Thai kitchen, and were brought by Portuguese traders more than 400 years ago.

Curries

For many people, *gaang* (curries; it rhymes with 'gang') are the definitive Thai dish, but few visitors have met the real McCoy. A well-made curry should possess a balance of the four main flavours: salty, fishy, spicy and a little sweet. Usually restaurants with a Western clientele will overdose on coconut milk and sugar to cater to their customers' sweet tooths.

All chilli-based *gaang* start as fresh – not powdered – ingredients that are smashed, pounded and ground in a stone mortar and pestle to form a thick, aromatic and extremely pungent paste. Typical ingredients include dried or fresh chilli, galangal (also known as Thai ginger), lemon grass, kaffir lime

> Curries and soups are generally ladled onto a plate of rice, rather than eaten directly out of the bowl.

CURRYING FAVOUR

Every morning at 4.30am, Paa Som, the owner of a nondescript but popular curry shop in Nakhon Sri Thammarat gets up to prepare a variety of curries, fried dishes, soups and spicy salads. On an average day she'll make immense servings of at least 12 different dishes, which, when finished, will sit in stainless steel bowls for the rest of the day, waiting to be consumed.

This is the typical routine of a curry shop owner in southern Thailand. Due to the importance of curries in southern Thai cooking, *ráhn kôw gaang*, literally 'rice and curry shops', are the most common eating places in this part of the country. Found in virtually every town, *ráhn kôw gaang* can range from proper air-conditioned restaurants to basic roadside shacks, but are always inexpensive and are never far away.

Although the Thai word *gaang* tends to get translated into English as curry, it actually encompasses a variety of dishes that can range from watery soups to thick stews. These dishes are the heart of southern Thai cooking and differ from curries in other parts of the country in several ways. To begin with, southern-style curries are generally much spicier, their curry pastes liberally employing small dried chillies as opposed to the larger and milder ones used elsewhere. Coconut, one of the largest cash crops in southern Thailand, finds its way into many dishes in the form of coconut milk. And many southern Thai curries have a distinct yellow hue, a result of the use of turmeric, a bright orange root.

At Paa Som's stall, you simply point to the two or three dishes you want, and they will be served, usually at room temperature, over a plate of steaming rice. Each table has a small bowl of *prík nám plah*, sliced chillies in fish sauce, if somehow you find the spice lacking. And as an added bonus, Paa Som will also give you a complimentary tray of fresh herbs and vegetables to help soothe the burn of her fiery handiwork.

SOMETHING'S FISHY

Westerners might scoff at the all-too-literal name of this condiment, but for much Thai food, fish sauce is more than just another ingredient, it is *the* ingredient.

Essentially the liquid obtained from salted and fermented fish, fish sauce takes various guises depending on the region. In northeastern Thailand, discerning diners prefer a thick, pasty mash of fermented freshwater fish and sometimes rice. Elsewhere, where people have access to the sea, fish sauce takes the form of a thin liquid extracted from salted anchovies. In both cases the result is highly pungent, generally salty (rather than fishy) in taste, and used in much the same way as the salt shaker is in the West.

---

zest, shallots, garlic, shrimp paste and salt. Certain curries employ dried spices such as coriander seeds or a touch of cumin.

During cooking, most *gaang* pastes are blended in a heated pan with coconut cream, to which the chef adds the rest of the ingredients. These include watery coconut milk, used to thin and flavour the *gaang,* although some recipes omit coconut milk entirely to produce a particularly fiery *gaang* known as *gaang ʾbàh* (forest curry).

Salads

Thai Food, by David Thompson, is widely considered the most authoritative book on Thai cooking, and includes authentic recipes from the country's south.

Standing right alongside *gaang* in terms of Thai-ness are *yam,* the ubiquitous hot and tangy salads combining a blast of lime, chilli and fresh herbs and a choice of seafood, roast vegetables, noodles or meats. Thais prize *yam* dishes so much that they are often eaten on their own, without rice, before the meal has begun. On Thai menus the *yam* section will often be the longest. The usual English menu translation is either 'Thai-style salad' or 'hot and sour salad'.

Lime juice provides the tang, while fresh chillies produce the heat. Other ingredients vary, but there are usually plenty of leafy vegetables and herbs present, including lettuce (often lining the dish) and Chinese celery. Lemon grass, shallots, kaffir lime leaves and mint may also come into play. Most *yam* are served at room temperature or just slightly warmed by any cooked ingredients.

Yam are the spiciest of all Thai dishes, and if you're not so chilli-tolerant, a good *yam* to start off with is *yam wún·sên*: mung bean noodles tossed with shrimp, ground pork, coriander leaves, lime juice and fresh sliced chillies.

Stir-fries & Deep-Fries

The simplest dishes in the Thai culinary repertoire are *pàt* (stir-fries), brought to Thailand by the Chinese, who are famous for being able to stir-fry a whole banquet in a single wok.

The wok and technique of stir-frying were probably brought to Thailand by Chinese immigrants.

The list of Thai dishes that you can *pàt* is seemingly endless. Many are better classified as Chinese, such as *néu·a pàt nám·man hǒy* (beef in oyster sauce). Some are clearly Thai-Chinese hybrids, such as *gài pàt prík kǐng,* in which chicken is stir-fried with ginger, garlic and chillies – ingredients shared by both traditions – but seasoned with fish sauce.

Tôrt (deep-frying in oil) is generally reserved for snacks such as *glôo·ay tôrt* (fried bananas) or *ʾbò·ʾbée·a* (egg rolls). One exception is *ʾblah tôrt* (crisp fried fish). Only a very few dishes require ingredients to be dipped in batter and then deep-fried, including *gài tôrt* (fried chicken) and *gûng chúp ʾbâang tôrt* (batter-fried shrimp).

Soups

Thai soups fall into two broad categories – *dôm yam* (also spelt as *tôm yam*) and *gaang jèut* – which are worlds apart in terms of seasonings. *Dôm yam* is almost always made with seafood, though chicken may also be used. It's often translated on English menus as 'hot and sour Thai soup', although this often leads non-Thais to mistakenly relate the dish to Chinese hot-and-sour soup, which is thinner in texture, milder and includes vinegar. *Ðôm yam* is meant to be eaten with rice, not alone, and the first swallow often leaves the uninitiated gasping for breath.

In contrast, *gaang jèut* (mild soup with vegetables and pork) is a soothing broth seasoned with little more than soy or fish sauce and black pepper. It isn't a very interesting dish by itself, but provides a nice balance when paired with other spicier dishes. It is also a good option if your tummy is feeling tender.

One of the most popular breakfasts in southern Thailand is *kôw yam*, a 'salad' of rice topped with thinly sliced herbs, bean sprouts, dried shrimp, toasted coconut and powdered red chilli served with a sour-sweet fish-based sauce.

Fruit

Thai fruits are so decadent and luscious that some visitors concoct entire meals of the different varieties. Common fruits that are in season all year include *má·prów* (coconut), *fa·ràng* (guava), *kà·nŭn* (jackfruit), *má·kăhm* (tamarind), *sôm* (orange), *má·lá·gor* (papaya), *sôm oh* (pomelo), *đaang moh* (watermelon) and *sàp·Ђà·rót* (pineapple).

Seasonal fruits to look for include: *chom·pôo* (rose apple; April to July), *mang·kút* (mangosteen; April to September), *má·môo·ang* (mango; several varieties and seasons), *ngó* (rambutan; July to September) and *nóy·nàh* (custard apple; July to October).

Thais are among the biggest consumers of garlic in the world.

Sweets

Sweets mostly work their way into the daily Thai diet as between-meal snacks and are typically sold by market or street vendors.

SOUTHERN FLAVOUR

Fans of subtle flavours beware: southern Thai cooking is undoubtedly the spiciest regional cooking style in a country of spicy regional cuisines. The food of Thailand's southern provinces also tends to be very salty, and seafood, not surprisingly, plays an important role, ranging from fresh fish that is grilled or added to soups, to fish or shrimp that have been pickled or fermented and served as sauces or condiments. Two of the principal crops in the south are coconuts and cashews, both of which find their way into a variety of dishes. In addition, southern Thais love their greens, and nearly every meal is accompanied by a platter of fresh herbs and veggies and a spicy 'dip' of shrimp paste, chillies, garlic and lime. Specific southern greens to look out for include *sà·đor* (a pungent green beanlike vegetable), *lôok nee·ang* (a round dark-green bean) and *mét ree·ang* (similar to large, dark-green bean sprouts).

Dishes you are likely to come across include the following:

- *Gaang đai Ђlah* – an intensely spicy and salty fish curry that includes *đai Ђlah* (salted fish stomach); much better than it sounds.
- *Kà·nŏm jeen nám yah* – this dish of fermented rice noodles served with a fiery currylike sauce is always accompanied by a tray of fresh vegetables and herbs.
- *Kôw yam* – this popular breakfast includes rice topped with thinly sliced herbs, bean sprouts, dried shrimp, toasted coconut and powdered red chilli served with a sour-sweet fish-based sauce.
- *Gaang sôm* – known as *gaang lĕu·ang* (yellow curry) in central Thailand, this sour-spicy soup gets its hue from the copious use of turmeric, a root commonly used in southern Thai cooking.
- *Ngóp* – something of a grilled curry, this dish takes the form of a coconut milk and herb paste containing seafood that is wrapped in a banana leaf and grilled until firm.
- *Gài tôrt hàht yài* – the famous deep-fried chicken from the town of Hat Yai gets its rich flavour from a marinade containing dried spices.

Not everything in your bowl of *dôm yam* is edible. Like bay leaves, the ingredients with the texture of bark are only there for flavouring.

Ingredients for many *kŏrng wăhn* (Thai sweets) include grated coconut, coconut milk, rice flour, cooked sticky rice, tapioca, mung-bean starch, boiled taro and fruits. For added texture and crunch some may also contain fresh corn kernels, sugar-palm kernels, lotus seeds, cooked black beans and chopped water chestnuts. Egg yolks are a popular ingredient in Thai sweets, particularly in the ubiquitous *fŏy torng* ('golden threads' that actually look like strands of gold), a sweet of Portuguese origin.

Thai sweets similar to the European concept of 'sweet pastry' are called *kà·nŏm*. Probably the most popular *kà·nŏm* are bite-sized items wrapped in banana or pandanus leaves, especially *kôw dôm mát*, which consists of sticky rice grains steamed with coconut milk inside a banana-leaf wrapper to form a solid, almost toffeelike, mass.

DRINKS
Coffee & Tea

For the best of Lonely Planet's culinary wisdom, seek out *World Food Thailand*, by Joe Cummings.

Thais are big coffee drinkers, and good-quality Arabica and Robusta are cultivated in hilly areas of northern and southern Thailand. The traditional filtering system is nothing more than a narrow cloth bag attached to a steel handle. The bag is filled with ground coffee and hot water poured through, producing *gah·faa tŏong* (traditional filtered coffee) or *gah·faa boh·rahn* (traditional coffee).

Black tea, both local and imported, is available at the same places that serve real coffee. *Chah tai* derives its characteristic orange-red colour from ground tamarind seed added after curing. *Chah rórn* (hot tea), like coffee, will almost always be served with condensed milk and sugar, so specify if you want black tea. Chinese-style tea is *nám chah*. *Chah yen* is a tall glass of Thai iced tea with sugar and condensed milk, while *chah má·now* (chilled black tea) comes without milk, and usually with a slice of lime.

Fruit Drinks

The all-purpose term for fruit juice is *nám* (water/juice) *pŏn·lá·mái* (fruit). When a blender or extractor is used, you've got *nám kán* (squeezed juice), hence *nám sàp·bà·rót kán* is freshly squeezed pineapple juice. *Nám ôy* (sugar-cane juice) is a Thai favourite and a very refreshing accompaniment to *gaang* dishes. A similar juice from the sugar palm, *nám·dahn sòt*,

---

COFFEE, SOUTHERN STYLE

In virtually every town or city in southern Thailand you'll find numerous old-world cafés known locally as *ráhn goh·bêe*. The shops are almost exclusively owned by Thais of Chinese origin, and often seem suspended in time, typically sporting the same décor and menu for decades. Characteristics of *ráhn goh·bêe* include marble-topped tables, antique mugs and dishes, and an almost exclusively male clientele that also seems not to have budged since opening day. Some of the most atmospheric *ráhn goh·bêe* in Thailand can be found in the town of Trang (p359).

The beans used at *ráhn goh·bêe* are sometimes grown abroad, but are roasted domestically, and although they're as black as the night, the drink typically tends to lack body. This may be due to the brewing method, which involves pouring hot water through a wind-socklike piece of cloth that holds the loose grounds. Typically, *goh·bêe* is served over a dollop of sweetened condensed milk and a tablespoon (or more) of sugar in small, handleless glasses. For those lacking a sweet tooth, try *goh·bêe or* (black coffee), or just ask them to hold the sugar. All hot coffee drinks are served with a 'chaser' of weak green tea.

Ráhn goh·bêe are also a great place for a quick bite. Upon arriving at the more traditional ones, you'll be greeted by a tray of steamed Chinese buns or sweet snacks, such as sticky rice wrapped in banana leaf or baked goods.

is also very good and both are full of vitamins and minerals. Mixed fruit blended with ice is *nám 'ɓàn* (mixed juice) as in *nám má·lá·gor 'ɓàn,* a papaya shake.

Beer & Whisky

Advertised with such slogans as *'ɓrà·têht row, bee·a row* (Our Land, Our Beer), the Singha label is considered the quintessential 'Thai' beer by faràng and locals alike. Pronounced 'sing' (not 'sing-*hah*'), it claims about half the domestic market, and has an alcohol content of 6%. Singha is sold in bottles and cans, and is also available on tap as *bee·a sòt* (draught beer) in many pubs and restaurants. Dutch-licensed but Thailand-brewed Heineken and Singapore's Tiger brand are also popular selections. You'll find other, even cheaper, Thai beers in supermarkets, but rarely in restaurants.

Rice whisky is a favourite of the working class because it's more affordable than beer. Most rice whiskies are mixed with distilled sugar-cane spirits and thus have a sharp, sweet taste not unlike rum, with an alcohol content of 35%. The most famous brand, Mekong, costs around 120B for a *glom* (large bottle) or 60B for a *baan* (flask-sized bottle). More popular nowadays is the slightly more expensive Sang Som.

WHERE TO EAT & DRINK

All restaurants, large and small, are referred to by the single Thai term *ráhn ah·hăhn* ('food shop', the term for restaurants). Decoration may be limited to a few beer posters and a small shrine or something more incongruous, such as a faded picture of the Swiss Alps. Fluorescent lighting – cheap and cool – is the norm. Such restaurants typically specialise in a single cuisine, whether local or regional.

At the more generic *ráhn ah·hăhn đahm sàng* (food-to-order shop), cooks can whip up almost any Thai dish you can name, including any kind of rice or noodle dish as well as more complex multidish meals. Most of the standard Thai dishes are available, including those in the *đôm yam, yam* and *pàt* categories. You can recognise this type of restaurant by the raw ingredients displayed out front.

More upmarket restaurants have printed menus, usually with broken English translations, where you'll find tablecloths, air-con and the Western idea of 'ambience'. Average Thais prefer to order their favourite dishes without referring to a menu at all, so these more expensive restaurants only cater to an upper-class clientele with international tastes.

Check out the international message board at www.chowhound.com, where culinary hobbyists post reviews of Thailand's restaurants.

Quick Eats

One of the simplest, most pleasurable venues for dining out in Thailand is the night market, which can vary from a small cluster of metal tables and chairs alongside the road to more elaborate affairs that take up whole city blocks. What they all have in common is a conglomeration of *rót kĕn* (vendor carts) whose owners have decided that a particular intersection or unused urban lot makes an ideal location to set up their mobile kitchens.

There are two types of night markets: the *đà·làht yen* (evening market) sets up just before sunset and stays open until around 9pm or 10pm – possibly later in large cities. The second type is the *đà·làht đôh rûng* (open until dawn), which begins doing business around 11pm and keeps going until sunrise. Typical places to look for both types of night market include in front of day markets, next to bus or train stations and at busy intersections.

Thai Hawker Food, by Kenny Yee and Catherine Gordon, is an illustrated guide to recognising and ordering street food in Thailand.

VEGETARIANS & VEGANS

The website www.happy cow.net has a searchable index of vegetarian restaurants across the world, including entries for Thailand.

The number of vegetarian restaurants in Thailand is increasing, thanks largely to Bangkok's former governor Chamlong Srimuang, whose strict vegetarianism inspired a nonprofit chain of *ráhn ah·hăhn mang·sà·wí·rát* (vegetarian restaurants) in Bangkok and several provincial capitals. The food at these restaurants is usually served buffet-style and is very cheap. Dishes are almost always 100% vegan; that is, no meat, poultry, fish, dairy or egg products have been used in their creation.

Chinese restaurants are also a good bet because many Chinese Buddhists eat vegetarian food during Buddhist festivals. Other easy, though less common, venues for vegetarian meals include Indian restaurants, which usually feature a vegetarian section on the menu.

The phrase 'I'm vegetarian' in Thai is *pŏm gin jair* (for men) or *dì·chăn gin jair* (for women). Loosely translated this means 'I eat only vegetarian food', which includes no eggs and no dairy products – in other words, totally vegan.

HABITS & CUSTOMS

There are no 'typical' times for meals, though the customary noon to 1pm lunch break tends to cluster diners in local restaurants at that hour. Nor are certain genres of food restricted to certain times of day. Practically anything can be eaten first thing in the morning, whether it's sweet, salty or chilli-ridden.

THE MUSLIM INFLUENCE

Muslims are thought to have first visited southern Thailand during the late 14th century. Along with the Koran, they brought with them a meat and dried spice–based cuisine from their homelands in India and the Middle East. Nearly 700 years later, the impact of this culinary commerce can still be felt. While some Muslim dishes such as roti, a fried bread similar to the Indian *paratha*, have changed little, if at all, others such as *gaang mát·sà·màn* are a unique blend of Thai and Indian/Middle Eastern cooking styles. In more recent years, additional Muslim dishes have arrived via contact with Thailand's neighbour to the south, Malaysia.

Typical Muslim dishes include the following:

- *Kôw mòk* – biryani, a dish found across the Muslim world, also has a foothold in Thailand. Here the dish is typically made with chicken and is served with a sweet/sour sauce and a bowl of chicken broth.

- *Sà·đé (satay)* – these grilled skewers of meat probably came to Thailand via Malaysia. The savoury peanut-based dipping sauce is often mistakenly associated with Thai cooking.

- *Má·đà·bà* – known as *murtabak* in Malaysia and Indonesia, these are roti that have been stuffed with a savoury or sometimes sweet filling and fried until crispy.

- *Súp hăhng woo·a* – oxtail soup, possibly another Malay contribution, is even richer and often more sour than the 'Buddhist' Thai *đôm yam*.

- *Sà·làt kàak* – literally 'Muslim salad' (*kàak* is a slightly derogatory word used to describe people or things of Indian and/or Muslim origin), this dish combines iceberg lettuce, hearty chunks of firm tofu, cucumber, hard-boiled egg and tomato, all topped with a slightly sweet peanut sauce.

- *Gaang mát·sà·màn* – 'Muslim curry' is a rich coconut milk–based dish, which, unlike most Thai curries, gets much of its flavour from dried spices. As with many Thai-Muslim dishes, there is an emphasis on the sweet.

Thais tend to avoid eating alone, especially for the evening meal. When forced to fly solo – such as during a lunch break – a single diner usually sticks to one-plate dishes such as fried rice or curry over rice.

If an opportunity presents itself, dining with a group of Thais will reveal more about Thai culture than watching canned classical dance performances. A big group means everyone has a chance to sample several different kinds of dishes. Traditionally, the party orders a curry, a fish, a stir-fry, a *yam,* a vegetable dish and a soup, taking care to balance cool and hot, sour and sweet, salty and plain.

When serving yourself from a common platter, put no more than one spoonful onto your plate at a time. Sometimes serving spoons are provided. If not, you simply dig in with your own spoon.

It is polite to leave a little rice on your plate to signal that you are full. To clean your plate to indicate that you are still hungry. This is why Thais tend to over-order at social occasions – the more food that is left, the more generous the host appears.

> Meals in southern Thailand are often accompanied by a complimentary tray of fresh herbs and vegetables and a fiery shrimp paste–based dipping sauce.

COOKING COURSES

The standard one-day course features a shopping trip to a local market to choose ingredients, followed by preparation of curry pastes, soups, curries, salads and desserts. Some of the better cooking classes in Bangkok and southern Thailand include the following:

Boathouse (p299) Phuket Town, Phuket.
Blue Elephant Cooking School (p89) In Bangkok.
KATI Culinary (p144) Ko Chang.
Koh Chang Thai Cooking School (p144) Ko Chang.
Krabi Thai Cookery School (p334) Ao Nang, Krabi.
Pum Restaurant & Cooking School (p346) Ko Phi-Phi.
Pum Thai Cooking School (p299) Hat Patong, Phuket.
Same Same Lodge Thai Cooking School (p217) Ko Pha-Ngan.
Samui Institute of Thai Culinary Arts (p197) Ko Samui.
Silom Thai Cooking School (p89) Bangkok.
Time for Lime (p353) Ko Lanta.

> *It Rains Fishes: Legends, Traditions and the Joys of Thai Cooking,* by Kasma Loha-Unchit, is both a cookbook and a charming culinary text.

EAT YOUR WORDS

Many travellers never experience the full wonder of Thai cuisine because they have difficulty negotiating the language barrier. The following guide should help you negotiate your way around some of the more common culinary options. Dishes are listed with Thai script and a transliterated pronunciation guide.

Useful Phrases

EATING OUT

restaurant
    ráhn ah·hǎhn   ร้านอาหาร

Can I see the menu please?
    kǒr doo rai gahn ah·hǎhn dâi mǎi?   ขอดูรายการอาหารได้ไหม

Do you have a menu in English?
    mee rai gahn ah·hǎhn ben pah·sǎh   มีรายการอาหารเป็น
    ang·grìt mǎi?   ภาษาอังกฤษไหม

I'd like ...
| *kŏr ...* | ขอ... |

What is that?
| *nán à·rai?* | นั่นอะไร |

I don't eat ...
pŏm/dì·chăn gin ... mâi dâi		ผม/ดิฉันกิน...ไม่ได้
meat	*néu·a sàt*	เนื้อสัตว์
chicken	*gài*	ไก่
fish	*blah*	ปลา
seafood	*ah·hăhn tá·lair*	อาหารทะเล
pork	*mŏo*	หมู

I'm allergic to ...
| *pŏm/dì·chăn páa ...* | ผม/ดิฉันแพ้... |

Does it contain ...?
| *nêe sài ... măi?* | นี่ใส่...ไหม |

Not too spicy please.
| *kŏr mâi pèt mâhk.* | ขอไม่เผ็ดมาก |

Can I have a (beer) please?
| *kŏr (bee·a) nòy* | ขอ(เบียร์) หน่อย |

Can you please bring me ...?
kŏr ... dâi măi?		ขอ...ได้ไหม
some water	*nám nòy*	น้ำหน่อย
some rice	*kôw nòy*	ข้าวหน่อย
a fork	*sôrm*	ส้อม
a glass	*gâa·ou*	แก้ว
a knife	*mêet*	มีด
a napkin	*grà·dàht chét bàhk*	กระดาษเช็ดปาก
a plate	*jahn blòw*	จานเปล่า
a spoon	*chórn*	ช้อน

This food is ...
ah·hăhn née ...		อาหารนี้
delicious	*a·ròy*	อร่อย
cold	*yen*	เย็น
undercooked	*mâi sùk*	ไม่สุก

Please bring the bill.
| *kŏr bin nòy* | ขอบิลหน่อย |

Food Glossary
MENU DECODER

ah·hăhn tá·lair	อาหารทะเล	**seafood**
gûng tôrt	กุ้งทอด	fried prawns
blah jĕe·an	ปลาเจี่ยน	whole fish cooked in ginger, onions and soy sauce

blah mèuk pàt pèt	ปลาหมึกผัดเผ็ด	spicy fried squid
blah brêe·o wǎhn	ปลาเปรี้ยวหวาน	sweet and sour fish
blah tôrt	ปลาทอด	crisp-fried fish

gaang	**แกง**	**curries**
gaang gà·rèe gài	แกงกะหรี่ไก่	mild, Indian-style curry with chicken
gaang kěe·ow wǎhn blah/gài/néu·a	แกงเขียวหวานปลา/ไก่/เนื้อ	green curry with fish/chicken/beef
gaang mát·sà·màn gài/néu·a	แกงมัสมั่นไก่/เนื้อ	Muslim-style curry with chicken/beef and potatoes
gaang pèt gài/ néu·a/mǒo	แกงเผ็ดไก่/เนื้อ/หมู	red curry with chicken/beef/pork
gaang pá·naang	แกงพะแนง	Penang curry (red curry with sweet basil)

kôw	**ข้าว**	**rice**
kôw man gài	ข้าวมันไก่	boned, sliced Hainan-style chicken with rice
kôw mǒo daang	ข้าวหมูแดง	red pork with rice
kôw nǎh gài	ข้าวหน้าไก่	chicken with sauce over rice
kôw nǎh bèt	ข้าวหน้าเป็ด	roast duck over rice
kôw pàt mǒo/ gài/gûng	ข้าวผัดหมู/ไก่/กุ้ง	fried rice with pork/chicken/shrimps

gǒo·ay đěe·o/bà·mèe	**ก๋วยเตี๋ยว/บะหมี่**	**noodles**
bà·mèe nám/hâang	บะหมี่น้ำ/แห้ง	wheat noodles with vegetables and meat in broth/dry
gǒo·ay đěe·o nám/hâang	ก๋วยเตี๋ยวน้ำ/แห้ง	rice noodles with vegetables and meat in broth/dry
pàt see·éw	ผัดซีอิ๊ว	fried noodles with soy sauce
pàt tai	ผัดไทย	thin rice noodles fried with tofu, vegetables, egg and peanuts

súp	**ซุป**	**soups**
gaang jèut	แกงจืด	mild soup with vegetables and pork
kôw đôm blah/gài/gûng	ข้าวต้มปลา/ไก่/กุ้ง	rice soup with fish/chicken/shrimps
đôm kàh gài	ต้มข่าไก่	soup with chicken, galangal root and coconut
đôm yam gûng	ต้มยำกุ้ง	prawn and lemon grass soup with mushrooms

ah·hǎhn èun	**อาหารอื่น**	**other dishes**
gài pàt bai gà·prow	ไก่ผัดใบกะเพรา	chicken fried with basil
gài pàt mét má·môo·ang	ไก่ผัดเม็ดมะม่วง	chicken fried with cashews

gài tôrt	ไก่ทอด	fried chicken
kài jee·o	ไข่เจียว	plain omelettes
kài yát sâi	ไข่ยัดไส้	omelette with vegetables and pork
kà·nŏm jeen nám yah	ขนมจีนน้ำยา	noodles with fish curry
gée·o gròrp	เกี๊ยวกรอบ	fried wonton
lâhp gài/néu·a	ลาบไก่/เนื้อ	spicy chicken/beef salad
néu·a pàt nám man hŏy	เนื้อผัดน้ำมันหอย	beef in oyster sauce
bò·bée·a	เปาะเปี๊ยะ	spring rolls
pàt pàk roo·am	ผัดผักรวม	stir-fried mixed vegetables
sà·đé (satay)	สะเต๊ะ	skewers of barbecued meat
sôm đam	ส้มตำ	spicy green papaya salad
tôrt man blah	ทอดมันปลา	fried fish cakes with cucumber sauce
yam néu·a	ยำเนื้อ	hot and sour, grilled beef salad
yam wún sên	ยำวุ้นเส้น	cellophane noodle salad

néu·a láa ah·hăhn tá·lair	**เนื้อและอาหารทะเล**	**meat & seafood**
néu·a	เนื้อ	beef
gài	ไก่	chicken
boo	ปู	crab
bèt	เป็ด	duck
blah	ปลา	fish
mŏo	หมู	pork
ah·hăhn tá·lair	อาหารทะเล	seafood
gûng	กุ้ง	shrimp/prawn
blah mèuk	ปลาหมึก	squid

pàk	**ผัก**	**vegetables**
má·rá jeen	มะระจีน	bitter melon
gà·làm blee	กะหล่ำปลี	cabbage
dòrk gà·làm	ดอกกะหล่ำ	cauliflower
đaang gwah	แตงกวา	cucumber
má·kĕu·a	มะเขือ	eggplant
grà·tee·am	กระเทียม	garlic
pàk gàht	ผักกาด	lettuce
tòo·a fàk yow	ถั่วฝักยาว	long bean
grà·jée·ap	กระเจี๊ยบ	okra
hŏo·a hŏrm	หัวหอม	onion
tòo·a lí·sŏng	ถั่วลิสง	peanuts
man fà·ràng	มันฝรั่ง	potato
fák torng	ฟักทอง	pumpkin
pèu·ak	เผือก	taro
má·kĕu·a têt	มะเขือเทศ	tomato

pŏn·lá·mái	ผลไม้	**fruit**
glôo·ay	กล้วย	banana
má·prów	มะพร้าว	coconut
nóy·nàh	น้อยหน่า	custard apple
tú·ree·an	ทุเรียน	durian
fa·ràng	ฝรั่ง	guava
kà·nŭn	ขนุน	jackfruit
má·now	มะนาว	lime
má·môo·ang	มะม่วง	mango
mang·kút	มังคุด	mangosteen
sôm	ส้ม	orange
má·lá·gor	มะละกอ	papaya
sàp·bà·rót	สับปะรด	pineapple
sôm oh	ส้มโอ	pomelo
ngó	เงาะ	rambutan
má·kăhm	มะขาม	tamarind
đaang moh	แตงโม	watermelon

kŏrng wăhn	ของหวาน	**sweets**
glôo·ay bòo·at chee	กล้วยบวชชี	banana in coconut milk
săng·kà·yăh má·prów	สังขยามะพร้าว	coconut custard
môr gaang	หม้อแกง	egg custard
glôo·ay kàak	กล้วยแขก	fried, Indian-style banana
kôw nĕe·o daang	ข้าวเหนียวแดง	sticky rice with coconut cream
săng·kà·yăh	สังขยา	Thai custard
đà·gôh	ตะโก้	Thai jelly with coconut cream

krêu·ang dèum	เครื่องดื่ม	**beverages**
bee·a	เบียร์	beer
kòo·at	ขวด	bottle
nám kòo·at/deum	น้ำขวด	bottled drinking water
nám chah	น้ำชา	Chinese tea
gah·faa tŏong (go·bée)	กาแฟถุง (โกปี๊)	coffee (traditional filtered)
gah·faa rórn	กาแฟร้อน	hot coffee with milk and sugar
gâa·ou	แก้ว	glass
nám kăang	น้ำแข็ง	ice
oh·lée·ang	โอเลี้ยง	iced coffee with sugar, no milk
nom jèut	นมจืด	milk
nám blòw	น้ำเปล่า	plain water
nám soh·dah	น้ำโซดา	soda water
chah rórn	ชาร้อน	tea with milk and sugar
chah dam rórn	ชาดำร้อน	hot black tea
wai	ไวน์	wine

Environment

THE LAND

Thailand's odd shape – bulky and wide up north, with a long pendulous arm draping to the south – has often been compared to the head of an elephant. Roughly the size of France, about 517,000 sq km, Thailand stretches an astounding 1650km along a north–south axis and experiences an extremely diverse climate, including monsoons from both the southwest and northwest. The north of the country rises into high forested mountains, while the south consists of a long ridge of limestone hills, covered in tropical rainforest.

Bound to the east by the shallow Gulf of Thailand and to the west by the Andaman Sea, an extension of the Indian Ocean, Thailand possesses one of the most alluring coastlines in the world, with exquisitely carved limestone formations above water and tremendously rich coral reefs below. Hundreds of tropical islands of all shapes and sizes adorn the coast, from flat sand bars covered in mangroves to looming karst massifs licked by azure waters and ringed by white sand beaches. Both coasts have extensive coral reefs, particularly around the granitic Surin Islands (p274) and Similan Islands (p279) in the Andaman Sea. More reefs and Thailand's most dramatic limestone islands sit in Ao Phang-Nga (p281) near Phuket. The west coast is of particular interest to divers because the waters are stunningly clear and extremely rich in marine life.

WILDLIFE

With its diverse climate and topography, it should come as no surprise that Thailand is home to a remarkable diversity of flora and fauna. What is more surprising is that Thailand's environment is still in good shape, particularly considering the relentless development going on all over the country; although see also opposite on endangered species and p62 on marine environmental issues.

Animals

Animals that live on the coasts and islands of Thailand must adapt to shifting tides and the ever-changing mix of salt and freshwater. Rather than elephants and tigers, keep your eyes open for smaller creatures, like the odd little mudskipper, a fish that leaves the water and walks around on the mud flats when the tide goes out; or the giant water monitor, a fearsome 350cm lizard that climbs and swims effortlessly in its search for small animals.

Without a doubt you will see some of the region's fabulous birdlife – Thailand is home to 10% of the world's bird species – especially sandpipers and plovers on the mud flats, and herons and egrets in the swamps. Look overhead for the sharply attired, chocolate brown and white Brahminy kite, or scan low-lying branches for one of the region's many colourful kingfishers. You are likely to spot a troop of gregarious and noisy crab-eating macaques, but don't be surprised to see these monkeys swimming from shore. With luck you may glimpse a palm civet, a complexly marbled catlike creature, or a serow, the reclusive 'goat-antelope' that bounds fearlessly among inaccessible limestone crags.

The oceans on either side of the Thai peninsula are home to hundreds of species of coral, and the reefs created by these tiny creatures provide the perfect living conditions for countless species of fish, crustaceans and tiny invertebrates. You can find one of the world's smallest fish (the 10mm-long goby) or the largest (an 18m-long whale shark), plus reef denizens such as

The famous white sands of Thailand's beaches are actually tiny bits of coral that have been defecated by coral-eating fish.

If anyone in Thailand comes across a white elephant, it must be reported to the Bureau of the Royal Household, and the King will decide whether it meets the criteria to be a royal white elephant.

The estuarine crocodile was one of Thailand's most formidable predators, reaching over 6m in length and 1000kg, but they are now thought to be extinct in the kingdom.

IT'S ALL CORAL

If there's one thing visitors to Thailand notice right away, it's the dramatically sculpted lime-stone formations towering over land and water throughout the country. These formations are the fossilised remains of sea shells and coral reefs, and their widespread presence in Thailand demonstrates that much of the region lay underwater more than 200 million years ago. Pushed upward by the crushing forces of two earth plates colliding 30 million years ago, these limestone formations are now exposed to rain and waves that dissolve calcium carbonate in the limestone creating bizarre towers and caves of all sizes. Sometimes the roof of a limestone chamber will collapse, forming a hidden *hôrng* (also spelt *hong*) that lets in sunlight or sea water.

Not only is Thailand the site of a massive fossil reef, it is also one of the best places in the world to see living corals (over 250 species of coral can be found on the Andaman coast alone). Whether old or young, reefs are composed of the skeletal remains of tiny marine organisms that extract calcium carbonate from sea water to build mineral homes. Coral reefs are biologically complex and diverse habitats for countless sea creatures. See p62 for the environmental issues surrounding coral degradation.

---

clownfish, parrotfish, wrasse, angelfish, triggerfish and lionfish. Deeper waters are home to larger species such as grouper, barracuda, sharks, manta rays, marlin and tuna. You might also encounter turtles, whales and dolphins.

ENDANGERED SPECIES

Thailand is a signatory to the UN Convention on International Trade in Endangered Species (Cites) but the enforcement of these trade bans is notoriously lax – just walk around the animal section of Bangkok's Chatuchak Weekend Market (p108) to see how openly the rules are flouted. Due to habitat loss, pollution and poaching, a depressing number of Thailand's mammals, reptiles, fish and birds are endangered, and even populations of formerly common species are diminishing at an alarming rate. Rare mammals, birds, reptiles, insects, shells and tropical aquarium fish are routinely smuggled out to collectors around the world or killed to make souvenirs for tourists.

Many of Thailand's marine animals are under threat, including whale sharks, seen in Thai waters in ever-decreasing numbers, and sea turtles, which are being wiped out by hunting for their eggs, meat and shells. Many other species of shark are being hunted to extinction for their fins, which are used to make shark-fin soup.

The rare dugong (also called manatee or sea cow), once thought extinct in Thailand, is now known to survive in a few small pockets, mostly around Trang in southern Thailand, but is increasingly threatened by habitat loss and the lethal propellers of tourist boats.

The Thai government is slowly recognising the importance of conservation, perhaps due to the efforts and leadership of Queen Sirikit, and many of the kingdom's zoos now have active breeding and conservation programs. Wildlife organisations such as the Phuket Gibbon Rehabilitation Centre (p324) are working to educate the public about native wildlife and have initiated a number of wildlife rescue and rehabilitation projects.

Bird-lovers will definitely want to carry *A Guide to Birds of Southeast Asia* by Craig Robson.

When threatened, the lionfish spreads its set of multicoloured fins into an impressive mane, giving fair warning not to touch this poisonous fish.

Plants

Southern Thailand is chock-full of luxuriant vegetation, thanks to its two monsoon seasons. The majority of forests away from the coast are evergreen rainforests, while trees at the ocean edge and on limestone formations are stunted due to lack of fresh water and exposure to harsh minerals.

The most beautiful shoreline trees are the many species of palm trees occurring in Thailand, including some found nowhere else in the world. All

Palm trees have been around for over 100 million years.

have small tough leaves with characteristic fanlike or featherlike shapes that help dissipate heat and conserve water. Look for the elegant cycad palm on limestone cliffs, where this 'mountain coconut' *(ʼblông)* grows from cracks in the complete absence of soil. Collected for its beauty, this common ornamental plant is disappearing from its wild habitat.

Thailand is also home to nearly 75 species of salt-tolerant mangroves – small trees highly adapted to living at the edge of salt water. Standing tiptoe-like on clumps of tall roots, mangroves perform a vital ecological function by trapping sediments and nutrients, and by buffering the coast from the fierce erosive power of monsoons. This habitat serves as a secure nursery for the eggs and young of countless marine organisms, yet Thailand has destroyed at least 50% of its mangrove swamps to make way for shrimp farms and big hotels.

NATIONAL PARKS

National parks in Thailand are a huge draw for beach visitors. The popular island getaways of Ko Chang and Ko Samet sit just off the mainland along the eastern gulf coast. Ko Tarutao Marine National Park is remote and undeveloped for real back-to-nature vacations. Ao Phang Nga, north of Phuket, competes for one of the most photogenic awards: limestone cliffs jut out of the aquamarine water while knotted roots of mangroves cling to thick mud flats. Similan Islands and Surin Islands National Parks, off the coast of Phuket, have some of the world's best diving.

Islands along the Andaman coast are one of the few places in the world where you can find living reefs growing on the edges of limestone cliffs that were themselves once coral reefs.

Approximately 13% of Thailand is covered by 112 national parks and 44 wildlife sanctuaries, which isn't bad going by international standards. Of Thailand's protected areas, 18 parks protect islands and mangrove environments. Thailand's parks and sanctuaries contain more than 850 resident and migratory species of birds and dwindling numbers of tigers, clouded leopards, kouprey, elephants, tapirs, gibbons and Asiatic black bears, among other species.

Despite promises, official designation as a national park or sanctuary does not always guarantee protection for habitats and wildlife. Local farmers, well-monied developers, and other business interests easily win out, either legally or illegally, over environmental protection in Thailand's national parks. Islands that are technically exempt from development often don't adhere to the law and there is little government muscle to enforce regulations. Ko Chang, Ko Samet and Ko Phi-Phi are all curious examples of national parks with development problems.

For detailed descriptions of all of Thailand's protected areas, the definitive text is *National Parks and Other Wild Places of Thailand*, by Stephen Elliot. The book has loads of colour pictures and covers conservation projects around the country.

Parks charge entry fees of 200B per adult and 100B for children under 14 years. These rates were recently doubled, then rescinded on a case-by-case basis, so what you pay may differ from park to park. In some cases the **Royal Forestry Department** (Map pp70-1; ☎ 0 2561 4292/3; www.forest.go.th/default_e.asp; 61 Th Phahonyothin, Chatuchak, Bangkok 10900) rents out accommodation; make reservations in advance as this is a popular option for locals. All parks are best visited in the dry season, particularly marine national parks which can have reduced visibility in the water during the monsoon.

ENVIRONMENTAL ISSUES

Environmental issues in Thailand are a mixed bag, with many issues kept (perhaps intentionally) off the radar screen of tourists. Simple issues, such as pollution and development, are easily observed in Thailand because basic infrastructure, such as sewage treatment and garbage collection, isn't always in place and land use is at a different developmental stage than in Western countries. But consider a hidden issue such as Thailand's phenomenal economic boom, which most visitors take for granted, and peel back the

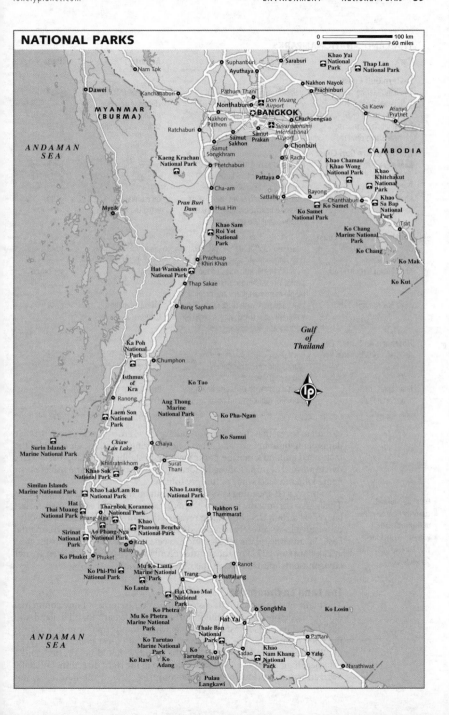

NATIONAL PARKS

0 — 100 km
0 — 60 miles

Nam Tok
Suphanburi
Saraburi
Khao Yai National Park
Thap Lan National Park

Dawei
Ayuthaya
Nakhon Nayok
Prachinburi

Kanchanaburi
Pathum Thani
Don Muang Airport

MYANMAR (BURMA)
Nonthaburi
BANGKOK
Chachoengsao
Sa Kaew
Aranya Prathet

Nakhon Pathom
Suvarnabhumi International Airport

ANDAMAN SEA
Ratchaburi
Samut Sakhon
Samut Prakan
Chonburi
CAMBODIA

Kaeng Krachan National Park
Samut Songkhram
Si Racha
Khao Chamao/ Khao Wong National Park
Khao Khitchakut National Park

Phetchaburi
Pattaya
Rayong
Chanthaburi
Khao Sa Bap National Park

Cha-am
Sattahip
Ko Samet
Trat

Pran Buri Dam
Hua Hin
Ko Samet National Park

Myeik
Khao Sam Roi Yot National Park
Ko Chang Marine National Park

Ko Chang

Prachuap Khiri Khan
Ko Mak

Hat Wanakon National Park
Ko Kut

Thap Sakae

Bang Saphan

Gulf of Thailand

Ka Poh National Park
Chumphon

Isthmus of Kra
Ko Tao

Ranong
Ang Thong Marine National Park
Ko Pha-Ngan

Laem Son National Park
Chaiya
Ko Samui

Surin Islands Marine National Park
Chiaw Lan Lake
Khirirathnikhom

Surat Thani

Similan Islands Marine National Park
Khao Sok National Park

Hat Thai Muang National Park
Khao Lak/Lam Ru National Park
Khao Luang National Park

Tharnbok Korannee National Park
Nakhon Si Thammarat

Phang-Nga

Sirinat National Park
Khao Phanom Bencha National Park

Ao Phang-Nga National Park
Krabi

Railay

Ko Phuket
Phuket

Ranot

Ko Phi-Phi National Park
Mu Ko Lanta Marine National Park
Trang
Phattalung

Ko Lanta

Hat Chao Mai National Park
Songkhla
Ko Losin

Ko Phetra
Mu Ko Phetra Marine National Park

ANDAMAN SEA
Hat Yai
Pattani

Ko Tarutao Marine National Park
Thale Ban National Park

Ko Rawi · Ko Adang
Ko Tarutao
Sadao
Khao Nam Khang National Park
Yala

Satun
Narathiwat

Pulau Langkawi

THAILAND'S NATIONAL PARKS

Park	Features	Activities	Page
Eastern Gulf Coast			
Ko Chang Marine National Park	archipelago marine park with virgin rainforests, waterfalls beaches and coral reefs	snorkelling, diving, elephant trekking, hiking	p138
Ko Samet National Park near-shore coral reefs	marine park with beaches; boat trips, sailboarding	snorkelling, diving,	p129
Northwestern Gulf Coast			
Kaeng Krachan National Park	mainland park with waterfalls and forests; plentiful birdlife and jungle mammals	bird-watching	see boxed text, p168
Khao Sam Roi Yot National Park	coastal park with caves, mountains cliffs and beaches; serow, Irrawaddy dolphins and 300 bird species	cave tours, bird-watching, kayaking	p180
Southwestern Gulf Coast			
Ang Thong Marine National Park	40 scenic tropical islands with coral reefs, lagoons and limestone cliffs	sea kayaking, hiking, snorkelling	p240
Khao Luang National Park	mainland park with forested mountain peaks, streams and waterfalls; jungle mammals, birds and orchids	hiking	see boxed text, p249
Khao Sok National Park	mainland park with thick rainforest, waterfalls and rivers; tigers, monkeys, *rafflesia* and 180 bird species	hiking, elephant trekking, tubing	p244
Northern Andaman Coast			
Ao Phang-Nga National Park	coastal bay with limestone cliffs, islands and caves; coral reefs and mangroves	sea kayaking, snorkelling, diving	p283
Khao Lak/Lam Ru National Park	coastal park with cliffs and beaches hornbills, monkeys and bears	hiking, boat trips	p276

curtain to reveal that the energy for this explosive growth comes from massive dams being built in Laos and other neighbouring countries. Or consider the fact that Thailand's marine parks were first established to stop destructive dynamite and cyanide fishing by local villagers, but those same fish are now being killed to feed scads of hungry tourists.

So many well-meaning laws have been put on the books that it might seem Thailand is turning the corner towards greater ecological consciousness, but lawyers at a 2008 UN conference revealed that corruption and lack of political resolve have severely hampered efforts to enforce these environmental laws. Meanwhile, plans for gigantic projects, such as the new deep-sea port at Pak Bara (see p372) on the southern Andaman coast, suggest even greater environmental destruction in the near future.

For a colourful and comprehensive overview of Thailand's natural ecosystems check out *Wild Thailand* by Belinda Steward-Cox.

The Land Environment

The main area in which Asia exceeds the West in terms of environmental damage is deforestation, though current estimates are that Thailand still has about 25% of its forests remaining, which stands up favourably against the UK's dismal 5%. The government's National Forest Policy, introduced in 1985, recommended that 40% of the country should be forested, and a complete logging ban in 1989 was a big step in the right direction. Officially decreed 'conservation forests' now comprise 79% of the land area, but

Park	Features	Activities	Page
Northern Andaman Coast (continued)			
Laem Son National Park	coastal and marine park with 100km of mangroves; jungle and migratory birds	bird-watching, boat trips	p270
Similan Islands Marine National Park	marine park with granite islands; coral reefs and seabirds; underwater caves	snorkelling, diving	p279
Sirinat National Park	coastal park with casuarina-backed beaches; turtles and coral reefs	walking, snorkelling, diving	p322
Surin Islands Marine National Park	granite islands; coral reefs, whale sharks and manta rays	snorkelling, diving	p274
Southern Andaman Coast			
Hat Chao Mai National Park	coastal park with sandy beaches, mangroves, lagoons and coral islands; dugong and mangrove birds	sea kayaking, snorkelling, diving	p363
Ko Phi-Phi Marine National Park	archipelago marine park with beaches, lagoons and sea-cliffs; coral reefs and whale sharks	sea kayaking, snorkelling, diving	p343
Khao Phanom Bencha National Park	mainland mountain jungle with tumbling waterfalls; monkeys	hiking	see boxed text, p330
Ko Tarutao Marine National Park	archipelago marine park with remote jungle islands and tropical beaches; monkeys, jungle mammals and birds	snorkelling, hiking, diving	p374
Mu Ko Lanta Marine National Park	archipelago marine park with scenic beaches; coral reefs and reef sharks	sea kayaking, elephant trekking, hiking, snorkelling, diving	p352
Mu Ko Phetra Marine National Park	rarely visited archipelago marine park; dugong, birds and coral reefs	sea kayaking, snorkelling	see boxed text, p374
Tharnbok Korannee National Park	coastal park with mangrove forests and limestone caves; monkeys, orchids and seabirds	sea kayaking	p332

predictably the logging ban simply shifted the need for natural resources elsewhere. Illegal logging persists in Thailand, plus a great number of logs are being illegally slipped over the border from neighbouring countries, putting a huge burden on countries with lax enforcement. Raw building materials, once provided by cheap lumber, are now replaced with cement obtained by dynamiting Thailand's spectacular karst formations.

Despite Thailand being a signatory to Cites, all sorts of land species are still smuggled out of Thailand either alive or as body parts for traditional Chinese medicines. Tigers may be protected by Thai law, but the kingdom remains the world's largest exporter of tiger parts to China (tiger penis and bone are believed to have medicinal effects and to increase libido). Other animal species are hunted (often illegally) to make souvenirs for tourists, including elephants, jungle spiders, giant insects and butterflies; and along the coast clams, shells and puffer fish.

The government has cracked down on restaurants serving *ah·hăhn Ъàh* (jungle food), which includes endangered wildlife species such as barking deer, bear, pangolin, gibbons, civet and gaur. A big problem is that national park officials are underpaid and undertrained, yet they are expected to confront armed poachers and mercenary armies funded by rich and powerful godfathers. Rising unemployment after the economic crisis of 1997 has made profitable wildlife poaching all the more attractive.

For ideas on ecotourism destinations and venues, see www.thailand.com /travel/eco/eco.htm.

The widely touted idea that ecotourism can act as a positive force for change has been extensively put to the test in Thailand. In some instances tourism has definitely had positive effects. The expansion of Thailand's national parks has largely been driven by tourism. In Khao Yai National Park, all hotel and golf-course facilities were removed to reduce damage to the park environment. As a result of government and private-sector pressure on the fishing industry, coral dynamiting has been all but eliminated in the Similan and Surin Islands, to preserve the area for tourists.

However, tourism can be a poison chalice. Massive developments around and frequently in national parks have ridden roughshod over the local environment in their rush to provide bungalows, luxury hotels, beach-bars and boat services for tourists. Ko Phi-Phi (p343) and Ko Samet (p129) are two national parks where business interests have definitely won out over the environment. In both cases, the development began in areas set aside for *chow lair* (sea gypsies, the semi-nomadic people who migrate up and down the coast; see boxed text, p353). Ko Lipe in Ko Tarutao Marine National Park (p374) and Ko Muk in Hat Chao Mai National Park (p364) now seem to be heading the same way.

Rubbish and sewage are growing problems in all populated areas, even more so in heavily touristed areas where an influx of visitors overtaxes the local infrastructure. For example, 80% of the freshwater wells at Ko Phi-Phi proved to be contaminated in recent tests due to the sheer number of tourists (and in 2004 all of Thailand's beaches ranked far below satisfactory health standards for similar reasons). One encouraging development was the passing of the 1992 Environmental Act, which set environmental quality standards, designated conservation and pollution-control areas, and doled out government clean-up funds. Pattaya built its first public wastewater treatment plant in 2000 and conditions have improved ever since.

Ordinary Thai people are increasingly environmentally aware and many are taking direct action to prevent environmental damage, stopping developers from accessing forests and demonstrating against bad environmental practices. The filming and destruction of a favourite beach by the movie *The Beach* in Ko Phi-Phi National Park triggered demonstrations around the country and the filming of the US TV show *Survivor* in Ko Tarutao Marine National Park provoked a similar outcry. The construction of a petroleum pipeline to Songkhla in 2002 created a remarkable level of grass-roots opposition by ordinary village people.

A group of ecologically engaged Buddhist monks, popularly known as Thai Ecology Monks, have courageously set one of the best examples by using their peaceful activism to empower local communities in their fight against monolithic projects. One such project was saving trees around the Elephant Nature Park in Chiang Mai.

The Marine Environment

Thailand's coral reef system, including the Andaman coast from Ranong to northern Phuket and the Surin and Similan Islands, is one of the world's most diverse. Some 600 species of coral reef fish, endangered marine turtles and other rare creatures call this coastline home.

The 2004 tsunami caused high-impact damage to about 13% of the Andaman coral reefs. However, damage from the tsunami was relatively minor compared to the ongoing environmental degradation that accompanies an industrialised society. It is estimated that about 25% of Thailand's coral reefs have died as a result of industrial pollution and that the annual loss of healthy reefs will continue at a rapid rate. Even around the dive centre of Phuket, dead coral reefs are visible on the northern coast. The biggest threat to corals is sedimentation from coastal development: new condos, hotels,

---

Producers of the Hollywood movie *The Beach* had a protected beach in Ko Phi-Phi National Park bulldozed for the film, while paying the lead actor US$2 million for his role in the film.

Students at Dulwich International College in Phuket collected 5000kg of garbage from the beach in a single day; help them out by picking up trash whenever you can.

roads and houses. High levels of sediment in the water stunts the growth of coral. Other common problems include pollution from anchored tour boats or other marine activities, rubbish and sewage dumped directly into the sea, and agricultural and industrial run-off. Even people urinating in the water as they swim creates by-products that can kill sensitive coral reefs.

The environmental wake-up call from the tsunami emphasised the importance of mangrove forests, which provide a buffer from storm surges. Previously mangroves were considered wastelands and were indiscriminately cut down. It is estimated that about 80% of the mangrove forests lining the gulf coast and 20% on the Andaman coast have been destroyed for conversion into small-scale fish farms, tourist development or to supply the charcoal industry. Prawn farms constitute the biggest threat because Thailand is the world's leading producer of black tiger prawns, and the short-lived, heavily polluting farms are built in pristine mangrove swamps at a terrific environmental and social cost. Many are run by a mafia of foreign investors and dodgy politicians. These farms are such big business (annual production in Thailand has soared from 900 tonnes to 277,000 tonnes in the past 10 years) that protesting voices are rapidly silenced.

Contributing to the deterioration of the overall health of the ocean are Thailand and its neighbours' large-scale fishing industries, frequently called the 'strip-miners of the sea'. Fish catches have declined by up to 33% in the Asia-Pacific region in the past 25 years and the upper portion of the Gulf of Thailand has almost been fished to death. Most of the commercial catches are sent to overseas markets and rarely see a Thai dinner table. The seafood sold in Thailand is typically from fish farms, another large coastal industry for the country.

Fragile mud flats are so full of life that on a low tide it is common to see a hundred local villagers out gathering seafood for their meals.

Making a Difference

It may seem that the range of environmental issues in Thailand is too overwhelming, but there is actually much that travellers can do to minimise

---

RESPONSIBLE TOURISM

What can the average visitor to Thailand do to minimise the impact of tourism on the environment? While many of Thailand's environmental issues are dependent upon the enforcement of environmental regulations, there are small measures you can take that will leave less of a footprint during a visit.

■ Reduce your garbage. Buy drinking water in returnable glass bottles, which are available in some restaurants. Alternatively, reuse plastic bottles by refilling them when drinking water is provided from returnable containers.

■ Refuse the plastic straws and plastic bags that are provided every time you buy a drink in Thailand.

■ Don't toss cigarette butts into the ocean or on the beach; dispose of them in designated receptacles.

■ Try to double up with other travellers for snorkelling outings to conserve fuel.

■ Avoid restaurants serving exotic wildlife species, including endangered marine life, bird's nest soup and shark-fin soup. Report offending restaurants to the Tourist Authority of Thailand (TAT) or Royal Forest Department.

■ On boat trips or visits to islands – including while diving – collect any rubbish you see and dispose of it properly on the mainland.

■ Never buy souvenirs made from rare plants or animals, including anything made from ivory, mounted giant insects, sea shells, turtle products and shark teeth.

the impact of their visits, or to even leave a positive impact. The way you spend your money has a profound influence on the kingdom's economy and on the pocketbooks of individual businesses. Ask questions up front and take your money elsewhere if you don't like the answers. For instance, a number of large-scale resorts that lack road access transport clients across fragile mud flats on tractors (a wantonly destructive practice), so when booking a room inquire into transport to the hotel. Of the region's countless dive shops, some are diligent about minimising the impact their clients have on the reefs; however, if a dive shop trains and certifies inexperienced divers over living reefs, rather than in a swimming pool, then it is causing irreparable harm to the local ecosystem. As a rule, do not touch or walk on coral, monitor your movements so you avoid accidentally sweeping into coral, and do not harass marine life (any dead puffer fish you see on the beach probably died because a diver poked it until it inflated).

A growing number of overseas tourism companies now insist that Thailand's tourism operators have environmental policies in place before doing business with them.

Make a positive impact on Thailand by checking out one of the many environmental and social groups working in the kingdom. If you do some research and make arrangements before arriving, you may connect with an organisation that matches your values, but here are some favourites to start the juices flowing.

The **Wild Animal Rescue Foundation of Thailand** (Map pp70-1; WAR; ☎ 0 2712 9715; www.warthai.org; 65/1 3rd fl, Soi 55, Th Sukhumvit, Bangkok 10110) is one of the leading advocates for nature conservation in Thailand and currently runs four wildlife sanctuaries that use volunteers to rehabilitate and return former pets to the wild.

The **Bird Conservation Society of Thailand** (Map pp70-1; ☎ 0 2691 4816; www.bcst.or.th /eng/; 43 Vipawadi 16/Th Vipawadi-Rangsit, Sam sen nok, Din Daeng, Bangkok 10400) provides a plethora of information about the birds of Thailand, offering field trip reports, sightings of rare birds, bird festivals and bird surveys.

Make a big change by checking out the **Sanithirakoses-Nagapateepa Foundation** (www.sulak-sivaraksa.org), which was started by the 1995 Alternative Nobel Prize winner, Sulak Sivaraksa. This umbrella group is associated with numerous environmental and social justice groups in Thailand including the Foundation for Children, Forum of the Poor, the Thai-Tibet Centre, and Pun Pun, an organic farm and sustainable living centre. These groups offer countless opportunities to help empower local communities, and to get involved in issues important to the people of Thailand. They have also started an alternative college called Spirit in Education Movement (SEM) that offers a spiritually based, ecologically sound alternative to mainstream education.

Other groups promoting environmental issues in Thailand:

Thailand Environment Institute (☎ 0 2503 3333; www.tei.or.th)

Wildlife Friends of Thailand (☎ 0 3245 8135; www.wfft.org)

World Wildlife Fund Thailand (☎ 0 2524 6168; www.wwfthai.org)

Bangkok

Unlike Thailand's famously chilled islands and beaches, there's something about Bangkok that never fails to get the blood pumping. This big, crowded, polluted and seemingly chaotic Asian mega-city is many things to many people, but you wouldn't call it boring.

For the visitor, the impact is immediate. Your first move is likely to be joining the cacophonous arteries of metal that pump – just barely – almost eight million people around the region's biggest city. Everywhere you look the streets and waterways are alive with commuters. Schoolkids run without sweating, smiling vendors create mouth-watering food in push-away kitchens, monks rub bare shoulders with fashionistas in air-conditioned malls… Whether it's in one of Bangkok's famous golden temples, riding in the back of its roguish túk-túk or just walking down the street, something odd and inexplicable will happen at the most unexpected time. Hey, was that an elephant with a tail light?

If all you want to do is kick back on a peaceful beach, at first glance Bangkok will seem like a transit burden full of concrete towers instead of palm trees. But once you tire of sea breezes, you'll better appreciate Bangkok's conveniences and breakneck pace. With its mix of the historic and contemporary, and some of the most delicious and best-value eating on earth, the City of Angels is surely one of the most invigorating in Asia.

HIGHLIGHTS

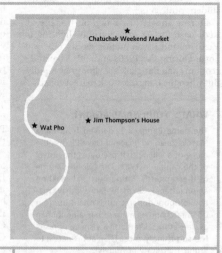

- Getting lost in quirky **Wat Pho** (p83), with its serene reclining Buddha, then finding yourself a massage

- Touring **Jim Thompson's House** (p87), one of the best-preserved examples of traditional Thai art and architecture

- Stocking up on exotic souvenirs at the vast **Chatuchak Weekend Market** (p108)

- Taking the lift to one of Bangkok's unique rooftop bars for a **sky-high sundowner** (p102) and unbeatable sunset views.

- Eating delicious **Thai cuisine** (p98) in what is one of Asia's best food cities.

★ Chatuchak Weekend Market

★ Jim Thompson's House

★ Wat Pho

- DRY SEASON: NOVEMBER-APRIL
- WET SEASON: MAY-OCTOBER

HISTORY

As capital cities go, Bangkok is a fairly recent invention. Following the sacking of Ayuthaya by the Burmese (p24), King Taksin established the Thai capital at Thonburi, on the west bank of Mae Nam Chao Phraya (Chao Phraya River). But in 1782 King Rama I founded the Chakri dynasty (p24) and promptly moved his capital across the river to the modest village of Bang Makok (current-day Bangkok).

Buddhist relics from Ayuthaya, Thonburi and Sukhothai were re-enshrined in towering new temples and the city expanded rapidly around the royal compound at Ko Ratanakosin. Under Rama IV (King Mongkut) and his son Rama V (King Chulalongkorn), Bangkok and the country began to modernise, adopting and integrating Western customs, styles and architecture. Europeans flocked to the city to negotiate trade contracts and increase their influence in the region.

In 1932 Bangkok saw the end of absolute monarchy and the beginnings of a turbulent political era. From 1932 to the present day, Bangkok has witnessed 19 coup attempts, half of which half have resulted in a change of government. The latest, in September 2006, saw Prime Minister Thaksin Shinawatra ousted without a shot being fired following months of protests in the capital. However, previous political ructions were not so peaceful and on several occasions mass demonstrations have ended in the military massacring student protesters.

During the 1970s, Bangkok became an R&R base for American troops fighting in Vietnam and its reputation as 'sin city' was born. During the 1980s and '90s Thailand's economy and Bangkok's skyline grew rapidly. But when the Bangkok stock market collapsed in 1997 the city, the country and indeed most of the region ground to an economic halt.

After some rocky years, Bangkok has bounced back and is now every bit the modern Asian metropolis, if not quite the 'world city' it so wants to be. Despite the uncertainty following the 2006 coup d'etat and economic sluggishness, construction is progressing apace and cranes are prominent on the skyline. Large infrastructure projects, such as the Skytrain and Metro urban railways and the Suvarnabhumi International Airport, have all made the city a less-congested and more enjoyable place.

ORIENTATION

Bangkok is a vast sprawling mess of a city and the urban chaos can be pretty intimidating at first. Concrete towers as far as the eye can see make it difficult to discern any real centre. But the capital does have several distinctly different districts. For the sake of simplicity, however, it makes sense to divide the city into two areas: 'old Bangkok', which has most of the royal palaces and historic temples, and 'new Bangkok', which is dominated by towering skyscrapers, shopping malls and a growing number of luxury hotels.

Old Bangkok straddles the Mae Nam Chao Phraya, with the original royal centre of Ko Ratanakosin occupying a man-made island on the east bank and the former capital of Thonburi now serving as a suburb on the west bank. To the north of the royal district, still on Ko Ratanakosin, is Banglamphu. This is one of Bangkok's oldest neighbourhoods and was once a home to officials and members of the royal court. Today it's the main budget travellers' centre in Bangkok with an increasing local art and bar scene. Northeast of Ko Ratanakosin is Dusit, the new royal district. The riverside district south of Ko Ratanakosin is home to the Indian neighbourhood of Phahurat and Bangkok's Chinatown, near the main train station of Hualamphong.

Surrounding the old city and stretching for at least 20km in every direction, 'new Bangkok' is a modern creation and quite unfathomable amounts of concrete, divided by massive congested highways and soaring flyovers. It's best to think of this part of the City of Angels in terms of its main streets. Th Charoen Krung runs south from Chinatown along the eastern edge of Mae Nam Chao Phraya. Running east from this road are Th

---

WHAT'S YOUR NAME AGAIN?

The name Bangkok is derived from Bang Makok, meaning 'Place of Olive Plums', the name of a village that pre-dates the arrival of the capital in 1782. The full official title of the capital is 'Krungthep mahanakhon amon rattanakosin mahintara ayuthaya mahadilok popnopparat ratchathani burirom udomratchaniwet mahasathan amonpiman avatansathit sakkathattiya visnukamprasit'. Not surprisingly, most Thais abbreviate it to Krung Thep (City of Angels).

BANGKOK IN ...

Two Days

In two days you can explore Bangkok's famous sights: the **Grand Palace & Wat Phra Kaew** (p83); **Wat Pho** (p83), home to the largest reclining Buddha in Thailand; and missile-shaped **Wat Arun** (p84). If you are jet lagged on day two, get up early and head to **Lumphini Park** (p87) to see the locals practising t'ai chi. Then chase away the heatstroke with a visit to the shopping centres on Th Phra Ram I and Th Ploenchit. Don't forget to follow the Thai crowds to the busy **Erawan Shrine** (p86). In the afternoon, visit **Jim Thompson's House** (p87) for an introduction to traditional Thai architecture. Take in the sunset from one of the **sky-high bars** (p102), before finding somewhere with better food for a lot less money for dinner.

Four Days

With more time, factor in a visit to the **National Museum** (p84) then the **amulet market** (p86), and take the **Chinatown Walking Tour** (p88). Take a detour up to Dusit to see **Vimanmek Mansion Museum** (p85), built entirely from golden teak, and get out on the river in a long-tail or the ferry. After dark, head to Th Sukhumvit to experience modern Bangkok at one of the fashionable restaurants or clubs, such as **Bed Supperclub** (p103). If you're here on the weekend juggle this plan to fit in the **Chatuchak Weekend Market** (p108)

Surawong (Surwongse) and Th Silom, which are lined with hotels, restaurants, shopping centres and an eye-popping dose of sleaze, and then Th Sathon, which adds embassies and consulates to the hotel mix.

Head north of the Silom neighbourhood along Th Phayathai or Th Ratchadamri and you'll reach Th Phra Ram I and the Siam Square and Th Ploenchit shopping districts. East of here Th Sukhumvit hosts hotels, restaurants and a rather seedy reputation at its start, before becoming more sophisticated and expensive east of Soi 21 (Soi Asoke).

Bangkok's Suvarnabhumi International Airport is about 30km east of the centre, while the old Don Muang airport is about 25km north and has a lot of (but not all) domestic flights to island and beach destinations.

Maps

From the moment you enter Thailand – literally right after you've passed immigration – you'll see your first free maps. Get used to it – Thailand is full of them. Quality varies between useful and utter rubbish, but unless you're planning to explore off the beaten track they should be good enough.

There are also several maps for sale that are worth your money. One that is often imitated but never equalled is *Nancy Chandler's Map of Bangkok* (www.nancychandler.net; 250B), a colourful hand-drawn map with useful inset panels for Chinatown, Th Sukhumvit and Chatuchak Weekend Market. To master

the city's bus system, purchase Roadway's *Bangkok Bus Map* (150B). For visitors who consider eating to be sightseeing, check out Ideal Map's *Good Eats* series, which has mapped mom-and-pop restaurants in three of Bangkok's noshing neighbourhoods.

If travelling to districts outside central Bangkok, Thinknet's *Bangkok City Atlas* is a wise investment for 250B.

INFORMATION
Bookshops

Bangkok is well-stocked with bookshops selling new titles in English and, less often, other languages. Virtually every major mall has branches of **Asia Books** (www.asiabook.com), **Kinokuniya** (www.kinokuniya.com), **Bookazine** (www.bookazine.co.th) and/or **B2S** (www.b2s.co.th). Tourist areas also have second-hand bookstores, and those on Th Khao San have the most diverse range of titles in the country (though they're not all that cheap). Recommended bookshops include:

Asia Books (www.asiabook.com) Soi 15 (Map p82; 221 Th Sukhumvit, Soi 15); Siam Discovery Center (Map pp80-1; 4th fl, Th Phra Ram I)

Dasa Book Café (Map p82; ☎ 0 2661 2993; btwn Soi 26 & 28, Th Sukhumvit).

Kinokuniya (☎ 0 2255 9834) Emporium (Map p82; 3rd fl, 622 Th Sukhumvit); Siam Paragon (Map pp80-1; 4th fl, Siam Paragon, Th Phra Rama I)

Shaman Bookstore (Map pp74-5; ☎ 0 2629 0418; D&D Plaza, 68-70 Th Khao San & 127 Th Tanao, Banglamphu) Used books galore.

Emergency

For an ambulance, call one of the hospitals listed under Medical Services (right).

Fire (☎ 199)

Police (☎ 191) Ordinary Thai police don't usually speak English.

Tourist Police (☎ 1155; ⊗ 24hr) An English-speaking unit that handles crime involving tourists, including gem scams. It can also act as a bilingual liaison with the regular police.

Immigration

For visa extensions or applications, visit the **Immigration Office** (Map pp72–3; ☎ 0 2287 3101-10; Th Sathon Tai, 507 Soi Suan Phlu; ⊗ 8.30am-4.30pm Mon-Fri, 8.30am-noon Sat). Most applications and extensions require two photos and a photocopy of the photo and visa pages on your passport. See p402 for details.

Internet Access

Bangkok has literally hundreds of internet cafés and plenty of wi-fi hotspots where you can get online free (or for the price of a coffee). Internet cafés come and go so we haven't recommended specific places. Rates are generally pretty cheap, and charges are similar within certain neighbourhoods. For example, Th Khao San and around have some of the cheapest rates in town, starting at about 40B an hour; 60B to 120B an hour is common elsewhere. Most internet cafés can also print and upload digital camera files, but fewer have CD-burning capabilities. You'll find independent internet cafés or guesthouse terminals along Th Sukhumvit and Th Silom, and in all the big shopping centres.

Almost every hotel listed in this chapter offers some level of internet access, from in-room wi-fi to a lonely machine in the corner of the lobby. Prices are also diverse, ranging from free (in many midrange places) to outrageous in some top-end places; check rates before you make a booking. Free wi-fi is available in a growing number of cafés, including chains such as Gloria Jean and Starbucks.

Media

Bangkok has well-established English-language media. The *Bangkok Post* (www.bangkokpost.net) is the major daily broadsheet, with local and international news as well as articles on culture, entertainment, dining and events. The *Nation* (www.nationmultimedia.com) is now a business paper published in conjunction with a free paper called *Daily Xpress*. The *International Herald Tribune* is widely available, as are all major international magazines.

Medical Services

Bangkok is the leading health-care centre in the region and the better hospitals have become major centres of elective 'medical tourism'. They can also handle medical and dental emergencies.

Bangkok Christian Hospital (Map pp78–9; ☎ 0 2235 1000-07; www.bkkchristianhosp.th.com; 124 Th Silom)

Bangkok Hospital (Map pp70–1; ☎ 0 2310 3000; www.bangkokhospital.com; 2 Soi 47, Th Phetburi Tat Mai, Bangkapi)

BNH Hospital (Map pp78–9; ☎ 0 2686 2700; www.bnhhospital.com; 9 Th Convent)

Bumrungrad International Hospital (Map p82; ☎ 0 2667 1000; www.bumrungrad.com; 33 Soi 3, Th Sukhumvit)

Money

You won't need a guide to find an ATM in Bangkok – they're everywhere. Bank ATMs accept major international credit cards and many will also cough up cash for accounts linked to the Cirrus and Plus networks. In tourist areas, such as the Siam Square shopping district and Th Khao San, you'll often find small money-exchange counters outside banks; these can change cash and cheques in major currencies and are typically open from about 9am or 10am to 8pm daily.

Post

Services at the huge **main post office** (Map pp78–9; Th Charoen Krung; ⊗ 8am-8pm Mon-Fri, 8am-1pm Sat & Sun) include poste restante and packaging within the main building. Do not send money or valuables via regular mail. The easiest way to get here is via Chao Phraya express boat to Tha Si Phraya.

There are convenient **post office branches** (⊗ 8am-5pm Mon-Fri, 9am-noon Sat) on Th Rambutri, opposite Wat Bowonniwet (Map pp74–5), and on the alley immediately north of Th Ratchadamnoen Klang, just east of Th Tanao (Map pp74–5).

Telephone

Many Bangkok internet cafés have Skype and this or similar programs are easily the cheapest way to make international calls; see p399 for more details. Internet cafés often also have their own phones with competitive rates, starting at about 10B a minute to Europe, North America and Australia. The online *Yellow Pages* (www .yellowpages.co.th) can be handy. For information on mobile phones, see p399. If you need a new mobile phone, **MBK** (Mahboonkrong Shopping Center; Map pp80-1; 4th fl, Th Phra Ram I) has millions of them. Staff can also 'unlock' phones here.

Communications Authority of Thailand (CAT; Map pp78-9; ☎ 0 2614 1000; Th Charoen Krung; ☷ 8am-8pm) Small, quiet, air-conditioned international call centre outside the main post office.

Telephone Organization of Thailand (TOT; Map pp80-1; ☎ 0 2251 1111; Th Ploenchit; Skytrain Chitlom) For long-distance calls.

Toilets

If you don't want to pee against a tree like the túk-túk (pronounced đúk đúk; three-wheeled motorcycle) drivers, use a public toilet in a shopping centre, hotel or fast-food restaurant. Shopping centres might charge 1B to 2B for a visit; some newer shopping centres have toilets for the disabled. In modern Bangkok squat toilets are positively difficult to find – expect to be greeted by a throne.

Tourist Information

Bangkok has two organisations that handle tourism matters: TAT for countrywide information, and Bangkok Tourist Division for city-specific information. Note that these offices do not make travel arrangements. Also be aware that travel agents in the train station and near tourist centres co-opt TAT as part of their name to lure in commissions.

Targeting the young ones, *Guru* is a lifestyle insert in the Friday edition of the *Bangkok Post*. For new restaurants, current happy hours, band dates and which DJs are in town, there are two good-quality independent publications: the free and irreverent weekly *BK Magazine* (www.bkmagazine .com), and the monthly *Bangkok 101* (www .bangkok101.com), which has photo features and handy reviews of sights, restaurants, nightclubs and theatres; it costs 100B.

Bangkok Tourist Division (Map pp74-5; ☎ 0 2225 7612-4; www.bangkoktourist.com; 17 Th Phra Athit; ☷ 8am-7pm Mon-Fri, 9am-5pm Sat & Sun) Immediately south of Saphan Phra Pinklao, it's fantastically well organised with hundreds of brochures and free booklets. Green kiosks around town are less useful, but do have maps. Look for the symbol of a mahout on an elephant.

TAT (for assistance 8am-8pm ☎ 1672; www.tourism thailand.org) Head Office (Map pp72-3; ☎ 0 2250 5500; 1600 Phetburi Tat Mai; ☷ 8.30am-4.30pm); Banglamphu (Map pp74-5; ☎ 0 2283 1555; cnr Th Ratchadamnoen Nok & Th Chakrapatdipong; ☷ 8.30am-4.30pm) opposite the boxing stadium; Suvarnabhumi International Airport (☎ 0 2134 4077; 2nd fl, btwn Gate 2 & 5; ☷ 8am-4pm).

Travel Agencies

Travel agents along Th Khao San and other streets where tourists gather often offer heavily discounted plane tickets, but there are plenty of sharks out there so be careful. Flight tickets will usually be OK, but unbelievably cheap tickets to the islands will often prove to be scams; see the boxed text, p83 for more scams information. Generally, it's best to buy long-distance bus and train tickets directly at stations instead of travel agents.

Reliable agents include:

Diethelm Travel (Map pp72-3; ☎ 0 2255 9150; www .diethelm-travel.com; 140/1 Th Withayu, Kian Gwan Bldg)

STA Travel (Map pp78-9; ☎ 0 2236 0262; www.statravel .com; 14th fl, Wall Street Tower, 33/70 Th Surawong; Silom)

DANGERS & ANNOYANCES

As you might expect for a city of seven million, Bangkok has its fair share of con artists, many of whom specifically target foreigners. Most of the scams involve touts who try to lure foreigners into jewellery and tailor shops in exchange for a commission, the cost of which will be tacked on to your bill. For more information, see the boxed text, p83.

Although the city may seem entirely lawless, the police discriminately enforce certain rules on those who can pay the fine. That means you. Don't litter (even cigarette butts), jaywalk (at least in front of the brown-suits) or cut down trees (tempting as it may seem).

Scams

The most common con artists are the taxi and túk-túk drivers who steer foreigners towards 'gem sales' or promotions at souvenir shops. The offer of a cheap ride with a short stop at a gem shop will always result in a drawn-out attempt to separate you from your money – see p108 for more on buying gems.

Be wary of smartly dressed men who approach you asking where you're from and where you're going. Rather than becoming your new and exotic Thai friend, they will almost certainly be trying to con you. Don't

(Continued on page 83)

BANGKOK

GREATER BANGKOK

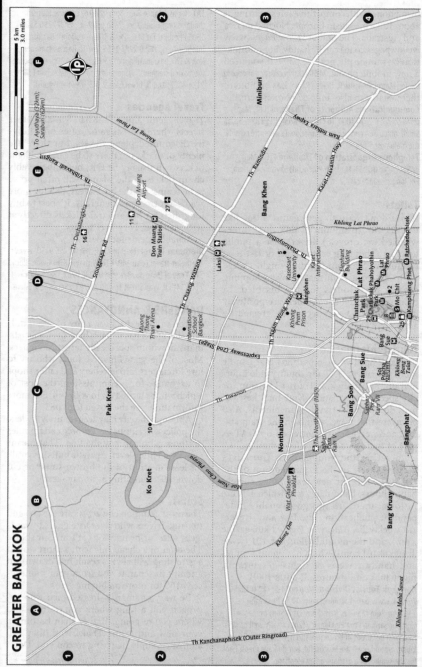

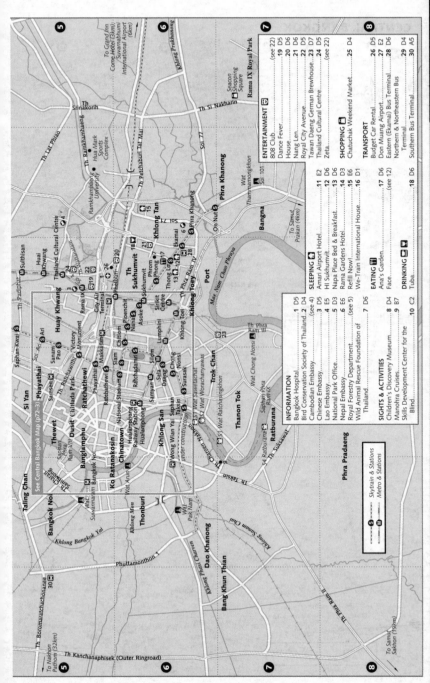

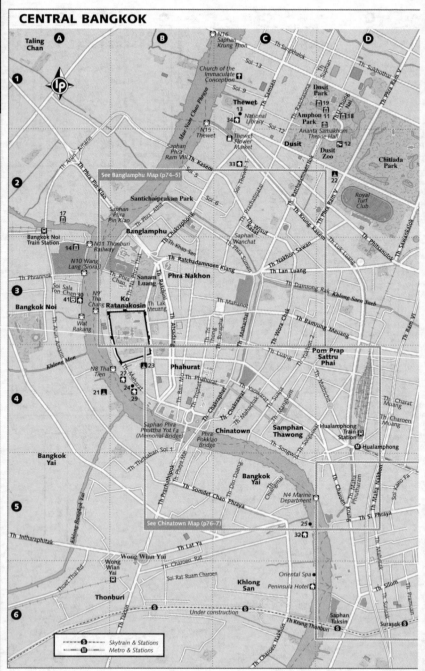

CENTRAL BANGKOK

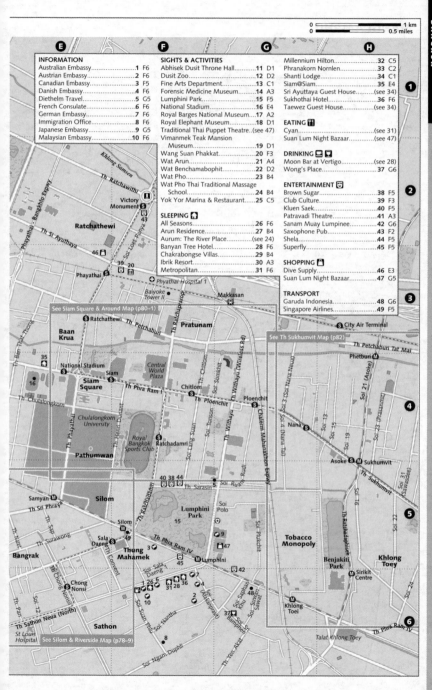

INFORMATION
Australian Embassy.....................1 F6
Austrian Embassy.......................2 F6
Canadian Embassy......................3 F5
Danish Embassy..........................4 F6
Diethelm Travel..........................5 G5
French Consulate........................6 F6
German Embassy.........................7 F6
Immigration Office......................8 F6
Japanese Embassy.......................9 G5
Malaysian Embassy....................10 F6

SIGHTS & ACTIVITIES
Abhisek Dusit Throne Hall.........11 D1
Dusit Zoo.................................12 D2
Fine Arts Department................13 C1
Forensic Medicine Museum........14 A3
Lumphini Park..........................15 F5
National Stadium......................16 E4
Royal Barges National Museum...17 A2
Royal Elephant Museum............18 D1
Traditional Thai Puppet Theatre..(see 47)
Vimanmek Teak Mansion
    Museum...............................19 D1
Wang Suan Phakkat.................20 F3
Wat Arun.................................21 A4
Wat Benchamabophit...............22 D2
Wat Pho..................................23 B4
Wat Pho Thai Traditional Massage
    School.................................24 B4
Yok Yor Marina & Restaurant....25 C5

SLEEPING
All Seasons...............................26 F6
Arun Residence........................27 B4
Aurum: The River Place..........(see 24)
Banyan Tree Hotel....................28 F6
Chakrabongse Villas..................29 B4
Ibrik Resort..............................30 A3
Metropolitan............................31 F6

Millennium Hilton.....................32 C5
Phranakorn Nornlen..................33 C2
Shanti Lodge............................34 C1
Siam@Siam..............................35 E4
Sri Ayuttaya Guest House.......(see 34)
Sukhothai Hotel........................36 F6
Taewez Guest House.............(see 34)

EATING
Cyan....................................(see 31)
Suan Lum Night Bazaar.........(see 47)

DRINKING
Moon Bar at Vertigo..............(see 28)
Wong's Place............................37 G6

ENTERTAINMENT
Brown Sugar............................38 F5
Club Culture............................39 F3
Kluen Saek..............................40 F5
Patravadi Theatre.....................41 A3
Sanam Muay Lumpinee..............42 G6
Saxophone Pub........................43 F2
Shela.......................................44 F5
Superfly...................................45 F5

SHOPPING
Dive Supply.............................46 E3
Suan Lum Night Bazaar............47 G5

TRANSPORT
Garuda Indonesia.....................48 G6
Singapore Airlines....................49 F5

BANGLAMPHU

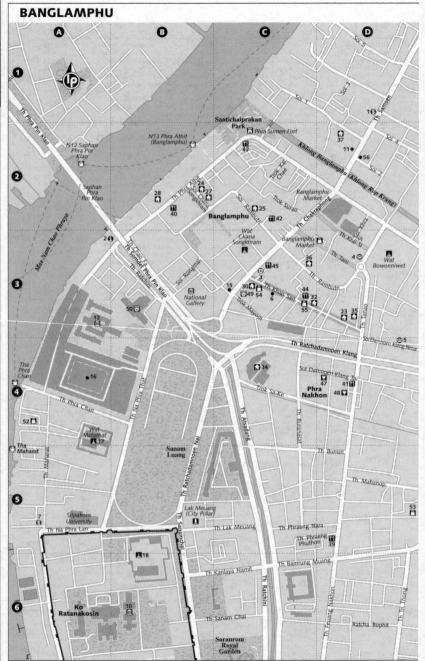

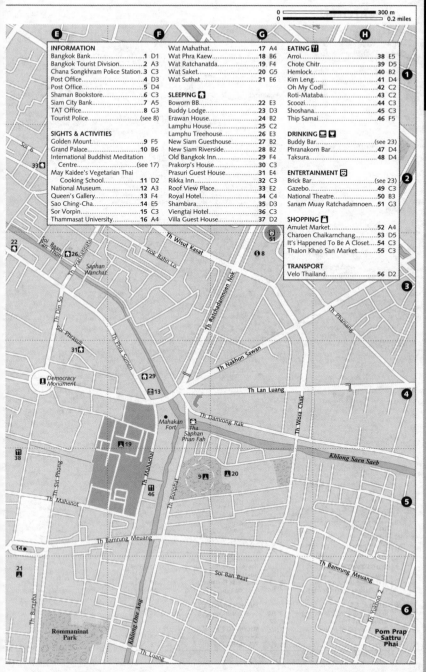

INFORMATION
Bangkok Bank...........................1 D1
Bangkok Tourist Division............2 A3
Chana Songkhram Police Station..3 C3
Post Office...............................4 D3
Post Office...............................5 D4
Shaman Bookstore.....................6 C3
Siam City Bank.........................7 A5
TAT Office................................8 G3
Tourist Police........................(see 8)

SIGHTS & ACTIVITIES
Golden Mount...........................9 F5
Grand Palace...........................10 B6
International Buddhist Meditation
  Centre...............................(see 17)
May Kaidee's Vegetarian Thai
  Cooking School....................11 D2
National Museum......................12 A3
Queen's Gallery.......................13 F4
Sao Ching-Cha.........................14 E5
Sor Vorpin..............................15 C3
Thammasat University...............16 A4

Wat Mahathat.........................17 A4
Wat Phra Kaew........................18 B6
Wat Ratchanatda......................19 F4
Wat Saket..............................20 G5
Wat Suthat.............................21 E6

SLEEPING
Boworn BB..............................22 E3
Buddy Lodge...........................23 D3
Erawan House..........................24 B2
Lamphu House.........................25 C2
Lamphu Treehouse....................26 E3
New Siam Guesthouse................27 B2
New Siam Riverside...................28 B2
Old Bangkok Inn.......................29 F4
Prakorp's House.......................30 C3
Prasuri Guest House..................31 E4
Rikka Inn................................32 C3
Roof View Place.......................33 E2
Royal Hotel............................34 C4
Shambara..............................35 D3
Viengtai Hotel........................36 C3
Villa Guest House.....................37 D2

EATING
Arroi....................................38 E5
Chote Chitr............................39 D5
Hemlock...............................40 B2
Kim Leng...............................41 D4
Oh My Cod!............................42 C2
Roti-Mataba...........................43 C2
Scoozi..................................44 C3
Shoshana..............................45 C3
Thip Samai.............................46 F5

DRINKING
Buddy Bar..........................(see 23)
Phranakorn Bar.......................47 D4
Taksura................................48 D4

ENTERTAINMENT
Brick Bar...........................(see 23)
Gazebo................................49 C3
National Theatre.....................50 B3
Sanam Muay Ratchadamnoen...51 G3

SHOPPING
Amulet Market........................52 A4
Charoen Chaikarnchang...........53 D5
It's Happened To Be A Closet.....54 C3
Thalon Khao San Market..........55 C3

TRANSPORT
Velo Thailand.........................56 D2

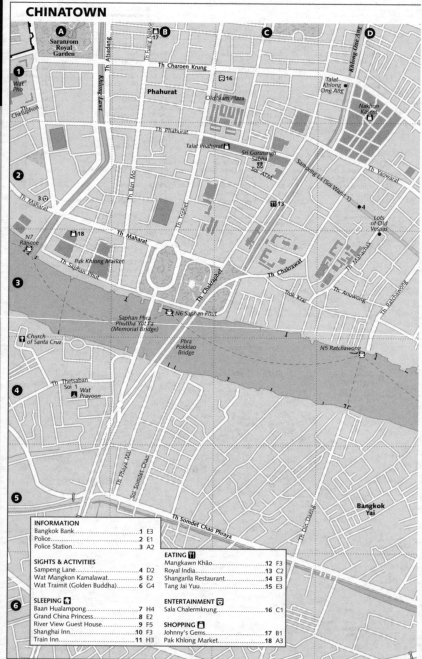

CHINATOWN

INFORMATION	
Bangkok Bank	1 E3
Police	2 E1
Police Station	3 A2

SIGHTS & ACTIVITIES	
Sampeng Lane	4 D2
Wat Mangkon Kamalawat	5 E2
Wat Traimit (Golden Buddha)	6 G4

SLEEPING 🛏	
Baan Hualampong	7 H4
Grand China Princess	8 E2
River View Guest House	9 F5
Shanghai Inn	10 F3
Train Inn	11 H3

EATING 🍴	
Mangkawn Khåo	12 F3
Royal India	13 C2
Shangarila Restaurant	14 E3
Tang Jai Yuu	15 E3

ENTERTAINMENT 🎭	
Sala Chalermkrung	16 C1

SHOPPING 🛍	
Johnny's Gems	17 B1
Pak Khlong Market	18 A3

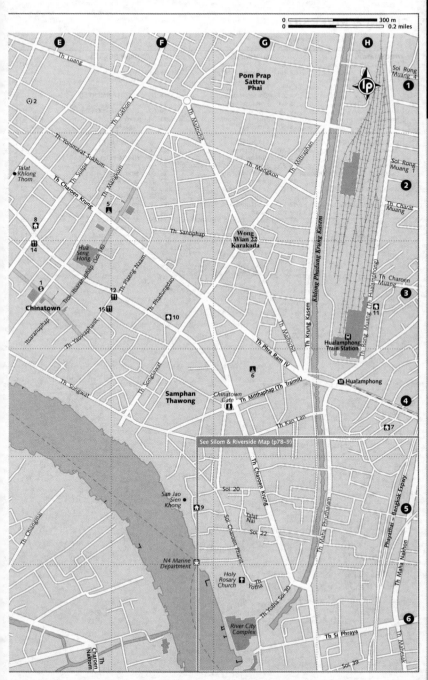

SILOM & RIVERSIDE

INFORMATION
Bangkok Christian Hospital	1	G3
BNH Hospital	2	H4
Communications Authority of Thailand Office	3	B3
French Embassy	4	A4
Main Post Office	5	B4
Myanmar Embassy	6	E6
Singapore Embassy	7	G5
STA Travel	8	G2

SIGHTS & ACTIVITIES
Blue Elephant Thai Cooking School	(see 23)	
H Gallery	9	E5
Loy Nava	10	A3
Queen Saovabha Memorial Institute (Snake Farm)	11	G2
Silom Thai Cooking School	12	E5
Sri Mariamman Temple (Wat Phra Si Maha Umathewi)	13	D4
Wan Fah	(see 10)	

SLEEPING
Dusit Thani Hotel	14	H3
La Résidence Hotel	15	E3
Lub*D	16	E3
New Road Guesthouse	17	B4
Oriental Hotel	18	A4
P&R Residence	19	A3
Rose Hotel	20	G2
Triple Two Silom	21	D4
Urban Age	22	G3

EATING
Blue Elephant	23	D6
Chennai Kitchen	24	D5
Home Cuisine Islamic Restaurant	25	A4
Khrua Aroy Aroy	26	D4
Le Bouchon	27	G3
Le Normandie	(see 18)	
Mizu's Kitchen	28	G3
Ran Nam Tao Hu Yong Her	29	F5
Scoozi	30	F3
Soi Pradit Day & Night Market	31	D4
Somboon Seafood	32	E3

DRINKING
Molly Malone's	33	H3
Sirocco & Sky Bar	34	B5
Telephone	35	G3

ENTERTAINMENT
DJ Station	36	H3
G.O.D (Guys On Display)	37	H3
Lucifer	38	G3
Tapas Room	39	G3

SHOPPING
House of Chao	40	E4
Niks/Nava Import Export	41	E4
River City	42	A2
Silom Village Trade Centre	43	D4
Sunny Camera	44	B4
Sunny Camera	45	F4
Thai Home Industries	46	B4

TRANSPORT
Air Canada	47	F5
Air France	48	D4
Air New Zealand	49	F4
KLM-Royal Dutch Airlines	(see 48)	

See Chinatown Map (p76–7)

Tha Si Phraya

N3 Si Phraya

Bangrak

Soi Yotha

Soi 30

Soi 41

Soi 43 (Soi Saphan Yao)

Soi 32

Soi Phutta Osot

Th Naret

Soi 45

N2 Wat Muang Kae

Soi 34

Soi 47

Th Mansak

Manohra Hotel

Soi 16

Soi 22

Soi 20 (Soi Pradit)

Old Customs House

Soi 36

Soi 38

Phayathai-Bangkok Expwy

Th Charoen Krung

Soi 18

Soi 26

Soi 21

Th Surawong

Soi 40

N1 Oriental

Assumption Cathedral

Peninsula Pier

Th Silom

Silom Galleria

Th Surasak

Soi 19

Th Pan

Soi 42/1 (Soi Wat Suan Phlu)

Shangri-La Hotel

State Tower

Soi 44

Soi 46

Th Si Wiang

Phayathai-Bangkok Expwy

Soi 21

Saphan Taksin

Soi 50

Th Charoen Wiang

Surasak

Saphan Taksin

Tha Sathon (Central Pier)

Charat Wiang

Th Charoen Krung

Th Sathon Tai (South)

Th Sathon Neua (North)

Th Pramuan

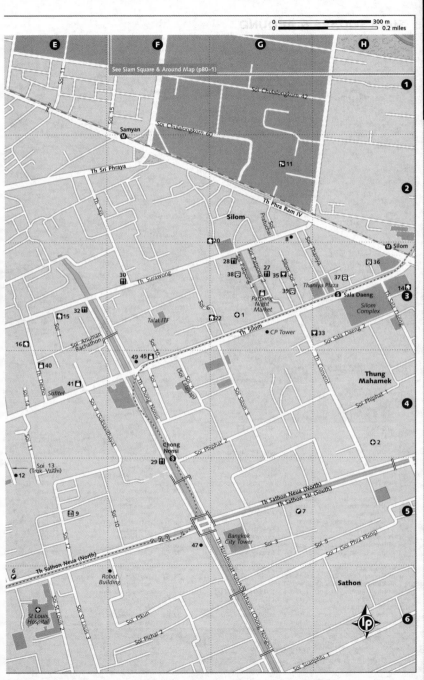

0 _____ 300 m
0 _____ 0.2 miles

See Siam Square & Around Map (p80–1)

Sol Chulalongkorn 42

Samyan

Sol Chulalongkorn 60

Th Sri Phraya

Th Phra Ram IV

Silom

20

8

11

Silom

28
38

27
35

37
36

30

Th Surawong

39

Thaniya Plaza

14

Sala Daeng

S Sala Daeng

32

15

1

22

Talat ITF

Silom
Complex

16

Th Silom

CP Tower

33

40

Th Dech

49 45

41

Sofitel

Soi Silom 3

**Thung
Mahamek**

Soi Convent

2

Chong
Nonsi

Soi Phiphat 2

29

12

Soi 13
(Trok Vaithi)

Th Sathon Neua (North)
Th Sathon Tai (South)

7

9

Sathon

Bangkok
City Tower

47

Robot
Building

Th Sathon Neua (North)

6

St Louis
Hospital

Soi Pikun

Soi Pichai 2

Soi Suanphlu 1

LP

BANGKOK

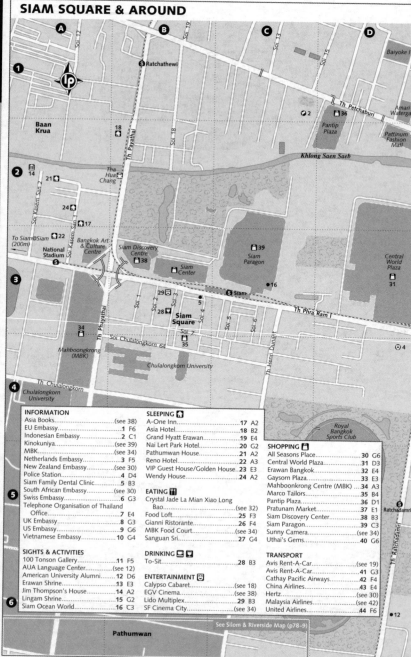

SIAM SQUARE & AROUND

See Silom & Riverside Map (p78–9)

Pathumwan

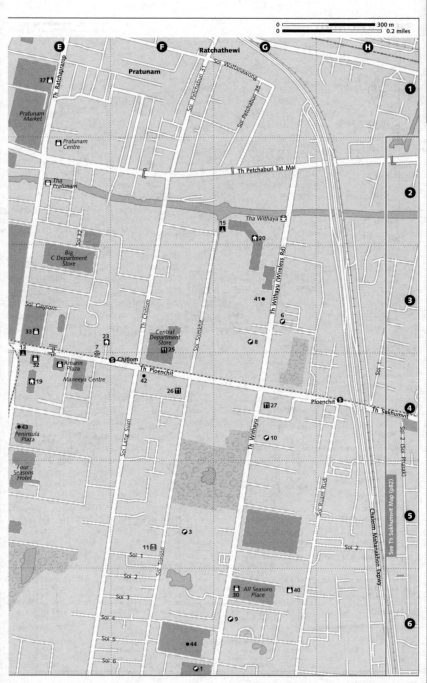

BANGKOK

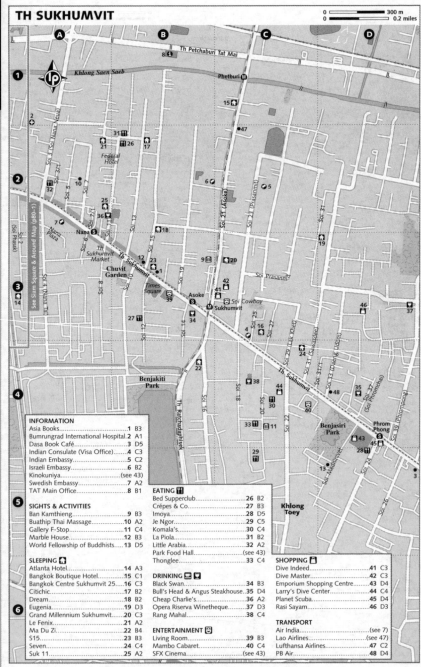

TH SUKHUMVIT

0 — 300 m
0 — 0.2 miles

(Continued from page 69)

automatically assume that female Thais are trustworthy – Bangkok has plenty of con women! Popular hunting grounds for scammers include around the Erawan Shrine, Th Khao San, the Grand Palace and Wat Pho.

SIGHTS

Thailand's islands and beaches are not particularly well-stocked with traditional Thai 'sights', so it's well worth taking in a few while you're in Bangkok. Fortunately, the capital is home to some of the most impressive wát (temples) and palaces in the country. Many are conveniently concentrated on Ko Ratanakosin, Thonburi and nearby Dusit, all of which abut the Banglamphu hotel district.

Ko Ratanakosin & Thonburi

These two districts are in the old part of Bangkok and are filled with historic wát, atmospheric shophouses and fine views of the river.

WAT PHRA KAEW & GRAND PALACE
วัดพระแก้ว/พระมหาราชวัง

Thailand's most famous attractions are **Wat Phra Kaew** (Temple of the Emerald Buddha) and the **Grand Palace** (Map pp74–5; ☎ 0 2222 6889; Th Na Phra Lan; admission to both & Dusit Park 250B; ☷ 8.30am–

3.30pm), occupying the same expansive walled compound south of Sanam Luang. The temple buildings are extravagant, with golden *chedi* (Thai-style stupas), ornate statues of mythical beings and incredible amounts of gold inlay. Only the exterior façades of the Grand Palace structures are open to the public.

Housed in the main *bòht* (chapel), the so-called Emerald Buddha (Phra Kaew) – actually made of nephrite jade – dates back to at least the 15th century. The image is only 66cm high but has repeatedly been a high-profile spoil of war. It spent more than 200 years in Laos before it was won back in 1778 and has been in Bangkok ever since. The image has three sets of robes, which are ceremonially changed by the King (or the crown prince) to mark the changing seasons.

Guides can be hired at the ticket kiosk; ignore anyone outside. Wat Phra Kaew and the Grand Palace are best reached either by a short walk south from Banglamphu, via Sanam Luang, or by Chao Phraya express boat to Tha Chang. From the Siam Sq area (in front of MBK, Th Phra Ram I) take bus 47.

WAT PHO
วัดโพธิ์

Bangkok's largest and oldest temple, **Wat Pho** (Wat Phra Chetuphon; Map pp72–3; ☎ 0 2622 3533; www.watpho.com; Th Sanam Chai; Th Tharawat; admission 50B;

JUST SAY NO: BANGKOK SCAMS

If your travel funds are ample, it might seem like a bother to resist the various scams that siphon off negligible sums. But diligence to fair and honest business benefits the travellers who follow in your footsteps. As a gift to future visitors, stop the scam cycle by just saying 'no'. For details of gem scams, see p390.

- **Closed today** – Ignore any 'friendly' local who tells you that an attraction is closed for a Buddhist holiday or for cleaning. These are set-ups for trips to a bogus gem sale.
- **Túk-túk rides for 10B** – Say goodbye to your day's itinerary if you climb aboard this ubiquitous scam. These alleged 'tours' bypass all the sights and instead cruise to all the fly-by-night gem and tailor shops that pay commissions.
- **Flat-fare taxi ride** – Flatly refuse any driver who quotes a flat fare (usually between 100B and 150B for in-town destinations), which will usually be three times more expensive than the very, very reasonable meter rate. Walking beyond the tourist area will usually help in finding an honest driver. If the driver has 'forgotten' to put the meter on, just say 'meter, kráp/kâ'.
- **Tourist buses to the south** – On the long journey south, well-organised and connected thieves have hours to comb through your bags, breaking into (and later re-sealing) locked bags, searching through hiding places and stealing credit cards, electronics and even toiletries. One traveller reported that his stolen credit card was used to pay for the trip's petrol. How generous. This scam has been running for years but is easy to avoid simply by carrying valuables with you on the bus.

TEMPLE DRESS RULES

Temples in Bangkok have dress codes and those with royal credentials enforce them with some gusto. Especially at Wat Phra Kaew and the Grand Palace and in Dusit Park, you won't be allowed to enter unless you're well covered. Shorts, sleeveless shirts or spaghetti strap tops, capri pants – basically anything that reveals more than your arms (not shoulders) and head – are not allowed. This applies to men and women. If you're flashing too much skin expect to be shown into a dressing room and issued with a sarong before being allowed in. For walking in the courtyard areas you are supposed to wear shoes with closed heels and toes. Sandals and flip-flops are not permitted. Also remember to take your shoes off whenever you enter a temple building and be sure point your feet away from sacred Buddha images.

8am-5pm) was founded in the 16th century and is quieter, less touristy and thus more enjoyable than Wat Phra Kaew. The most famous sight at Wat Pho is the **Reclining Buddha**. Thailand's largest, this 46m-long and 15m-high golden figure includes 3m-high feet bearing fantastic mother-of-pearl inlays.

The surrounding compound has a number of temples with huge golden Buddha images and dozens of colourful mosaic *chedi* (brick stupa). The interior of the main chapel, **Phra Uposatha**, is just as impressive as the Temple of the Emerald Buddha. Towering statues of Chinese mythical heroes guard the doorways within the compound, including figures in European dress said to represent Marco Polo.

Wat Pho is also the national headquarters for the teaching and preservation of traditional Thai medicine, particularly Thai massage. For more information, see p87. The nearest Chao Phraya Express pier is Tha Tien.

NATIONAL MUSEUM
พิพิธภัณฑสถานแห่งชาติ

The **National Museum** (Map pp74-5; ☎ 0 2224 1402; www.thailandmuseum.com; Th Na Phra That; admission 50B; 9am-4pm Wed-Sun) is one of the largest in Southeast Asia and has a vast collection of Thai antiquities and ceremonial objects. Don't miss the incredible ornate golden chariots used in the funeral parades of royal family members. The museum runs highly recommended free tours in English and French on Wednesday and Thursday, Japanese on Wednesday and German on Thursday; all start from the ticket pavilion at 9.30am.

WAT ARUN
วัดอรุณฯ

This striking **wát** (Temple of Dawn; Map pp72-3; ☎ 0 2891 1149; www.watarun.org; Th Arun Amarin; admission 20B; 8am-6pm) consists of four stupas around an

elongated Khmer *brahng* (tower), all covered with broken Chinese ceramics and seashells. Visit early in the morning or late in the afternoon to avoid the crowds. Cross-river ferries run over to Wat Arun every few minutes (3.50B per person) from Tha Tien (N8) to Tha Thai Wang.

ROYAL BARGES NATIONAL MUSEUM
เรือพระที่นั่ง

Over in Thonburi, on the west side of the Chao Phraya River, this interesting **museum** (Map pp72-3; ☎ 0 2424 0004; Khlong Bangkok Noi; admission 30B; still/video camera fee 100/200B; 9am-5pm) is the dry dock for Thai royal barges, which are still used by the royal family for important ceremonies of state. The ornately decorated *Suphannahong*, or 'Golden Swan', is the king's personal barge. At 45m long and made from a single piece of timber, it is the largest dugout in the world. To get here, take the tourist boat from Tha Phra Athit (Banglamphu, N13), which stops at the pier for the museum.

Banglamphu & Dusit

The old residential neighbourhood of Banglamphu that sits just north of the royal Ko Ratanakosin district has a more local feel in some parts, and an almost unfeasibly cosmopolitan atmosphere around the Th Khao San area of guesthouses, hotels, restaurants and bars. If your trip to Thailand is more about partying than sightseeing, then this is the place for you. Further north, Dusit is the current royal district and has several Victorian-era attractions.

WAT SAKET & GOLDEN MOUNT
วัดสระเกศ

The man-made **Golden Mount** (Map pp74-5; ☎ 0 2223 4561; off Th Boriphat; admission to summit 10B; 7.30am-5.30pm) and adjoining **Wat Saket** offer fine views over the old city. If you're a sunset buff, a walk up here before it closes will make you fall in love with Bangkok. Wat Saket is walkable from Banglamphu along Th Ratchadamnoen Klang. From eastern parts of the city, take the *klong* (often spelt as *khlong*; canal) boat to its western terminus at Tha Saphan Phan Fah.

WAT RATCHANATDA
วัดราชนัดดา

A mix of every imaginable temple style, **Wat Ratchanatda** (Map pp74-5; ☎ 0 2224 8807; 2 Th Mahachai; admission free; ☽ 8am-5pm) is most stunning at night when the 37 spires of the all metal Loha Prasat (Metal Palace) are lit up like a medieval birthday cake; at night, though, you'll have to look from outside. This temple is near Wat Saket and worth a detour for its quiet amulet market with more Hindu religious paraphernalia than the amulet market at Wat Mahathat.

WAT SUTHAT
วัดสุทัศน์

The truly remarkable Buddha image, colourful floor-to-ceiling murals and relative tranquillity make **Wat Suthat** (Map pp74-5; ☎ 0 2224 9845; Th Bamrung Meuang; admission 20B; ☽ 8.30am-9pm) arguably the most attractive of Bangkok's Buddhist wát. The main attraction is Thailand's largest *wí-hǎhn*, or main chapel, housing the 8m-high Phra Si Sakayamuni, Thailand's largest surviving Sukhothai-period bronze. Opposite the north entrance is **Sao Ching-Cha**, the Giant Swing, a tall, red swing formerly used in a death-defying (or sometimes not) Brahmin religious ritual. Wat Suthat is an easy walk from Banglamphu, or take the *klong* boat to Tha Saphan Phan Fah and walk from there.

DUSIT PARK
สวนดุสิต

Dusit Park (Map pp72–3) is a former palace estate of King Chulalongkorn, who took great inspiration from his turn-of-the-century tour of Europe. On the grounds, **Vimanmek Teak Mansion Museum** (Phra Thii Nang Wimanmek; ☎ 0 2628 6300-9; Th Ratchawithi; admission 100B or free with Grand Palace ticket; ☽ 9.30am-4pm) is said to be the world's largest golden teak building and is full of royal treasures. It was reportedly built without a single nail, held together by tiny wooden pegs. Compulsory tours (in English) leave every half-hour between 9.30am and 3pm and last about an hour. Free performances of Thai classical dances are staged in a pavilion on the side of the mansion at 10am and 2pm.

Nearby is the **Abhisek Dusit Throne Hall** (Phra Thii Nang Aphisek Dusit), a smaller but even more ornate structure with a strong Moorish influence. The façade is amazing, and the museum behind it contains regional handicrafts. Several other buildings have royal treasures on display and the **Royal Elephant Museum**, near the Th U Thong Nai gate, showcases two large stables that once housed three white elephants.

This is royal property so you must dress appropriately; see the boxed text, opposite. To get here from Banglamphu, take bus 70 from Th Ratchadamnoen Klang.

WAT BENCHAMABOPHIT
วัดเบญจมบพิตร

Built of shimmering white marble from Carrara in Italy, this renowned **wát** (Marble Temple; Map pp72-3; cnr Th Sri Ayuthaya & Th Phra Ram V; admission 20B; ☽ 8.30am-5pm) is grand if not as intimate of some of Bangkok's older wát. The courtyard behind the *bòht* has 53 Buddha

---

THANŎN KHAO SAN

Almost 30 years after locals on the Khao San Rd, as it's known, first started converting their homes into guesthouses for smelly backpackers – known jokingly in Thai as faràng *kêe ngók* ('stingy foreigners') – Banglamphu has evolved into a clearing house of travellers unlike anywhere else on earth. At any time of day or night, Th Khao San is mobbed by travellers from across the globe, mingling with beggars, hawkers, transvestites and street performers, and surrounded by stallholders offering hair-braiding, body-piercing, pirated CDs, hippy jewellery, handicrafts, fake brand-name clothes, Thai fast food, cold beers and croaking wooden frogs, among other things. Think of it as a backpacker cabaret in which you are both a spectator and a participant.

Critics claim Th Khao San cocoons travellers from the real Thailand. It's true that many people leave Bangkok having seen just this short stretch of road, but it's not really fair. Today, Banglamphu has become a major entertainment district for young Bangkokians, who add the Thai spice long missing from this dish.

FREAKY BANGKOK

Bangkok can be a weird and wonderful place without even trying. But if you need to go beyond the ordinary strangeness, here is a list of its more unusual sights (see p85 for the weirdness of Th Khao San).

The **amulet market** (Map pp74–5; Th Phra Chan) is the commercial side of Thai Buddhism, part animistic and part antiquities. The most common amulets are small ceramic plaques, produced by important Buddhist monasteries, but there are also tiny Buddha images, phallic symbols, bone fragments and other potent objects. If you fancy buying an amulet, several stalls can fit it into a metal pendant case for about 30B.

Perhaps Bangkok's strangest religious site is the **Lingam shrine** (Saan Jao Mae Thap Thim; Map pp80–1; Soi Somkhit, Th Withayu) hidden away behind the Nai Lert Park Hotel. Scattered around a spirit house and a 3m-high phallus statue are hundreds of wooden and stone representations of the male organ. Women pray here when they hope to become pregnant (hold on to your daughters).

For a creepy exploration of human mortality, the **Forensic Medicine Museum** (Map pp72–3; ☎ 0 2419 7000; 2nd fl, Forensic Medicine Bldg, Siriraj Hospital; admission 40B; ☽ 9am-4pm Mon-Sat) features evidence from many of Bangkok's most heinous murder cases, including the preserved body of serial child-killer and cannibal Si Ouey. To get here, take the cross-river ferry from Tha Chang (N9) or Tha Phra Chan to Tha Wang Lang (Siriraj, N10).

---

images representing every mudra (gesture) and style from Thai history, making this the ideal place to compare Buddhist iconography. The surrounding grounds are a pleasant place for a wander.

Chinatown

Bangkok's Chinatown (Map pp76–7) is centred on bustling Th Yaowarat, which is lined with gold shops, herbalists and banquet restaurants, all with loud neon signs in Chinese characters. The whole district is great for aimless wandering through crowded markets, charismatic old soi lined with shophouses and some of the best street food in the city. The old markets along **Sampeng Lane** (Soi Wanit; between Th Ratchawong and Th Chakrawat) and **Trok Itsaranuphap** are the most interesting and congested of all – mornings in Trok Itsaranuphap are like a mosh pit. See the walking tour (p88) for directions. Elsewhere there are dozens of little wát, some of them distinctively Chinese in style, dotted around the backstreets.

WAT TRAIMIT
วัดไตรมิตร
Right in the heart of Chinatown, between Th Traimit and Th Yaowarat, **Wat Traimit** (Temple of the Golden Buddha; Map pp76–7; ☎ 0 2225 9775; Th Mitthaphap (aka Th Traimit); admission 20B; ☽ 8am-5pm) houses an incredible Buddha image made from 5.5 tonnes of solid gold (that's a hefty US$190 million's worth at early 2008 prices).

The Sukhothai-era image was covered in plaster back in the Ayuthaya period to protect it from Burmese marauders, and its full worth was discovered only in 1955, when the image was accidentally dropped from a crane. Avoid the tour groups by visiting early in the morning or late in the afternoon. It's an easy walk from Hualamphong Metro station.

New Bangkok

In the new part of the city, the religious monuments and museums get crowded out by skyscraping offices and hotels and chic shopping malls the size of small suburbs. There are, however, a few sights that are made more interesting by their juxtaposition amid shiny modern Bangkok.

SRI MAHARIAMMAN
วัดพระศรีมหาอุมาเทวี
This colourful Hindu **temple** (Map pp78–9; Th Silom; ☽ 6am-8pm) is an important place of worship for Bangkok's Indian community as well as for many Thai Buddhists. The temple was built in 1879, and the ornate *gopura* (South Indian tower) is covered in figures from the Mahabharata. You can enter the compound (without your shoes), but photography is prohibited.

ERAWAN SHRINE
ศาลพระพรหม
In spite of all the temples, modern Bangkok might not seem to be a particularly spiritual

place, but there are all sorts of interesting shrines hidden away among the skyscrapers. Most famous is this **shrine** (Saan Phra Phrom; Map pp80-1; cnr Th Ploenchit & Th Ratchadamri; ☺ 6am-10.30pm), next to the Erawan Grand Hyatt. When the Erawan Hotel was first built in the 1950s a series of construction disasters stopped soon after this shrine to the Hindu god Brahma was erected. The hotel was a huge success and ever since people have come here to pray for luck and fortune. For an idea of just how revered the Erawan shrine is, when a mentally disturbed man attacked it in 2006, bystanders promptly beat him to death. You can see shrine dancers performing traditional lá·kon gâa bon dances here.

JIM THOMPSON'S HOUSE
บ้านจิมทอมป์สัน

This complex of traditional **teak buildings** (Map pp80-1; ☎ 0 2216 7368; www.jimthompsonhouse.org; 6 Soi Kasem San 2, Th Phra Ram I; adult/child 100/50B; ☺ 9am-5pm Mon-Sat) is the legacy of the American spy-cum-silk-mogul Jim Thompson. The traditional wooden houses were collected from as far away as northern Thailand and as near as the Muslim village of Baan Krua, just across the klong (where silk is still woven today), and reassembled as a private mansion on the edge of Khlong Saen Saep. Guided tours of the mansion with English-, French- and Japanese-speaking guides leave every 20 minutes. Photography is prohibited inside the mansion. Admission proceeds go to charities supported by the James Thompson Foundation. The mansion is a short walk from the National Stadium Skytrain stop and an even shorter walk from the Hua Chang klong boat pier.

LUMPHINI PARK
สวนลุมพินี

Named after Buddha's birthplace in Nepal, Bangkok's largest and most popular public **park** (Map pp72-3; ☺ 5am-8pm) is crisscrossed by walking trails and has tranquil lawns, wooded glades and a large artificial lake with pedalos for hire. It's a great place to watch Bangkokians unwind; practising t'ai chi in the early morning, running, working out, taking part in outdoor aerobics classes or just unleashing their kids on the grass. From mid-February to April, Lumphini is a favourite spot for kite fighting. The main entrance to the park is on Th Phra Ram IV, but there are also entrances on Th Sarasin, Th Withayu and Th Ratchadamri. It's well connected by Metro at Lumphini and Silom and by Skytrain stations Sala Daeng and Ratchadamri.

ACTIVITIES
Massage

Bangkokians regard traditional massage as a vital part of preventative health care and they frequent massage parlours more regularly than gyms. You'll have no trouble finding a massage shop (rather, they'll find you), but after a few visits to the backpacker hangars, you may want a more focused, professional experience. A good sign is a small shop off the main path. Note that for men asking for an 'oil massage' can sometimes lead to techniques that aren't on the curriculum at

---

EXHIBIT ONE

In recent years, Bangkok has seen an explosion in the number of galleries, and the number of people interested in them, meaning you should be able to catch an interesting exhibition at any time. To find out what's on, look for *BAM!* (Bangkok Art Map) from the *Bangkok 101* people, and *Thailand Art & Design Guide* (www.thailandartanddesignguide.com), or check the lifestyle magazines for exhibition opening nights.

Galleries worth looking out for include the **Queen's Gallery** (Map pp74-5; ☎ 0 2281 5360; 101 Th Ratchadamnoen Klang; admission free; ☺ 10am-7pm Thu-Tue), for conservative contemporary fare; **100 Tonson Gallery** (Map pp80-1; ☎ 0 2684 1527; www.100tonsongallery.com; 100 Soi Tonson, off Th Ploenchit; ☺ 11am-7pm Thu-Sun), regarded as the city's top commercial gallery; **H Gallery** (Map pp78-9; ☎ 0 2234 7556; www.hgallerybkk.com; 201 Soi 12, Th Sathon, Silom; ☺ noon-6pm Thu-Sat), a private gallery specialising in young Asian artists; and **Gallery F-stop** (Map p82; ☎ 0 2663 7421; www.galleryfstop.com; Tamarind Café, 27 Soi 20, Th Sukhumvit; ☺ 3pm-midnight Mon-Fri, 10am-midnight Sat & Sun), which mixes photographic and painted exhibitions.

OFF THE BEATEN PATH

There are some lovely, easily reached attractions within the city limits where you'll likely have the whole place to yourself. If you loved Jim Thompson's house, there are at least five other museums in old teak houses, including **Ban Kamthieng** (Map p82; ☎ 0 2661 6470; 131 Soi Asoke; admission 100B; ☿ 9am-5pm) and **Wang Suan Phakkat** (Lettuce Farm Palace; Map pp72-3; ☎ 0 2245 4934; Th Sri Ayuthaya; admission 100B; ☿ 9am-4pm). Both have collections of Thai artworks and handicrafts and you rarely see a soul, much less a tour bus full of camera slingers.

Wat Pho. If you're not looking for a 'happy ending', avoid parlours where the masseuses are young and wearing short skirts.

Depending on the neighbourhood, prices for massages tend to stay fixed: about 200B to 300B for a foot massage and 350B to 500B for a full-body massage. Recommended massages include:

Buathip Thai Massage (Map p82; ☎ 0 2251 2627; 4/13 Soi 5, Th Sukhumvit; ☿ 10am-midnight) Not in the most wholesome part of Bangkok, on a sub-soi behind the Amari Boulevard Hotel, but this crew are the real thing.

Marble House (Map p82; ☎ 0 2651 0905, 3rd fl, Ruamchit Plaza, 199 Th Sukhumvit at Soi 15; ☿ 10am-midnight) No 'happy endings' from these masseurs, either.

Skills Development Centre for the Blind (sŏon pá·tá·nah sà·màt·tà·pâhp kon đah bòrt; Map pp70-1; ☎ 0 2583 7327; Pak Kret) A government programme that trains the blind in Thai massage. Getting there is an adventure; take bus 33 from Sanam Luang to Pak Kret and hire a motorcycle taxi from there.

Wat Pho Thai Massage School (Map pp72-3; ☎ 0 2221 3686; Soi Penphat, Th Sanamchai; ☿ 8am-5pm) Thailand's primary massage school; open-air pavilions are also available in the southeast corner of the temple complex.

WALKING TOUR

Despite the traffic, the best way to discover much of Bangkok is by foot. And in some cases, such as the claustrophobic alleys of chaotic commerce in Chinatown, it's the only way. We recommend starting this tour after lunch so you can finish with a sunset drink. Remember that the river ferries stop about 7pm.

Starting from the river ferry at Tha Saphan Phut (Memorial Bridge Pier), walk north along Th Chakraphet and into **Phahurat (1)**, aka Little India. Turn right into narrow **Trok Huae Med (2)**, a largely-Indian market that extends east into **Sampeng Lane (3)**, signposted as Soi Wanit 1, the original Chinatown market that has been trading since 1782. Today it deals in useful stuff such as bulk Hello Kitty pens or tonnes of stuffed animals.

Turn left on Th Mahachak, walk 30m and turn left again through a covered passage to rows of photogenic, stuccoed yellow **Chinese shophouses (4)**; a peaceful intermission in the market tour. Return to Sampeng Lane and avoid the trolleys as far east as Th Mangkon, where you'll see two of Bangkok's oldest commercial buildings, the **Bangkok Bank (5)** and **Tang To Kang (6)** gold shop, both more than 100 years old.

Turn left (north) on Th Mangkun and walk up to manic Th Yaowarat, Chinatown's main drag. Turn right past the street's famous gold shops and after about 100m cross Th Yaowarat into super-crowded **Trok Itsaranuphap (7)**; you'll know it by the people shuffling into the alley one at a time. Not far along the alley is **Talat Leng-Buai-la (8)**, which was once the city's central vegetable market but today sells mainly Chinese ingredients such as fresh cashews, lotus seeds, and shiitake mushrooms. You will, eventually, pop out the far end of Trok Itsaranuphap onto Th Charoen Krung. Cross over a road and on Soi Charoen Krung 21 is **Wat Mangkon Kamalawat (9)**, one of Chinatown's largest and liveliest temples.

Head back to Th Charoen Krung, turn left (east) and then right into **Th Plaeng Naam (10)**. This atmospheric street of shophouses and street food makes a good pit stop, particularly at the two streetside kitchens at the north end. Turn left onto **Th Yaowarat (11)** and after passing a couple of old Art Deco buildings turn left at the Odeon Circle, with its distinctive Chinese gate, onto Th Mitthaphap (aka Th Traimit) for the **Wat Traimit and the Golden Buddha (12, p86)**. Head back to Odeon Circle, cross and walk past the machine shops of Soi Yaowarat 1 onto Soi Charoen Phanit and the atmospheric **Talat Noi (13)** neighbourhood. You deserve a drink now, so follow the signs to the River View Guest House (p94), where the 8th-floor restaurant-bar

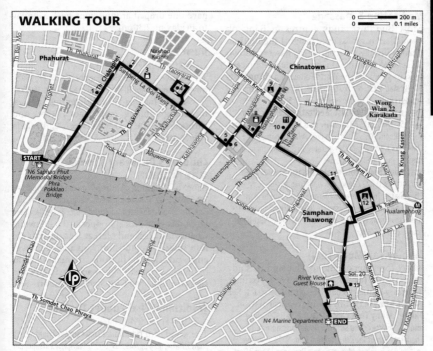

WALKING TOUR

WALK FACTS

Start Tha Saphan Phut (Memorial Bridge, river ferry N6)

End Tha Marine Department (river ferry, N4) or Hualamphong Metro

Distance 4km

Duration Three hours

Fuel Stop Streetside kitchens on Th Plaeng Naam

has cheap beer and amazing sunset views. Take either the ferry or the Metro to get your lodgings.

COURSES

There are some interesting courses available if you don't mind spending a little longer in the capital.

Cooking

Several luxury hotels offer expensive but memorable gourmet Thai cooking courses. Other recommended courses include:

Blue Elephant Thai Cooking School (Map pp78-9; ☎ 0 2673 9353; www.blueelephant.com; 233 Th Sathon Tai; lessons ⏲ 8.45am-12.30pm, 1.15-5pm Mon-Sat; 3276B) Bangkok's most renowned Thai cooking school offers two lessons daily. The morning class squeezes in a visit to a local market, while the afternoon session includes a detailed introduction to Thai ingredients.

May Kaidee's Vegetarian Thai Cooking School (Map pp74-5; ☎ 0 2281 7699; www.maykaidee.com; 33 Th Samsen, Banglamphu; ⏲ 9am-1pm & 2-5pm; 1200B) A truly meat-free cooking experience; learn veggie versions of 10 Thai classics.

Silom Thai Cooking School (Map pp78-9; ☎ 0 84726 5669; www.bangkokthaicooking.com; 68 Soi 13, Th Silom; lessons ⏲ 9.30am-1pm; 1000B) With a market trip and instruction in six dishes, this is the best bang for your baht.

Language

The most intensive language course in Bangkok is held at **AUA Language Center** (Map pp80-1; ☎ 0 2252 8170; www.auathai.com; 179 Th Ratchadamri; per hr 102B), which offers rolling classes from 7am to 8pm Monday to Friday; go whenever you like.

Meditation & Massage

Most Buddhist study centres in Bangkok specialise in *vipassana* (insight) meditation. **Dharma Thai** (www.dhammathai.org) has a rundown on several prominent wát and meditation centres, or speak to the **World Fellowship of Buddhists** (WFB; Map p82; ☎ 0 2661 1284; www.wfb-hq.org; 616 Benjasiri Park, Soi Medhinivet, Soi 24, Th Sukhumvit).

International Buddhist Meditation Center (Map pp74-5; ☎ 0 2623 6326; www.mcu.ac.th/IBMC/; Vipassana Section Room 106, Mahachula Bldg, Wat Mahathat, Th Pra Chan) Holds twice-monthly lectures on Buddhist topics in English, and meditation classes.

Wat Pho Thai Traditional Massage School (Map pp72-3; ☎ 0 2221 3686; www.watpomassage.com; Soi Phenphat 1, Th Maharat) By far the best place to learn traditional massage. Courses are held at school headquarters across from Wat Pho, just off Th Maharat. A 30-hour course costs 8500B.

Moo·ay Tai (Muay Thai)

Many foreigners come to Thailand to study *moo·ay tai* (or *muay thai*; Thai boxing). Training regimens can be *extremely* strict. See www.muaythai.com for more information.

Fairtex Muay Thai Camp (☎ 0 2755 3329; www .muaythaifairtex.com; 99/8 Soi Boonthamanusorn, Th Theparak, Samut Prakan) Training from 500B a session to 7700B-a-week residence. Samut Prakan is about 25km southeast of central Bangkok.

Sor Vorpin (Map pp74-5; ☎ 0 2282 3551; www.thai boxings.com; 13 Trok Kasap, Th Chakkaphong) Around the corner from Th Khao San, it offers training for foreigners. More serious training is held at a second facility outside the city. Half-day/weekly/monthly training costs 500/2500/9000B.

BANGKOK FOR CHILDREN

Bangkok has loads to offer children. Most malls have diverse and appealing attractions for kids of various ages: shopping for the tweens and rides for preschoolers. The website www.bambiweb.org is a useful resource for parents.

Queen Saovabha Memorial Institute (Snake Farm)
สถานเสาวภา

Lovers of things that slither will be fascinated by this working **snake farm** (Map pp78-9; ☎ 0 2252 0161; 1871 Th Phra Ram IV, Lumphini; adult/child 200/50B; ⊙ 9.30am-3.30pm Mon-Fri, 9.30am-1pm Sat & Sun), which provides antivenin for Thai hospitals. You can see deadly snakes being milked for their venom at 11am daily, or have one draped around your neck Monday to Friday at 2.30pm.

Dusit Zoo
สวนสัตว์ดุสิต(เขาดิน)

This above-average **zoo** (Map pp72-3; ☎ 2281 9027; www.zoothailand.org; Th Ratchawithi; adult/child 100/50B; ⊙ 8am-6pm) has loads of indigenous species, including banteng, gaur, tigers, serow and rhinoceros. The zoo is between Chitralada Palace and the National Assembly Hall.

Children's Discovery Museum
พิพิธภัณฑ์เด็ก

Bangkok's leading children's **museum** (Map pp70-1; ☎ 0 2616 6509; www.bkkchildrenmuseum.com; Queen Sirikit Park, Th Kamphaeng Phet 4; adult/child 70/50B; ⊙ 9am-5pm Tue-Fri, 10am-6pm Sat & Sun) is opposite the sprawling Chatuchak Weekend Market. The displays are fully interactive, and both kids and adults will enjoy pressing the buttons and making giant bubbles with the bubble machine. Follow the signs from the Mo Chit Skytrain station.

Traditional Thai Puppet Theatre
โรงละครโจหลุยส์

The wonderful **Traditional Thai Puppet Theatre** (Joe Louis Theatre; Map pp78-9; ☎ 0 2252 9683; www.thaipuppet .com/en/; Suan Lum Night Bazaar; adult/child 7-15/child under 7 900/300B/free; ⊙ shows 8pm) is great fun for adults and kids and provides a rare chance to see the ancient Thai art of puppetry. The future of the Suan Lum Night Bazaar is in doubt, so call ahead or check online that it hasn't moved.

Siam Ocean World
สยามโอเชี่ยนเวิร์ล

Southeast Asia's largest oceanarium, **Siam Ocean World** (Map pp80-1; ☎ 2687 2000; www.siamocean world.com; basement, Siam Paragon, Th Rama 1; adult/child 750/600B; ⊙ 9am-10pm, last entry 9pm) has hundreds of species of fish, crustaceans and even penguins. The main tank is the highlight, with an acrylic tunnel allowing you to walk beneath sharks and rays. Time your trip to coincide with the shark and penguin feedings; usually at 12.30pm and 1pm, and 4pm and 4.30pm.

TOURS
Cruises

Chao Phraya dinner cruises are hugely popular, with boats ranging from century-old rice barges to neon-clad cruisers taking in the brightly lit riverside sights, passing Wat

Arun, the Grand Palace and Saphan Phra Ram IX. Larger vessels often have dance floors and live bands, which might be less romantic than you hoped. Day trips to Ayuthaya are also possible. Book in advance. Options include:

Loy Nava (Map pp78–9; ☎ 0 2437 4932; www.loynava .com; set menu 1618B; 🕑 6-8pm & 8-10pm) Travels from River City shopping centre (Map pp78-9) aboard a converted rice barge.

Manohra Cruises (Map pp70–1; ☎ 0 2477 0770; www .manohracruises.com) These restored wooden rice barges are the grandest of all. Departing the Marriott Resort & Spa, take a hotel boat from Tha Sathon; there is a sunset cruise (900B, 🕑 6-7pm) that includes one cocktail, and a dinner cruise (2342B; 🕑 7.30pm-10pm). The Thai food is well above average.

Wan Fah (Map pp78-9; ☎ 0 2222 8679; www.wanfah .com; dinner cruise 1200B; 🕑 7-9pm) Reasonably priced cruises on a fine converted Chinese rice barge leaving from River City.

Yok Yor Restaurant (Map pp78-9; ☎ 0 2439 3477; www.yokyor.co.th; dinner 300-320B plus 120B surcharge; 🕑 8-10pm) This famous old restaurant beside the Hilton in Thonburi also runs a dinner cruise for the average folks, mainly Thais celebrating birthdays.

Other Tours

Every travel agent and most hotels can arrange guided tours of important sites.

Long-tail boats can be chartered for tours of the Thonburi *klong*, particularly Khlong Bangkok Yai and Khlong Bangkok Noi. Shop around for a tour that doesn't include Wat Arun and the Royal Barge Museum, both of which can be more easily (and, let's be honest, more cheaply) visited independently.

Tha Chang pier (Map pp74–5), close to Thammasat University, is the best place to go and hire a boat. They can also be booked at Tha Saphan Phut (Map pp76–7), Tha Oriental (Map pp78–9) and Tha Si Phraya (Map pp78–9); rental costs from about 400B to 800B an hour (it costs more the closer you are to an expensive hotel).

If you want a custom tour with an expert guide, and money is no objective, **Bangkok Private Tours** (www.bangkokprivatetours.com) is earning a reputation for its food tours, among others.

FESTIVALS & EVENTS

As well as the main countrywide festivals (see p19), Bangkok has a few celebrations of its own.

Kite Festival (March) Kite fights at Bangkok's public parks and Sanam Luang.

Royal Ploughing Ceremony (May) Ceremonial plough-ing by the king (or more recently the crown prince) at Sanam Luang to forecast the coming rice harvest.

Bangkok International Film Festival (July, but dates vary; www.bangkokfilm.org) In cinemas across town.

Thailand International Swan-Boat Races (Septem-ber) During the middle of the month on Chao Phraya River, near Saphan Rama IX.

Vegetarian Festival (September/October) Centred on Soi 20, Th Charoen Krung, Chinatown becomes an orgy of veg food.

Fat Festival (November) Popular alternative radio station hosts up-and-coming Thai bands at this annual music event.

King's Birthday (5 December) Illuminations and parades around the Grand Palace, Banglamphu.

Bangkok Jazz Festival (December; www.bangkokjazz festival.com) Features international and Thai performers.

SLEEPING

Bangkok boasts more than 400 hotels and guesthouses, ranging from cheap backpacker joints to some of the most luxurious lodgings on earth. Hotels of a type tend to congregate in certain neighbourhoods.

In 'old Bangkok', Banglamphu and the fa-mous (or should that be infamous?) Th Khao San are a virtual tractor beam for backpackers. This area is very convenient for the river and the monuments and museums of old Bangkok. A long walk north is Thewet, which is refreshingly laid-back and handy for the palaces in Dusit. Further south, Chinatown is a lively but often-overlooked part of Bangkok that has a couple of decent options, while nearby Hualamphong has some good budget choices.

In 'new Bangkok', the riverside boasts super-luxurious properties with spectacular views, while Th Silom and more recently Th Sathon are home to midrange and some funky top-end places. The area around Siam Sq also has several upmarket hotels, plus a handful of budget options. Th Sukhumvit, where you'll find sleaze and class in plentiful supply de-pending on which soi you're in, is home to most of the new boutique places plus loads of tourist-class midrangers. See p380 for more on accommodation in Thailand.

Ko Ratanakosin & Thonburi

Bangkok's oldest districts make an ideal base for exploring the city's major historic sights. It's best to book well ahead.

Arun Residence (Map pp72-3; ☎ 0 2221 9158; www .arunresidence.com; 396 Th Maharat; Ko Ratanakosin; d 3100-5000B; 🖳 🖵) Near Wat Pho, this romantic

---

BANGKOK ROOMS: WHAT YOUR MONEY WILL BUY

Bangkok suffers from capital-city syndrome and room rates can be considerably higher than elsewhere in Thailand. We have divided rooms into the following three categories:

Budget: under 1000B
Midrange: 1000B–4500B
Top-end: over 4500B

These are the walk-in rates we were quoted, but it's well worth noting that big, sometimes huge, discounts can be found by booking online or in advance by phone; see p382 for details.

So what do you get for your money? At the **budget** end, the days of 50B beds in Banglamphu are over but those on wafer-thin budgets can still get a dorm bed for between 150B and 400B with a shared bathroom. More comfortable and stylish rooms are available for upwards of 800B, with prices rising with size and location.

The **midrange** is where you'll find the biggest discounts for advance bookings. Rooms listed at up to 4500B will often go for between about 2500B and 4000B. More modest properties have more modest rates – modesty seemingly defined by the style of the décor. Thus the older places are often quite cheap, while trendier new places more pricey. If you're on a lower midrange budget, some very nice rooms can be had for between about 1500B and 2500B.

Bangkok's growing array of **top-end** hotels start at about 4500B per room and climb much higher. In the top tier rooms start at more than 10,000B, but in most of the luxurious design and boutique hotels, and the vast majority of the international brands, you're looking at about 6000B to 9000B, before hefty online discounting.

---

retreat appeals as much for the Deck restaurant, the bar and views of Wat Arun as the appealingly decorated but rather dark rooms (with wi-fi and cable broadband). The suite is the pick.

Ibrik Resort (Map pp72-3; ☎ 0 2848 9220; www.ibrik resort.com; 256 Soi Wat Rakhang, Th Arun Amarin, Thonburi; d with breakfast 3200-3500B; ❀) In a white wooden house that's literally right on the river on the Thonburi side, Ibrik has just three romantic rooms with silks and four-poster beds. It's not exactly luxurious, but it's very private. The Moonlight room has no view.

Aurum: The River Place (Map pp72-3; ☎ 0 2622 2248; www.aurum-bangkok.com; 396 Th Maharat; Ko Ratanakosin; tw/d with breakfast 3600/4100B; ❀) At the river-end of a row of old Chinese godowns, the attractive and very comfortable faux-Parisian–style Aurum has 12 tastefully furnished rooms with not-wholly-uninterrupted river views.

Chakrabongse Villas (Map pp72-3; ☎ 0 2622 3356; www.thaivillas.com; 396 Th Maharat; Ko Ratanakosin; villas 10,000-25,000B; ❀ ❀) Prince Chakrabongse Bhuvanath's 19th-century mansion has been converted into a luxurious, personal destination in itself. Four villas of varying ages (some quite new) are set around a garden and pool. The riverside dining pavilion is super romantic; meals are cooked to order. Delightful.

Banglamphu

The days of Th Khao San (p85) being all about supercheap flophouses are almost over. As hippies have been replaced by flashpacking couples so the tiny, boxlike fan rooms featured in the movie *The Beach* have been replaced by larger, air-conditioned rooms with private bathrooms starting at about 500B. Most places have attached restaurants serving faràng-oriented food and screening nightly movies.

Calmer guesthouses and a growing number of midrange places have spread in a 1km radius from Th Khao San, and these are where more experienced travellers prefer to stay. From December to February, competition for rooms is intense and many places are full by 10am. Staff usually won't reserve a room unless you pay in advance.

Th Khao San has all the life-support systems a traveller needs. Get here by public bus, the Chao Phraya River express to Tha Phra Athit (Tha Banglamphu, N13) or Airport Express bus from Suvarnabhumi.

BUDGET

There are now close to 100 guesthouses and hotels in Banglamphu. If one is not listed here, that doesn't mean it's no good – look around and use your own discretion. Remember that most of the best (and cheapest) places are not actually on Th Khao San, and the street can get pretty noisy. Look along Soi Rambutri, which bends around Wat Chana Songkhram west of Th Khao San; in the soi off Th Samsen north of Khlong Banglamphu; and if you're going supercheap the alley running parallel between Th Khao San and Th Ratchadamnoen Klang where you'll find a handful of old-style wooden guesthouses offering rooms with fan and shared bathroom (200B to 400B) or with fan and private bathroom (400B to 600B).

Prakorp's House (Map pp74–5; ☎ 0 2281 1345; fax 0 2629 0714; 52 Th Khao San; s/d with shared bathroom 160/250B) One of few remaining old-style guesthouses on Th Khao San. The simple rooms in an old wooden house are best, while the homely café is a highlight.

Villa Guest House (Map pp74–5; ☎ 0 2281 7009; 230 Soi 1, Th Samsen; s 300B, d 400-600B) In a garden oasis amid the village life of Soi 1, this historic 19th-century nobleman's teak house has 10 rooms with fan and shared bathroom; reservations strongly recommended.

Roof View Place (Map pp74–5; ☎ 081-805 8846; Soi 6, Th Samsen; s 450B, d 550-800B; ⚡ 🖵) These white, sparsely stylish rooms and a friendly young crew make the Roof View worth the 10-minute walk to Th Khao San. Guests can use the kitchen.

Lamphu House (Map pp74–5; ☎ 0 2629 5861; www.lamphuhouse.com; 75-77 Soi Rambutri, Th Chakraphong; d from 590B; ⚡ 🖵) Lamphu House creates a mellow mood with its hidden, relatively quiet location and clean, smartly decorated rooms. Cheaper rooms with fans and shared bathrooms are also available.

Boworn BB (Map pp74–5; ☎ 0 2629 1073; www.bowornbb.com; 335 Th Phra Sumen; r 600-700B; ⚡ 🖵) Boworn has bland but clean rooms but it's the familial atmosphere centred around the café-lobby and the garden rooftop that are most attractive.

Rikka Inn (Map pp74–5; ☎ 0 2282 7511; www.rikkainn.com; 259 Th Khao San; r 600-950B; ⚡ 🖵 ⚡) With a rooftop pool, small but mainly stylish rooms and a central Khao San location, the new Rikka is great value.

Shambara (Map pp74–5; ☎ 0 2282 7968; www.shambarabangkok.com; 138 Th Khao San; r 700-950B; ⚡ 🖵) Just off Th Khao San, this century-old wooden home has nine tiny rooms that share two clean showers and toilets. Great atmosphere. Book ahead.

Others include:

Prasuri Guest House (Map pp74–5; ☎ 0 2280 1428; prasuri_gh_bkk@hotmail.com; Soi Phrasuli; s 220-380B, d 280-420B; ⚡ 🖵) Simple, family-run – if a little tired – guesthouse in a quiet soi.

New Siam Guest House (Map pp74–5; ☎ 0 2282 4554; www.newsiam.net; 21 Soi Chana Songkhram, Th Phra Athit; s 280B, d 380-650B; ⚡) The original New Siam. Relaxed, backpacker atmosphere; bathrooms are shared.

MIDRANGE

Midrange places are popping up in Banglamphu faster than mushrooms at a Ko Pha-Ngan full-moon party.

Erawan House (Map pp74–5; ☎ 0 2629 2121; www.erawanhouse.net; 17 Soi Chana Songkhram, Th Phra Athit; r 1000B; ⚡ 🖵) A dash of 'boutique' in this soi of veteran guesthouses, the Erawan has comfortable rooms with modest fittings for an excellent price.

ourpick New Siam Riverside (Map pp74–5; ☎ 0 2629 3535; www.newsiam.net; 21 Th Phra Athit; d with breakfast 1190-2190B; ⚡ 🖵 ⚡) The fourth member of the New Siam guesthouse empire, this 104-room hotel on the riverfront has a pool (get some tanning in before the beach) and vaguely stylish rooms; those with views (from 1590B) are best. The New Siams II and III are also popular.

ourpick Lamphu Treehouse (Map pp74–5; ☎ 0 2282 0991-92; www.lamphutreehotel.com; Soi Baan Pan Thom, 155 Wanchat Bridge, Th Prachatipatai; s/d 1250/1450B; ⚡ 🖵 ⚡) Accessed via a *klong*-side footpath a few minutes northeast of Khao San, the Lamphu is no treehouse but with a pool and 40 colourful new rooms it's good value.

Buddy Lodge (Map pp74–5; ☎ 0 2629 4477; www.buddylodge.com; 265 Th Khao San; r 2400-2900B; ⚡ 🖵) The leader of Th Khao San's gentrification, Buddy has 76 airy, tropical-manor style rooms, a rooftop pool, a middle-of-the-action location…and…emm a Maccas in the lobby.

Old Bangkok Inn (Map pp74–5; ☎ 0 2629 1787; www.oldbangkokinn.com; 609 Th Phra Sumen; d with breakfast 3190-3990B, f 6590B; ⚡ 🖵) In several evocatively furnished old shophouses, this 10-room boutique hotel offers both charisma and warm service in a historic setting.

Also try:

Viengtai Hotel (Map pp74–5; ☎ 0 2280 5434-45; www.viengtai.co.th; 42 Th Ramburti; s/tw 2000/2200B; ⚡ 🖵 ⚡) A Banglamphu fixture since 1953; now a 200-room, reliable but fairly soulless midrange place.

Royal Hotel (Hotel Ratanakosin; Map pp74–5; ☎ 0 2222 9111-26; fax 0 2224 2083; cnr Th Ratchadamnoen Klang & Th Atsadang; d 1200-1700B; ⚡ 🖵) Old, comfortable but variable rooms; be sure to see a few.

Thewet

North of Banglamphu near the National Library, a strip of family-run budget places actually pre-dates Th Khao San but has managed to maintain a genuinely local feel, with no nightclubs and the only fast food coming from the nearby wet market. Thewet appeals particularly to repeat travellers who are 'over' Th Khao San. These places, plus the ecofriendly midrange Phranakorn Nornlen, are a (longish) walk to Th Khao San, Ko Ratanakosin and Dusit, but not that convenient to other areas. To get here, take a Chao Phraya express boat (get off at Tha Thewet, N15) or public buses 3, 30 and 53 along Th Samsen.

Shanti Lodge (Map pp72-3; ☎ 0 2281 2497; Th Sri Ayuthaya; dm 200, s/d 400/750-850B; 🞩 🖳) Stylish and self-assured, Shanti Lodge has a variety of rooms from simple affairs to the newer concrete wing with artful wall murals and bathrooms. The downstairs café and restaurant is popular with people hanging out, strumming guitars and not doing too much. Very chilled.

Taewez (Map pp72-3; ☎ 0 2280 8856-58; 23 Soi 12, Th Sri Ayuthaya; s/d 250/430B; 🞩 🖳) This popular place down a lane has an easy, family-oriented atmosphere. The fan rooms aren't fantastic but the air-conditioned rooms are excellent value.

Sri Ayuttaya Guest House (Map pp72-3; ☎ 0 2282 5942; Th Si Ayuthaya; s 350B, d 600-850B) Not quite as social as the neighbouring Shanti, but still superior to many Khao San joints. Rooms are attractive and fair value.

Phranakorn Nornlen (Map pp72-3; ☎ 0 2628 8188-90; www.phranakorn-nornlen.com; 46 Soi Thewet 1, Th Krung Kasem; s/d 1800/2200B; 🞩 🖳) Everyone loves this arty, rustically charming boutique hotel set in a garden and converted wooden building. Social and environmental responsibility is atop the agenda. Delicious organic breakfasts are served, but the helpful staff will also encourage you to spend your money at local restaurants and markets. Recommended.

Chinatown & Hualamphong

Bangkok's Chinatown is noisy, hectic and full of energy. Most hotels are institutional affairs suffering from the sort of total charisma bypass familiar in hotels in, ahm, China. However, change is coming and some of the budget places around Hualamphong train station are quite appealing.

There are several very rundown dosshouses beside Hualamphong train station, on Th Rong Muang (aka Th Hualamphong), but avoid them and try for one of these first two.

Baan Hualampong (Map pp76-7; ☎ 0 2639 8054; www.baanhualampong.com; 336/20 Soi 21, Th Charoen Krung; dm 220B, s 290B, d 520-700B; 🞩 🖳) A short walk from the station, this old-style wood-and-concrete guesthouse has developed a loyal following among those seeking a mix of family atmosphere and backpacker self-sufficiency. The owner is a font of knowledge.

Train Inn (Map pp76-7; ☎ 0818-195 544; www.thetraininn.com; 428 Th Rong Muang; r 450-900B; 🞩 🖳) The new, clean, secure and relatively funky Train Inn is a breath of fresh air. Owner Jana maintains a young, friendly and helpful atmosphere and her 41 rooms are hostel-style compact; ask to see a few.

River View Guest House (Map pp76-7; ☎ 0 2234 5429; www.riverviewbkk.com; 768 Soi Phanurangsi, Th Songwat; r 450-900B; 🞩) The aptly named River View has some rooms (on upper floors) and a rooftop bar-restaurant with views you'd pay thousands for in nearby hotels. Rooms are big and mostly with fan; air-con costs more. It's in a local neighbourhood and hard to find; start at the Maritime Department ferry stop, and follow the signs north.

Most hotels in Chinatown are in the midrange price bracket and these are the best.

Grand China Princess (Map pp76-7; ☎ 0 2224 9977; www.grandchina.com; 215 Th Yaowarat; r 2200-4200B; 🞩 🖳 🞩) A certifiable monstrosity to look at, this hotel in the heart of Chinatown is popular with groups and has nondescript but comfortable rooms buoyed by great views.

Shanghai Inn (Map pp76-7; ☎ 0 2221 2121; www.shanghai-inn.com; 479 Th Yaowarat; r with breakfast 2800-4000B; 🞩 🖳) The Shanghai is a genuine boutique hotel that brings a technicolour interpretation of '30s Shanghai to manic Th Yaowarat. The 55 Chinese-style rooms have four-poster beds, bright-painted walls and as many as 10 hanging silk lights. Wi-fi is available throughout. Chinatown's best, by far.

Siam Square & Around

This is Bangkok's retail heart so if working your way through half-a-dozen huge air-conditioned malls sounds like a good time, look no further. Several big international chains have hotels on or around Th Ploenchit and Th Withayu, and a few midrange places are dotted about. For budgeteers there is Soi Kasem

San 1. This area is easily reached by Skytrain, or via a boat along Khlong Saen Saep.

BUDGET & MIDRANGE

If you prefer to spend your baht shopping than sleeping, the places along Soi Kasem San 1 are for you. This dead-end soi is off Th Phra Ram I just before the intersection with Th Phayathai, a five-minute walk to Siam Sq and Jim Thompson's House.

A-One Inn (Map pp80-1; ☎ 0 2215 3029; www.aoneinn .com; 25/13-15 Soi Kasem San 1, Th Phra Ram I; d 600-850B; ✄ ▯) This friendly family operation has 25 cosy rooms (with hot showers and TVs) that live up to it's advertising, offering value 'in the heart of town'. A-One is a wi-fi hotspot.

Wendy House (Map pp80-1; ☎ 0 2214 1149-50; www .wendyguesthouse.com; Soi Kasem San 1; Th Phra Ram I; s/tw with breakfast 900/1100B; ✄ ▯) Wendy is a cheery backpacker joint with 20 small but well-scrubbed rooms and tiled bathrooms; all are nonsmoking. Desk staff are sweet and the well-lit lobby quietly social.

VIP Guest House/Golden House (Map pp80-1; ☎ 0 2252 9535-8; www.goldenhouses.net; 1025/5-9 Th Ploenchit; r with breakfast from 1400B; ✄) The 27 clean, quiet and mainly bright rooms make this a good lower-midrange choice in this otherwise pricey part of town.

Reno Hotel (Map pp80-1; ☎ 0 2215 0026; www.reno hotel.co.th; 40 Soi Kasem San 1, Th Phra Ram I; d 1180-1550B; ✄ ▯) This Vietnam War veteran has embraced the new millennium with colour and some flair, keeping some attitude with its retro features (check out the monogrammed pool) and funking up the foyer and café. The 70 rooms remain fairly simple, the best being those overlooking the pool.

Other reliable midrange options include:

Pathumwan House (Map pp80-1; ☎ 0 2612 3580; www .pathumwanhouse.com; 22 Soi Kasem San 1, Th Phra Ram I; d 1200-2300B, monthly 15,000-34,000B; ✄) Mainly a long-term hotel but lots of dailies cycle through after striking out elsewhere.

Asia Hotel (Map pp80-1; ☎ 0 2215 0808; www.asiahotel .co.th; 296 Th Phayathai; r from 2600B; ✄ ▯) The classic Asian midranger; busy, faux-luxurious, reliable. Connects to Ratchathewi Skytrain.

TOP END

These and several other top-end hotels gather around this central commercial area.

Siam@Siam (Map pp72-3; ☎ 0 2217 3000; www.siam atsiam.com; 865 Th Phra Ram I; d from 5700B; ✄ ▯) This world of concrete, rust, copper and railway sleepers, with dashes of orange, takes industrial design to the limit. The 203 rooms occupy the 14th to 25th floors and have city views. Rates include breakfast and wi-fi internet.

Nai Lert Park Hotel (Map pp80-1; ☎ 0 2253 0123; www .swissotel.com/bangkok-nailertpark; 2 Th Withayu (Wireless Rd); d from US$185; ✄ ▯) A mishmash of bygone styles, the Nai Lert is a bit disappointing in the cramped rooms, but glorious underneath a shady tree in its private garden-park. There are ponds, palms, walking trails and a lovely tree-shaded swimming pool.

Grand Hyatt Erawan (Map pp80-1; ☎ 0 2254 1234; www.bangkok.hyatt.com; 494 Th Ratchadamri; d from 8800B; ✄ ▯) The Erawan's neoclassical lobby, embellished with mature tropical trees, sets the establishment tone in what is one of Bangkok's most-respected hotels. The 320 rooms are relatively big and well-designed. Wi-fi internet is unnecessarily expensive.

Riverside

The riverside area along Th Charoen Krung has several of Bangkok's top hotels, plus a couple of cheaper options. A combination of the Skytrain to Saphan Taksin and either a walk or ferry ride on the complimentary hotel ferries is the way to reach the top-end places.

New Road Guesthouse (Map pp78-9; ☎ 0 2630 6994-98; www.jysk-rejsebureau.dk; 1216/1 Th Charoen Krung; dm 90B, d 600-1300B, f 2500B; ✄ ▯) This Danish-run guesthouse is the go-to budget lodging in this part of town, with a wide range of rooms, a social communal area and bar. The JYSK tourist office here offers quality tours. Good choice.

P&R Residence (Map pp78-9; ☎ 0 2639 6091-93; pandr residence@gmail.com; 34 Soi 30, Th Charoen Krung, Bangrak; r 1000-1200B; ✄) Comfortable, clean and very fairly priced midrange option in an atmospheric old part of town. Ask for a front room for embassy views. Cash only.

Millennium Hilton (Map pp72-3; ☎ 0 2442 2000; bang kok.hilton.com; 123 Th Charoennakorn, Klongsan; d from 6000B; ✄ ▯) This new kid on the riverside block is usually cheaper than its neighbours, but has a more relaxed atmosphere and 543 rooms all with cinemascopic views. The Beach (sunbeds by the pool) and ThreeSixty (jazz, penthouse views) add to the package. A private ferry connects it to River City shopping centre and Saphan Thaksin Skytrain.

Oriental Hotel (Map pp78-9; ☎ 0 2659 9000; www .mandarinoriental.com; 48 Soi Oriental, Th Charoen Krung; r from US$360; ✄ ▯) Bangkok's answer to

---

BANGKOK'S TOP BOUTIQUE HOTELS

Bangkok has seen an explosion in the number of small hotels that have embraced a different idea of design and décor. These are our pick:

Money is No Object
Dream (p98) Rock star in blue.
Eugenia (p98) Explorer chic.
Ma Du Zi (p98) Design masterpiece.
Sukhothai Hotel (right) Modern classic Thai.

Won't Break the Bank
Phranakorn Nornlen (p94) Green smiles.
Refill Now! (opposite) The hostel redefined.
Seven (opposite) Six rooms, seven colours.
Shanghai Inn (p94) Old China kaleidoscope.

Raffles in Singapore or the Peninsula in Hong Kong, this classic hotel is also one of the finest in Southeast Asia. The original Author's Wing is steeped in colonial-era charm. Since those days, two vast new wings have been added, and there are several fine restaurants, including Le Normandie (p101). The hotel also has dinner cruises, a dinner show and a cooking school.

Thanon Silom & Thanon Sathon

Although the infamous Soi Patpong is right on the doorstep, the sleaze is limited to that area and is easy enough to avoid if desired.

BUDGET & MIDRANGE

This area has few budget places but a good selection of good-value midrange hotels, most of which are family friendly.

Urban Age (Map pp78-9; ☎ 0 2634 2680; theurbanage@ hotmail.com; 130/6 Soi 8, Th Silom; dm 250B, d 800B; ✳ ▣) A New Age version of the classic Bangkok budget haunt. Rooms are small but attractive, bathrooms are shared and the women who run the place are friendly. The dorms are six storeys up, all stairs.

Lub*D (Map pp78-9; ☎ 0 2634 7999; www.lubd.com; 4 Th Decho, Th Surawong; dm 550B, d 1800B; ✳ ▣) This 'boutique hostel' has four-storeys of dorms (including a ladies-only wing) and rooms (with and without bathrooms) in industrial chic style. It has free internet, tight security and a streetside bar-cum-lobby.

ourpick Rose Hotel (Map pp78-9; ☎ 0 2266 8268-72; www.rosehotelbkk.com; 118 Th Surawong, Silom; r from 1700B;

(P) (✳) (▣) (▩)) After a much-needed facelift, the veteran Rose has been reborn as one of the best-value hotels in Bangkok. Its 70 spacious, stylish rooms are complemented by a small gym, sauna and Thai restaurant in an old teak house set around an oasis-like pool.

All Seasons (Map pp72-3; ☎ 0 2343 6333; www.all seasons-asia.com; 31 Th Sathon Tai; r 1800-2500B; ✳ ▣) The 78 spacious, high-ceilinged rooms in this newly made over hotel have a contemporary feel and are well-equipped, with desk, free wi-fi and cable broadband. Superior and deluxe rooms are best. Good value. Note that it's not on All Seasons Pl.

ourpick La Résidence Hotel (Map pp78-9; ☎ 0 2233 3301; www.laresidencebangkok.com; 173/8-9 Th Surawong; d/ste 2000/3700B; ✳) La Résidence is a charming boutique inn with 26 playfully and individually decorated rooms that are both casually sophisticated and fantastic value.

Triple Two Silom (Map pp78-9; ☎ 0 2627 2222; www .tripletwosilom.com; 222 Th Silom; r/ste 4500/5900B; ✳ ▣) Once a bland shopping mall, this is now a classy, 75-room boutique hotel in a pleasing pan-Asian mode. Rooms are large and well-kitted out with both wi-fi and ADSL internet at the desk.

TOP END

Many of Bangkok's finest and most-interesting luxury hotels are in this area.

Banyan Tree Hotel (Map pp72-3; ☎ 0 2679 1200; www .banyantree.com; Thai Wah Tower II, 21/100 Th Sathon Tai; d from 10,500B; ✳ ▣ ▩) This tall, wafer-thin and ultramodern hotel appeals for its spa-like atmosphere, larger luxurious rooms and, indeed, its six storeys of well-respected spa facilities. Then, of course, there is the dreamy Moon Bar and Vertigo grill (p102) on the roof.

Sukhothai Hotel (Map pp72-3; ☎ 0 2344 8888; www .sukhothai.com; 13/3 Th Sathon Tai; r 14,000-100,000B; ✳ ▣ ▩) Architect Ed Tuttle's uniquely Thai modernism embraces both classic Thai features – think winged roofs, hardwood floors and six acres of garden full of Sukhothai-style brick stupas – and a modern minimalism that is deeply satisfying.

Other good luxury hotels in this area include:

Metropolitan (Map pp72-3; ☎ 0 2625 3322; www .metropolitan.como.bz; 27 Th Sathon Tai; d from US$290; ✳ ▣ ▩) Uber-cool urban chic; excellent C'yan restaurant (p101); pricey rooms.

Dusit Thani (Map pp78-9; ☎ 0 2200 9000; www.dusit .com; 946 cnr Th Phra Ram IV & Th Silom; r from 6100B;

🔀 ▣ 🔁) This '60s landmark has embraced global Zen with mixed results. Great location and D'Sens restaurant.

Thanon Sukhumvit

Th Sukhumvit has been the centre of a hotel building boom in recent years. Many of the new places are boutique and design hotels, mostly in the midrange and top-end, though there are a couple of decent budget places scattered about. Alongside the new places are several 1970s cheapies catering largely to middle-aged Western men with teenage Thai girlfriends or boyfriends in tow, or long-termers gathering material for 'novels'. Intense competition at the upper end means big discounts can be found online.

BUDGET

Suk 11 (Map p82; ☎ 0 2253 5927-28; www.suk11.com; sub-soi off Soi 11, Th Sukhumvit; dm 250B, d 480-800B; 🔀 ▣) Sukhumvit's predominant outpost of backpacker culture, Suk 11 creates an atmosphere of convivial post-beach chill amid the concrete jungle. The small, garden-guarded entrance opens Tardis-like to 80 upstairs rooms along a wooden hallway. Rooms come with and without bathrooms.

HI Sukhumvit (Map pp70-1; ☎ 0 2391 9338; www.hisukhumvit.com; 23 Soi 38, Th Sukhumvit; dm 300B, d 800-900B, f 1200B; 🔀 ▣) Out east near the Ekamai bus station, the clean, simple dorms and rooms and welcoming family owners make this budget place a real find. The breezy rooftop and nearby night food market add to the appeal.

Atlanta Hotel (Map p82; ☎ 0 2252 1650; fax 0 2656 8123; 78 Soi 2, Th Sukhumvit; d from 800B; 🔀 🔁) Sukhumvit's first hotel is (in the lobby, at least) like a time capsule of 1950s décor, with old-fashioned writing desks and a grand-entrance staircase sweeping up five floors (there's no lift). The rooms are functional and those on the top floor aren't good at all, but they're fair value. Note: 'The Atlanta does not welcome sex tourists and does not try to be polite about it.'

Bangkok Centre Sukhumvit 25 (Map p82; ☎ 0 2259 6869; www.thailandhotel.com; Soi 25, Th Sukhumvit; dm 390B, s/d with breakfast 1200/1500B; 🔀 ▣) This place looks a bit institutional but feels friendly and communal and is very good value. The large, clean rooms and dorms are well-equipped (though dorms need three people for the air-con to be turned on). Prices here are for nonmembers of HI, but sign up for 200B per person and save 100/300/500B on a dorm/single/double.

Refill Now! (Map pp70-1; ☎ 0 2713 2044; www.refillnow.co.th; 191 Soi Pridi Banhom Yong 42, Soi 71, Th Sukhumvit; dm 560B, s/d 1085/1470B; 🔀 ▣ 🔁) Refill promises and delivers 'high-style low-cost', with spotless white private rooms and dorms that have flirtatious pull screens between each double-bunk; women-only dorms are also available. It's inconveniently located and pricey for shared bathrooms, but the hip-and-unpretentious vibe has made it hugely popular. Take a taxi or mototaxi from the Phra Kanong Skytrain down Soi 71, turn right on Soi 42 and left.

MIDRANGE

Citichic (Map p82; ☎ 0 2342 3888; www.citichichotel.com; 34 Soi 13, Th Sukhumvit; r from 2300B; 🔀 ▣ 🔁) Everything from the foyer, to the rooms, the gym and the rooftop pool is small in this new midranger. The self-applied 'boutique' classification might be stretching credulity a little, but it is very good value, with 'chic'-enough design, broadband internet included and smiling service.

Le Fenix (Map p82; ☎ 0 2305 4000; www.lefenix-sukhumvit.com; 33 Soi 11, Th Sukhumvit; r 2590B; 🔀 ▣) Accor's foray into the hip-design-boutique market has 147 rooms at the end of busy Soi 11 and is aimed at young, party-oriented tourists. It is reasonable value, though bear in mind that the small rooms all come with two single mattresses on one base, pushed together or separated by a few inches. Rooms have both wi-fi and cable internet.

Napa Place Bed & Breakfast (Map pp70-1; ☎ 0 2661 5525; www.napaplace.com; 11/3 Yaek 2, Soi 36, Th Sukhumvit; d 2750-4800B; 🔀 ▣) Tucked away in a quiet soi seven minutes walk from Thong Lo Skytrain, the 12-room Napa has a homely B&B atmosphere and appeals to families because it has huge rooms (36 to 67 sq m), plenty of communal space, solid security and free buffet breakfasts. Cable broadband is also free. Superb value.

Bangkok Boutique Hotel (Map p82; ☎ 0 2261 2850; www.bangkokboutiquehotel.com; 241 Soi Asoke, Th Sukhumvit; r from with breakfast 2900B; 🔀 ▣) This low-rise place combines a minimalist, polished-concrete mode with hi-tech gadgetry (free internet and wireless keyboards plugged into the big flatscreen TVs so you can surf from bed). Superior rooms are the best value; ask for one away from the cacophonous street.

Seven (Map p82; ☎ 081-616 2636; www.sleepatseven.com; 3/15 Soi 31, Th Sukhumvit; r 3100-6000B; 🔀 ▣) Six rooms, seven colours. From the designers of London's Ministry of Sound, this design hotel applies to its six rooms and lobby the Thai idea that each day has its own colour (eg Monday is yellow; the King was born on a Monday, hence the yellow shirts on Mondays). Rooms are quite small but well appointed with free wi-fi and mobile phones and iPods to use during the stay. Good for hip young singles and couples.

TOP END

Eugenia (Map p82; ☎ 0 2259 9017-19; www.theeugenia .com; 267 Soi 31, Th Sukhumvit; r 5800-7200B; ✕ ▢ ▣) This unique 12-room boutique place is modelled on the colonial mansions of Africa and the Subcontinent. Think Livingston, Hemingway, Indian Raj and rooms packed full of art, books, antique furniture, beaten copper bathtubs and stuffed animals. Rooms aren't huge (the Siam suites are tiny), but it's the ambience you're here for. Ask about the vintage-car airport transfers.

Dream (Map p82; ☎ 0 2254 8500; www.dreambkk .com; 10 Soi 15, Th Sukhumvit; r from US$200; ✕ ▢ ▣) Call it 'boutique' or 'design', but this hotel in two adjacent buildings is a rock-star world of cream leather, mirrors, silver and blue motifs and, in the uber-chic Flava lounge bar-cum-restaurant, a white tiger (with blue stripes). Blue is the theme, and 195 rooms are blue-lit (for deeper sleep, apparently). Suites are way overpriced, though.

Ma Du Zi (Map p82; ☎ 0 2615 6400; www.maduzihotel .com; cnr Th Ratchadapisek & Sukhumvit Soi 16; r 15,000B-33,000B; ✕ ▢) This 41-room luxury hotel is a masterpiece of design. The fittings, restrained but very stylish décor and service are all top notch – everything works. Rooms are huge and, in fairness, so too are the prices. But they include everything, from airport pickup through wi-fi to the minibar. The French restaurant is also excellent. Reservations only, no walk in.

Also worth considering:

S15 (Map p82; ☎ 0 2651 2000; www.s15hotel.com; 217 Th Sukhumvit, cnr Soi 15; d 4500-6000B, ste 7700B; ✕ ▢) New boutique place with reasonably sized, Zen-styled rooms.

Grand Millennium Sukhumvit (Map p82; ☎ 0 2204 4111; www.grandmillenniumskv.com; 30 Soi Asoke, Th Sukhumvit; r from 7500B, ste 13,500B; ✕ ▢ ▣) Bright, spacious and tastefully furnished rooms in one of Bangkok's more interesting new buildings.

EATING

Nowhere else is the Thai reverence for food more evident than in Bangkok. The city's

---

AIRPORT ACCOMMODATION

Most people will use the new Suvarnabhumi International Airport, which takes all international flights, but old Don Muang airport still hosts some domestic services, many of which fly to the islands and beaches of the south.

Suvarnabhumi International Airport

Grand Inn Come Hotel (☎ 0 2738 8189-99; www.grandinncome-hotel.com; 99 Moo 6, Th Kingkaew, Bangplee; s/tw from 1800/2000B; ✕ ▢) Solid midranger a few minutes by shuttle bus east of the airport, with 'lively' karaoke bar.

Novotel Suvarnabhumi Airport Hotel (☎ 0 2131 1111; www.novotel.com; r from 5000B; ✕ ▢) Has 600-plus luxurious rooms in the airport.

Refill Now! (see p97) Nearest good budget option.

Don Muang Airport

Amari Airport Hotel (Map pp70-1; ☎ 0 2566 1020; www.amari.com; 333 Th Choet Wutthakat; r from US$90; ✕ ▣) Opposite Don Muang, it's the most popular airport hotel and has well-equipped day-use rooms from US$85.

Rama Gardens Hotel (Map pp70-1; ☎ 0 2561 0022; www.ramagardenshotel.com; 9/9 Th Vibhavadi Rangsit; r from 4700B; ✕ ▣) Tranquil garden setting and very comfortable deluxe wings with deep-soak tubs. Shuttle buses to airport.

We-Train International House (Map pp70-1; ☎ 0 2967 8550-54; www.we-train.co.th; 501/1 Muu 3, Th Decha-tungkha, Sikan, Don Muang; dm 200B, r 800-1100B; ✕ ▣) Quiet place with good-value rooms 3km from airport, run by the Association for the Promotion of the Status of Women. Take a taxi (about 80B) from outside Amari Hotel.

characteristic body odour is a unique blend of noodle stall and car exhaust, and in certain parts of town, restaurants appear to form the majority of businesses, typically flanked by streetside hawker stalls and mobile snack vendors. To outsiders, the life of an average Bangkokian can appear to be little more than a string of meals and snacks punctuated by the odd job, not the other way around. If you can adjust your gutteral clock to fit this schedule, we're confident your stay in Bangkok will be a happy one indeed.

Despite the global infatuation with Thai food, many visitors go from one mediocre meal to another, mainly at guesthouse kitchens and tourist-oriented restaurants catering more to a Western definition of ambience than food. In order to break the bonds of so-so meals, we strongly urge you to break out of the ghetto mentality and explore the small eateries and street stalls of this great city. Virtually every regional Thai cuisine can be found in Bangkok.

The standard opening hours for restaurants here are 11am to 11pm daily, but many midrange places close from 2.30pm to 6pm.

Banglamphu

Despite encompassing faràng-dominated Th Khao San, Banglamphu is home to some of the city's most legendary Thai eats. The foreign influence has resulted in an abundance of cheap Western-style and vegetarian restaurants.

Arroi (Map pp74-5; 152 Th Din So; mains 20-30B) Employing a variety of tasty meat substitutes and sticking to a repertoire of classic Thai dishes, even dedicated flesh-eaters will be happy at this tiny restaurant.

Thip Samai (Map pp74-5; ☎ 0 2221 6280; 313 Th Mahachai; mains 25-120B; ☽ dinner) Less than a five-minute túk-túk drive away from Th Khao San is Thip Samai, home to the most legendary pàt tai in town. For something a bit different, try the delicate egg-wrapped version, or the pàt tai fried with man gûng, shrimp fat.

Kim Leng (Map pp74-5; ☎ 0 2622 2062; 158-160 Th Tanao; mains 40-80B; ☽ lunch & dinner Mon-Sat) Kim Leng is a true Bangkok eatery and, as with much of the food of the capital, sweet intermingles with spicy. You can't go wrong with the hòr mòk (steamed curry) or nám prík gà·bì (shrimp paste dip served as a set with veggies and deep-fried fish).

Roti-Mataba (Map pp74-5; ☎ 0 2282 2119; 136 Th Phra Athit; mains 50-90B; ☽ Tue-Sun) This classic eatery serves tasty Thai-Muslim dishes such as roti, gaang mát·sà·màn (Muslim curry), a brilliantly sour fish curry, and má·tà·bà (a sort of stuffed Indian pancake). An upstairs air-conditioned dining area provides barely enough seating for its loyal fans.

our pick Chote Chitr (Map pp74-5; ☎ 0 2221 4082; 146 Th Phraeng Phuton; mains 60-150B; ☽ lunch & dinner) Combining just six tables and two talented cooks, Chote Chitr (pronounced chôht jìt), puts out delicious, dictionary-definition Central Thai fare. The second-generation restaurant is particularly renowned for its mèe gròrp, sweet-and-spicy crispy fried noodles, still made the old-school way, but just about anything from the expansive menu will bring a smile.

Oh My Cod! (Map pp74-5; ☎ 0 2282 6553; 95d, Rambuttri Village Inn, Soi Rambuttri I; mains 70-200B) Fish and chips fried to perfection, not to mention all-day breakfast and a sunny courtyard dining area where parched Anglophiles can enjoy a proper cuppa.

Hemlock (Map pp74-5; ☎ 0 2282 7507; 56 Th Phra Athit; mains 80-200B; ☽ dinner Mon-Sat) The classiest of Banglamphu's bohemian Thai restaurants, Hemlock offers sublime Thai cuisine in stylish surroundings. As well as more familiar dishes such as gaang pá·naang gài (Penang curry with chicken), this place serves ancient and unusual dishes you won't find elsewhere.

Shoshana (Map pp74-5; ☎ 0 2282 9948; 88 Th Chakraphong; mains 90-150B) The 'I heart Shoshana' T-shirts worn by the wait staff may be a hopelessly optimistic description of employee morale, but the gut-filling chips-falafel-and-hummus plates leave nothing to be desired.

Chinatown

There are surprisingly few formal restaurants in Chinatown, and those that exist specialise in shark fin and bird's nest soup and dim sum. At night much of the neighbourhood is taken over by hawkers serving some of Bangkok's finest street food. Seafood is also great value – you can get gûng pow (grilled prawns) for a fraction of the cost of many Bangkok restaurants.

Chinatown becomes a major culinary destination during the Vegetarian Festival in September or October, when every restaurant in the area turns out special veg dishes.

During the day in nearby Phahurat heaps of tiny shops serve Indian food including fresh chapattis and Indian-style chai (tea), catering to Bangkok's small Indian community.

Mangkawn Khao (Map pp76-7; cnr Th Yaowarat & Th Yaowaphanit; meals 25-40B; ☻ dinner) Mangkawn Khao (White Dragon), a popular street stall, is a respected vendor of bà·mèe, Chinese-style wheat noodles, and gée·o, wontons, both served with generous slices of bacon-like barbecued pork.

Royal India (Map pp76-7; ☎ 0 2221 6565; 392/1 Th Chakraphet; mains 100-250B; ☻ lunch & dinner) This legendary north Indian place continues to draw local foodies despite the lack of aesthetics. Try any of the delicious breads or saucy curries, and finish with a homemade Punjabi sweet.

Tang Jai Yuu (Map pp76-7; ☎ 0 2224 2167; 85-89 Th Yaowaphanit; mains 100-300B; ☻ lunch & dinner) This Chinatown legend specialises in Teo Chew and Chinese–Thai specialties with an emphasis on seafood. You can't go wrong choosing a fresh fish from the tank out front and letting the experts grill it for you.

Shangarila Restaurant (Map pp76-7; ☎ 0 2224 5933; 306 Th Yaowarat; mains 220-500B; ☻ lunch & dinner) Roast duck, red pork and freshly steamed seafood feature prominently on the menu at this popular Chinese banquet restaurant. Chow down on some dim sum at lunchtime or Peking duck in the evening.

Thanon Silom & Thanon Sathon

The business heart of Bangkok has dozens of upscale restaurants for business lunches and dinners, and fast-food eateries catering to hungry office workers. Don't immediately assume that restaurants in malls will serve mediocre food. In fact many of Bangkok's leading eateries are tucked away in shopping arcades or hotels.

Th Charoen Krung and the river end of Th Silom near Th Charoen Krung, are good places for Indian and Muslim food.

BUDGET

Several cheap food markets set up at lunchtime or in the evenings. Opposite the Sri Mahariamman temple is the setting for a lively **day and night market** (Soi Pradit; Map pp78-9). Most of the stalls here serve Hainanese and Muslim dishes for around 30B to 50B, catering to local workers and devotees from the nearby Masjid Mirasuddeen mosque. Numerous fast-food outlets can be found at the Th Phra Ram IV end of Th Silom.

Khrua Aroy Aroy (Map pp78-9; ☎ 0 2635 2365; Th Pan, Th Silom; mains 30-70B) Prepare yourself for the trip down south at this authentic southern-style curry shack. The richest curries around and interesting daily specials make Khrua Aroy Aroy ('Delicious Delicious Kitchen') live up to its lofty name.

Ran Nam Tao Hu Yong Her (Map pp78-9; ☎ 0 2635 0003; 68 Th Narathiwat, Silom; mains 40-205B; ☻ lunch & dinner) The emphasis here is on northern Chinese cuisine – a rarity in Bangkok. Try the Shanghainese specialty xiao long bao (described on the menu as 'Small steamed bun') steamed dumplings encasing a pork filling and rich hot broth that pours out when you bite into them.

Home Cuisine Islamic Restaurant (Map pp78-9; ☎ 0 2234 7911; 196-198 Soi 36, Th Charoen Krung; mains 45-130B; ☻ lunch & dinner) This bungalow-like restaurant does tasty Thai–Muslim with an endearing Indian accent. Sit out on the breezy patio and try the simultaneously rich and sour fish curry, accompanied ideally by a flaky roti or three.

Chennai Kitchen (Map pp78-9; ☎ 0 2234 1266; 10 Th Pan, Th Silom; mains 50-120B; ☻ lunch) This thimble-sized restaurant near the Hindu temple puts out solid southern Indian vegetarian nosh. If you're feeling indecisive go for the banana-leaf thali that seems to incorporate just about everything in the kitchen.

Suan Lum Night Bazaar (Map pp72-3; Th Phra Ram IV; meals 60-120B; ☻ dinner) Find a seat (preferably as far from the tacky stage music as possible if you value your eardrums), order a draft hefeweizen and a dish of deep-fried soft-shell crabs, and settle down for an evening of typically tasty Thai entertainment. There is talk that Suan Lum is slotted for the wrecking ball in 2008, but until the bulldozers arrive, we're remaining sceptical.

Mizu's Kitchen (Map pp78-9; ☎ 0 2233 6447; 32 Soi Patpong 1, Th Silom; mains 90-400B; ☻ lunch & dinner) This certifiable hole-in-the-wall oozes character, not to mention the beefy essence of thousands of steaks served over the decades. The house steak is a winner, and you'll be hard-pressed to find a better macaroni and cheese in Bangkok.

MIDRANGE & TOP END

Scoozi (Map pp78-9; ☎ 0 2234 6999; 174 Th Surawong, Silom; mains 150-350B; ☻ lunch & dinner) At this trendy pizzeria you can witness your pie be skilfully tossed and topped before being blistered in a

FOOD COURT FRENZY

Every Bangkok mall worth its escalators has some sort of food court. In the recent past these were the abode of working-class Thais; the food was cheap, the settings bland, and you were even expected to serve yourself. In recent years, however, food courts have moved upscale, and the setting, cuisine and service have elevated accordingly. Expect to pay 30B to 150B for a meal at one of these.

Food Loft (Map pp80-1; 7th fl, Central Chidlom, 1027 Th Ploenchit) This new concept in food court serves up fresh Thai, Chinese, Vietnamese, Indian and Italian prepared by staff from some of Bangkok's better restaurants. Upon entering, you'll be given a temporary credit card and will be led to a table. You have to get up again to order, but the dishes will be brought to you. Paying is done on your way out.

ourpick **MBK Food Court** (Map pp80-1; 6th fl, Mahboonkrong Centre, cnr Th Phra Ram I & Th Phayathai) A virtual crash-course in Thai food, MBK's Food Court offers tens of vendors selling eats from virtually every corner of the country and beyond. Standouts include an excellent vegetarian food stall (stall C8), whose mock-meat mushrooms almost taste better than the real thing, and a very decent Isan food vendor (C22). The Fifth, on the 5th floor of the same mall, emphasizes international eats in a slightly more upscale setting.

Park Food Hall (Map pp70-1; 5th fl, Emporium Shopping Centre, 622 Th Sukhumvit, cnr Soi 24) Park brings together some of the city's most-loved international food vendors. Emporium Food Hall, on the same floor, features cheaper, mostly Chinese/Thai food, and what must be the cheapest meal with a view in town. Paying is done by buying coupons at the windows in the entrance. Be sure to leave these in your pocket until the next day when it's too late to get a refund; it's an integral part of the food court experience.

wood-burning oven from Italy. The Scoozi empire has other branches, including one at Th Khao San (Map pp74-5; ☎ 0 2280 5280; 201 Soi Sunset).

Le Bouchon (Map pp78-9; ☎ 0 2234 9109; Soi Patpong 2, Th Silom; mains 150-350B; lunch & dinner) This homey bistro smack-dab in the middle of one of Bangkok's more 'colourful' districts is a capable and fun introduction to French cooking. Choose your dishes from a chalkboard menu of Gallic faves toted about by the cheery wait staff.

Somboon Seafood (Map pp78-9; ☎ 0 2233 3104; cnr Th Surawong & Th Narathiwat Ratchanakharin; mains 150-250B; dinner) As with all good Thai seafood restaurants, your fish should be enjoyed with as many friends as you can get together, and an immense platter of *kôw pàt bŏo* (fried rice with crab).

Blue Elephant (Map pp72-3; ☎ 0 2673 9353; 233 Th Sathon Tai, Silom; mains 200-500B; lunch & dinner) If you're going to do upscale Thai, you can do no worse than the Blue Elephant. Set in a stunning Sino-Portuguese colonial building with service fit for royalty, the restaurant also features an impressive cooking school.

Le Normandie (Map pp78-9; ☎ 0 2236 0400; Oriental Hotel, Soi 38, Th Charoen Krung; 3-/7-course meals 1000/4000B; lunch & dinner, closed for lunch Sun) This elegant glass case overlooking the Chao Phraya River is the epitome of the French culinary tradition. Michelin-starred chefs and decadent

ingredients are flown in from all corners of the world, making reservations and formal attire (including jackets) a necessity.

ourpick **Cy'an** (Map pp72-3; ☎ 0 2625 3333; Metropolitan Hotel, 27 Th Sathon Tai, Silom; 7-course meal 2800B) Resembling the sleekest school cafeteria that Philippe Starck never designed, Cy'an is the perfect forum for the mix-and-match creations of Australian chef Daniel Moran. Combining vibrant Mediterranean and Moroccan flavours, a healthy obsession with the finest seafood, and a chic yet intimate atmosphere, the result is quite possibly the most faultless fine dining experience in town.

Siam Square & Thanon Ploenchit

This shopping area has lots of fast-food-type places that cater to diners on the run, plus a handful of posher options.

Sanguan Sri (Map pp80-1; ☎ 0 2252 7637; 59/1 Th Withayu, Th Ploenchit; mains 60-150B; lunch Mon-Sat) This restaurant can afford to remain decidedly *cheu-i* (old-fashioned) simply because of its reputation. Follow the lead of the local hungry office staff and try the excellent *gaang pèt bèt yaang*, red curry with grilled duck breast served over snowy white *kà-nŏm jeen* noodles.

Crystal Jade La Mian Xiao Long Bao (Map pp80-1; ☎ 0 2250 7990; Urban Kitchen, Basement, Erawan Bangkok, 494 Th Ploenchit; mains 120-300B; lunch & dinner) The tongue-twistingly long name of this Singaporean chain refers to the restaurant's signature wheat noodles *(la mian)* and Shanghainese steamed dumplings *(xiao long pao)*.

Gianni Ristorante (Map pp80-1; ☎ 0 2252 1619; 34/1 Soi Tonson; mains 260-600B; ☯ lunch & dinner) This classy restaurant nearly single-handedly upped the bracket for Italian dining in Bangkok. Homemade sausages, lobster-stuffed raviolis, and braised lamb shank transport tastebuds to the Adriatic. Wine lovers rave about the huge and unique selection.

Thanon Sukhumvit

Stretching east all the way to the city limits, Th Sukhumvit attracts equal numbers of business travellers and monkey-business travellers. This is where to go to eat foreign food, as the majority of expats and immigrants claim a Sukhumvit address.

BUDGET

Imoya (Map pp70-1; ☎ 0 2663 5185; 3rd fl, Terminal Shop Cabin, 2/17-19 Soi 24, Th Sukhumvit; mains 40-120B; ☯ dinner) A visit to this well-hidden Japanese restaurant, with its antique advertisements, wood panelling and wall of sake bottles, is like taking a trip in a time machine. Even the prices of the better-than-decent Eastern-style pub grub haven't caught up with modern times.

Thonglee (Map p82; ☎ 0 2258 1983; Soi 20, Th Sukhumvit; mains 40-70B; ☯ closed 3rd Sun of the month) Thonglee, the epitome of a typical Thai restaurant, offers a few dishes you won't find elsewhere, such as *môo pàt ga·bi* (pork fried with shrimp paste) and *mèe gròrp* (sweet-and-spicy crispy fried noodles).

Komala's (Map p82; ☎ 0 2663 5971; 15 Soi 20, Th Sukhumvit; mains 80-200B; ☯ lunch & dinner) If you can forgive the form-fitting plastic furniture and reckless use of teal, this Singaporean chain puts out some tasty south Indian vegetarian staples.

Je Ngor (Map p82; ☎ 0 2258 8008; 68/2 Soi 20, Th Sukhumvit; mains 90-600B; ☯ lunch & dinner) Je Ngor proffers banquet-size servings of tasty Thai-Chinese dishes in a banquet-like setting. The relatively brief seafood-heavy menu features rarities such as *sôm·dam bòo dorng* (papaya salad with preserved crab), and baked rice with preserved olive.

MIDRANGE

Ana's Garden (Map pp70-1; ☎ 0 2391 1762; 67 Soi 55, Th Sukhumvit; mains 150-250B; ☯ dinner) Ana's lush garden of broad-leafed palms and purring fountains will almost make you forget about the urban jungle on the other side. The spicy *yam tòo·a ploo* (wing bean salad), on the other hand, will leave no doubts about which city you're in.

Crêpes & Co (Map p82; ☎ 0 2653 3990; 18/1 Soi 12, Th Sukhumvit; mains 150-350B) The homey setting and excellent service, not to mention a menu that offers much more than the restaurant's name suggests, keep the desperate housewives of Bangkok's diplomatic corps coming back.

Little Arabia (Map p82; Soi 3/1, Th Sukhumvit) Packed full of Middle Eastern restaurants, Little Arabia provides a delicious respite from rice and noodles. *Shishah* (water pipe) smoke perfumes the air while concentrating couples devour sesame-flecked flatbread, creamy hummus and flawless falafels.

SKY-HIGH SUNDOWNERS

Bangkok is one the few places in the world where nobody seems to mind if you set up a bar or restaurant on top of a skyscraper. Except for Rang Mahal, the views are considerably more memorable than the pricey meals, so it's worth opting for a sundowner or two and then go and eat elsewhere.

Rang Mahal (Map p82; ☎ 0 2261 7100; Rembrandt Hotel, Soi 18, Th Sukhumvit; mains 195-595B) Sheltered from the elements, Rang Mahal still claims the altitude high on the top floor of the Rembrandt Hotel and delivers majestic Indian sets and buffets.

Sirocco/Sky Bar (Map pp78-9; ☎ 0 2624 9555; 63rd fl, State Tower, 1055 Th Silom; dishes 500-1000B) A sweeping staircase provides a Hollywood-style entrance to Sirocco. The connected Sky Bar is poised on the roof's edge and pours shots of vertigo; reservations and smart casual dress are required.

Moon Bar at Vertigo (Map pp72-3; ☎ 0 2679 1200; Banyan Tree Hotel, 21/100 Th Sathon Tai) Perched near the clouds on the 61st floor with the roar of Bangkok traffic far below, Vertigo has a front-row view of virtually the entire city.

TOP END

Face (Map pp70-1; ☎ 0 2713 6048; 29 Soi 38, Th Sukhumvit; mains 150-400B; 🕑 dinner) This handsome dining complex is essentially two very good restaurants in one: Lan Na Thai does excellent domestic (with an emphasis on regional) Thai dishes, while Hazara dabbles in exotic-sounding 'North Indian frontier cuisine'.

La Piola (Map p82; ☎ 0 2250 7270; 31/4 Soi 11, Th Sukhumvit; small/full set menu 900/1200B; 🕑 dinner Tue-Sat) They've recently gone à la carte, but the highlight at this homey Italian is still the fixed menu that has been known to punish even the biggest eater.

Bed Supperclub (Map p82; ☎ 0 2651 3537; 26 Soi 11, Th Sukhumvit, set menu 1000B; 🕑 Sun-Thu three seatings per evening, Fri & Sat one seating at 8.30pm) Think breakfast in bed, except that it's not breakfast, and your 'bed' is a gigantic white tube that you share with other diners. Come on Fridays when Kiwi Head Chef Paul Hutt takes the best of what he can get his mitts on and transforms it into a surprise four-course menu.

DRINKING

Bangkok's girlie-bar scene may still be going just as strong as it has for the last 30 years, but having a good time in the city doesn't have to involve ping-pong balls or bar fines. Just like any other big international city, Bangkok's drinking and partying scene ranges from classy to trashy, and touches on just about everything in-between.

Bangkok's nightlife took a serious hit in 2004 when the Thaksin administration decided that the city's residents needed to go to bed at a respectable hour. A gradual moving back to pre-2004 hours was halted by a renewed crackdown in 2008.

The good news is that everything old is new again. Th Khao San, that former outpost of foreigner frugality, has undergone something of an upscale renaissance, and is now more popular with the locals than ever. And RCA (Royal City Avenue), a suburban nightclub zone previously associated with gum-snapping Thai teenagers, is drawing in dancers and drinkers of all ages and races.

Buddy Bar (Map pp74-5; ☎ 0 2629 4477; Th Khao San) Buddy Lodge's clean and cool colonial-themed bar is perfect for folks who find Bangkok too dirty. Brick Bar, the subterranean live-music den, features nightly performances of Teddy Ska, one of Bangkok's most energetic live bands.

ourpick Cheap Charlie's (Map p82; Soi 11, Th Sukhumvit) An outdoor wooden shack decorated with buffalo skulls and wagon wheels, Charlie's is refreshingly out of place on image-conscious Th Sukhumvit, and draws a staunchly foreign crowd that doesn't mind a bit of kitsch and sweat with their Singha.

Opera Riserva Winetheque (Map p82; ☎ 0 2258 5601; 53 Soi 39, Th Sukhumvit) You're more than likely to find a vintage you'll fancy from this sleek den's weekly wine pics, and an attractive and extensive menu of wine-friendly Italian-style meals and snacks is also available.

Phranakorn Bar (Map pp74-5; ☎ 0 2282 7507; 58/2 Soi Damnoen Klang Tai) Students and arty types make Phranakorn Bar a home away from hovel with eclectic décor, gallery exhibits and, the real draw, a rooftop terrace with great views over old Bangkok.

Taksura (Map pp74-5; ☎ 0 2622 0708; 156/1 Th Tanao) There are no signs to lead you to this seemingly abandoned almost 100-year-old mansion in the heart of old Bangkok. Take a seat outside to soak up the breezes, and go Thai and order some spicy nibbles with your drinks.

To-Sit (Map pp80-1; ☎ 0 2658 4001; Soi 3, Th Phra Ram 1, Siam Sq) Live, loud and sappy music; cheap and spicy food; good friends and cold beer: To-Sit epitomises everything a Thai university student could wish for on a night out.

Tuba (Map pp70-1; ☎ 0 2622 0708; 30 Soi 21, Soi 63 (Ekamai), Th Sukhumvit) Used furniture store by day, Italian restaurant-slash-bar by night. Oddly enough, this business formula is not entirely unheard of in Bangkok.

Wong's Place (Map pp72-3; 27/3 Soi Sri Bumphen, off Soi Ngam Duphli, Th Phra Ram IV) A time warp into the backpacker world of the early 1980s, Wong's works equally well as a destination or a last resort, but don't bother knocking until midnight.

Every expat neighbourhood has an Irish-style pub where the lads can catch the game on a big-screen TV and drink Guinness amid North Atlantic temperatures. On Silom there's **Molly Malone's** (Map pp78-9; ☎ 0 2266 7160; 1/5-6 Th Convent) and on Th Sukhumvit, **Bull's Head** (Map p82; ☎ 0 2259 4444; 595/10-11 Soi 33/1, Th Sukhumvit) and **Black Swan** (Map p82; ☎ 0 2626 0257; 326/8-9 Th Sukhumvit) are two homey places to knock back a pint or three.

GAY & LESBIAN BANGKOK

Is there a gay-friendlier city on the planet? While stepping off the Western shelf is a gamble for many gays, Bangkok's male-gay nightlife is out and open with bars, discos and gà·teu·i (also spelt kàthoey; ladyboys) cabarets, but night spots for Thai lesbians (torm·dee) aren't as prominent or as segregated.

Utopia, the well-known gay information provider, publishes the Utopia Guide to Thailand, covering gay-friendly businesses in 18 Thai cities, including Bangkok. More listings and events can be found at www.fridae.com. Both gays and lesbians are well advised to visit Bangkok in mid-November, when the city's small but fun **Pride Festival** (www.bangkokpride.org) is in full swing. Dinners, cruises, clubbing and contests are the order of the week.

Some recommended bars:

DJ Station (Map pp78-9; ☎ 0 2266 4029; 8/6-8 Soi 2, Th Silom) Massively popular with the younger crowd, and among the most well known gay destinations in town, this place has pounding dance music, flamboyant costume parties and gà·teu·i cabaret at 11pm.

G.O.D. (Guys On Display; Map pp78-9; ☎ 0 2632 8032; Soi 2/1, Th Silom; cover 280B; ⊙ 11.30pm-late) The former Freeman has been reincarnated as this popular after-hours destination. Open late and, as the name suggests, not averse to a bit of shirtless dancing. Located on the tiny alley between Soi 2 and Soi Thaniya.

Kluen Saek (Map pp72-3; ☎ 0 2254 2962; 297 Th Sarasin) One of a strip of bars along Th Sarasin that is becoming gayer by the day, Kluen Saek is barely able to contain a mixed crowd of ravers in its cool grey grip.

Shela (Map pp72-3; ☎ 0 2254 6463; 106/12-13 Soi Lang Suan (cnr Soi Lang Suan & Soi Sarasin)) Owned by the same ladies who run Zeta, Shela draws a slightly more mature crowd with live music, a pool table and food. Women only.

Telephone (Map pp78-9; ☎ 0 2234 3279; 114/11-13 Soi 4, Th Silom) Bangkok's oldest gay bar-restaurant still features telephones so that patrons can 'ring' each other. The cafélike seating in front is probably the best place from which to watch the virtual gay pride parade that is Soi 4.

Zeta (Map pp70-1; ☎ 0 2203 0994; 29 Royal City Ave (RCA), off Phra Ram IX) This exceedingly popular lesbian club on the quiet end of RCA is packed to the gills with young torm-dee on weekends. Women only.

ENTERTAINMENT

Bangkok is a mature metropolis with lots of entertainment options for both culture vultures and cosmopolitan clubbers. To get an idea of what's going on, check out the entertainment listings in the daily Bangkok Post and Nation newspapers, the excellent weekly listings rag BK and the monthly Bangkok 101.

Discos & Nightclubs

Fickleness is the reigning characteristic of the Bangkok club scene, and venues that were pulling in thousands a night just last year are often only vague memories today. What used to be a rotating cast of hotspots has slowed to a few standards on the sois off Sukhumvit, Silom, Ratchadapisek and RCA (Royal City Ave), the city's 'entertainment zones' that qualify for the 2am closing time. You'll need an ID to prove you're legal (20 years old); they'll card even the grey hairs. Cover charges run as high as 600B and usually include a drink. Most places don't begin filling up until midnight.

To get an idea of current happenings around town, go check out Bangkok Spin (www.bangkokspin.com), as well as the entertainment press, in particular BK and the Bangkok Post's Friday supplement, Guru, and the Bangkok Recorder's online mag (www.bangkokrecorder.com).

808 Club (Map pp70-1; www.808bangkok.com; Block C, Royal City Ave (RCA), off Th Phra Ram IX) Named after the infamous beat machine, this club fills the space previously occupied by Astra and looks to follow the tradition of big-name DJs and insanely crowded events.

Club Culture (Map pp72-3; ☎ 0 89497 8422; www.club-culture-bkk.com; Th Sri Ayuthaya; ⊙ 7pm-late Wed, Fri & Sat) Housed in a unique 40 year-old Thai-style building and run by the same folks who ran RCA's popular Astra, Culture is the biggest recent arrival on Bangkok's club scene.

Dance Fever (Map pp70-1; ☎ 0 2247 4295; 71 Th Ratchadaphisek) Like taking a time machine back to the previous decade, Dance Fever is a holdover from the days when a night out in Bangkok meant live stage shows, wiggling around the whisky set table, and neon, neon, neon.

Nang Len (Map pp70-1; ☎ 0 2711 6564; 217 Soi 63 (Ekamai), Th Sukhumvit) Nang Len (literally 'Sit

Around') is a ridiculously popular sardine tin of live music and uni students on popular Th Ekamai. Get in before 10pm or you're not getting in at all.

Superfly (Map pp72-3; ☎ 0 2633 9990; cnr Phra Ram 4 & Soi 1, Th Sala Daeng) The gargantuan dance hall is a decent middle ground in the jungle of Bangkok clubs; not achingly trendy, with music that the majority of us can shake to.

Although not as hot as it once was, Soi 4 off Th Silom still boasts a few intimate dance clubs, such as **Tapas Room** (Map pp78-9; ☎ 0 2234 4737; 114/17-18 Soi 4, Th Silom). A few streets down, **Lucifer** (Map pp78-9; ☎ 0 0234 6902; 76/1-3 Soi Patpong 1; ☺ 9pm-1am) is a less devilish alternative to Patpong's ping-pong shows.

Live Music

Bangkok's live-music scene is fairly diverse: international jazz in the high-end hotels, blues in funky closet pubs, Thai pop in shiny kitchen clubs and Thai folk in cosy art bars. The website www.bangkok gigguide.com lists the city's music calendar. The Bangkok symphony plays every Sunday (5.30pm to 7.30pm) between mid-December and mid-February at Lumphini Park; see www.bangkoksymphony.net.

Brown Sugar (Map pp72-3; ☎ 0 2250 1825; 231/19-20 Th Sarasin) Cosy Brown Sugar mingles jazz musicians and listeners into an intimate embrace of good times and good music. The pub is the longest-running spot along a strip of bars on Th Sarasin, just north of Lumphini Park.

Gazebo (Map pp74-5; ☎ 0 2629 0705; 3rd fl, 44 Th Chakraphong) Like an oasis above Th Khao San, this Middle Eastern–themed pub draws in backpackers and locals alike with fun cover bands and fez-topped sheesha attendants. Its elevated location also appears to lend it some leniency with the city's strict closing times.

our pick Living Room (Map p82; ☎ 02 649 8888; Level I, Sheraton Grande Sukhumvit, 250 Th Sukhumvit) Every night this deceptively bland hotel lounge transforms into one of the city's best venues for live jazz, attracting a dedicated following of regulars. Contact ahead of time to see which sax master or hide hitter is currently in town.

Saxophone Pub (Map pp72-3; ☎ 0 2246 5472; 3/8 Th Phayathai) A live-music institution, good old Saxophone is worth the trip from your Banglamphu buffer zone for jazz, blues and beyond.

Tawan Daeng German Brewhouse (Map pp70-1; ☎ 0 2678 1114; 462/61 Th Narathiwat Ratchanakharin, cnr Th Phra Ram III) Despite its hangar-like girth, this Thai version of a Bavarian beer hall manages to pack 'em in just about every night with live music and fresh beer.

Cabaret

Bangkok is famous with tourists for its *gà·teu·i* (ladyboys; see p127 for more details) cabarets that are basically lip-syncing dance routines performed by Thailand's third gender.

Calypso Cabaret (Map pp80-1; ☎ 0 2653 3960-2; 1st fl, Asia Hotel, 296 Th Phayathai; tickets 1000B; ☺ shows 8.15pm & 9.45pm) Bangkok's most popular *gà·teu·i* cabaret, this place is half Moulin Rouge, half Broadway show.

Mambo Cabaret (Map p82; ☎ 0 2259 5715; Washington Sq, Th Sukhumvit btwn Soi 22 & Soi 24; tickets 600-800B; ☺ shows 8.30pm & 10pm) This is a less flashy operation than at the Calypso, but the show is still entertaining.

Cinemas

You might think that only film fanatics would want to see a movie overseas, but Bangkok's love of excess makes the glitzy cinemas worth a visit in their own right. VIP seats ring in at a mere 500B and include reclining seats (some with electric massage) and seatside service. Most cinemas are housed in the big shopping centres around Th Phra Ram I and Th Ploenchit. Hollywood blockbusters in English, and Thai movies (sometimes subtitled in English), are the usual staples. Many of Bangkok's cultural centres also screen movies for the benefit of expats, and various annual film festivals ensure going to the movies is a social event.

The royal anthem is played before every screening and you are expected to stand respectfully.

For movie listings and show times, see the *Bangkok Post* or www.movieseer.com; some reviews of Thai movies are available at www.thaicinema.org.

EGV Cinema (Map pp80-1; ☎ 0 2812 9999; www .egv.com; Siam Discovery Center, cnr Th Phra Ram I & Th Phayathai) Bangkok's poshest cinema shows international and Thai films in English.

SF Cinema City (Map pp80-1; ☎ 0 2611 6444; www .sfcinemacity.com; 7th fl, MBK Centre, Th Phra Ram I) This place has comfortable VIP seats and shows international blockbusters in English and Thai films with English subtitles.

Lido Multiplex (Map pp80-1; ☎ 0 2252 6498; Siam Sq, Soi 2) This retro cinema shows some European and art house films as well as US blockbusters.

SFX Cinema (Map p82; ☎ 0 2260 9333; www.sfx cinemacity.com; Emporium Shopping Centre, Th Sukhumvit) This is a convenient cinema for the Sukhumvit hotels.

House (Map pp70-1; ☎ 0 2641 5177; www.houserama.com; 3rd fl, UMB Cinema, RCA, Th Phra Ram IX) Arty and avant-garde flicks are on the menu here.

Go-Go Bars

Bangkok is legendary for its go-go bars, and lonely foreign men still flock here in huge numbers to take advantage of Thailand's liberal attitude towards love for sale. For some people this is paradise, for others it's pitiable.

Most visitors to Bangkok put in an appearance at Soi Patpong 1 and Soi Patpong 2, between Th Silom and Th Surawong, for the spectacle, but few stay here for any longer than it takes to buzz around the pirated goods market and sink a cold beer at one of the circus-like 'sex' shows.

These days the serious sex business has mainly shifted to the streets off Th Sukhumvit, particularly Soi Cowboy (Soi 23) and Nana Plaza (Soi 4), and the long strip of vast 'entertainment complexes' along Th Ratchadaphisek, which cater to an Asian clientele.

Moo·ay Tai

No-holds-barred *moo·ay tai* (often spelt *muay thai*) can be seen at two boxing stadiums in central Bangkok. Admission fees vary according to seating. Ringside seats are the most expensive and where the VIPs usually sit, backpackers usually opt for the 2nd-class seats while die-hard *moo·ay tai* fans bet and cheer from the bleachers in 3rd class. At some programmes a ticket mafia tries to steer every tourist into buying an expensive ringside seat. Don't believe anyone who says that the cheap seats are sold out unless you hear it directly from a window ticket vendor.

Sanam Muay Lumpinee (Map pp72-3; ☎ 0 2252 8765; Th Phra Ram IV; admission 1000-2000B; ☽ bouts 6.30-11pm Tue & Fri, 5-8pm & 8.30-11.30pm Sat) This large, popular stadium is close to Lumphini Park.

Sanam Muay Ratchadamnoen (Map pp74-5; ☎ 0 2281 4205; 1 Th Ratchadamnoen Nok; admission 1000-2000B; ☽ bouts 5-8pm & 8.30pm-midnight Sun, 6.30-11.30pm Mon, Wed & Thu) The best-matched bouts are held here on Thursday nights.

Theatre

Several theatres around town show modern and classical Thai theatrical performances, including traditional *lá·kon* and *kŏhn* performances (Thai mask dramas based on stories from the Ramayana) and modern plays. The following theatres are worth a look.

National Theatre (Map pp74-5; ☎ 0 2221 0171; Th Ratchini, Ko Ratanakosin; tickets 40-80B) Thailand's National Theatre is the country's centre stage for Thai drama and *kŏhn*. Exhibitions of Thai classical dancing and music are held on the last Friday and Saturday of each month.

Patravadi Theatre (Map pp72-3; ☎ 0 2412 7287; www.patravaditheatre.com; 69/1 Soi Wat Rakhang, Thonburi; tickets 300-800B; ☽ shows 7pm Fri-Sun) Patravadi is Bangkok's leading modern-dance venue. The theatre is also the primary venue for the Bangkok International Fringe Festival, held in January or February.

Sala Chalermkrung (Map pp76-7; ☎ 0 2222 0434; www.salachalermkrung.com; 66 Th Charoen Krung, Chinatown; tickets 1000-2000B; ☽ shows 8.30pm Fri & Sat) This art-deco Bangkok landmark, a former cinema dating back to 1933, is one of the few remaining places to witness *kŏhn*.

Thailand Cultural Centre (Map pp70-1; ☎ 0 2247 0028; www.thaiculturalcenter.com; Th Ratchadaphisek btwn Th Thiam Ruampit & Th Din Daeng) Bangkok's primary performing arts facility, the Thailand Cultural Centre is the home of the Bangkok Symphony Orchestra and hosts the International Festival of Dance and Music in September.

SHOPPING

Hope you brought your credit card; hardly a street corner in Bangkok is free from a vendor, hawker or impromptu stall, and the city is also home to one of the word's largest outdoor markets and Southeast Asia's largest mall. There's something here for just about everybody, and often the real and the knock-off live happily side-by-side. Although the tourist brochures tend to tout the upscale malls, Bangkok still lags slightly behind Singapore and Hong Kong in this area, and the open-air markets are where the best deals and most original items are found.

Antiques

Real Thai antiques are rare and costly, but many shops sell good reproductions, made using traditional techniques, which are far cheaper. The most popular genuine antiques are woodcarvings, furniture, celadon porce-

---

BUYING BUDDHAS

The government of Thailand places strict controls on the export of Buddha images and antiquities. Reproductions of antiquities and modern Buddha images can be exported with a permit from the Fine Arts Department (Map pp72–3). You should contact the **Office of Archaeology and National Museums** (☎ 0 2226 1661) for more information. If you don't have the appropriate paperwork and a Buddha image is discovered in your bags when you are leaving the country, it will be confiscated.

---

lain and lacquerware. Be warned that many shops in Thailand sell souvenirs made of turtle shell and ivory, in spite of international treaties restricting the sale of these items. If you try to bring these into Australia, Europe, the UK or the USA, they will be confiscated.

You might need a permit to take antiques out of Thailand, and you'll definitely need one for any Buddha images – see the boxed text, above, for details.

House of Chao (Map pp78-9; ☎ 0 2635 7188; 9/1 Th Decho) This three-storey antique shop, located (appropriately) in an antique house, has everything necessary to deck out your fantasy colonial-era mansion.

River City (Map pp78-9; ☎ 0 2237 0077; 23 Th Yotha, off Th Charoen Krung; ☺ many shops close Sun) This multistorey centre is an all-in-one stop for old-world Asiana, much of it too large to fit in the bag of most travellers. There's a free boat service from Saphan Taksin pier. Note that any Angkorian artefacts are most likely reproductions or being sold illegally, as the export of artefacts from Cambodia is banned.

Cameras & Electronics

Contrary to popular belief, Bangkok is not a good place to invest in electronic gadgetry. Import taxes make the prices probably more than you'd pay at home, and the selection doesn't compare with that of places such as Tokyo or Hong Kong. Where the city does excel is in the grey-market trade of pirated software and DIY recycling of computer peripherals.

Pantip Plaza (Map pp80-1; ☎ 0 2656 5030; 604 Th Phetburi) The best place to browse for tech gear and software, Pantip has five storeys of computer stores and dozens of stalls selling

computers and peripherals (both genuine and openly pirated software). **IT City** (☎ 0 2656 5030), on the 5th floor of the plaza, is a reliable computer megastore that is used to providing VAT refund forms for tourists.

Niks/Nava Import Export (Map pp78-9; ☎ 0 2235 2929; www.niksthailand.com; 166 Th Silom; ☺ 11am-4pm Mon-Fri) Thailand's biggest camera importer sells all types of professional equipment, including Nikon, Mamiya and Rollei. It's also the best place to bring your sick Nikon for a check-up.

Sunny Camera (Map pp78-9; ☎ 0 2236 8365; 144/23 Th Silom; ☺ Mon-Sat) Dedicated Nikon-heads should head directly to Sunny Camera to satisfy their gear addiction. There are other branches on the 3rd floor of MBK (Map pp80-1; ☎ 0 2620 9293) and at 1267-1267/1 Th Charoen Krung (Map pp78-9; ☎ 0 2235 2123).

Clothing

Once you realise everything you packed completely disagrees with Thailand's tropical heat, you'll need Bangkok's fashion-focused stores to fill the gaps. Clothes and food are typically sold side-by-side in Thai markets, but the sizes are far too petite for most foreigners; Pratunam and Chatuchak Weekend Market (see p108) are notable exceptions, selling sizes and styles geared towards Westerners.

Central World Plaza (Map pp80-1; ☎ 0 2635 1111; cnr Th Phra Ram I & Th Ratchadamri, Ploenchit) Boasting seven floors of unadulterated commercial bliss, we fancy the concrete-floored Section F that features cool domestic brands with barely pronounceable names such as Playground!, Manga, Qconceptstore and Flynow III.

Gaysorn Plaza (Map pp80-1; ☎ 0 2656 1149; cnr Th Ploenchit & Th Ratchadamri) More haute than the catwalk, Gaysorn is a manicured showroom for vogue fashions. The 2nd-floor 'Urban Street Chic' zone highlights the handiwork of local designers.

It's Happened To Be A Closet (Map pp74-5; ☎ 0 2629 5271; 32 Th Khao San; ☺ 1-11pm) Bright colours and bold patterns rule among the Thai designed and made togs, and the elegant multistorey shop even features a restaurant and café, a hair and nail salon, and private rooms for movie viewing.

Mahboonkrong Centre (MBK) (Map pp80-1; ☎ 0 2620-9111; cnr Th Phra Ram I & Th Phayathai) The energy of a Thai market is in full force in Bangkok's most popular mall. Just about everything is

BANGKOK

available here, and the 6th floor holds one of the city's best food courts (see p101).

Marco Tailors (Map pp80-1; ☎ 0 2251 7633; 430/33 Soi 7, Siam Sq; ☻ 10am-5pm Mon-Fri) Dealing solely in men's suits, this longstanding and reliable tailor has a wide selection of banker-sensibility wools and cottons.

Siam Discovery Center (Map pp80-1; ☎ 0 2658 1000-19; Th Phra Ram I) Clothes, furniture and books round out Siam Discovery's subdued corridors. The mall is also, somewhat incongruously, one of the best places in town to stock up outdoor gear. Within tent-pitching distance of each other on the 3rd floor are Pro Cam-Fis, Equinox Shop, Rockcamp Climbing Shop and the North Face.

Gems & Jewellery

Bangkok is a major centre for the gem trade, but amateurs should tread very carefully as many gem dealers are notorious for their underhanded sales techniques. Flawed or even glass gems are passed off as top quality, and many stores offer big commissions to túk-túk drivers and other touts who bring in foreigners off the street or offer phoney 'sales' to entice customers (for more information see p390). Above all beware of the infamous gem scam, where shopkeepers try to persuade customers to buy large quantities of gems to sell at a profit back home. Two longstanding and reputable shops are:

Johnny's Gems (Map pp76-7; ☎ 0 2224 4065; 199 Th Fuang Nakhon; ☻ Mon-Sat) A long-time favourite of Bangkok expats, Johnny's Gems is a reliable name in an unreliable business.

Uthai's Gems (Map pp80-1; ☎ 02 253 8582; 28/7 Soi Ruam Rudi, Th Ploenchit; ☻ Mon-Sat) With 40 years in the business, Uthai's fixed prices and good service, including a money-back guarantee, make him a popular choice among expats.

Handicrafts

Handicrafts are excellent value in Bangkok. The best place to start is Chatuchak Weekend Market (right), followed by the Suan Lum Night Bazaar (right), but the street markets on Th Khao San, Th Sukhumvit and Th Silom are also well stocked.

Some reliable shops selling handicrafts:

Rasi Sayam (Map p82; ☎ 0 2262 0729; 82 Soi 33, Th Sukhumvit) A step above Chatuchak, but not quite a Th Silom area antique shop, Rasi Sayam stocks a classy selection of handmade *objets d'art*. Particularly helpful are the in-

formative tags that describe the origin of your potential purchase.

Silom Village Trade Center (Map pp78-9; ☎ 0 2234 4448; 286 Th Silom) This complex of teak houses has been converted into a handicrafts market, with some decent open-air restaurants as well as nightly dance performances.

Thai Home Industries (Map pp78-9; ☎ 0 2234 1736; 35 Soi Oriental) A visit to this temple-like building is like discovering an abandoned attic of Asian booty. Despite the odd assortment of items and lack of order (not to mention the dust), it's heaps more fun than the typically faceless Bangkok handicraft shop.

Markets

In every tourist area, there are day and night markets for almost 24-hour souvenir shopping. Polite bargaining is expected and prices at Th Khao San market are more reasonable than at more upscale markets in Patpong, Th Silom and Th Sukhumvit.

Chatuchak Weekend Market (Jatujak Market; Map pp70-1; ☎ 0 2272 4440; Th Phahonyothin; ☻ 6am-6pm Sat & Sun) This gigantic market is the daddy of all Thai markets, with thousands of vendors selling everything from live rabbits to hill-tribe handicrafts.

Around 200,000 people mob the market every Saturday and Sunday. Pickpockets are common so keep an eye on your belongings. Many people make a day of it and eat at one of the many excellent covered restaurants and food stalls around the market. It's easy to get lost along the endless rows of covered booths, so a map can be helpful – *Nancy Chandler's Map of Bangkok* has a good Chatuchak panel. The best way to get to Chatuchak is by taking the Skytrain to Mo Chit or Metro to Kamphaeng Phet.

Suan Lum Night Bazaar (Map pp72-3; Th Phra Ram IV; ☻ 6pm-midnight) If you aren't in Bangkok for a weekend, Suan Lum is a fine alternative to Chatuchak. It is a huge government-sponsored night market with thousands of stalls selling slightly pricey modern Thai souvenirs, handicrafts and a few antiques.

Pak Khlong Market (Map pp76-7; off Th Maharat near Tha Saphan Phut (Memorial Bridge); ☻ 9pm-late) Orchids might not be on your gift-giving list, but Bangkok's wholesale flower market is a fascinating destination for flora lovers and people watchers. Keep an eye out for *poo·ang mah·lai* (flower garlands) that are offered to sacred Buddhas by merit-makers.

Pratunam Market (Map pp80-1; cnr Th Phetchaburi & Th Ratchaprarop) A virtual jungle of markets and shops that extends north from Th Phetchaburi, Pratunam is the paragon of the Thai market.

Religious Paraphernalia

Th Bamrung Muang, near Wat Suthat, is lined with dozens of emporia selling massive bronze Buddha statues and other votive objects used in Buddhist rituals.

To buy traditional Buddhist amulets, visit the amulet markets, see the boxed text, p86, or try at Wat Mahathat and Wat Ratchanatda (p85).

Charoen Chaikarnchang (Map pp74-5; ☎ 0 2222 4800; 87 Soi Nava, Bamrung Muang) This is easily the largest and most impressive religious shop in the area. The workshop in the back produces gigantic bronze Buddha images for wát all over Thailand.

Scuba Diving Supplies

Most of Bangkok's dive shops are located around Th Sukhumvit.

Dive Indeed (Map p82; ☎ 0 2665 7471; www.dive indeed.com; 14/2 Soi 21, Th Sukhumvit)

Dive Master (Map p82; ☎ 0 2259 3191; www.dive master.net; 16 Asoke Court, Soi 23, Th Sukhumvit)

Dive Supply (Map pp72-3; ☎ 0 2354 4815; www.dive supply.com; 457/4 Th Sri Ayuthaya)

Larry's Dive Center, Bar & Grill (Map p82; ☎ 0 2663 4563; www.larrysdive.com; 8/3 Soi 22, Th Sukhumvit)

Planet Scuba (Map pp70-1; ☎ 0 2261 4412/3; www.planetscuba.net; 666 Th Sukhumvit)

GETTING THERE & AWAY
Air

Bangkok has two main airports. Opened in late 2006, **Suvarnabhumi International Airport** (☎ 0 2132 1888; www2.airportthai.co.th) is the vast glass and concrete construction 30km east of central Bangkok that acts as the main international airport. After rather a lot of teething problems (see the boxed text, p32), at most times Suvarnabhumi (pronounced sù·wan·ná·poom) works fairly efficiently. The unofficial www.bangkokairportonline .com site has good, more up-to-date information and real-time details of airport arrivals and departures.

Don Muang Airport (Map pp70-1; ☎ 0 2535 1111; www2.airportthai.co.th) is 25km north of the city centre and after being temporarily retired it now serves some, but not all, domestic routes.

For hotels near the airports, see p98 for details. For transport details to the airports, see p110. Many airline offices appear on the various Bangkok maps.

Bus

A vast network of public and private bus services fan out from Bangkok all over the kingdom. Buses come in several varieties (see p411 for details). Ordinary and air-conditioned public buses are run by Baw Khaw Saw, the state-run bus company, which has three terminals around Bangkok. You can check departure times and fares at www.transport .co.th/Eng/HomeEnglish.htm, though it's not always completely up to date.

On all buses, and especially on buses catering to tourists and running to the beaches and islands in the south, keep valuables on your person or within reach; see p412 for details of bus scams.

PRIVATE BUS

The best private buses leave from the government bus stations (see below); tickets should be booked at the terminals themselves, not through a travel agent. It is not recommended you book tickets for pick-up at your hotel or from a tourist centre, particularly along Th Khao San. These services aren't always as prompt, fast, comfortable or safe as promised. Incidents of theft are also quite common.

See p411 and the regional chapters for more information about bus travel in Thailand.

PUBLIC BUS

There are three main public bus terminals in Bangkok:

Eastern Bus Terminal (Ekamai; Map p82; ☎ 0 2391 6846; Soi 40, Th Sukhumvit) Buses to cities on or near the eastern gulf coast such as Pattaya, Rayong, Chanthaburi and Trat. The Ekamai Skytrain station is right by the terminal.

Northern & Northeastern Bus Terminal (Mo Chit; Map pp70-1; ☎ northern office 0 2936 2852 ext 311/442, northeastern office 0 2936 2852 ext 611/448; Th Phahonyothin) This terminal is just north of Chatuchak Park (and the Weekend Market), and all buses to the north and northeast leave from here. From Mo Chit Skytrain station, you can take an ordinary bus 3; alternatively you can catch bus 3 from Th Phra Athit in Banglamphu.

Southern Bus Terminal (Sai Tai Mai; Map pp70-1; ☎ 0 2435 1200; cnr Th Boromaratchachonanee & Th Phuttamonthon 1, Chim Phli) Across Saphan Phra Pinklao in the far western suburbs, this new and refreshingly well organised station is the departure point for buses to all points south – hello Phuket, Surat Thani, Krabi, Hat Yai – as well as buses to Kanchanaburi and western Thailand. You can reach the station on bus 503 from Th Phra Athit.

Fares listed here are for government-run services from the Southern bus terminal that have air-con. Private companies also offer more expensive services on most of these routes:

Destination	Price	Duration	Frequency
Chumphon	211–500B	7hr	5 daily
Hat Yai	640–950B	14hr	10 daily
Hua Hin	99–171B	3½hr	half-hourly
Ko Samui	337–660B	15hr	6-8 daily
Krabi	357–710B	12hr	5 daily
Nakhon Si Thammarat	353–705B	12-13hr	7 daily
Pattaya	125B	2hr	half-hourly
Phetchaburi	80–120B	2½hr	every 20 minutes 9.20am-6pm
Phuket	596–900B	13-14hr	10 daily
Ranong	357–665B	10hr	6 daily
Satun	433–800B	14hr	4 daily
Songkhla	437–870B	15hr	4 daily
Surat Thani	295–590B	11hr	7 daily
Trang	377–750B	14hr	6 daily

Places on the eastern gulf coast are served by long-haul buses from the Eastern bus terminal. Rayong and Ban Phe are used for connections to Ko Samet and Chanthaburi, and Trat for Ko Chang.

Destination	Price	Duration	Frequency
Ban Phe	152B	3½ hr	hourly 5am-8pm
Chanthaburi	194B	4 hr	hourly 4.30am-midnight
Pattaya	117B	2 hr	hourly 5am-10pm
Rayong	152B	3½ hr	hourly
Trat	250B	5 hr	hourly 5am-midnight

Train

Centrally located just southeast of Chinatown, historic **Hualamphong train station** (Map pp76-7; ☎ 0 2220 4334, information & advance booking 1690; www.railway .co.th; Th Phra Ram IV) is Bangkok's – and indeed Thailand's – main rail hub and the station you'll use when heading south. Ordinary, rapid and express trains depart for Hua Hin, Surat Thani, Trang, Nakhon Si Thammarat, Hat Yai and then on to Malaysia. Ignore touts at the station who try to steer you towards travel agents (frequently using the name

'TAT'); it's better to book all train tickets directly at the station ticket desks or through a reputable agent. For more details on train travel in Thailand, see p417.

Infrequent trains to western Thailand (including Kanchanaburi) leave from **Bangkok Noi train station** (Map pp72-3; Thonburi), across the river from Banglamphu.

GETTING AROUND

Getting around Bangkok easily all depends on where you are, where you're going and what time it is. In the new part of town, you'll rely primarily on Skytrain and meter taxis. Taxis are cheap but during the many rush hours they can be excruciatingly slow. The rush hours are from about 7.30am to 10am and 5pm to 7.30pm. On Friday nights traffic in Bangkok is an immovable force of nature between about 4.30pm and 9.30pm. At these times the Skytrain, Metro, *klong* boat or river ferry are all better options.

If the traffic is bad and there isn't a non-road alternative, you might as well move painfully slowly in a bus as a taxi.

To/From the Airport

You can travel by taxi, bus and soon Skytrain between Suvarnabhumi and Bangkok. There are fewer services to Don Muang.

SUVARNABHUMI INTERNATIONAL AIRPORT
Airport Bus & Minivans

Airport Express runs four useful routes between Suvarnabhumi and Bangkok city. They operate from 5am to midnight for a flat 150B fare, meaning the price of a taxi will be comparable for two or more people heading to central Bangkok, but more expensive if you're going to Banglamphu. The Airport Express counter is near entrance 8 on level 1. Routes stop at Skytrain stations, major hotels and other landmarks.

AE-1 to Silom By expressway via Pratunam, Central World shopping centre, Ratchadamri Skytrain, Lumphini Park, Th Saladaeng, Patpong, Plaza Hotel and others, finishing at Sala Daeng Skytrain.

AE-2 to Banglamphu By expressway via Th Phetchaburi Soi 30, Democracy Monument, Royal Hotel, Th Phra Athit, Th Phra Sumen, Th Khao San.

AE-3 to Sukhumvit Soi 52, Eastern Bus Terminal, Soi 34, 24, 20, 18, 10, 6, Central Chidlom, Central World, Soi Nana.

AE-4 to Hualamphong train station Via Victory Monument, Phayathai Skytrain, Siam Sq, MBK, Chulalongkorn University.

If heading to the airport from Banglamphu, hotels and guesthouses can book you on air-conditioned minivans. These pick up from the front door and cost about 180B per person (you're better off using the AE bus).

Local Transport

With more time and less money, you could take the Skytrain to On Nut (40B), then from near the market entrance opposite Tesco take the BTS minivan (25B, about 40 minutes; look for the yellow BTS 552 Suvarnabhumi on the window) to the airport.

Several other air-conditioned local buses serve Suvarnabhumi for a 35B flat fare. Most useful are:

Bus 551 Siam Paragon Via Victory Monument.
Bus 552 Klong Toei Via Sukhumvit 101 and On Nut Skytrain.
Buses 554 & 555 Don Muang Airport
Bus 556 Southern Bus Terminal Via Democracy Monument (for Th Khao San) and Thammasat University.

Intercity buses to places including Pattaya, Rayong and Trat stop at the Public Transportation Centre, reached via a free shuttle from the airport.

Skytrain

From early 2009 (insha'Allah) a new Skytrain line will run from downstairs at the airport to a huge new City Air Terminal (Map pp72–3) in central Bangkok, near Soi Asoke and Th Phetchaburi. There will be an express service (the pink line) that will take 15 minutes, and a local service (the red line) taking 27 minutes.

Taxi

Ignore the touts and all the yellow signs pointing you to 'limousines' (which cost 800B flat), walk outside on the arrivals level and join the fast-moving queue for a public taxi. Cabs booked through this desk should always use their meter, but they often try their luck so insist by saying 'meter, please'. You must also pay a 50B official airport surcharge and reimburse drivers for any toll charges (up to 60B); drivers will usually ask your permission to use the tollway. Depending on traffic, a taxi to Asoke/Silom/Banglamphu should cost 200-250B/300-350B/350-425B per vehicle.

DON MUANG AIRPORT

There are no longer any express airport buses to/from Don Muang.

Bus

Slow, crowded public bus 59 stops on the highway in front of the airport and carries on to Banglamphu, passing Th Khao San and the Democracy Monument; luggage is not allowed. Buses with air-con are faster, and you might actually get a seat. Useful air-conditioned routes:

Bus 510 Victory Monument, Southern Bus Terminal.
Bus 513 Th Sukhumvit, Eastern Bus Terminal.
Bus 29 Northern Bus Terminal, Victory Monument, Siam Sq and Hualamphong train station.

Taxi

As at Suvarnabhumi public taxis leave from outside the arrivals hall and there is a 50B airport charge added to the meter fare. Fares are lower to Banglamphu but about the same to Sukhumvit and Silom.

Train

The walkway that crosses from Terminal 1 to the Amari Airport Hotel also provides access to Don Muang train station, which has trains to Hualamphong train station every one to 1½ hours from 4am to 11.30am and then roughly every hour from 2pm to 9.30pm (3rd-class ordinary/express 5/10B, one hour).

Boat

Although many of Bangkok's *klong* have been paved over, there is still plenty of transport along and across Chao Phraya River and up adjoining canals.

RIVER FERRIES

The **Chao Phraya Express Boat Co** (☎ 0 2623 6001; www.chaophrayaboat.co.th) operates the main ferry service along the Chao Phraya. The central pier is known as Sathorn or Saphan Taksin, and connects to the Skytrain's Saphan Taksin station, Riverside. Each pier is numbered consecutively from Sathorn.

Ferries run four stops south to Ratburana (S4), though tourists rarely use these. Much more useful are the services running to and from Nonthaburi (N30) in northern Bangkok; the maps in this book show the piers and their numbers. Fares are cheap and range from 10B to 34B. There are four different services, differentiated by the colour of the flags on their roofs. To avoid an unwanted trip halfway to Nonthaburi be sure to keep an eye on those flags.

Local Line (no flag) The all-stops service, operating every 15 to 20 minutes mornings and evenings.

Orange Express Stops at N1, N3, N4, N5, N6, N8, N9, N10, N12, N13, N15, N18, N21, N22, N24, N30. The most common service, departing every five to 20 minutes depending on the time of day.

Yellow Express Stops at N3, N5, N10, N12, N15, N22, N24, N30. Departing every five to 20 minutes depending on the time of day.

Blue Express Nonthaburi express, stopping N10 and N30 only. Just a couple of services in the morning 7am to 7.30am and evening at 5.35pm and 6.05pm.

A special tourist boat runs between Phra Athit in Banglamphu and Sathorn (Central Pier) every 30 minutes between 9.30am and 3pm. A one-day pass for unlimited travel costs 120B. There is also a boat that connects Tha Phra Athit with the Royal Barges Museum in Thonburi every hour from 10am to 3.35pm for 50B.

All this is best illustrated in the small, folding maps that detail routes, prices and times and are sometimes available at the ferry piers – ask for one – or on boards at the piers.

There are also dozens of cross-river ferries, which charge 3.50B and run every few minutes until late at night.

KLONG BOATS
Canal taxi boats run along Khlong Banglamphu and then Khlong Saen Saep (Banglamphu to Ramkhamhaeng) and are an easy way to get from Banglamphu to Jim Thompson's House, the Siam Square shopping centres (get off at Tha Hua Chang for both), and other points further east along Th Sukhumvit – after a mandatory change of boat at Tha Pratunam. These boats are mostly used by daily commuters and pull into the piers for just a few seconds – jump straight on or you'll be left behind. Fares range from 7B to 20B.

Bus
You can save a lot of money travelling in Bangkok by using the public buses, which are run by the **Bangkok Mass Transit Authority** (☎ 0 2246 4262; www.bmta.co.th); the website has incredibly useful information on all bus routes. Bangkok buses are cheap: air-conditioned fares typically start at 10B or 12B and increase depending on distance. Fares for ordinary (fan-con) buses start at 7B or 8B. Most of the bus lines run between 5am and 10pm or 11pm, except for the 'all-

night' buses, which run from 3am or 4am to midmorning.

Bangkok Bus Map, by Roadway, available at Asia Books (p67), is the most up-to-date route map available. Have small change and be careful with your belongings when riding on Bangkok buses. Bag-slashers and pickpockets are common on ordinary buses, particularly around Hualamphong train station.

Car
Renting a car just to drive around Bangkok is not a real good idea. Parking is impossible, traffic is frustrating, road rules can be mysterious and the alternative – taxis – are ubiquitous. If you are thinking of hiring a car to visit southern Thailand, you might be better off going south by plane or train and hiring a car when you get there. But if you still want to give it a go, all the big car-hire companies have offices in Bangkok and at Suvarnabhumi airport. Most can also provide chauffeur service (600B a day, 8am to 6pm), which gives local drivers a job and means you don't have to navigate, park or deal with overzealous police. Car-hire rates start at around 1500B per day for a small car. See p412 for more information on driving in Thailand.

Reliable car-rental companies include:

Avis Rent-A-Car (☎ 0 2255 5300; www.avisthailand .com; 2/12 Th Withayu) Also at Grand Hyatt Erawan Hotel (Map pp80–1).

Budget Car Rental (Map pp70–1; ☎ 0 2203 9200; www.budget.co.th; 19/23 Bldg A, Royal City Ave, Th Phetburi Tat Mai)

Hertz (Map pp80-1; ☎ 0 2654 1105; www.hertz.com; M Thai Tower, All Seasons Pl, 87 Th Withayu).

Metro (Subway) & Skytrain (BTS)
METRO (SUBWAY)
The first line of Bangkok's underground railway opened in 2004 and is operated by the **Metropolitan Rapid Transit Authority** (MRTA; www.mrta.co.th). Thais call the subway *rót fai đâi din* or 'Metro'. At the north end (Bang Sue) it connects with Chatuchak (with access to the Mo Chit Skytrain station), Thailand Cultural Centre, Sukhumvit (with access to Asoke Skytrain station), Queen Sirikit Convention Centre, Lumphini Park and Silom (with access to Sala Daeng Skytrain station) and terminates at Hualamphong. Altogether there are 18 stations with four that link up with the Skytrain.

Future extensions will connect Hualamphong to Chinatown and Thonburi. Fares cost 15B to 39B; child and concession fares can be bought at ticket windows. The trains run every seven minutes from 6am to midnight, except during peak hours – 6am to 9am and 4.30pm to 7.30pm – when frequency is less than five minutes. The main advantage for visitors is that the Sukhumvit hotel area is now easily connected to Hualamphong train station and Chinatown at one end, and Chatuchak weekend market and the northern bus terminal at the Bang Sue end.

SKYTRAIN (BTS)

The **BTS Skytrain** (rót fai fáh; ☎ 0 2617 6000; www .bts.co.th) allows you to soar above Bangkok's legendary traffic jams in air-conditioned comfort. Services are fast, efficient and relatively cheap, although you'll need to squeeze in during rush hours. There are two Skytrain lines, with another route to Suvarnabhumi airport scheduled for early 2009.

Silom Line Starting at National Stadium on Th Phra Ram I, near Siam Sq, it passes the Siam interchange station and bends around via the eastern section of Th Silom and western end of Th Sathon, on the river near at the intersection of Th Charoen Krung and Th Sathon. The final stop connects to the Chao Phraya river ferries (p111). A long-awaited extension across the river is due to come online in 2009.

Sukhumvit Line Running from On Nut, at distant Soi 81 of Th Sukhumvit, this line runs west right along Th Sukhumvit crossing over the Metro at Asoke. It continues into the shopping and commercial district and the main interchange station at Siam, where it meets the Silom line. From here the line turns north up to Mo Chit, near Chatuchak Weekend Market. Five more stations are to be built at the eastern end of the line.

Fares range from 15B to 40B and trains run from 6am to midnight. Ticket machines accept coins and notes; pick up change at the staffed kiosks. One-day (120B) passes are available, but the rechargeable cards (130B, with 100B travel and 30B card deposit) are more flexible.

Motorcycle Taxi

Motorcycle taxis serve two purposes in Bangkok. Most commonly and popularly they form part of the public transport network, running from the corner of a main thoroughfare, such as Th Sukhumvit, to the far ends of soi that run off that thoroughfare. Riders wear coloured, numbered vests and gather at either end of their soi, usually charging about 10B for the trip (without a helmet unless you ask).

Their other purpose is as a means of beating the traffic. You tell your rider where you want to go, negotiate a price (from 20B for a short trip up to about 100B going across town), strap on the helmet (they will insist on this for longer trips) and say a prayer to whichever god you're into. Drivers range from responsible to kamikaze, but the average trip involves some time on the wrong side of the road and several near-death experiences. It's the sort of white-knuckle ride you'd pay good money for at Disneyland, but is all in a day's work for these riders. Comfort yourself in the knowledge that there are good hospitals nearby.

Taxi

Bangkok's thousands of taxis are some of the best value cabs on earth. Most are new, air-conditioned and have working seatbelts in the front seat but less often in the back. You can flag them down anywhere in the city centre. The meter charge is 35B for the first 2km, then 4.50B for the next 10km, 5B for 13km to 20km and 5.50B for any distance greater than 20km, plus a small standing charge in slow traffic. Freeway tolls – 25B to 70B depending on where you start – must be paid by the passenger. Because of high fuel prices, there is talk of raising taxi rates.

Taxi Radio (☎ 1681; www.taxiradio.co.th) and other 24-hour 'phone-a-cab' services are available for 20B above the metered fare.

During the morning and afternoon rush hours, taxis might refuse to go to certain destinations because of the traffic; if this happens, just try another cab. Around Th Khao San and other tourist areas, some cabbies might refuse to use the meter and try to charge a flat fee; if this happens just walk away and find another cab.

You can hire a taxi all day for 1500B to 2000B, depending on how much driving is involved. Taxis can also be hired for trips to Pattaya (1500B), Hua Hin (2300B) and Phetchaburi (1700B), among others; see www .taxiradio.co.th for an idea of fares.

Túk-Túk

Bangkok's iconic túk-túk (like motorised rickshaws) are used by Thais as a traffic-jumper or for short hops not worth using a taxi for. For foreigners, however, these emphysema-inducing machines are notorious for taking little 'detours' to commission-paying gem and silk shops and massage parlours. En route to 'special' temples, you'll meet helpful locals who will steer you to even more rip-off opportunities. See the boxed text, p83, for more details about túk-túk scams, and ignore anyone offering too-good-to-be-true 10B trips.

The other problem is that túk-túk drivers always ask for too much baht from foreigners (partly because few expats use them, and the drivers figure tourists don't know what is a fair price). Expect to be quoted a 100B fare, if not more, for even the shortest trip. Still, it's an iconic experience to travel by túk-túk so it's worth bargaining down to about 40B for a short trip, preferably at night, when the pollution won't sour your alfresco trip as much. Once you've had the experience, you'll find taxis are cheaper, cleaner, cooler and quieter.

Eastern Gulf Coast

Thailand's eastern gulf coast is the ultimate smorgasbord of beach vacations. Not more than a few hours' hop from the Bangkok bustle, this diverse region offers a range of flavours that will surely suit the taste of every traveller.

Hot and spicy Pattaya sizzles under the neon lights long after the tropical sun plunges into the sea. There's a feast of sights, safaris and adrenaline-packed sports during the day, while the evenings feel like Patpong-by-the-sea, as thumping nightspots serve up a side order of sleaze.

For those short on time, try a seaside holiday to go on the powder-white sands of Ko Samet. This quieter spot is a great place to spend a weekend sampling Thailand's laid-back salt-sprayed beach life. Accommodation options run the gamut of the budget spectrum – you can get pampered at a luxury spa or play out your Robinson Crusoe fantasies in a lonely beachside shack.

For a hearty slice of rugged jungle, head further east to the Ko Chang Archipelago. Those who crave generous helpings of rustic solitude will be sated by the lonely tropical islands peppered across the churning sea. Divers and snorkellers will find fluorescent reefs and crystal waters that teem with every creature you would find at a sea food buffet. Although developers are gobbling up the large island of Ko Chang, the quieter Ko Kut and Ko Mak retain the naturalistic appeal of dining alfresco.

HIGHLIGHTS

- Delving deep within the inland rainforest to find hidden waterfalls throughout **Ko Chang** (p140)
- Glimpsing your smile reflecting back at you from the emerald waters surrounding **Ko Kut** (p157)
- Escaping the naughty and finding the nice in **Pattaya** (p119)
- Snorkelling through schools of colourful fish in the reefs near **Ko Mak** (p159)
- Joining weekending Bangkokians for a couple of days of sand and partying on **Ko Samet** (p129)

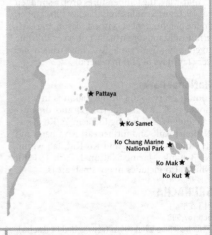

★ Pattaya

★ Ko Samet

Ko Chang Marine National Park ★

Ko Mak ★

Ko Kut ★

■ DRY SEASON: NOVEMBER-APRIL   ■ WET SEASON: MAY-OCTOBER

EASTERN GULF COAST

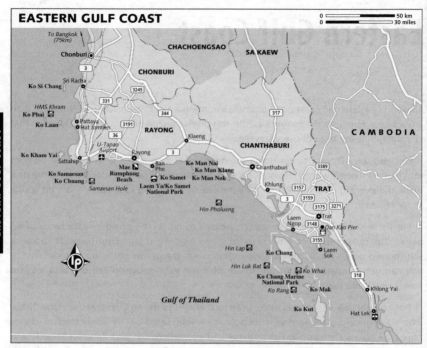

Climate
The eastern gulf coast experiences three seasons, or rather, three variations of hot. November to February are milder months with little rain. The hottest months are March to May, while in mid-May, the temperatures drop a smidgen to welcome the monsoons that last till October. In the height of the monsoon season, the easternmost islands are usually not accessible due to choppy waves, while Ko Samet usually has very few days of rain in general.

National Parks
Almost every island in the region is in a national park. Ko Samet (p129) and the surrounding islands belong to Laem Ya/Ko Samet National Park, and further east Ko Chang and its siblings, Ko Mak and Ko Kut, fall within Ko Chang Marine National Park (p138), which also includes many small areas.

SRI RACHA
ศรีราชา
pop 167,900
This bustling Thai town (also called Si Racha), two hours from Bangkok by bus, barely clings to its fishing village roots. The waterfront centre of Sri Racha is a veritable floating city – a maze of piers and interconnected stilt buildings housing hotels, restaurants and markets. It's no Venice, but there's a certain charm hidden deep within the layers of smog and garish modern construction.

Information
Krung Thai Bank (cnr Th Surasak 1 & Th Jermjompol) Has an ATM and exchange facilities.
Post office (Th Jermjompol) A few blocks north of the Krung Thai Bank.

Sights & Activities
Other than the wobbly waterfront piers, Sri Racha's sole downtown attraction is **Ko Loi**, a small rocky island that is connected to the mainland by a long jetty. A **Thai-Chinese Buddhist temple** (☼ dawn-dusk) inhabits the island and is surrounded by ponds of lethargic sea turtles.

The popular **Sriracha Tiger Zoo** (☎ 0 3829 6556-8; www.tigerzoo.com; 341 Moo 3, Nongkham; adult/child 250/150B; ☼ 8am-6pm) sits about 9km southeast of the city centre. The main attraction is the compound of 250 tigers that are involved with the zoo's remarkable breeding program. Visitors can get up close and personal with the cubs. Many people also come for the colourful array of performances, which include the **Scorpion Queen**, who poses for photos while covered in scorpions, the **Amazing Circus**, which features a variety of creatures doing bizarre tricks, and recently, the **dancing hog show**, which is getting tons of press.

Most of the zoo's visitors prefer to stay in nearby Pattaya and make the short 20km journey on a day trip.

Sleeping & Eating

In general, sleepovers in Sri Racha are uncommon and unnecessary since Pattaya, the uber-resort town, is only 27km down the road. If you decide to spend the night in this glorified transport interchange, you'll have a choice of rambling waterfront guesthouses or fancier spots that cater to local businesspeople.

Like most coastal towns in Thailand, Sri Racha specialises in seafood. Visitors have their pick of several memorable options

tucked within the maze of dangling sea shacks. Cheap eats are available at the colourful market near the town's clock tower, and at stalls along the Ko Loi jetty.

Siriwatana Hotel (☎ 0 3831 1037; 35 Th Jermjompol; r 160-200B) If you can avoid looking through the floorboards at the debris washed up by the tide, then you'll probably be smitten with Siriwatana's ramshackle charm. The innkeepers move as slowly as their motley gang of dogs, but smiles are plentiful and basic rooms are dirt-cheap and come with private bathrooms.

City Hotel (☎ 0 3832 2700; www.citysriracha.com; 6/126 Th Sukhumvit; r 3700-15,000B; ✿ ▣ ⬚ ✿) At the other end of the sleeping spectrum, the immaculate City Hotel is set back from Sri Racha's dockside clutter. The rooms are slightly Asian in theme, but the oriental austerity could be interpreted as being a bit sparse.

Grand Seaside Restaurant (☎ 0 3831 2537, 0 3832 3851; Soi 18; dishes 80-200B; ☯ lunch & dinner) This creaky, colonial-style restaurant leans over the curling sea with polished wooden floors that glisten in the sunset.

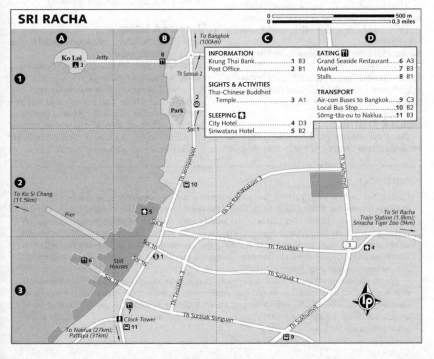

Getting There & Away

Buses bound for Sri Racha (ordinary/air-con 74/94B, two hours) leave every half hour from Ekamai in Bangkok. Ordinary direct buses stop near the pier for Ko Si Chang, while through buses and air-con buses stop along Th Sukhumvit (Hwy 3). Túk-túk (pronounced dúk dúk) can take you to the pier for 30B to 40B.

White sörng·tăa·ou (also spelt säwngthăew; small pickup trucks) bound for Naklua (north Pattaya; 30B, 30 minutes) leave from near the clock tower in Sri Racha throughout the day. Once you're in Naklua, you can easily catch another sörng·tăa·ou to central Pattaya for 10B.

KO SI CHANG
เกาะสีชัง
pop 5038

A hop, skip and jump from Bangkok, this green islet swimming in the Bight of Bangkok is a pleasant getaway from the big smoke. The scrubby little bump in the ocean isn't a white-sand paradise – Ko Si Chang attracts those who are charmed by hidden temples, fishing shanties, turquoise vistas and quiet evenings.

The island's sole settlement faces the mainland and doubles as the ferry terminus. Bumpy roads link the village with all the other sights.

Kasikornbank (99/12 Th Atsadang) Has an ATM and currency-exchange facilities.

Tourist Services Centre (☎ 0 3821 6201; Th Atsadang; ☽ 9am-4.30pm Mon-Fri) Opposite Sichang Palace hotel. Ask for the *Island Welcome* brochure.

Sights & Activities

A Buddhist meditation hermitage, **Tham Yai Phrik Vipassana Centre** (☎ 0 3821 6104; ☽ dawn-dusk) surrounds a series of meditation caves filled with Buddha images and swooping bats. These caves first came to the attention of monks when they discovered that some of the formations contained the natural likeness of Buddha. Today, monks from all over Thailand come here to take advantage of the peaceful environment for meditation. Faràng (foreigners of European descent) who are interested in studying here are also welcome; just be sure to phone ahead and be aware that you will need to follow the monastery's sober codes of conduct. Whether you visit for an hour or a month, please leave an appropriate donation with the monk who shows you around.

The ornate **San Jao Phaw Khao Yai** (Shrine of the Father Spirit of the Great Hill; ☽ dawn-dusk) is a stunning Chinese Temple believed to date back as far as China's Ming dynasty. Explore multiple shrine-caves and climb the several levels for splendid views of the sea.

Hat Tha Wang Palace (admission free; ☽ 9am-5pm) was used as a summer retreat by King Chulalongkorn (Rama V), but was abandoned when the French briefly occupied the island in 1893. Today, locals and visitors enjoy picnics on the perfectly manicured grounds.

Sleeping & Eating

Most places to stay have food available for guests and nonguests.

Rim Talay (☎ 0 3821 6237; 38/3 Mu 2, Th Devavongse; r 500-800B, 'houseboats' 1500B; ✹) Behind the Pan & David Restaurant, this waterside spot has simple but clean air-con rooms, and a selection of colourful Thai fishing boats that have been transformed into mini-apartments for up to five people. The bow of each 'houseboat' is a chill-out area with comfy couches.

GULF GOLF

Golfing has been a local pastime for over a century, but its popularity rose dramatically after Bangkok hosted the World Cup in 1975. Today, the warm climate and lush foliage have made the Land of Smiles one of the best places in the world to tee up. Most of the top-notch facilities lie within a three-hour drive from Bangkok, making it easy to escape the city for a relaxing weekend on the green. The best season for golfing along the eastern seaboard is generally November to March, when it's cooler and drier, but even during the wet season, the rainfall usually just comes in very short (but strong) bursts.

For more information on Thailand's many courses, or for details about package deals that include accommodation, check out www.golfinthailand.com. Apart from green fees (between 600B and 3000B), expect to pay about 200B for a caddy (although some of them only speak Thai). Equipment rental costs around 300B per day and cart hire is usually about 500B per day.

Sichang Palace (☎ 0 3821 6276; Th Atsadang 81; r 1050-1300B; ✕ ⊠) This central resort-style hotel starts with a gaudy golden lobby and ends with comfy sleeping options with all the mod cons. The better rooms come with balconies overlooking the island's bays and busy piers. Ask for a discount in the low season. Nonguests can use the pool for 50B.

Pan & David Restaurant (☎ 0 3821 6629; 167 Moo 3, Th Makhaam Thaew; dishes 40-280B; ✕ breakfast, lunch & dinner Wed-Mon) Friendly David and his wife Pan dish out the island's best eats. Nosh on top-notch Thai, European and vegetarian favourites. Wash it all down with a glass of wine, but make sure to leave room for the homemade ice cream.

Getting There & Around
Boats between Ko Si Chang (40B, 40 minutes) and Sri Racha depart hourly between 7am and 8pm. The last ferry costs 10B extra. Once you are on the island, motorcycle taxis can take you anywhere for 30B to 40B. Island tours are available for around 250B: be prepared to haggle. Motorbikes are available to rent from Tiewpai-Park Resort for 250B per day.

PATTAYA
พัทยา
pop 104,318
Oh Pattaya, land of the three 'S's: sun, sea and sex. PR pundits are working overtime to erase the city's sordid history of slow boats and fast women, but the saucy reputation still looms large. Once a lonely fishing village, Pattaya started to morph into its present state during the Vietnam War, when American GIs were looking for love on their break from war. Since then, this tourist metropolis has become a living testament to unchecked development.

It's the total lack of subtlety that sets Pattaya apart from other 'red light' areas around the world. Yes, Amsterdam has scantily clad women who dance in red-tinted windows, but Pattaya's sexual innuendos are much harsher and more terse – nothing is left to the imagination. The streets in Pattaya have names such as Soi BJ, and there are nightclubs called Cockswell and Shagfest. Even Hooters, the popular American food chain, pretends to have a double meaning; no such luck in ol' Pattaya.

Holiday purists may scoff at the name, but this beachside Bangkok is truly starting to change. Today, there's a new, fourth 'S' – 'sights' – that is very much a part of the ·

Pattaya experience. Fantastic temples, wild zoos, live shows and quirky museums fan out across the cobble sands and beyond. With a dash of gumption and a pinch of adventure, a trip to Pattaya might just turn out to be the most memorable part of your vacation.

If you're after a smidgen more tranquillity, head to Hat Jomtien, a 6km stretch of attractive beach just 2km south of Hat Pattaya. Hat Naklua, a smaller beach 1km north of Pattaya, is also quiet and quite tastefully developed. The small headland separating Pattaya and Hat Jomtien is a beautiful enclave with the region's top resorts.

Orientation
Pattaya proper is about four McDonalds' long and five Starbucks' wide. The heart of the city is a commercial jungle straddling a blonde stretch of scenic sand. Th Hat Pattaya (Pattaya Beach Rd) follows the perfect curvature of the bay, and turns into Walking St, a pedestrian mall chock-a-block with restaurants and nightclubs. Heading inland, you'll come across lanes thick with lodgings, restaurants, bars and travel agencies that snake their way towards the town's main traffic artery, Th Pattaya 2.

Information
BOOKSHOPS
Book Corner (Map p120; Soi Post Office; ✕ 10am-10pm) Decent selection of English-language fiction and travel guides.
Bookazine (Map p120; 1st fl, Royal Garden Plaza, Th Hat Pattaya; ✕ 11am-11pm) Has loads of travel books, literature and magazines. There's also a branch at Hat Jomtien (Map p122).

EMERGENCY
Tourist Police (Map p120; ☎ 0 3842 9371, emergency 1155; tourist@police.go.th; Th Pattaya 2) The head office is on Pattaya's busy main artery. There are also police boxes along the Pattaya and Jomtien beaches.

IMMIGRATION
Immigration office (Map p120; ☎ 0 3825 2751; Soi 8, Th Pattaya Klang) Handles visa extensions.

INTERNET ACCESS
There are several internet options around Soi Praisani (aka Soi Post Office), at the Royal Garden Plaza and along Th Pattaya 2. At Hat Jomtien, they pop up every couple of blocks or so along Th Hat Jomtien.

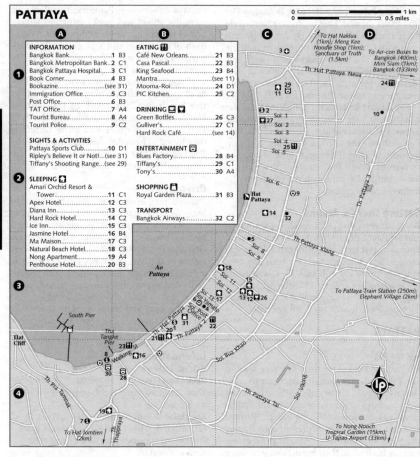

PATTAYA

INFORMATION	
Bangkok Bank...................**1** B3	
Bangkok Metropolitan Bank..**2** C1	
Bangkok Pattaya Hospital......**3** C1	
Book Corner.......................**4** B3	
Bookazine.....................(see 31)	
Immigration Office.............**5** C3	
Post Office........................**6** B3	
TAT Office........................**7** A4	
Tourist Bureau...................**8** A4	
Tourist Police....................**9** C2	

SIGHTS & ACTIVITIES	
Pattaya Sports Club..........**10** D1	
Ripley's Believe It or Not!...(see 31)	
Tiffany's Shooting Range...(see 29)	

SLEEPING	
Amari Orchid Resort &	
Tower.........................**11** C1	
Apex Hotel.....................**12** C3	
Diana Inn.......................**13** C3	
Hard Rock Hotel...............**14** C2	
Ice Inn..........................**15** C3	
Jasmine Hotel..................**16** B4	
Ma Maison.....................**17** C3	
Natural Beach Hotel...........**18** C3	
Nong Apartment................**19** A4	
Penthouse Hotel...............**20** B3	

EATING	
Café New Orleans.............**21** B3	
Casa Pascal....................**22** B3	
King Seafood..................**23** B4	
Mantra.......................(see 11)	
Mooma-Roi....................**24** D1	
PIC Kitchen....................**25** C2	

DRINKING	
Green Bottles..................**26** C3	
Gulliver's.......................**27** C1	
Hard Rock Café..............(see 14)	

ENTERTAINMENT	
Blues Factory..................**28** B4	
Tiffany's.........................**29** C1	
Tony's...........................**30** A4	

SHOPPING	
Royal Garden Plaza...........**31** B3	

TRANSPORT	
Bangkok Airways..............**32** C2	

INTERNET RESOURCES
Pattaya At Night (www.pattaya-at-night.com)

MEDIA
The weekly *Pattaya Mail* (www.pattayamail.com) publishes articles on political, economic and environmental developments in the area.

MEDICAL SERVICES
Bangkok Pattaya Hospital (Map p120; ☎ 0 3825 9911, emergency 1719; 301 Moo 6, Th Sukhumvit, Naklua; 24hr) Pattaya's premier health-care provider.

MONEY
There are banks all over Pattaya and Hat Jomtien; all have ATMs and most also have foreign exchange booths that stay open late (usually to 8pm).
Bangkok Bank (Map p120; ☎ 0 3822 2370; Th Hat Pattaya; 9.30am-7pm Mon-Fri)
Bangkok Metropolitan Bank (Map p120; ☎ 0 3842 8418; Th Hat Pattaya; 8.30am-3.30pm Mon-Fri)

POST
Post office (Map p120; ☎ 0 3842 9341; Soi Post Office)

TOURIST INFORMATION
Almost every establishment in Pattaya and Hat Jomtien has a variety of tourist rags and pamphlets, packed with ads and info. The bimonthly *What's On Pattaya* is a good resource with several maps, articles and a crossword to do while you relax at the beach. In addition to

the TAT office, there is a small tourist bureau near the police booth on Walking St.

Pattaya Call Centre (☎ 1337, 0 3841 0393) Provides vital information regarding accommodation, attractions, restaurants and shopping.

Tourism Authority of Thailand (TAT; Map p120; ☎ 1672, 0 3842 8750; tatchon@tat.or.th; 609 Moo 10, Th Pra Tamnak; ☺ 8.30am-4.30pm) Located at the northwestern edge of Rama IX Park. Offers mountains of brochures.

Danger & Annoyances

If you are arriving by bus, there will be several sŏrng·tǎa·ou waiting to cart you off to your hotel. Many of these drivers are unscrupulous and will try to scam you by taking you to the wrong part of the city, and then forcing you to pay extra to bring you to the correct location.

(We'll refrain from stating the obvious warnings about the booming skin trade in Pattaya.)

Sights

Pattaya probably has the most sights and activities of any resort destination in Thailand. There's so much to do, you might not have time to catch some rays on the beach.

If you're only going to visit one temple in Thailand, make it the **Sanctuary of Truth** (off Map p120; ☎ 0 3836 7229; www.sanctuaryoftruth.com; 206/2 Moo 5, Naklua; admission 500B; ☺ 8am-5pm). Although not technically a temple, this stunning teakwood palace details the pan-Eastern school of thought regarding the order of the universe. It's like the Thai version of Barcelona's Sagrada Familia (minus the crowds) – the structure is not yet complete, but visitors will undoubtedly be awestruck when they glimpse this incredible rambling fortress.

The **Nong Nooch Tropical Garden** (off Map p120; ☎ 0 3842 9321; 163 Th Sukhumvit, Sattahip; admission 400B; ☺ 9am-sunset) is a popular attraction located south of Pattaya. The perfectly manicured grounds feature four daily elephant and Thai dancing shows (between 9am and 3.45pm). The dancing shows demonstrate different movement styles from around the kingdom, and the elephant spectacles display the gentle giants' hidden talents, such as picture painting, bike riding and basketball.

Just 2.5km out of town, **Pattaya Elephant Village** (off Map p120; ☎ 0 3824 9818; www.elephant-village-pattaya.com; ☺ according to show & trek times) is a nonprofit sanctuary for former working elephants. There's a 2.30pm elephant show (adult/child 500/400B) that demonstrates training techniques, and daily elephant treks (adult/child 2000/1300B).

Many tourists also visit the **Tiger Zoo** in nearby Sri Racha (see p116).

Located at the Royal Garden Plaza mall, **Ripley's Believe It or Not!** (Map p120; ☎ 0 3871 0294; admission 580B; ☺ 11am-11pm) provides fun for the whole family. This museum of oddities has bizarre artefacts and body parts from all over the world. There's also a 4-D simulator, a tricky maze and a haunted house adventure.

Mini Siam (off Map p120; ☎ 0 3872 7333; 387 Moo 6, Th Sukhumvit; adult/child 250/120B; ☺ 7am-10pm) is – you guessed it – a scaled-down set of replicas of Thailand's ancient and famous sights. It's about 1.5km east of town.

Activities

Pattaya has a huge range of outdoor activities, including but by no means limited to **bowling**, **snooker**, **archery**, **target-shooting**, **softball**, **horse-riding** and **tennis**. Many of these activities are available at the **Pattaya Sports Club** (Map p120; ☎ 0 3836 1167; www.pattayasports.org; 3/197 Th Pattaya 3) or can be organised by most hotels.

You can take target practice at **Tiffany's Shooting Range** (Map p120; ☎ 0 3842 9642; ground fl, Tiffany's, Th Pattaya 2; admission 250B plus ammunition; ☺ 9am-10pm), or at Hat Jomtien you can visit an enclave of businesses offering adrenaline junkies their fix. There's a 56m bungee jump at **Pattaya Bungee Jump** (Map p122; ☎ 0 3830 1209; Soi 9, Th Thep Prasit; jumps 1500B; ☺ 9am-6pm) and the nearby **Paintball Park Pattaya** (Map p122; ☎ 0 3830 0608; www.paintballpark-pattaya.com; 248/10 Moo 12, Th Thep Prasit; 50 bullets starting at 500B; ☺ 10am-6pm) lets you run around and take your anger out on your friends with paint-filled bullets. To gratify your need for speed, drop in to the **Pattaya Kart Speedway** (Map p122; ☎ 0 3842 2044; 248/2 Soi 9, Th Thep Prasit; admission from 250B; ☺ 9am-6pm), where you can race go-karts around an impressive 1km loop.

There are several islands off the coast of Pattaya that are worth the short boat trip if you need an afternoon away from the city. **Ko Laan**, about 45 minutes away, is a popular choice – many visitors go on glass-bottom boat tours for views of the coral reef. **Ko Sak** and **Ko Phai** have powder sand beaches, and **Ko Krok** is a hot spot for divers. Ferry tickets can be booked at the large pier in South Pattaya. Tickets are around 20B to 85B.

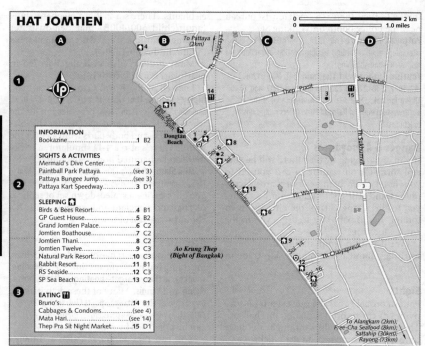

HAT JOMTIEN

INFORMATION
Bookazine...............................1 B2

SIGHTS & ACTIVITIES
Mermaid's Dive Center...........2 C2
Paintball Park Pattaya............(see 3)
Pattaya Bungee Jump.............(see 3)
Pattaya Kart Speedway...........3 D1

SLEEPING
Birds & Bees Resort.................4 B1
GP Guest House......................5 B2
Grand Jomtien Palace..............6 C2
Jomtien Boathouse..................7 C2
Jomtien Thani........................8 C2
Jomtien Twelve......................9 C3
Natural Park Resort.................10 C3
Rabbit Resort........................11 B1
RS Seaside............................12 C3
SP Sea Beach.........................13 C2

EATING
Bruno's................................14 B1
Cabbages & Condoms..............(see 4)
Mata Hari.............................(see 14)
Thep Pra Sit Night Market.........15 D1

DIVING & SNORKELLING

With 20 dive sites orbiting the coast, Pattaya is a good spot for scuba if you can't make it down the coast to the southern part of Thailand. Diving in the region is split up into three sections: the Near Islands, the Far Islands and Samesan.

The **Near Islands** have experienced overfishing and heavy boat traffic, so these sites can be barren with poor visibility. Nearby Ko Laan, Ko Sak and Ko Krok are fine for beginners. In most places expect 3m to 9m of visibility under good conditions, or, at more remote sites, 5m to 12m.

The **Far Islands**, located about 90 minutes from town, feature bright coral reefs including the popular artificial reef created by the shipwrecked HMS *Kram*.

Samesan is a small fishing village south of Pattaya with some of the best diving in the region. The shipwrecked *Petchburi Bremen* and *Hardeep* have created artificial reefs and are interesting dive sites. One of the best dive sites around is an old US Navy ammunition dump called Samesan Hole. This advanced dive goes down to 87m and has a gentle slope covered thickly with coral where you can see barracuda and large rays. The visibility here is pretty good, up to 20m on a good day.

A two-dive excursion costs between 2500B and 3500B, including the boat, equipment, underwater guide and lunch. Snorkellers may join these day trips for around 1000B. PADI Open Water certification, which takes three to four days, can cost anywhere between 11,000B and 15,000B, including all instruction and equipment. Certification costs are considerably less on Ko Tao (see p230).

There are several dive operators in town, including the following. It's best to organise these by phone, or through your hotel.

Adventure Divers (☎ 0 3836 4453; www.pattaya divers.com; 391/77-78 Th Thappraya)

Aquanauts Dive Centre (☎ 0 3836 1724; www.aqua nautsdive.com; Soi 6, Th Pattaya 1) Operates separate snorkelling and boat tours as well (1000B).

Mermaid's Dive Center (Map p122; ☎ 0 3823 2219; www.mermaiddive.com; Soi White House, Hat Jomtien)

Pattaya Dive Centre (☎ 0 3871 0918; www.dive centrepattaya.com; 219/3 Moo 10, Soi 6, Th Pattaya 1)

OTHER WATER SPORTS

Pattaya and Hat Jomtien have some of the best water sports facilities in Thailand and operators line the main beach roads competing for your custom. **Water-skiing** costs around 1000B per hour including equipment, boat and driver. **Parasailing** is 300B to 400B a shot (about 10 to 15 minutes). **Game-fishing** is also possible; rental rates for boats, fishing guides and tackle are reasonable. Hat Jomtien is the best spot for **windsurfing** (500B to 600B per hour), not least because you're a little less likely to run into people parasailing or jet-skiing.

The four main islands off the coast of Pattaya also provide countless hours of fun in the water (see p121).

Sleeping

There's no shortage of fantastic accommodation in Pattaya, however, most of it falls into the top-end category. Almost every international chain has set up shop along the sand, pushing lower-end options away from the beach. The proximity to Bangkok means that weekends tend to be quite crowded and prices usually rise accordingly.

Know the rooming rules at your hotel should you decide to bring an 'extra sleeper' back to your room. Hotel staff members are completely desensitised to such situations, so it's best to be frank, especially at small establishments, where unannounced guests could lead to prompt expulsion.

PATTAYA

Budget

Apex Hotel (Map p120; ☎ 0 3842 8281; www.apex hotelpattaya.com; 216/2 Soi 11; r 450-500B; 🞵 🞵) Rome wasn't built in a day, but Apex probably was – its prefabricated façade looks like a stack of grey Lego bricks. The cheapest rooms are doled out on a first-come basis, although forking out an extra 50B isn't that big a hassle considering the tidy rooms come with faux-marble flooring, air-con and cable TV. There's a swimming pool and private car park on the ground level.

Ice Inn (Map p120; ☎ 0 3872 0671; www.iceinnpattaya .com; 528/2-3 Th Pattaya 2; r 450-715B; 🞵 🞵) Tucked behind a shop stuffed with sundry Asian collectibles (and an oddly placed internet kiosk), this smaller setup offers midrange rooms with a budget price tag. The whole place is pathologically clean, yet the staff are remarkably laid-back.

Jasmine Hotel (Map p120; ☎ 0 3842 4590; www .jasminehotel-pattaya.com; 547/34 Moo 10; r 650-800B; 🞵 🞵) If you're seeking accommodation in the thick of things, look no further. Jasmine's low tariffs are an undeniable bargain for lodging on Walking St. Behind the orange façade, guests will enjoy prim tiled rooms with large kitchenettes, free internet and new cabinetry. Accessible to people in wheelchairs.

Midrange

Ma Maison (Map p120; ☎ 0 3871 0433; www.mamaison -hotel.com; 386 Moo 10, Soi 13; r 900-1400B; 🞵 🞵) Ma Maison feels a bit more personal than most of the other lodging options around town – the décor is rife with rows of potted flowers and hanging collectables, such as splayed fans and antique farming equipment. Rooms wind around the central pool, which acts like an oasis attracting weary guests after a long night among buzzing lights. Reservations recommended.

Natural Beach Hotel (Map p120; ☎ 0 3842 9239; www.naturalbeach.com; 216 Moo 10, Soi 11; r 950-1550B; 🞵 🞵) This is as close as you'll get to the beach without dropping some serious cash (not that the beach in Pattaya is by any means idyllic). A low-key spot with a cosy garden and pool patio, Natural Beach has dated furnishings lending an accidental '80s feel to the otherwise standard sleeping setup.

Diana Inn (Map p120; ☎ 0 3842 9675; www.diana pattaya.co.th; btwn Soi 11-12, 216/6-20 Th Pattaya 2; r 990-1500B, ste 3500; 🞵 🞵 🞵) This self-aggrandising hotel is popular with Thai tourists and offers the hook up for golfers. The betters rooms have sparkling hardwood floors and overlook the swimming pool with its big cursive 'D' carved in white tiles at the bottom. Complimentary buffet breakfasts are served in the lobby's coffee shop, and don't forget to grab your welcome drink when you check in.

Penthouse Hotel (Map p120; ☎ 0 3842 9639; www .penthousehotel.com; Soi Pattaya Funland; r incl breakfast 1000-5000B; 🞵 🞵) The Penthouse Hotel will definitely get you into the Pattaya spirit. The lobby is awash with every garish *objet d'art* tossed away during a Parisian *vide grenier*. Upstairs, rooms retain the French flea market theme and include additional amenities such as disco lighting, Jacuzzis, a dance area and a 'health swing' (?). Ignore the in-house TV channel where you can browse 'nightly companions' to be delivered to your room (which other places do too). It sounds pretty extreme, but we did see a couple of British grannies checking in…

Nong Apartment (Map p120; ☎ 0 3871 3371; www.pattayavacation.com; 373/5-6 Moo 10, Soi Yensabai; ste 1200-2200B; ✂ ☐) Nong is a fantastic deal for small groups, families and those who are looking to stick around town for a while. Apartment-style units are arranged around a long rectangular courtyard stuffed with a vivid assortment of enormous potted plants. Guests can retreat to their private patios, or lounge in the common areas covered with portraits of US naval cruisers.

Top End

Almost every international hotel chain has an outpost in Pattaya, which means that most of the accommodation around town falls into the top-end category. Count on paying a 10% service charge and a 7% value-added tax (VAT) for these places.

Amari Orchid Resort & Tower (Map p120; ☎ 0 3841 8418; www.amari.com/orchid; Th Hat Pattaya Neua; r/ste from US$89/200; ✂ ☐ 🏊) Amari has over 500 rooms spread between a low-rise garden complex and the brand spankin' new 'Ocean Tower'. There is a noticeable difference between the two buildings since the garden rooms are considered 'four star' (according to some unknown standard), while the tower units are 'five star'. Don't miss Mantra – this on-site restaurant is the hippest spot in town (see p126).

our pick **Hard Rock Hotel** (Map p120; ☎ 0 3842 8755; www.hardrockhotels.net/pattaya; 429 Moo 9, Th Hat Pattaya; r US$125-175; ✂ ☐ 🏊) Hard Rock is a fun, friendly way to spend a vacation in Pattaya. The excellent staff offer unparalleled smiles and service amid funky design details, including dangling guitars, giant music-related murals and awesome headboards featuring a Warhol-esque image of a rock legend. In the evening, the towering façade blinks with hundreds of multicoloured lights as though a lighthouse was hosting a disco party. Drop the kids off at the Lil' Rock childcare program, a fantastic service that takes the tykes to the on-site climbing wall, swimming pool (with floating trampoline), and arts and crafts centre. If you're staying on one of the top floors, you'll have access to the King Club, a private lounge serving up unlimited pre-dinner drinks in the early evening – not a bad way to kick off the night around town.

HAT JOMTIEN

Quieter Jomtien is only about a 15-minute sŏrng·tǎa·ou ride from the throng and bustle of Pattaya.

Budget

RS Seaside (Map p122; ☎ 0 3823 1867; fax 0 3823 1882; 125/19 Moo 10, Th Hat Jomtien; r 460-2300B; ✂ ☐ 🏊) The best budget option on Jomtien beach, RS has a vast selection of room types, from closet-like spaces that look out at an adobe wall, to spacious digs sporting balconies and sea views. But it doesn't matter if you're booked into the cheapest room, since everyone benefits from the swimming pool, Jacuzzi and caffeine at the espresso bar.

GP Guest House (Map p122; ☎ 0 3875 6072; fax 0 3875 6245; 144/126-128 Moo 12, Th Hat Jomtien; r 500-600B; ✂) Off the main drag and set among a colourful sandwich of narrow tenements, GP offers generic crash pads linked through a maze of weaving concrete hallways. Monthly rentals are also negotiable.

Midrange

Jomtien Boathouse (Map p122; ☎ 0 3875 6143; www.jomtien-boathouse.com; 380/5-6 Th Hat Jomtien; r 900-1250B; ✂) The lobby at Jomtien Boathouse looks like the beachside abode of a crusty sea captain, with schools of taxidermic fish, scrolls of lambskin maps and models of wooden frigates. On deck, you'll find a terrace for tan-lovers and a cosy pub that serves hearty fare fit for a sailor. The simple rooms upstairs do not retain the nautical theme, but they're clean and cosy. Go for the beachside rooms – the 'Garden View' accommodation has extremely tiny windows.

SP Sea Beach (Map p122; ☎ 0 3823 6101; www.spvillagepattaya.com/spseabeach/index.html; Th Hat Jomtien; r 1000-1800B; ✂) This white, cube-shaped inn is a great choice along Jomtien's main drag. The lobby looks like a futuristic ice cream parlour – everything's crisp white with pompous lime-green touches, such as bucket-seat bar stools. The sun-drenched rooms are slightly more demure, but still proffer traces of quirkiness in the Warhol-like pop art. Monthly rates are also available.

Jomtien Twelve (Map p122; ☎ 0 3875 6865; jomtien twelve@gmail.com; 240/13 Moo 12, Th Hat Jomtien; r 1100-1550B; ✂) Jomtien Twelve is trying to pull off 'boutique chic': the exterior incorporates teak slatting into a contemporary design scheme, and the lobby is dripping with trendy goodness. After that, however, it seems like the designer got a tad lazy – the rooms are well kept (especially the bathrooms), but they're noticeably devoid of that yuppie sensibility set loose downstairs.

Natural Park Resort (Map p122; ☎ 0 3823 1561; www .naturalparkresort.com; 412 Th Hat Jomtien; r 1500B, ste 2200-7500B; ❄ ▯ ⓢ) Natural Park changes things up along Jomtien's beach boulevard with its lush jungley property punctuated by mini hotel blocks. The lagoonlike swimming pool has an adorable island smack in the middle with two frizzy palms. Rooms are bedecked in a charming blend of teak beams, wicker lounge chairs and Japanese sliding screens.

Grand Jomtien Palace (Map p122; ☎ 0 3823 1405; www.grandjomtienpalace.com; 356 Th Hat Jomtien; r/ste 1600/3800B; ❄ ▯ ⓢ) Remember when hotels used to make their drapes and bed comforters from the same patterned material? Even though the rooms at Grand Jomtien Palace are in need of a designer's eye, they offer sweeping views of the area, and some have fresh hardwood floors. The 14-storey hotel isn't quite a 'palace', as the name suggests, but there's loads of professional service and hoards of amenities.

Jomtien Thani (Map p122; ☎ 0 3823 2990; www .jomtienthanihotel.com; 75/261 Moo 12, Th Hat Jomtien; r 1870-2675B, ste 5900B; ❄ ▯ ⓢ) The lobby here looks like a Siamese railway station from a vintage Bond flick. The rooms are a bit less showy, and could benefit with a framed picture, or maybe by changing the wall colours so that they're not identical to the floor tiles. Don't be bashful about requesting to see several different options – some rooms have excellent sea views and plasma TVs. Jomtien Thani's major perk is its cache of facilities and services: a gym, billiards, massage parlours, convention rooms, fine dining and the list goes on.

Top End
Birds & Bees Resort (Cabbages & Condoms; Map p122; ☎ 0 3825 0035; www.cabbagesandcondoms.co.th; 366/11 Moo 12, Th Phratamnak 4; r 4000-7000B, ste 6000-12,000B; ❄ ▯ ⓢ) It's hard to believe that a tranquil tangle of jungle lies between the bustle of Pattaya and Jomtien. There are two garden paths here – the Communist Walk and the Capitalist Walk – that lead guests towards the beach and the hidden pods of multistorey rooming units. Most of the resort's proceeds go to the **Population & Community Development Association** (www.pda.or.th), an important not-

for-profit organisation that contributes to Thailand's HIV/AIDS education and rural development, among many other endeavours. PDA, as it's often known, was the recipient of the Gates Award for Global Health in 2007.

Rabbit Resort (Map p122; ☎ 0 3830 3303; www .rabbitresort.com; Th Hat Dongtan 4; r 4200-5200B; ❄ ▯ ⓢ) Situated on a prime slice of Pattaya property, Rabbit Resort is a refreshing change from the clunky chain hotels nearby. This family-run operation offers forested cottages featuring Thai-style furnishings and hand-made, rustic textiles. The separate kids' pool and private beach area are added perks.

Eating
Western food rules the culinary roost, with several noteworthy establishments that have been around for decades. Pattaya's also the perfect place to step off the beaten path and explore some local haunts. There are some fantastic night markets and seafood joints that serve up excellent dishes for less baht than the usual tourist magnets.

PATTAYA
Meng Kee Noodle Shop (off Map p120; ☎ 0 3822 5262; Th Naklua, opposite Baan Suan Rung Roj; dishes 30-100B; ⓥ 9am-3pm) Leave the neon lights behind and venture north into Naklua for some authentic Chinese noodles and roasted duck. This open-air mom-and-pop stop also dishes out unusual finds such as salty-sweet bamboo soup. It'll be one of your cheapest meals in Pattaya, even with the 10B sŏrng·tǎa·ou ride.

Mooma-Roi (Map p120; ☎ 0 3841 4801; 15/15 Moo 6, Th Pattaya 3; dishes 50-150B; ⓥ dinner) The name says it all: Mooma-Roi is Thai for 'delicious corner'. With nary a faràng in sight, this outdoor bistro teams with locals who gather within the spacious cloister to savour classic Thai dishes around an ornamental pond.

King Seafood (Map p120; ☎ 0 3842 9459; king_sea food@hotmail.com; 94 Walking St; dishes 80-300B; ⓥ lunch & dinner) Yes, the prices are higher than at the hidden local fish markets, but this seafood mothership is a classic Walking St establishment. The tome-like menu is a veritable al-manac of edible marine life.

PIC Kitchen (Map p120; ☎ 0 3842 8374; 10 Soi 5, Th Pattaya 2; dishes 110-290B; ⓥ lunch & dinner) This teak-lined place has an intimate atmosphere with open-sided rooms, fluffy cushions and low wooden tables. Sample the Thai menu and sneak upstairs to the Jazz Pit for some post-repast tunes.

Café New Orleans (Map p120; ☎ 0 3871 0805; www .cafeneworleans.info; Soi Pattaya Funland; dishes 150-750B; ☻ 3pm-midnight) Café New Orleans has perfectly synthesized the unique Bourbon St atmosphere that mixes baroque and bayou charm. A lengthy menu echoes the ambience with juicy steaks and Creole onion soups. It's hard to believe that this romantic setup is just seconds away from Pattaya's other articulations of 'love'.

ourpick Mantra (Map p120; ☎ 0 3842 9591; www .mantra-pattaya.com; Th Hat Pattaya Neua; dishes 240-800B; ☻ dinner Mon-Sat, brunch & dinner Sun; ☒) Undoubtedly the coolest address in town, this two-storey behemoth oozes chic from every intricately arranged design detail. The interior combines Arabian and oriental elements in steady bursts of jet black and slick, lipstick red. The terrific restaurant has seven kitchens, each one dedicated to a specific cuisine; there's a sushi counter, Indian ovens and a homemade pasta station, to name just a few. It's always nice when the food lives up to the remarkable décor.

Casa Pascal (Map p120; ☎ 0 3872 3660; www.restau rant-pattaya.com; 485/4 Moo 10, Th Pattaya 2; mains 270-490B; ☻ lunch & dinner Mon-Sat, lunch Sun) Owned and operated by the former executive chef of Pattaya's Dusit Resort, Casa Pascal is an elegant dining experience set under a colonnade of large wooden pillars. Loosen your belt for the never-ending Sunday brunch buffet (799B), complete with a fanfare of napkin sculptures, cooking stations and delicious samplers, such as rock lobster and beef Tatar. The regularly changing menu features gourmet French, Italian and Thai dishes.

HAT JOMTIEN

Thep-Pra-Sit Night Market (Map p122; Th Sukhumvit; dishes from 20B; ☻ 6-10pm) Low prices and small portions make this popular night market the perfect spot to sample some local faves – just choose your 'delicacies' wisely. While nibbling on your street cuisine, browse stalls of knockoff clothes, shoes, accessories and CDs. To get here, grab a taxi or sŏrng·tăa·ou.

Pree-Cha Seafood (off Map p122; ☎ 0 3870 9439; Ban Amphur; dishes 30-200B, lobster 650B/kg; ☻ dinner) Make the pilgrimage to Pree-Cha for some of the cheapest (and tastiest) seafood around, in an area sans tourists. Take a taxi or hire a sŏrng·tăa·ou and head south of Jomtien for

about 20 minutes, turn right at the first intersection after the Ambassador Hotel, keep left and you'll happen upon an ungodly number of cars in front of the restaurant on the right-hand side of the road.

Cabbages & Condoms (Map p122; ☎ 0 3825 0035; www.cabbagesandcondoms.co.th; 366/11 Moo 12, Th Phratamnak 4; snacks from 50B, set menu 600-900B; ☻ breakfast, lunch & dinner) This saucily named restaurant hides along the secluded beach at the Birds & Bees Resort. Charming lamps, crafted from fish traps and coconuts, cast a romantic hue over sated diners. If that gets you in the mood, you'll be happy to know that the standard bin of farewell breath mints has been appropriately replaced with a bucket of prophylactics.

Bruno's (Map p122; ☎ 0 3836 4600; 306/63 Chateau Dale Plaza, Th Thappraya; lunch mains 100-200B, dinner mains 360-390B, pasta dishes 210-280B; ☻ lunch & dinner) The walk-in wine cellar makes Bruno's the go-to place for those seeking vino with their victuals. Lunchtime is a bargain – the team of gourmet chefs prepares scrumptious steaks and seafood courses for less than 200B.

Mata Hari (Map p122; ☎ 0 3825 9799; 482/57 Moo 12, Th Thappraya; mains 200-600B; ☻ dinner Tue-Sun) Mata Hari has been a Pattaya staple for over 40 years, serving *haute cuisine* to visitors and faithful expat patrons. The menu largely focuses on European fare, with a couple of exotic flavours tossed in to tempt the palate.

Drinking & Entertainment

Nightlife in Pattaya is an ever-evolving creature. While the southern part of town is chock-a-block with go-go bars, new venues are popping up all over the place, offering tourists and locals a more PG-13 experience. Nowadays there are ice bars, blues lounges, live-music venues and thumping discos. Walking St is the heart of Pattaya's nightlife, and it overloads the senses with trance music, gyrating bodies and buzzing neon signs advertising every fetish imaginable. Down the street, the convoluted Soi 1, 2 and 3 are collectively known as 'Pattayaland', and consist of wall-to-wall bars blaring the latest pop tunes. Most of the establishments in the area cater to the skin trade, especially along Soi BJ (duh). Soi 3 calls itself 'Boyztown' and is the centre of gay nightlife in Pattaya. At Jomtien, there's a growing gay beach scene along the northern end of the sand called Dongtan (pun actually not intended).

LADYBOYS

In most busy nightlife districts in Thailand, you're likely to come across Thailand's third sex, the ladyboy. Known in slang as a *gà·teu·i*, men who identify as women are surprisingly common throughout the Land of Smiles, though no-one is sure why. Although tolerance is widespread in Buddhist Thailand, concealed homophobia prevails; for *gà·teu·i*, this can be a challenging life, with the entertainment and sex industries the only lucrative career avenues open.

Female hormones are typically taken by *gà·teu·i* in early puberty to restrain the growth of masculine traits. Later on, many will have breast implants and some will complete their transformation by undergoing sex-reassignment surgery. Experience with this type of surgery means that Thailand now has some of the most advanced transgender clinics in the world – so much so that patients fly in from all over the globe for operations. After undergoing surgery, the transformation can be very convincing; there are even operations available to remove the telltale Adam's apple.

Hard Rock Café (Map p120; ☎ 0 3842 8755; www.hardrockhotels.net/pattaya; 429 Moo 9, Th Hat Pattaya) Hard Rock's beachside restaurant is a great place to chill out with a glass of wine and listen to some of the best cover bands in town.

Green Bottles (Map p120; ☎ 0 3842 9675; 216/6-20 Th Pattaya 2) Charmingly cosy and retro (you can even request your favourite songs from the band), Green Bottles has been on the scene since 1988 and is one of Pattaya's more traditional pubs.

Blues Factory (Map p120; ☎ 0 3830 0180; www.thebluesfactorypattaya.com; Soi Lucky Star) Off Walking St, Pattaya's best venue for no-nonsense live music features at least two bands every night and a hassle-free atmosphere just metres from the heavier hype of Walking St.

Gulliver's (Map p120; ☎ 0 3871 0641; Th Hat Pattaya; ⏰ 11.30am-2am) At the northern end of Pattaya, Gulliver's has pool tables, free wi-fi and a big international drinks menu. Before 7pm, take advantage of happy hour with discounted beer and cocktails.

our pick **Tiffany's** (Map p120; ☎ 0 3842 1700-5; www.tiffany-show.co.th; 464 Moo 9, Th Pattaya 2; VIP seat 800B, standard seat 700B; ⏰ shows 6pm, 7.30pm & 9pm, plus 10.30pm on holidays) Coming to Pattaya and missing a transvestite cabaret would be like going to Paris and not visiting the Louvre. OK, not really, but these spectacles really are a work of art. The costumes are the definition of glitz and glam, and every feminine nuance has been practised and perfected. Stick around after the show to take photographs with the lovely 'ladies'.

Tony's (Map p120; ☎ 0 3842 5795; www.tonydisco.com; 139/15 Walking St; admission free; ⏰ 8.30pm-2.30am) Run by Tony, a well-to-do Bangkok type, this club-conglomerate has it all: a deafeningly loud, neon-lit disco, pool tables and an in-house Thai boxer. Tony also runs a spa, gym, brewery and dog shelter.

Alangkarn (off Map p122; ☎ 0 3826 6000; www.alangkarnthailand.com; admission 1000B; ⏰ by performance) Located a couple of kilometres southeast of Pattaya, this large theatre features a variety of flashy performances involving elaborate costumes, dancing elephants and pyrotechnics.

Getting There & Away

It's important to note that buses heading between Bangkok and the eastern provinces do not swing through Pattaya, as it is not on the main eastbound highway. If you plan on travelling between Pattaya and Trat (500B), for example, you will have to use a minivan service (easily bookable at any agency or your hotel). There are trains that run between Bangkok and Pattaya, but the frequent buses are much more convenient.

There are air-con buses to Pattaya (113B, two hours, every 40 minutes from 4.45am to 9pm) from Bangkok's Ekamai station. Dozens of private minivans also ply this route for 150B. In Pattaya the air-con bus stop is on Th Hat Pattaya Neua, near the intersection with Th Sukhumvit. Cramped minivans from Th Khao San typically cost 200B per person. Once you reach the main Pattaya bus terminal, waiting red sŏrng·tăa·ou will take you to the main beach road for 20B per person.

Flights with **Bangkok Airways** (Map p120; ☎ 0 3841 2382; www.bangkokair.com; 75/8 Moo 9, Th Pattaya 2) from U-Tapao airport (about 33km south of Pattaya) head to Phuket four times weekly, and to Samui every day. The fare is around 3000B each way to Ko Samui and 3500B to Phuket.

DETOUR: KHAO CHAMAO/KHAO WONG NATIONAL PARK

อุทยานแห่งชาติเขาชะเมา–เขาวง

Although less than 85 sq km, **Khao Chamao/Khao Wong National Park** (☎ 0 3889 4378; reserve@ dnp.go.th; admission 400B; ◷ 8.30am-4.30pm) is famous for limestone mountains, high cliffs, caves, dense forest and waterfalls. Secreted in the rugged landscape are wild elephants, bears, gaur, gibbons and deer. The park features a few waterfalls and over 80 limestone caves and is a good spot for hiking – there are several trails that wind through it. The park is inland from Ban Phe, 17km north of the Km 274 marker off Hwy 3. To get to here, take a sŏrng·tăa·ou (40B) from Ban Phe to the marker, and another sŏrng·tăa·ou (20B) to the park.

You can stay at a camp site (per person 50B) or rent a two-person bungalow (600B to 800B). To book, email reserve@dnp.go.th, or phone ☎ 0 2562 0760.

Getting Around

CAR, JEEP & MOTORCYCLE

Jeeps can be hired for around 2500B per day, and car hire generally starts at 1500B, though you can pay as little as 1000B for a 4WD Suzuki in the low season. Motorcycle rentals usually cost between 200B and 300B per day. There are motorcycle rental places along Th Hat Pattaya and Th Pattaya 2.

SŎRNG·TĂA·OU

Sŏrng·tăa·ou cruise up and down Th Hat Pattaya and Th Pattaya 2 – just hop on and when you get out pay 10B anywhere between Naklua and South Pattaya, or 20B if you take the truck from Pattaya to Jomtien (or vice versa). A chartered sŏrng·tăa·ou to Jomtien should be no more than 40B.

Many readers have complained about riding the 10B sŏrng·tăa·ou with local passengers and then being charged a higher 'charter' price of 20B to 50B or more when they get off. In some instances drivers have threatened to beat faràng passengers when they wouldn't pay the exorbitant fares. It's little use complaining to the tourist police unless you can give them the licence plate number of the offending driver's vehicle. See p121 for more information.

RAYONG & AROUND

อ.เมืองระยอง

pop 522,133

Almost every visitor to Rayong Province, 200km southeast of Bangkok, comes for a beach getaway on sunny Ko Samet (opposite). Travellers will rarely have to stop in the region's capital, as there is a regular bus service from Bangkok to Ban Phe, the ferry port to Ko Samet. We don't want to discourage you from contributing to Rayong town's tourism industry, but besides the bus station and a few

barking dogs, your precious vacation time is better spent elsewhere.

The quaint fishing village of **Ban Phe** has managed to remain small despite its ferry monopoly. Should you decide to blaze your own tourist trail, this seaside shantytown is also the jumping-off point to several lesser-known beach destinations in the area. The province actually has over 100km of coastline, but the lack of tourist development and transport infrastructure means that most of these beaches have slipped under the tourism radar. From Ban Phe, sŏrng·tăa·ou can take you along the coast to the 'resort towns' (and we use that term lightly) of **Laem Charoen**, **Laem Mae Phim**, **Hat Sai Thong** and **Hat Mae Rampeung**. Ferries from near Ban Phe go to private resorts on the secluded islands of **Ko Man Klang** and **Ko Man Nok** (see the boxed text, p132); advance bookings are highly recommended.

Information

Rayong's **TAT office** (☎ 0 3865 5420; 153/4 Th Sukhumvit) is inconveniently positioned 7km east of Rayong town on Hwy 3. A sŏrng·tăa·ou can take you there for about 20B, but we recommend stopping by Ban Phe's police bureau instead. Located just east of Nuan Thip Pier in a pistachio-coloured building, the station has many brochures about the region, although the officers only speak Thai.

There are several banks scattered along Rayong's main drag (Th Sukhumvit) and Ban Phe has a few ATMs attached to convenience stores.

Sleeping & Eating

RAYONG

Should you somehow get stuck in Rayong town, there are a couple of lodging choices within eyeshot of the bus station, but most of the quality options are a short cab ride away. The bus terminal is set within a large market, so there are plenty of food options nearby.

Rayong President Hotel (☎ 0 3862 2771; www .rayongpresident.com; 16/8 Th Phochanakon; r incl breakfast 500-600B; 🛄) Located halfway between the bus station and Wat Khod Thimtaram, this large, white hotel is a quiet place to catch a couple of 'Z's.

BAN PHE

It's officially impossible to miss the boat to Ko Samet; the ferries run through the evening, and water taxis are available in the middle of the night (of course it'll be quite pricy if you're chartering a boat at 3am in the morning). Should you decide to stay in this little port village, there are a couple of options around town and one fully fledged resort a few kilometres down the road.

Christie's Guesthouse (☎ 0 3865 1975; fax 0 3865 2103; 280/92 Soi 1; d/tr 500/700B; 🛄) Crash at Christie's if you want to break up the journey to Ko Samet. Try the hearty Western breakfast, or take your lunch to go for a nibble on the ferry ride. In the evening, the restaurant becomes a popular hang-out for local expat English teachers.

Rayong Resort (☎ 0 3865 1000; www.rayongresort .com; 186 Moo 1, Th Ban Phe; r 3800-12,000B; 🛄 🖵 🛄) Located along the coast between Rayong town and Ban Phe, Rayong Resort is a popular option with Thai tourists seeking a more subdued beach holiday. There's a huge pool, green grounds and boats to Ko Samet – which you can ride for free if you stay for at least three nights.

Getting There & Around

See p135 for information regarding ferries from Ban Phe to Ko Samet. If you are heading straight to Ko Samet from Bangkok, take a direct bus to Ban Phe (157B, three hours, hourly), which depart from Bangkok's Ekamai Station between 5am and 8pm. Aircon buses to Rayong (146B, 2½ hours, every 30 minutes) leave from Ekamai between 4am and 10pm. Sŏrng·tǎa·ou between Rayong bus station and Ban Phe shouldn't cost more than 25B. Rayong has comprehensive bus services to destinations further east, such as Chanthaburi and Trat.

Minivan services connect the pier in Ban Phe to a variety of popular holiday destinations such as Pattaya (250B) and Ko Chang (300B), with a stop at the ferry pier in Laem Ngop. These can be booked at many resorts and travel agencies along the east coast.

KO SAMET
เกาะเสม็ด

If Goldilocks were a Bangkokian socialite, she'd probably spend her weekends here – Pattaya's too close and noisy, Ko Chang's too far and rugged, but Ko Samet is just right. This dagger-shaped island off the coast of quiet Rayong Province features a sun-bleached coastline scalloped by beige dunes. Statistically, this little isle boasts the most days of sunshine out of any beach retreat in the kingdom, which gives tourists and locals the green light almost every day of the year.

Lately, faràng visitors are becoming increasingly irked by the mandatory 400B entry fee (Ko Samet is technically a national park). This required donation is supposed to protect the island's natural virtues. However, there is no proper infrastructure for collecting rubbish on Ko Samet, which means that several areas are becoming rather unsightly. Please do your part in helping the overtaxed ecosystem by conserving valuable water and being mindful of your refuse.

Even though many of the beaches (particularly in the northeast) have been beaten silly with the 'development stick', pristine coves are still in abundance. For those seeking a more sociable vacation, the busier tracts of sand host weekend parties that rage on through the night.

Orientation

Most of the action on the 8km-long island takes place along the northern half of the eastern shore. Boats arrive at Na Dan, the island's only village, which is linked to the east coast by a built-up ribbon of road replete with 7-Elevens, internet cafés, noodle stalls and bars. A large gate (think the entrance to Jurassic Park) lies at the end of the street – this is where faràng pay their 400B entrance fee. Passengers arriving at other piers usually dodge the park tax.

Ko Samet's small size makes it a great place to explore on foot. A network of difficult dirt roads connects the western beach and most of the southern bays, while walking trails snake over the boulders and headlands that separate beaches.

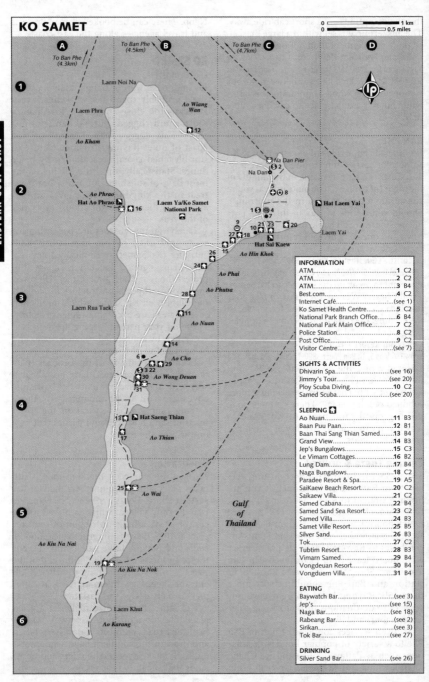

KO SAMET

INFORMATION	
ATM	**1** C2
ATM	**2** C2
ATM	**3** B4
Best.com	**4** C2
Internet Café	(see 1)
Ko Samet Health Centre	**5** C2
National Park Branch Office	**6** B4
National Park Main Office	**7** C2
Police Station	**8** C2
Post Office	**9** C2
Visitor Centre	(see 7)

SIGHTS & ACTIVITIES	
Dhivarin Spa	(see 16)
Jimmy's Tour	(see 20)
Ploy Scuba Diving	**10** C2
Samed Scuba	(see 20)

SLEEPING	
Ao Nuan	**11** B3
Baan Puu Paan	**12** B1
Baan Thai Sang Thian Samed	**13** B4
Grand View	**14** B3
Jep's Bungalows	**15** C3
Le Vimarn Cottages	**16** B2
Lung Dam	**17** B4
Naga Bungalows	**18** C2
Paradee Resort & Spa	**19** A5
SaiKaew Beach Resort	**20** C2
Saikaew Villa	**21** C2
Samed Cabana	**22** B4
Samed Sand Sea Resort	**23** C2
Samed Villa	**24** B3
Samet Ville Resort	**25** B5
Silver Sand	**26** C2
Tok	**27** C2
Tubtim Resort	**28** B3
Vimarn Samed	**29** B4
Vongdeuan Resort	**30** B4
Vongduern Villa	**31** B4

EATING	
Baywatch Bar	(see 3)
Jep's	(see 15)
Naga Bar	(see 18)
Rabeang Bar	(see 2)
Sirikan	(see 3)
Tok Bar	(see 27)

DRINKING	
Silver Sand Bar	(see 26)

Information

Ko Samet is part of a national park and there is an entry fee of 400B for adults, and 200B for children aged three to 14 (keep your ticket for proof of payment – you should only have to pay for admission once).

EMERGENCY

Police Station (☎ 0 3864 1111, emergency 1155) Next to Ko Samet Health Centre. There's also a smaller station at Ao Wong Deuan.

INTERNET ACCESS

All of the internet access on Ko Samet costs a whopping 2B per minute with a 20B minimum. There are several choices between Na Dan and Hat Sai Kaew. Opening hours are completely dependant on staff availability.

Best.com (per min 2B; 🖳) Across from the internet café listed following. Has wi-fi access.

Internet café (per min 2B; 🖳) Opposite the National Park Office, providing air-con/high-speed/flat-screen surfing bliss.

MEDICAL SERVICES

Ko Samet Health Centre (☎ 0 3861 2999; 🕐 8.30am-8pm Mon-Fri, to 4.30pm Sat & Sun) Small public clinic midway between the village harbour and Hat Sai Kaew. English-speaking doctors are on hand to help with problems such as heat rash or bites from snakes or poisonous sea creatures. The doctors use native vegetation to cure jellyfish stings.

MONEY

There are three ATMs on Ko Samet; two are attached to 7-Elevens. You'll find one of the 7-Eleven ones at the pier and the other opposite the National Park Office. The third is connected to a convenience store called '108' on Ao Wong Deuan.

POST

Post office (Ao Hin Khok) Small office next to Naga Bungalows; offers a poste restante service and internet access. It also buys/sells second-hand books.

TOURIST INFORMATION

The national park offices are located near Hat Sai Kaew and Ao Wong Deuan. The 'tourist office' (which deserves its quotation marks as it's really a visitors centre) is an empty room with a couple of photos of the different bays. There's a smiley man who works at the booth.

Dangers & Annoyances

The roads on Ko Samet are poorly paved and are easily flooded after monsoon rains. The island also has heaps of stray dogs. These mangy beasts can be quite annoying when they park themselves nearby and stare longingly at your food.

Sights & Activities

In addition to Ko Samet, there are several other islands that belong to Laem Ya/Ko Samet National Park. They include **Ko Man Klang**, **Ko Man Nok** and **Ko Man Nai**. Like on Ko Samet, this official park status hasn't deterred development. Ko Man Nai is home to the Rayong **Turtle Conservation Centre** (☎ 0 3861 6096; 🕐 9am-4pm), which is a breeding place for endangered sea turtles. Ask at Christie's Bar & Restaurant (attached to Christie's Guesthouse; p129) about visiting from Ban Phe, or join one of the many boat tours departing from Ko Samet.

You can also volunteer to work at the centre by contacting **Starfish Ventures** (www .starfishventures.co.uk). Activities include monitoring the progress of the turtles, releasing young turtles into the ocean and explaining the project to day-tripping tourists. You'll be expected to work two to three hours per day for four days a week; in your downtime there are good beaches nearby to explore.

There are plenty of **water sports** off Samet's silky sands, but if you're looking for a hardcore diving and snorkelling scene, head further east to the Ko Chang Archipelago (or better yet, Ko Tao and the Similan Islands further south). The best diving around Ko Samet is at **Hin Pholeung**, about halfway between the island and Ko Chang. This isolated spot is well away from destructive boat traffic and has two towering underwater rock pinnacles with excellent visibility (up to 30m) and a great assortment of marine life, such as manta rays, barracuda, sharks and, if you brought your four-leaf clover, whale sharks. A two-dive day trip generally costs 2500B, while an Open Water course will set you back 14,500B.

The following are two of the more reputable dive operations on the island:

Ploy Scuba Diving (☎ 0 3864 4212/3; www.ployscuba .com; 🕐 9am-5pm) Found at Ploy Talay in Hat Sai Kaew. Ploy also has branches in the Ko Chang Archipelago.

Samed Scuba (☎ 0 3864 4100-3; aopraodivers@ hotmail.com) Based at both the Ao Prao and SaiKaew Beach resorts.

EASTERN GULF COAST

KO HABITATION

If you're looking for peace and quiet, and Ko Samet doesn't quite cut it, check out some of the smaller islands nearby. The secluded **Ko Man Klang** and **Ko Man Nok** offer upmarket accommodation packages that include boat transport and meals. These vacations should be arranged by phone in advance through the Bangkok reservation numbers.

Public transport to the pier departure points for Ko Man Klang and Ko Man Nok can be arranged in Ban Phe. On weekends and holidays there may be sŏrng·tăa·ou out to the piers; otherwise charter a vehicle from the market for around 100B one way, and arrange a pickup for your return.

Ko Nok Island Resort (☎ in Bangkok 0 2860 3025; www.munnorkislandresort.com; packages per person 3500-4500B; 🔀) On Ko Man Nok, this classy resort has one-night, two-day packages in a variety of villas. The island is 15km off Pak Nam Prasae (53km east of Ban Phe).

Raya Island Resort (☎ in Bangkok 0 2316 6717; 1-night, 2-day packages per person 1400B; 🔀 🖳) This comfortable getaway has 15 bungalows and plenty of hush. It is 8km off Laem Mae Phim (27km east of Ban Phe), on Ko Man Klang.

Tours

There are tons of low-key tour operators around the island with giggle-worthy names such as 'Happy Fun Safe Tour'. Most excursions are for three hours, and they usually involve snorkelling, eating, some beach-bumming and a visit to the nearby Turtle Conservation Centre (p131). If you're a serious snorkeller, consider heading further east to the Ko Chang Archipelago (p138). Head to Ao Phai for some other options.

Jimmy's Tours (☎ 08 9832 1617/27) runs a variety of trips around Ko Samet and the neighbouring islands. A six-hour boat tour (10am to 4pm) of the neighbouring islets, including the Turtle Conservation Centre on Ko Man Nai, costs 1000B per person (with a minimum group size of 12 people), while a one-hour quad-bike trip around the island costs 1200B per person. Jimmy's Tours has booking offices at both the Ao Prao and SaiKaew Beach resorts.

Sleeping

Ko Samet's status as the 'it' weekend getaway spot means that prices skyrocket on Fridays and Saturdays (and go even higher on long weekends). It's also common to find rising prices as different places start to fill up – one bungalow could go from 500B on Friday morning to 800B by the end of the day. Most bungalow operations have an attached restaurant and/or bar. They can also help you arrange boats to the mainland or many of the activities that are available on the island.

HAT SAI KAEW

The most crowded strip of sand, Hat Sai Kaew (Diamond Beach) is set on a lovely 800m stretch of sand. Each night the whole seafront lights up like a Christmas tree, with beachside restaurants and bars.

Saikaew Villa (☎ 0 3864 4139-48; www.saikaew .com; bungalows 700-2500B; 🔀 🖳) This sprawling campus of bungalows near the nicest part of the beach is popular with large groups. The bungalows differ little from the rest of Sai Kaew's standard offerings, but breakfast is included in the price.

Samed Sand Sea Resort (☎ 0 3865 1126, 08 7508 3250; www.samedsandsea.com; r 2400-4000B; 🔀) The last new place on Hat Sai Kaew (since there's now officially no more room to build), Samed Sand Sea has beautiful wooden bungalows with refreshing air-con that's borderline cryogenic.

SaiKaew Beach Resort (☎ 0 2438 9771/2; www .samedresorts.com; r 3600-4800B, bungalows 4800-14,500B; 🔀) One of many links in the 'Samed Resort' chain, this woodsy retreat has a chipper summer camp vibe with bright blue shutters and teeny picket fences. The ever-grinning staff troll around in golf buggies helping guests move around the massive garden complex.

AO HIN KHOK

The island's backpacker ghetto, Hin Khok is a pleasant stretch of beach just south of the Sai Kaew bustle. These sleeping spots are pretty much the same: all have decent beachside restaurants and bars that vie for your attention with fire shows and drink specials.

Naga Bungalows (☎ 0 3864 4034; bungalows 300-400B; 🔀 🖳) A giant snake-shaped banister

EASTERN GULF COAST

leads beach-aholics up the hill to the simple huts. Naga draws in swarms of backpackers like moths to a really cheap flame. There's one-stop shopping near the reception area, featuring a pool table, a bookshop and the island's only post office.

Tok (☎ 0 3864 4072; bungalows 300–800B; ✗) Same same, but different (Tok has air-con rooms). These basic bungalows are flung up a jungley hillside. The cheaper huts have shared bathrooms and could use a face-lift.

Jep's Bungalows (☎ 0 3864 4112; www.jepbungalow.com; r 300–1200B; ✗ ▢) Jep's is hard to miss – there are giant banners strung up around the jungle announcing the 50% discounts on weekdays. The bungalows are a cheery mix of mahogany and magenta, although there are better options around if you're going to fork out more than 600B. Guests staying in the pricier pads get free breakfast. Mosquito repellent is a must.

AO PHAI

Accommodation here is slightly more upmarket than at Ao Hin Khok.

Silver Sand (☎ 08 6530 2417; www.silversandresort.com; bungalows 300–1800B; ✗) Silver Sand's bungalows are a mix of smooth whites and soft greens – kinda like they've been covered with pistachio ice cream. The verdant property is perfectly manicured, while the evening bar action throws a little chaos into the mix.

Samed Villa (☎ 0 3864 4094; www.samedvilla.com; r incl breakfast 1800–2800B; ✗) Top of the heap in the comfort stakes, the bungalows here are spotless, snug and fitted with frilly touches. There's oodles of shade around the restaurant and a welcome feeling of seclusion. Some of the better bungalows have great sea views and include breakfast.

AO PHUTSA & AO NUAN

At Ao Phutsa, you start to feel the seclusion of the island since the bustle of the pier is several coves away. Amble through a convoluted path from the road, or hike over a rocky crag to reach the teeny cove of Ao Nuan.

Ao Nuan (bungalows 600–1000B) Hidden among thick foliage, the simple wooden bungalows have the whole beach to themselves. The funky restaurant is packed with colourful books and board games, while dishing out delicious home-cooked faves. There's no phone and it doesn't take reservations.

Tubtim Resort (☎ 0 3864 4025; www.tubtimresort.com; Ao Phutsa; r 600–2000B; ✗) Tubtim has five rows of bungalows climbing a rugged hill from the beach up into the jungle. Spend the extra 200B and go for an upgraded fan bungalow – they have sparkling bathrooms and varnished fixtures, and are noticeably better than the rickety cheapies. The restaurant serves up some fantastic dishes within 3m of the crashing tide.

AO CHO (AO LUNGWANG)

A five-minute walk across the next headland from Ao Nuan, this bay can also be reached by road from Hat Sai Kaew, or you can take a boat directly from Ban Phe to Ao Wong Deuan and walk.

Grand View (☎ 0 3864 4219, 0 3864 4220; www.grandviewgroup.net; bungalows incl breakfast from 1800B; ✗ ▢) A solid choice for the midrange traveller, Grand View's name is a bit of a false moniker, but the villa-style pads are fastidiously clean and stocked with handsome furnishings and modern amenities.

AO WONG DEUAN

Wong Deuan is the island's southern hub with a fat dock jutting out from the powdery sand. The beach is lined with rows of bars and restaurants.

Vongduern Villa (☎ 0 3865 2300; www.vongduernvilla.com; bungalows 1000–3500B; ✗) Sprawling along the bay's southern edge are bungalows, either near the beach or higher on the clifftop for better views. The Beach Front Bar is a sociable spot for sundowner cocktails, but romantic couples may prefer the subdued ambience of the Rock Front Restaurant.

Vimarn Samed (☎ 08 6330 4002; www.vimarnsamed.com; r 1800–2200B; ✗) Hugging the rocky northern headland, Vimarn Samed looks like a rambling Thai temple with curving, skyscraping roofs and loads of teak accents.

Vongdeuan Resort (☎ 0 3865 1777; www.vongdeuan.com; r 2000–3500B; ✗) Setting a refined midrange scene, this rather extravagant spread has teak Thai-style houses decked out with beautiful bits of furniture. The resort has a front-and-centre beach property and also offers slightly cheaper and less attractive concrete cottages out the back.

Samed Cabana (☎ 0 3864 4320; www.samedcabana.com; r 2400B) At the quieter northern end of the beach, Samed Cabana has chic Asian styling and swish concrete floors. Private porches provide seclusion from the nearby bar scene across the bay.

AO THIAN (CANDLELIGHT BEACH)

Lung Dam (☎ 08 1659 8056; bungalows 600-1200B; ✖) Lung Dam looks like a forgotten settlement of castaways marooned on a deserted island. The quirky huts have been scraped together using sundry bits and bobs.

Baan Thai Sang Thian Samed (☎ 08 1305 9408; r 1800-2500B; ✖) This newer address, featuring traditional Thai architecture, represents the evolution of quiet Candlelight Beach away from its backpacker origins.

AO WAI & AO KIU NA NOK

These bays are right near the tip of the dagger-shaped island.

Samet Ville Resort (☎ 0 3865 1682; www.samet villeresort.com; r 980-3780B; ✖) Hidden under a thick emerald canopy, Samet Ville is a private getaway where guests can enjoy upscale accommodation and isolation. The shaded restaurant is a lovely spot for a romantic dinner. Staff can arrange speedboat transfers from Ban Phe.

Paradee Resort & Spa (☎ 0 2438 9771; www.samed resorts.com; villas 15,000B; ✖ 💻 ⊠) The price tag is high, but you do get your own self-contained, beachfront villa on what is probably Ko Samet's best beach. There's gorgeous Thai furniture, a personal plunge pool, DVD player, espresso maker – even your own butler. Speedboats from Ban Phe are arranged – you'll be way too busy getting pampered to have time to plan a ferry connection.

WEST COAST (HAT AO PHRAO)

Le Vimarn Cottages (☎ 0 2438 9771/2, Dhivarin Spa 0 3864 4104-7; www.samedresorts.com; r 8000-10,500B; ✖ 💻 ⊠) Vying for top luxury hotel laurels with Paradee Resort (even though it's owned by the same people), Le Vimarn sits on perfectly manicured grounds punctuated by the occasional water feature. The rooms and villas are adorned with a blend of elegant Thai and modern conveniences and an absolutely stunning pool. There are loads of facilities, including the lavish Dhivarin Spa. The name Dhivarin means 'sun and water'; the spa features a wide array of intensive massage and treatments.

NORTH COAST (AO WIANG WAN)

This beach won't make any postcards, but the solitude is refreshing.

Baan Puu Paan (Lizzy's; ☎ 0 3864 4095; bungalows 500-1000B; ✖) This Scottish-run place is a great choice for some R&R away from the east coast hustle. The pod of charming bungalows is scattered along the sand – a few even jut out into the sea. Delicious Indian food is served in the quaint on-site restaurant.

Eating & Drinking

Most accommodation has attached restaurants and bars. Typical Thai favourites go for around 30B to 100B. European flavours range from 60B to 300B. It's worth looking out for the nightly beach barbecues, particularly along Ao Hin Khok and Ao Phai. There are several food stalls along the main drag between Na Dan pier and Sai Kaew Beach. Most places toss around noodles in a wok for 40B.

Hat Sai Kaew offers the biggest range of places to down some cold ones, or check out **Naga Bar** (dishes 50-160B; ⏲ breakfast, lunch & dinner) and **Tok Bar** (dishes 40-150B; ⏲ breakfast, lunch & dinner), both on Ao Hin Khok, for some post-dinner shenanigans. Ao Wong Deuan is so packed with wall-to-wall bars, it's difficult to know where one ends and the next begins – but does it really matter?

Rabeang Bar (Na Dan; dishes 40-120B; ⏲ breakfast, lunch & dinner) Opposite Na Dan's main pier, this nondescript joint is a bit overpriced, but it's a decent place to grab a bite while killing time between ferries.

BYOB

As you haul around your ever-expanding luggage, you'll probably become jealous of the weekending Bangkokians toting one skimpy Louis Vuitton bag containing all the necessities for their quick two-day beach escape. You may notice, however, that certain Thai nationals have way more luggage than you. These savvy visitors are taking advantage of Thailand's unspoken BYOB rule: on Ko Samet (as well as many other destinations in the kingdom), you're allowed to bring your own booze to the table as long as you purchase something from the establishment. So for those who are tight on baht but big on luggage space, consider purchasing your beverage of choice before being subjected to the inflated island prices.

Jep's (Ao Hin Khok; dishes 60-400B; ☺ breakfast, lunch & dinner) If you're going to leave your bungalow in search of other restaurants, try Jep's. It's on the pricier side, but the almanac-sized menu offers everything from Thai staples to Indian and French faves. Tables are strewn along the sand, and there's plenty of covered outdoor seating just in case it rains. Later on, cocktail specials prevail and the music escalates as diners transform into drinkers who later morph into beachside dancers.

Baywatch Bar (☎ 08 1826 7834; Ao Wong Deuan; ke-babs 190-290B; ☺ breakfast, lunch & dinner) Sorry fellas, Pam Anderson is nowhere to be found, but the delicious cocktails and international dishes are good consolation prizes.

Sirikan (☎ 08 1782 0274; Ao Wong Deuan; dishes 200-300B; ☺ lunch & dinner) Tucked deep within the jumble of seaside restaurants, little Sirikan has an excellent assortment of fresh seafood – you even get to pick your prey.

Silver Sand Bar (☎ 0 6530 2417; Ao Phai; ☺ 1pm-2am) As the clock ticks towards the witching hour, the island's night owls congregate here under trippy spherical lights to watch the fire twirlers, grind to cheesy dance music and knock back over 35 types of cocktails (all served in buckets, of course).

Getting There & Away

Many Th Khao San agencies in Bangkok offer transport to Ko Samet, including the boat trip, for around 250B to 300B. This is more expensive than doing it on your own, but it's convenient for travellers who don't plan to go anywhere else on the east coast.

Nuan Thip Pier (☎ 0 3865 1508, 0 3865 1514) in Ban Phe is the pier behind the 7-Eleven where the direct bus from Bangkok drops you off. Purchase your ticket from the counter and wait until there are 20 other passengers wanting to go. The rustic ferries travel to five different stops along the Ko Samet coast, but most (one hourly) stop at Tha Na Dan (100B round trip), and five scheduled departures (every other hour between 8.30am and 4.30pm) arrive at Ao Wong Deuan (120B round trip). Boats will stop at other piers on the island if there is a quorum of passengers.

Alternatively, you can charter a speedboat to any of the island's beaches. They are quite expensive (1200B to Na Dan or 1600B to Ao Wai), but they take up to 10 passengers for this price, so it's worthwhile if you're travelling in a group. If you book ahead at one of

Ko Samet's ritzier resorts, speedboat transfers may be included in the price.

Getting Around

Ko Samet's small size makes it a great place to explore on foot. It's only a 15-minute walk from Na Dan to Hat Sai Kaew, but if you are carting luggage or want to go further, sŏrng·tăa·ou meet arriving boats at the pier and provide drop-offs all along the length of the island. Set fares for transport around the island from Na Dan are posted on a tree in the middle of a square in front of Na Dan harbour, but nobody pays them any attention; still, you shouldn't have to pay much more than 20B to get to Hat Sai Kaew, 30B to go halfway down the island, or 40B to reach the southern beaches. If drivers don't have enough people to fill the vehicle, they either won't go, or they will charge passengers 200B to 500B to charter the whole vehicle.

Motorcycles and mountain bikes can be rented from almost every bungalow operation on the island. Expect to pay about 300B per day or an hourly rate of 100B. The dirt roads are *very* rough – you may want to walk or rent a mountain bike (100B per hour) instead.

CHANTHABURI & AROUND
จันทบุรี
pop 500,000

The virgin coastline between Ko Samet and the Ko Chang Archipelago belongs to the quiet province of Chanthaburi. Tourists often overlook these hushed coral sands and sleepy fishing villages as they beeline for livelier beach holidays. Chanthaburi town has earned a global reputation as the centre for gem trading in Southeast Asia. Gem dealers line the streets during the weekend. Great deals can be clinched by the savvy, but amateurs are likely to go home with a bagful of worthless rocks. If you grab a taxi or local bus from Chanthaburi town, you can reach the quiet provincial villages along the water. The **Tha Mai** district has the area's nicest beaches, the most charming being **Hat Chao Lao**, which is stocked with delicious seafood restaurants. Our readers have also enjoyed the laid-back ambience in the lagoonside town of **Khlung**. The jagged peninsula of Laem Singh is a picturesque beach option and home to the region's most popular tourist destination, **Oasis Sea World** (☎ 0 3936 3238; Laem Singh; admission 400B). Dolphins are the main attraction and the

EASTERN GULF COAST

price of admission includes the opportunity to get in the water with the lovable creatures and assist the trainers with tricks and feeding. Visits can be arranged by most tour operators between Pattaya and Ko Chang.

Sleeping

River Guest House (☎ 0 3932 8211; Th Si Chan 3/5-8, Chanthaburi; r 150-350B; ❄ ☐) Chanthaburi town's real gem is the friendly team that runs this relaxed place beside the river. The rooms with air-con at the front are a bit noisy, so if you're happy with a fan ask for a room at the back. Downstairs is a good restaurant that does its best to overcome its proximity to the town's busiest bridge.

Le Village de Napoleon (☎ 0 3944 4575; www .napoleonvillage.net; Laem Singh; r from 1500B; ❄ ☐ ☎) Situated on the quiet cape of Laem Singh, about 30km from Chanthaburi town, Le Village de Napoleon is a small, five-room hotel with all the conveniences of a luxury resort. Spend the day poolside with a delicious cocktail, savour delicious international cuisine for dinner, and relax in the evening while watching cult classics in the cinema room.

Getting There & Away

Buses operate between Chanthaburi town (187B, 4½ hours) and Bangkok's Eastern bus terminal every half hour throughout the day and less frequently at night. Buses also travel to Rayong (90B, 2½ hours, five daily) and Trat (70B, 1½ hours, hourly). Taxis from Bangkok cost around 2300B.

TRAT & AROUND
อ.เมืองตราด
pop 219,345

Trat town, the provincial capital, is a major transfer hub for anyone heading to or from Cambodia or the Ko Chang Archipelago. Unlike many of the other transport junctions, Trat has slightly more to offer than buses and barking dogs. The town's main road, Th Sukhumvit, is a roaring drag-way of honking sŏrng·tăa·ou, but you just have to step into a side street to appreciate the gentle pace of everyday life along the slithering canal. The city's architecture is a striking cornucopia of styles: hidden pedestrian alleys are lined with century-old teak houses, while loud colours are splashed across the boxy department stores nearby. If you have an afternoon to kill, try exploring the area's

thriving markets, and if you decide to stay the night, you'll find some of the cheapest lodging in all of Thailand. The port villages of Laem Ngop and Laem Sok are purely devoted to moving tourists between the archipelago and aren't worth an extra look.

Information

Bangkok Trat Hospital (☎ 0 3953 2735; Th Sukhumvit; ☒ 24hr)

Immigration Office (☎ 0 3959 7261; Laem Ngop; ☒ 8.30am-noon & 1-4.30pm Mon-Fri) Can handle visa extensions and immigration issues. It's a short walk from Laem Ngop pier.

Krung Thai Bank (Th Sukhumvit, Trat) Has an ATM and currency exchange.

Police Station (☎ 1155, 0 3959 7033; Laem Ngop) Near the pier.

Police Station (☎ 1155, 0 3951 1035; cnr Th Santisuk & Th Wiwatthana, Trat) Located a short walk from Trat's centre.

Post Office (Th Tha Reua Jang) East of Trat's commercial centre. The telephone office is nearby.

TAT Office (☎ 0 3959 7255) Near the pier in Laem Ngop.

Sleeping

Trat has a small and charming super-budget guesthouse scene; just take a stroll through the quiet lanes lining Lak Meuang and pick one that tickles your fancy. There are only a few midrange options in town, most along or just off busy Th Sukhumvit.

There are also bungalows at the piers in Laem Ngop and Laem Sok, although it's impossible to get stuck in these places since ferries run during the day and Trat is only 20km away.

Ban Jaidee Guest House (☎ 0 3952 0678; 6 Th Chaimongkol; r 120-150B) Meaning 'good heart', this lovely Thai-style home is easily one of the best deals this side of Bangkok. The simple rooms share a bathroom and the whole place abounds with leafy greens and beautiful wooden objects (handmade by one of the artsy owners).

Pop Guest House (☎ 0 3951 2392; popson1958@ hotmail.com; 1/1 Th Thana Charoen; r 120-600B; ❄ ☐) Over the last few years, Pop has transformed into a veritable village – there are now over 40 comfy rooms spread around four tidy properties. The owner is part businessperson, part mother figure: she wheels and deals with one hand and pampers you with the other. Check out her handy hand-drawn map of Trat.

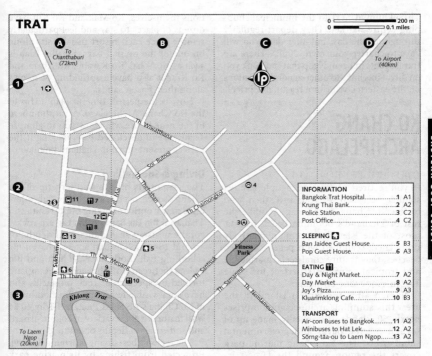

TRAT

Eating

Trat's surplus of vibrant day and night markets means that you're just steps away from a tasty (and *cheap*) meal. Both Laem Ngop and Laem Sok have an unremarkable restaurant at their pier, just in case you didn't have time to stock up on tasty noodles in Trat.

Kluarimklong Cafe (☎ 0 3952 4919; Soi Rimklong; dishes 70-100B; ☺ breakfast, lunch & dinner) This café has been around in some form for over 20 years. Its latest incarnation is as a smooth, lounge-style, atmospheric place that serves up some of the top Thai dishes in Trat.

Joy's Pizza (☎ 0 3952 2551; 49-51 Th Thana Charoen; pizzas 110-150B; ☺ lunch & dinner) When he's not making pizzas, the expat owner dishes out essential tourist info and maintains an unfathomably large collection of MP3s. The restaurant doubles as an art gallery for the quirky installations created by Joy, his wife.

Getting There & Around

To reach the islands in the Ko Chang Archipelago, travellers will have to transfer to one of the piers along the coast. Most tourists will end up around Laem Ngop. Sǎhm·lór

(also spelt as sǎamláw; three-wheeled pedicabs) around Trat cost between 10B and 15B per person.

TRAT

Bangkok Airways (☎ in Bangkok 0 2265 5555, Trat Airport 0 3952 5767; www.bangkokair.com) flies three times a day to/from Trat and Bangkok (2550B). The airport is 40km from town; minibuses and taxis meet all flights.

Air-conditioned buses from Bangkok to Trat (200B to 300B, five to six hours) leave hourly from the Eastern bus terminal between 8.30am and 10.30pm and stop along Th Sukhumvit; the price and frequency for the return trip to Bangkok are the same.

Direct minibuses from Trat to Hat Lek (115B, one hour) leave every 45 minutes from the bus station. Sǒrng·tǎa·ou (around 50B) also trundle from the bus station to Hat Lek, but you will have to wait for enough people to show up.

LAEM NGOP

Sǒrng·tǎa·ou for Laem Ngop and Centrepoint Pier (30B to 55B) leave Trat from a stand on

Th Sukhumvit next to the municipal shopping centre market. They depart regularly throughout the day, but after dark you will have to charter your own (200B). There are travel agents in Laem Ngop that can book you on direct bus links to other major destinations on the eastern coast (for a reasonable price).

KO CHANG ARCHIPELAGO

อุทยานแห่งชาติเกาะช้าง

If you're tired of hearing people say 'ya shoulda been here 10 years ago', then head to the Ko Chang Archipelago. Unlike the rest of Thailand's booming beach resorts, most of the islets here remain relatively untouched; scalloped with peach-coloured beaches, they feature coral reefs, marine life and tropical rainforests perfect for some Tarzan-esque vine-swinging.

Named after the largest island in the area, this stunning archipelago comprises nearly 50 islands. It's actually made up of several marine parks and governmental subdistricts. The Ko Chang marine park covers the region around the largest island, Ko Chang. Further along, there's the Mu Ko Rung park that guards the area's best coral reefs. A lack of freshwater on these smaller islands means that there is no commercial development. The quasi-autonomous government body called the Ko Kut Subdistrict controls most of the islands further away from the coast. There are only about 2500 inhabitants spread across these furry specks of jungle.

Ko Chang is the darling of southeast Thailand and has a one-two punch of beach and forest that will knock the socks off most visitors. Other islands have recently begun throwing their hats into the tourist ring and are quickly becoming idyllic tropical destinations themselves. Ko Mak and Ko Kut have dozens of places to stay and feel particularly remote since each resort usually sits alone on one of the myriad bays. Smaller islands such as Ko Whai, Ko Rayang, Ko Kham and Ko Kradat also have a sprinkling of resorts along their flaxen sands.

Now is the perfect time to plan a trip to the Ko Chang Archipelago. A vacation here in the near future will allow you to glimpse Thailand's undeveloped past, making it the perfect present on your Thailand holiday.

Diving & Snorkelling

The seamounts off the southern tip of Ko Chang stretch over 32km to Ko Kut, offering a new frontier of diving opportunities in Thailand. **Hin Luk Bat** and **Hin Lap** are rocky, coral-encrusted seamounts with depths of around 18m to 20m that act as a haven for schooling fish. Both **Hin Phrai Nam** and **Hin Gadeng** (between Ko Whai and Ko Rang) are formed by spectacular rock pinnacles and have coral visible to around 28m. Southwest of Ko Chang's Ao Salak Phet, reef-fringed **Ko Whai** features a good variety of colourful hard and soft corals at depths of 6m to 15m.

The region's best diving is around **Ko Rang**. Protected from fishing by its marine park status, this mini archipelago has some of the most pristine coral in Thailand. Visibility here is much better than near Ko Chang and averages between 10m and 20m. In the area, **Ko Yak** and **Ko Laun** are shallow dives perfect for beginners. These two small rocky islands can be circumnavigated and have lots of coral, schooling fish, puffer fish, morays, barracuda, rays and the occasional turtle. **Hin Kuak Maa** (also known as Three Finger Reef) is probably the top dive and is home to a coral-encrusted wall sloping from 2m to 14m and attracting swarms of marine life.

Most dive operators are based on Ko Chang, the largest island in the archipelago (see p142).

Tours

The best way to explore this quiet realm is by joining a live-aboard tour. Although there are very few operators at the moment, one company stands out for its off-the-beaten-path approach to holiday travel. The **JYSK Sea Safari** (☎ 0 2630 9371; www.jysk-rejsebureau.dk; 4-day trip 10,600B) takes passengers on an authentic fishing vessel for a four-day adventure

---

KEEPING YOU ABREAST

Topless sunbathing is not just considered to be offensive to Thais – it is forbidden by law in all of Thailand's national parks. This includes Ko Chang Marine National Park and all beaches on Ko Chang, Ko Kut, Ko Mak, Ko Whai etc.

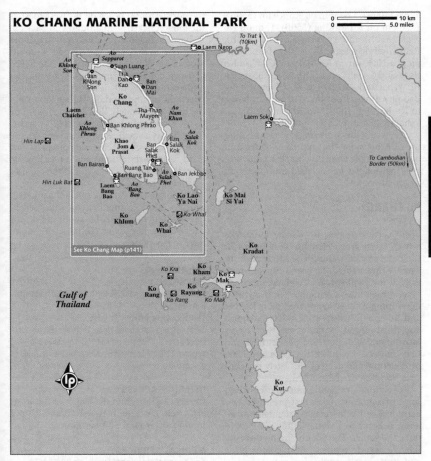

KO CHANG MARINE NATIONAL PARK

EASTERN GULF COAST

around the archipelago with sea kayaks and snorkelling equipment. This isn't a holiday cruise – there's one teeny bathroom and everyone sleeps on thin mattresses on the roof deck, but it's a fantastic way to experience life at sea and to take in the majestic vistas. You can decide where you prefer to end your voyage. Prices include transport from Bangkok, and these can be renegotiated for those who only want to do the boat portion of the trip.

Getting There & Around

Boat services to Ko Chang are year-round; between May and October, ferries to the smaller islands become irregular and often nonexistent.

In the high season, **Bang Bao Boat** (☎ 08 7054 4300; Bang Bao) and **Interisland Hopper** (☎ 08 1865 0610; Bang Bao) run a fleet of ferries linking many different islands in the archipelago. Boats leave Ko Chang every morning at 9am, stopping at 10am on Ko Whai (300B), 10.30am on Ko Kham (400B), 10.45am on Ko Rayang (400B) and 11am on Ko Mak (400B). The boat pauses until 1.30pm and continues on to Ko Kut (700B), arriving at 2pm. The return journey is as follows: a 10am departure from Ko Kut, alighting at 10.30am on Ko Mak; after a break, the boat stops at 12.05pm on Ko Rayang, 12.10pm on Ko Kham, 1pm on Ko Whai and 2pm on Ko Chang.

Speedboat services depart daily from Bang Bao at noon, stopping at 12.25pm on Ko

Whai (400B), 12.35pm on Ko Kham (550B), 12.45pm on Ko Rayang (550B), 1pm on Ko Mak (550B) and 2pm on Ko Kut (900B). Return services leave Ko Kut at 10am, stopping at 10.30am on Ko Mak, 10.35am on Ko Rayang, 10.45am on Ko Kham, 10.55am on Ko Whai and 11.20am at Ko Chang's Bang Bao pier. Prices from Ko Mak are as follows: to Ko Rayang (200B), Ko Kham (300B), Ko Whai (350B) and Ko Kut (400B).

See p137 for information concerning moving between the mainland piers and other parts of Thailand. Each island section that follows has detailed transportation information.

KO CHANG
เกาะช้าง

From certain angles, Ko Chang looks like a mammoth green elephant cooling off in the clear coastal waters. The locals seem to agree – they named the island *chang*, which is Thai for elephant. As Thailand's second-biggest island, Ko Chang has relatively little development when compared with Phuket and Ko Samui, which are Thailand's largest and third-largest islands respectively. This lush jungle, with postcard-perfect bays and fiery sunsets, was protected for many years by governmental decrees, but lately the construction ban has been lifted.

Ko Chang's rugged landscape conceals some of Southeast Asia's best-preserved wilderness. The island's craggy mountainous interior is home to a veritable Jurassic Park of flora and fauna. The abounding biodiversity includes exotic reptiles, technicolour birds and even some friendly elephants.

Recently, the mega-island has found itself firmly in the sights of developers and its coasts are quickly turning into a holiday habitat. Regardless, the impenetrable rainforests and wild coastal mangroves manage to hold their own and provide a counterbalance to the small beachside metropolis that fringes the island's western shore. Each holiday season brings new development, but rest assured, many years remain before Ko Chang will no longer be synonymous with 'paradise'.

Orientation
Most of Ko Chang's development straddles the western coastline, while the majority of the rest of the island remains a dripping rainforest. Hat Sai Khao (White Sands Beach),

the northernmost beach on the west coast, is the longest beach strip around and packs in the most bungalows, bars and restaurants per kilometre on Ko Chang. Ao Khlong Phrao sits around a rocky headland from White Sands and focuses on more upmarket digs, while Hat Kaibae, further south, is lost in transition between the up-and-coming Khlong Phrao and the uber-chill Lonely Beach, which is home to the island's burgeoning backpacker scene. Bang Bao is a small fishing settlement in the far south with several charming places to stay, good seafood restaurants and a pier hosting several dive shops and ferries to the region's smaller islands.

If you plan to venture off the main road into the island's interior, you will need to pay the 400B park entry fee at one of the four park offices. Keep your receipt so you don't have to pay twice.

Information
EMERGENCY
Police Station (☎ 0 3958 6191, 0 3952 1657) Based at Ban Dan Mai.
Tourist Police Office (☎ 0 3965 1351, emergency 1155) Based in Ban Khlong Phrao. There are also smaller police boxes at the northern end of Hat Sai Khao and between Khlong Phrao and Hat Kaibae on the west side of the road.

INTERNET ACCESS
Internet facilities run the length of the western coast, charging between 1B and 2B per minute, or around 50B per hour.

MEDICAL SERVICES
Ko Chang International Clinic (☎ 0 3955 1555, emergency 1719; Hat Sai Khao; ⊗ 24hr during high season) Related to the Bangkok Hospital Group and can handle most minor emergencies and arrange for emergency evacuations.

MONEY
There's a continuous chain of banks and ATMs between Hat Sai Khao and Lonely Beach.

POST
Ko Chang post office (☎ 0 3955 1240; ⊗ 8.30am-3.30pm) At the south end of Hat Sai Khao.

TELEPHONE
Mobile phones work along the coasts, although you may lose reception on treks into the centre of the island.

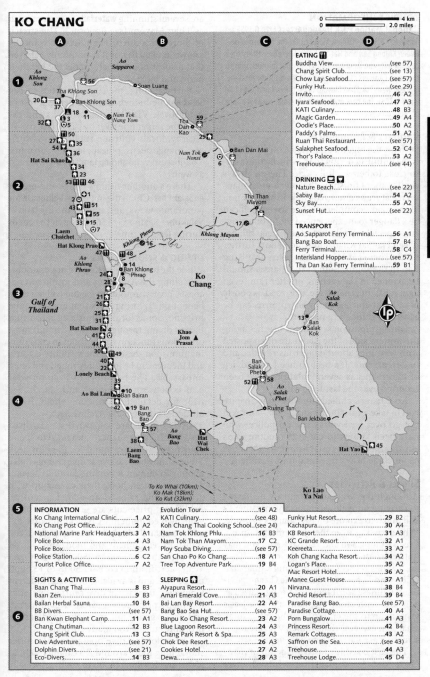

KO CHANG

EATING 🍴
Buddha View.............................(see 57)
Chang Spirit Club.....................(see 13)
Chow Lay Seafood...................(see 57)
Funky Hut................................(see 29)
Invito.......................................**46** A2
Iyara Seafood...........................**47** A3
KATI Culinary...........................**48** B3
Magic Garden...........................**49** A4
Oodie's Place............................**50** A2
Paddy's Palms...........................**51** A2
Ruan Thai Restaurant................(see 57)
Salakphet Seafood....................**52** C4
Thor's Palace............................**53** A2
Treehouse.................................(see 44)

DRINKING 🍷 🍸
Nature Beach...........................(see 22)
Sabay Bar.................................**54** A2
Sky Bay....................................**55** A2
Sunset Hut...............................(see 22)

TRANSPORT
Ao Sapparot Ferry Terminal...........**56** A1
Bang Bao Boat..........................**57** B4
Ferry Terminal..........................**58** C4
Interisland Hopper......................(see 57)
Tha Dan Kao Ferry Terminal......**59** B1

INFORMATION
Ko Chang International Clinic...........**1** A2
Ko Chang Post Office...................**2** A2
National Marine Park Headquarters.**3** A1
Police Box..................................**4** A3
Police Box..................................**5** A1
Police Station.............................**6** C2
Tourist Police Office....................**7** A2

SIGHTS & ACTIVITIES
Baan Chang Thai........................**8** B3
Baan Zen...................................**9** B3
Bailan Herbal Sauna...................**10** B4
BB Divers..................................(see 57)
Ban Kwan Elephant Camp..........**11** A1
Chang Chutiman........................**12** B3
Chang Spirit Club.......................**13** C3
Dive Adventure..........................(see 57)
Dolphin Divers...........................(see 21)
Eco-Divers.................................**14** B3

Evolution Tour...........................**15** A2
KATI Culinary............................(see 48)
Koh Chang Thai Cooking School.(see 24)
Nam Tok Khlong Phlu................**16** B3
Nam Tok Than Mayom...............**17** C2
Ploy Scuba Diving......................(see 57)
San Chao Po Ko Chang..............**18** A1
Tree Top Adventure Park............**19** B4

SLEEPING 🛏
Aiyapura Resort.........................**20** A1
Amari Emerald Cove...................**21** A3
Bai Lan Bay Resort.....................**22** A4
Bang Bao Sea Hut......................(see 57)
Banpu Ko Chang Resort..............**23** A2
Blue Lagoon Resort....................**24** A3
Chang Park Resort & Spa............**25** A3
Chok Dee Resort........................**26** A3
Cookies Hotel............................**27** A2
Dewa.......................................**28** A3

Funky Hut Resort.......................**29** B2
Kachapura.................................**30** A4
KB Resort..................................**31** A3
KC Grande Resort......................**32** A1
Keereeta...................................**33** A2
Koh Chang Kacha Resort............**34** A2
Logan's Place.............................**35** A2
Mac Resort Hotel.......................**36** A2
Manee Guest House...................**37** A1
Nirvana....................................**38** B4
Orchid Resort............................**39** B4
Paradise Bang Bao.....................(see 57)
Paradise Cottage........................**40** A4
Porn Bungalow..........................**41** A3
Princess Resort..........................**42** B4
Remark Cottages.......................**43** A3
Saffron on the Sea.....................(see 43)
Treehouse.................................**44** A3
Treehouse Lodge.......................**45** D4

TOURIST INFORMATION

National Marine Park Headquarters (☎ 0 3955 5080; ⏰ 8.30am-4.30pm Mon-Fri) On the main road between Khlong Son and Hat Sai Khao. Friendly staff try their best, despite the language barrier, to offer as much info as they can. Campers can book a site in the brush beyond the office at Nam Tok Than Mayom or on the isolated isle of Ko Rang (p163). The park entrance fee is 400B, payable at one of these offices.

Dangers & Annoyances

Perhaps the biggest annoyance on Ko Chang is the unfinished 'ring road', which comes oh-so close to being a full circle. There's always chatter about finishing the loop – most maps even feature a completed circle in anticipation of the road's completion. The street itself can be a danger to inexperienced motorbike drivers, especially on the extremely steep hill between Hat Sai Khao and Khlong Son, further north. There's another rough patch near Bang Bao in the south. Both of these areas should be avoided in the evening or after rain (even light rain). In general, the 'ring road' is poorly lit at night and the many sharp turns can be especially difficult to navigate.

During monsoon season, the beaches along the western side of the island are often posted with warnings about dangerous riptides and undercurrents. It's best to heed the advice of these signs as several fatalities have been reported over the last few years.

Ko Chang's chilled-out vibe may inspire you to take a toke of the local herb – this will not go over well with the local police, who have been known to conduct random raids at various bungalow establishments. Penalties can include heavy fines and imprisonment.

Sights & Activities

Although the west coast is mostly dedicated to thriving bungalow establishments, there's still much to explore on Ko Chang's east side. While passing over the steep mountain between Khlong Son and Hat Sai Khao, you may notice that drivers will honk their horns. They are paying respect to Ko Chang's guardian spirit who lives at **San Chao Po Ko Chang** – a vibrant Chinese spirit temple. A long staircase, adorned with stone elephant statues, leads visitors up to the entrance, although a small Thai sign explains that women who are menstruating are barred from entering.

The east coast is mostly made up of mangrove forests and plantations. Inland, there are several stunning **waterfalls** to explore, such as Than Mayom (see opposite). The stretch of shoreline south of Than Mayom is locally known as **Ghost Bay**, as it's commonly believed that a spirit of a woman roams the beach at night and looks out at the sea.

Further along, the rustic shanties of **Ban Salak Kok** lie hidden within a dense forest of mangroves. Visit the rickety docks and explore the serpentine river by kayak (see p144). Nearby, locals cultivate rubber trees, durians, mangosteens, pineapples and coconuts. You'll see several **shrimp farms** along the road as well.

There's another fishing village and pier at **Ao Salak Phet**. Climb the imposing **lighthouse** for panoramic views, and stop by the **fish farm** at Salakphet Seafood (p156) to watch the chaos during feeding time.

DIVING & SNORKELLING

While the best sites in Thailand are undoubtedly along the Andaman and southern Gulf coasts, divers around Ko Chang will have the benefit of exploring reefs that are still quite pristine. Some local enthusiasts claim that there's diving throughout the year, but most operations function with a skeleton crew during monsoon season as the visibility is lousy and the seas can be incredibly rough and often impassable. The best time to strap on your gear is between December and March. See p138 for detailed information about diving around the Ko Chang Archipelago.

Diving prices are somewhat standardised across Ko Chang so there's no need to spend your time hunting around for the best deal. You can, however, ask your operator of choice about discounted accommodation – several companies often hook their clients up with great lodging rates as an added incentive. Additional price cuts are given if you bring your own equipment. A typical fun-dive excursion usually includes two guided dives, transport, equipment and food, and will set you back about 2200B to 2500B. PADI Open Water certification costs 12,500B to 13,500B per person, and is available in several different languages. Be wary of dive centres that offer too many price cuts – safety is paramount, and a shop giving out unusually good deals is probably cutting too many corners.

The following dive operations also offer snorkelling tours around Ko Chang (500B to 550B) and Ko Rang (650B to 700B), especially during the low season when the visibility and sea conditions are often poor. Prices include snorkel gear and lunch. Evolution Tour (right) also offers full-day snorkelling trips.

BB Divers (☎ 0 3955 8040, 08 6129 2305; www .bbdivers.com) Based in Bang Bao, with a swimming pool at the south end of Lonely Beach.

Dive Adventure (☎ 08 1762 6482; www.thedive kochang.com) Also based in Bang Bao. Offers captained boat rentals from 8000B per day.

Dolphin Divers (☎ 08 7028 1627; www.scubadiving kohchang.com) Based in Khlong Phrao and also has a small booking office at the Amari Resort. Offers a variety of other water sports including surfing, kayaking and wake boarding.

Eco-Divers (☎ 0 3955 7296; www.ecodivers.fr) Main office also located at Khlong Phrao, with additional locations on most of the other west coast beaches.

Ploy Scuba Diving (☎ 0 3955 8033; www.ployscuba .com) Has a shop on nearly every beach in Ko Chang; the main office is in Bang Bao.

ELEPHANT TREKKING

Chang means elephant, so it's not surprising that there are three operations on the island offering travellers the opportunity to play with these gentle giants.

Ban Kwan Elephant Camp (☎ 08 9815 9566, 08 1919 3995; changtone@yahoo.com; 40-/90-min adventure 500/900B; ⏰ 8.30am-4.30pm), about 2km inland from Ban Khlong Son, takes in older pachyderms that were once used for labour and helps them live out their days close to nature. The informative 1½ hour 'experience' involves feeding, bathing, an elephant ride and the chance to learn about the creatures' lives in a wild setting.

Chang Chutiman (☎ 08 9939 6676, 08 7135 7424; 1-/2-hr ride 500/900B; ⏰ 8am-5pm) and **Baan Chang Thai** (☎ 0 3955 1474; 1-/2-hr ride 500/900B) are both based in Khlong Phrao and offer similar programs to Ban Kwan in a less dramatic setting.

Transfers are included in these prices, but make sure you book in advance. Most accommodation can arrange these adventures within a day's notice.

HIKING

If your muscles are starting to shrivel after one too many days of beach bumming, try stretching your legs in Ko Chang's breathtaking inland jungle of soaring mountain vistas, lush vegetation and gushing waterfalls.

Many consider **Nam Tok Khlong Phlu** (park admission 400B; ⏰ 8am-5pm) to be Ko Chang's most impressive waterfall. It's easily accessible from the resorts at Khlong Phrao on the western coast. Set amid striking jungle scenery, the chute is quickly reached by walking 600m along a well-marked jungle path. Khlong Phu dumps out into a cool pool; it's the perfect place to dunk your body after a sweaty day's adventure.

Another stunning cascade, **Nam Tok Than Mayom** (park admission 400B; ⏰ 8am-5pm) can be reached via Tha Than Mayom or Ban Dan Mai on the east coast. The view from the top is marvellous and there are inscribed stones bearing the initials of Rama V, Rama VI and Rama VII nearby.

There are many freelance guides on the island who charge reasonable prices for a rewarding day hike. Should you decide to set off on your own adventure (which is not particularly advisable), steer clear of the mountainous area between Bang Bao and Ao Salak Phet, unless you are an experienced tropical hiker with moderate orienteering skills. If you don't get lost, this rewarding hike will take four to six hours and you may find the isolated **Hat Wai Chek**. If you do get lost, try to find a stream and follow the current – it will usually take you either to the sea or a village, then you can either follow the coast or ask for directions.

If you plan to do several hikes, make sure you hold on to your park fee receipt, as you only have to pay once to access the park. The following operations offer all-inclusive tour packages. Your hotel can probably book you on similar trips as well.

Evolution Tour (☎ 0 3955 1058; www.evolutiontour .com; Khlong Phrao) Offers a huge assortment of hiking and boating trips. Snorkelling tours are also available.

Jungle Way (☎ 08 9223 4795; www.jungleway.com) Runs one- and two-day excursions (800B to 1000B) through the island's interior, including an intense hike through the Chang Noi peninsula; book through your hotel.

Trekkers of Koh Chang (☎ 08 1578 7513) Offers ornithological day trips (1200B to 1400B); book through your hotel.

OTHER SPORTS

The newly opened **Tree Top Adventure Park** (☎ 08 4310 7600; www.treetopadventurepark.com; admission 900B; ⏰ 9am-5pm), near Ao Bai Lan, is an exciting obstacle course suspended high in the trees. The price includes a couple of hours of jungle fun and complimentary hotel transfers. Last entry at 3pm.

A unique kayaking experience awaits visitors at the small fishing community of Salak

Kok. The **Chang Spirit Club** (☎ 08 1919 3995; ⏱ 8am-5pm) hires out kayaks by the hour (100B) for exploring a dense forest of mangroves along the inner river. Charming wooden crafts are also available (200B), and dinner cruises are another enchanting option (see p156).

Some of the bungalows between Hat Sai Khao and Hat Kaibae rent out **kayaks**, **sailboards** and **boogie boards**. Dolphin Divers (p143) can set you up with virtually every type of nautical craft. Several operations at Bang Bao, including Buddha View (p156) and Dive Adventure (p143) lease captained boats (8000B to 16,000B) for those who want to plan their own marine adventure.

SPA & YOGA

The proliferation of top-end resorts has meant a similar increase in the number of spas. Today there are places to get pampered on every beach on the west coast.

If you're into yoga, reiki, bamboo massage and/or meditation, look no further than **Baan Zen** (☎ 08 6530 9354; www.baanzen.com) in Khlong Phrao. Run by a friendly French couple, this serene teak retreat sits on a quiet lagoon near the ocean. It's a relaxing place where clients can indulge in an intimate holiday led by an experienced Sivananda yoga instructor.

When the natural humidity isn't enough to cleanse your pores, try a sauna treatment at **Bailan Herbal Sauna** (☎ 0 6252 4744; www.bailan-kohchang.com; admission 200B; ⏱ 3-9pm). Sweat to a variety of herbs including kaffir lime, lemon grass and *prai*. Mud masks and salt scrubs are also on offer in a lush garden setting.

Courses

Thai cooking classes are available at **KATI Culinary** (☎ 0 3955 7252, 08 9028 9969; kati_culinary@hotmail.com; lunch courses 1000B; ⏱ 10.30am-3pm) and **Koh Chang Thai Cooking School** (☎ 08 1940 0649; info cookingschool@yahoo.com; Blue Lagoon Resort; afternoon courses 1000B). Both are fun and friendly options that include transportation, a cookbook and, of course, your meal.

Sleeping

Accommodation on Ko Chang continues to multiply with every season, but it still has a long way to go before approaching the grandeur of Phuket or Ko Samui. Recently, the west coast bungalows have started to swap bamboo huts for newer, sleeker cottages. Prices have been climbing as well, and even though several cheapies remain, the island's prices are more inflated than similar island destinations such as Ko Tao and Ko Pha-Ngan.

Most development has been limited to the west coast, as the east coast has mangroves instead of beaches. Hat Sai Khao is the busiest strip of sand on the island, and development continues in a steady string down to the end of the coastline. There's a great backpacker scene at Lonely Beach (although the beach is far from lonely), and further south there are a few unique lodging choices that sit over the water on Bang Bao pier.

During the low season, the ferries usually stop servicing all of the piers on Ko Chang except Ao Sapparot, Tha Dan Kao and several remote resorts close their doors.

KHLONG SON

At the northern tip of the island is the largest village, Ban Khlong Son, which has a network of piers, a wát, a school and several noodle shops.

Manee Guest House (☎ 08 1863 2108, 08 1843 0977; puk_35@yahoo.com.hk; huts 150-600B) Now that 'Lonely Beach' has become a false moniker, budget backpackers are spreading out in search of quieter retreats. Some have found a second home at friendly Manee, where rustic wooden huts sit on stilts over a snaking river. Month-long stays are also available starting at 4000B.

Aiyapura Resort (☎ 0 3955 5111; www.aiyapura.com; bungalows 4000-14,000B; 🍴 🖥 🏊) If you want to be treated like a king or queen, then Aiyapura is the perfect place to drop your luggage. The unbelievably friendly staff don perfectly pressed uniforms and ear-to-ear smiles. This rambling resort sits alone on a hilly promontory and fashionable bungalows are nestled in-between shivering coconut palms and fruit-bearing trees. Amenities include a long jogging track, state-of-the-art spa, gargantuan pool and beachside restaurant.

HAT SAI KHAO (WHITE SANDS BEACH)

If you're arriving on Ko Chang from Trat, busy White Sands will be your first stop after coming over the steep northern headland. This long sandy strip isn't one of Ko Chang's best, but it's convenient to a plethora of dining and nightlife options. The southern end of the beach is known as Hat Kai Muk (Pearl Beach).

(Continued on page 153)

THREE DIMENSIONS OF PARADISE

You'd be excused for being suspicious of terms such as 'beach paradise', 'outrageous sunset' and 'underwater wonder' as being tourist-brochure puffery. But when it comes to the islands and beaches of Thailand, the superlatives are justified. And there's more than 'just' sun-kissed stretches of white sand and swaying palms. Roll out of the hammock, and off the most well-trodden paths, and you'll discover national parks protecting everything from enormous flowers to gigantic whale sharks. Or sit down to a local dinner for a chance to redefine Thai spice. Best of all...the experience almost always outdoes the adjectives.

Beach Paradises

It isn't fair really – there are over 200 countries around the globe and Thailand has managed to snag a disproportionate amount of the world's top beaches. These aren't your average stretches of sand; you're about to uncover perfect powder-soft dunes and dramatic limestone crags that pop straight out of the impossibly clear waters. Robinson Crusoe, eat your heart out!

1 Hat Phra Nang, Railay

This beauty will shock and awe. Perfect sand, limestone cliffs and caves, emerald water and colourful long-tail boats make this photographic bliss. It's little more than a cosy nook, and tends to get crowded in high season (p338).

2 Hat Khao Lak

On this seemingly endless swath of golden, boulder-studded beach, expect outrageous sunsets and lazy days (p276). The Surin and Similan Islands as well as inland jungle parks are an easy boat or road trip away.

3 Ko Tao

Trying to decide between a slice of lively sand and hermitic retreat? Ko Tao offers plenty of both. Hit the island's west side for tiki-torched beach bars, and escape to the eastern shores to re-enact your favourite scenes from TV's *Lost* (p227).

4 Ko Mak & Ko Kut

Take your pick on quiet Ko Mak: sling your hammock up on a desolate beach or the next one over, which is just as perfect and pristine (p159). Jungle-ier Ko Kut next door has an excellent spread of flaxen sand as well (p157).

5 Ko Ngai

Cook on the slender, powder-white beach, dip in the sandy-bottomed shallows then slip over the reef for clear water, healthy corals and fish aplenty (p363). Knobby karst islands fill the horizon towards the Krabi mainland in the distance.

6 Ao Bang Thao, Phuket

With 8km of white sand, expect calm seas in the high season and surfable waves during the low season. Don't let the posh Laguna Complex scare you; this laid-back yet lively beach has something for everyone (p321).

7 Ko Pha-Ngan

Every month, on the night of the full moon, pilgrims pay tribute to the party gods with trancelike dancing and neon body paint. Join the legions of bucket-sippers on the infamous Sunrise Beach for the ultimate gathering that eclipses all other celebrations around the world (p211).

Southern Thai Cuisine

You may think you know Thai food, but a trip to Thailand's south is a new stamp in your culinary passport. With palpable influences from China and Malaysia, copious fresh seafood, and an obsession with bold flavours, the food of Thailand's beaches and islands is dynamic and diverse, not to mention intense.

1 Thai-Muslim Food

From satay to biryani, Thailand's Muslim minority makes some mean dishes (see p50). The emphasis is often on meat, but even vegetarians can dig into *sà·làt kàak*, a salad of lettuce, tomato, cucumber and hearty chunks of tofu, all topped with a sweet peanut sauce.

2 Kôw Yam

Where else is the cheapest dish also among the most delicious? For less than a packet of gum back home you get a dish of *kôw yam*, rice steamed with purple flowers and topped with toasted coconut, shredded herbs and a sweet/spicy fish sauce.

3 Night Markets

Southern Thailand's night markets are among the best in the country. In particular, the ones in Songkhla (p252), Satun (p371) and Trang (p361) are particularly good places to sample authentic southern Thai dishes such as *kà·nŏm jeen* (noodles served with curry) or local sweets.

4 Hat Yai–Style Fried Chicken

Legendary across the entire Kingdom, Hat Yai's deep-fried bird gets its special flavour from a marinade spiked with dried spices – a rarity in most schools of Thai cooking. A dry texture and a red hue round out the package (p256).

5 Coffee Shops & Mŏo Yâhng, Trang

The unassuming town of Trang has several atmospheric *ráhn goh·bêe* (coffee shops) that haven't changed in decades, a healthy addiction to *mŏo yâhng* (crispy barbecued pork) and, to top it off, one of Thailand's tastiest night markets (p361).

6 Bang Po Seafood

The native cuisine of Ko Samui can be difficult to find. To truly taste the island, visit Bang Po Seafood (p208), a popular local seaside shack where you can dig in to local specialties such as a salad of sea urchin eggs or grilled turmeric-coated flying fish.

7 Roti

Real roti are nothing like the guesthouse menu cliché. Whether served on the street and drizzled with sweetened condensed milk, or paired with a bowl of curry, they're a taste of southern Thailand.

National Parks & Protected Areas

Some of southern Thailand's most visited areas are its out-of-this-world national parks and protected areas. The range is enormous: far-out islands with virgin corals to little-visited mangrove swamps. The most popular areas are stressed environmentally by the number of visitors they receive each year, so please tread lightly.

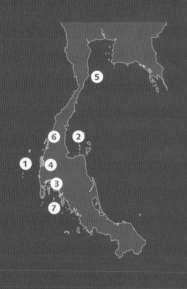

2

❶ Surin & Similan Islands Marine National Parks

These tiny islands 60km offshore, though astoundingly beautiful above water, are known more for their underwater wonders. Whale sharks are elusive but you're sure to see sea turtles, myriad healthy corals and multicoloured fish (see p274 and p279).

❷ Ang Thong Marine National Park

The ultimate cache of unspoiled lands, Ang Thong Marine Park is a stunning collection of easily anthropomorphised islets stretching along the cerulean waters like an emerald necklace (p240).

❸ Ao Phang-Nga National Park

Motor or paddle through a seemingly endless maze of steep, limestone isles to visit cave paintings, a rickety Muslim fishing village and the hide-out of Scaramanga, James Bond's old nemesis. Don't expect to get any of it to yourself though (p283).

❹ Khao Sok National Park

Perhaps the oldest rainforest in the world, Khao Sok is a dripping, juicy jungle overflowing with lurking beasts, gushing waterfalls and an alien flora, including the largest flower in the world (almost 1m in diameter!; p244).

❺ Khao Sam Roi Yot

Khao Sam Roi Yot is known as the 'land of the 300 peaks' for its stunning, seemingly endless expanse of chunky limestone crags. Walk quietly as you trudge between the hidden temples deep within – you may hear the distant rustle of dusky langur monkeys dangling in the trees above (p180).

❻ Laem Son National Park

Find the easy pace of yesteryear's Thailand in this mangrove-laden park (p270). Ko Phayam has a groovy, reggae-inspired beach scene while on Ko Chang life moves in slow motion. Snorkelling isn't great, although divers can go on trips to the Surin islands.

❼ Ko Phi-Phi Marine National Park

Phi-Phi deserves its fame for being one of Thailand's most beautiful protected areas. The fine sand, limestone cliffs and turquoise waters mean excellent diving, climbing and beach-side relaxation, but you'll have to share the experience with throngs of other travellers (p343).

A tranquil sunset at Big Buddha Beach, Ko Samui (p191)

(Continued from page 144)

Remark Cottages (☎ 0 3955 1261; www.remark cottage.com; bungalows 2000-3300B; 🐕) A wonderfully overgrown garden conceals 15 Balinese-style bungalows that may look simple at first, but are actually accented with intricate design details. Relax in the wooden spa pool or treat yourself with a course of shower spray therapy.

Mac Resort Hotel (☎ 0 3955 1124; www.mac -resorthotel.com; r & bungalows 2000-3500B; 🐕 🖳 🌐) Ponder the intended meaning of Mac's motto – 'the natural lover's stay' – while soaking up the sun in the large infinity pool. The resort feels noticeably modern compared with some of the other choices on Hat Sai Khao; ritzier rooms have faux marble tiles and large porthole windows over the tub.

Cookies Hotel (☎ 0 3955 1107; www.kohchang cookieshotel.com; r 2000-4000B; 🐕 🖳 🌐) Cookies occupies two horseshoe-shaped buildings: a two-storey structure along the beach, and a three-floor building bordering the jungle across the road. Most of the action goes down at the bustling pool area in the 'U' of the beach-facing unit. It's worth dropping the extra 500B to 1000B to grab a breezy room near the pool.

Keereeta (☎ 0 3955 1304; www.keereeta.com; r 2500B; 🐕 🌐) Even though little Keereeta sits away from the beach, it's one of our favourite hideaways on Hat Sai Khao. The charming rooms are arranged around a Mediterranean-inspired cloister, and each unit has a secret rooftop balcony offering views of the distant turquoise waves.

KC Grande Resort (☎ 0 3955 1199; www.kckohchang .com; r & bungalows 2500-6500B; 🐕) The first place you'll see as you tumble down the mountain into Sai Khao, KC is 'grande' indeed. It seems that this metropolis adds new accommodation every season – when we visited, it was completing a fancy-schmancy hotel with 60 units.

Other notable accommodation options include the following:

Koh Chang Kacha Resort (☎ 0 3955 1224; www .kohchangkacha.com; r 1400-1600B; 🐕 🌐) A charming mix of wood and brick overlooking the sea.

Banpu Ko Chang Resort (☎ 0 2580 3596; www.banpu resort.com; bungalows incl breakfast 1500-1800B; 🐕 🌐) Situated in a shady garden that slopes down to the beach.

Saffron on the Sea (☎ 0 3955 1253; r 1500-1800B; 🐕) Nestled in the pebbled cove. Saffron strives for boutique beauty.

Logan's Place (☎ 0 3955 1451; r 1600B; 🐕) Efficient service and oh-so-Scandinavian Ikea styling.

KHLONG PHRAO

About 4km south of Hat Sai Khao is Ao Khlong Phrao (Coconut Bay). It stretches south of Laem Chaichet and features the growing village of Ban Khlong Phrao.

Chok Dee Resort (☎ 0 3955 7064, 08 1910 9052; bungalows 400-1000B; 🐕) The bungalows at Chok Dee may remind you of the little house on a cuckoo clock where the bird hides between hours. It's a good budget choice on Khlong Phrao; just make sure you pick a hut without a squat toilet (unless you're looking for an authentic Thai experience).

Blue Lagoon Resort (☎ 08 1940 0649; r 600-1200B; 🐕) There's no false advertising at Blue Lagoon – the bungalows actually sit along a small lagoon that draws its blue water from the nearby sea. To find the beach, tug yourself across the ravine with an adorable pulley contraption. The smiley owners also run a small culinary school (see p144).

The Dewa (☎ 0 3955 7339; www.thedewakohchang .com; r & bungalows 4500-14,500B) The pitched roofs of The Dewa's beachside villas have piles of tan thatch, yet they look like the metal helmets of medieval chevaliers. This unique dual style permeates the interiors as well – rooms are adorned with velvet day beds and dark teak panelling.

Amari Emerald Cove (☎ 0 3955 2000; www.amari .com; r incl breakfast from 6000B; 🐕 🖳 🌐) Stunning gardens and eye-catching architecture make Amari feel like a secret paradise, even though this hotel is one of the largest operations on the island. The enormous lap pool, trimmed in white sandstone, frames the fiery tropical sunsets. Rates include a scrumptious breakfast feast that will easily fuel you until dinner.

KAIBAE

As Hat Kaibae becomes quite developed, most of the bungalow operations have gone upscale.

Porn Bungalow (☎ 08 9251 9233; huts 500-800B) Huts here range from beat-up shacks to comfortable wooden options and almost everything is covered in thatch. There's a multilevel chill space where idlers watch the sun bleed red as it dips behind four jagged islands. (It took an incredible amount of self-restraint to tell you about Porn without tossing in an obvious joke.)

KB Resort (☎ 0 3955 7125, 08 1862 8103; www
.kbresort.com; bungalows 1150-5000B; ☒) KB jetti-
soned the backpacker crowd when it added
'resort' to its name and popped an extra '0' on
the bill. Nowadays, the new fleet of wooden
bungalows caters mostly to families, although
everything is blatantly overpriced.

Chang Park Resort & Spa (☎ 0 3955 7100; www
.changpark.co.th; bungalows from 2500B, r from 3300B;
☒ ☐ ☒) We wouldn't exactly describe
Chang Park as 'ritzy', but it's one of the nicest options on this stretch of sand. There's a
variety of accommodation including motel
units and bungalows, and the *pièce de résist-
ance* is a small collection of beachside homes
that look like gingerbread houses. The seafood
restaurant proudly proclaims 'if it swims, we
have it'.

LONELY BEACH (HAT THA NAM)

For those who want to stay up all night and
sleep all day, head straight to this relaxed oasis
of backpackers. Although the beach is by no
means lonely, it's still considerably quieter
than the buzz on White Sands.

Treehouse (☎ 08 1847 8215; bungalows 220-500B)
We heard unconfirmed rumours that the HQ
of hippydom was closing down and moving
its entire operation to its second property on
the east coast. It's worth stopping by to see
if the original Treehouse is alive and kicking – there's a great vibe here, even though
the bungalows are crude and the communal shower looks a bit like a Chinese water
torture chamber.

Paradise Cottage (☎ 0 3955 8122, 08 1773 9337; bungalows 300B) The reception area here is a modern
combustion of polished concrete and bamboo
thatch. The pale green bungalows are a bit
more basic and sit along a shaded path where
ripe bananas droop like idle fingers. Laze the
day away in a private gazebo and listen to
relaxing, smooth jazz as gushing water over-
flows from overturned urns.

Kachapura (☎ 0 3955 8020; bungalows 500-2800B;
☒) If you're digging the Lonely Beach mojo
but can't live without hot showers and air-con,
then Kachapura's a dream come true.

BAI LAN BAY

Little Bai Lan is just south of Lonely Beach
and considerably quieter.

Orchid Resort (☎ 0 3955 8137; www.kohchangorchid
.com; bungalows 400-1000B; ☒ ☒) True to its
name, this wooded retreat is thick with wild

orchids – even the towels in the deluxe cabins are folded in the shape of a flower. The
older bungalows are smothered with stripes
of yellow and black paint – it's like sleeping
inside a giant bee.

Bai Lan Bay Resort (☎ 0 3955 8022, 08 1782 1710;
bungalows 600B) Padlocks on the doors make the
cabins feel more like a shed, but the interiors
are surprisingly fresh and tidy for a rustic
bamboo hut. The 20-odd bungalows mingle
with a patch of gnarled mangroves along the
shore, and there's a little snack shack further
up the hill along the road.

Princess Resort (☎ 0 3955 8055; www.royalprincess
.com; r 6000-8000B, bungalows 9000B; ☒ ☐ ☒)
Dusit's done it again: the well-respected
hotel chain has spawned another opulent
resort. Spirals of jade stones line the white
walkways as they snake by a luxuriant free-
form swimming pool and several sunken
Jacuzzis. The rooms are accented with similar swirling mosaics that offset the clean
90-degree angles.

BANG BAO

Bang Bao is a picturesque village floating on
stilts above the sea. It may feel like the edge
of the world, but the delightful pier accommodation is worth the trek.

Paradise Bang Bao (☎ 0 9934 8044; r with shared
bathroom 250-400B) A bewitching alternative
to the standard A-frame huts, this wooden
complex teeters above the tide water on
chiselled tree trunks. You'll feel like a Thai
fisherman while taking an afternoon snooze
in your tiny sea shack.

Bang Bao Sea Hut (☎ 0 3955 8098, 08 9759 7550;
www.bangbaoseahut.com; bungalows incl breakfast 1600-
2200B; ☒) These 'shanty-chic' bungalows look
like bobbing octagonal buoys connected by
an intricate network of thin planks. The
ebbing ocean curls under your cabin floor
and fresh ocean breezes float through
wooden shutters.

Nirvana (☎ 0 3955 8061; www.nirvanakohchang.com;
r 4620-9240B; ☒ ☐ ☒) Find your inner bliss
at this charming resort hidden on a quiet
peninsula of rambling vegetation. 'Balinese'
was the initial design concept, but each bungalow is furnished in muted earth tones with
subtle Asian accents. Make sure you bring
along your airline's phone number – there's
a good chance you'll be calling them to catch
a later flight.

EAST COAST

This part of the island is less developed than the west coast, mostly due to the lack of beaches.

Treehouse Lodge (☎ 08 1847 8215; Hat Yao; huts 100-300B) You may as well drop your watch in the ocean, 'cause this rustic enclave is a bohemian booby trap for backpackers. The offspring of Lonely Beach's legendary hangout of the same name, this village of simple huts is popular with those who seek something that's actually 'lonely'. Most taxis avoid the treacherous path down to this secluded beach, so it's best to grab the shuttle that links the sister properties, or you can take Laem Ngop's afternoon ferry to Ko Whai (which stops nearby along the way).

Funky Hut Resort (☎ 0 3958 6177; www.funky hut-thailand.com; Ao Dan Kao; r 1750-2250B; ☒ ☐ ☒) Staying at Funky Hut is as close as you'll get to time travel – this secluded east coast fave lets visitors experience life on Ko Chang before it became a giant construction site. Choose from an assortment of charming cream-coloured huts, and don't worry about bringing along the noisy kids – there's plenty of hushed jungle to go around. The resort is a couple of kilometres south of Tha Dan Kao.

Eating & Drinking

Virtually every place to stay has a place to eat. Independent restaurants are quickly becoming popular, and there are several special options throughout the island. After dinner, things start to pick up along White Sands and Lonely Beach.

WHITE SANDS BEACH (HAT SAI KHAO)

Thor's Palace (mains 70-170B; ☒ breakfast, lunch & dinner) Only on Ko Chang is Thor the name of a camp *gà·teu·i* (also spelt *kàthoey*; ladyboy) instead of a burly Scandinavian lumberjack. Savour excellent dishes in an upbeat atmosphere of pumping tunes and colourful knick-knacks. Sadly, this beachside haunt is only open in the high season.

Paddy's Palms (☎ 08 4930 3240; mains 150-300B; ☒ breakfast, lunch & dinner) Well, it finally happened. The Irish have landed on Ko Chang and they've brought with them a whole bunch of goodies with them: draft Guinness and Kilkenny, lamb stew, beef marinated in beer and shepherd's pie. Yum. Too bad they left the angioplasty equipment back home.

Oodie's Place (☎ 0 3955 1193; pizzas 170-260B; ☒ dinner) It's almost as though chunks of wood, brick, rattan, kitschy trinkets and metal sheeting all rolled together and somehow formed this special place. After the nightly movie, Mr Oodie straps on the guitar and plays to the crowd as they sling back French and Thai dishes, or Mongolian barbecue with a couple of beers.

ourpick Invito (☎ 0 3955 1326; mains 320-490B; ☒ lunch & dinner) Warning: conversation may be limited to expressions of gustatory delight. Set in a charming teak house, Invito offers wood-fired pizzas, handmade pasta, braised beef dishes and mouth-watering desserts. It's everyone's favourite *ristorante* on the island, and they'll even deliver to your bungalow.

Bustling Sai Khao has a lively night scene relative to the rest of the island. **Sabay Bar** (☎ 0 3955 1098) has a great night-time vibe and a daily onslaught of talented Filipino bands. **Sky Bay** (☎ 0 3955 1319), towards Khlong Phrao, is a popular pub choice with a plastic cartoon elephant that greets patrons out the front.

KHLONG PHRAO

KATI Culinary (☎ 0 3955 7252, 08 9028 9969; mains 40-120B; ☒ dinner) This charming twig hut is swathed in warm rosy lighting as the gruff serenades of Serge Gainsbourg drift through the thick jungle air. Dishes burst with fresh ingredients, and essential side orders of rice are served in an adorable variety of shapes – we got a heart. If you enjoy your meal (and we're pretty sure you will), enrol in KATI's Thai cooking course.

Iyara Seafood (☎ 0 3955 1353, 08 1751 0058; mains from 100B; ☒ 10am-10pm) Iyara isn't your standard island seafood warehouse: after dining in the lovely bamboo *săh·lah* (often spelt *sala*; open-sided room), guests are invited to kayak along the adjacent lagoon to watch the flickers of wild fireflies.

LONELY BEACH (HAT THA NAM)

Treehouse (☎ 08 1847 8215; mains 30-80B; ☒ breakfast, lunch & dinner) We can't think of a better name for this awesome wooden hang-out. Actually, 'Blackhole' might be more apropos, as once you hunker down on a bed-sized cushion, you'll never want to leave. After negotiating the sea of colourful flip-flops left at the entrance, make sure you watch your step while finding a place to relax: the planks of wood are weathered and uneven after years of wear and tear.

Magic Garden (☎ 0 3955 8027; mains 60-120B; Ⓨ dinner) If you're not up for a night of thumping tribal beats and jungle pyrotechnics, Magic Garden's stop-sign-shaped pagoda is probably the best place on Ko Chang to chill out and watch a movie. The open-air pavilion has six enormous beds arranged around the large projection screen. You have to get up to grab some grub – most people get seduced by the squishy pillows and fall asleep.

For some post-dinner partying, check out the DJ-ed beats at **Sunset Hut** (☎ 08 1377 5545) or the funky discotheque at **Nature Beach** (☎ 0 3955 8027).

BANG BAO

Buddha View (☎ 08 9936 1848; www.thebuddhaview .com; mains 80-250B; Ⓨ breakfast, lunch & dinner) A newer venture at the end of the pier, Buddha View is a great place to relax with a cocktail, play some pool and watch the waves roll in at sunset. Potted jungle flowers abound and the furniture is made from various incarnations of tubular bamboo.

Chow Lay Seafood (☎ 0 3955 5081, 08 1917 9084; www.chowlayseafood.com; mains 100-300B; Ⓨ breakfast, lunch & dinner) When the fishing boats pull into Bang Bao, they unload their seafood by the bucketful at Chow Lay. This bustling wooden shanty, halfway down the pier, is very popular with visitors, but it's hardly a tourist trap – its vast assortment of fresh seafood is delish. Fishing trips and boat rentals are also on tap.

Ruan Thai Restaurant (☎ 08 9833 5117; mains 100-300B; Ⓨ breakfast, lunch & dinner) Another option on Bang Bao's rickety pier, Ruan Thai is Chow Lay's neighbour and clone.

EAST COAST

Salakphet Seafood (☎ 0 3955 3099, 08 1429 9983; www.kohchangsalakphet.com; Ao Salak Phet; mains 40-200B; Ⓨ breakfast, lunch & dinner) This lonely restaurant hit it big when Thailand's prime minister rolled up, strapped on a bib and declared the food 'delicious'. Since then, other celebrities have stopped by to sample the seafood and pose for an obligatory photograph to go on the 'wall of fame'. Salakphet also has a large fish farm with submerged nets full of humungous critters – feeding time is a memorable frenzy.

Funky Hut (☎ 0 3958 6177, 08 9936 7750; www .funkyhut-thailand.com; Ao Dan Kao; mains 120-350B; Ⓨ breakfast, lunch & dinner) A lazy lunch at Funky Hut is a good choice for those who want a taste of the pace on Ko Chang's quieter east coast. Take your pick from Thai floor seating or Western tables, order a juicy 'Funky Hut Burger' and watch the fishing boats idle by under the midday sun. It's 1km east of the Centrepoint ferry pier.

Chang Spirit Club (☎ 08 1919 3995; set menu 1200B; Ⓨ dinner) Based at the rustic fishing village of Salak Kok, this unique dining experience is a romantic sunset adventure aboard a wooden catamaran. Fresh seafood is served as the quiet craft meanders through gnarled mangroves.

Getting There & Away

There is year-round service between the mainland and Ko Chang. During the high season, Tha Laem Ngop is the main pier to many of the Ko Chang Marine Park islands. There is a passenger (backpacker) ferry that runs hourly to Tha Dan Kho in Ko Chang (80B, one hour), but this rusty fishing boat often gets overcrowded and it's not the safest option.

From Tha Ko Chang Centrepoint, 4km from Laem Ngop, there are hourly ferries to and from Ko Chang's Tha Dan Kao (90B to 120B, 45 minutes) from 7am until 7pm daily. This is also a vehicle ferry – cars and motorbikes can ride this ferry free with every paying passenger. This is a faster, cheaper and safer option than the backpacker ferry and will drop you off closer to the main beaches. A sŏrng·tăa·ou from Trat to Tha Ko Chang Centrepoint costs around 60B per person.

Another way to get to Ko Chang is via the hourly vehicle ferry from Tha Thammachat. This ferry arrives at Ao Sapparot pier (per person/car 100/150B, 30 minutes) and may be the only boat running during rough seas.

For transport information to the smaller islands in the archipelago, consult the section of your desired destination.

Getting Around

There are loads of places along the west coast that rent out motorbikes for 200B to 250B per day. Jeeps can be hired for around 2000B per day in the high season. See p142 for important safety protocols.

The sŏrng·tăa·ou meeting the boats at Tha Dan Kao and Ao Sapparot charge from 40B to 100B per person, depending on how far

---

LOCAL VOICE: PRESERVING KO KUT

Louis Thompson is the Deputy Project Manager of Ko Kut's up-and-coming Soneva Kiri Resort. His primary focus is to limit the environmental impact of new tourism on the island.

What were your initial thoughts about Ko Kut when you arrived? Well, it was almost the low season, so there was a big storm and kick-ass waves – I thought I was in *Deadliest Catch 3* on *National Geographic*.

How do you feel about the island now? It's paradise. Ko Kut is the last remaining authentic tropical island in Thailand. I love the place and the people.

What are your thoughts about tourism development on Ko Kut? I hope that the island develops slowly and intelligently and I really hope that there's no infusion of Pattaya sleaziness. The island needs to insure that a car ferry doesn't come here from the mainland. If we can limit the number of cars, or only use electric vehicles and motorbikes, the island will maintain much of its pristine environment. A reservoir will also be required in the future, and a waste management strategy will need to be conceived. I sincerely hope that much of the island will be granted national park status, so that we can keep much of Ko Kut pristine.

How are the island's residents reacting to tourism development? Pretty well, in general; everyone is excited about the new influx of jobs, which will boost the economy and encourage environmental endeavours.

Any special tips for travellers? Visitors should definitely bring a phrasebook, as English is pretty scarce around certain parts. Have a look at the villages in Ao Yai – it's an authentic fishing cove and was a favourite destination for pirates. My favourite place to visit is the dense forest in Khao Din Daeng. Bikes and long-tail boats are the best ways to get around the island.

As told to Brendon Presser

---

down the west coast you want to go. Expect to pay between 50B and 80B for east coast deliveries.

KO KUT
เกาะกูด

Ko Kut is Thailand's last large island frontier and a veritable blank canvas for developers. Numerous operations are already up and running, but there are some big plans in store for this rugged speck of jungle. The topography of this quiet islet is quite similar to Ko Chang, with rainforest and waterfalls hidden deep within its interior; however, its location at the edge of the archipelago means that the coastal waters have a unique emerald tint.

Orientation

Almost all of the resorts are located along Ko Kut's western beaches. A dirt road runs through the west side, connecting the villages of Ban Khlong Hin Dam and Ban Khlong Chao, and then turns northeast before ending in Ao Salat on the other side of the island.

Information
EMERGENCY
Police Station (☎ 0 3952 3125, 08 1861 1677; Ban Khlong Chao) Near the hospital.

INTERNET ACCESS
If you're addicted to checking your email, then Ko Kut might not be the place for you. Access is very limited – there are no internet cafés and resorts with a computer generally have poor satellite-enabled connections.

MEDICAL SERVICES
Koh Kood Hospital (☎ 0 3952 1852; Ban Khlong Chao) Near the police station. A masseur affiliated with the hospital can visit your resort for a reasonable price.

MONEY
There are no banks or ATMs on the island, and credit cards are not accepted due to the lack of fixed telephone lines. Some bungalow operators can exchange small amounts of foreign currency, but it's best to withdraw plenty of cash beforehand. There are many banks and ATMs in Trat, Laem Ngop and Ko Chang.

POST
Ko Kut does not have an official post office, however, most resorts can organise mail.

TELEPHONE
Despite the dearth of working land lines, mobile phones work surprisingly well throughout the island.

Sights

If you have your sights set on finding a secluded strip of sand, you can pretty much
choose from any beach on the island. The
main attraction on Ko Kut is **Nam Tok Khlong
Chao**. It's considerably more impressive during
the rainy season when tourists aren't around,
but there's always more than just a trickle to
be seen. Ask the manager of your bungalow
about getting to the falls – they'll probably take
you there for a small fee and lead you around
on a mini jungle trek. **Ao Salat** and **Ao Yai**, two
east coast bays, both have small shanty-filled
fishing villages. Most of the residents are
Cambodians who earn their living by catching an assortment of crabs, prawns and fish. In
the early evening, visitors can purchase freshly
caught seafood as it's coming off the boat.

Activities

Ploy Scuba Diving, next to Away Resort, runs
programs from Ao Salat and Ban Khlong
Chao. For detailed information about **diving**
around Ko Kut and the other islands of the Ko
Chang Archipelago, see p138. The crystalline
waters just off the coast are the perfect place
to pop on a mask and frolic with fish. Most
bungalow operations have rentable **snorkelling**
equipment for around 100B to 200B.

Sleeping & Eating

Prepaid all-inclusive vacations tend to dominate Ko Kut's tourism, although an independent visit is definitely doable. It should be
noted, however, that while a majority of places
warmly welcome walk-in bookings (when
they aren't stuffed with package tourists), Ko
Kut isn't suited for spontaneity. The island is
vast and the 20-odd resorts have the luxury
of being spread far apart from one another.
Advance reservations are also advantageous
because speedboat operators will usually drop
you off at your accommodation.

Besides the lone Thai restaurant near the
police station in Ban Khlong Chao, dining
on Ko Kut is limited to resorts. The food
will probably be tasty, but the island is by
no means a destination for foodies. You can,
however, ask your resort staff about ordering
freshly caught seafood from one of the fishing villages, or you can retrieve it yourself
(see above).

Siam Beach (☎ 08 1945 5789, 08 1899 6200; sb_koh
kood@yahoo.com; Ao Bang Bao; r 500-1200B; 🞩) An appealing blend of fan and air-con bungalows

lies beneath curving palm trees. Dangle your
legs on the rickety dock and then jump into
the crystal sea to play with quixotic sardines.
Most of the staff speak only Thai.

The Beach Natural Resort (☎ 08 6009 9420, in
Bangkok 0 2222 9969; www.thebeachkohkood.com; Ao
Bang Bao; bungalows incl breakfast 1200-1900B; 🞩 🖳)
Balinese-style bungalows sit among loads of
vegetation on a private beach that's great for
kayaking. The thatched massage *săh·lah* along
the ocean are a great place to unwind in the
shade and watch small fish dance through the
perfectly clear waters. Thais pack this place
for karaoke-fuelled fun on the weekend, so
try and come on a weekday if you're after
some hush.

Away Resort (Bai Kood Shambala; ☎ 08 1835 4517,
08 7147 7055, in Bangkok 0 2696 8239; www.awayresorts
.com; Ban Klong Chao; bungalows incl breakfast 1500-4350B;
🞩 🖳) Hidden within a jungle of shivering
palms, Away's elegant wooden cottages are
just steps away from the curling sea. A philosophy of tranquillity pervades the resort, as
guests swing slowly in their hammocks and
listen to the waves roll in. The staff organises
a variety of activities and programs including
scuba outings.

ourpick Koh Kood Beach Bungalows (☎ in Bangkok
0 2630 9371; www.kohkoodbeachbungalows.com; Ao Bang
Bao; r 1500-3000B; 🞩 🖳) This stunning, sloping
resort has perfectly maintained grounds that
rest beneath a canopy of skyscraping palms.
There are two types of bungalows: the Balinese
cottages have slanted roofs with plenty of
thatch, and the Thai-style units have private
outdoor whirlpools. It's the only resort on the
island with a swimming pool (although with
continuous construction, this may no longer
be true). Free snorkelling gear and delicious
food are extra bonuses. Reserve in advance.

Shantaa (☎ 08 1817 9648, 08 1826 4077; www.shantaa
kohkood.com; Ao Yai Kee; bungalows incl breakfast 3700B; 🞩)
One of the more elegant options on Ko Kut,
Shantaa has stylish bungalows with sea-view
balconies and polished wood throughout.
This hillside retreat is owned and operated
by a local family, and they speak remarkably
good English.

Other quality options available include the
following:

Ngamkho Resort (☎ 08 1825 7076, 08 4653 4644;
www.kohkood-ngamkho.com; Ao Ngam Kho; tents 200B;
bungalows 300-650B) A great budget option with simple
huts or flashier fan bungalows. Campers can pitch a tent
for 200B. Guaranteed sea views from every hammock.

THE 7-ELEVEN GAME

According to the 7-Eleven website (www.7eleven.co.th), there are almost 5000 franchised conven- ience stores throughout Thailand, and this astonishing total continues to grow. In Bangkok you'll often be given directions such as 'take a right at the 7-Eleven, and then turn left at the corner that has a 7-Eleven on either side of the street', but as you venture further afield, these palpable markers of globalisation start to disappear – it's like an off-the-beaten-path-o-meter.

If you're stuck on a long bus ride with nothing to do, play the 7-Eleven Game: try to recall the number of superettes seen in each place you visited. We counted five on Ko Chang, four on Ko Tao and three on Ko Samet. You'll be happy to know that there are zero on Ko Mak and Ko Kut (for now).

Sai Dang Beach Paradise (☎ 0 2511 3313; r & bunga- lows 400-600B) Bamboo bungalows on a rolling lawn with swaying palms. There's also a large wooden house containing a few additional rooms.

Khlong Chao Resort (☎ 08 1403 6174; bungalows 400- 800B; ✷) A pretty good deal since it's located along a lazy river rather than the beach. Near Nam Tok Khlong Chao.

S-Beach Resort (☎ 08 1949 6093; www.s-beach.net; bungalows 500-1000B; ✷) The tin-roofed bungalows are a tad drab from the exterior, but the insides are comfy and clean.

Dusita (☎ 0 3951 2902; bungalows 700-2000B; ✷) Pleasant fan and air-con bungalows near the sandy beach. An all-inclusive vacation fave.

Captain Hook (☎ 0 2966 1800, 08 1826 1188; www .captainhookresort.com; 2- or 3-night packages 3000- 6000B; ✷) A popular pick for an all-in-one vacation. Has a fantastic on-site restaurant.

Getting There & Away

The best way to access Ko Kut is from either Laem Sok or Ko Chang's Tha Bang Bao. As a general rule, all boats stop on Ko Mak as they make their journey (a trip from Ko Mak to Ko Kut is 400B). During the high season, daily ferries depart Ko Chang at 9am, arriving on Ko Kut (700B) at 2pm. The daily return trip leaves Ko Kut at 10am and arrives back on Ko Chang around 2pm. Speedboats (900B) from Ko Chang depart at noon and arrive at 2pm. The reverse trip begins at 10am on Ko Kut, alighting at Ko Chang at 11.20am.

Passenger ferries (350B) from the small pier at Laem Sok make the two-hour trek to Ko Kut at 8am. The one-hour speedboat (550B) departs daily at 1pm. Leaving from Ko Kut, the ferry takes off at 11am, while the speedy service jets away at 10am.

If you are taking a speedboat, there's a good chance that the driver will take you to the beach near your resort, so it's a good idea to book ahead.

See p139 for more information about mov- ing around the archipelago.

Getting Around

Most visitors tend to stay close to their ac- commodation since there is no transportation infrastructure on the island. Resorts usually offer tours of the various natural attractions, and transportation is always included in the price. You can rent a motorbike for 400B, although good luck finding a petrol station.

KO MAK
เกาะหมาก

This cross-shaped island makes up the third- largest landmass in the Ko Chang Archipelago, measuring 16 sq km. Ko Mak can trace its his- tory back to the late 1800s during the reign of Rama V. The Thai king briefly ceded the island to French Indochina and many of to- day's locals can trace their lineage back to the original Chinese ambassadors. Although Ko Mak is smaller and less populated than Ko Kut, its flat topography has made it easier for resorts to flourish. The island now has over two dozen resorts, most with 24-hour electricity, although much of the island's other modern infrastructure is still in development. Most of Ko Mak remains covered with co- conut and rubber plantations, leaving many cobble beaches untouched.

Looking for even more seclusion? Try one of the resorts on Ko Rayang or Ko Kham – the two furry isles orbiting Ko Mak. The larger Ko Kradat, slightly further afield, is also easily reachable from Ko Mak by ferry or boat taxi. See p162 for additional info about vacationing on these smaller satellites.

Orientation

Ko Mak is shaped like a plus sign, and most of the tourist development has evolved along

EASTERN GULF COAST

the western arm. The eastern part of the island has a small town with around 50 families, but remains rather quiet despite the main passenger pier at Ao Nid.

Information

Serious medical emergencies must be handled in Trat or Ko Chang, as Ko Mak does not have a hospital. There is, however, a small **clinic** (☎ 08 9093 4629, 08 9403 5986) on the main road to Tha Ao Nid, which is operated by three health officials during normal business hours. A **police station** (☎ 08 1663 2410) is located in the exact centre of the island (just up the street from the clinic) – hours are known to vary, as crime is rather uncommon on the island, and the station is often empty during random boat checks.

There is a small post office at KohMak Resort along Ao Suan Yai, with one postie who delivers mail throughout the island. The hours of operation tend to fluctuate – your resort manager can also collect your outgoing mail and hand it to the postman when he passes through.

A network of land lines has been installed on the island, however, due to maintenance problems and frequent monsoon winds, there are currently no functioning public telephones and the network is too fragile to support high-speed internet. Most people use mobile phones, which get very good reception throughout the island. Email is starting to become more widely accessible and can be checked at KohMak Resort, Koh Mak Villa, Monkey Island and at a couple of eating establishments around Tha Maka Thanee and Tha Ao Nid. Expect to pay the usual 1B or 2B per minute.

There are no banks or ATMs on the island, so it's best to plan in advance and withdraw extra baht before arriving. The occurrence of theft is extremely low on Ko Mak, although caution should always be taken with liquid assets. Only a few resorts accept credit cards.

Sights

Ko Mak's two longest beaches, **Ao Suan Yai** and **Ao Kao**, are scenic stretches of beige sand on the western portion of the island. They are great spots for a leisurely stroll or swim, and offer excellent sunset vistas (watch out for sandflies!). The pier at **Ao Nid** is worth a visit in the early morning if you can muster the energy to wake up for a tropical sunrise. A small wát, **Wat Samakkeetham**, sits right near the dock. **Coconut and rubber plantations** occupy most of the island's flat terrain. Informal visits can usually be organised at your resort for a nominal fee.

Activities

Diving has become a popular pastime on the island, and the locally run **Koh Mak Divers** (☎ 08 3297 7724) is a reputable choice. Divers can also suit up with Ploy Scuba Diving at its satellite locations at Monkey Island or Panorama Resort on the island's southern leg (it's based out of Ko Chang). For detailed information about diving around Ko Mak and the other islands of the Ko Chang Archipelago, see p138. Most resorts have rentable **snorkelling** equipment (100B to 200B) for an impromptu afternoon of blowing bubbles.

On land, visitors can explore the island with **bicycles** or **motorbikes**. Several resorts offer bike rentals – it's usually between 100B and 200B for a bicycle (per day) and around 250B to 400B for a motorbike. Scooters can also be rented near the pier at Ao Nid.

Tours

Tripmaker (☎ 08 9804 2595; khunrano@yahoo.com) is a friendly local company offering a glimpse at life on Ko Mak. Walking, biking and car tours (200B) explore the island's history, fishing culture, rubber plantations and coconut farms. Snorkelling boat trips (550B) stop at two smaller islands and three separate sites. Rates include snorkel equipment, lunch and a guide.

Sleeping & Eating

Although Ko Mak once garnered a reputation as a 'package destination', recent resort expansion has made it easy for tourists of every ilk to scout out their own lodging. There are now over two dozen places to stay ranging from A-frame hovels to chic incarnations of adobe, teak and thatch. Most of the accommodation is located on the western half of the island, where the beaches tend to be that quintessential mixture of beige cobble sand and emerald water.

Walk-in bookings are definitely doable; however, if you're eyeing a particular resort, it's best to book in advance, especially during the high season. If you make a reservation, an employee from the resort will most likely pick you up when you arrive at the pier. Low

EASTERN GULF COAST

season sees a dramatic decrease in tourism as the waves are quite choppy and the skies are often overcast. Several bungalows close down during these months, and the ones that stay open often offer hefty discounts.

Restaurants on Ko Mak are largely affiliated with bungalows; however, there are a few stand-alone options that are slightly cheaper than resort fare. A few chow shacks gather near Tha Maka Thanee, where a mixed bag of locals and tourists feasts on an assortment of cheap noodles and barbecued seafood. **Ball Café** (☎ 08 1925 6591) has a dainty assortment of light nibbles, and the owner can help you out with local accommodation and transportation to other islands.

Island Hut Resort (☎ 08 7139 5537; huts 350-500B) Twig-and-thatch huts, over-water swings and lazy hammocks give this simple spot a funky feel. The friendly owners have been on the island for many generations and they'll make you feel like part of the family.

Monkey Island (☎ 08 9501 6030; www.monkey islandkohmak.com; bungalows 400-3000B; ✕) Monkey's funky bungalows are a popular choice for vacationing Thais, and range from simple bamboo affairs with shared bathrooms to deluxe wooden villas with bay windows and outdoor lounge settings.

Koh Mak Cococape Resort (☎ 08 1937 9024; www .kohmakcococape.com; r 500-4500B; ✕) Cococape's whitewashed cottages have coolie-hat-like roofs lavished with thick thatch. Scraps of sun-bleached fronds dangle like a visor over the 2nd-storey balconies of the more opulent villas. The 500B bungalows have shared bathrooms and are noticeably more rustic. The abounding hammocks are made from pearls of smooth rope.

KohMak Resort (☎ 0 3950 1013; www.geocities.com /kohmaak; bungalows 600-4000B) On the northwestern bay amid a coconut and rubber plantation, friendly KohMak has some pricier, large, two-room sleeping options. A windsurfing school on the beach offers courses and rents out equipment.

Baan Koh Mak (☎ 0 3952 4028; www.baan-koh-mak .com; bungalows 1400B; ✕) These spacious and sundrenched bungalows feel a bit like Wisteria Lane (of *Desperate Housewives* fame) – each of the 18 cottages is encased by a white picket fence. Snorkel gear, beach volleyball and bicycles are on offer.

Good Time Resort (☎ 08 3118 0011; www.goodtime -resort.com; villas 2500-3000B; ✕ 🖳) Fifteen gorgeous two- and three-bedroom Thai-style villas are nestled in an expansive tropical garden. Relax by the pool, enjoy the spa services or journey to the owner's other resort on teeny Ko Rayang.

Other worthy options to check out include the following:

Holiday Beach Resort (☎ 08 1937 9024, 0 2319 6714; info@kohmakholiday.com; bungalows 100-1500B) Good smattering of room types; the pricier picks have ocean views.

TK Huts (☎ 08 7134 8435; www.tk-hut.com; bungalows 400-800B) A sociable setting with spartan huts set amid shady trees.

Ko Mak Buri Hut (☎ 08 9888 8355; bungalows 1200-3800B) Variety of air-con bungalows scattered along a general stretch of sand.

Koh Mak Villa (☎ 08 1925 6591; bungalows 1500-2500B) Spacious villas with hilltop views of the sandy beaches below.

Makathanee (☎ 08 7600 0374; www.makathanee.com; bungalows 2500B) A newer retreat with deservedly popular Thai-style bungalows.

Getting There & Away

In the high season, there are daily departures to Ko Mak from Laem Ngop and Tha Bang Bao on Ko Chang. The ferry (300B) leaves Laem Ngop at 3pm and arrives on Ko Mak around 6pm. Speedboat services (450B) leave Laem Ngop at 1.30pm and 4pm, arriving on the island at 2.30pm and 5pm respectively. To reach Laem Ngop from Ko Mak, take the daily three-hour ferry at 8am, or try the one-hour speedboat at 8am and 10am. Also, all of the boats from Laem Sok to Ko Kut stop at Ko Mak halfway through the journey (see p159).

From Ko Chang's Tha Bang Bao, there are daily ferries (400B) departing at 9am and noon, arriving around 11am and 2pm respectively. A speedboat (550B) leaves at noon daily and alights on Ko Mak at 1pm. Boats going in the opposite direction take off at noon and 3pm, and land on Ko Chang at 3pm and 6pm. The one-hour speedboat service leaves Ko Mak at 10.30am. All boats can stop at Ko Kham and Ko Rayang if you let the captain know in advance. These teeny islands are a 15-minute hop from Ko Mak.

See p139 for more information about moving around the archipelago.

Getting Around

The terrain on Ko Mak is quite flat, making it relatively easy to get around by motorbike, bicycle or foot. A few vans troll the island in search of passengers – no specific schedules or prices have been established. See p160 for bike and motorbike rental info.

OTHER ISLANDS

If you thought there was nothing to do on Ko Kut and Ko Mak, then you'll really feel like a castaway on the smaller islands of the Ko Chang Archipelago. Between June and October, boats stop running and most bungalow operations close down. In addition to the following islands, there is also accommodation on the wee islets of **Ko Kradat** (☎ 08 9099 7917, in Bangkok 0 2368 2675), **Ko Lao Ya Nai** (☎ 0 3951 2818), **Ko Mai Si Yai** (☎ 08 7077 2018) and **Ko Sai Kao** (☎ 08 1929 8669). See p139 for transport queries not addressed in the following sections.

Ko Whai

This 'L'-shaped isle has two sandy coves and a few places to spend the night. An attractive palm-fringed sand bar holds the two arms of the island together, creating captivating lagoons on either side – the perfect place to park your boat for the night. A vast network of shallow coral reefs radiates around Ko Whai, making it a good choice for avid snorkellers. BB Divers (p143) has an on-site outpost and can hook you up with scuba equipment.

Friendly staff and tasty food come with simple wooden bungalows on the beach at **Ko Wai Paradise** (☎ 08 1762 2548; bungalows from 250B; 𝕏). **Kla Thom Yai Ma** (☎ 08 1841 3011; bungalows from 250B) is another option on little Ko Whai –

it's the usual facsimile of white sand, tall palms and rustic huts. The fan bungalows at **Ko Wai Pakarang** (☎ 08 4113 8945; www.kohwaipaka rang.com; bungalows 600-2000B) are as flash as it gets on Ko Whai. Nightly movies offset the ennui of island life.

One-hour ferries to Ko Whai (300B) depart from Ko Chang's Tha Bang Bao at 9am and noon. Speedboats (400B) depart Ko Chang at noon. Return trips leave at 1pm, 4pm and at 10.55am for speedboats. Ferries from Laem Ngop (250B) depart at 3pm and arrive at 5pm, while speedboats (450B) take one hour and depart at 1.30pm and 4pm. All return trips depart at 8.30am and 10am.

Ko Kham & Ko Rayang

Little Ko Kham and Ko Rayang bob like brilliant green apples just 1km off the coast of Ko Mak. Braids of hardened lava suggest the presence of ancient volcanic activity, but today these islands boast shimmering turquoise vistas, swimmable beaches and vibrant coral reefs. These quiet spots are easily accessible by speedboat from Ko Mak, and during the high season there are daily passenger ferries that stop through.

Ko Kham Resort (☎ 08 1303 1229; bungalows from 800B) is so close to Ko Mak, you could kayak across from Ao Suan Yai. Enjoy quiet starlit evenings, although there tend to be a lot of day-tripping snorkellers in the afternoon. **Rayang Island Resort** (☎ 08 3118 0011, 0 3955 5082; www.rayang-island.com; bungalows from 1600B) is a serene place with 15 refurbished one- and

---

CAMBODIAN BORDER CROSSING

The border at Hat Lek between Cambodia and Thailand is open between 7am and 8pm daily. Motorcycles and minivans are available from Hat Lek to the border for 50B. There is accommodation on Koh Kong in Cambodia, but little to keep you there. If you plan to continue further, there is one boat to Sihanoukville per day (US$25, four hours) leaving at 8am; if you don't get across the border early enough you may have to spend a night on Koh Kong (the best bet is to leave Hat Lek at 6am). There are also minibuses to Sihanoukville (600B) and Phnom Penh (700B) that usually depart before 9.30am.

Before arriving at the border, check in at the Cambodian Embassy in Bangkok – prices and rules are always changing. A visa is usually available at the border for 1200B (US dollars are no longer preferred). It's cheaper to get a Cambodian visa in Bangkok as many of the border guards impose extra 'mystery' charges. Thailand grants most nationalities a one-month visa on entry (or re-entry) to Thailand. If your nationality is not on the instant-visa list, or if you've exhausted your entry-exit allowance, you will find yourself stuck in Cambodia (see p401 for more information on Thai visas).

If this all sounds a little tricky, and you don't want to risk a visa mess-up, there are plenty of travel agencies in Trat and Ko Chang that can arrange the trip for a few hundred extra baht.

two-bedroom bungalows. There are no day trippers, so it's wonderfully quiet. It's owned by the same family that runs the Good Time Resort on Ko Mak.

Boats leave from Ko Chang's Tha Bang Bao at 9am and noon, alighting on Ko Kham at 10.30am and 2pm respectively, and arriving 15 minutes later at Ko Rayang. These trips cost 400B. Speedboat services depart at noon (also from Bang Bao) and costs 550B. Ferries back to Ko Chang leave just after noon on both islands, and speedboats return around 10.30am. Contact the two resorts for additional information about transport, including water taxis.

Ko Rang

Dazzling Ko Rang is the largest landmass of an island chain called Mu Ko Rang (Ko Rang Archipelago). This area boasts one of the best strings of coral in the region and a long stretch of sand called **Hat San Chao**. Although there are no resorts on the island, campers are allowed to pitch a tent as long as they register with the **national park office** (☎ 0 3955 5080; ☺ 8.30am-4.30pm Mon-Fri) on Ko Chang. There is a 400B fee per person to access the marine park. Crude washrooms and running water have been set up; however, visitors must bring their own consumables.

TRAT TO CAMBODIA

A thin necklace of sandy beaches lines the skinny scrap of land between Trat town and the Cambodian border. **Hat Sai Si Ngoen** (Silver Sand Beach) lies just north of the 41km marker off Hwy 3. Nearby, at the 42km marker, is **Hat Sai Kaew** (Crystal Sand Beach), while at the 48km marker you'll find **Hat Thap Thim** (Sapphire Beach); neither one quite lives up to its whimsical name. The most promising

beach is **Hat Ban Cheun**, a long stretch of clean sand near the 63km marker.

In the little town of Khlong Yai, travellers can stop by the **immigration office** (☎ 0 3958 8108) to have their passport stamped upon re-entry from Cambodia. The small border outpost of **Hat Lek** is the departure point for boats to Koh Kong in Cambodia. There's a popular casino in the vicinity, and loads of touts to guide you through the visa process. For information on crossing to Cambodia, see the boxed text, opposite.

EASTERN GULF COAST

Northwestern Gulf Coast

NORTHWESTERN GULF COAST

Thai vacationers have been flocking to Thailand's northwestern gulf coast for decades, yet somehow foreign tourists never got the memo. This thin isthmus connecting the Asian continent to the Malay Peninsula offers sleepy seaside towns and rugged shell-strewn sand dunes, making it a great place to slough off Bangkok's urban smog.

Most tourists will only experience the region through the window of a speeding train destined for the kingdom's southern treasures. Those who decide to stop will enjoy a unique vacationing experience steeped in local tradition.

Quiet Phetchaburi makes for a pleasant afternoon of temple gazing. Stop in Cha-am to master the lyrics of your favourite Thai pop-rock song as it blares along the beach during the usual weekend bustle. Countless guesthouses and resorts are crammed along the beachfront thoroughfare, much like in Hua Hin, further south, which is the favoured resort destination of the royal family.

The dramatic crags of Khao Sam Roi Yot National Park are definitely worth a visit, especially for wildlife enthusiasts. And at the southernmost point of the region, Chumphon earns its spot on the map as the official gateway to southern Thailand and the obligatory transfer point for the diving-centric Ko Tao.

While transport between major destinations is a cinch, navigating the quieter regions requires a little ingenuity and may put your independent travel spirit to the test.

HIGHLIGHTS

- Smiling at the sea while lounging in the shade of myriad beachside umbrellas in **Cha-am** (p169)
- Living like royalty in one of the swish seaside hotels around **Hua Hin** (p172)
- Ogling crumbling temples scattered around **Phetchaburi** (opposite)
- Listening for rustling leaves while trying to spot a furry monkey at **Khao Sam Roi Yot National Park** (p180)
- Pressing binoculars against your face while anticipating the arrival of a rare bird in **Kaeng Krachan National Park** (p168)

★ Phetchaburi

Kaeng Krachan ★
National Park

★ Cha-am

★ Hua Hin

★ Khao Sam Roi Yot
National Park

■ DRY SEASON: NOVEMBER-MAY ■ WET SEASON: JUNE-OCTOBER

Climate
The northwestern gulf coast shares its weather patterns with the rest of central Thailand. Temperatures peak in the March to May hot season, followed by monsoon rains falling in the June to October wet season. November through February is known as the 'cool' season and is the best time to visit. The afternoon temperatures seem to hover around 32°C throughout the year, but evenings tend to be cooler and there is little rain.

National Parks
Kaeng Krachan (p168) is the largest national park in Thailand, covering nearly half of Phetchaburi Province. This unending expanse of jungle is known for the Pala-U waterfall and excellent bird-watching. The undulating hills of Khao Sam Roi Yot (p180) offer breathtaking views of the gulf amid limestone cliffs. This is another spot bird fanatics can check off their lists.

PHETCHABURI (PHETBURI)
อ.เมืองเพชรบุรี
pop 47,200

Unlike many other centres of worship around the world, quiet Phetchaburi (also called Phetburi) feels surprisingly devoid of tourist traffic. Dozens of temples lie frozen within the city's slowly paced quotidian life, each one a relic reflecting the achievements of empires that flourished long ago. The Khmer first settled here in the 11th century, and since then the town has seen a steady stream of inhabitants that have used the convenient riverside location as a central trading post. Today, the town has barely changed, and a stroll through the city centre will reveal a burg teeming with crumbling wát mixed with old teak houses and misplaced concrete indicators of a modern future.

If you're light on time, the sleepy religious town can be tackled in an afternoon visit – glimpse the diverse array of wát along the eastern riverbank during a half-day walking tour (see the boxed text, p167). The underground Buddhist shrine at the Khao Luang caves is also worth a visit.

Orientation & Information
If you've come by bus, you'll be getting off close to Khao Wang and will have to take a motorcycle taxi into the centre of town. Train users should follow the road southeast of the

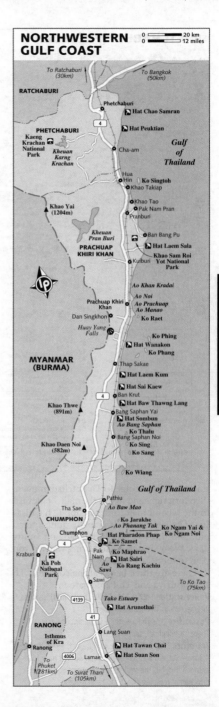

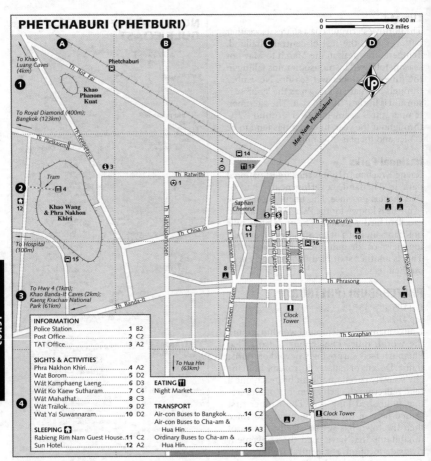

PHETCHABURI (PHETBURI)

INFORMATION
Police Station...................................1	B2
Post Office.......................................2	C2
TAT Office..3	A2

SIGHTS & ACTIVITIES
Phra Nakhon Khiri.........................4	A2
Wat Borom......................................5	D2
Wát Kamphaeng Laeng..................6	D3
Wát Ko Kaew Sutharam.................7	C4
Wát Mahathat.................................8	C3
Wát Trailok......................................9	D2
Wat Yai Suwannaram....................10	D2

SLEEPING
Rabieng Rim Nam Guest House...11	C2
Sun Hotel..12	A2

EATING
Night Market...................................13	C2

TRANSPORT
Air-con Buses to Bangkok...........14	C2
Air-con Buses to Cha-am &	
Hua Hin......................................15	A3
Ordinary Buses to Cha-am &	
Hua Hin......................................16	C3

tracks until you come to Th Ratchadamnoen, then turn right and follow the main boulevard to the second major intersection (Th Chisa-In). The city centre is actually quite spread out, and there is very little shade on sunny days. Wear sunscreen and bring water if you plan to tour the temples.

There are three banks at the corner of Th Phongsuriya and Th Panichjaroen.

Police station (☎ 0 3242 5500; Th Ratwithi) Near the intersection of Th Ratchadamnoen.

Post office (cnr Th Ratwithi & Th Damnoen Kasem) There's a telephone centre upstairs.

TAT office (☎ 0 3240 2220; Th Ratwithi; ☼ 8.30am-4.30pm) Set in a wát-like structure, it doesn't have loads of brochures, but the smiley staff can point you in the direction of temples, cheap food and lodging.

Sights & Activities

Looming west of the city, **Khao Wang** is studded with wát and topped by various components of King Mongkut's 1860 palace, **Phra Nakhon Khiri** (Holy City Hill; ☎ 0 3240 1006; admission 40B; ☼ 9am-4pm). You can make the strenuous upward climb along the cobblestone paths or head to the west side of the hill and take a funicular straight to the peak (adult one way 40B). The views here are great, especially at sunset, and the entire hill teems with meandering monkeys looking for attention. The ticket office will sell you an information pamphlet (5B) that includes a map of the palace grounds.

The cave sanctuary of **Khao Luang** (donation encouraged; ☼ 8am-6pm) is 5km north of Phetchaburi. The caverns here are filled with

WALKING TOUR: WÁT TO SEE IN PHETCHABURI

Sleepy Phetchaburi is known throughout Thailand for its collection of varied wát. The following tour ambles through some of the town's most striking relics from previous empires.

Start Wat Yai Suwannaram
Finish Wat Mahathat
Distance 2.7km
Duration 1½ hours

Wat Yai Suwannaram (1)

After crossing Mae Nam Phetchaburi (Phetchaburi River), walk about 300m along Th Phongsuriya until you come to a big temple on the right. This is Wat Yai Suwannaram, originally built during the 17th century and renovated during the reign of King Rama V (r 1868–1910). Legend has it that the gash in the ornately carved wooden doors dates to the Burmese attack of Ayuthaya. The main *bòht* (central sanctuary) is surrounded by a cloister filled with sombre Buddha images. The murals inside the *bòht* date back to the 1730s and are in good condition. Next to the *bòht*, set on a murky pond, is a beautifully designed old *hŏr đrai* (Tripitaka library).

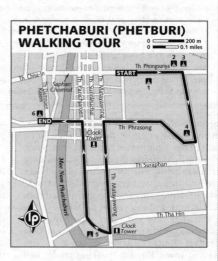

Wat Borom (2) & Wat Trailok (3)

These wát are next to each other opposite Wat Yai Suwannaram on Th Phongsuriya, a little to the east. They aren't especially attractive, but they do have distinctive monastic halls and long, graceful wooden 'dormitories' on stilts.

Wat Kamphaeng Laeng (4)

South of the two wàts, on Th Phokarong, is this pleasant, 13th-century Khmer site. It has five *brahng* (Khmer-style chimney-like towers) and part of the original *kamphaeng laeng* (laterite wall) is still standing. The front *brahng* contains a Buddha footprint. Two others contain images dedicated to famous *lŏo-ang pôr* (venerated monks), and two have been restored. If you're feeling peckish, there's a decent on-site restaurant that serves up the usual assortment of Thai treats.

Wat Ko Kaew Sutharam (5)

Follow Th Phrasong back towards the town centre, turning left onto Th Matayawong. After about 800m turn right at the clock tower and look for signs to the Ayuthaya-period Wat Ko Kaew Sutharam (Wat Ko). The *bòht* features early-18th-century murals that are among the best in Thailand. One panel depicts what appears to be a Jesuit priest wearing the robes of a Buddhist monk, while another shows other foreigners undergoing Buddhist conversion. There is also a large wooden monastic hall on stilts – similar to the ones at Wats Borom and Trailok but in much better condition.

Wat Mahathat (6)

Follow Th Panichjaroen in front of Wat Ko towards central Phetchaburi and turn left onto Th Phrasong; soon you'll reach Wat Mahathat. Its large white *brahng* can be seen from a distance – a typical late Ayuthaya–early Ratanakosin adaptation of the *brahng* of Lopburi and Phimai.

If you have extra time, continue along Th Phrasong, turn left on Th Ratchadamneon, a quick right on Th Banda-It, and make a right at Th Keeleetaya. You'll find the cobbled staircase up to the top of Khao Wang, which provides stunning views of all the temples you've just visited.

NORTHWESTERN GULF COAST

DETOUR: KAENG KRACHAN NATIONAL PARK

The largest national park in Thailand and home to the gorgeous Nam Tok Pala-U, **Kaeng Krachan** (adult/child 400/200B) is easily reached from Phetchaburi. There are caves to explore, mountains, a huge lake and excellent bird-watching opportunities (see the boxed text, p182) to be had in the evergreen forest that blankets the park. Kaeng Krachan has fantastic trekking, and it is one of the few places to see elephants roaming wild. To reach the park by car, drive south on Hwy 4 about 20km from Phetchaburi, and at the Kern Pet Junction, turn right and go 38km to Pet Dam, then 3km more to the park headquarters. Alternatively you can arrange a tour in Hua Hin (see p175). In Phetchaburi, contact Rabieng Rim Nam Guest House (below), which arranges day trips (2000B per person, minimum four people, or 6000B for a group of two) and overnight visits in rustic bungalows (2400B per person, minimum four people).

---

ageing Buddha images in various stances, many of them originally placed by King Rama IV. The best time to visit is around 5pm, when evening light pierces the ceiling, surrounding artefacts below with an ethereal glow. There are multiple chambers to wander through, which feature easily anthropomorphised rock formations, and showers of stalactites.

Another cave sanctuary – perhaps even more magical than Khao Luang – is at **Khao Banda-It** (donation encouraged; ◷ 9am-4pm), 2km west of town. English-speaking guides will lead you through the caves and answer your questions. A săhm·lór (also spelt săamláw; three-wheeled pedicab) from the city centre to either site costs about 55B; a motorcycle taxi is 40B.

Festivals & Events

The **Phra Nakhon Khiri Fair** (◷ early Feb) centres on Khao Wang and the city's historic temples. Festivities include a sound-and-light show held at the Phra Nakhon Khiri palace, temples festooned with lights, and performances of lá·kon chah·đree (classical Thai dance-drama), lí·gair 'bàh (folk dance-drama) and modern-style historical dramas. A twist on the usual beauty contest provides a showcase for Phetchaburi widows.

Sleeping & Eating

Phetchaburi is a popular stop for temple oglers, so it's surprising that such a small collection of lodging and dining options exists. Western tourists have yet to make their mark, so most chow houses are hidden in the urban fray. Try the night market on Monday evenings for cheap, tasty treats.

The town is famous for its local cuisine, which includes kôw châa pét·bù·ree (moist, chilled rice served with sweetmeats – a hot-season speciality) and the widely known môr gaang (egg custard).

Rabieng Rim Nam Guest House (☎ 0 3242 5707; 1 Th Shesrain; s/d 120/240B) Set in a large, creaky teak structure sitting along the lazy river, this popular backpacker choice has simple rooms that are nothing fancier than a wooden closet with a mattress. If you aren't impressed with the rooms, the owner will point across the bridge to the Jomklow Hotel, which is the same price. Don't bother walking over there; the place feels like a prison. Rabieng's riverside restaurant is open for all three meals, serving an enormous selection of Thai staples. Go for a yam (spicy salad) – it's yum. The wafting '70s music matches the record jackets glued to the walls (think ABBA and Elvis). Extras include laundry service (5B per piece) and motorcycle rental (250B). Trips to Kaeng Krachan National Park (above) can be organised from here.

Sun Hotel (☎ 0 3240 0000; 43/33 Soi Phetkasem 1; r 800-1500B, ste 1700B; ☒) Located opposite the funicular to Phra Nakhon Khiri, Sun Hotel is backcountry Thailand's attempt at bou-tique sophistication. The enormous rooms are mostly painted in cool greys and browns, with one brightly coloured accent wall. There's a restaurant in the open-air lobby that's quite popular with the Thai guests. The professional staff will turn your food order into room serv-ice for an extra 5B. Discounted room rates are usually given.

Royal Diamond (☎ 0 3241 1061; www.royaldiamond hotel.com; 555 Moo 1, Th Phetkasem; r 1200-2000B; ☒) It's a bit of a hike to get there, but Royal Diamond has a good selection of comfort-able lodging. The rates are pretty good value, especially for the roomy cheaper (standard) rooms, which come with wall-to-wall car-peting. The attached karaoke bar is a good place to make some noise during your visit to quiet Phetchaburi.

Getting There & Away

Buses pulling into town make several stops depending on travellers' requests. Most buses stop at the Big C (a multistorey shopping centre) and a large lime-coloured hospital. It is best to get off at the hospital (just west of Khao Wang), as it is closer to the town's sites. There are frequent air-con bus services to/from Bangkok's Southern bus station (120B, 2½ hours). The bus terminal for air-con buses to/from Bangkok is across from the night market. Figure on around 1B per kilometre to reach nearby destinations such as Cha-am (35B) and Hua Hin (50B).

Trains are less convenient than buses, unless you factor in the time taken to get to or from Bangkok's bus terminals. There are frequent services to/from Bangkok's Hualamphong train station. Fares vary depending on the train and class (2nd class around 200B, 3rd class around 100B, three hours).

Getting Around

Sǎhm·lór and motorcycle taxis go anywhere in the town centre for 30B; you can also charter them for the whole day (from 300B). Sǒrng·tǎa·ou (small pickup trucks) cost 10B to 20B around town. Rabieng Rim Nam Guest House rents out motorcycles (250B per day).

CHA-AM

อำเภอชะอำ

pop 65,500

After Hua Hin struck it big when the king moved in, the quiet fishing town was transformed into a cosmopolitan beach destination. Little Cha-am, just 20km up the coast, has managed to escape a similar fate – this sandy stretch of casuarinas and umbrellas caters mostly to weekending Thais. It can be a great alternative to a beach vacation further south: the prices are cheaper, the cuisine is geared towards Thai tastebuds and you'll have the chance to practise your bargaining skills.

Each weekend a stream of tour buses expels giddy revellers who grab a shaded spot under the millions of beachside parasols for days filled with picnics and frenzied chatter. On weekdays, Cha-am is virtually deserted, making it a great time to cash in on the lowered room rates and quiet sands.

Lately, Cha-am has become a popular stop for touring Scandinavians – you'll find countless restaurants and guesthouses proudly waving Nordic flags at the entrance.

Orientation

On the west side of Phetkasem Hwy (the 'highway') you'll find all of the civic facilities: the main post office, the train station, the police station and government offices. The road that fronts the beach, Th Ruamjit, about 2km from the train station, is a long string crammed with hotels, restaurants, souvenir stalls and public bathhouses.

Information

There are large clusters of banks and ATMs at the intersections of Th Phetkasem and Th Narathip, and Th Narathip and Th Ruamjit.

Cha-am Hospital (☎ 0 3247 1808; Th Leapkhlong) Northwest of the beach.

CV.Net (Th Ruamjit; per hr 40B; ☻ 9am-10pm) An internet café on the main drag.

Post office (Th Ruamjit) This small branch is on the main beach strip; the main office is near the train station.

TAT office (☎ 0 3247 1005; tatphet@tat.or.th; 500/51 Th Phetkasem; ☻ 8.30am-4.30pm) Has English-speaking staff and information on Cha-am, Phetchaburi, Hua Hin and Prachuap Khiri Khan.

Tourist police (☎ 0 3251 5995, emergency 1155; cnr Th Ruamjit & Th Narathip)

Sights & Activities

The beautiful **Wat Nerancharama**, on Th Chaolai, features an unusual six-armed Buddha statue. Each hand covers a sensory organ in a symbolic gesture denying the senses – kinda like 'see no evil, hear no evil, speak no evil'.

Colourful Cha-am is largely the domain of Thai tourists who spend their holidays under giant parasols along the beach. If you abide by the 'when in Rome…' philosophy, you can hire a beach chair anywhere along the sand. At the end of the day, follow your fellow travellers to one of the many **public bathhouses** along the main strip (5B to 10B).

Volunteering

If you love animals and aren't afraid of a bit of hard work, then consider a stint at the **Wildlife Friends of Thailand Rescue Centre** (☎ 0 3245 8135; rescue centre www.wfft.org, volunteering www.wildlifevolunteer.org). Based 35km northwest of Cha-am, the centre cares for an entire menagerie of creatures

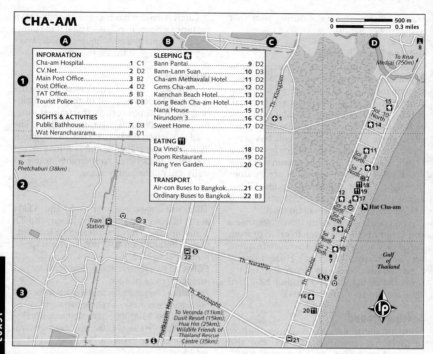

CHA-AM

INFORMATION	
Cha-am Hospital	1 C1
CV.Net	2 D2
Main Post Office	3 B2
Post Office	4 D2
TAT Office	5 B3
Tourist Police	6 D3

SIGHTS & ACTIVITIES	
Public Bathhouse	7 D3
Wat Neranchararama	8 D1

SLEEPING	
Bann Pantai	9 D2
Bann-Lann Suan	10 D3
Cha-am Methavalai Hotel	11 D2
Gems Cha-am	12 D2
Kaenchan Beach Hotel	13 D2
Long Beach Cha-am Hotel	14 D1
Nana House	15 D1
Nirundorn 3	16 C3
Sweet Home	17 D2

EATING	
Da Vinci's	18 D2
Poom Restaurant	19 D2
Rang Yen Garden	20 C3

TRANSPORT	
Air-con Buses to Bangkok	21 C3
Ordinary Buses to Bangkok	22 B3

rescued from animal shows and exploitative owners. An average day could involve feeding sun bears, building enclosures for macaques and establishing island refuges for gibbons. Volunteering costs US$140 per week, including all accommodation and meals. Volunteers are expected to stay for two to three months.

Sleeping

Sleeping options run from hovel-like guest-houses to futuristic boutique hotels. The seaside lodging in central Cha-am is tightly packed and generally in need of renovation (some exceptions to the rule are listed following). Consider booking ahead on the weekend, and expect prices to increase or decrease for any number of seemingly illogical reasons.

BUDGET

Nirundorn 3 (☎ 0 3247 1038, 0 3243 3450; www.nirundorn.com; 247/7 Th Ruamjit; r 300-1000B; ⊠) Nirundorn is an endearing spot with clean cottages, friendly managers and cute décor details that play with positive and negative space. Fan accommodation is rather lacklustre – go for an upper-floor room for the best views.

Nana House (☎ 0 3243 3632, 0 3247 1357; www.nanahouse.net; 203/3-4 Th Ruamjit; r 700-800B; ⊠) Seems like pink and purple paint was on sale when this place was under construction. But don't let the cutesy pastels put you off; inside you'll find the best budget rooms in town. Nana House has spread across several buildings at the northern end of the strip, but all of the accommodation is comfy and sparkling clean.

MIDRANGE

Bann-Lann Suan (☎ 0 3243 3171, 0 3247 1893; www.bannlannsuan.com; 261/2 Th Ruamjit; r 800-1500B; ⊠) This trendy address is easily the most stylish midrange option squished along Cha-am's beachside road. Remember to keep your curtains shut in the evening as the rooms face one another along a narrow scrap of synthetic jungle.

Gems Cha-am (☎ 0 3243 4060-79; www.gemscha-am.com; 251 Th Chaolai; d 1400-2260B; ⊠ ☒) A large billboard at the entrance gate boldly announces that Gems was awarded a silver medal for being a 'healthy and nice hotel'. The owners seem a little too proud of their second-place finish, especially since we have a hunch that they won the title quite a while ago (it's the excessive use of speckled turquoise carpeting that clued us in). The 17th floor, also known as the 'health floor', features a comprehensive fitness centre, a sauna and an egg-shaped swimming pool.

Sweet Home (☎ 0 3241 1039; 279/1 Th Ruamjit; bungalows 1500B; ☒) It must have taken an entire forest to build Sweet Home – everything's been constructed from beautiful burnished teak. The bathrooms are surprisingly basic, but everything else oozes rustic charm, including the shaded picnic table contraptions in front of each bungalow.

Kaenchan Beach Hotel (☎ 0 3247 0777; www .kaenchanbeach.com; Th Ruamjit; bungalows 1500B, r 2150-3300B; ste 5700B; ☒ ☒) This tangerine tower is a popular midrange choice for vacationing Thais and expats. Kaenchan's spacious rooms boast loads of lacquered cherry wood furnishings and windows that face the sea. Additional bungalow-style accommodation sits behind the hotel for those who aren't too fussed about ocean views. The complimentary breakfast feels a bit like an anthropological study – it's a Thai interpretation of a Western buffet. Walk-ins can usually score 50% discounts even on the busiest weekends of the year.

Long Beach Cha-am Hotel (☎ 0 3247 2444; www .longbeach-chaam.com; 225/75 Th Ruamjit; r from 2600B; ☒ ☐ ☒) This towering, Miami-style hotel is smothered in pastels. Guests can worship the sun at the 3rd-floor outdoor pool or on the rooftop garden 11 storeys up. Long Beach is the first resort in Phetchaburi Province to be recognized as a 'green hotel' by the Green Leaf Foundation, which promotes eco-friendly tourism.

TOP END
There are numerous top-end options around Cha-am, but the most lavish resorts are located several kilometres south. Most of the pricey places in the area offer taxi shuttles to and from Hua Hin nearby.

Cha-am Methavalai Hotel (☎ 0 3243 3250-3; www .methavalai.com; 220 Th Ruamjit; r 3200-4200B, ste 6500-10,400B; ☒ ☐ ☒) Methavalai doesn't compete with the armada of sleek boutique resorts popping up along the king's coast, but there's something very charming about this older stalwart. Flowers spill from the white, terraced balconies like green pom-poms, and Thai-

style cottages hide throughout the campus of manicured foliage.

Bann Pantai (☎ 0 3243 3111; www.bannpantai.com; Th Ruamjit; r 4000-8000B; ☒ ☐ ☒) The sexiest option in the heart of Cha-am, Bann Pantai is a chic village oozing trendy décor details yanked straight out of a magazine. Sleek hotel pods sit on the edge of the amoeba-like pool, which drips a refreshing turquoise tint.

Dusit Resort (☎ 0 3252 0009; http://huahin.dusit .com; 1349 Th Phetkasem; r 7000-8000B, ste 14,000-58,000B; ☒ ☐ ☒) This stunning, colonial-style resort pretends to be in Hua Hin, however, it's technically within Cha-am's city limit, despite being several kilometres south of town. Dusit is one of the most respected names in Thai vacation luxury, and this beachside avatar is probably the flagship. Amenities include a fitness centre, minigolf course, horse-riding facilities, a pool, tennis and squash courts and polo grounds.

Veranda (☎ 0 3270 9000-99; www.verandaresortand spa.com; 737/12 Th Mung Talay; r 8400-9800B, ste 19,800B, villa 35,000-45,000B; ☒ ☐ ☒) If the Starship *Enterprise* were disassembled and turned into a beachside resort, it would probably look a bit like sleek Veranda. Muted tones and trendsetting details permeate the plush oasis, while Speedo-clad jetsetters lounge around the pool absorbing sunrays and the chic ambiance in equal measure.

Eating
There are loads of options along the main coastal drag – some are affiliated with hotels, while others are stand-alone venues and beachside food stalls.

Rang Yen Garden (☎ 0 3247 1267; 259/40 Th Ruamjit; dishes 50-180B; ☽ lunch & dinner Nov-Apr) This lovely patio-style restaurant serves up Thai favourites under the stars. It's only open in the high season.

Krua Medsai (☎ 08 1763 6070, 0 3243 0196; dishes 60-280B; ☽ dinner) This fantastic local haunt rarely registers on Cha-am's tourism radar because it sits just north of the beachside burg. Try succulent *ʿboo nim* (soft-shell crab) and order a bowl of spicy *ɖôm yam gûng* (prawn and lemongrass soup) with coconut. To find Krua Medsai, go north along the main ocean road until the rows of accommodation end; you'll pass over a small bridge and a few hundred metres later there's a large blue billboard pointing to the restaurant on the right-hand side of the road.

ourpick Poom Restaurant (☎ 0 3247 1036; 274/1 Th Ruamjit; dishes 100-200B; ☺ lunch & dinner) Poom is the restaurant of choice for weekending Thais – there's copious indoor and outdoor seating, and the long tables are conducive to a sociable evening with a large group of friends. It's slightly pricier than similar establishments, but the portions are massive, and, according to the lengthy menu, everything's 'cooked the way you lick it'. We 'licked' everything we ate.

Da Vinci's (☎ 0 3247 1871; 274/5 Th Ruamjit; mains 120-400B; ☺ lunch & dinner) Trimmed with a Euro-Asian mix of old-style lamps and shady palms, Da Vinci's chic patio is easily the classiest spot to dine in Cha-am.

Getting There & Away

All of the luxury hotels, as well as some of the midrange hotels, have shuttles to Hua Hin. Expect to pay about 300B to 450B one way.

Ordinary and air-conditioned buses stop in the town centre, on Phetkasem Hwy. Some air-conditioned buses to/from Bangkok go to the beach, stopping on Th Chaolai a few hundred metres south of the Th Narathip intersection.

Frequent bus services operating to/from Cha-am include Bangkok (around 150B, three hours), Phetchaburi (35B, 40 minutes) and Hua Hin (25B, 30 minutes).

The train station is inland on Th Narathip, west of Phetkasem Hwy, and a 30B motorcycle ride to/from the beach. From Bangkok, three train stations have daily services to Cha-am: Hualamphong (3.50pm), Sam Sen (9.27am) and Thonburi (7.15am, 1.30pm and 7.05pm). Tickets cost from 60B to 180B and the journey is around four hours. Cha-am isn't listed on the English-language train schedule – ask at the ticket counter in Bangkok to be sure the train is stopping at Cha-am.

Getting Around

From the city centre to the beach it's a quick motorcycle taxi (30B) or share taxi (10B) ride. Motorcycle taxis around town cost 30B.

Bicycles and motorbikes are available for rent all along Th Ruamjit. Motorcycles generally go for 300B per day, while the hot-pink bicycles are 20B per hour or 100B per day. They're a great way to get about town.

HUA HIN
อำเภอหัวหิน
pop 49,800

The humble fishing village of Hua Hin became the poster child for a traditional Thai beach holiday back in 1922 when King Rama IV chose the quiet site for his rambling summer palace. Today, his teak fortress is still used by his progeny when they need to unwind from the daily chore of ruling a nation. Western developers have followed suit, creating highrise skyscrapers and rambling resorts offering visitors the chance to live like the royalty up the road.

Growing development has encroached on government land, completely obstructing the ocean view from the beach road of Th Naresdamri. Girlie bars are starting to make an appearance and, although they are relegated to a few small side streets, it may be a sign of things to come. Many beachseekers are heading to nearby towns such as Cha-am (p169) or Pranburi (p179) for a quieter vacation closer to the sand. Adventure types might want to try Khao Sam Roi Yot National Park (p180).

Although the city is light on sights, there are plenty of activities to keep you busy throughout the day. Play a round of golf at one of the nearby private courses, or go horse riding on the nearby polo grounds. Make mealtime an event and try a leisurely lunch at one of the seafood restaurants jutting out over the bay along the pier. Dinners can be easily arranged at one of the charming colonial hotels around town. Evening drinks can last through the night until the sun prepares itself for another day of casting rays over this urban jungle by the sea.

Orientation

Th Naresdamri is the tourist backbone and home to a cacophony of restaurants, souvenir stalls and persistent tailors, some of whom try to get passers by into an 'original' Armani suit. Guesthouses and busy outdoor restaurants line the waterfront area, and it's here that the catches of the day flounder, awaiting a tasty fate. Small *soi* (lanes) veer off this thoroughfare and hide more guesthouses, antique teak houses, jumping bars (of the girlie and nongirlie variety) and travel agencies. It's a lively place to visit, but if you want some quiet time it may be best to stay elsewhere.

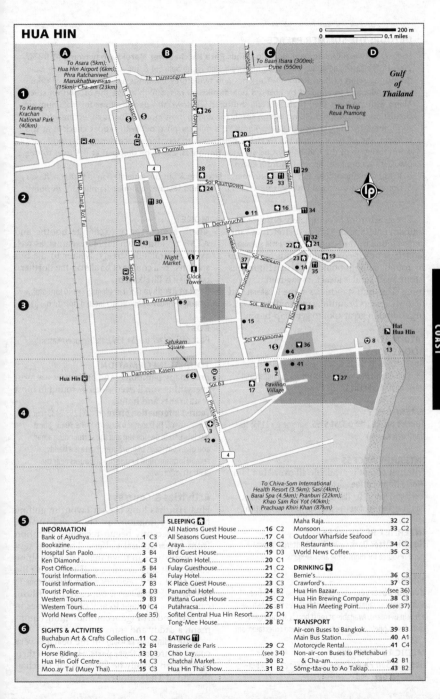

HUA HIN

INFORMATION

Bank of Ayudhya	**1** C3
Bookazine	**2** C4
Hospital San Paolo	**3** B4
Ken Diamond	**4** C3
Post Office	**5** B4
Tourist Information	**6** B4
Tourist Information	**7** B3
Tourist Police	**8** D3
Western Tours	**9** B3
Western Tours	**10** C4
World News Coffee	(see 35)

SIGHTS & ACTIVITIES

Buchabun Art & Crafts Collection	**11** C2
Gym	**12** B4
Horse Riding	**13** D3
Hua Hin Golf Centre	**14** C3
Moo.ay Tai (Muey Thai)	**15** C3

SLEEPING

All Nations Guest House	**16** C2
All Seasons Guest House	**17** C4
Araya	**18** C2
Bird Guest House	**19** D3
Chomsin Hotel	**20** C1
Fulay Guesthouse	**21** C2
Fulay Hotel	**22** B2
K Place Guest House	**23** C3
Pananchai Hotel	**24** B2
Pattana Guest House	**25** C2
Putahracsa	**26** B1
Sofitel Central Hua Hin Resort	**27** D4
Tong-Mee House	**28** B2

EATING

Brasserie de Paris	**29** C2
Chao Lay	(see 34)
Chatchai Market	**30** B2
Hua Hin Thai Show	**31** B2
Maha Raja	**32** C2
Monsoon	**33** C2
Outdoor Wharfside Seafood Restaurants	**34** C2
World News Coffee	**35** C3

DRINKING

Bernie's	**36** C3
Crawford's	**37** C3
Hua Hin Bazaar	(see 36)
Hua Hin Brewing Company	**38** C3
Hua Hin Meeting Point	(see 37)

TRANSPORT

Air-con Buses to Bangkok	**39** B3
Main Bus Station	**40** A1
Motorcycle Rental	**41** C4
Non-air-con Buses to Phetchaburi & Cha-am	**42** B1
Sŏrng-tăa-ou to Ao Takiap	**43** B2

DETOUR: THE SUMMER PALACE

Midway between Cha-am and Hua Hin stands **Phra Ratchaniwet Marukhathayawan** (☎ 0 3247 2482; Th Phetkasem; admission 90B; ☼ 8.30am-4pm Mon-Fri, to 5pm Sat & Sun), a summer palace built during the reign of King Rama VI. The one- and two-storey buildings are constructed of prime golden teak and interlinked by covered boardwalks, all raised high above the ground on stilts. Along with the high, tiled roofs and tall, shuttered windows, this design allows for maximum air circulation – a tropical building design sorely missing in most modern Thai architecture. It's now surrounded by the grounds of Camp Rama VI, a military post, but with proper check-in at the gate you should have no trouble receiving permission to tour the palace during opening hours. If you take one of the half-hourly Cha-am–Hua Hin buses, ask to be dropped at the road to this place; it's a couple of kilometres from there.

If you don't have time to visit the summer palace, check out the train station in Hua Hin. It was designed to be the royal waiting room for the king, and features a similar flamboyant design.

The beachfront is completely obscured by tourism enterprises – the best stretch of sand can be found by the Sofitel resort. This pleasant stretch of peach-coloured beach is broken up by round, smooth boulders (Hua Hin means 'stone head') and is ideal for year-round swimming. The train station lies at the western end of town, and its beautifully restored royal waiting room is a great spot to get snap-happy.

Information

BOOKSHOPS
Bookazine (☎ 0 3253 2071; 166 Th Naresdamri; ☼ 9am-10pm) Has tons of maps, books in English and travel books, including Lonely Planet guides.

EMERGENCY
Tourist police (☎ 0 3251 5995, emergency 1155; Th Damnoen Kasem)

INTERNET ACCESS
Internet access is available all over Hua Hin. **World News Coffee** (Th Naresdamri; per hr 40B; ☼ 8am-11pm; ✷) This café has fast internet connection in air-con comfort (see p177 for more information).

INTERNET RESOURCES
Hua Hin After Dark (www.huahinafterdark.com) A good resource for night-time shenanigans.

MEDIA
Hua Hin Observer (www.observergroup.net) A free, home-grown magazine with short features in English (and a few in German). Available at most hotels around town, it contains snippets on eating out, culture and entertainment.

MEDICAL SERVICES
Hospital San Paolo (☎ 0 3253 2576; 222 Th Phetkasem) For basic and emergency care.

MONEY
There are currency exchange booths and ATMs up and down Th Naresdamri, as well as on several side streets. Nearer to the bus stations are a couple of banks on the northern part of Th Phetkasem.
Bank of Ayudhya (Th Naresdamri; ☼ 10am-8pm) Exchange window conveniently located close to the beach.

POST
Post office (☎ 0 3251 1350; Th Damnoen Kasem)

TOURIST INFORMATION
Free maps, pamphlets and brochures – almost everything you'll need – can be found in most restaurants and hotels.
Tourist information office (☎ 0 3253 2433; cnr Th Phetkasem & Th Damnoen Kasem; ☼ 8.30am-8pm) Has lots of info on Hua Hin and the surrounding areas, and gives out loads of brochures. There is a handy, second location right beside the Starbucks near the central clock tower.

Activities & Courses
Hua Hin has long been a favourite golfing holiday destination for Thais and royalty, and has recently begun receiving attention from international golfers. There are several companies in town that rent out golfing equipment and arrange golf tours. **Hua Hin Golf Centre** (☎ 0 3253 1096; www.huahingolf.com; Th Naresdamri; ☼ noon-10pm), opposite the Hilton, can tailor a package to any of the courses in the area and arrange accommodation, equipment, a caddy and transfers.

Horse riding (per hr 450B) on the beach is very common around these parts. Horses and their owners can usually be found at the beach at the end of Th Damnoen Kasem.

Muay thai (Thai boxing; ☎ 0 3251 5269; 8/1 Th Phunsuk; admission 300B) matches take place every Tuesday and Friday at 9pm. The fighters aren't pros by any stretch of the imagination, but they put on a good show. If you're inspired by the *moo-ay tai* (or *muey thai*) matches and feel like partaking in a little kick boxing yourself, there's a **gym** (Th Phetkasem) south of town – just south of the hospital and market – that gives lessons (300B). Daily admission to the gym is 180B.

For some serious pampering, head to the **Barai Spa** (☎ 0 3251 1234; www.thebarai.com; 91 Th Khao Takiap) at the Hyatt Hotel, a couple of kilometres south of the city centre. This stunning, state-of-the-art retreat is so proud of its unique design details that it offers regular free guided tours of the facility.

If you wish to re-create some of the scrumptious dishes you've eaten in Thailand, visit **Buchabun Art & Crafts Collection** (☎ 0 1572 3805; www.siambeing.com/restaurant/cookingcourse; 22 Th Dechanuchit) where you can sign up for a half-day Thai cooking class with Ratthreeya Buchabun. Classes cost 1000B and include a market visit and recipe book – but they're only run if several people are interested.

Tours

Hua Hin has loads of travel agencies, most of which offer day trips to nearby places such as Phetchaburi (p165), Khao Sam Roi Yot (p180) and Kaeng Krachan (p168). You may have to wait a day or two before a quorum of tourists signs up for your desired trip.

Hua Hin Adventure Tour (☎ 0 3253 0314; www.hua hinadventuretour.com; Th Naep Khehat; 8.30am-7pm) Runs kayaking trips in the Khao Sam Roi Yot National Park (1900B), amongst several other things. Tours include pick-up from your hotel.

Ken Diamond (☎ 0 3251 3863; www.travel-huahin .com; 4/34 Th Naresdamri) A German-run outfit that has dozens of trips to destinations in the vicinity, including waterfalls, national parks, and diving and snorkelling locations. It also arranges car rentals.

Western Tours (☎ 0 3253 3303; www.westerntours huahin.com; 11 Th Damnoen Kasem) Has tours to surrounding attractions, golf packages (including equipment rentals), hotel bookings, bus tickets and help with local transportation. It's an authorised agent for Thai Airways. There's another branch on Th Amnuaysin.

Festivals & Events

The annual **Hua Hin Jazz Festival** (http://jazzfestival huahin.com; mid-Jun) is held near the beachfront and showcases Thailand's best jazz talent.

Sleeping

Lodging in Hua Hin generally falls on the extreme ends of the pricing spectrum. There are some great deals around town for the budget traveller, and some of Thailand's best boutique hotels for those who can drop the big bucks. Cha-am and Pranburi lie around 20km north and south respectively, and offer some fantastic sleeping options as well.

Hua Hin's proximity to Bangkok means that rates sometimes skyrocket on weekends (especially holiday weekends), while weekdays are noticeably less expensive.

BUDGET

All Nations Guest House (☎ 0 3251 2747; www.geocities .com/allnationsguesthouse; 10-10/1 Th Dechanuchit; d with shared bathroom 350-600B) All Nation's backpacker lodging is simple, but it gets the job done. The lobby bar is decorated with foreign flags and currencies, and the televisions are conveniently stuck on the sports channel. Single travellers get a 50% discount.

Pattana Guest House (☎ 0 3251 3393; huahinpat tana@hotmail.com; 52 Th Naresdamri; r 350-600B) Blink and you'll miss the narrow soi that leads to little Pattana. This charming teak habitat is adorned with a variety of colourful collectibles, including a giant wooden rooster, toy ships and endless stacks of tattered paperbacks.

Bird Guest House (☎ 0 3251 1630; birdguesthousehua hin@hotmail.com; 31/2 Th Naresdamri; r 400-600B;) Bird doesn't sing like it used to, but it's a decent budget choice if you're seeking out a charming, pier-shanty ambiance. It's a bit smaller than some of the other guesthouses nearby, so there's a homely, relaxed atmosphere.

Tong-Mee House (☎ 0 3253 0725; 1 Soi Raumpown; r 550B;) This hidden gem is tucked away along a quiet residential *soi*. Fresh potted plants cheer the stairwell, and although the rooms are cosy (ie small), they have polished wooden floors and immaculate bathrooms. There's a neat little café, a small library and plenty of genuine smiles.

Panuchai Hotel (☎ 0 3251 1707, 0 3251 1633; 71 Th Naep Khehat; d incl breakfast 650B;) Panuchai feels like a small European hotel with its teeny check-in desk and thin, rickety elevator. The rooms have small windows and are decked out in faded floral patterns.

K Place Guest House (☎ 0 3251 1396; kplaceus@yahoo .com; 116 Th Naresdamri; r 800-1000B;) Smack in the heart of things on Th Naresdamri, but tucked away behind the associated minimart,

---

LIVE LIKE A KING

The king made Hua Hin his royal summer residence back in 1922, and today, you too can find your very own palace in the form of a stunning, world-class resort. While the following options may break the bank, they are sure worth the splurge.

- **Chiva-Som International Health Resort** (right; Hua Hin)
- **Evasons** (p179; Pranburi)
- **Veranda** (p171; Cha-am)
- **Putahracsa** (right; Hua Hin)
- **Asara** (right; Hua Hin)

K Place's spacious rooms are good value, but not all have natural light.

MIDRANGE

Fulay Guesthouse (☎ 0 3251 3145; www.fulay-huahin .com; 110/1 Th Naresdamri; r 750-1500B; 🔀) One of the best pier guesthouses jutting out over the sea, Fulay has charming marine-themed rooms with fresh coats of white and blue paint, and the odd framed portrait of a wooden frigate. Guests fall asleep to the soft crashing of the waves below.

Fulay Hotel (☎ 0 3251 3670, 0 3251 3145; fishshop@ hotmail.com; 110/1 Th Naresdamri; r 850-1500B; 🔀) Across from Fulay Guesthouse is this narrow, teak-façade hotel right in the thick of things. The hotel is good value, and there's also a romantic, fancy-looking restaurant downstairs.

Chomsin Hotel (☎ 0 3251 5348; www.chomsin huahin.com; 130/4 Th Chomsin; r 900-1200B; 🔀) Friendly Chomsin is a great addition to the spread of low-priced accommodation in Hua Hin. The rooms are immaculate, and feature polished hardwood floors, modern bathrooms and sun-filled picture windows.

All Seasons Guesthouse (☎ 0 3251 5151; Soi 63, 77/18-19 Th Phetkasem; r 1000-1300B; 🔀) All Seasons has spacious, sun-soaked rooms with enormous bathrooms befitting a top-end resort. The friendly, UK-born owner rents out DVD players, so you can finally watch any purchases you pirated. The seven rooms can fill up quickly so it's best to call ahead.

Araya (☎ 0 3253 1130, 08 6339 9563; www.araya -residence.com; 15/1 Th Chomsin; r 1200-1700B; 🔀 🖳) The shiny, tangerine façade is very hard to miss. On the inside, guests will be pleased to find beautiful hardwood floors and modern furni-

ture that feels a bit like 'IKEA meets Thailand'. There's complimentary wi-fi throughout and each room's lavatory sparkles with a different primary colour (we liked the vibrant, radioactive lettuce colour the most).

TOP END

Dune (☎ 0 3251 5051; www.dunehuahin.com; 5/5 Th Naep Kaehat; r incl breakfast from 5800B; 🔀 🖳 🛒) Little Dune has five luxurious suites stocked with a cache of boutiquey design details. Cool club beats gently waft through the air as guests recline on imported furniture made from handcrafted textiles.

Putahracsa (☎ 0 3253 1470; www.putahracsa.com; 22/65 Th Naep Khehat; r from 7000B; 🔀 🖳 🛒) How do you say 'swanky' in Thai? It's 'Putahracsa'. This stunning complex features a variety of structures shaped like cubic Tetris pieces, which sit along a beachfront lawn with blades of bright green grass. The design is elegant yet simple, with teak veneers covering smooth white walls. This terrific resort is hard to spell, but definitely easy to love.

Asara (☎ 0 3254 7555; www.asaravillaandsuite.com; 35 Hua Hin Soi 5; r from 8000B; 🔀 🖳 🛒) Beautiful Asara is a veritable village of modern villas. Located just north of the city centre, this lagoon-filled property boasts ocean vistas, private plunge pools, two restaurants and a vast spa offering world-class spa packages. The friendly staff tend to guests with ear-to-ear smiles.

Sofitel Central Hua Hin Resort (Hua Hin Railway Hotel; ☎ 0 3251 2021-38; www.accorhotels.com/asia; 1 Th Damnoen Kasem; r from 8000B, ste from 12,000B; 🔀 🖳 🛒) In 1922 the State Railway of Thailand (then the Royal Thai Railway) extended the national rail network to Hua Hin to allow easier access to the Hua Hin summer palace. The area proved to be a popular vacation spot with the general population too, so in the following year the Hua Hin Railway Hotel was built – a graceful colonial-style inn by the sea. Today the property is under the management of Accor's Sofitel branch, and it remains a beautiful campus with plenty of beach views, three pools, rolling grounds and first-class spa services. Discounts of up to 40% may be possible during the week and in the low season.

Chiva-Som International Health Resort (☎ 0 3253 6536; www.chivasom.com; 73/4 Phetkasem Hwy; 3-night package US$1650-4500; 🔀 🖳 🛒) Set along seven acres of beach, Chiva-Som is the ultimate vacation playground for the overworked, overstressed and overpaid. The name means 'haven of life' in Thai-Sanskrit, and the staff of 200 fuse Eastern and Western approaches to wellness with planned nutrition, step and aqua aerobics, and Thai, Swedish or underwater massage. Rates include three meals per day along with health and fitness consultations, spa treatments and recreational activities. Lengthier packages are also available (up to one month), as are specialized detox and fitness regimes.

Eating

Seafood rules the culinary roost in Hua Hin and fresh delights from the sea are available all over town. You can get seafood snacks on the beach throughout the day; cracked crab and cold Singha beer can be ordered without leaving your deckchair. The best seafood to eat in Hua Hin is *Ƀlah săm·lee* (cotton fish or kingfish), *Ƀlah grà·pong* (perch), *Ƀlah mèuk* (squid), *hŏy má·laang pôo* (mussels) and *Ƀoo* (crab). The concentration of wharfside outdoor seafood restaurants on Th Naresdamri, at the intersection of Th Dechanuchit, offers the widest choice in ocean fare.

Chao Lay (☎ 0 3251 3436; 15 Th Naresdamri; dishes 60–400B; ☼ breakfast, lunch & dinner) Probably the best of the wharf restaurants, this place certainly manages to fill its two levels of pier seating. There's a veritable fish market out front where you can choose your catch of the day, and a small army of waiters to deliver the end product.

Maha Raja (☎ 0 3253 0347; 25 Th Naresdamri; dishes 80–200B; ☼ lunch & dinner) With gaudy décor fit for a king, this place provides officious service typical of Indian restaurants in Thailand. The dining room has a pink theme throughout with ostentatious chandeliers, and solid Indian cuisine at respectable prices. You'll get a free welcome drink, too.

Baan Itsara (☎ 0 3253 0574; 7 Th Naebkhehars; dishes 90–400B; ☼ lunch & dinner) Baan Itsara is a destination for aficionados of the ocean's produce. Considered by some to be one of the best seafood places in town, this restaurant has tables right on the ocean and a small imported-wine list. The tiger prawns in sweet basil sauce are a perennial favourite.

Monsoon (☎ 0 3253 1062; 62 Th Naresdamri; dishes 100–250B, set menu 390B; ☼ lunch & dinner) Beautiful Monsoon feels like a far-flung railway station deep within IndoChine. There are large leather chairs plucked directly from a posh lodge and the menu offers imported teas and a mix of regional and foreign cuisine. The 50B water surcharge was the only thing that marred the experience.

World News Coffee (Th Naresdamri; breakfast 150B, coffee 60–120B; ☼ breakfast, lunch & dinner) This Starbucks-esque, popular breakfast venue is run by the nearby Hilton. Breakfasts and bagels are proffered here, as are various coffee drinks. There's an excellent selection of newspapers and magazines to digest with your morning brew. Internet access is available for 40B per hour.

Brasserie de Paris (☎ 0 3253 0637; 3 Th Naresdamri; dishes 180–500B; ☼ breakfast, lunch & dinner) An actual French chef serves up real French food (crab Hua-Hin is a speciality) in this lovely, light and airy restaurant. There's a good view of *la mer* from upstairs.

Hua Hin Thai Show (☎ 08 1400 7030, 0 3251 1423; 67/2 Dechanuchit; set menu 350–450B; ☼ dinner) Just off the main night-market street, this open-air Thai restaurant draws in the crowds with free nightly performances – try to make the Wednesday night classical and folk Thai dance show. The food's not bad either, and there's nice mood lighting with tables set around Thai-style pagodas – it's only mildly cheesy.

Sasi (☎ 08 1880 4004, 0 3251 2488; Th Khao Takiap; set menu 350–450B; ☼ dinner) Located near the Hyatt Regency Hotel, Sasi is another pleasant option for a traditional Thai dinner accompanied by a performance featuring Thai theatre and dance.

Chatchai Market (Th Dechanuchit) This colourful and inexpensive market is one of Hua Hin's major attractions. Vendors gather nightly in the centre of town (off Th Phetkasem) to fry, steam, grill, parboil or bake fresh gulf seafood for hordes of hungry Thais. Don't leave town without trying the famous *roti Hua Hin* (10B) served at this market, a delicious snack made with special dough and filled with sweets such as strawberries, custard or raisins.

Drinking

Countless faràng bars can be found at the Hua Hin Bazaar and on the little soi off Th Naresdamri and Th Damnoen Kasem. Some of these offer a Thai-hostess atmosphere, but a few bill themselves as sports bars and have a widescreen TV tuned to events around the world.

Hua Hin Brewing Company (Th Naresdamri) This maze of barges, decks and masts is one of the most popular entertainment venues around. There's often live music and it attracts a mix of hotel guests, expats, tourists and some

MOO·AY TAI (MUAY THAI)

Moo·ay tai (often spelt as *muay thai*; Thai boxing) is the most popular spectator sport in Thailand. When watching a *moo·ay tai* match, it seems like the only goal is to butcher your opponent. However, this ancient sport is steeped in tradition, and its meaning goes beyond the cacophony of flying limbs.

Moo·ay tai is derived from an early martial art known as *grà·bèe grà·borng* (stick and sword), which originated in Southeast Asia more than 2000 years ago. Thankfully the sticks and swords are left behind in today's popular ring-based version. *Moo·ay tai* is known as the 'science of eight limbs' because fighters can use not only their hands and feet, but elbows and knees as well. In the ring, boxing techniques are used, as well as hard kicking, elbows, knees and stand-up grappling – the low kick to the thigh is a distinguishing technique frequently used in *moo·ay tai*. Points are awarded for every landed blow and even blows below the belt are allowed, though a hit to the groin is not considered a 'valid' target.

Before each bout, opponents will perform the *wâi kroo*. Also known as the *ram moo·ay* (boxing dance), these varied performances are elaborate recitals that pay respect to the fighter's instructor, as well as acting as a warm up and often stirring up the crowd. Each *wâi kroo* is unique, and if two fighters execute the same *wâi kroo*, they will not fight because it is understood that they have the same teacher.

Young Thai men all over the country train as *moo·ay tai* fighters; for many it's their only way out of poverty. The sport of *moo·ay tai* is highly revered and is intertwined with religion and cultural history – championship fighters become instant national heroes.

Moo·ay tai matches take place all over Thailand, particularly during festivals and public holidays. Most Tourism Authority of Thailand (TAT) agencies have information about upcoming matches and training programs.

local 'ladies of the night'. It's not at all sleazy, however – it's attached to one of the classiest hotels in town.

Bernie's (Hua Hin Bazaar, Th Damnoen Kasem) A British-run sports bar – the owner is a big golf nut with loads of info on swinging a club in the area.

Hua Hin Meeting Point (☎ 0 3253 1132; 3 Th Phunsuk) The corner location ensures this place sees plenty of action. It serves meals but is also a popular place for a few drinks. There's indoor seating around a slick, modern white bar (in the comfort of air-con) or sit on the outside patio, which has a giant projection screen.

Crawford's (☎ 0 3251 1517; 5 Th Phunsuk) Hua Hin's favourite Irish bar has imported everything directly from the motherland (minus the cold weather). There are two wood-finished levels of air-conditioned, Guinness-drinking comfort. It's not too rowdy and there's a friendly expat 'drink with your mates' mood here, as well as the occasional sports match on one of its many televisions.

Getting There & Away

SGA (☎ in Hua Hin 0 3252 2300, in Bangkok 0 2134 3233; www.sga.aero) flies a 12-seat shuttle three times a day (one-way 3100B, 40 minutes,

11.45am, 3pm and 6.30pm) from Bangkok's Suvarnabhumi airport to Hua Hin.

There are air-con buses to/from Bangkok's Southern bus station (171B, 3½ hours, every half hour). These leave Hua Hin 70m north of Rajana Garden House on Th Sasong (outside the Siripetchkasem Hotel).

The main government bus station, on Th Liap Thang Rot Fai, has air-con buses to many destinations throughout the country. Be sure to ignore the touts here and go to the window for assistance and ticket purchase. There is at least one air-con bus per day to each destination: Phetchaburi (80B, 1½ hours), Cha-am (40B, 30 minutes), Prachuap Khiri Khan (80B, 1½ hours), Chumphon (160B, four hours), Phuket (378B, eight hours), Krabi (389B, eight hours), Koh Samui (320B, nine hours) and Songkhla (457B, 11 hours). Frequent non-air-con buses to Phetchaburi (50B, 1½ hours) and Cha-am (25B, 30 minutes) leave from near the intersection of Th Chomsin and Th Phetkasem.

There are several trains running to/from Bangkok's Hualamphong train station (2nd class 292B to 382B, 3rd class 234B to 294B, four hours) and other stations on the southern railway line.

Getting Around

The airport is 6km north of town – about a 150B taxi ride away.

Local buses (10B) and sŏrng·tǎa·ou (10B) to Ao Takiap, for resorts south of Hua Hin, leave from the corner of Th Sasong and Th Dechanuchit.

Even though sǎhm·lór fares in Hua Hin have been set by the municipal authorities, haggling is still often required. Some sample fares: from the train station to the beach, 20B; from the air-con bus terminal to Th Naresdamri, 30B to 40B (depending on the size of your bags); and from Chatchai Market to Tha Thiap Reua Pramong, 20B. Most drivers will ask for at least twice this much.

Motorcycles and bicycles can be rented from a couple of places on Th Damnoen Kasem near the Sofitel Central Hua Hin Resort. Motorcycle rates are reasonable: 200B to 250B per day for 100cc to 125cc bikes. Occasionally, larger bikes (400cc to 750cc) are available for 600B to 700B a day. Car and 4WD rental can also be arranged at most travel agencies, including Ken Diamond (p175) and Western Tours (p175). Expect to pay around 1300B to 1500B for a small Suzuki 4WD. Bicycle rental costs 50B to 100B per day.

PRANBURI
ปราณบุรี
75,000

Pranburi, about 35km south of Hua Hin, is quickly becoming the choice destination for high-end travellers heading along the king's coast. Flanked by verdant pineapple orchards and creamy brown sands, this little hamlet has caught the eye of cinematographers capitalising on the area's natural beauty and seclusion.

The region of Pranburi sits slightly inland from the ocean, while the beach area is commonly known as Pak Nam Pran. A long, sandy road snakes directly along the coast cutting a path between the seaside resorts and the cool, crashing tides.

Pranburi Hospital (☎ 0 3262 1757, 0 3262 1767)
Tourist Police (☎ 0 3251 5995, emergency 1155)

Sleeping & Eating

As the region continues to increase in popularity, several new hotels are popping up. There are a few independent restaurants and bars along the main beach street, but most guests tend to dine at the fantastic resort restaurants.

Huaplee Lazy Beach (☎ 0 3263 0555; www.huapleelazybeach.com; 163 Moo 4; r 3500-7000B; 🗷) Charming, sun-drenched rooms line a miniature pasture by the sea. The interiors are white-on-white with an occasional blue accent that feels distinctly Mediterranean. Handcrafted furniture and little knick-knacks such as seashell mobiles and colourful teapots give the Lazy Beach an extra pinch of *je ne sais quoi*.

Evasons (☎ 0 3262 2111; www.sixsenses.com/evason-huahin; 9 Moo 5, Pak Nam Pran; r & bungalows 5500-18,000B; 🗷 🖳 🗷) This stunning resort is actually made up of two different properties: one section offers charming hotel-style lodging and the other zone features ultraprivate villas, some with exquisite plunge pools. The super-smiley staff don pastel uniforms while catering to guests' every whim and shuttling them around the campus and beyond. Several fantastic adventure activities can be

NORTHWESTERN GULF COAST

MANAGING MANGROVES

In 1996 the king and queen visited the quiet region of Pranburi and were shocked to find that extensive shrimp farming had marred the land. The ground conditions were inhospitable, turning this once thriving estuary into a veritable desert. A reclamation project was immediately implemented to restore the coastal forest and, after 12 long years, the **mangrove park** (☎ 0 3263 2255; Rte 4, Pranburi Estuary; admission free; ⏰ 8.30am-4.30pm) has finally opened its doors to visitors.

Local environmentalists have now taken on a new role – they have become guides who lead informal tours through the state-of-the-art interpretive centre and then continue along the raised boardwalk that winds through the forest of gnarled branches. On our tour, the guide offered personal stories detailing the reclamation of sullied land. He was raised in a nearby town and worked on a shrimp farm as a youth. When the land became exhausted many people lost their jobs, which prompted him to become interested in sustainable endeavours. 'It's important', he said, 'for Thailand to develop better habits when harvesting the kingdom's natural products. If we continue to disrespect the land, we will soon have nothing left to reap.'

arranged, including biking, hiking, diving and other water sports. There are two on-site spas offering an eclectic assortment of treatments in a garden setting that blends in with the naturally occurring foliage. The resort has an entire department dedicated to environmental management and conversation; the primary focus is limiting the impact of tourism and fishing on the surrounding nature.

Aleenta (☎ 0 2508 5333; www.aleenta.com; 183 Moo 4; r 5700-20,000B; ❷ ▣ ▨) Delicate Aleenta offers villas and suites set within an adobe-and-thatch fortress. Rambling staircases cross the sandy grounds like an Escher print, and the quiet rooms fuse modern amenities and natural textiles. This place prides itself on providing a secluded getaway – almost to the point of snootiness.

Getting There & Away

There are two **minivan services** (☎ 08 6007 4742, 08 5242 5268) that transport passengers between Bangkok and Pranburi (220B). The communication might be a little tricky over the phone since the operators speak very little English. The pick-up and drop-off site is Pranburi's sole 7-Eleven, and in Bangkok, plan to get out at the Victory Monument. It is best to book ahead as these shuttles can fill up rather quickly. If you are trying to connect to a city between Pranburi and Bangkok, simply inform the driver of your intended destination. Taxis from Hua Hin cost 400B, or 500B from Hua Hin airport.

KHAO SAM ROI YOT NATIONAL PARK
อุทยานแห่งชาติเขาสามร้อยยอด

Long ago, a wooden merchant ship was trolling the coast, and when it reached this region it sprang a leak and rapidly began to sink. Miraculously, all 300 individuals aboard swam to shore escaping a watery grave. From then on, the area became known as Khao Sam Roi Rot, which roughly means 'land of the 300 saved'. After many retellings, this nickname started to change – the memory of the ancient ship became overshadowed by the region's natural virtues, which include myriad skyscraping mountains. The 'rot' ('saved') changed to 'yot' and today this jagged jungle is known as the land of the 300 peaks.

Recently, this tropical realm was given a national park status preserving the stunning mounds, caves and trails from developers' hands. The area is home to a vibrant ecosystem that includes friendly dusky langur monkeys, barking deer, Javan mongooses, otters and palm civets. Bird-watchers also hold the park in high esteem, since over 300 species of migratory birds descend on the region's ponds and mangroves each year (see the boxed text, p182).

Other wildlife you may be able to spot around Khao Sam Roi Yot includes the crab-eating macaque, slow lorises, Malayan pangolins, fishing cats, serows and monitor lizards. Unfortunately, as is the case with many of Thailand's natural resources, the encroachment of industry (in this case shrimp farms) is taking its toll on the natural habitat of the park's varied fauna.

Information

There are three park headquarters (Hat Laem Sala, Ban Rong Jai and Ban Khao Daeng) and three visitors centres (Hat Laem Sala, Hat Sam Phraya and Ban Khao Daeng) where you can obtain information on the area. A nature study centre lies at the end of a 1.5km road leading north from Ban Rong Jai. There are a couple of checkpoints – one on the road south from Pranburi and the other on the road east of Hwy 4. You'll have to pay admission (adult/child under 14 years 400/200B) at these checkpoints or, if you've left the park and are returning, show proof that you've already paid.

Sights & Activities

Well worth the steep 45-minute climb, the **Khao Daeng viewpoint** is reached by a well-marked trail beginning 500m from Ban Khao Daeng. The views from the top are breathtaking and the vista spans the length of the park, from the limestone cliffs to the wiggling coastline below.

BEACHES

Both of the park's beaches have plenty of facilities, including food stalls, picnic areas and washrooms.

Hat Laem Sala, a sandy beach flanked on three sides by dry limestone hills and casuarinas, has a small visitors centre, a restaurant, bungalows and a camping area. The trail to Tham Phraya Nakhon starts here. Boats to the beach (250B return), which take up to 10 people, can be hired from Bang Pu. You can also reach the beach from Bang Pu via a steep trail (20 minutes' walk).

Hat Sam Phraya, 5km south of Hat Laem Sala, is about 1km in length and has a restaurant and washrooms.

CAVES

The three main caves in this park are all worth a detour.

Tham Phraya Nakhon is probably the most photographed cave in Thailand and can be reached by boat or foot. The boat trip takes about 30 minutes there and back, while it's 30 minutes each way by foot along a steep, rocky 430m trail from Hat Laem Sala. The cave is made up of two large sinkholes, and when the sun shines through in the early morning the effect is truly mystical. In one cave there's a royal *săh·lah* (often spelt *sala;* an 'open room' with a roof but no walls). It was built for King Chulalongkorn, who would stop off here when travelling back and forth between Bangkok and Nakhon Si Thammarat. Check out 'Pagoda Rock', covered with colourful talismans, and 'Crocodile Rock', which actually looks more like an alligator.

Tham Kaew, 2km from the Bang Pu turn-off, features a series of chambers connected by narrow passageways; you enter the first cavern by a ladder. The stalactites and limestone formations glitter with calcite crystals as though they were encrusted with diamonds (hence the cave's name, Jewel Cave). Tham Kaew is best visited in the company of a park guide because of the dangerous footing. Guides can be arranged at Bang Pu.

Tham Sai is a hill cave near Ban Khung Tanot, about 2.3km from the main road between Laem Sala and Sam Phraya beaches. You can rent lamps for a small fee from a shelter near the cave's mouth. A 280m trail leads up the hillside to the cave, which features a large single cavern. Be mindful of steep drop-offs in the cave.

Sleeping & Eating

Just outside the northerly checkpoint, roads turn off towards a long sandy bay and Hat Sam Roi Yot. Here, several private resorts offer midrange to top-end accommodation along the uninterrupted and spotless beach. This bay is supposedly a breeding ground for a school of dolphins.

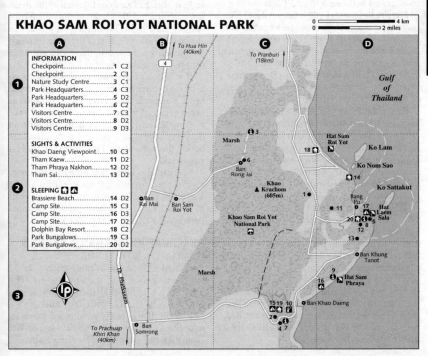

KHAO SAM ROI YOT NATIONAL PARK

INFORMATION	
Checkpoint	1 C2
Checkpoint	2 C3
Nature Study Centre	3 C1
Park Headquarters	4 C3
Park Headquarters	5 D2
Park Headquarters	6 C2
Visitors Centre	7 C3
Visitors Centre	8 D2
Visitors Centre	9 D3

SIGHTS & ACTIVITIES	
Khao Daeng Viewpoint	10 C3
Tham Kaew	11 D2
Tham Phraya Nakhon	12 D2
Tham Sai	13 D2

SLEEPING	
Brassiere Beach	14 D2
Camp Site	15 C3
Camp Site	16 D3
Camp Site	17 D2
Dolphin Bay Resort	18 C2
Park Bungalows	19 C3
Park Bungalows	20 D2

To Hua Hin (40km)
To Pranburi (18km)
To Prachuap Khiri Khan (40km)

Gulf of Thailand

Marsh
Ban Rong Jai
Khao Krachom (605m)
Khao Sam Roi Yot National Park
Ban Rai Mai
Ban Sam Roi Yot
Marsh
Ban Somrong
Hat Sam Roi Yot
Ko Lam
Ko Nom Sao
Ko Sattakut
Bang Pu
Hat Laem Sala
Ban Khung Tanot
Hat Sam Phraya
Ban Khao Daeng

0   4 km
0   2 miles

FOR THE BIRDS

Kaeng Krachan and Khao Sam Roi Yot National Parks both vie for the title of Thailand's top bird-watching spot. We'll leave the battle for that honour to the ornithologists, but there's no denying that these world-renowned birding sites are a feast for avid avian-spotters' eyes.

Kaeng Krachan is so huge it is still largely unexplored. So far, over 250 bird species have been recorded in the tropical, broad-leaved evergreen forests of this national treasure. The best places for bird-watching are in the northern parts of the park, particularly around Huai Nam Yen. With a bit of patience, birds you're likely to see here include the rufous-bellied eagle, oriental hobby, wreath hornbill, silver-breasted broadbill, banded broadbill, yellow-vented pigeon, chestnut-breasted malkoha, great barbet, white-throated laughing thrush, white-hooded babbler, black-thighed falconet, brown fish owl, grey peacock-pheasant, bay woodpecker, grey treepie, large scimitar-babbler, blue pitta, yellow-bellied warbler and narcissus fly-catcher.

In Khao Sam Roi Yot National Park the best locales to look are around marshland areas, both along the coast and near the nature study centre. The park lies at the intersection of the East Asian and Australian fly ways, and as many as 300 migratory and resident bird species have been recorded here. Spotters can see the yellow bittern, cinnamon bittern, purple swamp hen, water rail, ruddy-breasted crake, bronze-winged jacana, grey heron, painted stork, whistling duck, spotted eagle and black-headed ibis. The park has Thailand's largest freshwater marsh, along with mangroves and mudflats, and is one of only three places in the country where the purple heron breeds.

You can pitch your own tent at camp sites near the Khao Daeng Viewpoint, at Hat Laem Sala or at Hat Sam Phraya. There are basic restaurants at all these locations, serving decent food priced between 30B and 120B.

Forestry Department (☎ in Bangkok 0 2562 0760; camp site per person 30B, bungalows per 5-6 people 1200-1400B, per 6-9 people 1600-2200B) The forestry department hires out yellow and green bungalows with metal roofing at Hat Laem Sala and at the visitors centre near the Khao Daeng viewpoint. Two-person tents are available for rent at these spots for 150B per night.

Dolphin Bay Resort (☎ 0 3255 9333; www.dolphinbay resort.com; 227 Moo 4, Phu Noi; r & bungalows 1290-11,000B; 🏊 🍴) This well-priced option is a great place to take the family. There's plenty of space to frolic around and the large swimming pool has a slippery slide. A wide range of trips is on offer to nearby islands and peaks around the national park.

our pick Brassiere Beach (☎ 0 3263 0555, 0 2511 1397; brassierebeach@hotmail.com; 210 Moo 5, Tambol Samroiyod; villas from 4000B; 🏊 🍴) When you check into Brassiere Beach, the first thing you'll notice are two breastlike islands bobbing just off the coast (hence the name). The second thing you'll notice is the key to your room – it's attached to a colourful miniature bra. Each of the stunning Mediterranean-style villas has loads of personalised charm. When we visited, a Thai pop star was getting ready to shoot a music video on the premises.

Getting There & Away

The park is approximately 40km south of Hua Hin and is best seen by car or motorcycle. From Hua Hin take Hwy 4 (Th Phetkasem) to Pranburi. In Pranburi turn left at the main intersection and 4km later, at the police substation, turn right. From there, it's 19km to the park's entrance. If you're trying to reach the park from the south, there's an entrance off Hwy 4 – make a right at Km 286.5.

If you don't have your own wheels, catch a bus or train to Pranburi (possible from both Bangkok and Hua Hin, as well as other regional places). From Pranburi, take a sŏrng·tăa·ou (50B, every half-hour during daylight hours) to Bang Pu, a small village inside the park. Bang Pu is virtually on Hat Laem Sala.

You can also hire a taxi for 350B, or a motorcycle taxi for 300B, from Pranburi all the way to the park. Be sure to mention you want to go to the ù·tá·yahn hàang châht (national park) rather than Ban Sam Roi Yot.

PRACHUAP KHIRI KHAN & AROUND
อ.เมืองประจวบคีรีขันธ์

Prachuap town is the administrative centre for the province with the same name. The little burg is light on attractions, but it's an OK place to stretch your legs and grab a bite to eat. If you really need some exercise, hike the 418 steps to the golden-spired **Wat Thammikaram**, established by King Rama IV.

Hordes of monkeys provide endless entertainment along the way. The view from the top stretches west to Myanmar's border, only 11km away.

Fishing still provides the main source of income for the town's inhabitants and you're likely to see brightly painted vessels bobbing up and down the coastline like rainbow-coloured sea birds. Not surprisingly, the seafood here is excellent and considerably cheaper than at the more popular tourist hang-outs along the coast.

Uncrowded beaches and broad bays sweep north and south around town, and locals are always happy to see the few faràng that make the effort to get off the well-trodden tourist trail. **Ao Manao** and **Hat Wa Kaw**, both south of Prachuap town, and **Ao Noi**, to the north, all have calm casuarina-lined dunes along quiet rolling waters.

Orientation & Information

The city of Prachuap Khiri Khan stretches along the 8km-long Ao Prachuap. While the bay isn't the best for swimming, a well-lit esplanade runs the length of the town, and is ideal for morning or twilight ambling.

There are two unsigned internet cafés (open 8am to 10pm) right next to each other on Th Sarachip, charging 30B per hour.

Bangkok Bank (cnr Th Maitri Ngam & Th Sarachip)

Kasikorn Bank (Th Phitak Chat)

Police station (☎ 0 3261 1148; Th Kong Kiat) Just west of Th Sarachip.

Post office (cnr Th Maitri Ngam & Th Suseuk) Right by a telephone office with internet access.

Tourist office (☎ 0 3261 1491; Th Chai Thaleh) At the northern end of town. The staff speak good English and offer detailed information of the town.

Sleeping

The accommodation options in Prachuap Khiri Khan leave a lot to be desired, but there are a few passable establishments here and some better ones a few kilometres north and south of town, in particular at Ao Manao.

Yuttichai Hotel (☎ 0 3261 1055; 115 Th Kong Kiat; r from 200B) Yuttichai offers large, old decent rooms with fan, and has friendly and informative staff. The squeaky clean units are fine for a kip, but the mattresses are on the stiff side.

Hadthong Hotel (☎ 0 3260 1050-6; www.hadthong .com; 21 Th Suseuk; r 700-1600B; 🛜) Right on the beach, this place has a light and airy lobby and is hands down the best option in town.

Some rooms have views of Khao Chong Krajok and others have windows facing the sea.

Eating

Prachuap Khiri Khan has a well-deserved reputation for fine seafood. One of the must-try specialities is *blah săm·lee dàat dee·o* – whole cotton fish that's sliced lengthwise, left to dry in the sun and then fried in a wok. It's often served with mango salad on the side, and it tastes way better than it sounds. An all-day market lines the street on Th Maitri Ngam daily, starting at around 6am.

Pan Phochana Restaurant (☎ 0 3261 1195; 11 Th Suseuk; dishes 40-300B; 🕑 lunch & dinner) This is one of the best seafood restaurants around town. Its speciality is *hòr mòk hŏy* (ground-fish curry with steamed mussels).

Shiew O Cha (☎ 0 3260 1732; cnr Th Phitak Chat & Th Thetsaban Bamrung; meals 50-160B; 🕑 breakfast, lunch & dinner) This big, modern and airy Chinese-Thai restaurant offers plenty of alternatives to seafood and occasionally hosts live music. There's no roman-script sign but you can't miss the large cream and green building.

Getting There & Away

There are frequent air-con buses to/from Bangkok (around 250B, five hours), Hua Hin (around 100B, 1½ hours), Cha-am (around 100B, 2½ hours) and Phetchaburi (around 100B, three hours) leaving from Th Phitak Chat near the centre. For southern destinations such as Phuket or Krabi, hike 2km northwest out to the police station on the highway to catch passing buses (motorcycle taxis will take you for 40B). Ordinary buses to Hua Hin (70B), Bang Krut (60B), Bang Saphan (65B) and Chumphon (160B, 3½ hours) leave from the southeast corner of Th Thetsaban Bamrung and Th Phitak Chat.

There are frequent train services to/from Bangkok (2nd class 317B to 357B, 3rd class 250B, six hours). Trains also run to Ban Krut (one hour) and Bang Saphan Yai (1½ hours).

Getting Around

Prachuap is small enough to get around on foot, but you can hop on a motorcycle taxi around town for 30B. Other destinations include Ao Noi (50B) and Ao Manao (40B). At Ao Manao motorcycles aren't permitted past the gate unless both driver and passenger are wearing helmets.

STAR LIGHT, STAR BRIGHT, FIRST SQUID I SEE TONIGHT...

After the fiery equatorial sun plunges deep into the ocean, stars begin to emerge overhead and a strange concentration of greenish lights materialises on the horizon. The brilliant lights look like a flotilla of UFOs as they illuminate the night sky with their powerful beams – these are the squid fishermen of Thailand, and you are likely to see them ply their trade along the length of the country.

Squid are best fished after dark. The powerful lights mimic sunlight and are used to attract plankton and small fish that usually feed in the daytime to the surface. Squid, which feed on these organisms, follow their mobile meals into waiting nets. The lights are so powerful that they can be seen in satellite photos taken 800km from earth. That's a lot of candle power.

As fishing techniques improve collection rates, overfishing is becoming a growing problem in Thailand and the government has attempted to impose limits, much to the chagrin of fishermen. Regardless, squid fishing is a huge industry and you are likely to see these galaxies of bobbing beams for a while yet.

You can rent motorbikes in front of the Hadthong Hotel for 200B per day. The roads in the area are very good and it's a great way to see the surrounding beaches. Opposite the post office, bicycles can be rented for 100B per day.

BAN KRUT & BANG SAPHAN
หาดบ้านกรูด/บางสะพานใหญ่

Things start to get quiet between the administrative centres of Prachuap Khiri Khan and Chumphon. This wooded realm is dotted with plantations and rice fields that spread between the flaxen shoreline and the Myanmar border. The long strings of sand are popular holiday spots for weekending Thai tourists. During the week, the beaches are virtually deserted, save for a few colourful long-tail vessels.

The main beach of Hat Ban Krut is right beside a road, making the 10km beach handy to cars and services, but detracting from a 100% peaceful beach experience. Sitting atop a headland to the north, **Wat Tan Sai** has multiple golden spires that reach to the sky like a fantasy Disneyland castle. You can clamber up to the top for sensational views of the area. Just beyond, there's **Hat Sai Kaew**, which is quieter but slightly out of the way, making it a better beach experience.

Bang Saphan Yai, 20km south of the town, is starting to experience development. Accommodation is also strung along the sand between Bang Saphan Yai and Bang Saphan Noi, 15km further south. Islands off the coast to the south, including **Ko Thalu** and **Ko Sing**, offer good **snorkelling** and **diving** from the end of January to mid-May. Coral Hotel in Bang Saphan Yai can arrange half-day

diving excursions to these islands, as well as outings to virtually every site in the region.

Sleeping & Eating
There are plenty of places to spend the night in Ban Krut and Bang Saphan. Big-spenders won't find five-star palaces, and penny-pinchers will be hard-pressed to track down dirt-cheap shacks, but there are a couple of unique options within this zone of decidedly midrange places. If you know where you want to stay, it's best to book ahead – public transport is a bit rough around these parts, and the resort of your choice can probably arrange some of your transport. Virtually all beachside accommodation options offer a place to eat.

BAN KRUT
Banito Beach Resort (☎ 0 2964 2175; www.banito beach.com; bungalows 1300-9000B; 🅿 🛈) Colourful Banito feels like it was plucked from a Caribbean island and set down in sleepy Ban Krut. Accommodation is arranged in houses along a long street that connects the ocean to a large swimming pool bizarrely placed at the back of the resort. Have a look at a couple of rooms before plopping down your bags – some options have been renovated more recently than others.

Rachavadee Resort (☎ 0 3269 5155; www.rachav adee.com; bungalows 1800-4800B; 🅿) Rachavadee offers a rugged serenity within its faux-brick walls and skyscraping cantilevered roofs. Free bus transfers are also on offer.

Baan Klang Aow Beach Resort (☎ 0 3269 5123; www.baanklangaowresort.com; bungalows 1800-5200B; 🅿 🖳 🛈) Further south on the same beach as Suan Bankrut, the one- and two-bedroom bungalows here have large verandas and are hidden in leafy thickets. Bicycles, kayaks and two swimming pools will get you hungry for your next meal at the resort's scenic restaurant.

Suan Bankrut Beach Resort (☎ 0 3269 5217; www.suanbankrut.com; bungalows 2200-6400B; 🔀) Suan Bankrut offers charming bungalows with plenty of thatch that squat beneath furry palms.

BANG SAPHAN

Vanveena Hotel (☎ 0 3269 1251; www.vanveena.com; r 270-1500B; 🔀) Vanveena's rooms are noticeably spartan, with a few stencil drawings to liven up the walls, but this cookie-cutter hotel is beach-adjacent and there's a charming bamboo restaurant on the sand.

Western Hotel (☎ 0 3269 1015; r 600-700B; 🔀) If the bungalows along Bang Saphan are full, try the Western Hotel. The drab décor feels a bit like 'Soviet Gulag takes a tropical holiday', but the rooms are clean enough if you're on a tight budget.

Coral Hotel (☎ 0 3269 1667; www.coral-hotel.com; 171 Moo 9; r 1525B, bungalows 2730-3525B; 🔀 🖳) Set amid a coconut grove, this upmarket French-managed hotel is right on the beach. There's a huge pool, a very good restaurant and all rooms have TV, fridge and hot water. Fill your days with water sports, or exploring the area on an organised tour. Four-person bungalows are also available for families.

Sailom Resort (☎ 0 3269 1003; www.sailomresort bangsaphan.com; r 1900-4900B; 🔀 🖳) Manicured grounds, a huge swimming pool, Asian chic décor – this new spot has certainly shaken things up in sleepy Bang Saphan.

I-Ta-Lay (☎ 08 9905 8512; dishes 40-150B; 🕑 lunch & dinner) A small white cottage, just south of Coral Hotel, I-Ta-Lay is a tasty local joint right along the beach. Not a drop of English is spoken, but the seafood is great and there are plenty of smiles. There are also a couple of bungalows out the back for 1500B per night.

Getting There & Around

From Chumphon, there are many connections to Ban Krut and Bang Saphan, departing Chumphon every day at 8am, 9.30am, 11.45am, 1pm, 4pm, 6pm, 7pm and 8pm (70B). Buses from every direction usually stop in front of the Rama Inn, a white hotel

in the heart of Bang Saphan. The towns are positioned along the main train artery between Bangkok and the south; however, you will need to hire a motorcycle taxi to get you to the beach.

There is one **motorcycle shop** (☎ 0 3269 1059) in Bang Saphan Yai that rents out automatic and manual bikes (250B and 300B respectively). Its rows of scooters are hard to miss. Other than that, transport can be a bit of a problem. Once you get to the beaches, however, most resorts can hook you up with bike rental for a similar price.

When booking transport, don't confuse Bang Saphan Yai with Bang Saphan Noi, which is 15km further south.

CHUMPHON

อ.เมือง ชุมพร

pop 81,700

Chumphon doesn't pretend to be a destination in itself. The air is thick with anticipation: tourists are eager to arrive in Ko Tao, or they're wrapping up an island getaway and want to get back to Bangkok. Either way, Chumphon feels like a border town. There's even a big, vanilla archway near the train station welcoming passengers to Thailand's south. The sleepy town has embraced its status as a link in the transport chain – it's one of the few cities in Thailand with more travel agencies than 7-Elevens.

Information

There are dozens of travel agencies around town that can organise all of your booking needs, such as transport, lodging, even scuba lessons on Ko Tao. Most agencies offer internet access for 40B per hour, and complimentary wi-fi for those with laptops. There are numerous banks and ATMs scattered around town.

Chumphon Hospital (☎ 0 7750 3672; Th Phisit Phayaban) The main hospital in town.

Chumphon Tourist Services Centre (Th Sala Daeng) This bureau has recently moved to its present location, and the office hours are a bit unstable. The agencies usually offer better tourism details.

Kiat Travel (☎ 0 7750 2127; www.chumphonguide.com; 115 Th Tha Taphao) One of the better full-service agencies. Friendly and knowledgeable staff who are more than happy to answer questions.

New Infinity Travel (☎ 0 7757 0176; new_infinity@ hotmail.com; 68/2 Th Tha Taphao) Extremely helpful and friendly agency with loads of information on the area.

NORTHWESTERN GULF COAST

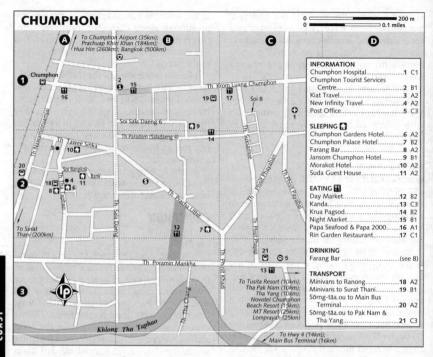

CHUMPHON

INFORMATION
Chumphon Hospital..................1 C1
Chumphon Tourist Services
  Centre...................................2 B1
Kiat Travel..............................3 A2
New Infinity Travel..................4 A2
Post Office.............................5 C3

SLEEPING
Chumphon Gardens Hotel..........6 A2
Chumphon Palace Hotel............7 B2
Farang Bar.............................8 A2
Jansom Chumphon Hotel..........9 B1
Morakot Hotel.......................10 A2
Suda Guest House..................11 A2

EATING
Day Market...........................12 B2
Kanda..................................13 C3
Krua Pagsod.........................14 B2
Night Market........................15 B1
Papa Seafood & Papa 2000.....16 A1
Rin Garden Restaurant...........17 C1

DRINKING
Farang Bar........................(see 8)

TRANSPORT
Minivans to Ranong...............18 A2
Minivans to Surat Thani.........19 B1
Sŏrng·tăa·ou to Main Bus
  Terminal............................20 A2
Sŏrng·tăa·ou to Pak Nam &
  Tha Yang...........................21 C3

Purchase a second-hand book for some entertainment on the journey to your next destination.

Post office (☎ 0 7751 1012; Th Poramin Mankha) In the eastern part of town.

Festivals & Events

The city hosts the **Chumphon Marine Festival** some time in March – it features cultural and folk art exhibits, a sailboarding competition at Hat Thung Wua Laen and a marathon. **Lang Suan Buddha Image Parade & Boat Race Festival** is a five-day festival that includes a procession of temple boats and a boat race on the Mae Nam Lang Suan. It's held in October.

Sleeping

The accommodation options in Chumphon are quite utilitarian, as the city is mostly used as a transfer centre. There are a few resorty places a few kilometres away along the coast.

CITY CENTRE

Farang Bar (☎ 0 7750 1003; farangbar@yahoo.com; 69/36 Th Tha Taphao; r 150B) The cheap rooms at Farang Bar could definitely use a fix-up, but the hip staff foster a great backpacker vibe, and they can answer virtually every travel query. Showers cost 20B.

Suda Guest House (☎ 0 7750 4366; 8 Soi Bangkok Bank; r 200-500B; ✷) A fantastic little find hidden within the urban chaos, this little guesthouse has a homey vibe and a low price tag. The owner, Suda, speaks perfect English and keeps her rooms spick-and-span. It's best to book ahead.

Morakot Hotel (☎ 0 7750 3628-32; fax 0 7757 0196; Th Tawee Sinka; r 310-600B; ✷) The staff here don't speak much English, but the rooms are spotless and some have great views. It's in a large green structure and the reception is located behind a motorcycle showroom that rents out motorcycles for 150B per day.

Chumphon Palace Hotel (☎ 0 7757 1715-22; 328/15 Th Pracha Uthit; r 450-600B; ✷) Keep an eye out for a purple sign saying 'Hotel', and you'll find the pink, frilly Chumphon Palace Hotel hiding just off the main drag. Upstairs, the rooms are clean and crisp, and the beds have rose-coloured ruffles at granny's house.

Chumphon Gardens Hotel (☎ 0 7750 6888; 66/1 Th Tha Taphao; r 540-700B; ste 2000B; ✷) The new kid on the block, Chumphon Gardens is the go-to spot for businesspeople passing through town. The lobby is a bit drab, but the rooms are sparkling clean.

Jansom Chumphon Hotel (☎ 0 7750 2506-11; 188/138 Th Sala Daeng; r 550-1600B; ❄) From the outside, Jansom could double as an abandoned warehouse, but the interior has some passable rooms – just make sure you find one that doesn't reek of stale air-con. The advertised rates are ludicrously high; however, you'll often find touts at the train station offering units with TV and hot water for around 350B.

SEASIDE

MT Resort (☎ 0 7755 8153; www.mtresort-chumphon .com; Hat Tummakam Noi; bungalows incl breakfast 1500B; ❄) This low-key hang-out, right beside the Lomprayah ferry pier, is a scenic option if you'd rather stay outside of Chumphon's grimy downtown core while waiting for the boat to Ko Tao. There are free kayaks for wandering around the nearby islands and mangroves. Call ahead to organise transport, or grab a cab for around 300B.

Novotel Chumphon Beach Resort (☎ 0 7752 9529; info@novotel-chumphon.com; 110 Moo 4, Hat Paradonpab; r from 2500B; ❄ ▭ ▨) The brand new Novotel is breathing new life into Chumphon's quiet coast nearby. Despite its chain status, this plush getaway is a great place to hang your hat if you want to turn a layover into a mini vacation.

Tusita Resort (☎ 0 7757 9073; www.tusitaresort.com; 259/9 Moo 1, Paktako, Tungtako; bungalows 6900-18,500B; ❄ ▭ ▨) A worthy option if you're not yet ready to hit the islands, this Indian-style resort features large teak *săh·lah* dotting the windswept sand, and private bungalows hidden among a patchwork of coconut palms and jungle vines. Tusita is 10km from the city centre – take a taxi to Kaao Pii junction (30B to 45B) and then call the resort for a free pick-up. There are no public phones, so you'll need a mobile phone or ask to use someone else's.

Eating & Drinking

Krua Pagsod (☎ 0 7757 1731; 110/32 Th Paradorn; dishes 50-200B; ☽ lunch & dinner) Delicious vegetarian options are available at this prim, modern establishment that blows cool gusts of air-conditioning over weary travellers.

Papa Seafood & Papa 2000 (☎ 0 1569 6161, 0 7751 1972; 188/181 Th Krom Luang Chumphon; dishes 80-200B; ☽ lunch & dinner) This large patio restaurant right in the heart of town dishes out tasty barbecued seafood and steak under flickering Christmas lights. As the evening turns to night, Papa fills up with locals who toss back a few beers before heading to the adjacent Papa 2000 discotheque.

Farang Bar (☎ 0 7750 1003; 69/36 Th Tha Taphao) A good place to meet other backpackers in transit, Farang Bar has cheap eats and frosty beer in a tiki-torched ambiance.

Rin Garden Restaurant (☎ 0 7751 1531; ☽ lunch & dinner) and **Kanda** (☎ 0 7751 1707; ☽ lunch & dinner) both have good local reputations if you want to chow down off the tourist trail.

Chumphon's **night market** (Th Krom Luang Chumphon) can be a little hit-or-miss depending on the day of the week (and the weather), but when things start to get moving, it can be a good distraction while waiting for the next link in your chain of transport. The food isn't fantastic, but it's dirt-cheap. A bustling day market runs north–south between Th Pracha Uthit and Th Poramin Mankha.

Getting There & Away

There are Lomprayah and Seatran Discovery bus/boat packages from Bangkok to Ko Tao, Ko Samui and Ko Phan-Ngan via Chumphon. Taking a train/boat combination is another way of getting to these islands. If you're arriving in Chumphon from Ko Tao, the Lomprayah shuttle from the ferry drops passengers off at either Fame Travel Agency or New Infinity, depending on the day.

BOAT

The small island of Ko Tao (p227), north of Ko Samui and Ko Pha-Ngan, can be reached by boat from one of three piers south of town. Services continue to Samui and Pha-Ngan.

The *Lomprayah Express* catamaran (550B, 1½ hours) leaves from Tha Tummakam (25km from town) at 7am and 1pm, and returns from Ko Tao at 10am and 3pm. Transfers between Chumphon and Tha Tummakam are included in the ticket price. The *Songsrem Express* (400B, three hours) leaves Tha Yang (7km from town) at 7am, returning from Ko Tao at 2.30pm. Most travel agencies will provide free transfers to this pier as well.

There is also a midnight boat (200B) that leaves from Tha Pak Nam (10km from town) and arrives at Ko Tao at 6am. Consider nixing this option if there's a chance of rain. A shared taxi to Tha Pak Nam costs 50B. Sŏrng·tăa·ou to Tha Pak Nam or Tha Yang are 15B.

BUS

The main bus terminal is inconveniently located on the main highway, 16km from Chumphon – it's better to take the train if you are arriving from Bangkok. To get here you can catch a local bus or sŏrng·tǎa·ou from a stop on Th Nawaminruamjai for 20B. There are several buses travelling daily from Bangkok to Chumphon: one VIP bus (500B, seven hours, departs 9.30pm), three regular air-conditioned buses (around 350B, seven hours) and three 2nd-class buses (250B). From Bangkok, all buses leave from the Southern bus terminal. There are several private bus companies running buses to Bangkok for around 400B; tickets can be bought at any travel agency and include a free pick-up from your hotel.

Figure on around 1B per kilometre when paying for your ticket on government buses. Destinations include Hua Hin (230B, five hours), Bang Saphan (100B, two hours), Prachuap Khiri Khan (160B, 3½ hours), Ranong (130B, three hours), Surat Thani (170B, 3½ hours), Krabi (270B, eight hours), Phuket (320B, eight hours) and Hat Yai (310B, 10 hours). Tickets can be bought at travel agencies.

MINIVAN

Air-conditioned minivans run hourly to/from Ranong (100B to 200B, three hours) and leave from a stop on Th Tha Taphao. Half-hourly minivans to/from Surat Thani (150B to 200B, 3½ hours) run all day and leave from a stop just off Th Krom Luang Chumphon.

TRAIN

The southern line has several trains a day to/from Bangkok. If you catch the train in mid-afternoon, you will arrive in Chumphon in time to find a room and crash for the night. Early evening trains arrive in the wee hours of the morning; however, you may miss your connection to Ko Tao and be forced to lounge around Chumphon until the afternoon ferry. If this is the case, scout out a travel agency that has comfy chairs and plenty of space for your luggage.

Trains to and from towns all along the southern line leave and arrive several times a day. Third-class trains head out to Prachuap Khiri Khan (40B, three hours), Surat Thani (45B, three hours) and Hat Yai (90B, 12 hours). Southbound rapid and express trains – the only trains with 1st and 2nd class – are much less frequent and can be difficult to book out of Chumphon in the high season (November to April).

Getting Around

Motorcycle taxis around town cost a flat 20B per trip. Most travel agencies can arrange motorbike rentals, as can the Morakot Hotel (p186), which has dozens of bikes sitting around the lobby.

Southwestern Gulf Coast

This stunning coast features a Thailand holiday trifecta: Ko Samui, Ko Pha-Ngan and Ko Tao. This family of spectacular islands lure millions of tourists every year with their powder-soft sands and emerald waters. Ko Samui is the oldest brother, with a business-minded attitude towards vacation. High-class resorts operate with Swiss efficiency as uniformed butlers cater to every whim. Ko Pha-Ngan is the slacker middle child with tangled dreadlocks and a penchant for hammock-lazing and all-night parties. Baby Ko Tao has plenty of spirit and spunk – offering high-adrenaline activities including world-class diving and snorkelling.

A thin archipelago of pin-sized islets creates a small barrier between these three busy destinations and the quieter beachside towns along the coast. Known as Ang Thong Marine National Park, this ethereal realm of greens and blues offers some of the most picture-perfect moments in the entire kingdom. As the rugged coastline swerves south, the ancient rainforest of Khao Sok rises up into the clouds as it dominates the inner terrain and drips with gushing waterfalls and exotic wildlife. Urban Nakhon Si Thammarat buzzes with booming trade and religious devotees.

Thailand's southwestern gulf coast also has the kingdom's most intriguing social and religious dynamic. The region is a fascinating crucible of Buddhist and Muslim cultures, where you're as likely to wake up to the Muzennin's call to prayer as you are to see a monk wandering in saffron robes. Unfortunately, at the time of research, tensions between Muslim separatists and Thai authorities meant that the far southernmost provinces were experiencing some civil unrest.

HIGHLIGHTS

- Cavorting with a school-bus-sized whale shark off the coast of **Ko Tao** (p230),
- Praying to the party gods while howling at the full moon on **Ko Pha-Ngan** (p211)
- Kayaking between jagged jungle islands in **Ang Thong Marine Park** (p240)
- Discovering all the perks of a world-class resort on **Ko Samui** (p198)
- Traipsing through the veritable Jurassic Park of **Khao Sok National Park** (p244)
- Stepping off the tourist trail and practicing your Thai in the temple town of **Nakhon Si Thammarat** (p246)

- DRY SEASON: DECEMBER-APRIL
- WET SEASON: MAY-NOVEMBER

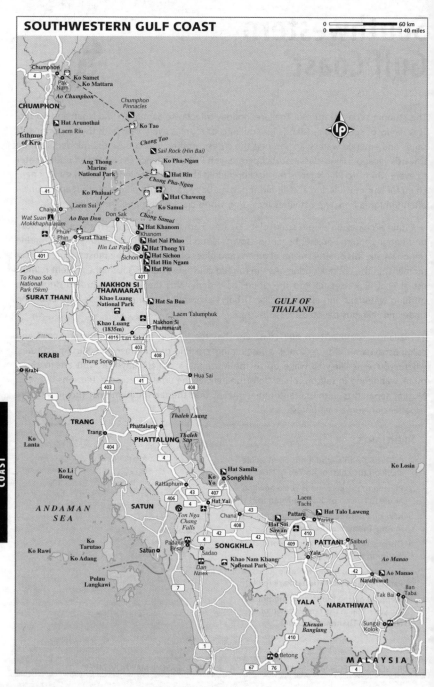

SOUTHWESTERN GULF COAST

0   60 km
0   40 miles

Chumphon

Ko Samet
Pak Nam   Ko Mattara
CHUMPHON
Ao Chumphon

Chumphon Pinnacles

Isthmus of Kra   Hat Arunothai
Laem Riu   Ko Tao

Chong Tao
Sail Rock (Hin Bai)
Ko Pha-Ngan

Ang Thong Marine National Park   Hat Rin

Chong Pha-Ngan
Ko Phaluai
Laem Sui   Hat Chaweng
Chaiya   Ko Samui
Wat Suan Mokkhaphalaram   *Ao Ban Don*   Don Sak   *Chong Samui*
Phun Phin   Surat Thani   Hat Khanom
                                          Khanom
Hin Lat Falls   Hat Nai Phlao
                       Hat Thong Yi
                       Sichon   Hat Sichon
                                      Hat Hin Ngam
SURAT THANI   401   Hat Piti

To Khao Sok National Park (5km)   41

NAKHON SI THAMMARAT   Hat Sa Bua   *GULF OF THAILAND*

Khao Luang National Park

Khao Luang (1835m)   Laem Talumphuk
4015   Lan Saka   Nakhon Si Thammarat

KRABI   403   408

Thung Song

Krabi   41   Hua Sai   408

Thaleh Luang

TRANG   Phattalung
Trang   Trang   *Thaleh Sap*
Ko Lanta   404   **PHATTALUNG**

Ko Losin

Ko Li Bong   4   Hat Samila
Rattaphum   Ko   Songkhla
SATUN   406   Yo
A N D A M A N   43   407   Laem Tachi
S E A   4   Hat Yai   Hat Talo Laweng
Ton Nga Chang Falls   Chana   43   Pattani   Yaring
Ko Rawi   Ko Tarutao   408   Hat Soi Sawan   410
Ko Adang   Padang   42   Saiburi
        Besar   42   **PATTANI**
Satun   Sadao   **SONGKHLA**   409   Yala   *Ao Manao*
Pulau Langkawi   Dan Nawk   Khao Nam Khang National Park   Ao Manao
                                                        42
        7   Narathiwat   Tak Bai
                                                        Ban Taba
YALA   **NARATHIWAT**
Kheuan Banglang   Sungai Kolok
        410
        1
        Betong
67   76   **M A L A Y S I A**   4

Climate

The best time to visit islands around Samui is during the hot, dry season from February to April. From May to October, during the southwest monsoon, it can rain intermittently, and from October to January, during the northeast monsoon, there can be strong winds. However, many travellers have reported sunny weather (and fewer crowds) in September and October. November tends to get some of the rain that affects the east coast of Malaysia at this time.

The overall lack of tourism south of the Samui archipelago is mostly because the southwestern gulf's best season (climatically) runs from April to October – the exact opposite of Thailand's typical tourist season.

National Parks

There are many national parks in the region; three stand out as particularly stunning. Ang Thong Marine Park (p240), the setting for the perfect beach in the movie *The Beach* (although much of the movie was actually filmed on Ko Phi-Phi), is a breathtaking archipelago with 42 jagged islands. Khao Sok (p244) is a thick, virgin rainforest with surreal numbers of fauna and flora. Khao Luang National Park (p249) is known for its beautiful mountain trails, gushing waterfalls and indigenous wildlife.

KO SAMUI
เกาะสมุย
pop 45,800

The Gulf Coast's answer to the Andaman's Phuket (that's '*p-h*' as in '*p*'), Ko Samui is the ultimate pleasure island, boasting crystal waters and bleach-blonde sands. Its undeniable appeal has captured the hearts of its visitors, and with each passing year there are newer resorts and higher price tags to keep up with the insatiable demand. This rampant development has transformed much of the coastline into a continuous string of bungalows, sending seclusion-seekers to quieter islands as they say 'phuket' to Samui (that's '*p-h*' as in '*f*').

Once upon a time, the upside-down 'Q'-shaped island was settled by Chinese merchants from Hainan Island, who earned their keep by cultivating the millions of indigenous coconut palms. These unique roots have encouraged an island-specific culture that remains hidden beneath the glossy holiday veneer. Although three million palm trees remain, the island's number one industry is tourism. Today, there are thousands of different rooms and bungalows, from twig huts to rambling palaces. You can eat foie gras on fine china or grab a bag of roasted crickets at a local food stand. Try a cheap massage in a shaded shack along the beach, or pamper yourself silly in a lavish spa. Whatever your vacation type may be, Samui tries its best to satisfy.

Orientation

Ko Samui is quite large – the ring road around the island is almost 100km in total. The island has been blessed with picturesque beaches on all four sides. The most crowded are Hat Chaweng (Map p194) and Hat Lamai (Map p197), both on the eastern side of the island.

The beaches on the island's northern coast, which include Choeng Mon, Mae Nam, Bo Phut, Bang Po, and Big Buddha Beach (Bang Rak), are starting to become quite busy as well, but the prices are still acceptable and secluded nooks can still be found. For a quieter experience, try the secluded beaches along the southern coast, and western shore south of Na Thon.

The *Siam Map Company Samui Guide Map* is fantastic, free, and easily found throughout the island.

Information
BOOKSHOPS

There are several places around the island where you can snag a paperback to read in your hammock. Many hotels also have libraries or book trades.

Bookazine (Map p194; ☎ 0 7741 3616; Hat Chaweng; ☻ 10am-9pm) Chain outlet selling new books and magazines.

Saai Bookshop (Map p194; ☎ 0 7741 3847-9; Hat Chaweng; ☻ 10am-11pm) Friendly small bookstore selling new and used books, and magazines in several languages.

EMERGENCY

The Samui International Hospital (see p193) has a 24-hour ambulance service.

Tourist police (Map p192; ☎ 0 7742 1281, emergency 1155) Based at the south of Na Thon.

IMMIGRATION OFFICES

During high season, the Bangkok Samui Hospital (see p193) also has an immigration booth and can offer small extensions on tourist visas.

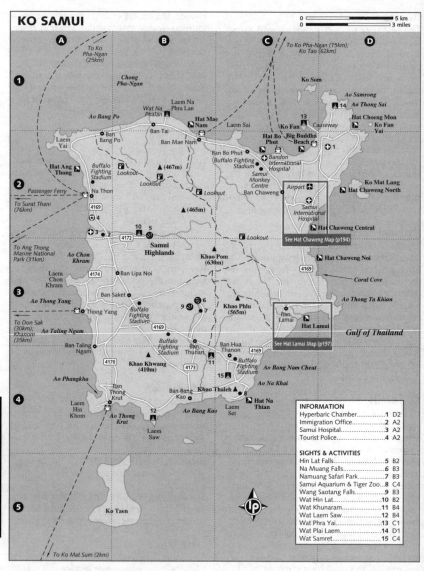

KO SAMUI

INFORMATION

Hyperbaric Chamber	1 D2
Immigration Office	2 A2
Samui Hospital	3 A2
Tourist Police	4 A2

SIGHTS & ACTIVITIES

Hin Lat Falls	5 B2
Na Muang Falls	6 B3
Namuang Safari Park	7 B3
Samui Aquarium & Tiger Zoo	8 C4
Wang Saotang Falls	9 B3
Wat Hin Lat	10 B2
Wat Khunaram	11 B4
Wat Laem Saw	12 B4
Wat Phra Yai	13 C1
Wat Plai Laem	14 D1
Wat Samret	15 C4

Immigration Office (Map p192; ☎ 0 7742 1069; ☼ 8.30am-noon & 1-4.30pm Mon-Fri) Offers 10-day tourist visa extensions. Located about 2km south of Na Thon.

INTERNET ACCESS

There are countless places all over the island for internet access, even at the less popular beaches. Prices range from 1B to 2B per minute. Keep an eye out for restaurants that offer complementary wi-fi service.

INTERNET RESOURCES

There are several useful internet sites that cover sleeping, transport and sights on Ko Samui.

Sawadee.com (www.samui.sawadee.com)
Tourism Association of Koh Samui (www.samui
tourism.com)

MEDICAL SERVICES

Ko Samui has four private hospitals, all near
the Tesco-Lotus supermarket on the east coast
where most of the tourists tend to gather.
The government hospital near Na Thon
(Map p192) has seen significant improvements in the last couple years but the service
is still a bit grim since funding is based on
the number of Samui's legal residents (which
doesn't take into account a heap of illegal
Burmese workers).

Bangkok Samui Hospital (Map p194; ☎ 0 7742 9500,
emergency 0 7742 9555; Hat Chaweng) Your best bet for
just about any medical problem.

Hyperbaric Chamber (Map p192; ☎ 0 7742 7427; Big
Buddha Beach) The island's dive medicine specialists.

Samui International Hospital (Map p194; ☎ 0 7742
2272, fax 0 7723 0049; www.sih.co.th; Hat Chaweng)
Emergency ambulance service available 24 hours and credit
cards are accepted. Near the Amari Resort.

MONEY

Changing money isn't a problem on the east
and north coasts, and in Na Thon. Multiple
banks and foreign-exchange booths offer daily
exchange services and there's an ATM every
couple of hundred metres.

POST

In several parts of the island there are privately
run post office branches charging a small commission. You can almost always leave your
stamped mail with your accommodation.

Main post office (Na Thon) Near the TAT office; not
always reliable.

TELEPHONE

Many private phone offices around the island charge an additional rate above the usual
Communications Authority of Thailand
(CAT) prices. Mobile-phone service works
well throughout the island.

CAT Office (Na Thon; ☼ 7am-10pm) Provides economical international phone service at the main post office.

TOURIST INFORMATION

The Siam Map Company puts out quarterly
booklets including a *Spa Guide*, *Dining Guide*,
and an annual directory, which lists virtually
thousands of companies and hotels on the
island. *Essential* (www.essential-samui) is a

pocket-size pamphlet focused on promoting
Samui's diverse activities. *Samui Guide* looks
more like a magazine and features mostly restaurants and attractions. Another booklet,
Passport, proffers insider information about
each beach, and there are coupons and postcards stuffed at the back.

TAT office (☎ 0 7742 0504; Na Thon) At the northern
end of Na Thon; is friendly, helpful and has handy brochures and maps.

TRAVEL AGENCIES

Basically every resort and bungalow operation
has travel services that can book you tours and
transport. Booking directly with a tour operator will usually save you a bit of baht.

Asia Travel (☎ 0 7723 6120; Th Thawi Ratchaphakdi,
Na Thon; ☼ 8.30am-6pm Mon-Sat) Deals especially with
airline tickets.

Dangers & Annoyances

As on Phuket, the rate of road accident fatalities on Samui is quite high. This is mainly
due to the large number of tourists who rent
motorcycles only to find out that the winding roads, sudden tropical rains, and frenzied
traffic can be lethal. If you decide to rent a
motorcycle, protect yourself by wearing a helmet, and ask for one that has a plastic visor.
Shoes and appropriate clothing are also a must
when driving – jeans will save you from skin-
ning your knees if you wipe out. Even if you
escape unscathed from a riding experience,
we've heard reports that some shops will claim
that you damaged your rental and will try to
extort you for some more serious cash. Car rental
is another option on the island – we suggest
leasing a vehicle from a reputable and internationally recognized name brand.

Lately, jet-ski rentals are the newest avatar
of the motorbike scam. Incidents of injury are
high on these water scooters, and leasers will
claim that you damaged their goods in order
to collect some extra money.

Another scam that's rapidly gaining popularity involves timeshares. It's best to avoid
anyone who approaches you offering a vacation deal that seems too good to be true.

Beach vendors are registered with the
government and should all be wearing a
numbered jacket. No peddler should cause
an incessant disturbance – seek assistance if
this occurs.

Theft is a continuing problem, particularly
around the more populated parts of the island

SOUTHWESTERN GULF COAST

lonelyplanet.com

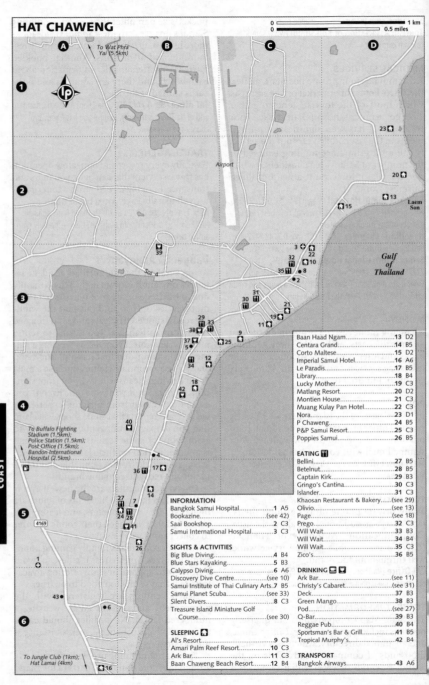

HAT CHAWENG

To Wat Phra Yai (5.5km)

Airport

Gulf of Thailand

Laem Son

Sol 4

To Buffalo Fighting Stadium (1.5km); Police Station (1.5km); Post Office (1.5km); Bandon International Hospital (2.5km)

To Jungle Club (1km); Hat Lamai (4km)

INFORMATION
Bangkok Samui Hospital.....................1 A5
Bookazine..(see 42)
Saai Bookshop......................................2 C3
Samui International Hospital..............3 C3

SIGHTS & ACTIVITIES
Big Blue Diving.....................................4 B4
Blue Stars Kayaking............................5 B3
Calypso Diving.....................................6 A6
Discovery Dive Centre......................(see 10)
Samui Institute of Thai Culinary Arts.7 B5
Samui Planet Scuba...........................(see 33)
Silent Divers...8 C3
Treasure Island Miniature Golf
    Course...(see 30)

SLEEPING
Al's Resort...9 C3
Amari Palm Reef Resort.....................10 C3
Ark Bar...11 C3
Baan Chaweng Beach Resort..........12 B4

Baan Haad Ngam................................13 D2
Centara Grand.....................................14 B5
Corto Maltese.......................................15 D2
Imperial Samui Hotel.........................16 A6
Le Paradis...17 B5
Library..18 B4
Lucky Mother.......................................19 C3
Matlang Resort....................................20 D2
Montien House....................................21 C3
Muang Kulay Pan Hotel.....................22 C3
Nora..23 D1
P Chaweng...24 B5
P&P Samui Resort...............................25 C3
Poppies Samui.....................................26 B5

EATING
Bellini...27 B5
Betelnut..28 B5
Captain Kirk...29 B3
Gringo's Cantina.................................30 C3
Islander..31 C3
Khaosan Restaurant & Bakery......(see 29)
Olivio..(see 13)
Page..(see 18)
Prego..32 C3
Will Wait..33 B3
Will Wait..34 B3
Will Wait..35 C3
Zico's..36 B5

DRINKING
Ark Bar...(see 11)
Christy's Cabaret...............................(see 31)
Deck..37 B3
Green Mango..38 B3
Pod..(see 27)
Q-Bar..39 B3
Reggae Pub...40 B4
Sportsman's Bar & Grill.....................41 B5
Tropical Murphy's................................42 B4

TRANSPORT
Bangkok Airways.................................43 A6

such as Chaweng and Lamai. If you're staying in a beach bungalow, consider depositing your valuables with the management while on excursions around the island or while you're swimming at the beach. Consider asking for a receipt listing the items stored with the staff.

Lastly, never give your passport to anyone as collateral. If a company demands identification, give them your driver's license or any other form of ID. A fraudulent operation can try to extort money from you, or track you down when filing for a new passport.

TRANSPORT
There are over 400 registered taxis on Samui, which means that the competition for passengers is fierce. Unlike Bangkok, cabs will refuse to use their meters so you must *always* negotiate your price before stepping into a cab. A 35B taxi ride in Bangkok will probably set you back about 350B on Samui. It's a flagrant rip-off, but there's not much you can do other than taking a sŏrng·tǎa·ou (also spelt sǎwngthǎew; pick-up truck) instead.

Take care when making train and bus reservations: bookings are sometimes not made at all, or the bus turns out to be far inferior to the one expected. In another scam involving air tickets, agents claim that the economy-class seating is fully booked and force tourists to book in business class – when the customer boards the plane, they find out that they've been allotted an economy seat but paid for a business-class ticket.

Sights
Even though the island has over 500 resorts, there are still some interesting things hidden among the island's three million coconut palms.

Ko Samui is one of Thailand's premiere beach destinations and there's a reason why **Hat Chaweng** is the most popular spot – it's the longest and most beautiful beach on the island. The sand is powder soft, and the water is surprisingly clear, considering the number of boats and bathers. Picture opps are best from the southern part of the beach, with stunning views of the hilly headland to the north.

At the south end of **Hat Lamai**, the second-largest beach, you'll find the infamous **Hin-Ta and Hin-Yai** (Map p197) stone formations (also known as Grandfather and Grandmother Rocks). These genitalia-shaped rocks provide endless mirth to giggling Thai tourists.

Hua Thanon, just beyond, is home to a vibrant Muslim community, and their anchorage of high-bowed fishing vessels is a veritable gallery of intricate designs.

Although the **northern beaches** have coarser sand and aren't as striking as the beaches in the east, they have a laid-back vibe and stellar views of Ko Pha-Ngan. **Bo Phut** stands out with its charming Fisherman's Village; a collection of narrow Chinese shophouses that have been transformed into trendy resorts and boutique hotels.

Many visitors spend the day on the wild, rugged beaches of **Ang Thong Marine National Park** (p240). This stunning archipelago might just have the most beautiful islands in all of Thailand.

WATERFALLS
At 30m, **Na Muang Falls** (Map p192) is the tallest waterfall on Samui and lies in the centre of the island about 12km southeast of Na Thon. The water cascades over ethereal purple rocks, and there's a great pool for swimming at the base. This is the most scenic – and somewhat less frequented – of Samui's falls. There are two other waterfalls in the vicinity; a smaller waterfall called **Na Muang 2**, and recently, improved road conditions have also made it possible to visit the high drop at **Wang Saotong Falls**. These chutes are just north of the ring road near Hua Thanon.

Hin Lat Falls (Map p192), near Na Thon, is worth visiting if you have an afternoon to kill before taking a boat back to the mainland. After a mildly strenuous hike over streams and boulders, reward yourself with a dip in the pool at the bottom of the falls. Keep an eye out for the Buddhist temple that posts signs with spiritual words of moral guidance and enlightenment. Sturdy shoes are recommended.

WÁT
For temple enthusiasts, **Wat Laem Sor** (Map p192), at the southern end of Samui near Ban Phang Ka, has an interesting, highly venerated old Srivijaya-style stupa. At Samui's northern end, on a small rocky island linked by a causeway, is **Wat Phra Yai** (Temple of the Big Buddha; Map p192). Erected in 1972, the modern Buddha (sitting in the Mara posture) stands 15m high and makes an alluring silhouette against the tropical sky and sea. Nearby, a new temple,

---

BUFFALO TANGO

Thai villagers just love to watch their buffaloes tussle. You won't find any pompous matadors here though – unlike its Spanish counterpart, Thai bullfighting involves two male water buffaloes being pitted against each other in a fairly harmless contest of wills.

Thai bullfighting is known to take on circus proportions. Flowers are placed on the bull's horns and sacred ropes are hung around their necks. The animals are then released to engage in a battle of wits, attempting to establish territory with shows of bravado and intimidating ground-stomping. Eventually the two contestants will lock horns and connect in a brief bout of head wrestling – the first animal to turn and run is declared the loser. Fights are usually over in minutes and the animals are rarely injured.

Crowds get seriously riled up and wild hollering is the norm when a popular animal takes centre stage. Gambling is a big sideline activity – you can understand the passion when you know that millions of baht might be hanging on the outcome.

On Samui, bullfights mostly take place during festivals and public holidays. Events are arranged on a rotating basis at several rustic fighting rings around the island. Tourists are usually charged about 200B.

Wat Plai Laem (Map p192), features an enormous 18-armed Buddha.

On the eastern part of Samui, near the waterfalls of the same name, **Wat Hin Lat** (☎ 0 7742 3146) is a meditation temple that teaches daily *vipassana* courses. Several temples have the mummified remains of pious monks including **Wat Khunaram** (Map p192), which is south of Rte 4169 between Th Ban Thurian and Th Ban Hua. The monk, Luang Phaw Daeng, has been dead for over two decades but his corpse is preserved sitting in a meditative pose and sporting a pair of sunglasses.

At **Wat Samret** (also known as the Secret Hall of Buddhas; Map p192), near Hua Thanon, you can see a typical Mandalay sitting Buddha carved from solid marble – a common sight in India and northern Thailand, but not so common in the south.

Activities
DIVING
If you're serious about diving, head to Ko Tao and base yourself there. If you're short on time and don't want to leave Samui, there are plenty of operators who will take you to the same dive sites (at a greater fee, of course). Try to book with a company that has their own boat (or leases a boat) – it might be slightly more expensive, but you'll be glad you did it. Companies without boats often shuttle divers on the passenger catamaran to Ko Tao, where you need to board a second boat to reach your dive site. These types of trips are arduous, time-consuming, meal-less, and rather impersonal.

Certification courses tend to be twice as expensive on Ko Samui as they are on Ko Tao, largely due to use of extra petrol, since tiny Tao is significantly closer to the best diving locations. You'll drop between 16,000B to 20,000B on an Open Water certification, and figure between 3200B and 6200B for a diving day-trip depending on the location of the site.

The island's hyperbaric chamber is at Big Buddha Beach (Hat Bang Rak). For other important details about diving in Thailand, see p383.

100 Degrees East (☎ 0 7742 5936; www.100degrees east.com; Hat Bang Rak) Highly recommended.

Big Blue Diving Samui (Map p194; ☎ 0 7742 2617; www.bigbluedivingsamui.com; Hat Chaweng)

Calypso Diving (Map p194; ☎ 0 7742 2437; www .calypso-diving.com; Hat Chaweng)

Discovery Dive Centre (Map p194; ☎ 0 7741 3196; www.discoverydivers.com; Hat Chaweng) Based at the Amari Resort. Recommended.

Samui Planet Scuba (SIDS; Map p194; ☎ 0 7723 1606; samuiplanetscuba@planetscuba.net)

Silent Divers (Map p194; ☎ 0 7742 2729; www.silent divers.com; Hat Chaweng)

OTHER WATER ACTIVITIES
For those interested in snorkelling and kayaking, book a day-trip to the stunning **Ang Thong Marine Park** (p240). For some instant gratification, head to Chaweng – from there you can hire sailboats, catamarans, snorkelling gear, boats for water-skiing, and so

forth. Be wary of scams involving jet-ski rentals (see p193 for details).

SPA & YOGA

Competition by Samui's five-star resorts is fierce, which means that their spas are of the highest calibre. Pick up the Siam Map Company's free booklet, *Spa Guide* (www .siamspaguide.com), for a detailed list of the island's top centres. The following retreats include some of the finest places to be pampered on Samui (if not the world).

Anantara Spa (p205; Bo Phut) Stunning private massage suites spread across a 3000-sq-m spa complex hidden in the jungle.

Bandara Spa (p204; Bo Phut) An extensive selection of massage treatment from around the world including aqua therapy.

Hideaway Spa (p203; Choeng Mon) At the Sila Evason, it's a rambling retreat of sumptuously designed spa villas scattered along a rocky cliffside. Pure elegance and relaxation.

Spavilion (p202) At the Pavilion Resort, it's a mix of modern and oriental stylistic elements complimenting an array of full-body and facial treatments.

Tamarind Springs (p202; Lamai) Guests choose from traditional massage in a large open-air *säh-lah* (sala), or a

forest spa treatment set deep within the hilly jungle amid mammoth boulders and trickling waterfalls.

For straight up yoga without the frilly spa perks, check out Bo Phut's **Absolute Yoga** (☎ 0 7743 0290; www.absoluteyogasamui.com), which offers hot and flow yoga classes. There's no need to reserve in advance, just show up 15 minutes early. Sessions are 500B, or cheaper if you sign up for several classes.

The **Spa Resort** (p201), in Lamai, is the island's original health destination, and is still known for its effective 'clean me out' fasting regime.

Courses

The **Samui Institute of Thai Culinary Arts** (Sitca; Map p194; ☎ 0 7741 3434; www.sitca.net; Hat Chaweng) has daily Thai-cooking classes, and courses in the aristocratic Thai art of carving fruits and vegetables into intricate floral designs. Lunchtime classes begin at 11am, while dinner starts at 4pm (both cost 1850B for a three-hour course with three or more dishes). Of course you get to eat your projects, and even invite a friend along for the meal.

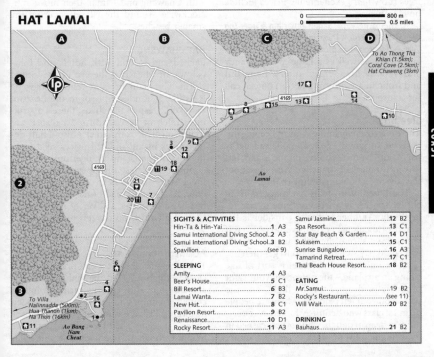

HAT LAMAI

DVDs with Thai cooking instruction are also available so you can practise at home.

The **Health Oasis Resort** (p205) offers one- to eight-day courses and certification in Thai and Swedish massage, aromatherapy, reiki, meditation and yoga for 5500B to 9000B. The length and tuition of all courses can be adjusted to suit the individual.

Samui for Children

If seawater and sand castles just aren't enough to keep the tykes entertained, there are plenty of family-friendly activities around the island.

At Choeng Mon, there's a new creation called **'football golf'** (☎ 08 9771 7498) where you 'putt' your football into a trash-bin-sized hole. It's great for the kids and each game (300B) comes with a complimentary soft drink. It's a par 66.

Namuang Safari Park (Map p192; ☎ 0 7742 4098), near Na Muang Falls, has safari options and packages galore. Adventure tours (from 900B) vary in length and can include elephant trekking, monkey shows, 4WD rides, and even a visit to a rubber plantation to drain the trees (now *that's* excitement). Prices include hotel transfer.

In the same vein, **Samui Aquarium & Tiger Zoo** (Map p192; ☎ 0 7742 4017; orchid@sawadee.com; admission 350B; ⏲ 9am-6pm) has picture-worthy aquariums and tigers, as well as a large aviary. Nancy and Woody, two 'crazy' otters, hang out and frolic in a swimming pool. You can call for transport.

Sleeping

There is an overwhelming array of sleeping options on Ko Samui. We've compiled a lengthy list of our favourite choices on the island, but this by no means exhaustive. Also check out the advice on booking online (p382).

The breed of no-frills backpackers is an elusive species as prices continue to rise relentlessly. Another factor to consider is the island's ridiculously expensive taxis. Even if you score a slice of heaven for under 800B, you could pay well over 300B to get there.

Accommodation on Samui is sort of like riding an airplane – the person on your right probably paid more for the flight, and the person on your left paid less. There are people up in 1st class who definitely forked over a significant heap of dough, while others cashed in their frequent flyer points, or maybe they are

friends with the pilot. Prices on the island are at the whim of each establishment – unforseen crowds can make tariffs skyrocket, advance bookings could be double the walk-in price, or vice versa. Do your research if you're trying to get the biggest bang for your baht (and it never hurts to bargain).

If you're looking to splurge, there is definitely no shortage of top-end resorts sporting extravagant bungalows, charming spas, private infinity pools, and first-class dining; see the boxed text, opposite for some of our picks. In the same boxed text we've also compiled a list of our favourite accommodations at prices that won't force you to mortgage your house. Bo Phut, in the north, has a fantastic assortment of inexpensive boutique-style lodging. Chaweng and Lamai, with pumping nightlife scenes, are worthy options if you're looking to save on transport.

Private villas have become quite popular in recent years. Rental companies often advertise in the various tourist booklets that circulate on the island.

This large section is organised as follows: we start on the popular east coast with Chaweng and Lamai, then move anticlockwise around the island covering the smaller beaches.

HAT CHAWENG

Packed end-to-end with hotels and bungalows, this beach is the eye of the tourist storm. The main street in central Chaweng feels like a nondescript soi in the heart of Bangkok. Despite the chaos, there's a striking stretch of beach, and most resorts are well protected from street noise. High demand has meant inflated prices relative to the rest of the island. Budget options have almost completely disappeared, and midrange stays are the next ones to go out the door. At the south end of the beach, a small headland separates a sliver of sand (called Chaweng Noi) from the rest of the hustle.

Budget

P Chaweng (Map p194; ☎ 0 7723 0684; r 500-800B; ▨) This cheapie doesn't even pretend to be close to the beach, but the pink-tiled rooms are spacious and squeaky clean (minus a couple of bumps and bruises on the wooden furniture). Pick a room facing away from the street – it seems a tad too easy for someone to slip through an open window and pilfer

---

SAMUI'S TOP RESORTS

Taking a Splurge

There's no shortage of places on Samui willing to help you live the rock-star lifestyle. If the five-digit hotel prices don't give your accountant a heart attack, then check out the following.

Anantara (p205; Bo Phut)
Centara Grand (p201, Chaweng)
Four Seasons (p205; Laem Yai)
Library (p201, Chaweng)
Rocky Resort (p202; Lamai)
Sila Evason Hideaway (p203; Choeng Mon)
Tongsai Bay (p203; Choeng Mon)
Villa Nalinnadda (p202; Lamai)
White House (p203; Choeng Mon)
Zazen (p204; Bo Phut)

The Best of the Rest

Okay, chances are you're not looking to spend a billion baht on one night's worth of accommodation. So we've put together a list of our favourite spots on Samui that won't require you to sell your children on e-Bay. These options have rooms for under 2000B per night.

Jungle Club (below; Chaweng)
L'Hacienda (p204; Bo Phut)
Red House (p204; Bo Phut)
Wiesenthal (p206; Taling Ngam)

---

your stuff. P Chaweng shouldn't be confused with the so-so rooms at Bann Chaweng, one street over, which sits betwixt several rowdy late-night gay clubs.

Matlang Resort (Map p194; ☎ 0 7723 0468; www.mat langresort.com; bungalow 400–2000B; ❄ ❒) Matlang is a camp of several dozen bungalows dotted along a red brick path that winds through a shrubby garden. Older bungalows are made from charming vertical slats of timber with a thin skin of thatching on the roof. This budget operation occupies one of the prettiest stretches of sand in Chaweng.

Lucky Mother (Map p194; ☎ 0 7723 0931; bungalows 500–1500B; ❄) First, let's take a moment to giggle at the resort's name. OK, now we can appreciate the old utilitarian huts – a dying breed in Chaweng. For those wanting hot showers and air-con, modern hotel rooms are also available, but most of them look out onto a parking lot.

Jungle Club (Map p194; ☎ 0 1894 2327; bungalows 600–2900B; villas 3500B; ❄ ❒ ☎) The perilous drive up the slithering dirt road is totally worthwhile once you get a load of the awesome views from the top. This isolated mountain getaway is a huge hit among locals and tourists alike. There's a relaxed back-to-nature vibe – guests chill around the stunning horizon pool or

tuck themselves away for a catnap under the canopied roofs of an open-air *săh·lah* (often spelt *sala*; covered hall or resting place). You'll be talking about Jungle Club long after you've returned home from your trip. Call ahead for a pick-up – you don't want to spend your precious jungle holiday in a body cast.

Midrange

P&P Samui Resort (Map p194; ☎ 0 7742 2540; fax 0 7742 2324; r 1300–2000B; ❄) P&P is a pretty good choice for those doing a Chaweng beach holiday on a budget. More work has gone into sprucing up the exteriors, but the tiled rooms remain very clean and come with fridges. If you can, pop into a couple of different rooms before putting down your bags – some of the air-con units emit a faint unidentifiable smell.

Ark Bar (Map p194; ☎ 0 7742 2047; www.ark-bar.com; bungalows 1600–2500B; ❄ ☎) You'll find two of every creature at Ark Bar – hardcore partiers, chilled out hippies, teenagers, 40-somethings, even Canadians. Sky-blue motel units run along the thin verdant strip connecting the Bangkokian streets of Chaweng to the colourful restaurant on the beach. Despite our concerted effort not to use prison lingo when describing holiday destinations, we suggest getting a room in the A- or C-block for less noise.

Corto Maltese (Map p194; ☎ 0 7723 0041; www.corto-samui.com; r 2000-4000B, tr 3000B; 🟦 🖳) Owned by a Frenchman, this place looks like it just fell out of a comic book – maybe '*Tintin and the Mystery of Surprisingly Cheap Accommodation in Chaweng*'? Actually, the resort draws its name from a comic by Hugo Pratt. Rooms have monikers such as 'Pandora & Esmeralda', or 'Hugo & Flamingo', and are outfitted with cheerful pastels, wooden moulding, and the occasional stone feature. 'Corto' has a loft and a honey-coloured adobe thing goin' on.

Montien House (Map p194; ☎ 0 7742 2169; www.montienhouse.com; bungalows incl breakfast 2200-6000B; 🟦 🖳) Semidetached bungalows permeate the thick jungle-garden strewn with orchids and lanterns, while motel rooms linger further afield. The pool area has tonnes of beach chairs making it a great place to ogle unfortunate tan lines on Chaweng beach.

Al's Resort (Map p194; ☎ 0 7742 2154; www.alsresort.com; r 2750-6500B; 🟦 🖳 🖳) Go for a room that starts with a '2' – they're swathed in black and white, and are nothing short of chic. The resort is particularly sexy in the evening when golden moodlighting accents the sleek wooden walkways that cut symmetrical lines through the Zen-like austerity. The staff isn't big on smiles, which is a shame since everything else is quite charming.

Top End

Baan Chaweng Beach Resort (Map p194; ☎ 0 7742 2403; www.baanchawengbeachresort.com; bungalows 3800-7000B; 🟦 🖳 🖳) A pleasant option for those who want top-end luxury without the hefty bill, Baan Chaweng is one of the new kids on the block and is keeping prices relatively low. The immaculate rooms are painted in various shades of peach and pear, with teak furnishings that feel both modern and traditional.

Muang Kulay Pan Hotel (Map p194; ☎ 0 7723 0849-51; www.kulaypan.com; r incl breakfast 4725-13,540B; 🟦 🖳 🖳) No, that's not a rip in the wallpaper – it's all part of the design concept. The architect cites a fusion between Zen and Thai conceits, but we think the décor is indefinable – some beds are upholstered with logs, others have batik duvets and lie close to the ground under an opened parasol. Dramatic black-and-white photographs and simple bamboo-inspired murals cover the walls. The

charming grounds have been purposefully neglected to lend an additional sense of chaos to this unique resort.

Imperial Samui Hotel (Map p194; ☎ 0 7742 0220-36; www.imperialhotels.com; bungalows 5300-15,000B; 🟦 🖳 🖳) Built on a slope in the middle of quieter Chaweng Noi, this place is white adobe galore with accents of baby-blue wood finishing (à la Mediterranean). The restaurant and lounge area overflow with giant cushions and the rambling gardens burst with colour. There's a dash of rustic elegance here, but it might not be enough to warrant the hefty price tag.

Nora (Map p194; ☎ 0 7741 3999; www.norabeachresort.com; bungalows 6000-25,000B; 🟦 🖳 🖳) Nora is another large-scale resort resting along Chaweng's beige sand. If you're gonna drop the big bucks on a private pool villa, we suggest going with one of the more opulent resorts in Choeng Mon, but the lower-priced rooms are worth the baht – they're charming and spacious, and you have access to the wide array of on-site amenities. Keep an eye out for discount deals.

Baan Haad Ngam (Map p194; ☎ 0 7723 1500; 0 7723 1520; www.baanhaadngam.com; bungalows 6400-14,000B; 🟦 🖳 🖳) Vibrant Baan Haad Ngam shuns the usual teak and tan – every exterior is painted in an interesting shade of green – like radioactive celery. It's sassy, classy and a great choice if you've got the dime.

Le Paradis (Map p194; ☎ 0 7723 9041; fax 0 7723 9040; www.leparadisresort.com; bungalows 7000-10,100B; 🟦 🖳 🖳) Formerly the Princess Village, this silent sanctuary is still fit for royalty. Stunning Ayuthaya-period stilt homes crouch among lily ponds and lazy palms. For those with modern inclinations, there's a new set of villas sporting never-ending bathrooms and cheerful interiors. Paradis, indeed.

Poppies Samui (Map p194; ☎ 0 7742 2419; www.poppiessamui.com; r 7000-11,000B; 🟦 🖳 🖳) After passing through the marble lobby, a small staircase suddenly opens onto a juicy tropical paradise that feels miles away from the commotion in Chaweng. A small collection of charming bungalows lies hidden in the brush – only the opulent arched roofs poke through from between the patchwork of climbing ferns. The splashes of the swimming pool echo the small waterfall and gurgling stream in the garden. Small presents, such as designer soaps, are placed on the beds during the nightly turndown service.

SOUTHWESTERN GULF COAST

Centara Grand (Central Samui Beach Resort; Map p194; ☎ 0 7723 0500; www.centralhotelsresorts.com; r 8900-19,500B; ☒ ☐ ☒) This resort has recently undergone a name change, making it even trickier for the Thai employees to pronounce. We suggest they try something like 'Kid Heaven' – they'll avoid the trademark 'r' and 'l' switcheroo, and everyone will know that it's Samui's go-to resort for families. Centara is a massive, manicured compound in the heart of Chaweng, but the palm-filled property is so large that you can safely escape the streetside bustle. Rooms are found in a hotel-like building that is conspicuously Western in theme and décor. Parents can escape to the spa, or one of the four restaurants, and leave the children at the labyrinth of swimming pools under the watchful eye of an inhouse babysitter.

Library (Map p194; ☎ 0 7742 2407; www.thelibrary .name; bungalows 9000-12,000B; ☒ ☐ ☒) This place is too cool for school, which is ironic since it's called 'the Library'. The entire resort is a sparkling white mirage accented with black trimming and slatted curtains. Besides the futuristic iMac computer in each page (rooms are called 'pages' here), our favourite feature is the large monochromatic wall art – it glows brightly in the evening and you can adjust the colour depending on your mood. Lifesize statues are engaged in the act of reading, and if you also feel inclined to pick up a book, the on-site library houses an impressive assortment of colourful art and design books. The large rectangular pool is not to be missed – it's tiled in piercing shades of red, making the term 'bloodbath' suddenly seem appealing.

Amari Palm Reef Resort (Map p194; ☎ 0 7742 2015; reservations@palmreef.amari.com; www.amari.com; r & bungalows 9500-11,500B; ☒ ☒) Most of the accommodation is housed in a beautiful whitewashed hotel complex across the street from the beach. The pricier items are double-decker villas set in a gorgeous garden with plenty of trickling water features. Swimming pools and restaurants abound. Rooms are discounted 45% during low season.

HAT LAMAI

Whether you're looking to spend 200B, 2000B or 20,000B, Lamai has accommodation to suit every wallet size. This 'New Chaweng' is almost as busy as its neighbour up the coast, and while prices are still slightly less expensive, the beach at Chaweng

is undoubtedly nicer. South of Lamai, Hua Thanon is a small, quieter beach with a couple standout resorts.

Budget

New Hut (Map p197; ☎ 0 7723 0437; newhut@hotmail .com; huts 200-500B) New Hut is a rare beachfront cheapie with tiny-but-charming A-frame huts. The wooden structures, including the welcoming restaurant, are covered with layers of thick black paint.

Beer's House (Map p197; ☎ 0 7723 0467; bungalows 200-550B) These tiny shade-covered bungalows are lined up right along the sand. Some huts have a communal toilet, but all have plenty of room to sling a hammock and laze the day away. People with their own bathroom will be pleased to find freshly retiled surfaces. The lights take a little while to turn on after you flick the switch, so don't be too hasty when summoning the management.

Sukasem (Map p197; ☎ 0 7742 4119; bungalows 400-800B; ☒) Facing out on a sandy lot, Sukasem's sparkling bungalows are great value. There isn't much atmosphere, however, and some guests might find that there's a little too much traffic – the main road is a bit close, and heaps of small boats park on the beach out back.

Amity (Map p197; ☎ 0 7742 4084; bungalows 350-1500B; ☒) Amity offers alluring modern bungalows and a few ramshackle cheapies with shared bathroom – there's no theme, just a mishmash of accommodation that changes style depending on the price range (we liked the 700B huts). The air-conditioned cottages are a welcome addition to the repertoire.

Sunrise Bungalow (Map p197; ☎ 0 7742 4433; www .sunrisebungalow.com; bungalows 400-1300B; ☒) Steps away from the awkward giggles at Hin Ta Hin Yai (the island's infamous genital-shaped rocks), Sunrise offers budget travellers a relaxing place to hang their backpack. The owner is a sixth-generation Samui native.

Midrange

Spa Resort (Map p197; ☎ 0 7723 0855; www.spasamui .com; bungalows 900-3500B; ☒) This health spa has a bevy of therapeutic programs on offer, and no one seems to mind that the lodging is cheap by Lamai's standards. Programs include colonics, massage, aqua detox, hypnotherapy and yoga, just to name a few. The bathrooms leave a bit to be desired, but who needs a toilet when you're doing a week-long cleansing fast? Accommodation tends to book up quickly, so it's best to reserve in advance (by email). Nonguests are welcome to partake in the programs.

Bill Resort (Map p197; ☎ 0 7741 8870; www.billresort .com; r & bungalows 1000-5500B; 🅿) A tornado of colourful materials and textures, Bill Resort is a jungly spot set on a slope at the south end of Lamai. Don't be shy about wanting to see several types of cottages; some rooms are a bargain, while others are a bit of a rip-off. Ask about the free tours to Bill's nearby 'mountain garden' retreat.

Star Bay Beach & Garden (Map p197; ☎ 0 7742 4546; www.starbay-beach.com; houses 1500-2500B; 🅿🅿) If you're travelling in a small group, or looking to stay on the island for a while, Star Bay might be the right place for you. An on-site team manages these privately owned properties, and rents them out to tourists. Each villa has a living room, kitchen, and private gardens. You will be charged separately for electricity, so turn off your air-con during the day!

Lamai Wanta (Map p197; ☎ 0 7742 4550; 0 7742 4218; www.lamaiwanta.com; r & bungalows 1600-3400B; 🅿🅿🅿) The pool area feels a bit retro, with its swatchbook of beige- and blue-toned tiles, but there are modern motel rooms and bungalows in the back with fresh coats of white paint. On the inside, rooms tread a fine line between being 'minimal' and sparse.

Top End

Thai House Beach Resort (Map p197; ☎ 0 7723 2451; www.thaihousebeach-resort.com; bungalows 3500-5200B; 🅿🅿) If there weren't bikini-clad guests at the pool, Thai House Beach could be mistaken for a stunning seaside temple with wooden pavilions that pierce the green canopy of palms. Spend the extra 800B and go for a villa; the cheaper rooms are surprisingly spartan.

Tamarind Retreat (Map p197; ☎ 0 7723 0571; www .tamarindretreat.com; villas 3500-11,600B; 🅿🅿) Tucked away from the beach within a silent coconut palm plantation, Tamarind's small collection of villas are each elaborated with a different design schema. Some have granite boulders built into walls and floors; others offer private ponds or creative outdoor baths. There's a seven-night minimum stay (three nights in low season) and free pick-up at the airport is included. Advance reservations are a must.

Samui Jasmine Resort (Map p197; ☎ 0 7723 2446; www.samuijasmineresort.com; r & bungalows 3800-5000B;

🅿🅿) Pleasant Samui Jasmine is a great deal along Lamai's sun-bleached sands. Go for the lower-priced rooms – most have excellent views of the ocean and the crystal-coloured lap pool. The design scheme features plenty of varnished teak and frilly accessories such as lavender pillows.

Rocky Resort (Map p197; ☎ 0 7741 8367; www .rockyresort.com; Hua Thanon; r 4200-14,000B; 🅿🅿) Our favourite spot in Lamai, Rocky finds the right balance between an upmarket ambience and an unpretentious, sociable atmosphere. During the quieter months the prices are a steal, since ocean views abound, and each room has been furnished with beautiful Thai-inspired furniture that seamlessly incorporates a modern twist. The pool has been carved in between a collection of boulders mimicking the rocky beach nearby (hence the name). The attention to detail permeates the restaurant as well – don't miss out on Rocky's delicious dishes served throughout the day.

Renaissance (Map p197; ☎ 0 7742 9300; www.ren aissancekohsamui.com; bungalows 5900-12,600B; 🅿🅿) Rambling Renaissance expands over the entire northern headland of Lamai. The hilly property features stunning villas in a manicured garden that feels wild and charmingly overgrown. The sugar candies in the lobby are delicious.

Villa Nalinnadda (Map p197; ☎ 0 7723 3131; www .nalinnadda.com; Hua Thanon; bungalows 6000-6500B; 🅿🅿) Villa Nalinnadda's exterior walls are swathed in undulating waves of white adobe that mimic the bubbling water in the rectangular plunge pool. Seven suites of various shapes and sizes face out towards the swaying ocean, offering a blend of romantic solitude while also fostering a convivial atmosphere among guests. Our favourite thing about Nalinnadda is the service – genuine smiles abound and the exceptionally friendly staff do everything in their power to assure a pleasant stay – breakfast is even served on each room's private porch. They had us at hello, Renee Zellwegger would say.

Pavilion Resort (Map p197; ☎ 0 7742 4420; www .pavilionsamui.com; r & bungalows 10,000-28,000B; 🅿🅿) Pavilion has a sophisticated contemporary design with great lighting effects that 'promise romance' according to the brochures. Everything is sleek and perfectly planned; from the dangle of each paper lantern to the vertical angle of the potted alfalfa sprouts. The 'hydro pool villas' have gargantuan Jacuzzis, and water-spouting turtle statues surround the curling beachside pool. The room rates are astronomical, but 'special promotions' involving large discounts are often available.

NORTHERN BEACHES

Ko Samui's northern beaches have the largest range of accommodation. Choeng Mon has some of the most opulent resorts in the world, while Mae Nam and Bang Po cling to their backpacker roots. Bo Phut, in the middle, is the shining star.

Choeng Mon (Plai Lam)

While technically known as Plai Lam, this rugged outcropping is often called Choeng Mon after the largest beach in the area. If you happen to be the CEO of a *Fortune 500* company, Choeng Mon is where you'll stay. These resorts are locked in an unwavering battle to out-posh one another.

White House (☎ 0 7724 7921; 0 7724 5318; www .hotelthewhitehouse.com; r 5000-6600B; ✖ ✚) You can check Angkor Wat off your 'to do' list – the White House feels like the seat of an ancient empire hidden deep within the thickest jungle. Sandstone temples bleed luscious tropical ferns from every crevice, and the gazes of praying diety statues pierce the rambling foliage.

Imperial Boat House Hotel (☎ 0 7742 5041-52; www.imperialhotels.com; r 4000-5500B, boat ste 6000-6700B; ✖ ✚) This sophisticated retreat has a three-storey hotel, and several free-standing bungalows made from imported teak rice barges whose bows have been transformed into stunning patios. Oxidized copper cannons blast streams of water into the boat-shaped swimming pool.

Sala Samui (☎ 0 7724 5888; www.salasamui.com; bungalows US$360-1100; ✖ ▢ ✚) Look out folks, these guys mean business – they quote their room rates in US dollars instead of baht. Is the hefty price tag worth it? Probably. The design scheme is undeniably exquisite – regal whites and lacquered teaks are generously lavished throughout, while subtle turquoise accents draw on the colour of each villa's private plunge pool.

Tongsai Bay (☎ 0 7724 5480-5500; www.tongsaibay .co.th; ste 11,000-30,000B; ✖ ✚) For serious pampering, head to this secluded luxury gem. Expansive and impeccably maintained, the hilly grounds make the cluster of bungalows look more like a small village. Golf carts whiz around the vast landscape transporting guests

to various activities such as massages or dinner. All the extra-swanky split-level suites have day-bed rest areas, gorgeous romantic décor, stunning views, large terraces and creatively placed bathtubs (you'll see). Facilities include salt- and fresh-water pools, a tennis court, the requisite spa, a dessert shop, and several restaurants.

Sila Evason Hideaway (☎ 0 7724 5678; www.six senses.com/hideaway-samui/index.php; bungalows from 17,000B; ✖ ▢ ✚) We're not saying that you should sell all your earthly possessions (because then you'll have nothing to pack), but this hidden bamboo paradise is worth the once-in-a-lifetime splurge. Set along a rugged promontory, Sila Evason strikes the perfect balance between opulence and rustic charm, and defines the term 'barefoot elegance'. Most of the villas have stunning concrete plunge pools and offer magnificent views of the silent bay below. The regal, semi-outdoor bathrooms give the phrase 'royal flush' a whole new meaning. Beige golf buggies move guests between their hidden cottages and the stunning amenities strewn throughout the property – including a world-class spa and two excellent restaurants.

Big Buddha Beach (Bang Rak)

This area gets its moniker from the huge golden Buddha that acts as overlord from the small nearby quasi-island of Ko Fan. Its proximity to the airport means lower prices at the resorts.

Chez Ban-Ban Resort (☎ 0 7724 5135; cottages 500-1000B; ✖) A bit French, and a bit Thai (as the name would suggest), Chez Ban-Ban is a seaside jumble of burgundy brick cottages – each one named after a French herb. Green curries and petanque balls further contribute to the subdued East-meets-West motif.

Shambala (☎ 0 7742 5330; www.samui-shambala .com; bungalows 600-1000B; ✖) While surrounding establishments answer the call of upmarket travellers, this laid-back, English-run place is a backpacking stalwart with a subtle hippy feel. There's plenty of communal cushion seating, a great wooden sundeck, and the bungalows are bright and roomy. Staff doles out travel tips and smiles in equal measure.

Samui Mermaid (☎ 0 7742 7547; www.samui -mermaid.info; r 600-2500B; ✖ ▢ ✚) Samui Mermaid is a great choice in the budget category because it feels like a full-fledged resort. There are two large swimming pools, copious beach chairs, two lively restaurants and every room has cable TV. The landing strip at Samui's airport is only a couple of kilometres away, so sometimes there's noise, but free airport transfers sweeten the deal.

Maya Buri (☎ 0 7748 4656, 08 1539 4194; www.maya buri.com; r incl breakfast 1200-1600B; ✖ 🖳 🔊) Maya Buri's inland location near the airport means that these boutique bungalows would be four times more expensive if they were situated along Chaweng. The modern resort has been designed with finesse – airy rooms, stocked with teak furniture, are focused around a cooling infinity pool.

Bo Phut

The beach isn't breathtaking, but Bo Phut has the most dynamic lodging in all of Samui. A string of vibrant boutique cottages starts deep within the clutter of Fisherman's Village and radiates outward along the sand.

Khuntai (☎ 0 7724 5118; 08 6686 2960; r 600-850B; ✖) This clunky orange guesthouse is as cheap as decent rooms get on Samui. A block away from the beach, on the outskirts of Fisherman's Village, Khuntai's 2nd-floor rooms are drenched in afternoon sunshine and feature outdoor lounging spots.

Cactus (☎ 0 7724 5565; cactusbung@hotmail.com; bungalows 700-1590B; ✖) Cactus does a good job of keeping up with Bo Phut's boutique crowd by offering cavelike concoctions that sizzle with burnt reds and oranges. The palpable backpacker buzz means that rooms err on the basic side, but they're still clean, comfy and sport loads of charm (the fan bathrooms could benefit from an air freshener though). Fan huts are half price in low season.

Lodge (☎ 0 7742 5337; www.apartmentsamui.com; r 1350-1900B; ✖ 🔊) Another great choice in Bo Phut, the Lodge feels like a colonial hunting chalet with pale walls and dark wooden beams jutting across the ceiling. Every room has scores of wall hangings and a private balcony overlooking the beach. The 'pent huts' on the top floor are very spacious. Reservations are a must – this place always seems to be full.

L'Hacienda (☎ 0 7724 5943; www.samui-hacienda.com; r 1400-3000B; ✖ 🔊) The entrance is one cross short of looking like a Spanish mission (if you ignore the statues of praying oriental deities) – floors are tiled with polished terracotta and the white façade bursts with rounded archways. A similar design motif permeates the

eight adorable rooms, which sport loads of personal touches such as pebbled bathroom walls and translucent bamboo lamps. There's a charming surprise waiting for you on the roof, and we're pretty sure you'll love it as much as we did.

Red House (☎ 0 7742 5686; www.design-visio.com; r 2000B; ✖) To reach the small reception area at the back, guests must pass through a sleek shoe shop drenched in jet-black hues and set ablaze with flaming tints of red paint – think Carrie Bradshaw's closet if it were 2048 and she lived in a Chinese bordello. The four rooms upstairs are decorated with a similar spiciness. Intricate oriental patterns liven the walls and canopied beds are swathed in streamers of ruby and chartreuse. A cache of reclining beach chairs and potted plants is the perfect rooftop escape.

B1 Villa Spa (☎ 0 7742 7268; www.b1villa.com; ste 3500-5000B; ✖ 🔊) There's a refreshing burst of character at this inn-style option along the beach in Fisherman's Village. The earth's vital energy forces have been factored into the Feng Shui-ed design of the eight vibrant suites. Each room displays a unique collection of wall art, and has been given a special moniker – the 2nd-storey spaces are named after the stars in Orion's belt. Oh, and it's B1 as in 'B1 with yourself', get it?

Zazen (☎ 0 7742 5085; www.samuizazen.com; r 5300-12,800B; ✖ 🖳 🔊) Zazen is the boutique-iest boutique resort on Samui – every inch of this charming getaway has been thoughtfully and creatively designed. It's 'Asian minimalism meets modern Rococo' with a scarlet accent wall, lots of pillows, a dash of Feng Shui and generous smattering of good taste. Terracotta deities meditate beside flat-screen TVs, but our favourite accoutrement is the shiny amorphous blob sculpture in each villa – it kind of looks like the infamous 'Asahi Golden Poo' in Tokyo (which is meant to represent a bead of the froth from a freshly poured beer). Guests relax poolside on comfy beach chairs gently shaded by canvas parasols. The walk-in prices are pretty scary, so it's best to book in advance.

Bandara (☎ 0 7742 5337; www.bandararesort.com; r 6050-9350B; ✖ 🖳 🔊) Bandara's is different from the top-end bungalows on Samui. The design philosophy has refocused the accommodation away from the beach, into several hotel structures that collectively form a U-shape pointing towards the ocean. A central expanse of perfectly manicured grounds has a jungle theme, but incorporates order and symmetry by using thatched *săh·lahs,* wooden pilasters and stone figurines.

Anantara (☎ 0 7742 8300; www.anantara.com; r 7000-15,000B; 🔀 🖳 �) Anantara's stunning palanquin entrance satisfies every fantasy of a far-flung oriental kingdom. Low-slung torches spurt plumes of unwavering fire, and the residual smoke creates a light fog around the fanned palm fronds higher up. Clay and copper statues of grimacing jungle creatures abound on the property's wild acreage, while guests savour wild teas in an open-air pagoda, swim in the lagoon-like infinity-edged swimming pool, or indulge in a relaxing spa treatment. The 'deluxe' hotel-style rooms have moveable window-walls in the bathroom, but feel a tad small when considering the steep price tag.

Mae Nam

Mae Nam doesn't have the most beautiful tract of sand, but it offers cheap accommodation relative to the other beaches.

CocoPalm Resort (☎ 0 7742 5095; bungalows 450-1000B; 🔀) The bungalows at CocoPalm have been crafted with tonnes of rattan. A rectangular pool is the centrepiece along the beach – and the price is right for a resort-like atmosphere.

Maenam Resort (☎ 0 7742 5116; www.maenam resort.com; bungalows 1200-2700B; 🔀 🖳) Palm-bark cottages are set in several rows amid a private, jungle-like garden. The cottages are decked out in a mix of wicker and wooden furnishings, and vary in price according to their distance from the beach. Suites are a steal for families.

Harry's (☎ 0 7742 5447; www.harrys-samui.com; bungalows 1200-3000B; 🔀 🌺) Arriving at Harry's feels like entering sacred temple grounds. Polished teak wood abounds in the lobby and the classic pitched roofing reaches skyward. The concrete bungalows, stashed in a verdant garden, do not retain the flamboyant architectural theme out front, but they're cute and comfortable nonetheless.

Bang Po & Laem Yai

The small enclave of Bang Po has a cache of budget bungalows, and further west, the mountainous cape of Laem Yai has one ridiculous resort.

Sunbeam (☎ 0 7742 0600; bungalows 500-1000B) Quiet Sunbeam has just over a dozen rustic cottages by the sea. They're spacious, comfy, and offer beach views from the porch. Brick paths wind through a lush garden, and cool breezes pass through the shanty-like bar.

Moon (☎ 0 7724 7740; bungalows 600-1800B) Moon is a throwback to an earlier time when Samui was rife with seaside shacks. Several modern concrete cottages have recently sprung up on the property – they're comfortable and clean, and they don't detract from the general laid-back jungle-on-the-beach atmosphere. The large wood-beamed restaurant is the heart of the action.

Health Oasis Resort (☎ 0 7742 0124; www.health oasisresort.com; bungalows 800-4500B; 🔀) If you're lookin' to get 'cleansed' – whether it's your aura or your colon, then you've happened upon the right place. New Age is all the rage at the Health Oasis. Guests can choose from a variety of healing packages involving everything from meditation to fasting. Bungalows are modern and receive plenty of sunshine. There's also a vegetarian restaurant on site, of course.

Four Seasons (☎ 0 7724 3000; www.fourseasons.com /kohsamui; Laem Yai; villas 30,000B) Four Seasons Koh Samui feels more like a private village than a resort. The international company has purchased an entire peninsula on the island, and transformed it into a hilly enclave. A ridiculous amount of on-site amenities means that you'll probably never leave the grounds. Each villa has a large private plunge-pool and spacious sitting areas. Should you decide to be more social, there's a beautiful stretch of flaxen sand offering beach chairs and water sports. If you're into hotel provisions (ie soaps, slippers etc), each suite is loaded with designer fragrances, sandals, bathrobes – you name it, they have it – a klepto's dream place.

WEST COAST

Largely the domain of Thai tourists, Samui's west coast doesn't have the most picturesque beaches, but it's a welcome escape from the eastside bustle.

Na Thon

Na Thon is the island's main settlement – a large pier dominates the beach, and the town itself is far from picturesque.

Seaside Palace Hotel (☎ 0 7742 1079; r 400-500B; 🔀) If Seaside Palace were any closer to the pier, it would be a boat. We found the rooms to be smokey, but you won't find air-con cheaper than this. It's doable if you must spend the night in Na Thon, but go for the 500B rooms – they're larger and some have ocean views.

Jinta Hotel (☎ 0 7742 0630, 0 7723 6369; www .jintasamui.com; r 500-650B; 🅿 🖥) Another option near the pier, Jinta's white walls and linoleum floors feel a bit institutional, but the place gets the job done. All rooms have satellite TV.

Grand Sea View Hotel (☎ 0 7742 0441; www .grandseaviewbeachhotel.com; r 1000-2000B; 🅿 🖥) Na Thon's pick of the litter, this five-floor hotel is popular with visiting businessmen. Spacious rooms have sparkling tile floors, light wooden framing, air-con and cable TV. The higher levels have great views over the town and sea.

Thong Yang & Taling Ngam

Thong Yang is close to the ferry piers heading to Don Sak, although still a quiet place to relax. Taling Ngam is a quiet and charming hideaway further south with a quaint local village nearby.

Wiesenthal (☎ 0 7723 5165; fax 0 7741 5480; Taling Ngam; bungalows incl breakfast 1500-2500B; 🅿) The name sort of sounds like smokey German beer hall made from thick trunks of cedar, but this Thai-owned operation is a breezy beachside paradise. Cast modesty aside, spread your curtains wide, and welcome sunshine and sea views in through your floor-to-ceiling windows. Lounge-worthy porch furniture further contributes to the comfy, casual vibe established at the open-air restaurant and pool.

Big John (☎ 0 7742 3025; international@sawadee .com; Ao Chon Khram; r 2000B, bungalows 3000-5000B; 🅿 🖥 🏊) Big John is a casual place on a patch of beach not too far from Na Thon. Square, thatched-roof bungalows are dotted around a sandy lot. Inside, colourful sutra and *Veda* tapestries dangle throughout. The restaurant is quite popular.

Ban Sabai (☎ 0 7742 8200; Taling Ngam; www.bansabai sunset.com; bungalows 6800-25,000B; 🅿) Beautiful Baan Sabai has 20 rooms on a secluded stretch of sand and palms. Villas along the beach have multi-room bathrooms under a charming patchwork of thatching and starlight. Rooms have a private waterfall – the bathtubs receive water from a charming cascade-like faucet. The intimate common

spaces and semidetached cottages make this resort a great place to relax with friends.

Ao Phangkha

Around Laem Hin Khom on the southern end of Samui's west coast, this little bay is often known as Emerald Cove.

Phang Ka Paradise Resort (☎ 0 7733 4207, 08 4647 4632; www.samuixl.com/phangka-paradise; bungalows 2500-4500B; 🅿 🖥 🏊) A newbie on the Samui scene, Phang Ka's owner just returned to her native Samui after spending several decades working as a nurse in New York (so her English is pretty darn good). Each beachside bungalow is a facsimile of the next, but they're all immaculate, spacious and they still have that new-car smell. In-room internet, fridge and satellite TV are added perks.

Coconut Villa (☎ 0 7733 4069; bungalows 4000-6000B; 🅿 🖥 🏊) The perky huts that used to rest on this isolated bay have been recently replaced with an array of posh villas – now the price tags all have a newly added zero.

SOUTH COAST (HAT NA THIAN)

The southern end of Ko Samui is spotted with rocky headlands and smaller sandy coves. Accommodation is mostly midrange and top-end. These places are on Hat Na Thian.

Laem Set Inn (☎ 0 7723 3299; www.laemset.com; bungalows 1200-20,000B; 🅿 🖥 🏊) This secluded paradise offers accommodation to suit every budget. Cheaper huts have woven bamboo siding, and the midrange choices are gathered in blocks of units that have a homey vibe. The priciest options sport snazzy lacquered upholstery and are authentic southern Thai homes that were dismantled and reconstructed at the resort.

Centara Villas Samui (Central Samui Village; ☎ 0 7742 4020; www.centralhotelsresorts.com; bungalows 4500-5500B; 🅿 🖥 🏊) Driving through the remote dirt roads of the south coast feels like a trip through Jurassic Park. Centara Villas are set right where the wild thicket meets a deserted patch of boulder-strewn sand. Pavilions and terraced boardwalks, which climb over the rocky landscape, link the chic, wooden cottages.

Eating

If you thought it was hard to pick a place to sleep, Samui has even more options when it comes to dining. Lately, shmancy restaurants outnumber Thai food shacks, as opulent resorts continue to lure world-class chefs. The 'scene' changes with the wind – currently Italian joints are popping up left and right, but next year is anyone's guess. Most hotels and bungalow operations also have their own restaurants, so you rarely need to go far to grab a bite.

HAT CHAWENG

Dozens of the restaurants on the 'strip' serve a mixed bag of local bites, international cuisine, and greasy fast food. For the best ambience, get off the strip and head to the beach, where many bungalow operators set up tables on the sand and have glittery fairy lights at night.

Khaosan Restaurant & Bakery (Map p194; dishes from 60B; breakfast, lunch & dinner) From *filet mignon* to flapjacks and everything in between, this chow house is popular with those looking for a cheap nosh. Hang around after your meal and catch a newly released movie on the big TV. It's everything you'd expect from a place called 'Khaosan'.

Islander (Map p194; ☎ 08 1788 6239; dishes 100-250B; 8am-2am) This is a popular, pub-style shanty with Western and Thai food, a kids' menu, outdoor tables, billiards and sports on TV – something for everyone. Breakfast is a sausage fest (literally) – the stacks of greasy meat are perfect cure-all remedy for your Singha-induced hangover.

Gringo's Cantina (Map p194; ☎ 0 7741 3267; dishes 140-280B; 2pm-midnight) Wash down a Tex-Mex classic with a jug of sangria or a frozen margarita. We liked the *chimichangas* (deep-fried burritos) mostly because we like saying '*chimichanga*'. There are burgers, pizza and veggie options too, for those who don't want to go 'south of the border'.

Captain Kirk (Map p194; ☎ 08 1270 5376; dishes 140-480B; dinner) Beam yourself up to this beautiful rooftop garden for a vast selection of international eats. Patrons often lounge on the cushioned bamboo furniture and indulge in a post-repast cocktail.

Prego (Map p194; ☎ 0 7742 2015; mains 200-700B; lunch & dinner) This swankified ministry of culinary style serves up fine Italian cuisine in an ultra-stylish pagoda.

Page (Map p194; ☎ 0 7742 2767; dishes 180-850B; breakfast, lunch & dinner) If you can't afford to stay at the ultra-swank Library (p201), have a meal at their beachside restaurant. The food is overpriced (of course) but you'll receive glances from the beach bums on Chaweng as they try to figure out if you're a jetsetter or movie star. Lunch is a bit more casual and affordable, but you'll miss the designer lighting effects in the evening.

Bellini (Map p194; ☎ 0 7741 3831; dishes from 200B; dinner) A staple on Soi Colibri, Bellini sizzles under designer mood lighting. There's Italian on the menu, but not in a pizza-pasta kind of way – think veal, rock lobster and a dainty assortment of tapas.

Olivio (Map p194; ☎ 0 7723 1500; dishes 280-580B; lunch & dinner) The charming seaside restaurant at Baan Haad Ngam Resort (p200), Olivio is an elegant outdoor dining experience with an assortment of Italian and Thai treats. The decadent 'hot chocolate cake' scores the most yum's. Call ahead to arrange a complimentary transfer (if you're staying in Chaweng or along the north coast).

Betelnut (Map p194; ☎ 0 7741 3370; mains 600-800B; dinner) Betelnut's wooden benches and baby-blue flooring aren't much to look at – the focus here is the innovative Californian cuisine. Fusion favourites bait foodies, who come to savour a short menu of dishes with long names. Reservations recommended.

Zico's (Map p194; ☎ 0 7723 1560; menu 750B; dinner) This palatial *churrascaria* puts the '*carne*' in Carnaval. Vegetarians beware – Zico's is an all-you-can-eat Brazilian meat-fest complete with saucy dancers sporting peacock-like outfits.

HAT LAMAI

As Samui's second-most populated beach, Lamai has a surprisingly limited assortment of decent eateries compared to Chaweng. Most visitors dine wherever they're staying.

Will Wait (Map p197; ☎ 0 7742 4263; dishes 60-200B; breakfast, lunch & dinner) This joint's been around forever, and it never loses popularity, which says a lot in Samui's fickle eating market. The menu is stuffed with breakfast fare, Thai dishes, pizzas and cakes. There are several locations in Chaweng as well.

Mr Samui (Map p197; ☎ 0 7742 4630; dishes 100-180B; lunch & dinner) Enter Baan Soi Gemstones (look for the 'illy' sign out front) and pass the veritable garage sale of oriental knick-knacks to find a tiny cluster of tables and cushions. Savour your nutty *massaman* curry amid flamboyant Chinese wall art, dripping chandeliers and gaudy geometric pillows (everything's for sale).

Rocky's Restaurant (Map p197; ☎ 0 7741 8367; dishes 300-800B; ☺ lunch & dinner) Easily the top dining spot on Lamai, Rocky's gourmet dishes are actually a bargain when you convert the baht into your native currency. Try the signature beef tenderloin with bleu cheese – it's like sending your tastebuds on a Parisian vacation. On Tuesday evenings, diners enjoy a special Thai-themed evening with a prepared menu of local delicacies. Sunday night barbecues are quite popular too.

NORTHERN BEACHES

Some of Samui's finest establishments are located on the northern coast. Boho Bo Phut has several trendy eateries to match the string of yuppie boutique hotels.

Choeng Mon

our pick Dining On The Rocks (☎ 0 7724 5678; reservations-samui@sixsenses.com; menus from 1500B; ☺ dinner) The Sila Evason's (p203) ultimate dining experience takes place on nine cantilevered verandas of weathered teak and bamboo that yawn over the gulf. After sunset, guests feel like they're dining on a wooden barge set adrift on a starlit sea. The 'chef's table', located right beside the kitchen, is an unforgettable 10-course fiesta for the senses. Each serving is the brainchild of the experimental cooks who regularly dabble with taste, texture and temperature. You'll have to book well in advance if you want to sit at 'table 99' – the honeymooners' table – positioned on a private terrace.

Big Buddha Beach (Bang Rak)

BBC (☎ 0 7742 5264; dishes 60-200B; ☺ breakfast, lunch & dinner) No, this place has nothing to do with our parent company, or 'Dr Who' – BBC stands for Big Buddha Café. It's popular with local expats, and there's a large international menu and exquisite ocean views from the patio.

Elephant & Castle (☎ 0 7743 0394; dishes 80-250B; ☺ lunch & dinner) The ultimate hangout for homesick Brits, the Elephant & Castle is the perfect replica of a London pub. There's beer by the pint and the steak and kidney pies will give you meat sweats for days.

Antica Locanda (☎ 0 7724 5163; dishes 170-280B; ☺ 2pm-midnight) This friendly *trattoria* has pressed white tablecloths and caskets of Italian wine. Try the *vongole alla marinara* (clams in white wine) and don't forget to check out the succulent specials of the day.

Bo Phut

Coffee Junction (☎ 08 9866 1085; snacks from 30B; ☺ breakfast, lunch & dinner) This coffee shop will relieve you of your Starbucks craving without making you feel guilty for being an unadventurous tourist or a creature of habit.

Frog & Gecko Pub (☎ 0 7742 5248; dishes 60-200B; ☺ breakfast, lunch & dinner) Locals recommend this popular spot on the beach. Part sports bar, part restaurant, it serves full English breakfasts (along with the footy), as well as the usual assortment of Thai and English pub food. Quiz nights lure trivia buffs once a week.

Starfish & Coffee (☎ 0 7742 7201; mains from 120B; ☺ breakfast, lunch & dinner) This adorable eatery was probably named after the Prince song, since we couldn't find any starfish on the menu (there's loads of coffee though). Evenings feature warm candlelit dinners and sunset views of rugged Ko Pha-Ngan.

Villa Bianca (☎ 0 7724 5041, 08 9873 5867; dishes from 200B; ☺ lunch & dinner) Another fantastic Italian spot on Samui, Villa Bianca is a sea of crisp white tablecloths and woven lounge chairs. Who knew wicker could be so sexy?

Pier (☎ 0 7743 0681; dishes 200-390B; ☺ lunch & dinner) This sleek black box sticks out among Bo Phut's narrow Chinese tenements. It's the hippest address in Fisherman's Village, sporting multilevel terraces, a lively bar, and plenty of wide furniture to lounge around and watch the rickety fishing vessels pull into the harbour.

Zazen (☎ 0 7742 5085; dishes 550-850B; set menu from 1300B; ☺ lunch & dinner) The chef describes the food as 'organic and orgasmic', and the ambient 'yums' from elated diners definitely confirm the latter. This romantic dining experience comes complete with ocean views, dim candle lighting and soft music. Reservations recommended.

Mae Nam & Bang Po

Ko-Seng (☎ 0 7742 5365; Mae Nam; dishes 100-300B; ☺ dinner) Hidden down a narrow side street near Mae Nam's Chinese temple, Ko Samui's best kept secret is a welcome escape from the island's restaurants that fuss over the décor instead of their food. It's a local haunt that dishes out top-notch soft-shell crab and plump, flash-fried prawns in a peppery sauce.

Bang Po Seafood (☎ 0 7742 0010; Bang Po; dishes from 100B; ☺ dinner) A meal at Bang Po Seafood is a test for the tastebuds. It's one of the few restaurants that serve traditional Ko Samui fare (think of it as island roadkill, well, actually its more like local sea-kill): recipes call for ingredients such as raw sea urchin roe, baby octopus, sea water, coconut, and local tumeric.

WEST COAST

The quiet west coast features some of the best seafood on Samui. Na Thon has a giant **grocery** and a **day market** (Th Thawi Ratchaphakdi) – it's worth stopping by to grab some snacks before your ferry ride.

Wiesenthal (☎ 0 7723 5165; Taling Ngam; dishes 90-250B; ☼ breakfast, lunch & dinner) Wiesenthal is a casual open-air restaurant overlooking a quiet beach. Devour a scrumptious assortment of international cuisine in the shade of a bamboo umbrella.

Big John Seafood (☎ 0 7742 3025; Thong Yang; dishes 60-300B; ☼ breakfast, lunch & dinner) Big John's menu looks like an encyclopaedia of marine life. The seafood is freshly caught daily from various fishing hotspots off the coast. Dinnertime is particularly special – live entertainment kicks in around 6pm just as the sun plunges below the watery horizon.

our pick Five Islands (☎ 0 7741 5359, 08 1447 5371; Taling Ngam; dishes 150-500B; tours 5000-6500B; ☼ lunch & dinner) Five Islands defines the term 'destination dining' and offers the most unique eating experience on the island. Before your meal, a traditional long-tail boat will take you out into the turquoise sea to visit the haunting Five Sister Islands where you'll learn about the ancient and little-known art of harvesting bird nests to make bird's-nest soup – a Chinese delicacy. This perilous task is rewarded with large sums of cash – a kilo of bird's nests is usually sold for 100,000B to restaurants in Hong Kong (yup, that's five zeros). Upon returning to the beachside restaurant, you'll indulge in a *kan·đòk* featuring an assortment of dishes such as fried crab with garlic and pepper, roast duck curry, and lobster with cashew nuts. The lunch tour departs at 10am, and the dinner program leaves at 3pm. Customers are also welcome to dine without going on the tour.

Drinking & Entertainment

Samui's biggest party spot is, without a doubt, noisy Chaweng. Lamai and Bo Phut come in second and third respectively, while the rest of the island is generally quiet, as the drinking is usually focused around self-contained resort bars.

HAT CHAWENG

Making merry in Chaweng is a piece of cake. Most places are open until 2am and there are a few places that go strong all night long. Soi Green Mango has loads of girly bars. Soi Colibri and Soi Reggae Pub are raucous as well.

Christy's Cabaret (Map p194; ☎ 0 1894 0356) This flashy joint offers free *gà·teu·i* (also spelt *kàthoey*; transgender males) cabaret nightly at 11pm and attracts a mixed clientele of both sexes. Other ladyboys loiter out front and try to drag customers in, so to speak.

Pod (Map p194; ☎ 08 3692 7911, 08 4744 9207) Bathed in cool Prada greens, Pod feels like a hidden metropolitan lounge whose address is known only by the poshest of jet-setters.

Ark Bar (Map p194; ☎ 0 7742 2047) The 'it' destination for a Wednesday-night romp on Samui. Drinks are dispensed from the multi-coloured bar draped in paper lanterns, and guests lounge on pyramidal pillows strewn down the beach. The party usually starts around 4pm.

Green Mango (Map p194; ☎ 0 7742 2661) This place is so popular it has an entire soi named after it. Another Samui power-drinking house, it is cavernous, very loud and very faràng. Green Mango has blazing lights, soccer on TV, expensive drinks and masses of sweaty bodies swaying to dance music.

Reggae Pub (Map p194; ☎ 0 7742 2331) This fortress of fun sports an open-air dance floor with music spun by foreign DJs. It's a towering two-storey affair with long bars, pool tables, and a live-music stage. The whole place doubles as a shrine to Bob Marley.

Tropical Murphy's (Map p194; ☎ 0 7741 3614; dishes 50-300B) A popular faràng joint, Tropical Murphy's dishes out steak and kidney pie, fish and chips, lamb chops, and Irish stew. Come night-time, the live music kicks on and this place turns into the most popular Irish bar on Samui (yes, there are a few).

Q-Bar (Map p194; ☎ 08 1956 2742) Up on a hill overlooking the fray, sleek Q-Bar (an offshoot of the like-named bar in Bangkok) features a regular rotation of international DJs.

Deck (Map p194; ☎ 0 7723 0897) An open-air, multiterraced bar with comfortable lounging platforms and good views of the street scene below.

Sportsman's Bar & Grill (Map p194; ☎ 08 1079 1618) Down a small road away from the noise, the Sportsman's Bar is a giant yellow venue open all day long. Catch the latest sports match on the huge TVs, or grab a beer and check your email.

HAT LAMAI

In accordance with Lamai's reputation as a mini-Chaweng, this area has a smattering of girly bars and a couple of clubs, mostly along the road, rather than the beach.

Bauhaus (Map p197; ☎ 0 7741 8387/8) Lamai's long-running dance club, Bauhaus' DJ-ed beats are interspersed with short drag shows, Thai boxing demos and the occasional foam party.

NORTHERN BEACHES (BO PHUT)

Gecko (☎ 0 7724 5554) It's hard to believe that poured concrete could look so cool – these guys pull it off in slick, minimalist style. Fresh House music wafts through the air and guest DJs get things going on Sundays.

Billabong Surf Club (☎ 0 7743 0144) Billabong's all about Aussie rules – it's playing on the TV and the walls are smothered with memorabilia. This popular watering hole has great views of Ko Pha-Ngan and hearty portions of ribs and chops to go with your draught beer.

Frog & Gecko Pub (☎ 0 7742 5248) This tropical British watering hole and food stop is famous for its 'Wednesday Night Pub Quiz' competitions and its wide selection of music. Live sporting events are shown on the big screen.

Getting There & Away

AIR

Bangkok Airways has a flight every 30 minutes between Ko Samui and Bangkok (2000B to 4000B, one to 1½ hours). There is a **Bangkok Airways Office** (Map p194; ☎ 0 7742 0512-9) in Chaweng and another at the **airport** (Map p192; ☎ 0 7742 5011). The first and last flights of the day are always the cheapest.

Other destinations from Samui include Phuket (2000B to 3000B, 50 minutes, two daily) and Pattaya (3000B, one hour, three daily). There are flights to Krabi on Fridays and Sundays. During the high season, flights may be completely booked as much as six weeks in advance, so be sure to plan accordingly. If Samui flights are full, you can fly into Surat Thani and take a short ferry ride. Flights to Surat Thani are generally cheaper than a direct flight to the island.

At the time of research Thai Airways was announcing new flights connecting Ko Samui to various domestic and international destinations, which will hopefully add some competition and reduce flight prices.

BOAT

The ferry situation is rather convoluted: schedules and prices are always in flux, and there are tons of entry and exit points on Samui and the mainland. Where you leave and arrive will probably depend on what's available when you arrive in Surat Thani (after all, you probably don't want to hang around town). The main piers on the mainland are Ao Ban Don in town (for the night ferry), and Tha Thong and Don Sak (reachable by a bus/boat package) to the east of town. On Samui, the three oft-used ports are Na Thon, Mae Nam and Big Buddha. Service quality can also vary greatly within the same ferry company – some boats are rusty and rundown, others are much more modern and are even outfitted with TVs.

There are frequent daily boat departures between Samui and Surat Thani. The hourly Seatran ferry is a common option. Ferries cost 110B to 190B and take one to three hours, depending on the boat. A couple of these departures can connect with the train station in Phun Phin (for an extra 100B to 140B). The slow night boat to Samui (150B) leaves from central Surat Thani each night at 11pm, reaching Na Thon around 5am. It returns from Na Thon at 9pm, arriving at around 3am. Watch your bags on this boat.

Car ferries from Don Sak land at Thong Yang, about 10km south of Na Thon.

There are almost a dozen daily departures between Samui and Ko Pha-Ngan. These leave either from the Na Thong, Mae Nam or Big Buddha piers and take from 20 minutes to one hour (130B to 250B). On Ko Pha-Ngan there are two piers (Hat Rin and Thong Sala). The boats departing from Big Buddha service Hat Rin, and the other boats alight at Thong Sala. From the same piers, there are also around six daily departures between Samui and Ko Tao. These take 1¼ to 2½ hours and cost 350B to 600B. There are no car ferries from Samui to Ko Pha-Ngan.

BUS/TRAIN

A bus/ferry combo is more convenient than a train/ferry package because you don't have to switch transport in Phun Phin (a tiny town near Surat Thani). However, the trains are much more comfortable and spacious – especially at night. If you prefer the train, you can get off at Chumphon and catch the *Lomprayah Express* catamaran service the rest of the way to Samui.

The government-bus fares from Bangkok's Southern bus terminal include the cost of the ferry. These are 500B for 2nd-class passengers. Most private buses from Bangkok charge around 450B for the same journey and include the ferry fare. From Th Khao San in Bangkok it's possible to get bus/ferry combination tickets for as little as 350B, but service is substandard and theft is very common. If an agency on Th Khao San claims to be able to get you to Samui for less, it is almost certainly a scam as no profit can be made at such low prices.

Getting Around

See p193 for the dangers and annoyances concerning transport around the island, including motorcycle safety. You can rent motorcycles (and bicycles) from almost every resort on the island. The going rate is 200B to 300B per day, but for longer periods try to negotiate a better rate.

Sŏrng·tăa·ou drivers love to try to overcharge you, so it's always best to ask a third party for current rates, as they can change with the season. These vehicles run regularly during daylight hours only. It's about 30B to travel along one coast, and no more that 75B to travel halfway across the island. Figure about 20B for a five-minute ride on a motorcycle taxi.

TO/FROM THE AIRPORT

Taxi service on Samui is quite chaotic and prices can vary greatly depending on your driver's mood. Ask your resort about complimentary airport transfers or try the **Samui Shuttle** (www.samuishuttle.com).

KO PHA-NGAN

เกาะพะงัน

pop 12,100

While big Samui wheels and deals the big bucks, and little Tao revels in its status as the hyperactive brainchild of the diving industry, Ko Pha-Ngan quietly idles in between like a laid-back beach bum. For two decades (and still going strong) this steaming jungle island has been the go-to spot for party pilgrims. Thousands flock to Hat Rin every month for the eponymous full moon parties. These raucous events can be a 24-hour gig for those fuelled by adrenaline (and perhaps a couple other substances as well). This monthly influx of big baht has encouraged rapid growth, and now Ko Pha-Ngan is leaving its *raison d'etre* behind in search of a new reputation.

Hat Rin sees an exorbitant amount of visitors relative to the rest of the island. Party pilgrims flock to this peninsula for the legendary festivities on Sunrise Beach, and although most of them sleep through the daylight hours, the setting remains quite stunning despite the errant beer bottle in the sand.

Despite the prevalent backpacker vibe, the island is slowly creeping upmarket and becoming a choice destination for families. Each year, tired old shacks are replaced by crisp modern abodes. Soon, the phrase 'private infinity pool' and 'personal butler' will find a permanent place in the island's lexicon, replacing 'pass the dutch' and 'another whiskey bucket please'. But don't fret yet – the vast inland jungle continues to feel undiscovered, and there are still plenty of secluded bays on the northern and eastern coasts to string up a hammock and watch the tide roll in.

Orientation

Ko Pha-Ngan is the fifth-largest island in Thailand, measuring 193-sq-km. The town of Thong Sala is its administrative capital, Hat Rin is party central and little Chalok Lam, in the north, is starting to come into its own as another commercial centre.

Most of the island's visitors stay on the thin peninsula known as Hat Rin. This mountainous cape is flanked with beaches on either size, and is home to the infamous full moon parties held every month (p215). The rest of the island is noticeably quieter, although gradual development has meant an increase in population on the west and south coasts. The northern coast has a few good beaches that have modern amenities but feel relaxed and remote. The quiet eastern shore is virtually deserted.

About half of Ko Pha-Ngan's population lives in and around the small port of Thong Sala, where the ferries to and from Ko Tao, Surat Thani and Ko Samui dock.

Information

EMERGENCY

Police station (☎ 0 7737 7114) About 2km north of Thong Sala.

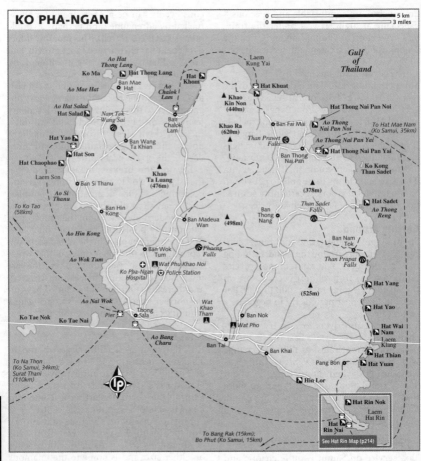

KO PHA-NGAN

INTERNET ACCESS

Hat Rin and Thong Sala are the main centres of internet activity, but every beach with development now offers access. Rates are generally 2B per minute, with a 10B to 20B minimum and discounts if you stay on for one hour. Places that offer a rate of 1B per minute usually have slower internet connections.

LAUNDRY

If you got neon body paint on your clothes during your full moon romp, don't bother sending them to the cleaners – the paint will never come out. Trust us, we tried. For your other washing needs, there are heaps of places that will gladly wash your clothes.

Prices hover around 40B per kilo, and express cleanings shouldn't be more than 60B per kilo.

MEDICAL SERVICES

Medical services can be a little dodgy in Ko Pha-Ngan – expect unstable prices and underqualified doctors. Serious medical issues and dental problems should be dealt with on nearby Ko Samui.

Ko Pha-Ngan Hospital (☎ 0 7737 7034; Thong Sala; ☯ 24hr) About 2.5km north of Thong Sala, offers 24-hour emergency services.

Sang's Clinic (☎ 0 1896 2195; Hat Rin; ☯ 5-10pm Mon-Fri, 10am-10pm Sat & Sun) Near the pier, Sang's is a trustworthy choice for fixing your 'Ko Pha-Ngan tattoo' (motorcycle muffler burn-mark) or other minor injuries.

MONEY

Thong Sala, Ko Pha-Ngan's financial 'capital', has plenty of banks, currency converters and several Western Union offices. Hat Rin has numerous ATMs and a couple of banks at the pier. There are a few ATMs dotted along the western and northern beaches.

POST

The main office is in Thong Sala and there's a smaller office right by the pier in Hat Rin.

TELEPHONE

There are many places offering long-distance phone services in the major tourist areas. Most internet cafés have calling services.

TOURIST INFORMATION & TRAVEL AGENCIES

There's no TAT office on Ko Pha-Ngan; we repeat: there is no TAT office on the island. Several travel agencies display signage claiming to be the official TAT outpost – these are bogus claims. That said, not everyone on the island is out to take advantage of you. There are a few agents on the island that have attained an official sanctioned status by the TAT; these shops will be more than happy to show you their license, and give you tourist information. Hat Rin has an ungodly amount of travel agencies, and there's also a cluster within eyeshot of Thong Sala pier terminus.

Several mini-magazines also offer comprehensive information about the island's accommodation, restaurants, activities and full moon parties. Our favourite option is *Phangan Info* (www.phangan.info).

Backpacker's Information Centre (Map p214; ☎ 0 7737 5535; www.backpackersthailand.com; Hat Rin) A must for travellers looking for info and tours, this standout operation is run by a gregarious Harley-riding expat. The UK-born owner has hung up his backpack in Ko Pha-Ngan and now helps others discover the island (and the rest of Thailand). He can hook you up with an assortment of quality activities such as scuba diving and live-aboard boat trips, and works hard to ensure that his customers are satisfied.

Dangers & Annoyances

Some of your fondest vacation memories may be forged on Ko Pha-Ngan; just be mindful of the following situations that can seriously tarnish your experience on this hot-blooded jungle island.

MOTORCYCLES

Ko Pha-Ngan has more motorcycle accidents than injuries incurred from full moon tomfoolery. Nowadays there's a system of paved roads, but much of it is a labyrinth of rutty dirt-and-mud paths. The island is also very hilly, and even if the road is paved, it can be very tricky for most to take on. The *very* steep road to Hat Rin is a perfect case in point. Too many injuries (and outrageous motorcycle damage fees) result from drivers being too proud to turn around and hail a sŏrng·tăa·ou instead.

DRUGS

If you're thinking about sampling some local herb, know this: Ko Pha-Ngan does not have tourist police. In other words, a force of locally appointed officers runs the island. Here's another important thing to remember: your travel insurance does not cover drug-related injury or treatment. There are always reports of travellers being offered and sold 'natural' drugs by locals, and promptly being busted by police who somehow know exactly who, when and where to check. The anti-drug laws in Thailand are taken extremely seriously and it's best to resist the call of the ganja.

When full moon fun is in full swing, the local police often set up inspection points on the road between Thong Sala and Hat Rin. All vehicles are stopped and the penalties for drugs on board are huge: five-digit fines and/or jail sentences.

Drug-related freak-outs *do* happen – we've heard first-hand accounts of partiers slipping into extended periods of delirium. Suan Saranrom (Garden of Joys) Psychiatric Hospital in Surat Thani has to take on extra staff during full-moon periods to handle the faràng who freak out on magic mushrooms, acid or other abundantly available hallucinogens.

SCAMS

As previously stated, there are no tourist police on Ko Pha-Ngan, which means that a greater percentage of tourists fall victim to various gimmicks. A common scam involves booking '1st-class' bus or boat tickets only to find that the transport is rickety at best, and you paid much more than anyone else. Many tourists have reported problems with the bus between Bangkok and Ko Pha-Ngan – operators often rifle through luggage placed underneath the bus.

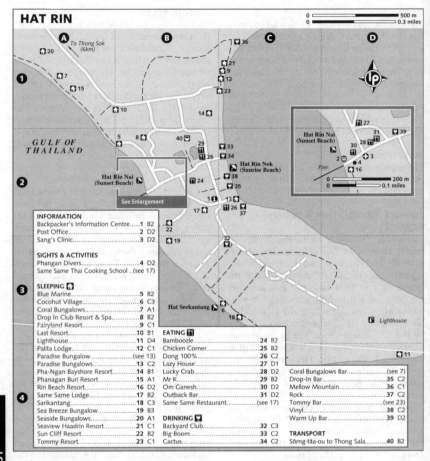

HAT RIN

0 — 500 m
0 — 0.3 miles

To Thong Sok (6km)

GULF OF THAILAND

Hat Rin Nai (Sunset Beach)

See Enlargement

Hat Rin Nok (Sunrise Beach)

Hat Rin Nai (Sunset Beach)

Pier

0 — 200 m
0 — 0.1 miles

Hat Seekantang

Lighthouse

INFORMATION
Backpacker's Information Centre.....1 B2
Post Office.................................2 D2
Sang's Clinic..............................3 D2

SIGHTS & ACTIVITIES
Phangan Divers............................4 D2
Same Same Thai Cooking School ..(see 17)

SLEEPING
Blue Marine................................5 B2
Cocohut Village...........................6 C3
Coral Bungalows..........................7 A1
Drop In Club Resort & Spa..............8 B2
Fairyland Resort..........................9 C1
Last Resort...............................10 B1
Lighthouse...............................11 D4
Palita Lodge.............................12 C1
Paradise Bungalow...................(see 13)
Paradise Bungalows.....................13 C2
Pha-Ngan Bayshore Resort............14 B1
Phanagan Buri Resort...................15 A1
Rin Beach Resort........................16 D2
Same Same Lodge.......................17 B2
Sarikantang.............................18 C3
Sea Breeze Bungalow...................19 B3
Seaside Bungalows......................20 A1
Seaview Haadrin Resort................21 C1
Sun Cliff Resort.........................22 B2
Tommy Resort...........................23 C1

EATING
Bamboozle...............................24 B2
Chicken Corner..........................25 B2
Dong 100%...............................26 C2
Lazy House...............................27 D1
Lucky Crab..............................28 D2
Mr K.....................................29 B2
Om Ganesh..............................30 C2
Outback Bar.............................31 C2
Same Same Restaurant...............(see 17)

DRINKING
Backyard Club...........................32 C3
Big Boom................................33 B2
Cactus...................................34 C2

Coral Bungalows Bar...................(see 7)
Drop-In Bar.............................35 C2
Mellow Mountain.......................36 C1
Rock.....................................37 C2
Tommy Bar............................(see 23)
Vinyl....................................38 C2
Warm Up Bar............................39 D2

TRANSPORT
Sŏrng-tǎa-ou to Thong Sala..........40 B2

WOMEN'S SAFETY

Female travellers should be extra careful when partying on the island. We've received many reports about drug- and alcohol-related rape (and these situations are not limited to full moon parties). Another disturbing problem is the unscrupulous behaviour of some of the local motorcycle-taxi drivers. Several complaints have been filed about drivers groping female passengers; there are even reports of severe sexual assault.

Sights

For those who tire of beach-bumming, this large jungle island has many natural features to explore including mountains, waterfalls and spectacular beaches.

BEACHES & WATERFALLS

There are many **waterfalls** throughout the island's interior, four of which gush throughout the year. Near the east coast, **Than Sadet** features boulders carved with the royal insignia of Rama V, Rama VII and Rama IX. King Rama V enjoyed this hidden spot so much that he returned over a dozen times between 1888 and 1909. The river waters of Khlong Than Sadet are now considered sacred and used in royal ceremonies. To the north, **Than Prawet** is a series of chutes that snake inland for about 2km.

Near the centre of the island, **Phaeng Falls** is protected by a national park and is a pleasant reward after a short-but-rough hike. Continue the adventure and head north to

FULL MOONING

The full moon party is sort of like smoking a cigarette – its obviously not healthy, it'll leave you looking older than you actually are, but for some unknown reason you kinda just have to try it.

No one knows exactly when and how these crazy parties got started – many believe it began in 1987 or 1988 as someone's 'going away party' – but none of that is relevant now. Today, thousands of bodies converge monthly on the powdery sand of Hat Rin Nok to bump, grind, sweat and drink their way through a lunar-lit night filled with thumping DJ-generated beats. Crowds can reach an outrageous 30,000 partiers in high season, while low season still sees 10,000 pilgrims.

If you can't make your trip coincide with a full moon but still want to cover yourself in fluorescent paint, fear not – enterprising locals organise a black moon party (at Ban Khai), a half moon party (at Ban Tai) and moon-set parties (held a couple of days before the full moon party) at Hat Chaophao on the west coast. There's something going on no matter what the moon is doing, though these parties tend to be more subdued.

Full Moon Party Dates

Religious protests have forced some of Hat Rin's full moon parties to take place either before or after the actual full moon date; these are related to Buddhist holidays that occur around the full moon about four times yearly. During periods of royal mourning, the parties are usually cancelled. Double-check if any changes are in store when you plan to attend the party. Dates are posted on www.fullmoon.phangan.info.

Accommodation

If you arrive on the day of the full moon party or even the day before, you can forget about finding a vacant room or bungalow anywhere near Hat Rin – many ravers nail down a room four or more days in advance.

Transport

Taxis to/from Hat Rin run throughout the night – try your best to locate transport that's nearly full or you'll have to wait until it brims with partiers before it hits the road. If you're coming over from Ko Samui, hop on a ferry from Big Buddha Beach. There are several Samui companies that organise full moon packages (400B to 600B), taking passengers over in the evening and picking everyone up around 6am. These operators use speedboats, which gets the job done much faster, especially in the morning when you're craving a pillow.

Safety

With a little bit of planning and forethought about personal safety, these parties can be a blast. At the risk of sounding like your mother, here's some helpful advice:

- Wear protective shoes – broken beer bottles always hobble several beach dancers.
- Try not to bring any bags, and carry what money you have in several secure pockets.
- Don't keep valuables in your bungalow – it's a big night for break-ins, especially at the cheaper huts.
- Don't swim under the influence of drugs or alcohol.
- If you're going pass out, try to do it in one of the designated 'passing out areas'. Yes, it sounds silly, but you'll shield yourself from the inebriated revelry going on.
- Don't accept consumables from strangers.
- Be sure to regularly check in with friends, and try not to walk home alone – especially if you're staying on another island.
- Oh, and remember to eat your vegetables.

Khao Ra, the highest mountain on the island at 625m. Those with eagle-eyes will spot wild crocodiles, monkeys, snakes, deer and boar along the way, and the **viewpoint** from the top is spectacular – on a clear day you can see Ko Tao. Although the trek isn't arduous, it is very easy to lose one's way, and we *highly* recommend hiring an escort in Ban Madeua Wan (near the falls). The local guides have crude signs posted in front of their homes, and, if they're around, they'll take you up to the top for 500B. Most of them only speak Thai.

Pha-Ngan's stunning **beaches** are definitely worth visiting; however caution should also be exercised for those travelling on foot. The 'Green Dot' trail from Hat Rin to Hat Yuan is completely overgrown, as is most of the route between Chalok Lam and Hat Khuat (Bottle Beach). Save yourself the strife and charter a water taxi.

Hat Khuat is a classic fave. Visitors flock to this shore for a relaxing day of swimming and snorkelling – some opt to stay the night at one of the several bungalow operations along the beach. For additional seclusion, try the isolated beaches on the east coast, which include: **Hat Yuan**, **Hat Thian** and **Hat Sadet**, and the teeny **Ao Thong Reng**. For more enchanting beaches, consider doing a day-trip to the stunning **Ang Thong Marine National Park** (p240).

WÁT

Remember to change out of your beach clothes when visiting one of the 20 **wát** on Ko Pha-Ngan. Most temples are open during daylight hours.

The oldest temple on the island is **Wat Phu Khao Noi**, near the hospital in Thong Sala. While the site is open to visitors throughout the day, the monks are only around in the morning. **Wat Pho**, near Ban Tai, has a free herbal sauna accented with natural lemongrass. The steam bath is open from 3pm to 6pm. The **Chinese Temple** is known to give visitors good luck. It was constructed about 20 years ago after a visiting woman had a vision of the Chinese Buddha who instructed her to build a fire-light for the island. **Wat Khao Tham**, also near Ban Tai, sits high on a hill and has resident female monks. At the temple there is a bulletin board detailing a meditation retreat taught by an American-Australian couple. For additional information, write to Wat Khao Tham, PO Box 8, Ko Pha-Ngan, Surat Thani 84280.

Activities

DIVING & SNORKELLING

With Ko Tao, the high-energy diving behemoth, just a few kilometres away, Ko Pha-Ngan enjoys a much quieter, more laid-back diving scene. Prices are about 2000B to 2500B cheaper on Ko Tao (for an Open Water certification), but group sizes can be smaller on Ko Pha-Ngan since there are usually fewer divers. Like the other islands in the Samui Archipelago, Pha-Ngan has several small reefs dispersed around the island. The clear favourite snorkelling spot is **Ko Ma**, a small island in the northwest connected to Ko Pha-Ngan by a charming sandbar. There are also some rock reefs of interest on the eastern side of the island. Several tour operators take snorkellers to **Ko Nang Yuan** off the coast of Ko Tao, and trips to **Ang Thong Marine National Park** are quickly gaining popularity.

A major perk of diving from Ko Pha-Ngan is the proximity to **Sail Rock** (Hin Bai), perhaps the best dive site in the Gulf of Thailand. This large pinnacle lies about 14km north of the island. An abundance of corals and large tropical fish can be seen at depths of 10m to 30m and there's a rocky vertical swim-through called 'The Chimney'. Your author was lucky enough to spend 45 minutes diving with an elusive whale shark the size of a school bus.

Dive shops on Ko Tao visit Sail Rock as well, although the focus tends to swing more towards the shark-infested waters at Chumphon Pinnacle. The other major sites in the region (including Chumphon Pinnacle) are closer to Ko Tao, but are still frequented by the companies on Ko Pha-Ngan.

Lotus Diving (☎ 0 7737 4142; www.lotusdiving.com) This terrific dive centre has world-class instructors, and owns two beautiful boats (that's two more vessels than most of the other operations on Ko Pha-Ngan). Two- and three-dive adventures run between 2300B to 3500B. The Open Water course will set you back 11,000B, but includes huge lunches between dives and a DVD of your experience (or a 20-minute wake-boarding session should you not want a DVD). Trips can be booked at their base in the northwestern part of the island, or at the Backpacker Information Centre (p213).

Phangan Divers (Map p214; ☎ 0 7737 5117; www.phangandivers.com), with their main office near the pier at Hat Rin (and a smaller office in Thong Sala), charges between 2500B and 2800B for two 'fun dives' including lunch. Three-dive daytrips cost 3600B, and stop at Chumphon Pinnacle, Southwest Pinnacle and Sail Rock. Open Water certification runs for 12,500B. A snorkelling set can be rented for 150B to 200B.

YOGA & MASSAGE

The yoga retreat on Hat Chaophao, **Agama Yoga** (☎ 08 1397 6280, 08 9233 0217; www.agamayoga .com; Hin Wong, r 500B, bungalows 1200B, 4- night minimum stay), gets rave reviews from our readers for its holistic approach to the study of tantric yoga. The centre is often closed from September to December while its instructors travel to India to work on their craft. On the east coast, the **Sanctuary & Wellness Centre** (p223) is another popular retreat for yoga enthusiasts.

If you're dropping the big bucks for lodging, then you probably have access to an onsite spa. Inexpensive massage parlours are aplenty in Hat Rin and Thong Sala. Others can be scouted along the main road connecting the two towns (although be wary of the shadier joints offering 'happy endings').

OTHER ACTIVITIES

Hiking day-trips to **Ang Thong Marine National Park** generally depart from Ko Samui, but recently tour operators are starting to shuttle tourists from Ko Pha-Ngan as well. Check out p240 for more info. **Pha-Ngan Safari Eco-Nature Tours** (☎ 0 7737 4159, 08 1895 3783) offers a variety of treks and trips including 30-minute or one-hour **elephant trekking**.

There are loads of opportunities to try your hand at water sports, including jet-skiing, kiteboarding, water-skiing, sea-kayaking, windsurfing and sailing. Back on land, alternative modes of transport include 4WDs or quadbikes. The friendly staff at the Backpacker's Information Centre (p213) can help you arrange any of these, and Coral Bungalows (p218) in Hat Rin has loads of sports equipment from snorkel masks to jet skis.

Courses

Same Same Lodge runs a **Thai Cooking School** (Map p214; ☎ 0 7737 5200; www.same-same.com) and has one-/three-/five-day courses for 900/2500/4200B.

Sleeping

Ko Pha-Ngan's lengthy history of laid-back revelry has solidified its reputation as *the* stomping ground for the gritty backpacker lifestyle. Recently, however, the island is starting to see a shift towards a more upmarket clientele. Many local mainstays have collapsed their bamboo huts and constructed newer, sleeker accommodation aimed at the ever-growing legion of 'flashpackers'. On other

parts of the island, new tracts of land are being cleared for Samui-esque five-star resorts. But backpackers fear not; it'll still be many years before the castaway lifestyle goes the way of the dodo. For now, Ko Pha-Ngan can revel in its three distinct classes of lodging: pinch-a-penny shacks, trendy midrange hangouts, and blow-the-bank luxury.

The following sleeping options are organised into five sections: we start in Hat Rin, move along the southern coast, head up the west side, across the northern beaches and down the quiet eastern shore.

HAT RIN

The thin peninsula of Hat Rin is unofficially divided into four sections. Hat Rin Nok (Sunrise Beach) is the epicentre of full moon tomfoolery. Hat Rin Nai (Sunset Beach) is the less impressive stretch of sand on the far side of the tiny promontory, while Hat Seekantang (also known as Hat Leela), just south of Hat Rin Nai, is a smaller, more private beach. The three beaches are linked by Ban Hat Rin (Hat Rin Town); a small inland collection of restaurants and bars.

Needless to say, the prices listed here are meaningless during periods of maximum lunar orbicularity. Also, during full moon events, bungalow operations expect you to stay for a minimum number of days. If you plan to arrive the day of the party (or even the day before), we strongly suggest booking a room in advance, or else you'll probably have to sleep on the beach (which you might end up doing anyway).

Budget

Some of the places listed here with midrange options have one cheap room/bungalow, which will most likely already be booked out.

Paradise Bungalows (Map p214; ☎ 0 7737 5244; Hat Rin Nok; bungalows 250-1200B; ✴) The world-famous full moon party was hatched at this scruffy bunch of bungalows, and the place has been living on its name fame ever since. Nowadays, the grounds look more like a junkyard than a resort. Paradise lost.

Sun Cliff (Map p214; ☎ 0 7737 5134; bungalows 250-2000B; Hat Rin Nai; ✴) Perched on a palm-studded knoll, Sun Cliff overlooks the sea and basks in the tropical sun amid huge boulders and rolling vegetation. Each bungalow is a completely different species; some are dipped in pastels, others embody the quintessential island hut.

Last Resort (Map p214; ☎ 08 3595 0085; Ban Hat Rin; sebastian_prct@yahoo.com.sg; bungalows 300-350B) Just minutes away from the beach, the Last Resort (which shouldn't be your last resort) is a great place to base yourself for some no-frills full moon fun. Concrete bungalows have been painted with warm earth tones, giving them a desert adobe vibe – a refreshing change from the exhausted bamboo beach shack. Spaz, the charismatic owner, will bend over backwards to make sure you have the best time possible in Hat Rin.

Seaside Bungalow (Map p214; ☎ 08 6940 3410, 08 7266 7567; Hat Rin Nai; bungalows 300-600B; ✕) Seaside sees loads of loyal customers who return for the mellow atmosphere, cheap drinks, free pool table, and comfy wooden bungalows staggered along Sunset Beach. At 500B, we're pretty sure that these huts are the cheapest air-conditioned rooms on the island.

Same Same Lodge (Map p214; ☎ 0 7737 5200; www.same-same.com; Ban Hat Rin; r 300-800B; ✕) This busy backpacker hangout is a Hat Rin institution. In the party-prone restaurant, the affable staff works around the clock making sure that smiles (and drinks) abound. Above the action, the no-frills motel rooms are cheery, but need some freshening up.

Coral Bungalows (Map p214; ☎ 0 7737 5023; www.coralhaadrin.com; Hat Rin Nai; bungalows 300-1500B; ✕ ▭ ▣) Coral Bungalows has firmly planted its flag in 'Backpackerland' as the go-to resort for a holiday on a shoestring. By day, sun-worshippers straddle beachside chaises or jet skis. Then, by night, like a superhero, Coral transforms into its alter ego; a pool-party machine fuelled by gregarious employees and a couple of vodka/Red-Bulls. The party-centric paradise has grown to almost 100 motel-style rooms clustered around an amoeba-shaped pool.

Lighthouse Bungalow (Map p214; ☎ 0 7737 5075; Hat Seekantang; bungalows 350-800B) Hidden at the far end of Hat Rin, this low-key collection of humble huts gathers along a sloping terrain punctuated by towering palms. The wood-planked restaurant is breezy (in both senses of the word) and offers ocean vistas ripped right off a postcard. To access this secluded resort, walk through Leela Beach Bungalows (don't bother stopping) and follow the wooden boardwalk as it curves to the left (southeast) around the sea-swept boulders.

Seaview Haadrin Resort (Map p214; ☎ 0 7737 5160; Hat Rin Nok; bungalows from 500B; ✕) If you want a front row seat for the full moon party then you've come to the right place. Bungalows are scattered right along the north end of beach; the cheaper huts have walls that look like tatami mats.

Sarikantang (Map p214; ☎ 0 7737 5055, 08 1444 1322; www.sarikantang.com; Hat Seekantang; bungalows 500-3500B; ✕ ▣) Don't get too strung out over trying to pronounce the resort's name – you can simply call this place 'heaven'. Cream-coloured cabins, framed with teak posts and lintels, are sprinkled amongst swaying palms and crumbling winged statuettes. Inside, the rooms look like the set of a photo shoot for an interior design magazine.

Sea Breeze Bungalow (Map p214; ☎ 0 7737 5162; bungalows 500-8000B; ✕) Sea Breeze gets a good report card from our readers, and we agree; the labyrinth of secluded hillside cottages is an ideal hammocked retreat for any type of traveller. Several bungalows, poised high on stilts, deliver stunning views of Hat Rin and the sea.

Blue Marine (Map p214; ☎ 0 7737 5079; Hat Rin Nai; bungalows 600-1200B; ✕) The shimmering blue-tiled roofs act like a beacon luring in curious backpackers in search of a good deal, and most of them stay since the cheery interiors sparkle as well. Try to nab a concrete cottage closer to the beach as a few affiliated bungalows have sprung up on the far side of the road.

Cocohut Village (Map p214; ☎ 0 7737 5368; www.cocohut.com; Hat Seekantang; r 600B, bungalows 1900-4500B; ✕ ▭ ▣) A super-social place unto itself, guests might forget that they are just up the street from the brouhaha on Sunrise Beach. The backpacker digs, with shared locker-room–styled toilets, are a bit sub-par, however the pricier options, such as the cliff villas and beachfront bungalows, are some of the best bets in Hat Rin.

Midrange & Top End
Many budget places offer midrange options as well.

Pha-Ngan Bayshore Resort (Map p214; ☎ 0 7737 5227, 0 7737 5224; www.phanganbayshore.com; Hat Rin Nok; bungalows 1000-3000B; ✕ ▭ ▣) At the time of research, this hotel-style option was getting a much-needed overhaul as the owners prime themselves for the ever-increasing influx of flashpackers.

Rin Beach Resort (Map p214; ☎ 0 7737 5112; www.kohphanganrinbeach.com; Hat Rin Nai; bungalows 1000-

3000B; 🏊 🖥) Giant amphorae, spewing forth gushes of water, welcome weary travellers as they tumble off the wooden ferry. Cottages are bright and airy with dark cherry wood accents and colourful sutra paintings. The enormous flower-shaped pool is a booby trap for sun-seekers.

Fairyland Resort (Map p214; ☎ 0 7737 5076, 08 5057 1709; www.haadrinfairyland.com; Hat Rin Nok; bungalows from 1400B; 🏊) Although the name sounds like a board game for six-year-old girls, these sparkling bungalows are serious competition for the older resorts on Sunrise Beach. Walk-ins might be lucky enough to score a 60% discount depending on the time of the month and year – be sure to ask the other vacationers how much they're paying before you check in.

Palita Lodge (Map p214; ☎ 0 7737 5172; www.palita lodge.com; Hat Rin Nok; bungalows 1500-4500B; 🏊 🖥) Smack in the heart of the action, Palita is a tribute to the never-ending party that is Hat Rin's Sunrise Beach. Spacious concrete bungalows, with wooden accents and modern design elements, are neatly pressed together on this beachy wedge of sand and shrubs. Week-long bookings are a must during full moon revelry.

Drop In Club Resort & Spa (Map p214; ☎ 0 7737 5444; www.dropinclubresortandspa.com; Bat Hat Rin; r 1500-12,000B; 🏊 🖥) The Drop In Club feels like a rambling Thai temple with detailed double-peaked architecture and a turquoise swimming pool. The proximity to Sunrise Beach means that things get pretty wild when the full moon rolls around. Although the resort is located in Ban Hat Rin (Hat Rin Town), most of the rooms offer glimpses of the sea.

Tommy Resort (Map p214; ☎ 0 7737 5215; www .phangantommyresort.com; Hat Rin Nok; r 1800-2200B; 🏊 🖥 🖥) Tommy is a trendy address in the heart of Hat Rin, striking a good balance between chic boutique and carefree backpacker hangout. The rectangular swimming pool can be jarring at first, since every other man-made body of water on the island looks like it was manufactured at the kidney-shaped pool factory.

Phangan Buri (Map p214; ☎ 0 7737 5481; www .phanganburiresort.com; Hat Rin Nai; bungalows from 2700B; 🏊 🖥) The front façade looks a bit like a drab oriental-themed hotel from the 1950s, but the 40 tight-knit bungalows along the orchid-lined beach are modern and charming. Soft-spoken staff members don identical uniforms

and greet guests with pressed palms and a gracious bow.

SOUTHERN BEACHES

Accommodation along the southern coast offers the best bang for your baht on Ko Pha-Ngan. There are fleeting views of distant Ang Thong Marine Park; however, the beaches aren't particularly stunning. This section starts in Thong Sala and heads east towards Hat Rin.

Thong Sala

There's really no reason to stay in Thong Sala, unless you're paranoid about missing a morning ferry, or feeling ill and seeking medical attention nearby.

Bua Kao Inn (☎ 0 7723 7226; buakao@samart.co.th; r 550-900B; 🏊) If you're looking for a town vibe rather than a strip of sand, Bua Kao isn't a bad choice. The rooms are well kept and the restaurant downstairs teems with chatty expats.

Pha-Ngan Chai Hotel (☎ 0 7737 7068, 0 7737 7286; r 700-1200B; 🏊 🖥) Think 'Soviet tenement meets tropical holiday' and you'll immediately spot this dowdy behemoth while landing at the Thong Sala pier. The convenient location is the hotel's best feature, although you'll need some taxi fare to find a swimmable beach.

Ao Bang Charu

There are some great bargains on this sandy stretch between Thong Sala and Ban Tai.

Chokana (☎ 0 7723 8085; bungalows 300-1200B; 🏊) Our favourite spot on Bang Charu is the Jabba the Hut of huts; these wooden beachside bungalows are shockingly large. The bubbly owner genuinely cares about her clientele – the cabins have loads of personal touches such as wooden carvings and mosaics, and it feels as though all of the guests are repeat customers.

Holiday Resort (☎ 0 7737 7468; www.holiday beachresort.net; bungalows 800-1700B) The owners aren't too fussed about landscaping, but the bungalows are kept very tidy – the best deals are the 900B bungalows (loaded with air-con and a TV) right along the water. There's a funky bar doused in fluorescent blues and greens, a couple of volleyball nets strung up, and a well-worn pool table hilariously positioned a mere 5m from the rolling tide.

Ban Tai

The waters at Ban Tai tend to be shallow and opaque, especially during low season, but lodging options are well-priced compared to other parts of the island.

Lifestyle Bungalows (☎ 08 5916 3852; bungalows 250-600B; 🌀) A skin artist by trade, the owner has tattooed each fan bungalow with a blazing palette of colours. Each elaborate design fuses tribal imagery with inspired patterns of swirling shapes. The cluster of sandy huts embodies the true essence of Ko Pha-Ngan; no capitalist nonsense here, just a sign saying 'eat, drink and chill'.

Phangan Beach Resort (☎ 0 7723 8809; phangan beachresort@hotmail.com; bungalows 450-1200B; 🌀) A solid backpacker pick, Phangan Beach's fan rooms ooze old-school bamboo charm while remaining prim. Air-conditioned rooms have been outfitted with hot water, a TV and fridge; however, they are otherwise identical to the fan rooms.

Phangan Great Bay Resort (☎ 0 7723 8659; fax 0 7723 8697; bungalows 1250-2000B; 🌀 🖥 🛆) Take your pick from motel rooms housed in a mauve structure, or comfy bungalows further afield that also make use of ostentatious colours such as radioactive carrot and lime. Idle away the day trying to anthropomorphize the curious shape of the pool, or catch a movie on the TV in the restaurant.

Milky Bay Resort (☎ 0 7723 8566; www.milkybay .com; bungalows 1200-8000B; 🌀 🖥 🛆) Milky white walls, which permeate the grounds, are peppered with large black stones resembling the spots on a cow. These bovine bulwarks snake through the resort, linking the airy thatched bungalows to the sea. The smart, semicovered swimming pool is a big hit with the kids, as are the hanging gardens, billiards, table tennis and beach volleyball.

Ban Khai

Like Ban Tai, the beaches aren't the most stunning, but the accommodation is cheap and there are beautiful views of Ang Thong Marine Park in the distance.

Lee's Garden (☎ 08 5916 3852; bungalows 250-600B) If Lee's Garden had a soundtrack it would probably be Bob Marley's greatest hits. The clump of comfy wooden huts is a welcomed throwback to a time when Pha-Ngan attracted a grittier backpacker who wasn't fussed about hot showers or air-con.

Mac Bay (☎ 0 7723 8443; bungalows 500-1500B; 🌀 🛆) Home to the Black Moon Party (another lunar excuse for Ko Pha-Ngan to go wild), Mac Bay is a sandy slice of Ban Khai where even the cheaper bungalows are spic and span. At beer o'clock, grab a shaded spot on the sand and watch the sun dance amorphous shadows over the distant islands of Ang Thong Marine Park.

Morning Star (☎ 0 7737 7756; morningstarkpn@yahoo .com; bungalows 1190-2490B; 🌀 🛆) This collection of wooden and concrete jungle cottages has spotless interiors; some rooms are furnished with noticeably ornate dressers and vanities, others have subtle dark wood trimming. A dozen white wooden beach chairs orbit the adorable kidney-bean–shaped swimming pool.

Hin Lor

Quiet Hin Lor sits along the coast right before the main road takes a dramatic plunge into Hat Rin.

Boom's Cafe Bungalows (☎ 0 7723 8318; www .boomscafe.com; bungalows 300-1000B; 🌀) Staying at Boom's is like visiting the Thai family you never knew you had. The friendly owners lovingly tend their sand acreage and dote on the contented clientele. No one seems to mind that there's no swimming pool, since the curling tide rolls right up to your doorstep.

WEST COAST BEACHES

The west coast has seen a lot of development in recent years, now that there's a smooth road between Thong Sala and Chalok Lam. The atmosphere is a pleasant mix between the east coast's quiet seclusion and Hat Rin's sociable vibe.

Ao Nai Wok

If you need to be near Thong Sala, consider staying along Nai Wok, only a few kilometres north.

Grand Sea Resort (☎ 0 7737 7777; www.grand searesort.com; bungalows 1200-3000B; 🌀 🛆) A good choice for those wanting a bit of sand close to Thong Sala, Grand Sea feels like a collection of wooden Thai spirit houses.

Ao Hin Kong to Hat Chaophao

After a quieter stretch of coastline, there's a continuous string of resorts that start at the northern end of Hin Kong. Like Hat Yao up the coast, Hat Chaophao's rounded beach is lined with a variety of bungalow operations. There's an inland lake further south, and a 7-Eleven to cure your midnight munchies.

Loy Fa (☎ 0 7737 7319; loyfabungalow@yahoo.com; Srithanu; bungalows 400-1200B) Loy Fa scores high marks for its friendly staff, charming gardens, and sturdy huts guarding sweeping ocean views. Modern bungalows tumble down the promontory onto an uber-private sliver of ash-coloured sand.

Sunset Cove (☎ 0 7734 9211; www.thaisunsetcove .com; Hat Chaophao; bungalows 1500-3350B; 🞬 🖳 🖭) There's a feeling of Zen symmetry among the forested assortment of boutique bungalows; the towering bamboo shoots are evenly spaced along the cobbled paths weaving through brush and boulders. The beachside abodes are particularly elegant, sporting slatted rectangular windows and barrel basined bathtubs.

Pha-Ngan Paragon (☎ 08 4728 6064; www.pha nganparagon.com; Hat Chaophao; bungalows 2500-13,000B; 🞬 🖳 🖭) A tiny hideaway with seven rooms, Paragon's décor incorporates stylistic elements from the ancient Khmer, India and Thailand, without forfeiting any modern amenities. The 'royal bedroom' deserves a special mention – apparently the canopied bed has been imported from Kashmir.

Hat Son

Little Hat Son sits between two rocky cliffs.

Tantawan Bungalows (☎ 0 7734 9108; www.tanta wanbungalow.com; bungalows 450-550B; 🖭) Little Tantawan sits high up in the jungle like a tree house, boasting soaring sea views from the sprinkle of rugged bungalows. Guests can take a dip in the trapezoidal swimming pool or enjoy the sunrise on their small bamboo porches. Don't forget to try the tasty French and Thai dishes at the on-site restaurant (see p225).

Haad Son Resort (☎ 0 7734 9104; www.haadson .info; bungalows 1000-8000B; 🞬 🖳 🖭) The word 'complex' has a double meaning at this vast resort; we suggest leaving a trail of breadcrumbs along the serpentine paths if you ever want to find the way back to your room. The poshest rooms aren't worth the baht, so go for the budget digs; they're simple, but you'll have access to all of the on-site amenities.

Hat Yao

One of the busier beaches along the west coast, Hat Yao sports a swimmable beach, numerous resorts and a few extra conveniences such as ATMs and convenience stores.

Ibiza (☎ 0 7734 9121; www.ibizabungalows.com; bungalows 150-1300B; 🞬) Ibiza brings Hat Rin's youthful backpacker vibe up the west coast to Hat Yao. The no-frills bungalows are run-

of-the-mill, but the friendly staff, appealing central garden, and cheap rates keep budget travellers coming back for more. An on-site ATM machine is an added perk, as are the free barbecue dinners on Saturday nights.

High Life (☎ 0 7734 9114; www.highlifebungalow .com; bungalows 500-2000B; 🞬 🖭) We can't decide what's more conspicuous: the dramatic ocean views from the infinity-edged swimming pool, or the blatant double entendre in the resort's name. True to its moniker, the 25 bungalows, of various shapes and sizes, sit on a palmed outcropping of granite soaring high above the cerulean sea. Advance bookings will set you back an extra 200B.

Long Bay Resort (☎ 0 7734 9057; www.long-bay .com; bungalows 1200-3000B; 🞬 🖳 🖭) The Long Bay is a solid midrange option that has all the bells and whistles of a top-end resort. Most of the action takes place at the large swimming pool, while golf carts plod around shuttling guests to various activities. The cheapest rooms are slightly ramshackle; we recommend upgrading to a 'deluxe' bungalow. Visitors staying in the air-conditioned accommodation receive complimentary breakfast.

Haad Yao Bay View (☎ 0 7734 9193, 0 7734 9141; www.haadyao-bayviewresort.com; r & bungalows 1500-5000B; 🞬 🖳 🖭) Sparkling after a recent facelift, this conglomeration of bungalows and hotel-style accommodation looks like a tropical mirage on Hat Yao's northern headland. Vacationers, in various states of undress, linger around the large turquoise swimming pool catching rays and Z's. Others nest in their private suites amid polished hardwood floors and wicker daybeds.

Hat Salad

One of the best beaches on the island, Hat Salad has a string of quality accommodation along the sand.

Cookies Salad (☎ 0 7734 9125, 08 3181 7125; www .cookies-phangan.com; bungalows 1200-2400B) The resort with a tasty name has delicious Balinese-styled bungalows orbiting a two-tiered lap pool tiled in various shades of blue. Shaggy thatching and dense tropical foliage gives the realm a certain rustic quality, although you won't want for creature comforts.

Green Papaya (☎ 0 7737 4182; www.greenpapaya resort.com; bungalows 4000-7500B; 🞬 🖳 🖭) The polished wooden bungalows at Green Papaya are a clear standout along the lovely beach at Hat Salad; however, they come at quite a hefty price.

Ao Mae Hat

The northwest tip of the island has excellent ocean vistas, and little Ko Ma is connected to Pha-Ngan by a stunning sandbar.

Pha-Ngan Utopia Resort (☎ 0 7737 4093; www .phanganutopia.com; bungalows 1500-3000B; 🛏 🖳 🕿) It's pretty audacious to name one's resort 'Utopia', but the owners have done an excellent job of creating an idyllic jungle retreat perched high above the sea. Our favourite rooms – the two-storey villas – slope down the mountainside and have an entire level dedicated to an extra-large Jacuzzi.

NORTHERN BEACHES

Stretching from Chalok Lam to Thong Nai Pan, the dramatic northern coast is a wild jungle with several stunning and secluded beaches.

Ao Chalok Lam (Chaloklum)

The cramped fishermen's village at Chalok Lam is like no other place on Ko Pha-Ngan. The conglomeration of teak shanties and huts is a palpable reminder that the wide-reaching hand of globalisation has yet to touch some parts of the world. The village has several restaurants and plenty of amenities such as grocery stores, laundry, internet, and motorbike-rental places. Sŏrng·tăa·ou ply the route from here to Thong Sala for 50B to 100B per person.

Malibu (☎ 0 7737 4013; bungalows 300-1300B; 🛏) The casual vibe around the large backyard lagoon sets Malibu apart from the other budget bungalows around Chalok Lam. A drink-wielding hut, stationed on the private sandbar, lures guests of every ilk. The cheapest huts are a bit rough around the edges – try the higher-priced air-conditioned rooms for a restful sleep.

Mandalai (☎ 0 7737 4316; www.mymandalai.com; r 2750-5600B; 🛏 🖳 🕿) Like a white-washed Riyadh from a distant Arabian land, this small boutique hotel quietly towers over the surrounding shantytown of fishermen's huts. Floor-to-ceiling windows command views of tangerine-coloured fishing boats in the bay and the intimate wading pool in the hidden cloister. The only palpable flaw is the oc-

casional stench of sun-drying squid in the village nearby.

Hat Khom

Hat Khom is smaller and more peaceful than Bottle Beach next door. There's a dirt road leading to Chalok Lam, and water taxis are available as well (50B to 100B).

Coconut Beach (☎ 0 7737 4298; www.coconutbeach -bungalows.com; bungalows 250-800B) Grab a Corona, 'cause this is the perfect place to shoot one of those idyllic beach beer commercials. Wooden and concrete bungalows, all with green metal roofing, lie splayed across a forested acreage of swaying palms and scraggly mangroves.

Hat Khuat (Bottle Beach)

This isolated dune, commonly known as Bottle Beach, has garnered a reputation as a low-key getaway, and has thus become quite popular. During high season, places can fill up fast so it's best to try and arrive early. Grab a long-tail taxi boat from Chalok Lam for 50B to 100B.

Bottle Beach I (☎ 0 7744 7572, 0 7744 5151; www .bottlebeach.com; bungalows from 400B; 🛏) These bungalows make up one-third of a lodging triumvirate, all with the same name (and all owned by different members of the same family). The best of the bunch, Bottle Beach I's older rooms offer excellent beach views while showing visible signs of wear and tear. Newer avatars are further field, but are spacious and constructed from polished wood and concrete.

The other Bottle Beach brothers are:

Bottle Beach II (☎ 0 7744 5156; www.bottlebeach.com; bungalows 200-600B) Rows of rustic huts.

Bottle Beach III (☎ 0 7744 5127; www.geocities.com /haadkhuad_resort; bungalows 800-3200B; 🛏) Newer but pricey.

Ao Thong Nai Pan

Thong Nai Pan sort of looks like buttocks, with two rounded bays separated by a thin promontory; Ao Thong Nai Pan Yai (*yài* means 'big') is the northern half, and Ao Thong Nai Pan Noi (*nóy* or *noi* means 'little') curves just below. There are no paved roads to Thong Nai Pan, although sŏrng·tăa·ou can make the trek for 100B to 200B depending on your departure point.

Dolphin (bungalows 500-700B) Dolphin gives yuppie travellers a chance to rough it in style, while granola-types will soak up every inch of the laid-back charm. Quiet afternoons are spent lounging on a comfy cushion in one of the small pagodas hidden throughout the jungle. Lodging is only available on a first-come basis.

Baan Panburi (☎ 0 7723 8599; www.baanpanburi village.com; bungalows 500-2500B; ✷) This swanky place still offers basic huts with shared bathroom. The midrange bungalows have gabled roofs with straw moustache-like awnings dangling over the front porches. The restaurant here is great.

Panviman Resort (☎ 0 7744 5101-9; www.pan viman.com; r & bungalows from 4900B; ✷ ▣ ▨) One of the most charming (and expensive) places on Ko Pha-Ngan, Panviman sits atop a narrow promontory separating two picturesque bays. The older rooms look like the captain's quarters on a wooden steam ship, while others incorporate the ashen rock face into the shape of the dwelling. Cheaper hotel options give off a '70s tropical hunting-lodge vibe, but are spacious and immaculate nonetheless.

Santhiya (☎ 0 7723 8333; www.santhiya.com; bungalows from 10,000B; ✷ ▣ ▨) Beautiful Santhiya feels a bit out of place on Ko Samui's shabby younger brother – Ko Pha-Ngan is accustomed to bamboo huts, not maid service and flamboyant gestures of Siamese design. Warm outdoor lighting flickers on after sunset and drenches the curving palms and thatched bungalows in a rich caramel hue.

EAST COAST BEACHES

Robinson Crusoe; eat your heart out. The east coast is the ultimate hangout for hermits. For the most part, you'll have to hire a boat to get to these beaches, but water taxis are available at every pier.

Than Sadet & Hat Thong Reng

The ultra-remote coast of Ao Thong Reng has a striking, intimate beach that has been visited by many of Thailand's kings. Most travellers only come to see the waterfalls, but basic accommodation is also available.

Than Sadet Resort (bungalows 150-300B) Hat Thong Reng's only accommodation, these huts are one of Ko Pha-Ngan's best-kept secrets. The friendly owners manage two classes of bungalows – primitive shacks, and sturdier cabins that are considerably more spacious. Seclusion seekers will love the boulder-strewn property, wild forest, and private beach.

Mai Pen Rai (☎ 0 7744 5090; www.thansadet.com; Than Sadet; bungalows 450-800B; ▣) 'Mai Pen Rai'

can be interpreted as the Thai 'don't worry, be happy', which isn't too surprising since this bay elicits nothing but sedate smiles. Bungalows have been constructed with panels of straw weaving, and some have aluminium sheeting on the gabled roofs.

Hat Thian & Hat Yuan

Geographically, Hat Thian is quite close to Hat Rin; however, there are no roads and the crude hiking trail is lengthy and confusing. Ferry taxis are available from Hat Rin for less than 100B. Hat Yuan has a few bungalow operations, and is quite secluded as there are no roads connecting this little beach to Hat Rin down the coast.

Barcelona (☎ 0 7737 5113; Hat Yuan; bungalows 200-600B) Solid wood huts come in two shades: natural wood or creamy white. They climb up the hill on stilts behind a palm garden and have good vistas and jovial staff.

Beam Bungalows (☎ 0 7927 2854, 08 6947 3205; Hat Thian; bungalows 300-500B) Beam is set back from the beach and tucked behind a coconut palm grove. Charming wooden huts have dangling hammocks out front, and big bay windows face the ocean through the swaying palms.

Sanctuary & Wellness Centre (☎ 08 1271 3614; www .thesanctuary-kpg.com; Hat Thian; bungalows 400-4000B) A friendly enclave promoting well-being and natural harmony, this relaxing retreat offers everything from yoga classes, to detox, dancing, and hydrotherapy. Accommodation, in various manifestations of twigs, is scattered around the resort, married to the natural surroundings. You'll want to Nama-stay forever.

Eating

Ko Pha-Ngan's no culinary capital, especially since most visitors quickly absorb the lazy lifestyle and wind up eating at their accommodation. If you're feeling adventurous, check out the tasty fare at independent restaurants scattered around the island. It's best to steer clear of the barbecue seafood stands – even though you're on a tropical island, the stuff that wasn't sold yesterday is kept on ice over night and sold again the following day.

HAT RIN

This bustling burb has the largest conglomeration of restaurants and bars on the island, yet surprisingly most of them are quite lacklustre. The infamous Chicken Corner is a popular intersection stocked with several poultry peddlers promising to cure the munchies, be it noon or midnight.

Dong 100% (Map p214; ☎ 0 7737 5245; dishes 40-100B; ☺ lunch & dinner) This vegetarian joint gets an honourable mention for its snicker-inducing name. The diner-cum-tattoo parlour seems like a bit of a mismatch at first, but what's better than a spicy curry to distract your mind from the sting of a bamboo needle? Oh, and don't worry, the food's not made with a 100% dong.

Mr K (Map p214; ☎ 0 7737 5470; dishes 50-80B; ☺ 24hr) Our favourite joint at 'Chicken Corner', Mr K offers local eats all night long. Cheesy Thai soap operas blare on the TV, and there's dirt-cheap beer to wash down your meal.

Same Same Restaurant (Map p214; ☎ 0 7737 5200; dishes 50-200B; ☺ breakfast, lunch & dinner) This raucous chow house gives the oft-heard phrase 'same same, but different' a whole new meaning – where else can you get *pàt tai* with a side of Frikadeller (Swedish meatballs)? Crowds gather for live music, pub-crawls, or to watch sports on the large TVs. If you like the food, enrol in the on-site cooking school (p217).

Bamboozle (Map p214; ☎ 08 7896 4941; dishes 70-180B; ☺ 3pm-midnight) Head up the steps and go 'south of the border' for nachos, burritos and chilli *rellenos*. The Mexican theme continues behind the bar – wash your meal down with a pitcher of margaritas.

Om Ganesh (Map p214; ☎ 0 7737 5123; dishes 70-190B; ☺ breakfast, lunch & dinner) At the entrance, 'Namaste' is written in blue tile. Customers meditate over curries, biryani rice, roti and lassis beneath a ceiling of painted clouds and cartoon murals of the Himalayas. Two-person platters cost 350B.

Lazy House (Map p214; ☎ 0 7737 5432; dishes 90-270B; ☺ lunch & dinner) This joint used to be the owner's apartment – everyone liked his cooking so much that he decided to turn the place into a restaurant and hangout spot. Today, Lazy House is easily one of Hat Rin's best places to veg in front of a movie with a scrumptious shepherd's pie.

Lucky Crab (Map p214; dishes 100-400B; ☺ lunch & dinner) Lucky Crab is your best bet for seafood in Hat Rin. Rows of freshly caught creatures are presented nightly atop miniature long-tail boats loaded with ice. Once you've picked your prey, grab a table inside amid dangling plants and charming stone furnishings.

Outback Bar (Map p214; ☎ 0 7737 5126; dishes 120-250B; ☺ breakfast, lunch & dinner; 🕱) Stop by this expat eatery and coat your stomach with international faves such as burgers and salad, before inhaling 'buckets', shooting some pool, and heading off into the night.

SOUTHERN BEACHES

Lately, the night market in the heart of Thong Sala is all the rage; prices hover around 30B per dish, there are heaps of BBQ stalls and plenty of plastic patio furniture for sitting.

Boom's Cafe (☎ 0 7723 8318; www.boomscafe.com; Hin Lor; dishes 30-100B; ☺ breakfast, lunch & dinner) A family-run operation nestled between impassable boulders, this secluded option promises scrumptious local meals, scraped together at a moment's notice as the super-smiley owner cheerfully clangs her weathered pots and pans.

Somtum Inter (☎ 0 7737 7334; Ban Tai; dishes 40-100B; ☺ breakfast, lunch & dinner) Right next door to Boat Ahoy (and owned by the same family), the Somtum announces its speciality in the restaurant's name: spicy papaya salad (pronounced *sôm·dam* in Thai). Other Isan favourites include spicy minced pork and grilled chicken.

A's Coffee Shop and Restaurant (☎ 0 7737 7226; Thong Sala; dishes 40-170B; ☺ breakfast, lunch & dinner Mon-Sat) The perfect place to spend a few hours if you're stuck in town waiting for the ferry, it offers everything from homemade breads to big breakfasts, and throws in sandwiches, pasta and salads for good measure.

Boat Ahoy (☎ 0 7723 8759, 0 7737 7334; www.firstvilla .com/boatahoy; Ban Tai; dishes 40-180B; ☺ breakfast, lunch & dinner) A compound of open-air pavilions encased in slats in mahogany wood, Boat Ahoy offers a night's worth of fun. After feasting on a variety of delicious Asian victuals, grab a drink at the boat-shaped bar, or re-enact the Spice Girls' reunion tour in your own private karaoke suite.

Ando Loco (☎ 08 6780 7200; Ao Bang Charu; meals from 59B; ☺ dinner) This outdoor Mexican hangout looks like an animation cell from a vintage Hanna-Barbera cartoon, with assorted kitschy accoutrements such as paper-maché cacti. Sling back a super-sized margarita and test for skills on the beach volleyball court.

Anahata (☎ 08 6952 4563; dishes 120-180B; Ban Khai; ☺ lunch & dinner) Sunday evening at Anahata is the ultimate gorge-fest; feast on an endless assortment of Mediterranean dishes including couscous, salads, pasta and meats for 290B. These dishes, and much more, are also served throughout the week. Anahata is sometimes closed for lunch during low season.

WEST COAST BEACHES

Sandy Bay Restaurant (☎ 0 7734 9119; Hat Yao; dishes 60–180B; ☯ breakfast, lunch & dinner) Sandy Bay Bungalow's long-running restaurant in the centre of Hat Yao gets good reviews for its Thai and Western dishes. Tables are sprinkled along the sand, some within arm's reach of the ocean.

Tantawan (☎ 0 7734 9108; www.tantawanbungalow .com; Hat Son; dishes 60–200B; ☯ lunch & dinner) This charming teak hut, nestled amongst jungle fronds, is dripping with clinking chandeliers made from peach coral and khaki-coloured seashells. Diners sit in a sea of geometric cushions while gobbling up some of the tastiest Thai and French-inspired dishes on the island.

Absolute Island (☎ 0 7734 9109; Hat Yao; dishes 60–250B; ☯ breakfast, lunch & dinner) The name sounds like a Swedish vodka ad, but it's only by coincidence that the menu has some Scandinavian classics. Actually, every traveller will find a dish from his or her native country – Absolute's menu is so vast it really needs an index. Try the egg sandwich baguette with a side of massaman curry (or maybe a taco) while staring out over the beautiful bay.

Me'n'u (☎ 08 9289 7133, 08 7897 0025; www.menu -phangan.com; Hin Kong; dishes 60–300B; ☯ dinner Tue-Sun) Me'n'u (get it?) is a newer addition to Pha-Ngan's palette (palate?). It's decidedly gourmet, with dishes such as grilled duck in a black currant sauce and crab salad with caviar dressing. There's a kids' menu too, so you can bring the brood along.

NORTHERN & EAST COAST BEACHES

Most of the dining options on this part of the island are affiliated with accommodation – the only exception being several small restaurants in the fishermen's village at Chalok Lam.

Bamboo Hut (☎ 0 7737 5139; Hat Yuan; dishes 40–180B; ☯ breakfast, lunch & dinner) High up the rocks at the northern end of the beach, this spacious eatery has awesome views of the bay. It's a good thing there are some comfy bungalows on the premises; you might like your dinner so much that you'll want to stay for breakfast.

Nong Nook (☎ 08 6953 1908; Chalok Lam; dishes from 60B; ☯ dinner) This little gem, hidden among the clutter of Chalok Lam, serves a fresh assortment of seafood with big smiles from the staff.

Cucina Italiana (Chalok Lam; pizza 180B; ☯ dinner) Cucina Italiana is starting to have a cult following on Ko Pha-Ngan. The friendly Italian chef is passionate about his food, and creates all of his dishes from scratch. On Thursday and Sunday, you can order unlimited toppings on your oven-roasted pizza for only 180B.

Drinking

Every month, on the night of the full moon, pilgrims pay tribute to the party gods with trance-like dancing, wild screaming, and glow in the dark body paint. The throngs of bucket-sippers and fire twirlers gather on the infamous Sunrise Beach (Hat Rin Nok) and party til the sun replaces the moon in the sky.

Recently, a few other noteworthy party spots have opened up around the island – they're definitely worth a look if you want something a bit mellower.

HAT RIN

Hat Rin is the beating heart of the infamous full moon fun, and the area can get pretty wound up even without the influence of lunar phases. There are loads of bars and dance clubs crammed along Hat Rin Nok; the following are some of our favourites.

Paradise Bungalows (Map p214; ☎ 0 7737 5244) The full moon's Garden of Eden, if you will, Paradise basks in its celebrity status as the genesis of the lunar *loco*-motion. Check out the guest DJs spinning international beats at the Paradise Shark Tent.

Drop-In Bar (Map p214; ☎ 0 7737 5374) A fan favourite during full moon festivities, this dance shack blasts the chart toppers that everyone knows and loves. The other nights of the year are equally as boisterous – someone's always twirling a fire stick, while others are winning 'buckets' of whisky by scoring football goals.

Tommy Bar (Map p214; ☎ 0 7737 5215) Tommy Bar, one of Hat Rin's largest venues, lures the masses with black lights and trance music blaring on the sound system. Drinks are dealt to partiers from a large wooden structure that looks a bit like Noah's ark.

Mellow Mountain (Map p214; ☎ 0 7737 5347) Also called 'Mushy Mountain' (you'll know why when you get there), this trippy hangout sits at the northern edge of Hat Rin Nok delivering stellar views of the shenanigans below.

Cactus (Map p214; ☎ 0 7737 5308) Smack in the centre of Hat Rin Nok, Cactus pumps out a healthy mix of old school tunes, hip hop and R&B.

Backyard Club (Map p214; ☎ too chill to have a phone) The Backyard Club separates the strong from the weak – only the most hardcore make it to their full moon after-parties. When Hat Rin Nok shuts down mid-morning, surviving 'Mooners' stumble over for a second round of slippery beats. And we all know there's nothing better than a beer to cure a hangover.

Warm Up Bar (Map p214; ☎ 08 9652 1778) Groove to DJ-generated beats or shoot some pool – this sit-down joint, in the heart of Hat Rin Town, is the perfect place to (yeah, you guessed it) warm up for a wild night out.

Coral Bungalows Bar (Map p214; ☎ 0 7737 5023; Hat Rin Nai) Back on Hat Rin Nai, Coral's pool-centric powwows are so raucous they might just eclipse the full moon parties.

Other places to hit up for full moon fun along Sunrise Beach:

Big Boom (Map p214) Heaps of house music.

Rock (Map p214; ☎ 0 7737 5244) Great views of the party.

Vinyl (Map p214) More trance and techno.

OTHER BEACHES

Mason's Arms (☎ 08 5884 7271; Thong Sala; ◷ 10.30am-11.30pm) Suddenly, a clunky structure emerges from the swaying palms; it's a Tudor-style cottage, plucked directly from Stratford-upon-Avon and plunked down in the steamy jungle. This lodge-like lair is one blood pudding away from being an official British colony.

Amsterdam (☎ 0 7723 8447; Ao Plaay Laem) Near Hat Chaophao on the west coast, Amsterdam attracts tourists and locals from all over the island who are looking for a chill spot to watch the sunset.

Pirates Bar (☎ 08 4728 6064; Hat Chaophao) This popular and wacky drinkery is a replica of a pirate ship built into the cliffs. When you're sitting on the deck and the tide is high (and you've had a couple of drinks), you can almost believe you're out at sea. These guys host the well-attended moon-set parties, three days before Hat Rin gets pumpin' for the full moon fun.

Eagle Pub (☎ 08 4839 7143; Hat Yao) At the southern end of Hat Yao, this drink-dealing shack, built right into the rock face, is tattooed with the neon graffiti of virtually every person

who's passed out on the lime-green patio furniture after too many *caiparinhas*.

Sheesha Bar (☎ 0 7737 4161; Chalok Lam) The antithesis of grungy Hat Rin, the Sheesha Bar swaps 'buckets' of radio music for designer drinks. The enticing patchwork of beige sandstone and horizontal slats of mahogany wood fit right in with the arabesque Mandalai Hotel across the street (owned by the same family).

Getting There & Away

The fastest way to get to Ko Pha-Ngan is to take an airplane to Ko Samui and then connect to a ferry.

The Lomprayah and Seatran Discovery service has bus/boat combination packages departing from Bangkok and passing through Chumphon. It is also quite hassle-free to take the train from Bangkok to Chumphon and switch to a ferry service (it works out to be about the same price). For detailed information about travelling through Chumphon, see p187.

There are about six daily departures between Ko Pha-Ngan's Thong Sala pier and Surat Thani (220B to 320B, 2½ hours) on the *Raja Car Ferry*, *Songserm ferry* or Seatran. These boats leave from 7am to 10pm.

You can also take a slow night ferry direct to Pha-Ngan from Ban Don in Surat at 11pm (200B, seven hours). The night ferry can be a rough ride – November is the worst month. As with the night ferry to Samui, don't leave your bags unattended on the boat and remember that you'll arrive *very* early in the morning.

There are usually around a dozen daily boat departures between Ko Pha-Ngan and Ko Samui (130B to 250B), depending on the time of year and sea conditions. These boats leave throughout the day and take from 30 minutes to an hour. All leave from either Thong Sala or Hat Rin on Ko Pha-Ngan and arrive either in Na Thon, Mae Nam or the Big Buddha pier on Ko Samui. The *Hat Rin Queen* is a popular ferry that shuttles passengers between Hat Rin and Big Buddha Beach on Ko Samui (150B). There are four daily departures. If the final location matters, state your preferences while buying your ticket.

There are no car ferries between Ko Pha-Ngan and Ko Samui; you must return to the mainland and take a separate boat.

Getting Around

See p213 for important information about the dangers of riding motorbikes around the island.

You can rent motorcycles all over the island for 150B to 250B per day. Always wear a helmet. Bicycle rentals are discouraged unless you're fit enough to take on Lance Armstrong. Car rentals are around 1000B a day.

Some places can only be reached by boat, such as Hat Khuat and some sections of the east coast. If you do find trails, keep in mind that they are often overgrown and not suitable for solo navigation.

Sŏrng·tăa·ou chug along the island's major roads and the riding rates double after sunset. Ask your accommodation about free or discount transfers when you leave the island. The trip from Thong Sala to Hat Rin is 50B, while further beaches will set you back around 100B.

Long-tail boats depart from Thong Sala, Chalok Lam and Hat Rin, heading to a variety of far-flung destinations such as Hat Khuat (Bottle Beach) and Ao Thong Nai Pan. Expect to pay anywhere from 50B for a short trip, to 300B for a lengthier journey. You can charter a private boat ride from beach to beach for about 150B per 15 minutes of travel.

KO TAO

เกาะเต่า

pop 5000

Ko Tao has a special place in the hearts of scuba divers worldwide. Once a favoured hideout for pirates who stashed their gems deep within the jungle, this magical island now has a reputation for its treasures under the sea.

Diving drives the island's economy; Ko Tao issues more diving certifications than any other place in the world (yes, even more than the Great Barrier Reef in Australia!) It's no surprise really; there are dozens of spectacular shallows reefs just off the shore. These colourful realms teem with marine life, from triangular angelfish to inconceivably large whale sharks, and everything in between – rays, sharks, barracuda etc. Even if you aren't into blowing bubbles underwater, this peaceful gem has lots to offer among the plentiful dramatic bays hidden along its craggy coast.

Ko Tao literary means 'Turtle Island,' but we think 'magnetic island' might be more apropos. During a visit to the small bump in the ocean, you'll undoubtedly meet local expats who came for a beach holiday with a side of diving, but fell in love with the island's undeniable charm and decided to stay. If you're planning a trip to Ko Tao, consider adding on a couple days to prolong your visit – trust us, you'll be happy you did.

Orientation

All ferries pull into Ban Mae Hat, on the western side of the island. This seaside town has all the tourist amenities one would need: travel agencies, dive shops, restaurants, shops, internet cafés and motorcycle rentals. The biggest village on the island is Hat Sai Ri, about 2km up the coast. Here, travellers will find similar amenities but in greater quantity. Also, Sai Ri's nightlife is the best on the island. On the southern end of the island, a third town, Chalok Ban Kao, is steadily growing as well.

The east and north coast of the island are fairly undeveloped, with only a few bungalow enterprises on each little bay. A 4WD should be used when navigating the rugged roads that link these bays. Just 1km off the northwestern shore is the picturesque Ko Nang Yuan, which

is really three islands joined by a sand bar during low tide.

About the only thing of historic interest on the island is a large boulder, which has the initials of King Rama V, commemorating his royal visit in 1900.

Information

EMERGENCY
Police station (☎ 0 7745 6631) Just north of Mae Hat near the beach.

INTERNET ACCESS
If your accommodation doesn't offer internet access, there are heaps of places to check your email in Hat Sai Ri and Mae Hat. You may find that certain useful tourism websites have been firewalled at internet cafés affiliated with travel agencies. Several restaurants offer wi-fi connections – most have a bright 'wi-fi' sticker or sign at the entrance. Rates are generally 2B per minute, with a 20B minimum and discounts if you log on for one hour.

LAUNDRY
After a few dives, you'll probably want to wash your swim trunks (especially if you saw a shark and 'accidentally' peed your wetsuit). Almost every bungalow operation (and even some restaurants) offers laundry service. One kilo of laundry should be 30B, although operations closer to the beach tend to charge 40B. You may want to ask your diving instructor where (s)he gets their washing done, as sometimes items get conveniently lost. Express service is usually available for 60B per kilo.

MEDIA
The ubiquitous *Koh Tao Info* booklet lists loads of businesses on the island and goes into some detail about the island's history, culture and social issues. The small section detailing nearby destinations is also quite helpful.

MEDICAL SERVICES
All divers must sign a medical waiver before exploring the sea. If you have any medical condition that might hinder your ability to dive (including mild asthma), you will be asked to get medical clearance from a doctor on Ko Tao. Consider seeing a doctor before your trip as there is no official hospital on the island and the number of qualified medical professionals is limited. Also, make sure your traveller's insurance covers scuba diving. **Badalveda**

(☎ 0 7745 6580, 08 6272 4618, for diving emergencies 08 1989 9482; www.badalveda.com; Mae Hat; ☼ on call 24hr) has a hyperbaric chamber and emergency evacuation services. It has a related physician's clinic in Hat Sai Ri. The **Ko Tao Evacuation Centre** (☎ 0 7745 6572; www.sssnetwork.com) is also on call.

MONEY
As a general rule, there are 24hr ATMs at every 7-Eleven on the island. We also found more than five ATMs orbiting the ferry docks at Mae Hat. Money-exchange windows are also at the pier, in Hat Sai Ri, and at the far end of Mae Hat near Ko Tao's main road. **Siam City Bank** (☎ 0 7745 61533, ☼ 8.30am-3.30pm Mon-Fri) In Mae Hat.

POST
Post Office (☎ 0 7745 6170, 0 7745 6555) A 10 to 15 minute walk from the pier; at the corner of Ko Tao's main road and 'Mae Hat Boulevard'.

TELEPHONE
There are numerous places in Mae Hat, Hat Sai Ri and Chalok Ban Kao offering long-distance phone services. Mobile-phone service can be a tad temperamental in the more remote portions of the east coast.

TOURIST INFORMATION
There's no official TAT office on Ko Tao.

Dangers & Annoyances
There's nothing more annoying than enrolling in a diving course with your friends and then having to drop out because you scraped your knee in a motorcycle accident. The roads on Ko Tao are horrendous, save for the main drag connecting Sai Ri to Chalok Ban Kao. While hiring a moped is extremely convenient, this is not the place to learn how to ride. The island is rife with abrupt hills and sudden sand pits along gravel trails. Even if you escape unscathed from a riding experience, we've heard reports that some shops will claim that you damaged your rental and will try to extort you for some serious bling. See p239 for information about renting a motorcycle.

Sights
Sightseeing on Ko Tao revolves around its scenic **beaches**. While the beautiful Hat Sai Ri offers spectacular sunset vistas, it's by no means the stunning, secluded beach

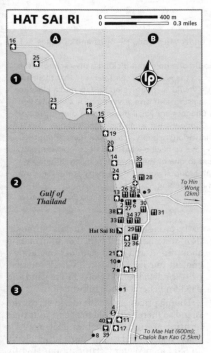

HAT SAI RI

0   400 m
0   0.3 miles

Gulf of Thailand

Hat Sai Ri

To Hin Wong (2km)

To Mae Hat (600m); Chalok Ban Kao (2.5km)

you were dreaming about. To find a hidden cove, venture through the jungle to the undeveloped east and northern coasts. Follow the weaving dirt road east from Sai Ri until you roll down the steep hill at **Hin Wong** – a stunning, rounded bay. There's no beach here, but the water is impossibly clear and the giant schools of black sardines look like an oozing oil spill as they swish through the sea. Hundreds of thick coconut palms bend over the cove as though they were trying to drink the water. The boulder-strewn inlet at **Ao Tanot** (Tanote Bay) has a similarly magical juxtaposition of jungle and sea. **Ao Leuk**, further south, is the choice retreat for many, and **Ao Thian Ok** (Shark Bay) is another stunning option, although despite the nickname, there are no sharks in the bay.

In the far north, **Ao Mamuang** (Mango Bay) has become a choice spot for scuba rookies – the bay is shallow and swimmable, with a picture-perfect backdrop featuring a rolling forest dotted with the occasional pitched roof of a hidden bungalow. In good weather you can get there by sŏrng·tǎa·ou; otherwise take a water taxi.

Just off the island's northwest coast, the rugged **Ko Nang Yuan** is a lonely island featuring three dramatic cone-shaped peaks connected by a remarkable sandbar. This idyllic beige strip is a stunning natural phenomenon that finds its way onto virtually every local postcard. Ferries from Mae Hat and water taxis from northern Sai Ri stop regularly at Ko Nang Yuan. There is a 100B levy to access the island.

LOCAL VOICE: DIVE SCHOOL ADVICE

Chris Clark is a videographer who specialises in underwater work. He owns and operates ACE Marine Images in Sai Ri.

With so many scuba centres on Ko Tao, how should one go about picking a dive school? As a videographer, I've worked with many dive centres on the island and can safely say that there are many great schools to choose from. My suggestion would be to arrive on Ko Tao, find a place to crash, and then chill out for a couple days before starting your dive adventure. This will give you plenty of time to have a look around the island. Chances are you'll bump into a dive instructor at a bar who can give you some insider advice. Chopper's Bar is always a good choice (p237). You'll also meet loads of divers already enrolled in various schools – they'll be frank about their experiences. When picking a dive shop, you also have to decide what kind of school you want. If you're looking for a family vibe, then don't head to one of the centres certifying 30 people a day – try a place that is only working with a small group. If you want the party scene there are tonnes of places offering a sociable bar scene in the evening.

As told to Brandon Presser

Activities

DIVING

If you've been toying with the idea of diving on your Thailand adventure, Ko Tao is the place to do it. The island certifies more divers than any other place in the world, which means that prices are low and quality is high as dozens of dive shops vie for your baht.

It's no surprise that this underwater playground has become exceptionally popular; the waters are crystal clear, there are loads of reefs and temperatures feel like bathwater. The best dive sites are found at offshore pinnacles within a 20km radius of the island (see the boxed text, opposite). The local marine wildlife includes grouper, moray eels, batfish, bannerfish, barracuda, titan triggerfish, angelfish, clownfish (Nemos), blue-spotted stingrays, a slue of sharks, and the occasional whale shark.

When you alight at the pier in Mae Hat, swarms of touts will try to coax you into staying at their dive resort with promises of a 'special price for you'. There are over 40 dive centres on the island, so it's best to arrive armed with the names of a few reputable dive schools. Remember: the success of your diving experience (especially if you are learning how to dive) will largely depend on how much you like and respect your instructor. There are other factors to consider as well, such as the size of your diving group, the condition of your equipment, and the condition of the dive site, to name a few. Smaller dive centres, such as New Way Diving, have familial atmospheres, while larger outfitters, such as Ban's Diving School or Big Blue, enjoy a party-prone vibe with on-site accommodation, restaurants and bars. For information about these, and other standout operations, consult our list (opposite). Check out also p291 for details on dive sites in Thailand and p383 for general diving information.

Diving prices are standardised across the island so there's no need to spend your time hunting around for the best deal. A PADI Open Water Certification course costs 9800B; an SSI Open Water Certification is slightly less (9000B because you do not have to pay for instructional materials). An Advanced Certification will set you back 8500B, a rescue course is 9500B, and the Divemaster program costs 25,000B. Fun divers should expect to pay 1000B per dive, or 7000B for a 10-dive package. These rates include gear, boat, instructor and snacks. Discounts are given if you bring your own equipment. Be wary of dive centres that offer too many price cuts – safety is paramount, and a shop giving out unusually good deals is probably cutting too many corners.

Most dive schools can hook you up with cheap (or even free) accommodation. Expect larger crowds between December and April, and a monthly glut of wannabe divers after the full moon party on Ko Pha-Ngan.

The following list includes a variety of standout operations on the island.

Ban's Diving School (Map p229; ☎ 0 7745 6466; www.amazingkohtao.com; Hat Sai Ri) A well-oiled dive machine and relentlessly expanding conglomerate, Ban's certifies more divers per year than any other scuba school in the world. Classroom sessions may be conducted in large groups, but there's good amount of individual attention in the water. A breadth of international instructors means that students can learn to dive in their native tongue. The affiliated resort is quite popular with party-seekers (see p233).

Big Blue Diving (Map p229; ☎ 0 7745 6415; 0 7745 6772; www.bigbluediving.com; Hat Sai Ri) This midsize diving centre gets praise for its awesome staff and youthful vibe. Big Blue usually hires videographers to create purchasable DVDs of the final dives of your Open Water certification. Divers of every ilk can score dirt-cheap accommodation at their resort (see p233).

Buddha View (☎ 0 7745 6074; www.buddhaview -diving.com; Chalok Ban Kao) Another big dive operation on Ko Tao, Buddha View offers the standard fare of certification and special programs for technical diving (venturing beyond the usual parameters of recreational underwater exploration). Discounted accommodation is available at their friendly resort.

Crystal (☎ 0 7745 6107; www.crystaldive.com; Chalok Ban Kao) Divers who choose this large scuba school will benefit from the friendly management, a multilingual staff, air-conditioned classrooms and an on-site swimming pool to learn the ropes. Groups are capped at six people, and there are spacious boats to shuttle divers to the sites. Crystal offers accommodation in both Mae Hat (see p234) and Sai Ri.

New Heaven (☎ 0 7745 6587; www.newheavendive school.com; Chalok Ban Kao) The owners of this small diving operation dedicate a lot of their time to preserving the natural beauty of Ko Tao's underwater sites by conducting regular reef checks and contributing to reef restoration. A special CPAD research diver certification program is available in addition to the regular order of programs and fun dives.

New Way Diving (Map p229; ☎ 0 7745 6527; www .newwaydiving.com, www.scubadivingkohtao.com; Hat Sai Ri) One of our favourite diving centres on Ko Tao, this small school has built an impressive reputation based upon small

diving groups and a friendly yet professional atmosphere. Their early-morning excursions depart before the larger schools, which means less traffic in the water and higher chances of seeing large pelagics. It's not too uncommon to go out for a post-dive dinner with the school. The manager can organise discounted accommodation nearby and there's free internet access at the dive shop.

Planet Scuba (☎ 0 7745 6110; www.planet-scuba.net /kohtao; Mae Hat) Planet Scuba is affiliated with a larger network of schools called the Samui International Diving School Group. They were the first company in Southeast Asia to be awarded PADI's Career Development Centre rating. Special courses using Nitrox (oxygen-enriched air tanks) are also on offer. Accommodation can be arranged at one of four locations around Mae Hat and Sai Ri.

Scuba Junction (Map p229; ☎ 0 7745 6164; www .scuba-junction.com; Hat Sai Ri) Scuba Junction guarantees a maximum of four people per diving group. 'Fun' divers get to use a Suunto diving computer for extra charge.

SNORKELLING

Snorkelling is a popular option for travellers. Orchestrating your own snorkelling adventure is simple, since the bays on the east coast have small bungalow operations offering equipment for 100B to 200B.

Almost every dive operation offers snorkelling day-trips tailored to the customers' desires. Prices range from 500B to 700B (usually including gear, lunch and a guide/boat captain) and stop at various snorkelling hotspots around the island. **Laem Thian** is popular for its small sharks, **Shark Island** has loads of fish (and ironically no sharks), **Hin Wong** is known for its crystalline waters, and **Light House Point**, in

---

TOP FIVE KO TAO DIVE SITES

- **Sail Rock** (34m max depth) Near Ko Pha-Ngan, features a massive rock chimney with a vertical swim-through, and large pelagics such as barracuda, kingfish and the occasional whale shark.

- **Chumphon Pinnacle** (36m max depth) West of Ko Tao, has a colourful assortment of sea anemones along the four interconnected pinnacles. The site is home to schools of giant trevally, tuna, and large grey reef sharks. Whale sharks are known to pop up once in a while.

- **Green Rock** (25m max depth) An underwater jungle gym featuring caverns, caves and small swim-throughs. Rays, grouper and triggerfish are known to hang around. It's a great place for a night dive.

- **Japanese Gardens** (12m max depth) Between Ko Tao and Ko Nang Yuan, it is a low-stress dive site perfect for beginners. There's plenty of colourful coral, and turtles, stingrays and pufferfish often pass by.

- **White Rock** (29m max depth) Home to colourful corals, angelfish, clown fish and territorial triggerfish. Another popular spot for night divers.

the north, offers a dazzling array of colourful sea anemones.

Don't forget to wear sunscreen on your back and consider wearing a T-shirt (very effective) – time quickly passes when you hover near the surface hobnobbing with pelagics. **AC Tours** (☎ 0 7745 6197; Mae Hat; 550-650B) Trips depart at 9am daily and stop at five different sites. Lunch included.

Golden Travel (☎ 0 7745 6978; Mae Hat; 550-700B) Day-long trips to some of the 20-odd snorkelling sites. Located across from the Songserm pier in Mae Hat. Rates include lunch, equipment and taxi service. Staff also organise fishing excursions, sunset cruises, and speedboat trips to stunning Ang Thong Marine Park.

OTHER WATER ACTIVITIES

In recent years, **underwater photography** and filmmaking has become quite popular on Ko Tao. Many scuba schools hire professional videographers to film the final dives of your Open Water diving certification. If this piques your interest, consider enrolling in an underwater video and film course. **ACE Marine Images** (Map p229; ☎ 0 7745 7054; www.acemarineimages.com), located beside Chopper's Bar & Grill in Sai Ri, is one of Thailand's leading underwater film-production companies. The exceptionally knowledgeable and friendly staff happily runs courses and internships for those who are serious about gaining field experience.

If hanging out underwater doesn't appeal to you, there are a few things you can do on the surface. Most bungalows and midsize dive centres offer sundry watersports such as kayaks or surfboards. Both **Black Tip Divers** (☎ 0 7745 6204; www.black-tip.com) and the friendly folks at **MV Sports** (☎ 0 7745 6065; www.mvsports.net) in Mae Hat can pull you behind a speedboat while you ride a variety of items including water skis, wakeboards or even an inflatable sumo suit. Two exhausting 10-minute sessions will cost you 1250B. Fishing enthusiasts can swing their tackle out at sea by contacting the **Adventure Centre** (☎ 08 9019 1761; Mae Hat), which arranges all-day fishing *sea*faris for around 1500B (minimum two people).

SPA & YOGA

If you are paying more than 2500B for your bungalow, then you probably have access to on-site spa services. Budget travellers looking to be pampered will find several good places to splurge. **Jamahkiri Resort & Spa** (☎ 0 7745 6400/1; www.jamahkiri.com), near Ao Tanot, does aloe-vera wraps (great for sunburn), massage and facials atop a huge island peak. While the spas on Ko Samui outshine it, Jamahkiri is one of the best on Ko Tao, and the prices are relatively cheap. Stunning cliffside bungalows are also available (see p236). Call for free transport, or swing by their wooden storefront near the Mae Hat pier. **Charm Churee Villa** (☎ 0 7745 6393; www.charm chureevilla.com), just south of Mae Hat, is another solid choice. Rejuvenation suites are dripping with Balinese decoration and sit close to the water's edge along a rugged escarpment of boulders. Seaside villas are on offer here as well (see p235). In the heart of Mae Hat, **Royal Thai Massage** (☎ 0 7745 6472) offers quality spa treatment at low prices. One-hour massages start at 250B, and aromatherapy costs 400B.

The Japanese-style bathhouse at **Yakuzen** (☎ 0 7745 6229, 08 4837 3385), in Mae Hat, changes things up by offering this unique form of relaxation and rejuvenation.

Ko Tao's only full-time yoga studio is a beautiful wooden *săh·lah* (often spelt *sala*) located on the forested grounds of **Blue Wind** (☎ 0 7745 6116, 0 7745 6015), a collection of budget bungalows along Sai Ri Beach (see opposite). Classes are 300B.

OTHER ACTIVITIES

Ko Tao Bowling & Mini Golf (☎ 0 7745 6316; ☽ noon-midnight), on the main road between Mae Hat and Chalok Ban, has several homemade bowling lanes where the employees reset the pins after every frame (300B per hour). The 18-hole mini-golf course has a landmark theme – putt your ball through Stonehenge or across the Golden Gate Bridge. Petanque is also available, and if you're feeling snackish, the restaurant dishes out finger food favourites suck as wings and ribs.

Sleeping

If you are planning to dive while visiting Ko Tao, your scuba operation might offer you discounted accommodation as an extra incentive. Some schools have on-site lodging, while others have deals with nearby bungalows. It's important to note that you only receive your scuba-related discount on the days you dive. So, if you buy a package, and decide to take a day off in the middle, your room rate will not be discounted on that evening. Also, a restful sleep is important in between dives, so scope out these 'great room deals' before saying yes – some of them are one roach away from being condemned. During the busier months, discounts are often unavailable and prices can spike when resorts are at full capacity.

There are also many sleeping options that have absolutely nothing to do with the island's diving culture. Ko Tao's secluded eastern coves are dotted with stunning retreats that still offer a true getaway experience, but these can be difficult to reach due to the island's dismal network of roads. You can often call ahead and arrange to be picked up from the pier.

HAT SAI RI (SAIREE BEACH)

Giant Sai Ri is the longest and most developed strip on the island, with a string of dive operations, bungalows, travel agencies, minimarkets and internet cafés. The narrow 'yellow brick road' stretches the entire length of the beach (watch out for motorcycles).

Budget & Midrange

Some of the places listed here with midrange options have one cheap room/bungalow, which will most likely already be booked out.

Here & Now (Map p229; ☎ 0 7745 6730; www.here andnow.be; bungalows 100-700B) At Here & Now, the crashing waves sound exactly like those ocean recordings people use to relax when they're not on vacation. The bungalows aren't particularly stellar, however there's something rather charming about climbing over gargantuan boulders to reach your teetering abode.

Big Blue Resort (Map p229; ☎ 0 7745 6050; www.big bluediving.com; r 200-1000B; ⚡ 💻) This scuba-centric resort has a summer camp vibe – diving classes dominate the daytime, while evenings are spent en masse, grabbing dinner or watching fire twirling. Both the basic fan bungalows and motel-style air-conditioned rooms offer little when it comes to views, but who has the time to relax when there's an ocean out there to explore?

Sunlord Bungalows (Map p229; ☎ 0 7745 6139; bungalows 300-400B) Just north of the action on the beach, these basic-but-sturdy bungalows trickle down a rugged escarpment that abruptly dumps into the sea. The owner, an older Thai lady, should host 'Let's Make a Deal' – she's ready at a moment's notice to strike a bargain for your lodging.

Blue Wind (Map p229; ☎ 0 7745 6116, 0 7745 6015; bluewind_wa@yahoo.com; bungalows 300-900B; ⚡) Hidden within a cluster of bodacious lodging options, Blue Wind offers a breath of fresh air from the high-intensity dive resorts strung along Sairee Beach. Sturdy bamboo huts are peppered along a dirt trail between the beachside bakery and a newly built yoga *săh.lah*. Large, tiled cabins are also available, boasting air-con, hot showers and TVs.

AC Resort (Map p229; ☎ 0 7745 6197; acresort@ yahoo.com; info@phoenix-divers.com; bungalows 300-1900B; ⚡ 💻 🌐) A large sign, half-covered by a manmade waterfall, welcomes vacationers to the party at AC Resort. Backpackers will find a standard issue of well-worn huts. The airconditioned cottages have gargantuan beds, but the bathrooms are microscopic. Divers get a 30% to 40% discount, which increases depending on how long you stay.

Sairee Cottage (Map p229; ☎ 0 7745 6126, 0 7745 6374; saireecottage@hotmail.com; bungalows 400-1500B; ⚡) The air-con bungalows are hard to miss since they've been painted in various hues of fuchsia. Low prices mean low vacancy – so arrive early to score one of the brick huts facing out onto a grassy knoll.

our pick Ban's Diving Resort (Map p229; ☎ 0 7745 6466, 0 7745 6061; www.amazingkohtao.com; r 400-3000; ⚡ 💻 🌐) This dive-centric party palace offers a palette of quality accommodation from basic backpacker digs to sleek hillside villas. Post-scuba chill sessions happen on Ban's prime slice of beach, or at one of the two swimming pools tucked within the strip of jungle between the two motel-like structures. Evenings are spent at the bar downing international cuisine and 'buckets' in equal measure.

Seashell Resort (Map p229; ☎ 0 7745 6299; www .seashell-resort.com; bungalows 450-3800B; ⚡) Several bungalows have ocean views from their porches (a rarity in Sai Ri), while others sit in a well-maintained garden of colourful vegetation and thin palm trunks. Seashell welcomes divers and non-divers alike.

In Touch (Map p229; ☎ 0 7745 6514; bungalows 500-1200B; ⚡) Older bungalows are a mishmash of bamboo and dark wood. Several rounded air-conditioned rooms have a cave theme – it's all very 'Flintstones', except the shower nozzle hasn't been replaced with the trunk of an elephant. The bustling restaurant can get a bit rowdy in the evening.

Pranee's (Map p229; ☎ 0 7745 6080; bungalows 500-2000B) Tidy budget bungalows, made of wood and rattan-woven walls, are shaded by coconut-wielding palms. A new fleet of aircon options are an uninspiring mix of white and blue, but some still have that new car smell. Afternoon excursions, like a visit to nearby Ko Nang Yuan, are easily executed since a few long-tail boat taxis park along Pranee's beachfront.

Bow Thong (Map p229; ☎ 0 7745 6266; bungalows 500-3400B; 🔀 ⚑) A member of the more up-scale northern section of Hat Sai Ri, Bow Thong has high prices but the rooms aren't up to snuff. This friendly resort is, however, worth a second look if you are planning to dive, as a couple of affiliated scuba schools can give you a hefty discount.

Sunset Buri Resort (Map p229; ☎ 0 7745 6266; bungalows 700-2500B; 🔀 ⚏ ⚑) A long beach-bound path is studded with beautiful white bungalows featuring enormous windows and flamboyant temple-like roofing. The kidney-shaped pool is a big hit, as are the large beach recliners sprinkled around the resort.

Top End
Koh Tao Cabana (Map p229; ☎ 0 7745 6250; www.kohtaocabana.com; bungalows 3000-6300B; 🔀) This prime piece of beachside property offers timber-framed villas and crinkled white adobe huts dotted along the landscape between sea-swept boulders and verdant bursts of luscious palms. Bric-a-brac cheers the colourful bungalows: bamboo message cylinders dangle at the doors and stone gnomes greet you with a naughty smirk as you shower in the indoor/outdoor bathrooms.

Thipwimarn (Map p229; ☎ 0 7745 6409; www.thipwimarnresort.com; bungalows 3100-4900B; 🔀 ⚑) Tucked away just north of the bustling beach, this cliff-side retreat is undisputedly the poshest address in the Sairee Beach neighbourhood. The steep curvature of the property promises dramatic evening panoramas from every balcony as the flaming equatorial sun plunges into the crystalline sea.

Koh Tao Coral Grand Resort (Map p229; ☎ 0 7745 6431; www.kohtaocoral.com; bungalows 3200-4500B; 🔀 ⚑) The plethora of pink façades at this family-friendly option feels a bit like Barbie's Thai beach dream house. Cottage interiors are coated in cheery primary colours framed by white truncated beams while pricier digs have a more distinctive Thai flavour, boasting dark lacquered mouldings and gold-foiled art. Guests can participate in an array of organised off-site activities such as fishing, hiking, kayaking and boat-

ing, although it might be hard to tear yourself away from the relaxing resort and large beachside pool.

HAT AO MAE (MAE HAT)
All ferry arrivals pull up at the pier of the busy village of Mae Hat. There are several guesthouses in town, but the more charming accommodation options extend in both directions along the sandy beach. The options to the south are much more secluded and relaxed.

North of the Pier
Mr J Bungalow (☎ 0 7745 6066, 0 7745 6349; bungalows 250-1000B) Even though Mr J tried to charge us 50B for his business card, we still think he's well worth the visit. The eccentric owner entangles guests in a philosophical web while tending to his flock of decent bungalows. Ask him about reincarnation if you want to hear some particularly twisted conjectures.

View Cliff Resort (☎ 0 7745 6353; www.viewcliff.com, www.kohtaoholiday.com; bungalows from 400, r 1500B; 🔀) A photogenic strip of Italianate double-decker bungalows links the narrow street with the rocky shoreline. The perfectly manicured lawns feel almost like the green of a golf course, and large rounded balconies overhead offer glimpses of the turquoise sea. If a competition was held for Ko Tao's biggest smile, the affable manager would surely win.

Tommy's Dive Resort (☎ 0 7745 6039; bungalows 700-2500B) Follow the undulating curve of the motel's porches as they slope down a hill, and check out the seaside views from the 700B rooms – these are the best bang for your baht at Tommy's. The convenient location between the bustle of Mae Hat and Sai Ri is a big plus.

Crystal (☎ 0 7745 6107; www.crystaldive.com; bungalows 800-1500B; 🔀 ⚑) At Crystal, you'll probably hear the phrase 'what a dive!' – the guests are talking about scuba, not the accommodation. Divers can grab a room for as little as 300B, and if you enrol in a course, they'll knock the price down to 200B (500B for air-con.)

South of the Pier
Take a right after exiting the main pier. Most of these establishments will require a taxi ride.

Sai Thong Resort (☎ 0 7745 6868; www.saithong-resort.com; bungalows 300-2500B; 🔀 ⚏ ⚑) As the rush of Hat Ao Mae dwindles away along the island's southwest shore, Sai Thong emerges along sandy Hat Sai Nuan. Bungalows, in various incarnations of weaving and wood, have colourful porch hammocks and palm-filled vistas. Guests frequent the restaurant's relaxing sun deck and open-air spa pagodas.

Tao Thong Villa (☎ 0 7745 6078; bungalows from 500B) Very popular with long-termers seeking peace and quiet, these funky, no-frills bungalows have killer views. Tao Thong actually straddles two tiny beaches on a craggy cape about halfway between Hat Ao Mae and Chalok Ban Kao. The pair of neighbouring swim spots is the perfect place for a hermitic afternoon.

Utopia Suites (☎ 0 7745 6729, 08 9816 5654; r 800-1600B, ste 1800-2800) Utopia's apartment-style accommodation is a stone's throw from the busy Mae Hat pier. The spacious suites have all the amenities you left behind at home: a kitchen, living room, TV, and the list goes on.

Sensi Paradise Resort (☎ 0 7745 6244; www.sensi paradise.com; bungalows 2500-9000B; ❄) There are one too many geckos in the bathroom to call this place 'natural chic', but if you like to be one with nature then you'll appreciate that these rustic cottages are somehow simultaneously upscale. Friendly caretakers and several airy teak *săh·lahs* add an extra element of charm.

our pick Charm Churee Villa (☎ 0 7745 6393; www .charmchureevilla.com; bungalows 3200-12,200B; ❄ 🖳 🖳) Tucked gently under sky-scraping palms, the luxuriant villas of Charm Churee are dedicated to the flamboyant spoils of the Far East. Gold-foiled oriental demigods pose in arabesque positions, with bejewelled eyes frozen in a Zen-like trance. Staircases, chiselled into the rock face, dribble down a palmed slope revealing teak huts strewn across smokey boulders. The villas' unobstructed views of the swishing indigo waters are nothing short of charm-ing.

CHALOK BAN KAO

Ao Chalok, about 1.7km south of Ban Mae Hat, is the third-largest concentration of accommodation on Ko Tao, but can feel a lot more crowded because the beach is significantly smaller than Hat Sai Ri and Mae Hat.

JP Resort (☎ 0 7745 6099; bungalows 400-700B) This little cheapie promises a colourful menagerie of prim motel-style rooms stacked on a small scrap of jungle across the street from the sea. Sun-soaked rooms have polished pastel-coloured linoleum floor, and many of the tiled bathrooms have been recently refurbished. The beachside restaurant, doused in blazing yellow paint, doubles as a restaurant and hangout spot.

Tropicana (☎ 0 7745 6167; www.koh-tao-tropicana -resort.com; r from 400) With some intense refurbishment underway, Tropicana is upping the ante when it comes to quality budget digs. Low-rise hotel units are peppered across a garden campus providing fleeting glimpses of the ocean between fanned fronds and spiky palms.

Viewpoint Resort (☎ 0 7745 6666; www.kohtaoview point.com; bungalows 800-1300B) A hot-shot architect from Bangkok allegedly designed this friendly, family-run retreat at the end of civilization. Cottages are spartan but airy and well maintained. Some have partial sea views; others quietly sit in a gorgeous hillside garden that thrums with cicadas at night.

New Heaven Resort (☎ 0 7745 6422; newheaven resort@yahoo.co.th; r & bungalows 1200-3900B) Just beyond the clutter of Chalok Ban Kao, New Heaven proffers colourful huts perched over impossibly clear waters. A steep path of chiselled stone tumbles down the shrubby rock face revealing unique bungalows with views ripped straight from the pages of *National Geographic*. The fan rooms are an unbelievable steal especially since evenings welcome cool gusts from the moonlit bay.

Ko Tao Resort (☎ 0 7745 6133; www.kotaoresort.com; r & bungalows 1600-3000B; ❄ 🖳 🖳) The entrance is a throwback to the days when taste and architecture weren't particularly synonymous (the '70s perhaps?), but the facilities themselves fit the true definition of a resort. The rooms are well stocked, water sports equipment is on offer, and there are several bars ready to serve you a variety of fruity cocktails.

EAST COAST BEACHES

The serene east coast is, without a doubt, one of the best places for escapists in this entire region of Thailand. The views are stunning, beaches are silent, yet all of your creature comforts are 10 minutes away. Accommodation along this coast is organised from north to south.

Hin Wong

A sandy beach has been swapped for a coast that is boulder-strewn, but the water is crystal clear. The road to Hin Wong is paved in parts, but sudden sand pits and steep hills can toss you off your motorbike.

Hin Wong Bungalows (☎ 0 7745 6006, 08 1229 4810; bungalows from 300B) Pleasant wooden huts are scattered across vast expanses of untamed tropical terrain – it all feels a bit like TV's 'Lost' (minus the body snatchers). A rickety dock juts out just beyond the breezy restaurant and dips into the lucent bay. This line of weathered wooden planks is the perfect place to dangle your legs and watch schools of black sardines slide through the cerulean water.

View Rock (☎ 0 7745 6548/9; viewrock@hotmail.com; bungalows 300-400B) When coming down the dirt road into Hin Wong, follow the signs as they lead you north (left) of Hin Wong Bungalows. View Rock is precisely that: views and rock; the hodge-podge of wooden huts, which looks like a secluded fishing village, is built into the steep rockface offering stunning views of the bay.

Laem Thian & Ao Tanot

Laem Thian is a scenic cape with a small patch of sand. Ao Tanot (Tanote Bay) is slightly more populated than some of the other eastern coves, but it's still quiet and picturesque. There are a couple of simple shops in the area.

Laem Thian (☎ 0 7745 6477; r & bungalows 400-1500B; ✷) Nestled far from civilization on a lush stretch of jungle, this small boulder-filled resort is the only operation on Laem Thain. The modern rooms tend to be better than the bungalows, so long as you don't mind the ugly façades. The road here is very rough; call for a pick-up.

Black Tip Dive Resort (☎ 0 7745 6488; www.blacktip -kohtao.com; Ao Tanot; bungalows 600-2800B; ✷ ▣) Part dive shop and water-sports centre, Black Tip also has a handful of lovely wooden bungalows with thatched roofing. The scuba centre is housed in a wacky structure made of rippling white adobe and strange geometric protrusions. Guests get a 50% discount when enrolled in a diving course and 'fun divers' get 25% off room rates.

Ao Leuk & Ao Thian Ok

The dirt roads to Ao Leuk and Ao Thian Ok are steep, rough and rutty, especially towards the end; don't attempt it on a motorcycle unless you're an expert. Both bays are stunning and serene.

Ao Leuk Bungalows (☎ 0 7745 6692; bungalows 400-1500B) Lodging at Ao Leuk comes in several shapes and sizes ranging from backpacker shacks to modern family-friendly options. The elevated restaurant is a tad cheesy but

has top views. Flickering torches and ambient cackles of curious cicadas accent the jet-black evenings.

Jamahkiri Resort & Spa (☎ 0 7745 6400; www .jamahkiri.com; bungalows 6900-13,900B) The flamboyant décor at this whitewashed estate is decidedly focused around tribal imagery. Wooden gargoyle masks and stone fertility goddesses abound amid swirling mosaics and multiarmed statues. Feral hoots of distant monkeys confirm the overarching jungle theme, as do the thatched roofs and tiki-torched soirees. The resort's seemingly infinite number of stone stairways can be a pain, so it's a good thing Ko Tao's most luxurious spa is located on the premises (see p232).

North Coast
Ao Mamuang

The isolated rocky bay of Ao Mamuang has great snorkelling and a dramatic backdrop of jungle and rocky hills.

Mango Bay Grand Resort (☎ 0 7745 6097; www .mangobaygrandresortkohtaothailand.com; bungalows 1400-3000B; ✷) Spacious mahogany villas with burgundy roofs are perched high on stilts above the ashen boulders surrounding the bay. A thin necklace of mosaic-lined paths winds through the tropical shrubbery, connecting the secluded cottages. The on-site restaurant offers delicious sea views from the wood-planked veranda.

Ko Nang Yuan

Little Ko Nang Yuan sits just off the coast of Ko Tao, easily accessible by regular ferry, by Lomprayah catamaran, and by water taxis that depart from Mae Hat and Sai Ri.

Ko Nangyuan Dive Resort (☎ 0 7745 6088, 0 7745 6093; www.nangyuan.com; bungalows 1500-7000B; ✷) While the obligatory 100B tax to access the island is a bit off-putting, and the inflated prices positively reek of a monopoly, Nangyuan Dive Resort is nonetheless a charming place. The rugged collection of wood and aluminium bungalows winds its way across three cooliehat-like conical islands connected by an idyllic beige sandbar. The resort also boasts the best restaurant on the island, but then again, it's the only place to eat…

Eating

With super-sized Samui lurking on the horizon, it's hard to believe that quaint little Ko Tao is a worthy opponent in the gastronomy category. Most resorts offer on-site dining, and stand-alone establishments are multiplying at lightning speed in Hat Sai Ri and Ao Hat Mae. The diverse population of the diver community means a broad range of international cuisine, including Mexican, French, Italian, and even African. On our quest to find the tastiest Thai fare on the island, we discovered, not surprisingly, that our favourite local meals were being dished out at small, unnamed restaurants on the side of the road.

HAT SAI RI (SAIREE BEACH)

Sairee Beach is tiny Tao's unofficial capital of cuisine, offering an impressive assortment of international flavours. In the evenings there are several foods carts scattered around the village serving tea and treats. Stop by the 7-Eleven beside Big Blue Resort to check out Ally The Pancake Man as he dances around, like an Italian chef making pizza, while cooking your tasty dessert. He's become quite the local legend and has even appeared on YouTube.

Budget

Coffee Boat (Map p229; ☎ 08 5784 4831; dishes 30-70B; ✹ breakfast, lunch & dinner) A perilous set of rickety steps hoists nibblers up into the tiny treehouse-like hut. The service isn't big on smiles, but the scrumptious curries and low prices will have you coming back for seconds.

Tong (Map p229; ☎ 0 7745 6458; dishes 30-70B; ✹ breakfast, lunch & dinner) The food doesn't win any awards, but the menu is vast and cheap. Ogle their hideous pet fish while waiting for your takeaway order, or grab a table in the large dining room. Laundry service is available for 30B per kilogram.

Café Corner (Map p229; dishes 30-100B; ✹ breakfast & lunch) The flaky *pain au chocolat* can easily be mistaken for a Parisian patisserie. Customers enjoy their desserts at swirling stainless steel countertops while watching movies on a swank plasma TV. Swing by at 5pm to stock up for tomorrow morning's breakfast; the scrumptious baked breads are marked down 50% before being tossed at the end of the night.

E-san Inter (Map p229; ☎ 0 7745 7003; dishes 40-90B; ✹ 10.30am-11pm) If you've never had *sôm-dam tai* (spicy papaya salad), here's the perfect place to start. The matronly owner caters each serving to meet her customer's tastes – ask for four chillies if you're feeling really adventurous (which is still milder than the original

Thai recipe). Try the recommended side order of sticky rice and BBQ chicken.

Blue Wind Bakery (Map p229; ☎ 0 7745 6116; dishes 40-150B; ✹ breakfast, lunch & dinner) This beachside shanty dishes out Thai favourites, Western confections and freshly blended fruit juices. Enjoy your thick fruit smoothie and flaky pastry while reclining on tattered triangular pillows.

Chopper's Bar & Grill (Map p229; ☎ 0 7745 6641; dishes 60-200B; ✹ breakfast, lunch & dinner) A great place to widen that beer belly, Chopper's offers live music, sports on the big-screen TVs, billiards, and a cinema room upstairs. Friday nights are particularly popular; the drinks are 'two for one', and dishes are half-priced as well. Cheers for scored goals are interspersed with the exaggerated chatter about creatures seen on the day's dive.

East Restaurant (Map p229; ☎ 0 7745 6416; dishes 75-250B; ✹ breakfast, lunch & dinner) Big Blue Resort's busy chow house, located about 2m from the crashing tide, dispatches the best personal pizzas on the island. The joint fills up around sunset with divers who chuckle at the daily dive bloopers shown on the big-screen TV.

El Gringo (Map p229; ☎ 0 7745 6323; dishes 80-150B; ✹ breakfast, lunch & dinner) As if there weren't already enough nicknames for white people in Thailand. The self-proclaimed funky Mexican joint slings burritos of questionable authenticity at two locations in Sai Ri and a third in Ao Hat Mae.

Portobello (Map p229; ☎ 0 7745 7029; dishes 80-250B; ✹ lunch & dinner) Portobello pays tribute to the boot-land by serving up favourites such as ravioli stuffed with shrimp and crab, or personal pizzas topped with scrumptious imported cheeses. Dessert enthusiasts can earn a place in the 'hall of fame' by devouring a slice of thick chocolate cake sans hands.

Papa's Tapas (Map p229; ☎ 0 7745 7020; papas .tapas.kohtao@gmail.com; plates 90-130B; ✹ dinner) Another member of Ko Tao's new designer diner army, this swish set-up takes a stab at nouveau cuisine with sample-sized platters. Those with a big wallet (and a little foresight) can order the Chef's Special – a menu of unique dishes that requires 24 hours to procure and prepare (2500B). Reservations recommended.

Zanzibar (Map p229; ☎ 0 7745 6452; dishes 90-140B; ✹ breakfast, lunch & dinner) Grab a seat in the sea of velvety cushions – Zanzibar's pressed sandwiches are a welcomed break from the endless supply of rice and noo-dles. The tribal spears have been hung on the burnt sienna walls, so there's no jungle fare at this joint, just an assortment of yup-pie condiments betwixt two slices of whole grain bread.

Midrange

Rim Lae (Map p229; ☎ 0 7745 6505; dishes 150-300B; breakfast, lunch & dinner) Ko Tao Cabana's *piece de resistance*, Rim Lae is perched high over the gaping bay offering exquisite views of the bobbing long-tail boats. Dinnertime is particularly special as scorching sunsets are on order almost every evening.

Morava (Map p229; ☎ 0 7745 6270; dishes 160-300B; dinner) This Sairee splurge has out-swanked the competition with the effective use of dark purples and Zen stepping stones. The food can be a little bit hit or miss, so have your friendly waiter educate you on the house favourites (the omelettes are a surprisingly good choice).

HAT AO MAE (MAE HAD)

Yang (☎ 0 7745 6226; dishes 30-70B; breakfast, lunch & dinner) For mounds of cheap Thai fare, try Yang – Tong's Mae Hat cousin (see p237).

Cappuccino (☎ 08 7896 8838; cappuccino_koh tao@hotmail.com; dishes 30-90B; breakfast & lunch) Cappuccino's décor falls somewhere between the New York deli on *Seinfeld* and a French *brasserie* – it's a great place to grab a coffee and croissant while waiting for the ferry.

Farango Pizzeria (☎ 0 7745 6205; dishes 60-220B; lunch & dinner) Ko Tao's first faràng restaurant spins tasty steaks, seafood and Italian dishes alongside matching wine selections. The cheery atmosphere drips with burnt yellows and Spanish-themed posters of flamboyant matadors.

Zest Coffee Lounge (☎ 0 7745 6178; dishes 70-190B; breakfast & lunch) Zest is a great spot to indulge in the street-café lifestyle. Idlers can nibble confections or nurse their cup of joe all the way 'til sunset. A second location has opened in Hat Sai Ri (Map p229).

Café del Sol (☎ 0 7745 6578; dishes 70-250B; breakfast, lunch & dinner; ▯) Even the pickiest eater will be satisfied with the menu's expansive selection of 'world cuisine'. The focus is namely European (French and Italian) with specialities such as homemade liver paté, bruscetta, and tender steaks imported from New Zealand. There's free wi-fi.

CHALOK BAN KAO

New Heaven Restaurant (☎ 0 7745 6462; lunch dishes 60-180B, dinner dishes 60-350B; lunch & dinner) The best part about New Heaven Restaurant is the awe-inducing view of Shark Bay (Ao Thian Ok) under the lazy afternoon moon. The turquoise waters below are so translucent that the curving reef is easily visible from your seat. The menu is largely international, and there are nap-worthy cushions tucked under each low-rise table.

Drinking

Ko Tao's favourite pastime, after diving, is drinking. And there's definitely no shortage of places to get tanked. Flyers detailing upcoming parties are posted on various trees and walls along the west coast (check at the 7-Elevens in Hat Sai Ri). Also keep an eye out for posters touting 'jungle parties' held on nondescript patches of scrubby jungle in the centre of the island. The tides also play an integral part in the island's night scene. On evenings when the tides are high, there tends to be less raucous revelling along Hat Sai Ri since there's not a lot of room to go and get wild.

Just remember: don't drink and dive.

Fizz (Dry Bar; Map p229; ☎ 08 7887 9495; Hat Sai Ri) Recline on mattress-sized pillows and enjoy designer cocktails while listening to Moby, or Enya, mixed with hypnotic gushes of the rolling tide.

Lotus (Map p229; ☎ 0 7745 6358) Lotus, next door to Fizz, is the de facto late-night hangout spot along the northern end of Hat Sai Ri. Muscular fire twirlers toss around flaming batons, and the drinks are so large there should be a life-guard on duty.

Whitening (☎ 0 7745 6199; Ao Hat Mae) Artsy folk will appreciate the venue's interesting use of positive and negative space. Drinkers will love the groovy atmosphere; the 'floors' are sandy, torches glow in the evening, and house music gently wafts in the background.

Dirty Nelly's Irish Pub (☎ 0 7745 6569; Ao Hat Mae) True to its name, Dirty Nelly's is unapologetically Irish; the draught beers, the managers – everything's been imported straight from the motherland (except the weather). There's billiards, sports on the big-screen TV and regular weekend BBQs.

Tattoo Bar (☎ 08 9291 9416; Ao Hat Mae) Just 30m south of Whitening (at the edge of town), Tattoo is a casual affair with a cosy area for TV-watching. If you're hungry, try the massive Aussie burger, homemade meat pies and sausage rolls.

Dragon Bar (☎ 0 7745 6423; Ao Hat Mae) This bar caters to those seeking snazzy, cutting-edge surroundings. There is a happening 'Communist chic' retro styling throughout, and everything's dimly lit, moody and relaxing. Dragon Bar is rumoured to have the best cocktails on the island.

Safety Stop Pub (☎ 0 7745 6209; Ao Hat Mae) A haven for homesick Brits, this pier-side pub feels like a tropical beer garden. Stop by on Sundays to stuff your face with an endless supply of barbecued goodness.

Clumped at the southern end of Sai Ri Beach, these three nightspots take turns reeling in the partiers throughout the week.

AC Party Pub (Map p229; ☎ 0 7745 6197)

In Touch (Map p229; ☎ 0 7745 6514)

Maya Bar (Map p229; ☎ 0 7745 6195)

Getting There & Away

As always, the cost and departure times are in flux. Rough waves are known to cancel ferries between October and December. Beware of travel agencies in Bangkok and on Ko Tao selling fake bus/boat or train/boat combinations.

The Lomprayah and Seatran Discovery service has bus/boat combination packages departing from Bangkok and passing through Chumphon. It is also quite hassle-free to take the train from Bangkok to Chumphon and switch to a ferry service (it's roughly the same price). For detailed information about travelling through Chumphon, see p187.

Many different types of ferries connect Ko Tao to the other oft-travelled destinations in the region. The **Lomprayah Catamaran** (☎ 0 7745 6176) shuttles passengers to Ko Pha-Ngan (1¼ hours) with continuing service to Ko Samui (two hours total). Daily boats depart Mae Hat at 9.30am and 3pm. The Ko Tao-bound catamarans leave Ko Samui at 8am and 12.30pm, and leave Ko Pha-Ngan at 8.30am and 1pm. **Seatran Discovery** (☎ 0 7745 6907) offers the exact same service, however, the boats are about 20 minutes slower, and the afternoon ferries headed to Ko Tao depart about an hour later than Lomprayah. The **Songserm Express** (☎ 0 7745 6274) is also similar, with a departure at 10am daily, stopping in Ko Pha-Ngan at 11.30am, Ko Samui at 12.45pm, and arriving at its final destination, Surat Thani, around 4.30pm. Boats heading to Ko Tao from Surat, leave

at 8am and arrive at 2.30pm. A **night ferry** departs Ko Tao at 10.30pm, and reaches Surat at 5.30am. Or, the boat leaves Surat at 11pm and alights at Ko Tao's Mae Hat pier around 8am.

Getting Around

Sŏrng·tǎa·ou crowd around the pier in Mae Hat as passengers alight. If you're a solo traveller, you will pay 100B to get to Sai Ri and Chalok Ban Kao. Groups of two or more will pay 50B each. Rides from Sai Ri to Chalok Ban Kao cost 80B per person, or 150B for solo tourists. These are non-negotiable prices, and passengers must wait until each sŏrng·tǎa·ou is full before it departs. If these taxis are empty, you will be asked to pay for the entire cab (300B to 500B). Prices double for trips to the east coast, but rain makes the roads harder to negotiate and drivers will raise the prices in these situations. If you know where you intend to stay, you can call ahead for a pick-up. Several guesthouses also send representatives to the pier offering free cab rides to the resort.

There is one paved road on Ko Tao, which connects Sai Ri to Chalok Ban Kao (stopping at Mae Hat in between). If you are planning to travel between these destinations then renting a motorcycle is a possibility (from 150B per day). The other roads on the island are rutty, sandy and often quite steep. See p228 for vital information about rentals and motorcycle safety.

Boat taxis depart from Ban Mae Hat, Chalok Ban Kao and the northern part of Hat Sai Ri (near Prawnee Bungalows). A boat ride to Ko Nang Yuan will set you back around 200B. Long-tail boats can be chartered for around 1500B a day, depending on the number of passengers.

MOTORCYCLE & 4WD

Ko Tao's noticeable lack of paved roads is a daredevil's dream. If you're one to throw caution (and common sense) to the wind (but, hopefully, not overmuch), then consider renting a motorbike or 4WD to explore the island's rugged jungle. There are loads of places to lease a vehicle, but be warned that scams are common (see p228). Go with **Lederhosenbikes** (☎ 08 1752 8994; www.lederhosenbikes.com; Ao Hat Mae; ❂ 8am-8pm Mon-Sat); this expat operation has a great selection of quality equipment, and promises honest service. Daily rental rates begin with 150/200B for manual/automatic scooters, larger bikes start at 350B, four-wheelers are 500B, and four-seater 4WDs will set you back 1800B.

ANG THONG MARINE NATIONAL PARK
อุทยานแห่งชาติหมู่เกาะอ่างทอง

When Alex Garland wrote his cult novel *The Beach* (which later became a movie with the same name), he must have been dreaming about Ang Thong Marine National Park. Known as 'Mu Ko Ang Thong' in Thai, this stunning archipelago contains 42 small islands featuring sheer limestone cliffs, hidden lagoons, perfect peach-coloured beaches and an interesting menagerie of animals, such as otters, crab-eating monkeys, bats, cobras, iguanas, wild boar and over 50 species of bird.

February to April are the best months to visit this ethereal realm of greens and blues; crashing monsoon waves means that the park is almost always closed during November and December.

Sights

Every tour stops at the park's head office on **Ko Wua Talap**, the largest island in the archipelago. The island's viewpoint might just be the most stunning vista in all of Thailand. From the top, visitors will have sweeping views of the jagged islands nearby as they burst through the placid green water in easily anthropomorphized formations. The trek to the lookout is an arduous 450m trail that takes roughly an hour to complete. Hikers should wear sturdy shoes and walk slowly on the sharp outcrops of limestone. A second trail leads to **Tham Bua Bok**, a cavern with lotus-shaped stalagmites and stalactites.

The **Emerald Sea** (also called the Inner Sea) on **Ko Mae Ko** is another popular destination. This large lake in the middle of the island spans an impressive 250m by 350m and has an ethereal turquoise tint. A second dramatic viewpoint can be found at the top of a series of staircases nearby.

Across from Mae Ko, kayakers can paddle under the naturally occurring stone bridge on **Ko Samsao**. Beach bums should head to **Ko Tai Plao**, **Ko Wuakantang** and **Ko Hintap**, all of which feature stunning powder-sand beaches. There's a shallow **coral reef** for snorkellers to explore just off the coast of Ko Tai Plao.

Tours

The best way to experience Ang Thong is through one of many guided tours departing from Ko Samui and Ko Pha-Ngan. The tours usually include lunch, hiking, snorkelling equipment, hotel transfers, and (fingers crossed) a knowledgeable guide. If you're staying in luxury accommodation, there's a good chance that your resort has a private boat for group tours. Some midrange and budget options also have their own boats, and if not, they can easily set you up with a tour operator. Dive centres on Ko Samui and Ko Pha-Ngan offer scuba trips to the park, although Ang Thong doesn't offer the world-class diving that can be found around Ko Tao.

The following companies represent a small fraction of the tour operators in the region:
Blue Stars Kayaking (Map p194; ☎ 0 7741 3231; www.bluestars.info; 2000B) Based in Chaweng Beach on Ko Samui, offers guided sea-kayak trips in the park.
Grand Sea Tours (☎ 0 7742 7001; adult/child 1800/900B) Departs from Thong Sala pier on Ko Pha-Ngan. Hotel transfers and park admission fee are not included. Tours run on Monday, Wednesday and Friday.
Island Discovery (☎ 0 7723 8363; www.island-discovery.com) Based on Ko Pha-Ngan, offers private boat charters; 15,000B for a 15-person boat.
Island Safari (☎ 0 7625 4501; www.islandsafaritour .com; adult/child 1900/1400B) Operates from Samui and departs from Na Thon pier.
Liquid Leisure (☎ 08 7889 4077) Located in Ban Tai on Ko Pha-Ngan.

Sleeping

Ang Thong does not have any resorts; however, the national park has set up five bungalows on Ko Wua Talap, which each house between two and eight guests. The marine park also allows campers to pitch a tent in certain designated zones. Advance reservations can be made with the **National Parks Services** (☎ 0 7728 6025, 0 7728 0222; www.dnp.go.th; bungalows 500-1400B). On-line bookings are possible, although customers must forward a bank deposit within two days of making the reservation. Check out their website for detailed information.

Getting There & Around

The best way to reach the park is to catch a private day-tour from Ko Samui or Ko Pha-Ngan (located 28km and 32km away, respectively). The islands sit between Samui and the mainland pier at Don Sak; however, there are no ferries that stop along the way. Smaller ferry 'tours' make the slow, two- to three-hour trip from Samui's northern coast and Na Thon town. They leave around 8am and the return trip departs Ang Thong at 2.30pm. There's officially an adult/child 400/200B admission fee for foreigners, although it should be included in the price of every tour. Private boat charters are also another possibility, although high petrol prices will make the trip quite expensive.

SURAT THANI
อ.เมืองสุราษฎร์ธานี
pop 126,900
Known in Thai as 'City of Good People', Surat Thani was once the seat of the ancient Srivijaya empire. Today, this busy junction has become a transport hub that indiscriminately moves cargo and people around the country. Travellers rarely linger here as they make their way to the deservedly popular islands of Ko Samui, Ko Pha-Ngan and Ko Tao.

Information
Scores of tourists pass through town every day sparking many unscrupulous travel agencies to develop innovative scams involving sub-standard buses, phantom bookings and surprise 'extra' fees. Not everyone's a crook, of course; just make sure to ask a lot of questions and trust your instincts. Traffic in Surat Thani flows both ways, so when you happen upon

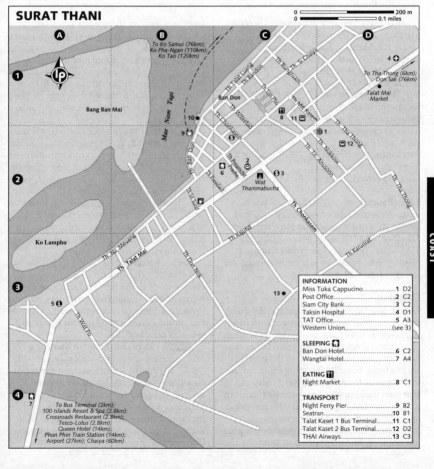

DETOUR: WAT SUAN MOKKHAPHALARAM

It's hard to believe that Chaiya, a sleepy town 60km north of Surat Thani, was once an important seat of the Srivijaya empire. These days, most foreigners who visit are on their way to the outstanding meditation retreats held at the progressive Suan Mokkhaphalaram monastery.

Surrounded by lush forest, **Wat Suan Mokkhaphalaram** (Wat Suanmokkh; www.suanmokkh.org), which means 'the Garden of Liberation', charges 1500B for a 10-day program that includes food, lodging, and instruction (although technically the 'teaching' is free). English-speaking retreats begin on the first day of every month and registration takes place the night before. Founded by Ajahn Buddhadasa Bhikkhu, arguably Thailand's most famous monk, the temple's philosophical teachings are ecumenical in nature, comprising Zen, Taoist and Christian elements, as well as the traditional Theravada schemata.

To reach the temple, located 7km outside of Chaiya, you can catch a 3rd-class local train from Phun Phin (10B to 20B, one hour), or catch a sŏrng·tăa·ou (40B to 50B, 45 minutes) from Surat's Talat Kaset 2 bus terminal. If you're heading to Surat Thani by train from Bangkok, you can get off before Surat Thani at the small Chaiya train station. Take a motorcycle taxi from the station for an additional 40B.

---

tourists travelling in the opposite direction, ask them about their experiences.

Th Na Meuang has a bank on virtually every corner in the heart of downtown. If you're staying near the 'suburbs', the Tesco-Lotus has ATMs as well.

Miss Tuka Cappucino (☎ 0 7721 2723; 442/307 Th Talat Mai; per hr 40B; 🕙 9am-midnight; 🖳) Not the cheapest internet in town, but with real coffee, sandwiches, air-con and smiles on tap it's one of the better places to get digital.

Post Office (☎ 0 7727 2013, 0 7728 1966; Th Talat Mai) Across from Wat Thammabucha.

Siam City Bank (Th Chonkasem) Has a Western Union office.

Taksin Hospital (☎ 0 7727 3239; Th Talat Mai) The most professional of Surat's three hospitals. Just beyond the Talat Mai Market in the northeast part of downtown.

TAT office (☎ 0 7728 8817-9; tatsurat@samart.co.th; 5 Th Talat Mai; 🕙 Sun-Fri) Friendly office southwest of town. Distributes plenty of useful brochures and maps, and staff speak English very well.

Sleeping

For a comfy night in Surat, escape the grimy city centre and hop on a sŏrng·tăa·ou heading towards the Phangna district. When you climb aboard, tell the driver 'Tesco Lotus', and you'll be taken over 2km out of the town centre to a large, box-like shopping centre. When looking away from the mall, head right, and as you start walking you'll spot the billboards of at least four hotel options that have low prices and refreshingly modern amenities.

Sleeping options in the downtown area are cheaper, but many tend to offer 'by the

hour' service, so things can get a bit noisy as clients come and go. If you're on a very tight schedule or budget, consider zipping straight through town and take the night ferry (see opposite). When the weather is nice, you may even sleep better on the boat than in a noisy hotel. But if there's a chance of rain, beware – you're likely to be wet and weary in the morning.

Queen Hotel (☎ 0 7731 1003; 916/10-13 Th Sri Sawat, Phun Phin; r 200-400B; 🖳) If you are stuck in the cruddy transport junction of Phun Phin, or want to catch a very early train, don't despair; there is one tolerable option. The Queen Hotel is just a block away from the train station. It's no luxury vacation, but at least you won't have to sleep on the streets. Have a look at a couple rooms before putting down your bags – some choices are larger and less dingy than others.

Ban Don Hotel (☎ 0 7727 2167; 268/2 Th Na Meuang; r 200-400B; 🖳) This quieter spot with squeaky-clean rooms is the best budget value in the heart of Surat Thani. Those with air-con are a great deal. The entrance is through a Chinese restaurant – quite a good one for inexpensive rice and noodle dishes.

ourpick 100 Islands Resort & Spa (☎ 0 7720 1150; www.roikoh.com; 19/6 Moo 3, Bypass Rd; r 590-1200B; 🖳 🖳 🖳) Across the street from the suburban Tesco-Lotus, 100 Islands is as good as it gets in Thailand for under 600B. This teak palace looks out of place along the suburban highway, but inside, the immaculate rooms surround an overgrown garden and lagoon-like swimming pool.

Wangtai Hotel (☎ 0 7728 3020; www.wangtaisurat .com; 1 Th Talat Mai; r 790-2000B; ❄ ▯ ⬙) Across the river from the TAT office, Wangtai tries its best to provide a corporate hotel atmosphere. Polite receptionists and tux-clad bellboys bounce around the vast lobby, and upstairs, rooms have unmemorable furnishings, but there are good views of the city from the upper floors.

Eating & Drinking

Surat Thani isn't exactly bursting with dining options. Head to the **night market** (commonly called Sarn Chao Ma; Th Ton Pho) for fried, steamed, grilled or sautéed delicacies – don't forget to try the crunchy insects, we hear they're a great source of protein. During the day many food stalls near the downtown bus terminal sell *kôw gài òp* (marinated baked chicken on rice), which is very tasty.

Crossroads Restaurant (☎ 0 7722 1525; Bypass Rd; dishes 50-200B; ⏱ 11am-1am) Located 2km southwest of Surat across from the Tesco-Lotus mall, Crossroads has a quaint bluesy vibe enhanced by dim lighting and live music. Try the oysters – Surat Thani is famous for their giant molluscs, and the prices are unbeatable.

GM Pub (30/16 Th Karunrat; dishes 40-140B; ⏱ lunch & dinner) GM has a good mix of locals and faràng English teachers who return time and time again for the mellow atmosphere, tasty international menu, and wide selection of beer and cocktails.

Getting There & Away

In general, if you are departing Bangkok or Hua Hin for Ko Samui, Ko Pha-Ngan or Ko Tao, consider taking the train or a bus/boat package that goes through Chumphon rather than Surat. You'll save time, and the journey will be more comfortable.

AIR

There are two daily shuttles to Bangkok on **Thai Airways International** (THAI; ☎ 0 7727 2610; 3/27-28 Th Karunarat) for around 3000B (70 minutes).

BOAT

In the high season there are usually bus/boat services to Ko Samui and Ko Pha-Ngan directly from the Phun Phin train station. These services don't cost any more than those booked in Surat Thani and can save you a lot of waiting around. There are also several ferry and speedboat operators that connect Surat Thani to Ko Tao, Ko Pha-Ngan and Ko Samui. All boat services to Samui depart from Don Sak (except the night ferry) and ticket prices include the price of the bus transfer. See the transport section of your desired destination for more details.

From Surat there are nightly ferries to Ko Tao (500B, eight hours), Ko Pha-Ngan (200B, seven hours) and Ko Samui (150B, six hours). All leave from the town's central night ferry pier at 11pm. These are cargo ships, not luxury boats, so bring food and water and watch your bags. If Thai passengers are occupying your assigned berth, it's best to grab a different one nearby rather than asking them to move.

BUS & MINIVAN

Most long-distance public buses run from the Talat Kaset bus terminals 1 and 2. Air-conditioned minivans leave from Talat Kaset 2 and tend to have more frequent departures than buses, although they're usually more expensive.

Air-conditioned buses and minibuses to Khao Sok National Park (two hours) can be booked through travel agencies and should cost no more than 100B. You can also catch certain Phuket-bound buses from the two bus terminals in town and ask to be let off at Khao Sok – a better option as some pushy minivan drivers double as touts for Khao Sok hotels.

TRAIN

When arriving by train you'll actually pull into Phun Phin, a cruddy town 12km west of Surat. From Phun Phin, there are buses to Phuket, Phang-Nga and Krabi – some via Takua Pa, a junction city further west. Transport from Surat moves with greater frequency, but it's worth checking the schedule in Phun Phin first – you might luck out and save yourself a slow ride between towns. Local orange buses chug between Phun Phin and Surat (a 25-minute ride) every 10 minutes (15B). Buses in Phun Phin line up along a white wall with a Pepsi symbol just south of the station.

Fares from Bangkok with fan/air-con: 297/397B in 3rd class, 438/578B for a 2nd-class seat, 498/758B in an upper 2nd-class sleeper, 548/848B in a lower 2nd-class sleeper, and 1279B in 1st class. If you take an early evening train from Bangkok you'll arrive here in the morning.

The train station has a 24-hour left-luggage room that charges 20B a day. The advance ticket office is open from 6am to 6pm daily (with a nebulous one-hour lunch break somewhere between 11am and 1.30pm).

Getting Around

Air-conditioned vans run to/from the Surat Thani airport cost around 70B per person and they'll drop you off at your hotel. Buy tickets at travel agencies or the **Thai Airways office** (☎ 0 7727 2610; 3/27-28 Th Karunarat).

To travel around town, sŏrng·tǎa·ou cost 10B to 30B, while sǎhm·lór (also spelt as sǎamláw; three-wheeled vehicles) charge from 30B to 40B.

Orange buses run from Phun Phin train station to Surat Thani every 10 minutes (15B, 25 minutes). For this ride, taxis charge 150B. Other taxi rates are posted just north of the train station (at the metal pedestrian bridge).

KHAO SOK NATIONAL PARK
อุทยานแห่งชาติเขาสก

If your leg muscles have atrophied after one too many days of beach-bumming, consider venturing inland to the wondrous Khao Sok National Park. Many believe this lowland jungle to be over 160 million years old, making it the oldest rainforest on the globe. This remarkable 646-sq-km reserve features dramatic limestone formations that pierce the sky, and waterfalls that cascade through juicy thickets drenched with rains and morning dew. A network of dirt trails snakes through the quiet park, allowing visitors to spy on the exciting array of indigenous creatures.

Information

The **park headquarters** (☎ 0 7739 5025; www.khaosok .com; admission 400B) and visitors centre are 1.8km off Rte 401, close to the Km 109 marker.

The best time of year to visit is between December and May – the dry season. During the June to November wet season, trails can be extremely slippery and waterlogged, and flash flooding is a common and sometimes fatal occurrence. On the other hand, animals leave their hidden reservoirs throughout the wet months, so you're more likely to stumble across some big fauna.

Sights & Activities

Khao Sok's vast terrain makes it one of the last viable habitats for **large mammals**. During the wetter months you may happen upon bear, boar, gaur, tapirs, gibbons, deer, wild elephants, and perhaps even a tiger. There are also over 180 species of bird, as well as the world's largest flower, the rare *Rafflesia kerrii*. Found only in Khao Sok, these **giant flowers** can reach 80cm in diameter. They have no roots or leaves of their own; instead they live as parasites inside the roots of the liana, a jungle vine.

The stunning **Chiaw Lan Lake** sits about an hour's drive east of the visitor's centre. The lake was created in 1982 by an enormous shale-clay dam called Ratchaprapha (Kheuan Ratchaprapha or Kheuan Chiaw Lan). The limestone outcrops protruding from the lake reach a height of 960m, over three times higher than the formations in the Phang-Nga area.

A cave known as **Tham Nam Thalu** contains striking limestone formations and subterranean streams, while **Tham Si Ru** features four converging passageways used as a hideout by communist insurgents between 1975 and 1982. The caves can be reached on foot from the southwestern shore of the lake. You can rent boats from local fishermen to explore the coves, canals, caves and cul-de-sacs along the lakeshore.

Elephant trekking, kayaking and rafting are popular park activities. The hiking is also excellent, and you can arrange park tours from any guesthouse – just be sure you get a certified guide (they wear an official badge). Various hiking trails from the visitors centre lead to the waterfalls of **Sip-Et Chan** (4km), **Than Sawan** (9km) and **Than Kloy** (9km), among other destinations.

Sleeping

The road leading into the park is lined with charming fan bungalows offering comfortable digs in natural surroundings. Try to arrive in the daytime, so you can walk along the short road leading up to the park and pick where you want to stay.

The following options are recommended:
Jungle Huts (☎ 0 7739 5160, 08 7264 6032; huts 150-350B) An excellent choice for backpackers. Free monkey and waterfalls tours are on offer.
Art's Riverview Jungle Lodge (☎ 0 7739 5009; bungalows 350-550B) Pricier huts have verandas and hammocks, in a very tranquil setting.
Khao Sok Rainforest Resort (☎ 0 7739 5006; www .krabidir.com/khaosokrainforest; bungalows 400-600B) Has huts perched high on stilts along the snaking river.

In-house conservation programs target low-impact hiking and forest restoration.

Tree Tops River Huts (☎ 0 7739 5000; www.treetops riverhuts.com; bungalows 420-1800B) A charming retreat with some bungalows built right into the trees.

Morning Mist Resort (☎ 0 7885 6185; bungalows 600B) Plenty of twigs and thatch with views of the jagged rock formations. Bookings should be made through the National Park Services.

Cliff & River Jungle Resort (☎ 08 7271 8787; www.thecliffandriver.com; bungalow 1800B) A beautiful property set just below the jagged silver cliffs. The plunge pool and steam spa are extra perks.

Getting There & Around
Minivans to Kho Sok from Surat Thani (80B, one hour, 100km) leave at least twice daily. Tickets can be arranged through most travel agents in Surat, but be aware that some minivan companies work with specific bungalow outfitters and will try to convince you to stay at that place. Otherwise, from the Surat Thani area you can catch a bus going towards Takua Pa – you'll be getting off well before hitting this destination. From the Andaman coast, there are buses from Takua Pa to the park (25B, one hour, nine daily) that drop you off along the highway, 1.8km from the visitors centre. If guesthouse touts don't meet you, you'll have to walk to your chosen guesthouse (from 50m to 2km).

To visit Chiaw Lan Lake, it is best to book a tour (which can be easily arranged at your guesthouse for 1000B to 3000B).

AO KHANOM
อ่าวขนอม
Halfway between Surat Thani and Nakhon Si Thammarat, little Khanom quietly sits along the blue gulf waters. Overlooked by tourists who flock to the jungle-islands nearby, this pristine region, simply called Khanom, is a worthy choice for those seeking a serene beach setting unmarred by enterprising corporations.

The police station and hospital are located just south of Ban Khanom at the junction leading to Kho Khao Beach. There's a 7-Eleven (with an ATM) in the heart of Ban Khanom.

Sights
The most unique feature in Khanom are the **pink dolphins** – a rare breed of albino dolphins that have a stunning pink hue. They are regularly seen from the old ferry pier and the electric plant pier around dawn and dust.

The area is also home to a variety of pristine geological features including **waterfalls and caves**. The largest falls, known as **Samet Chun**, has tepid pools for cooling off, and great views of coast. To reach the falls, head south from Ban Khanom and turn left at the blue Samet Chun sign. Follow the road for about 2km and after crossing a small stream, take the next right and hike up into the mountain following the dirt road. After a 15-minute walk, listen for the waterfall and look for a small trail on the right. The scenic **Hin Lat Falls** is the smallest cascade, but it's also the easiest to reach. There are pools for swimming and several huts providing shade. The falls are located south of Nai Phlao.

There are also two beautiful caves along the main road (Hwy 4014) between Khanom and Don Sak. **Khao Wang Thong** has a string of lights guiding visitors through the network of caverns and narrow passages. A metal gate covers the entrance; stop at the house at the base of the hill to retrieve the key (and leave a small donation). Turn right off the main highway at Rd 4142 to find **Khao Krot Cave**, which has two large caverns, but you'll have to bring a flashlight.

For a postcard-worthy vista of the undulating coastline, head to **Dat Fa Mountain**, located about 5km west of the coast along Hwy 4014. The hillside is usually deserted, making it easy to stop along the way to snap some photos.

Sleeping & Eating
In the last few years, construction in the area has started to take off. The area is far from booming, but large-scale development is definitely on the cards. A recent surge in gulf-oil rigging has meant that developers are eyeing Khanom as a potential holiday destination for nearby workers.

One More Beer (☎ 08 1396 4447; www.1morebeer .net; bungalows 800-1000B; ✪ 🖳) One More Beer is a chill spot to grab some delicious international cuisine. The tidy bungalows and friendly faràng staff make it a worthy option even though it's not directly on the beach.

Talkoo Beach Resort (☎ 0 7552 8397, 08 3692 2711; bungalows 800-1500B; ✪ ✪ ✪) This charming operation has dozens of snazzy white cottages featuring quirky fixtures such as sinks made from hollowed out tree trunks.

Khanom Hill Resort (☎ 0 7552 9403; bungalows 800-1800B; ❄ ⛱) The seven small, red-roofed bungalows overlook the sea from various angles along this hilly property. Adorable wicker furnishings abound, and when we visited, the construction of a swimming pool was underway.

Racha Kiri (☎ 0 7552 7847; www.rachakiri.com; bungalows 3500-12,500B; ❄ ⛱) Khanom's upscale retreat is a beautiful campus of rambling villas. The big price tag means no crowds, which can be nice, although the resort feels like a white elephant in low season.

For some cheap eats, head to **Kho Khao Beach** at the end of Rd 4232. You'll find a steamy jumble of BBQ stands offering some tasty favourites such as *mŏo nám đòk* (spicy pork salad) and *sôm·đam* (spicy papaya salad). On Wednesday and Sunday, there are markets further inland near the police station.

Getting There & Away

From Surat Thani, you can catch any Nakhon-bound bus and ask to be let off at the junction for Khanom. Catch a motorcycle taxi (70B) the rest of the way. You can get a share taxi from Nakhon Si Thammarat's share-taxi terminal to Khanom town for 85B. From Khanom town you can hire motorcycle taxis out to the beaches for about 60B. There are three separate bus stops in the vicinity. Ask your driver to stop near the fruit market or the hospital, as these are closer to the beach. Motorbikes can be rented at One More Beer for 300B per day.

NAKHON SI THAMMARAT
อ.เมืองนครศรีธรรมราช
pop 123,100

The bustling city of Nakhon Si Thammarat (usually shortened to 'Nakhon') won't win any beauty pageants. However, travellers who stop in this historic town will enjoy a decidedly cultural experience amid some of the most important *wát* in the kingdom. Hundreds of years ago, an overland route between the western port of Trang and eastern port of Nakhon Si Thammarat functioned as a major trade link between Thailand and the rest of the world. This ancient influx of cosmopolitan influences is still palpable today, and can be found in the recipes of local cuisine, or housed in the city's temples and museums.

There's an **OTOP** (Th Tha Chang) crafts centre a block away from TAT on the west side of Sanam Na Meuang Park (City Park).

Orientation & Information

Most of Nahkon's commercial activity (hotels, banks and restaurants) takes place in the northern part of the downtown. South of the old city wall ruins, visitors will find the city's historic quarter with the often-visited Wat Mahatat. Th Ratchadamnoen is the main thoroughfare and is loaded with cheap *sŏrng·tăa·ou* heading in both directions.

Several banks and ATMs hug Th Ratchadamnoen in the northern end of downtown. There is an English-language bookstore on the 3rd floor of the Robinson Ocean shopping mall.

Bovorn Bazaar (Th Ratchadamnoen) A mall housing a few internet cafés.

Police station (☎ 1155; Th Ratchadamnoen) Opposite the post office.

Post office (Th Ratchadamnoen; ⊗ 8.30am-4.30pm)

TAT office (☎ 0 7534 6515) Housed in a 1926-vintage building in the northern end of Sanam Na Meuang. Has some useful brochures in English.

Sights

The most important *wát* in southern Thailand, **Wat Phra Mahathat Woramahawihaan** (simply known as 'Mahathat') is a stunning campus boasting 77 *chedi* and an imposing 77m *chedi* crowned by a gold spire. According to legend, Queen Hem Chala and Prince Thanakuman brought relics to Nakhon over a thousand years ago, and built a small pagoda to house the precious icons. The temple has since grown into a rambling site, and today, crowds gather daily to purchase the popular Jatukham amulets (see p248). Mahathat's resident monks live across the street at **Wat Na Phra Boromathat**.

When the Tampaling (or Tambralinga) kingdom traded with merchants from Indian, Arabic, Dvaravati and Champa states, the region around Nakhon became a melting pot of crafts and art. Today, many of these relics are on display behind the run-down façade of the **national museum** (Th Ratchadamnoen; admission 30B; ⊗ 9am-4pm Wed-Sun), 1km south of the *wáts*.

Nakhon's noteworthy **shadow puppets** are also worthy of exploration. Traditionally, there are two styles of puppet: *năng đà·lung* and *năng yài*. At just under 1m tall, the former are similar in size to the Malay-Indonesian-style puppets and feature moveable appendages and parts (including genitalia); the latter are unique to Thailand, nearly life-sized, and lack moving parts. Both are intricately carved from buffalo-hide.

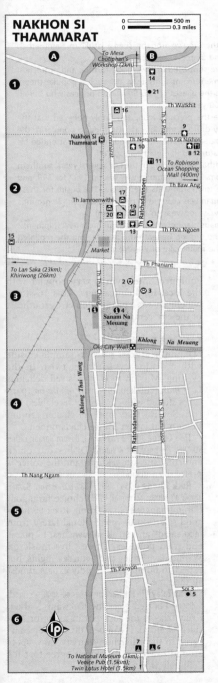

NAKHON SI THAMMARAT

0   500 m
0   0.3 miles

Nowadays puppet performances are rare and usually limited to festivals; however, there are two places in town where you can see the puppets being made and you can also make purchases.

The acknowledged Thai master of shadow puppet craft is **Suchart Subsin** (Suchaat Sapsin; ☎ 0 7534 6394; 110/18 Soi 3, Th Si Thammasok; ☺ shows usually around 8.30am & 5pm), and he runs a workshop near Wat Mahathat. Suchart has received several awards for his mastery and preservation of the craft and has performed for the king. His puppets are only purchasable at his studio – he refuses to sell them through distributors.

Another craftsperson, **Mesa Chotiphan** (☎ 0 7534 3979; 558/4 Soi Rong Jeh, Th Ratchadamnoen; ☺ 9am-4pm), has a workshop in the northern part of the city; visitors are welcome. Call if you would like to be picked up from anywhere in Nakhon Si Thammarat. To get there, go north from the city centre on Th Ratchadamnoen, and about 500m north of the sports field, take the soi opposite the Chinese cemetery (before reaching the golf course and military base).

SOUTHWESTERN GULF COAST

JATUKHAM RAMMATHEP

If you've spent more than 24 hours in Thailand then you've probably seen a Jatukham Rammathep dangling around someone's neck – these round amulets are everywhere.

The bearers of the Jatukham Rammathep are supposed to have good fortune and protection from any harm. The origin of the amulet's name remains a mystery, although a popular theory suggests that Jatukham and Rammathep were the aliases of two Srivajayan princes who buried relics under Nakhon's Wat Mahathat some 1000 years ago.

A notorious Thai police detective first wore the precious icon, and firmly believed that the guardian spirits helped him solve a particularly difficult murder case. He tried to popularise the amulet, but it wasn't a market success until his death in 2006. Thousands of people attended his funeral, including the crown prince, and the Jatukham Rammathep took off.

The talismans are commissioned at the Mahathat temple, and in the last several years, southern Thailand has seen an incredible economic boom. The first amulet was sold in 1987 for 39B, and today, over 100 million baht are spent on the town's amulets every *week*. The desire for these round icons has become so frenzied that a woman was crushed to death on the temple grounds during a widely publicised discount sale (she was not wearing her talisman).

Everyday, trucks drive along Nakhon's main roads blaring loud music to promote new shipments. These thumping beats have started to shake the ground beneath the temple, and the repeated hammering has, in an ironic metaphor, bent the main spire of Wat Mahathat.

Sleeping

Lodging options are limited to a few respectable places.

Thai Hotel (☎ 0 7534 1509; fax 0 7534 4858; 1375 Th Ratchadamnoen; r with fan 220-270B, r with air-con 340-450B, ste 750B; 🖭) The Thai Hotel is the most central sleeping spot in town – look for a small sign (which actually says 'Thai Hotet' in Thai) pointing down a busy sidestreet. The walls are thin, but the air-con options are a good deal for the price. Each room has a TV and the higher floors have good views of the urban bustle.

Nakorn Garden Inn (☎ 0 7532 3777; 1/4 Th Pak Nakhon; r 445B; 🖭) The motel-style Nakorn Garden Inn offers a pleasant alternative to the usual cement cube. Rooms are encased in exposed crimson brick and set around a sandy garden. Each unit is identical, sporting a TV and fridge; try to score a room that gets plenty of sunlight.

Grand Park Hotel (☎ 0 7531 7666-73; fax 0 7531 7674; 1204/79 Th Pak Nakhon; r 700-1700B; 🖭) The Grand Park offers fine, modern rooms with TV and fridge – nothing too fancy or luxurious. The rooms are on seven floors, some with sweeping vistas of the city. Guests can loiter in the spacious lobby and restaurant.

Twin Lotus Hotel (☎ 0 7532 3777; www.twinlotus hotel.net; 97/8 Th Phattanakan Khukhwang; r 1100-3000B; 🖭 🖭) Its age is starting to show, but Twin Lotus is still a nice spot for a little pampering while visiting Nakhon. The well-

equipped hotel gym is very popular with the local English teachers. This 16-storey behemoth sits several kilometres southeast of the city centre.

Eating & Drinking

Nakhon is a great place to sample cuisine with a distinctive southern twist. In the evening, Muslim food stands sell delicious *kôw mòk* (chicken biryani), *má·dà·bà* (pancakes stuffed with chicken or vegetables) and roti. Several tasty options cluster around Bovorn Bazaar on Th Ratchadamnoen.

Hao Coffee (☎ 0 7534 6563; Bovorn Bazaar; dishes 30-60B; 🕑 breakfast & lunch) Dishes out quick and convenient breakfasts, and the coffee is pretty darn good.

Rock 99 (☎ 0 7531 7999; 1180/807, Bavorn Bazaar; dishes 40-100B; 🕑 dinner) The choice faràng-hangout (faràng-hangout) in Nakhon, Rock 99 has a good selection of international fare – from taco salads and steak sandwiches, to pizzas and fried potatoes. There's live music on Wednesday, Friday and Saturday nights, but expect to bump into friendly expats almost all the time.

Krua Talay (Th Pak Nakhon; dishes 40-300B; 🕑 lunch & dinner) Located Near the Kukwang Market, Krua Talay is the top spot in town for succulent seafood. It can be a little pricey compared to the other non-touristy chow spots around town, but the locals agree that it's definitely worth it.

Khrua Nakhon (☎ 0 7531 7197; Bovorn Bazaar; dishes 60-200B ☺ breakfast & lunch) This joint, next to Hao Coffee, has a great selection of traditional Nakhon cuisine. Order one of the sharing platters, which comes with five types of curry (including an unpalatable spicy fish sauce), or try the *kôw yam* (southern-style rice salad). There's a second location in Robinson Ocean mall.

Country Home (☎ 08 1968 0762; 119/7 Th Ratchadamnoen) This large, open-air bar invokes the Wild West with saloon-style seating and an odd smattering of straw hats. There's live music every night and the joint gets packed with beer-toting locals.

For an all-night dance fest, head south towards the Twin Lotus Hotel and you'll find the popular Venice Pub. For a tamer evening of beers and pub grub, check out Bar 60 (known locally as 'Bar Hok Sip'), near the corner of Th Ratchadamnoen and Th Phra Ngoen.

Getting There & Away

Due to the burgeoning popularity of the Jatukham amulet (opposite), transport to Nakhon is booming.

Several small carriers (plus Thai Airways) fly from Bangkok to Nakhon every day. There are about six one-hour flights daily costing around 3500B.

There are two daily train departures from Bangkok to Nakhon (via Hua Hin, Chumphon and Phun Phin). They are both 12-hour night trains leaving at 5.35pm and 7.15pm. Second-class fares cost between 590B and 890B. These trains continue on to Hat Yai and Sungai Kolok.

Buses from Bangkok depart either between 6am and 8am, or between 5.30pm and 10pm. There are about seven daily departures (1st class/2nd class around 700/600B, 12 to 13 hours). Ordinary buses to Bangkok leave from the bus terminal, but a couple of private buses leave from booking offices on Th Jamroenwithi, where you can also buy tickets.

When looking for minivan stops to leave Nakhon, keep an eye out for small desks along the side of the downtown roads (minivans and waiting passengers may or may not be present nearby). It's best to ask around as each destination has a different departure point. Krabi and Don Sak minivans are grouped together – just make sure you don't get on the wrong one. Stops are scattered around Th Jamroenwithi, Th Wakhit and Th Yommarat. There are frequent minivans (that leave when they're full) to Krabi (180B to 240B, 2½ hours) and Phuket (175B to 275B, five hours), Surat Thani (100B, one hour), Khanom (85B, one hour) and Hat Yai (around 120B, three hours).

Getting Around

Sŏrng·tǎa·ou run north-south along Th Ratchadamnoen and Th Si Thammasok for 10B (a bit more at night). Motorcycle-taxi rides start at 20B and cost up to 50B for longer distances.

SONGKHLA & AROUND
สงขลา
pop 85,600
Unlike many of the urban centres in Thailand's deep south, Songkhla has enough going for itself to entertain visitors for a couple of days.

DETOUR: KHAO LUANG NATIONAL PARK

Known for its beautiful mountain and forest walks, cool streams, waterfalls and orchards, **Khao Luang National Park** (☎ 0 7530 9644-7; adult/child 400/200B) surrounds the 1835m peak of Khao Luang. This soaring mountain range reaches up to 1800m, and is covered in virgin forest. An ideal source for streams and rivers, the mountains show off impressive waterfalls and provide a habitat for a plethora of bird species – this place is a good spot for any budding ornithologist. Fans of flora will also get their kicks here; there are over 300 species of orchid in the park, some of which are found nowhere else on earth.

Park bungalows can be rented for 600B to 1000B per night and sleep six to 12 people. Camping is permitted along the trail to the summit.

To reach the park, take a sŏrng·tǎa·ou (25B) from Nakhon Si Thammarat to the village of Khiriwong, at the base of Khao Luang. The entrance to the park and the offices of the Royal Forest Department are 33km from the centre of Nakhon on Rte 4015, an asphalt road that climbs almost 400m in 2.5km to the office and a further 450m to the car park.

The city is surrounded by pleasant beaches, has several green parks and has a pretty historical centre. Due to the generous sea breezes, Songkhla manages to feel gracefully cool just about year-round, and also boasts some great food, including copious seafood and two vibrant night markets.

Orientation

Towards the north is a scenic promontory, Laem Songkhla; the eastern side of the jutting piece of land is Hat Son Awn, along which there is a lovely path for strolling. Further southeast is Hat Samila, which is comely and peaceful, too. If you enter town coming from the north or leave town heading north, you'll go through Ko Yo (see below) and cross the Tinsulanonda Bridges – the longest concrete bridges in Thailand.

Information

Banks can be found all over town.

Click Me! (cnr Th Phetchakhiri & Th Saiburi; per hr 15B; 8am-10pm) Internet service.

Corner Bookshop (0 7431 2577; cnr Th Saiburi & Th Phetchakhiri; 7am-7.30pm) Stocks a small selection of English-language novels, maps, newspapers, magazines and Lonely Planet guides.

Immigration office (0 7431 3480; Th Laneg Phra Ram; 8.30am-4.30pm Mon-Fri) File for visa extensions here.

Indonesian Consulate (0 7431 1544; Th Sadao)

Malaysian Consulate (0 7431 1062; 4 Th Sukhum)

Police station (0 7431 2133) North of the town centre.

Post office (Th Wichianchom) Opposite the market; international calls can be made upstairs.

Tourist Office (cnr Th Jana & Th Saiburi) Located in the same compound as Prem Tinsulanonda Museum, it has helpful staff and a variety of brochures and maps.

Sights & Activities

KO YO
เกาะยอ

A popular day trip from Songkhla, this island in the middle of Thale Sap is actually connected to the mainland by bridges and is famous for its cotton weaving industry. There's a roadside market selling cloth and ready-made clothes at excellent prices.

If you visit Ko Yo, the **Thaksin Folklore Museum** (0 74591 618; admission 60B; 8.30am-4.30pm) actively aims to promote and preserve the culture of the region, and is a must-see. The pavilions here are reproductions of southern Thai-style

houses and contain folk art, handicrafts and traditional household implements.

Frequent sŏrng·tǎa·ou to Ko Yo depart from Th Ramwithi in Songkhla (15B, 20 minutes). To stop at the small market ask for *nâh đà·làht* (in front of the market). To get off at the museum ask for *pí·pí·tá·pan*.

NATIONAL MUSEUM
พิพิธภัณฑสถานแห่งชาติ

The 1878 building that now houses the **national museum** (0 7431 1728; Th Wichianchom; admission 30B; 9am-4pm Wed-Sun, closed public holidays) was originally built in a Chinese architectural style as the residence of a luminary. This museum is easily the most picturesque national museum in Thailand and contains exhibits from all Thai art-style periods, particularly the Srivijaya. Also on display are Thai and Chinese ceramics and sumptuous Chinese furniture owned by the local Chinese aristocracy.

BEACHES

The residents are taking better care of the windy strip of white sand along **Hat Samila**, and it is now quite a pleasant beach for strolling along or for an early morning read. A **bronze mermaid**, depicted squeezing water from her long hair in tribute to Mae Thorani (the Hindu-Buddhist earth goddess), sits atop some rocks at the northern end of the beach. Nearby are the **cat and rat sculptures**, named for the Cat and Rat Islands (Ko Yo and Ko Losin).

A few kilometres south of Hat Samila is **Kao Seng**, a quaint beachfront Muslim fishing village – this is where the tourist photos of gaily painted fishing vessels are taken. Sŏrng·tǎa·ou run regularly between Songkhla (from near the stand to Ko Yo) and Kao Seng for 10B.

PREM TINSULANONDA MUSEUM
พิพิธภัณฑ์พธำนะรงค์

The minute **Prem Tinsulanonda Museum** (0 7431 2679; cnr Th Jana & Th Saiburi; admission free; 8.30am-4pm Tue-Sun) is touted as the birthplace of Thailand's 16th prime minister, who served from 1980 to 1988. It's actually a wooden house, built in the '90s, upon the site of Prem's birthplace and is a charming example of a traditional Thai house.

WAT MATCHIMAWAT (WAT KLANG)

This large temple compound typifies the Sino-Thai temple architecture in Songkhla

SONGKHLA

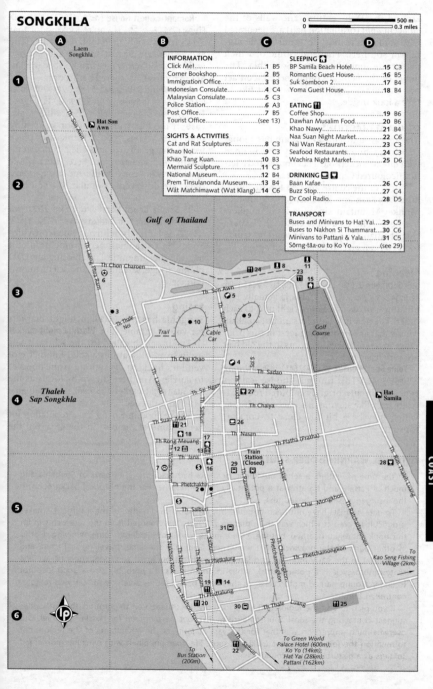

| 0 | 500 m |
| 0 | 0.3 miles |

INFORMATION
Click Me!.................................**1** B5
Corner Bookshop...................**2** B5
Immigration Office.................**3** B3
Indonesian Consulate.............**4** C4
Malaysian Consulate...............**5** C3
Police Station.........................**6** A3
Post Office..............................**7** B5
Tourist Office...................(see 13)

SIGHTS & ACTIVITIES
Cat and Rat Sculptures...........**8** C3
Khao Noi................................**9** C3
Khao Tang Kuan...................**10** B3
Mermaid Sculpture...............**11** C3
National Museum..................**12** B4
Prem Tinsulanonda Museum...**13** B4
Wát Matchimawat (Wat Klang)...**14** C6

SLEEPING
BP Samila Beach Hotel...........**15** C3
Romantic Guest House...........**16** B5
Suk Somboon 2.....................**17** B4
Yoma Guest House.................**18** B4

EATING
Coffee Shop...........................**19** B6
Dawhan Musalim Food...........**20** B6
Khao Nawy............................**21** B4
Naa Suan Night Market..........**22** C6
Nai Wan Restaurant...............**23** C3
Seafood Restaurants..............**24** C3
Wachira Night Market............**25** D6

DRINKING
Baan Kafae............................**26** C4
Buzz Stop..............................**27** C4
Dr Cool Radio........................**28** D5

TRANSPORT
Buses and Minivans to Hat Yai....**29** C5
Buses to Nakhon Si Thammarat...**30** C6
Minivans to Pattani & Yala......**31** C5
Sŏrng·tăa·ou to Ko Yo...............(see 29)

Laem
Songkhla

Hat Son
Awn

Gulf of Thailand

Th Son Awn

Th Chon Charoen

Th Laeng Phra Ram

Thaleh
Sap Songkhla

Golf
Course

Trail

Cable
Car

Th Chai Khao

Th Saen S

Th Sadao

Th Sai Ngam

Th Limai

Th Suan Mak

Th Rong Meuang

Th Jana

Th Chaiya

Th Saibun

Th Nasan

Th Platha (Pratha)

Train
Station
(Closed)

Th Phetchakhir

Th Chai Mongkhon

Th Siket

Th Ratchadamnoen

Th Phetkalung

Th Phattalung

Th Nakhon Nok

Th Nong Ngam

Th Nakhon Nai

Th Nakhon Nawk

Th Saibun

Th Chaimongkon
Phetchamongkhon

Th Phetchamongkon

Th Thale Luang

Th Thale Luang

Hat
Samila

To
Kao Seng Fishing
Village (2km)

To Green World
Palace Hotel (600m);
Ko Yo (14km);
Hat Yai (28km);
Pattani (162km)

To
Bus Station
(200m)

around the 18th-century. The walls of the adjacent *bòht* (ordination hall) are decorated with some of the most beautiful temple murals in southern Thailand, some of which depict life in 19th-century Songkhla. The doors of the *bòht* are often locked; contact one of the resident monks if you'd like to take a look inside.

OTHER ATTRACTIONS

The area around Th Nang Ngam has a long-standing Chinese community and is lined with quaint, rickety old Thai houses and a few multicoloured Chinese temples.

North of the centre are two forested hills, **Khao Tang Kuan** and **Khao Noi** (also known as Monkey Mountain, since hordes of monkeys live here). There's a cable car on the eastern side of Khao Tang Kuan and vendors selling food you can give to the little hairy guys.

Sleeping

Suk Somboon 2 (☎ 0 7431 3809-10; fax 0 7432 1406; 14 Th Saiburi; r 200-550B; ✿) This is actually two buildings, an old and a new, right next to each other. The new half has pleasant but smallish rooms that are among the nicest in this price range in town, while the rooms in the old half are very basic indeed.

Yoma Guest House (☎ 0 7432 6433; Th Rong Meuang; r 250-350B; ✿) This tiny guesthouse features ridiculously cute, brightly coloured rooms. It really feels like staying in somebody's home, which may be a bit too close to comfort for some.

Romantic Guest House (☎ 0 7430 7170; 10/1-3 Th Platha; r 250-380B; ✿) If you're looking for that 'fresh room smell' then look no further. The abodes here are massive and airy and all come with a TV and rather nice bamboo bed frames. Some rooms have shared bathrooms.

Green World Palace Hotel (☎ 0 7443 7900-8; fax 0 7443 7899; 99 Th Samakisuk 2; r 750-900B; ✿ ▢ ▣) Judging by the chandeliers, spiralling staircase in the lobby and 5th-floor swimming pool with views, you'd think this place would charge an arm and a leg. It doesn't – and the immaculate rooms here, with a whole stack of mod-cons in the more expensive ones, are deservedly popular. It's south of the town.

BP Samila Beach Hotel (☎ 0 7444 0222; www .bphotelsgroup.com; 8 Th Ratchadamnoen; r 1200-1150B; ✿ ▢ ▣) This beachfront hotel provides Songkhla's swankiest accommodation and has all the amenities, including an IDD phone, fridge, satellite TV and sea or mountain views.

Eating

Songkhla has two excellent night markets for you to sample. The **Wachira night market** (Th Thale Luang), so-called for the school it sets up in front of, features a solid kilometre of vendors hocking everything from noodles to curries. Another, known by locals as the **Naa Suan night market** (Th Saiburi), has a palpable Muslim influence.

The seafood in Ko Yo has a reputation for being some of the best in the area. On the

---

TRAVEL WARNING: DEEP SOUTH

At the time of writing, a series of violent incidents had made travel in parts of Songkhla and much of Pattani and Narathiwat a potentially risky enterprise. For the historical background to the insurgency, see the boxed text, p28.

To date, tourists have not been targeted but the haphazard nature of the insurgency makes it difficult to predict which way the situation will turn. We emerged from the research trip for this book entirely unscathed, but there were multiple violent incidents, some involving deaths, in other parts of the provinces that we visited. Generally speaking, travelling in Pattani and Narathiwat in the early morning and late evening is discouraged, and independent travel via rented motorcycle is a potential risk. While in urban areas, it's probably also a good idea not to linger around parked motorcycles, as they have been used as a vehicle for carrying remote-controlled bombs.

If you plan to visit the region and want to know the situation on the ground, the authorities suggest contacting the local Tourist Police or TAT, but be prepared for pessimistic spiel. Our overwhelming impression was that for the vast majority of the inhabitants of the region, not to mention the few tourists that trickle through, life goes on, albeit with machine gun-armed soldiers as a disturbing background.

mainland, there are several cheap, excellent seafood restaurants around the beach along Th Som Awm.

Coffee Shop (cnr Th Nang Ngam & Th Phattalung; dishes 10-15B; ☽ 6am-6pm) Experience the epitome of southern Thai city life – sipping coffee with the locals in an ancient café. Augment your java with a dish of still-warm *kà·nŏm bórk*, dumplings of flour or sticky rice rolled in coconut and sprinkled with sugar, made directly in front of the shop.

Khao Nawy (☎ 0 7431 1805; 14/22 Th Wichianchom; dishes 30-50B; ☽ breakfast & lunch) Songkhla's most lauded *ráhn kôw gaang* (curry shop) serves up an amazing variety of authentic southern-style curries, soups, stir-fries and salads. Look for the glass case holding several stainless steel trays of food just south of the sky-blue Chokdee Inn.

Nai Wan Restaurant (☎ 0 7431 1295; Th Ratchadamnoen; dishes 35-200B; ☽ lunch & dinner) Popular for its crab dishes (bring moist wipes!), the menu also offers Thai salads, soups and other seafood offerings, as well as a few veggie entries.

Dawhan Musalim Food (☎ 0 7431 5637; 140 Th Phattalung; dishes 40-60B; ☽ lunch & dinner) Praised by locals, Dawhan is located in the tall pink building. It has a small selection of Thai-Muslim soups, stir-fries and rich curries, as well as a popular chicken biryani. If you don't see anything you fancy here, there are several other similar Muslim restaurants along this strip of Th Phattalung.

Drinking

Several casual bars and restaurants are found on and around happening Th Sisuda. **Buzz Stop** (☎ 0 7444 0231; 24 Th Sisuda; ☽ 9am-1am), a quasi-Irish boozer, offers a variety of imported draft beers and an expansive menu of pub grub. **Baan Kafae** (☎ 08 6956 8066; Th Sisuda; ☽ 5pm-midnight) is an open-air garden where locals nibble on spicy snacks and drink beer over low tables.

There's a strip of quasi-beachfront restaurant-bars along Hat Samila. **Dr Cool Radio** (Th Rim Thaleh Luang) has great sea views and is filled most nights with Thai students listening to local DJs spinning pop hits.

Getting There & Away
BUS & MINIVAN

Songkhla is something of a Hat Yai transport satellite; from Songkhla, you'll have to go to Hat Yai to reach most long-distance destinations in the south. There are a few destinations with transport originating in Songkhla, though.

The bus station is located a few hundred metres south of the town centre. Three 2nd-class buses go daily to Bangkok (593B), stopping in Nakhon Si Thammarat (136B), Surat Thani (207B) and Chumphon (312B), among other places. One VIP bus to Bangkok leaves at 5pm (1125B).

To Hat Yai, buses (19B) and minivans (25B) take around 40 minutes and leave from Th Ramwithi.

Minivans to Pattani (90B) and Yala (100B) leave from 6am to 5pm from further south on Th Ramwithi.

Getting Around

Sŏrng·tăa·ou circulate around town or head to Ko Yo for 15B. Motorcycle taxis around town cost around 20B during the day; rates double at night.

HAT YAI
หาดใหญ่
pop 192,500

Hat Yai literally means 'Big Beach', but you won't find a drop of sea in this landlocked urban monstrosity that is a hive of activity. Instead, the city functions as a significant transit hub to virtually every other destination in the region. If you're heading to an island or beach in the deep south, you'll undoubtedly be passing through at some point.

Because of its proximity to the Malaysian border, only 60km away, much of the business in Hat Yai has developed to service cross-border trade. Despite all this, Hat Yai isn't a bad place to get stuck for a night, especially if you count shopping or eating among your hobbies. Markets are plentiful and the malls provide an escape from the heat. The nightlife scene also buzzes and you can hang out in some cosy pubs before heading off.

Information
EMERGENCY

Tourist police (☎ 0 7424 6733; Th Niphat Uthit 3; ☽ 24hr) Near the TAT office.

IMMIGRATION OFFICE

Immigration Office (☎ 0 7425 7019; Th Phetkasem) Near the railway bridge, it handles visa extensions.

INTERNET ACCESS

Idea.net (Th Chi Uthit; per hr 20B; 🕙 9am-11pm) Near OH (Oriental Hotel); offers internet and other computer-related services.

MEDICAL SERVICES

Bangkok Hatyai Hospital (☎ 0 7436 5780-9; bhhi mc@bgh.co.th; 75 Soi 15 Th Pechkasam) One of the best health-care providers in southern Thailand, it has English-speaking staff. It's northeast of the centre.

MONEY

Hat Yai is loaded with banks. Several after-hours exchange windows are located along Th Niphat Uthit 2 and 3 near the Th Thamnoonvithi intersection. If you have Malaysian

ringgit the banks won't take them, but many midrange and top-end hotels have exchange windows that will.

POST

Main post office (1 Th Niphat Songkhrao) At the very north of town. A more convenient post office lies two blocks northeast of the train station.

TELEPHONE

Telephone office (Th Niphat Songkhrao; 🕙 7am-11pm) Adjacent to the main post office.

TOURIST INFORMATION

Tourist maps and pamphlets are available at hotels throughout town.

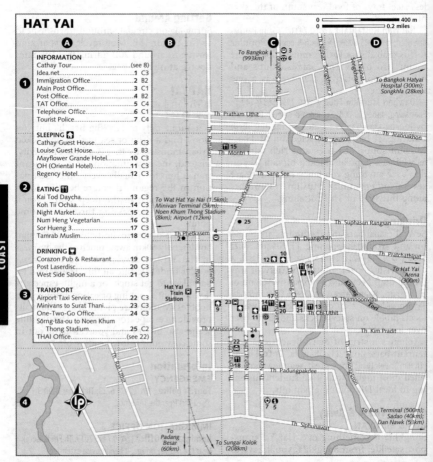

HAT YAI

INFORMATION
Cathay Tour.............................(see 8)
Idea.net..1 C3
Immigration Office......................2 B2
Main Post Office..........................3 C1
Post Office...................................4 B2
TAT Office....................................5 C4
Telephone Office........................6 C1
Tourist Police..............................7 C4

SLEEPING 🛏
Cathay Guest House....................8 C3
Louise Guest House.....................9 B3
Mayflower Grande Hotel...........10 C3
OH (Oriental Hotel)...................11 C3
Regency Hotel............................12 C3

EATING 🍴
Kai Tod Daycha...........................13 C3
Koh Tii Ochaa.............................14 C3
Night Market..............................15 C2
Num Heng Vegetarian...............16 C3
Sor Hueng 3................................17 C3
Tamrab Muslim............................18 C4

DRINKING 🍸
Corazon Pub & Restaurant.........19 C3
Post Laserdisc.............................20 C3
West Side Saloon........................21 C3

TRANSPORT
Airport Taxi Service....................22 C3
Minivans to Surat Thani.............23 C3
One-Two-Go Office....................24 C3
Sŏrng·tăa·ou to Noen Khum
   Thong Stadium.......................25 C2
THAI Office.............................(see 22)

ISLAM IN SOUTHERN THAILAND

At approximately 4% of the population, Muslims make up Thailand's largest religious minority, living side by side with the majority Theravadin Buddhists. There are some 3000 mosques in Thailand – over 200 in Bangkok alone. Of these mosques, 99% are associated with the Sunni branch of Islam (in which Islamic leadership is vested in the consensus of the Ummah, or Muslim community), and 1% with the Shi'ite branch (in which religious and political authority is given to certain descendants of the Prophet Mohammed).

Islam was introduced to Thailand's southern region between AD 1200 and 1500 through the influence of Indian and Arab traders and scholars. To this day, most of Thailand's Muslims reside in the south, concentrated in the regions of Pattani, Narathiwat, Satun and Yala. These southerners trace their heritage to the former Kingdom of Pattani, an Islamic kingdom whose territory straddled the present-day border between Thailand and Malaysia. Accordingly, the south shares both a border and a cultural heritage with its predominantly Muslim neighbour. Indeed, most of Thailand's southern Muslims are ethnically Malay and speak Malay or Yawi (a dialect of Malay written in the Arabic script) in addition to Thai.

These cultural differences, inflamed by a history of perceived religious and linguistic discrimination, have led to a feeling of disconnection with the Buddhist mainstream among a radical few of the southern Muslims (see the boxed text, p38). Some have called for secession, and fewer still have, in the past, taken up armed insurgency (see the boxed text, p28).

Proper etiquette in Thai Muslim communities is simple and predictable. Islam forbids the consumption of pork and alcohol. In very conservative communities, multigender groups will be split off into separate rooms upon arrival. Men and women will be reunited as they depart.

Just as is the case when visiting wát, mosques will not permit entry to those in shorts or shoes. Women should not wear short skirts, sleeveless tops or any particularly revealing clothing; simply think conservative. Unless invited to do so, avoid entering the mosque's main prayer hall, as this is a sacred space intended for Muslims. Do not bring cameras, and remember to turn off mobile phones.

Friday is the day of the Sabbath, with religious activities culminating between 11am and 2pm. Locals may be too busy on Friday for visitors and most restaurants close down during this time.

TAT Office (☎ 0 7424 3747; tatsgkhla@tat.or.th; 1/1 Soi 2, Th Niphat Uthit 3) Very helpful staff here speak excellent English and have loads of info on the entire region.

TRAVEL AGENCIES
Hat Yai is full of travel agencies, but **Cathay Tour** (☎ 08 9466 2491, 0 7423 2202; cathay_ontours@ hotmail.com; 93/1 Th Niphat Uthit 2; ☻ 9am-9pm) stands out for its super-friendly staff and full range of services, from tickets to tours to visa runs.

Sights

BULLFIGHTING
A more innocuous version than its Spanish equivalent, **bullfighting** (☎ 0 7438 8753; tickets 300-600B; ☻ 10am-3pm) revolves around two bulls butting heads in opposition, but the real sport here is gambling. Fights occur on the first Saturday of the month, or the second Saturday if the first Saturday is a *wan prá* (Buddhist worship day; full or new moon). The venue

changes from time to time, but lately they've been held at **Noen Khum Thong Stadium**, west of the city on the way to the airport (20/80B by sŏrng·tăa·ou/túk-túk). Check dates and venues with the TAT office.

WAT HAT YAI NAI
วัดหาดใหญ่ใน
About 1.5km west of town, on Th Phetkasem, this wát features a 35m reclining Buddha (Phra Phut Mahatamongkon). Inside the image's gigantic base is a curious little museum and mausoleum with a souvenir shop. To get here, get a motorcycle taxi (40B) or hop on a sŏrng·tăa·ou near the intersection of Th Niphat Uthit l and Th Phetkasem and get off after crossing the river – it costs about 12B.

Sleeping
Hat Yai has dozens of hotels within walking distance of the train station.

Cathay Guest House (☎ 0 7424 3815; fax 0 7435 4104; 93/1 Th Niphat Uthit 2; r 160-250B) Ludicrously helpful staff and plentiful information about onward travel make up for the run-down rooms at this popular cheapie.

Louise Guest House (☎ 0 7422 0966; 21-23 Th Thamnoonvithi; r 300-400B; 🗙) This place has more appealing rooms than the Cathay – though not its buzz. The numerous portraits of the Thai royal family on the walls and the apartment-style layout give the place a homey feel.

OH (Oriental Hotel; ☎ 0 7423 0142; fax 0 7435 4824; 135 Th Niphat Uthit 3; r 500-550B; 🗙) OH offers rooms with TV (no cable), hot water, a fridge and some truly psychedelic carpets. Lack of a writing desk is a downside if you plan to do any work.

Mayflower Grande Hotel (☎ 0 7423 4888; mayflowergrande@hotmail.com; 150 Th Saeng Chan; r 990-1190; 🗙 🖳) Blonde wood floors, full-length windows and minimalist design give the rooms here a real Scandinavian feel. Free wi-fi and a chic coffee shop seal the deal.

Regency Hotel (☎ 0 7435 3333-47; www.regency-hatyai .com; 23 Th Prachathipat; r 898-1398B; 🗙 🖳) This hotel has that grand old-world charm that's so very rare nowadays. The rooms in the old wing are smaller (and cheaper) and feature attractive wood furnishings, while rooms on the upper floors of the new wing boast amazing views.

Eating

Hat Yai is southern Thailand's gourmet mecca, offering Muslim roti and curries, Chinese noodles and dim sum, and fresh seafood.

The extensive **night market** (Th Montri 1) boasts heaps of local eats including several stalls selling the famous Hat Yai–style deep-fried chicken and *kà·nŏm jeen* (fresh rice noodles served with curry), as well as a couple of stalls peddling grilled seafood.

On Th Niyomrat, between Niphat Uthit 1 and 2, starting at Tamrab Muslim, is a string of casual and inexpensive Muslim restaurants open from about 7am to 9pm daily. Meals at these places cost between 20B to 60B.

Num Heng Vegetarian (☎ 0 7435 1032; 99/3-4 Th Prachathipatai; dishes 20-30B; 🕑 breakfast, lunch & dinner) Those who eschew flesh will appreciate this clean and yummy looking veggie corner.

Kai Tod Daycha (☎ 08 1098 3751; Th Chi-Uthit; dishes 30-50B; 🕑 lunch & dinner) Locals claim that Daycha does the best Hat Yai–style fried chicken. Enjoy your spicy bird over fragrant yellow rice, or with a plate of *sôm·đam*.

Koh Tii Ochaa (☎ 0 7423 4243; 134-136 Th Niphat Uthit 3; dishes 30-80B; 🕑 lunch) This classic eatery sells all your Sino favourites, including some you didn't even know about such as the delicious *bà·gùt·đĕh*, pork ribs in a fragrant dark broth.

Sor Hueng 3 (☎ 08 1896 3455; 79/16 Th Thamnoonvithi; dishes 30-120B; 🕑 4pm-3am) This popular local legend with branches all over town prepares heaps of delicious Thai-Chinese and southern Thai faves. Simply point to whatever looks good or order something freshly wok-fried from the extensive menu.

Drinking & Entertainment

Th Thamnoonvithi boasts a string of lively bars and pubs.

Post Laserdisc (☎ 0 7423 2027; 82/83 Th Thamnoonvithi; 🕑 9am-2am) Unlike most other places in town, this long-standing pub has no 'theme', but this makes it all the more authentic. The live music here is relatively good, and the happy hour is among the most generous in Thailand.

MAKING A (VISA) RUN FOR THE BORDER FROM HAT YAI

The Malaysian border is about 60km south of Hat Yai, and many travellers come through town just to extend their Thai visas.

To get an in-and-out stamp, head to Padang Besar, the nearest Malaysian border town. Buses cost 39B (two hours, every 25 minutes, 6am to 6pm) and minivans are 50B (1½ hours, hourly, 6am to 6pm). It's also possible to get a train, but this option is not very fast or frequent. The **immigration office** (☎ 0 7452 1020) on the Thai side is open from 5am to 9pm daily.

There's another border at Dan Nawk, south of Sadao, which can be reached by minivan (50B, 1½ hours, 6am to 6pm), but this route sees more through traffic than daytrippers. The **immigration office** (☎ 0 7430 1107) on the Thai side is open from 5am to 11pm daily.

If you need a longer Thai visa, you'll have to see the Thai consulate in Georgetown, on Penang Island (accessible through the mainland town of Butterworth). Buses from Hat Yai to Butterworth are run by private tour companies and start from 250B (four hours). Again, trains from Hat Yai to Butterworth are slower and less frequent.

West Side Saloon (☎ 0 7435 4833; 135/5 Th Thamnoonvithi; ☾ 6pm-midnight) This 'saloon' attracts Thais, Malays and fàràng to its dim, rustic, publike space. Tables are set in front of a stage, where live music rocks from 8.30pm nightly.

Corazon Pub & Restaurant (☎ 0 7435 0360; 41 Th Pracharom; ☾ 6pm-midnight) This is a cosy Latin disco-pub, eclectically but well decorated. There's live and DJ music of all kinds (including Latin), and Thai and Western foods are served.

Getting There & Away

AIR

THAI (☎ 0 7423 3433; 182 Th Niphat Uthit 1) operates three flights daily between Hat Yai and Bangkok (2500B, 90 minutes). Nearly all of the low-cost airlines now operate flights to and from Bangkok:

Air Asia (☎ 0 2515 9999; www.airasia.com) Six daily flights to and from Bangkok (1175B).

Nok Air (☎ 0 2900 9955; www.nokair.com) Five daily flights to/from Bangkok's Don Meuang Airport for 1090B.

One-Two-Go (☎ in Bangkok 1126, elsewhere 1141 ext 1126; www.fly12go.com; New World Hotel, Th 152-156 Niphat Uthit 2) One flight daily for 1850B.

BUS & MINIVAN

The bus terminal is 2km southeast of the town centre, though all inter-provincial buses and minivans make stops in town. Destinations from Hat Yai are shown in the table below:

Destination	Transport	Fare	Duration
Bangkok	air-con bus	740B	14hr
	VIP bus	783-1065B	14hr
Ko Samui	air-con bus	380B	8hr
Krabi	air-con bus	234B	5hr
Narathiwat	air-con bus	178B	4hr
	minibus	150B	3hr
Padang Besar	ordinary bus	39B	2hr
	minibus	50B	1½hr
Pattani	air-con bus	100B	3hr
	minibus	100B	2½hr
Phuket	air-con bus	371B	8hr
Sadao	minibus	45B	1hr
Satun	air-con bus	65B	2hr
	minibus	100B	1½hr
Songkhla	ordinary bus	19B	1hr
	minibus	25B	1hr
Sungai Kolok	air-con bus	250B	5hr
	minibus	150B	4hr
Surat Thani	air-con bus	240B	5hr
Trang	air-con bus	100B	3hr
	minibus	100B	2½hr
Yala	ordinary bus	90B	3hr

Most north-bound minivans now leave from a minivan terminal 5km west of town at Talat Kaset, a 60B túk-túk ride from the centre of town. Destinations and fares from here include Pak Bara (100B) and Surat Thani (250B).

Cathay Tour (☎ 0 7423 2202; 93/1 Th Niphat Uthit 2) also runs minivans to many destinations in the south.

TRAIN

There are four overnight trains to/from Bangkok each day, and the trip takes at least 16 hours. Sample fares include 339B for a 3rd-class seat, 455/675B (fan/air-con) for a 2nd-class seat, 605/945B for a 2nd-class sleeper (in the lower berth) and 1394B to 1594B for a 1st-class sleeper. There are also seven trains daily that run to Sungai Kolok (43B to 286B) and two daily trains running to Butterworth (180B to 322B) and Padang Besar (57B to 272B), both in Malaysia.

There is an advance booking office and left-luggage office at the train station; both are open 6am to 6pm daily.

Getting Around

An **Airport Taxi Service** (☎ 0 7423 8452; Uthit 1) makes the run to the airport four times daily (6.45am, 10am, 2pm and 5pm; 80B per person). A private taxi for this run costs about 300B.

Sŏrng·tăa·ou run along Th Phetkasem and charge 10B per person. Túk-túk and motorcycle taxis around town cost 20B to 40B per person.

PATTANI

อ.เมืองปัตตานี

pop 44,800

Once the centre of an independent Muslim principality that included Yala and Narathiwat, sprawling Pattani has never quite adjusted to being a part of the Kingdom of Thailand. The Portuguese established a trading post here in 1516, the Japanese in 1605, the Dutch in 1609 and the British in 1612. During these times Pattani's allegiances shifted several times and rebellions were not uncommon.

Despite the city's interesting past, there's little of interest in the town except its access to some excellent nearby beaches. Unfortunately, the ongoing insurgency (see the boxed text, p252) has made all but a few of these sandy destinations unsafe for the independent traveller.

Orientation & Information

The Mae Nam Pattani acts as a divider between the older town to the east, and the newer town to the west. Most services are in the older town.

There are several banks along the southeastern end of Th Pipit, near the Th Naklua Yarang intersection.

Internet café (cnr Th Peeda Talattewiwat 2 and Th Pipit; per hr 20B)

Le Rich Travel (☎ 0 7331 3699; fax 0 7331 3911; 78/13 Th Makrut) This friendly agency can help you arrange everything from safe beach destinations to good local eats.

Main post office (Th Pipit) The attached CAT office provides an overseas phone service from 7am to 10pm daily.

Pattani Hospital (☎ 0 7332 3411-14; Th Nong Jik)

Police station (☎ 0 7334 9018; Th Pattani Phirom) In a central location.

Sights

Along Th Ruedi you can see what is left of old Pattani architecture – the Sino-Portuguese style that was once so prevalent in this part of southern Thailand. West of San Jao Leng Ju Kieng Shrine on Th Arnoaru are several very old, but still quite intact Chinese-style homes.

BEACHES

If it wasn't for the ongoing violence, Pattani could be one of the better beach destinations in southern Thailand. Unfortunately exploring much of the area independently is not a safe option at this time.

However, there are a few beaches in the area that the locals still frequent. **Laem Tachi**, a sandy cape that juts out over the northern end of Ao Pattani, can be reached by boat taxi from Pattani harbour. **Hat Talo Kapo**, 14km east of Pattani near Yaring Amphoe, is a pretty beach that's also a harbour for *gow·lŏw*, the traditional fishing boats of southern Thailand. And although it's technically in Songkhla Province, **Thepha District**, located 35km northwest of Pattani, is the most developed beach destination in the area. There you'll find a few slightly aged resorts that cater mostly to middle-class Thais. At **Hat Soi Sawan**, near the Songkhla-Pattani provinces border, several families have set up informal beachfront restaurants that are popular with locals on the weekends.

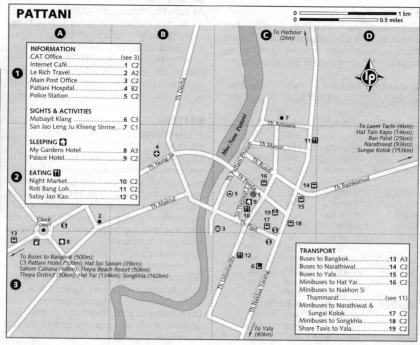

PATTANI

INFORMATION	
CAT Office	(see 3)
Internet Café	1 C2
Le Rich Travel	2 A2
Main Post Office	3 C2
Pattani Hospital	4 B2
Police Station	5 C2

SIGHTS & ACTIVITIES	
Matsayit Klang	6 C3
San Jao Leng Ju Khieng Shrine	7 C1

SLEEPING	
My Gardens Hotel	8 A3
Palace Hotel	9 C2

EATING	
Night Market	10 C2
Roti Bang Loh	11 C2
Satay Jao Kao	12 C3

TRANSPORT	
Buses to Bangkok	13 A3
Buses to Narathiwat	14 C2
Buses to Yala	15 C2
Minibuses to Hat Yai	16 C2
Minibuses to Nakhon Si Thammarat	(see 11)
Minibuses to Narathiwat & Sungai Kolok	17 C2
Minibuses to Songkhla	18 C2
Share Taxis to Yala	19 C2

To Harbour (2km)

To Laem Tachi (4km); Hat Talo Kapo (14km); Ban Palat (25km); Narathiwat (93km); Sungai Kolok (153km)

Mae Nam Pattani

Th Dejha
Th Arnoaru
Th Mayor
Th Ruedi
Th Pratani Phirom
Th Peeda
Th Ramkomud
Th Nong Jik
Th Makrut
Th Pipit
Th Ubomvithi
Th Naklua Yarang

Clock Tower

To Buses to Bangkok (500m);
CS Pattani Hotel (500m); Hat Soi Sawan (35km);
Sakom Cabana (40km); Thepa Beach Resort (50km);
Thepha District (90km); Hat Yai (134km); Songkhla (162km)

To Yala (40km)

0 ___ 1 km
0 ___ 0.5 miles

To reach Thepha, hop on any Songkhla-bound bus from Pattani (or vice versa) and mention the name of your resort – you'll be deposited at the side of the road for the brief walk the beach.

Dress modestly on or near the beaches.

MOSQUES

Thailand's second-largest mosque is the **Matsayit Klang** (Th Naklua Yarang), a traditional structure with a green hue that is probably still the south's most important mosque. It was built in the 1960s.

Sleeping & Eating

Palace Hotel (☎ 0 7334 9171; 10-12 Pipit Soi Talattewiwat 2; r 250-500B; ✵) Despite its location in a grubby market soi, the rooms here, in particular those with air-con on the lower floors, are neat and comfortable.

My Gardens Hotel (☎ 0 7333 1055-8; fax 0 7333 6217; 8/28 Th Charoenpradit; r 300-800B; ✵) A favourite with travelling businesspeople, My Gardens is good value. Rooms are well maintained and comfortable with satellite TV, bath, good hot-water showers and fridge.

The next three places are out of town.

Sakom Cabana (☎ 0 7431 8065; 136 Moo 4, Tambon Sakom; r 600-1000B; ✵) Located in Thepa District, 40km from Pattani, this basic resort features a clean compound with several attractive wooden duplex bungalows a short walk from the beach.

Thepa Beach Resort (☎ 0 7432 5551; 255 Moo 4, Tambon Thepha; bungalows 1140B; ✵ 🖳) Located near the Pattani-Songkhla border, this resort features attractive bungalows (get one by the lotus pond), not to mention a pool and calm stretch of ocean

CS Pattani Hotel (☎ 0 7333 5093/4; cspatani@cscoms .com; 299 Muu 4 Th Nong Jik; r 1500-5500B; ✵ 🖳 🖳) Pattani's poshest digs has a gorgeous colonial lobby, two pools, an excellent restaurant, a sauna and steam room…the list goes on. Breakfast is included. Ask about discounts. It's 3km southwest of town.

Roti Bang Loh (☎ 0 81096 9555; Th Naklua Yarang; dishes 15-20B; ✵ 6-9am & noon-8pm) This delicious roti vendor is known around town for the several prizes he's won – if you speak Thai or Yawi ask him about them and he'll go on for ages!

Satay Jao Kao (☎ 0 89737 5417; 37/20 Th Udomwithi; dishes 20-30B; ✵ 10am-6pm) This well respected open-air restaurant serves beef satay local style with cubes of rice and a sweet dipping sauce. Several other restaurants along this stretch of Th Udomwithi come highly recommended by Pattani's Muslim foodies.

A variety of food vendors convenes at the **night market** (Pipit Soi Talattewiwat 2).

Getting There & Around

Minivans are the most common way to get around this part of Thailand, and just to make things more difficult for visitors, there's no single minivan or bus terminal in Pattani. See Map p258 for pick-up and drop-off locations. All minivans and buses run from approximately 6am to 5pm.

Destination	Transport	Price	Duration
Hat Yai	minivan	100B	1½hr
Narathiwat	ordinary bus	55B	2½hr
	minivan	100B	2hr
Songkhla	minivan	90B	1½hr
Sungai Kolok	minivan	120B	2½hr
Yala	ordinary bus	21B	1hr
	share taxi	50B	40mins

Buses to Bangkok depart from the small lot beside a petrol station near the CS Pattani Hotel – call ☎ 0 7334 8816 for ticket purchase and reservations. The trip takes 15 to 16 hours and costs 1185B (VIP), 763B (1st class) and 615B (2nd class).

Sŏrng·tăa·ou go anywhere in town for 10B per person. **Zakee** (☎ 08 9655 3223), a native of Pattani, is a reliable driver who speaks English, has his own car and provides heaps of local knowledge.

NARATHIWAT
อ.เมืองนราธิวาส
pop 44,200

Sitting on the banks of the Bang Nara River, Narathiwat is probably the most Muslim large city in Thailand, and conversations in Yawi (a Malay dialect) and the daily calls to prayer are sounds you can expect to hear here. Some of the Sino-Portuguese buildings lining the riverfront are over a century old, and some of the prettiest beaches on southern Thailand's eastern coast are just outside town. Unfortunately the security situation in this part of the country (see the boxed text, p252) has suffocated the little tourism that this region used to see. Be sure to check the latest situation before travelling in this region.

Information

There's a bunch of banks in the town centre.

CAT office (Th Pichitbamrung; ☒ 8.30am-10pm Mon-Fri, 9am-5pm Sat & Sun) Same location as the post office.

Internet cafés (☒ 9am-9pm) There's a good café near the clock tower in town and another near the minivan stand for Yala.

Phanwiphaa (☎ 0 7351 1161; Th Puphapugdee; ☒ 8am-5pm) This ticket office, located across from the large Krung Thai Bank, arranges airline tickets as well as transport to the airport.

Post office (Th Pichitbamrung)

TAT (☎ 0 7352 2411; tatnara@cscoms.com) Inconveniently located a few kilometres southeast of town, just across the bridge, on the road to Tak Bai.

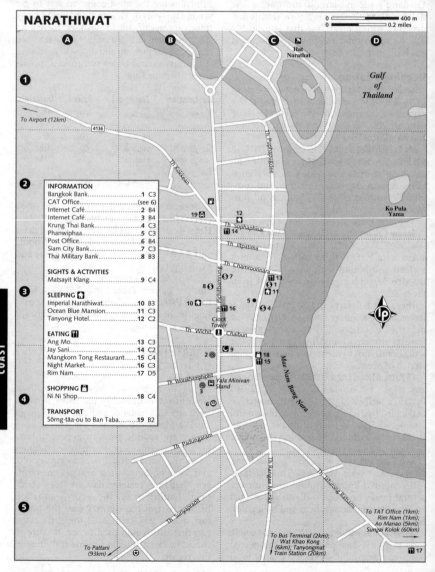

NARATHIWAT

0   400 m
0   0.2 miles

INFORMATION	
Bangkok Bank	1 C3
CAT Office	(see 6)
Internet Café	2 B4
Internet Café	3 B4
Krung Thai Bank	4 C3
Phanwiphaa	5 C3
Post Office	6 B4
Siam City Bank	7 C3
Thai Military Bank	8 B3

SIGHTS & ACTIVITIES	
Matsayit Klang	9 C4

SLEEPING	
Imperial Narathiwat	10 B3
Ocean Blue Mansion	11 C3
Tanyong Hotel	12 C2

EATING	
Ang Mo	13 C3
Jay Sani	14 C2
Mangkorn Tong Restaurant	15 C4
Night Market	16 C3
Rim Nam	17 D5

SHOPPING	
Ni Ni Shop	18 C4

TRANSPORT	
Sŏrng-tăa-ou to Ban Taba	19 B2

Hat Narathat

Gulf of Thailand

To Airport (12km)

4136

Ko Pula Yama

Th Kokkrau

Th Puphapugdee

Th Sophaphisai

Th Jitpatima

Th Chamroonnara

Th Pichitbamrung

Clock Tower

Th Wichit

Chaibun

Th Worathamphiphit

Yala Minivan Stand

Th Padungaram

Mae Nam Bang Nara

Th Rangae Munka

Th Jaturong Rachan

To Pattani (93km)

Th Suryapradit

To Bus Terminal (2km); Wat Khao Kong (6km); Tanyongmat Train Station (20km)

To TAT Office (1km); Rim Nam (1km); Ao Manao (5km); Sungai Kolok (60km)

Sights
BEACHES

Just north of town is **Hat Narathat**, a 5km-long sandy beach, which serves as a kind of public park for locals. The beach is only 2km from of the town centre – you can easily walk there or take a sǎhm·lór.

Five kilometres south of town, **Ao Manao** used to be a popular sun and sand destination, but today is mostly frequented by locals catching fish. Nonetheless, there's accommodation, and on weekends, basic food and drinks.

MATSAYIT KLANG
มัสยิดกลาง

Towards the southern end of Th Pichitbamrung stands this interesting old, wooden mosque built in the Sumatran style. It was reputedly built by a prince of the former kingdom of Pattani over a hundred years ago.

WAT KHAO KONG
วัดเขากง

The tallest seated-Buddha image in southern Thailand is at **Wat Khao Kong**, about 6km southwest on the way to the train station in Tanyongmat. The image is 24m high and made of reinforced concrete covered with tiny gold-coloured mosaic tiles that glint magically in the sun. A sǒrng·tǎa·ou to Wat Khao Kong costs 10B from the clock tower, while a motorcycle ride should cost 40B.

Sleeping & Eating

Most of the town's accommodation is located on and around Th Phupha Phakdi (signposted as 'Puphapugdee') along the Bang Nara River.

Ao Manao Resort (☎ 0 7354 2193; bungalows 300B; ✷) This accommodation, 5km southeast of town at Ao Manao, features large, clean cement cottages in a small compound. A motorcycle taxi here costs 40B.

Ocean Blue Mansion (☎ 0 7351 1109; 297 Th Puphapugdee; r 350-450B; ✷) This newish hotel is the only one in town to really take advantage of the riverfront view. Rooms include a huge fridge and cable TV.

Tanyong Hotel (☎ 0 7351 1477-79; fax 0 7351 1834; 16/1 Th Sophaphisai; r 550-750B; ✷) A few decades ago this was undoubtedly Narathiwat's most upscale hotel, but the passing of time has rendered it a competent, although slightly overpriced choice.

Imperial Narathiwat (☎ 0 7351 5041; narathiwat@imperialhotels.com; 228 Th Pichitbamrung; r 1000-2250B; ✷ ✷) Narathiwat's nicest accommodation features everything you'd expect in an upscale hotel. Cut rates make this excellent value.

Every evening a ragtag **night market** (Th Pichitbamrung) forms along the north of the clock tower.

Jay Sani (☎ 0 89657 1546; 50/1 Th Sophaphisai; dishes 30-60B; ✷ breakfast, lunch & dinner) This is where locals go for excellent Thai-Muslim food. Point to whatever curry or stir-fry looks good, but be sure not to miss the sublime súp néua (beef soup).

Ang Mo (cnr Th Phuphapugdee & Th Chamroonnara; dishes 30-80B; ✷ lunch & dinner) This exceedingly popular Chinese restaurant is both cheap and tasty, and has even fed the likes of members of the Thai royal family.

Mangkorn Tong Restaurant (☎ 0 7351 1835; 433 Th Puphapugdee; dishes 60-160B; ✷ lunch & dinner) This small seafood place, with a floating dining section out the back, does quite good food and its prices are reasonable.

Rim Nam (☎ 0 7351 1559; 45/6 Th Narathiwat-Tak Bai; dishes 70-200B; ✷ dinner) South of town on the way to Ao Manao, Rim Nam is well worth the ride. The service is warm and attentive, and dishes are artistically presented. Call for free transport.

Shopping

Ni Ni Shop (☎ 0 89736 3346; 439 Th Puphapugdee; ✷ 9am-8pm) This boutique offers a variety of local handicrafts including silks, batik and jewellery.

Community Handicraft Centre (☎ 0 7354 2255; 356/3 Moo 12, Ao Manao; ✷ 9am-4pm) Located near Ao Manao Resort, this community project combines a large showroom and workshop where you can witness batik items being painted by hand.

Getting There & Away
AIR

Air Asia (☎ 0 2515 9999; www.airasia.com) operates one daily flight to and from Bangkok at 11.10am (1496B).

BUS & MINIVAN

Air-conditioned buses to Bangkok and Phuket and most minivans leave from the bus terminal 2km south of town on Th Rangae Munka. The buses to Phuket (530B, 12 hours) originate in Sungai Kolok, pass Narathiwat three times daily (7am, 9am and 6.30pm) and continue via Pattani, Hat Yai, Songkhla, Trang, Krabi and Phang-Nga. Buses to Bangkok (VIP/1st/2nd class 1295/833/669B) take at least 15 hours and depart several times during the day.

Minivans heading to Hat Yai (150B, three hours), Pattani (100B, 1½ hours), Songkhla (150B, two hours), Sungai Kolok (70B, one hour) and Yala (100B, 1½ hours) generally leave on an hourly basis from 5am to 5pm.

TRAIN

Narathiwat's train station is in Tanyongmat, 20km west of town (40B by sŏrng·tăa·ou). The town is on the Southern Line, and there are two daily departures heading for Bangkok (174B to 863B) as well as several daily departures for Hat Yai (35B) and Yala (13B).

Getting Around

Phanwiphaa (☎ 0 7351 1161) offers a minivan service to the airport from its office on Th Puphapugdee at 9.30am daily (60B).

Narathiwat is easy to navigate on foot. If you don't feel like walking, motorcycle taxis will take you around for 15B to 30B. There is also a new bus system that circles the city from 7am to 6pm (9B), stopping near Hat Narathat. Look for the light-blue bus stop signs along Th Puphapugdee and Th Phichitbamrung.

SUNGAI KOLOK
สุไหงโกลก
pop 40,500

Although Narathiwat is officially the provincial capital, it's a skinny wimp compared to its bigger and brasher sibling, Sungai Kolok. This soulless border town is the main southern coastal gateway between Malaysia and Thailand, and the primary industries here revolve around border trade and catering to weekending Malaysian men who are often looking for sex. Every night Soi Phuthon and the small strip behind the Marina Hotel come alive with booming bars that make Pattaya or Patong look sedate in comparison.

The border is open from 5am to 9pm (6am to 10pm Malaysian time) and there are several passable sleeping options in town as well as money-changing facilities and good connections to the rest of Thailand.

Information

There are plenty of banks with ATMs in town as well as foreign-exchange booths, which are also open on weekends. There's one across from the train station.

CAT office (Th Thetpathom) Handles international calls.

CS Internet (Th Asia 18; per hr 20B; ☻ 10am-9pm) Offers internet service.

Easy Net (Soi 1, Th Charoenkhet; per hr 30B; ☻ 9am-6pm) Internet service.

Immigration offices Border (☎ 0 7336 1414; ☻ 5am-9pm); In town (☎ 0 7361 1231; Th Charoenkhet; ☻ 8.30am-4.30pm Mon-Fri) A larger office across from the Merlin Hotel.

Post office (Th Asia 18) A hike to the western edge of town.

Tourist Police (Th Asia 18) At the border, it has a small selection of free maps and brochures.

Sleeping & Eating

There's heaps of accommodation options here, but most hotels are pretty grubby and cater to the 'by the hour' market. Many places in Sungai Kolok will take Malaysian ringgit as well as Thai baht for food or accommodation.

Merlin Hotel (☎ 0 7361 8111; 68 Th Charoenkhet; r 390-450B; ⚡) Don't let the lobby fool you – the rooms here are very plain indeed, but a good choice if you need a cheap room with a view.

Genting Hotel (☎ 0 7361 3231-40; fax 0 7361 1259; 250 Th Asia 18; r 550-1520B; ⚡ ⚡) Geared towards the conference trade, this place comes equipped with a barber, a snooker room, entertainment venues, pub and a karaoke lounge. There are some good, only slightly scuffed, midrange rooms and it's away from the seedier areas.

Marina Hotel (☎ 0 7361 3881-5; fax 0 7361 3385; Soi Phuthon; r 580-780B; ⚡ ⚡) Don't be alarmed by the chirping in the lift; this hotel's elevator shaft doubles as a home to swifts whose nests are a Chinese delicacy. Located right in the epicentre of the entertainment district, the Marina also has multiple bars, clubs and a restaurant all on site.

Despite the mix of cultures and emphasis on tourism, Sungai Kolok is definitely not a culinary destination. A small night market unfolds next to the immigration office – exceptionally good and cheap eats can be got at the stall in the centre that only has Chinese writing.

Soon Ahaan Thai-Jeen (Thai-Chinese Food Centre; ☎ 0 7341 8207; cnr Th Charoenkhet & Soi Phuthon; dishes 20-60B; ☻ breakfast & lunch) This small food court serves a variety of mostly Chinese-style dishes.

Getting There & Away
BUS & MINIVAN

The **long-distance bus station** (☎ 0 7361 2045) is located west of downtown, and there are three

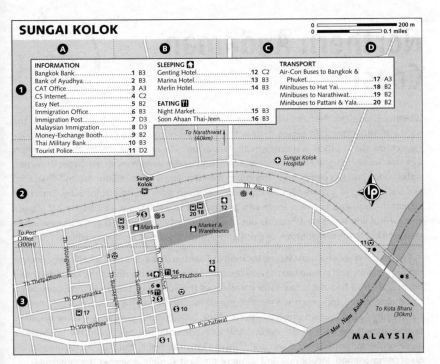

SUNGAI KOLOK

INFORMATION
Bangkok Bank.................................1 B3
Bank of Ayudhya...........................2 B3
CAT Office......................................3 A3
CS Internet.....................................4 C2
Easy Net...5 B2
Immigration Office.........................6 B3
Immigration Post............................7 D3
Malaysian Immigration..................8 D3
Money-Exchange Booth.................9 B2
Thai Military Bank........................10 B3
Tourist Police................................11 D2

SLEEPING
Genting Hotel...............................12 C2
Marina Hotel................................13 B3
Merlin Hotel.................................14 B3

EATING
Night Market...............................15 B3
Soon Ahaan Thai-Jeen..................16 B3

TRANSPORT
Air-Con Buses to Bangkok &
   Phuket......................................17 A3
Minibuses to Hat Yai....................18 B2
Minibuses to Narathiwat...............19 B2
Minibuses to Pattani & Yala..........20 B2

daily air-conditioned buses for the 18-hour trip to Bangkok; one VIP (1365B, noon), one 1st class (880B, 1pm) and one 2nd class (706B, 8.30am). From Bangkok, the VIP bus leaves at 5.15pm, three 1st-class buses leave between 9pm and 10pm, and the 2nd-class at 9pm. Buses head off to Phuket (579B) at 6am, 8am and 5.30pm via Krabi (446B).

Minivans to Narathiwat (80B) depart half-hourly from Th Asia 18, across from the train station. Minivans heading to Pattani (120B), Yala (90B) and Hat Yai (180B) depart hourly from 7am to 5pm, in front of and west of the Genting Hotel.

TRAIN

Trains from Bangkok to Sungai Kolok include the 1pm rapid and 3.10pm special express and take at least 20 hours (180B to 893B). Trains from **Sungai Kolok station** (☎ 0 7461 4060) back to Bangkok include the 11.30am rapid and the

2.20pm special express. Sample fares on these trains include 370B for a 3rd-class seat (fan, for sadomasochists only), 607B for a 2nd-class seat (fan), 677/917B for a 2nd-class sleeper (fan/air-con, lower berth) and 1753B for a 1st-class sleeper. There are also daily departures to Phun Phin, Nakhon Si Thammarat and Hat Yai.

Getting Around

The border is about 1km east of the centre of Sungai Kolok or the train station. Transport around town is by motorcycle taxi – it's 30B for a ride to the border or into the centre of town.

From Rantau Panjang (Malaysian side), a share taxi to Kota Bharu will cost about eight Malaysian ringgit per person (or 30 ringgit to charter the whole car yourself) and it takes about an hour. It costs four ringgit to Kota Bharu on the regular yellow and orange bus.

Northern Andaman Coast

Whether you've got designer villa wishes, bamboo hut desires or anything in-between, the northern Andaman coast serves it up hot with a shot of turquoise ocean to wash it down. Phuket, on the southern extremity, is the audacious starlet of the region, flaunting glitzy five-star hotels that grace soda-white beaches, and where sleep is an afterthought to parties, water sports and spa pampering. Ranong, to the far north, is a mix of Burmese and Thais who eke out a living in a dusty frontier town very removed from the tourist industry. Travel the 300km through and between these two provinces and you'll see it all: Muslim stilt villages and vertical limestone karsts; resorts out of the pages of *Architectural Digest* and bays abuzz with jet skis; tangled mangrove swamps and skittish clouds of nesting swallows.

Phuket is the second-most visited location in Thailand (Pattaya is first) and its fame for fine dining, cabarets and private beaches makes it easy to overlook the rest of this coast. But head north and you'll find the underwater paradises of the Surin and Similan islands, considered to be among the top seven wonders of the diving world. In Phang-Nga province several community based tourism projects – fruits of the 2004 tsunami wreckage – allow travellers to give something back to the cultural and environmental hotchpotch. In the low season, much of the far north shuts down and Phuket's beaches empty out, leaving fabulous deals on accommodation, lots of rain and some of the best surfing waves on the peninsula.

HIGHLIGHTS

- Searching for elusive whale sharks and swimming with the fish on a live-aboard cruise of the **Similan Islands** (p279) and **Surin Islands Marine National Parks** (p274)

- Experiencing Thai-Muslim culture via community-based projects around **Khuraburi, Khao Lak** or **Ko Yao** (p278)

- Cruising the art galleries and hole-in-the-wall restaurants and bars of colonial **Phuket Town** (p300)

- Kayak around the beautiful bay of **Ao Phang-Nga** (p281)

- Finding gluttonous hedonism in the hair-raising clubs and on the packed beaches of **Hat Patong** (p313) – love it or hate it

- Falling into the snoozy, beach-bar vibe and lounging on the white sand of **Ko Phayam** (p271)

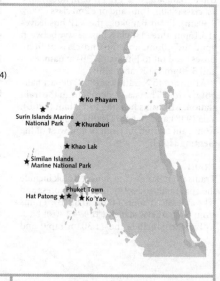

★ Ko Phayam
Surin Islands Marine National Park ★ Khuraburi
★ Khao Lak
Similan Islands Marine National Park
Hat Patong ★★ ★★ Phuket Town ★ Ko Yao

■ DRY SEASON: NOVEMBER-APRIL   ■ WET SEASON: MAY-OCTOBER

Climate

The Andaman coast is wetter than the southern gulf provinces with the low season months between May and October logging the highest rainfall. During this time, seas are rough and passenger boats to some islands, such as the Surin and Similan archipelagos, are suspended. On the upside, peninsular Thailand is narrow, so if the weather turns sour on the Andaman coast, you can always pack your bags and chase the sun to the eastern seaboard.

National Parks

Some of the northern Andaman coast's most visited areas are national parks. Ao Phang-Nga National Park (p283) swarms with day-trippers drawn by the expanse of turquoise water and pristine islands – it's no wonder Scaramanga (of *The Man with the Golden Gun* fame) chose to build his lair here. Divers and snorkellers are now flocking to Surin Islands Marine National Park (p274) and Similan Islands Marine National Park (p279), considered to be among the seven wonders of the diving world, mostly on two-day to week-long live-aboard cruises.

Even built up Phuket Province has its share of parks: Khao Phra Taew Royal Wildlife & Forest Reserve (p323) is a pristine rainforest in the heart of Phuket's concrete jungle and Sirinat National Park (p322) is one of the wildest stretches on the island.

Further off the beaten track in the far north is Laem Son National Park (p270), where you'll find mangrove forests, empty beaches and turtle nesting sites.

RANONG & AROUND

อ.เมืองระนอง

pop 25,000

The least charming of the Andaman coast's provincial capitals, Ranong lies on the east bank of tea-brown Pak Chan estuary, a short boat ride from Myanmar. This is a frontier town through and through, with a frenetic, downtrodden feel and a mix of Burmese and Thais scrambling for your tourist dollar. The town attempts to woo visitors not only with its interesting visa runs to Myanmar (Burma), but with a clutch of natural hot springs and a handful of tumbledown historic buildings. Even if you don't need to renew your visa, it's well

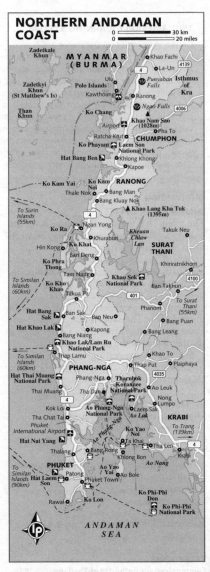

worth taking the opportunity to have a cup of tea in Myanmar – but the bleak town of Ranong doesn't entice a stay longer than a day or two.

There are also a number of dive operators using Ranong as a jumping-off point for live-aboard trips to the Burma Banks and the Surin Islands.

TSUNAMI EARLY WARNING SYSTEM

On the morning of 26 December 2004, an earthquake off the coast of Sumatra sent enormous waves crashing against much of Thailand's Andaman coast, claiming around 8000 lives and causing millions of dollars of damage to homes and businesses. In 2005, Thailand officially inaugurated a national disaster warning system, which was created in response to the country's lack of preparedness in 2004. The Bangkok-based centre anticipates that a tsunami warning can be issued within 30 minutes of the event being detected by existing international systems.

The public will be warned via the nationwide radio network, Channel 5 army TV network, the state-operated TV pool and SMS messages. For non-Thai speakers, the centre has installed warning towers along the high-risk beachfront areas that will broadcast prerecorded announcements in various languages accompanied by flashing lights. The **call centre** (☎ 1860) also handles questions and tips from the public regarding potential or unfolding disasters.

Information

IMMIGRATION OFFICES

The main Thai immigration office is on the road to Saphan Plaa, about halfway between town and the main piers, across from a branch of the Thai Farmer's Bank. If entering Thailand from Myanmar via Kawthoung, you'll have to visit this office to get your passport stamped with a visa on arrival.

There is also a smaller immigration post in the vicinity of Tha Saphan Plaa. If you're just going in and out of Myanmar's Kawthoung for the day, a visit to the small post will suffice.

For details on getting a new Thai visa or making a day trip to Victoria Point (Myanmar), see the boxed text, p268.

INTERNET ACCESS

J Net (☎ 0 7882 2877; Th Ruangrat; per hr 40B; ⏰ 9am-9pm)

MONEY

Most of Ranong's banks and ATMs are near the intersection of Th Tha Meuang and Th Ruangrat.

POST

Main post office (Th Chonrau; ⏰ 9am-4pm Mon-Fri, to noon Sat)

TELEPHONE

Communications Authority of Thailand (CAT; Th Tha Meuang; ⏰ 24hr) For phone services.

TRAVEL AGENCIES

Plenty of agencies along Th Ruangrat offer visa services, bus and boat tickets, accommodation arrangements for the nearby islands of Ko Chang and Ko Phayam, and day trips to Kawthoung (in Myanmar).

Pon's Place (☎ 0 7782 3344; Th Ruangrat; ⏰ 7.30am-midnight) Also rents out motorcycles and cars.

Tanatwan Tours (☎ 0 7782 2807; tanatwan@ hotmail.com; 16/8 Th Chonrau; ⏰ 9am-8pm) Visa trips cost 400B per person (plus visa costs) and depart at 9am daily.

Sights & Activities

HOT SPRINGS

บ่อน้ำร้อน

Ranong may lack the sophisticated pizzazz of your standard spa town, but it is well known for its hot springs. You can sample these famous waters at Wat Tapotaram, where **Ranong Mineral Hot Springs** (Th Kamlangsap; admission 10B; ⏰ 8am-5pm) offers pools hot enough to boil eggs in (65°C). Like the three bears of *Goldilocks* fame, the Thai names of the springs translate as Father Spring, Mother Spring and Baby Spring and each has its own distinct smell (all horrid). The water from the three springs is thought to be sacred as well as possessing miraculous healing powers.

Bathing occurs in rustic rooms where you can scoop water from separate hot and cool water tanks and sluice the mixed water over your body, Thai-style. Don't get inside the tanks and spoil the water. Several local hotels pipe water directly from the springs into rooms.

WAT HAT SOM PAEN

วัดหาดส้มแป้น

About 7km beyond the springs, the village of **Hat Som Paen** is a former tin-mining community. At **Wat Hat Som Paen**, visitors feed fruit to the huge *blah ploo·ang* (black carp) in the temple stream. The faithful believe these carp are actually *tair·wá·dah*, a type of angel, and it's forbidden to catch and eat them. Legend has it that those who do will contract leprosy.

NAI KHAI RANONG
ในค่ายระนอง

Nai Khai Ranong (Th Ruangrat; admission free; 9am-4.30pm) is the former home of Koh Su Chiang, a Hokkien who became governor of Ranong during the reign of King Rama V. These days, it is a combination clan house (clubhouse for Chinese who share the same surname) and shrine. It's on the northern edge of town and is worth a peep.

Of the three original buildings, one still stands and is filled with mementos of the Koh family's glory days. The main gate and part of the original wall also remain.

Several shophouses on Th Ruangrat preserve this old Hokkien style. **Koh Su Chiang's mausoleum** (Susaan Jâo Meuang Ranong) is set into the side of a hill a few kilometres north of Nai Khai Ranong, on the road to Hat Chandamri.

WATERFALLS
Of the several well-known waterfalls in Ranong Province, **Nam Tok Ngao** and **Nam Tok Punyaban** are within walking distance of Hwy 4. Ngao is 13km south of Ranong, while Punyaban is 15km north. Just take a sŏrng·tăa·ou (small pickup truck) in either

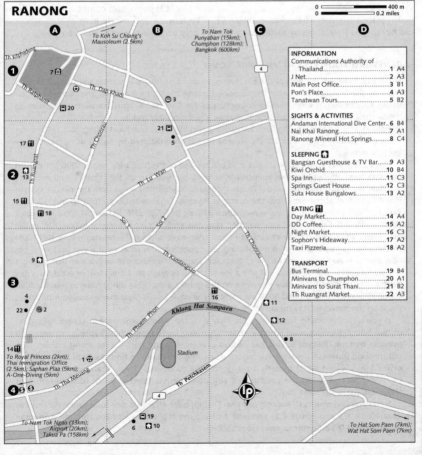

RANONG

INFORMATION
Communications Authority of
Thailand...................................1 A4
J Net..2 A3
Main Post Office........................3 B1
Pon's Place.................................4 A3
Tanatwan Tours..........................5 B2

SIGHTS & ACTIVITIES
Andaman International Dive Center..6 B4
Nai Khai Ranong.........................7 A1
Ranong Mineral Hot Springs.........8 C4

SLEEPING
Bangsan Guesthouse & TV Bar....9 A3
Kiwi Orchid..............................10 B4
Spa Inn....................................11 C3
Springs Guest House.................12 C3
Suta House Bungalows..............13 A2

EATING
Day Market..............................14 A4
DD Coffee.................................15 A2
Night Market............................16 C3
Sophon's Hideaway..................17 A2
Taxi Pizzeria.............................18 A2

TRANSPORT
Bus Terminal............................19 B4
Minivans to Chumphon.............20 A1
Minivans to Surat Thani............21 B2
Th Ruangrat Market..................22 A3

To Koh Su Chiang's Mausoleum (2.5km)

To Nam Tok Punyaban (15km); Chumphon (128km); Bangkok (600km)

Th Kitphadung
Th Ratphanit
Th Dap Khadi
Th Ruangrat
Th Chonlau
Th Lu Wan
Soi 1
Soi 2
Th Kamlangsap
Th Chonlau
Th Phoem Phon
Khlong Hat Sompaen
Stadium
Th Tha Meuang
Th Petchkasem

To Royal Princess (2km); Thai Immigration Office (2.5km); Saphan Plaa (5km); A-One-Diving (5km)

To Nam Tok Ngao (13km); Airport (20km); Takua Pa (158km)

To Hat Som Paen (7km); Wat Hat Som Paen (7km)

0 .... 400 m
0 .... 0.2 miles

direction and ask to be let off at the *nám dòk* (waterfall).

DIVING

Live-aboard diving trips run from Ranong to world-class bubble-blowing destinations, including the Burma Banks and the Surin and Similan islands. The speciality is four-day, four-night packages for around 15,900B. Try **A-One-Diving** (☎ 0 7783 2984; www.a-one-diving.com; 77 Saphan Plaa) or **Andaman International Dive Center** (☎ 0 7783 4824; Th Petchkasem; www.aidcdive.com) at the bus station.

Sleeping

Don't expect fireworks from Ranong's hotels; most offer little more than bare bones amenities. Everyone in town can help you arrange a visa run for 400B.

The places on or near Th Petchkasem (Hwy 4) can be reached from town by sǒrng·tǎa·ou 2.

Bangsan Guesthouse & TV Bar (☎ 0 8972 74334; bangsanbar@chaiyo.com; 225 Th Ruangrat; r from 150B) Looking like Greg Brady's psychedelic bedroom circa 1973, you'll need a few drinks at the streetside TV bar before the granite-hard beds upstairs will feel comfy. Shared bathrooms have a free-love style of nonprivacy, but the whole place is as clean as a preppy.

Springs Guest House (☎ 0 7783 4369; Th Kamlangsap; r 200B) This unassuming spot offers a pool table and satellite TV in the quiet bar-restaurant downstairs. The rooms are a little grubby and bathrooms are shared.

Kiwi Orchid (☎ 0 7783 2812; www.kiwiorchid.com; Th Petchkasem; r 250B) Right by the bus station – expect late night rumblings – this ramshackle backpackers has cardboard-like walls and dingy shared bathrooms. It's awfully convenient though, and comes with a mediocre restaurant and overly helpful staff who can help arrange activities and transport.

RENEWING YOUR VISA AT VICTORIA POINT

The dusty, tumbledown port at the southernmost tip of mainland Myanmar was named Victoria Point by the British, but is known as Ko Song (Second Island) by the Thais. The Burmese appellation, Kawthoung, is most likely a corruption of the Thai name. Most travellers come here to renew their visas, but the place also makes an interesting day trip.

Fishing and trade with Thailand keep things ticking over, but Kawthoung also churns out some of Myanmar's best kick boxers. Nearby islands are inhabited by bands of nomadic *chow lair* (sea gypsies).

The easiest way to renew your visa is to opt for one of the 'visa trips' (from 400B per person plus visa fees) offered by travel agencies in Ranong, but you can do the legwork yourself.

When the Thai–Myanmar border is open, boats to Kawthoung leave from the pier at Saphan Plaa (Pla Bridge) about 5km from the centre of Ranong. Take sǒrng·tǎa·ou (pickup truck) 2 from Ranong (10B) and get off at the **immigration office** (☎ 0 7782 2016; Th Ruangrat; ☉ 8.30am-6pm), 700m north of the pier, to get your passport stamped. Walk or take a motorcycle taxi (10B) to the pier where you'll find crowds of long-tail boats that leave when full (one-way/return 100/150B) to Myanmar immigration. When negotiating your price, confirm whether it is per person or per ride, and one-way or return. At the checkpoint, you must inform the authorities that you're a day visitor – in which case you will pay a fee of US$10 (it must be a crisp bill) or 600B for a day permit. It's also possible to stay overnight on this permit, although a dingy hotel in rough-edged Victoria Point will cost around 800B per night. If you have a valid Myanmar visa in your passport, you'll be permitted to stay for up to 28 days.

If you're just coming to renew your Thai visa, the whole process will take a minimum of two hours. Bear in mind when you are returning to Thailand that Myanmar's time is 30 minutes behind Thailand's. This has caused problems in the past for returning visitors who got through Burmese immigration before its closing time only to find the **Thai Immigration office** (☉ 8.30am-4.30pm) closed. It's a good idea to double-check Thai immigration closing hours when leaving the country – if you don't get stamped in you'll have to return to Myanmar again the next day.

Some visa-run agents in Ranong (try Kiwi Orchid) offer Myanmar day tours with visa services from 1000B; it's also possible to combine a diving day trip with a visa run through **Andaman International Dive Center** (above) from 5500B.

Spa Inn (☎ 0 7781 1715; fax 0 7782 3384; 25/11 Th Petchkasem; r 300-450B; ❄) The walls at this place could do with a rubdown with the local mineral water. That said, this so-so hotel takes a step up the quality (and price) escalator. Spa Inn has large rooms and pumps its water in from the springs. The rooms at the back look out over the lush green mountainside.

Suta House Bungalows (☎ 0 7783 2707; Th Ruangrat; r 395B; ❄) One of the more comfy choices and right in the town centre, this off-the-road place has a cluster of simple bungalows – and plenty of flowers – around a courtyard/car park. Beds are hard but the showers are hot.

Royal Princess (☎ 0 7783 5240; www.dusit.com; 41/144 Th Tha Meuang; r 990-3000B; ❄ ☐) Topping Ranong's accommodation options, this is about the best you can get on the hotel front. There's a gym, pool and mineral water bathrooms, but the trimmings are starting to look a little tatty.

Eating & Drinking

On Th Kamlangsap, not far from Hwy 4 and the Spa Inn, is a night market with several food stalls selling great Thai dishes at low prices; across the street from it is a modest noodle stand. The day market, on Th Ruangrat towards the southern end of town, offers inexpensive Thai and Burmese meals, as well as fresh produce, fish and meats. A cluster of decent eateries can also be found at the northern end of Th Ruangrat.

DD Coffee (☎ 0 7783 0111; Th Ruangrat; snacks 30-100B; ☾ breakfast, lunch & dinner) Promising 'the best coffee in Ranong', this vibrant café has teems of jabbering teenagers and good black stuff. At night it turns into a popular bar.

Taxi Pizzeria (☎ 0 7782 5730; Th Ruangrat; dishes 70-200B; ☾ lunch & dinner) Completed framed jigsaws provide the decoration at this spartan pizzeria. The food won't have mamma amending her recipe book, but the chef makes a reasonable attempt at rustling up a margarita.

Sophon's Hideaway (☎ 0 7783 2730; Th Ruangrat; mains 80-250B; ☾ 10am-midnight) This expat favourite has everything and then some, including internet access, a free pool table, a pizza oven, full bar, water features and rattan furnishings aplenty. The food isn't great but the sizzling ostrich steak is quite a change from pàt tai.

Getting There & Away

AIR

Ranong airport is located 20km south of town, just off Hwy 4. **Air Asia** (www.airasia.com) provides flights Tuesdays, Fridays and Sundays between Ranong and Bangkok (one-way 1200B).

BUS

The bus terminal is on Th Petchkasem towards the southern end of town, though some buses stop in town before proceeding on to the terminal. Sŏrng·tăa·ou 2 (blue) passes the terminal.

The bus terminal has services to destinations as shown below:

Destination	Bus type	Price	Duration
Bangkok	VIP	665B	10hr
	1st class	428B	
	2nd class	357B	
	ordinary	220B	
Chumphon	2nd class	120B	3hr
Hat Yai	2nd class	410B	5hr
Khuraburi	air-con	100B	1½hr
	ordinary	70B	
Krabi	air-con	190B	6hr
Phang-Nga	ordinary	150B	5hr
Phuket	air-con	240B	5-6hr
	ordinary	180B	
Surat Thani	1st class	180B	4-5hr
	2nd class	100B	

Minivans head to Surat Thani (150B, 3½ hours, four times daily) and Chumphon (120B, three hours, hourly from 6am to 5pm); see the map for departure locations.

Getting Around

Motorcycle taxis will take you almost anywhere in town for 20B, to the hotels along Th Petchkasem for 25B and to the pier for boats to Ko Chang, Ko Phayam and Myanmar for 50B. Pon's Place (p266) can assist with motorcycle and car rentals.

KO CHANG
เกาะช้าง

If you tell folks in Ranong and on Ko Phayam that you are planning on going to Ko Chang, they'll exclaim: 'Why do you want to go there? There's nothing to do!'.

And yes, it's blissfully true. This little visited rustic isle is a long way – in every respect – from its much more popular Trat Province namesake. Pass the time exploring the island's tiny village capital (where the boats dock during the dry season) or wend your way around the island on one of the dirt trails. Sea eagles, Andaman kites and hornbills all nest here and if you're lucky, you'll catch sight of them floating above the mangroves. The white, west coast beach of **Ao Yai** might entice you for sunbathing, but note that you'll risk getting devoured by sandflies.

Bungalow operations on the island can arrange **boat trips** to Ko Phayam and other nearby islands for around 200B per person (including lunch) in a group of six or more. Dive trips are also possible. **Aladdin Dive Cruise** (☎ 0 7782 0472; www.aladdindivecruise.de), on Ko Chang, runs PADI courses and offers a range of live-aboard dive safaris. A three-day live-aboard trip to the Surin Islands costs 18,400B; four-day trips to the Similan Islands cost 16,900B.

There are no banks, internet access or cars on Ko Chang so slow down even more with some yoga, t'ai chi and qi gong at **Omtao** (classes 250B; ◎ Oct-May), a German run 'studio' just north of Cashew Resort on Ao Yai.

Sleeping & Eating

Basic bamboo huts reign supreme on Ko Chang and, for the most part, they're only open from November to April. Electricity is limited and a few places have solar and wind power.

Ao Yai is the main beach where you'll find most lodging options and a few more places are tucked away on Ao Daddaeng, to the south, which is linked to Ao Yai via a short walking track. More isolated options can be found on the beaches to the north and far south of the island.

Golden Bee (Ao Yai; bungalows 150B) Uber-basic but spacious, central and clean beachfront huts are tended by some of the nicest folks on the island.

N & X Bungalows (☎ 0 7782 0180; huts 150B) Aspiring Robinson Crusoes should bed down in these no-frills huts. At the southern end of the island at Ao Lek (Small Bay), they're several giant strides off the beaten track.

Hornbill Bungalow (☎ 0 7783 3820; bungalows 150-250B) On an isolated beach in the island's north, this is a good spot for solitude seekers. It's a bit of a hike to get here, but the owner has a boat for ferrying guests around.

Mama's (☎ 0 7782 0180; mamasbungalows@yahoo .com; huts 200B) Tucked in a pretty corner on a rocky, hibiscus-laden hillside above Ao Daddaeng, the huts here are standard-basic but the restaurant serves some of the best Thai food around.

our pick Ko Chang Resort (☎ 0 7782 0177; Ao Yai; bungalows 200-300B) Bright colours and rustic bamboo chic are served on the rocks here above patches of white sand. The priciest bungalows have huge split-level decks and the bathrooms are some of the best around.

Cashew Resort (☎ 0 7782 4741; Ao Yai; bungalows 200-600B) Cashew is Ko Chang's most venerable resort. Choose from cheap A-frame huts or larger, more robust bungalows.

Sawadee (☎ 0 7782 0177; sawadeekochang@yahoo .com; Ao Yai; bungalows 300-400B) The slightly Bali-style, varnished wood bungalows here are the most comfortable you'll find on Ko Chang. Spring mattresses, vibrantly painted bathrooms and the very good alfresco restaurant add a touch of class.

Nature Resort Restaurant (Ao Yai; mains 50-150B) You can't miss this three-storey pagoda-style restaurant on the hillside. The Thai food is very good and don't leave without sampling the cashew or mango wine (50B). Basic bungalows are also available for 200B to 300B.

Little Italy (mains 120-200B) Meals from recipes from the owner's Sicilian grandma are served in the woods about 50m inland from Wat Pah Ko Chang on Ao Yai.

Getting There & Away

From Ranong take a sŏrng·tăa·ou (15B) from Th Ruangrat Market to Saphan Plaa. Alternatively most Ranong guesthouses will shuttle you to the pier for 50B.

Two boats to Ao Yai (per person 150B, 9am and 2pm) leave daily from late October to April – if there's not enough demand only the 2pm boat will run. During the highest season (December to March) there's also a regular daily noon departure. Boats return to Ranong at 8am the next day. During the monsoon months there's a once weekly boat, weather permitting, that stops at the east coast pier – it's a two-hour walk from here to Ao Yai. Chartering a long-tail boat to or from Ko Phayam is 1200B.

Getting Around

There are no cars on the island and only a couple of scooters, so if you're inspired to move, it's on foot or nothing. Some places, such as Hornbill, have boats too and will provide transfers.

LAEM SON NATIONAL PARK

อุทยานแห่งชาติแหลมสน

The **Laem Son National Park** (☎ 0 7782 4224; www.dnp .go.th; adult/child 200/100B) covers 315 sq km of the

Kapoe district of Ranong and Khuraburi district in Phang-Nga. This area includes about 100km of Andaman Sea coastline – the longest protected shore in the country – as well as over 20 islands. Much of the coast here is covered with mangrove swamps, home to various species of birds, fish, deer and monkeys (including crab-eating macaques) often seen while driving along the road to the park headquarters. Sea turtles lay eggs on Hat Praphat.

The most accessible beach is **Hat Bang Ben**, where the park headquarters are. This long, sandy beach, backed by shady casuarinas, is said to be safe for swimming year-round. From Hat Bang Ben you can see several islands, including the nearby Ko Kam Yai, Ko Kam Noi, Mu Ko Yipun, Ko Khang Khao and, to the north, Ko Phayam. The park staff can arrange boat trips out to any of these islands for 800B per boat per day. During low tide you can walk to an island just a couple of hundred metres from Hat Bang Ben.

Ko Phayam has plenty of places to stay and is a friendly, demure little island. It has only a few hundred inhabitants, mostly Thais and Burmese, with a smattering of expats and a few dozen *chow lair* (sea gypsies) thrown into the mix. Tourists congregate on the island's pretty beaches, but locals support themselves prawn fishing, cashew-nut farming or working on the rubber plantations. Interesting fauna in the area includes wild pigs, hornbills, monkeys and snakes. There's one 'village' on the island, where you will find the main pier, a couple of simple eateries, some small grocery stalls and a bar. From the pier area, motorcycle taxis scoot you to the bungalow operations around the island, almost all of which are located on one of the island's two picturesque bays and are pretty basic. The motorcycle 'highway', running down the middle of Ko Phayam, augments smaller concrete roadways and dirt driveways.

Ko Khang Khao is known for a beach on its northern end, which is covered with colourful pebbles. Although underwater visibility isn't great around the island, it's a little better than on Ko Chang as it's further from the mouth of the Mae Nam Chan. The beach on **Ko Kam Noi** has relatively clear water for swimming and snorkelling (April is the best month), plus the added bonus of fresh water year-round and plenty of grassy areas for camping. **Ko Kam Yai** is 14km southwest of Hat Bang Ben. It's a large island with some accommodation (camping

and bungalows), a pretty beach and great snorkelling. One island on the other side of Ko Kam Yai is **Ko Kam Tok** (also called Ko Ao Khao Khwai). It's only about 200m from Ko Kam Yai, and, like Ko Kam Noi, has a good beach, coral, fresh water and a camping ground.

About 3km north of Hat Bang Ben, across the canal, is another beach, **Hat Laem Son**, which is almost always deserted. The only way to get here is to hike from Hat Bang Ben. In the opposite direction, about 50km south of Hat Bang Ben, is **Hat Praphat**, very similar to Bang Ben with casuarinas and a long beach. There is a second park office here, which can be reached by road via Hwy 4 (Petchkasem Hwy).

In the canals you ford coming into the park, you may notice the large wooden racks that are used for raising oysters.

Sleeping & Eating
HAT BANG BEN
Small bungalow outfits tend to come and go, especially following the tsunami. Have a good scout around before settling on digs, or head for the better established outfits on Ko Phayam. Camping is allowed anywhere among the casuarinas for 80B per person (pay at the park office just inside the park entrance) or you can rent a tent from 300B per night. Many of these small family operations have basic on-site eateries.

National Park Bungalows (☎ 0 2562 0760; reserve@dnp.go.th; bungalows 100-1000B) The national park has the usual, slightly dowdy array of basic bungalows and bigger, concrete villas. Standards are basic, but fine if you are here to spend your time out in the great outdoors. Similar park accommodation is available on Ko Kam Yai and can also be arranged in advance by contacting the listed number.

KO PHAYAM
Fan-cooled, rustic bungalows are the staple on Ko Phayam and electricity is usually only available from sunset to 10pm or 11pm. Most of the bungalow operations stay open throughout the year – although the shutters will come down if business becomes too slow – and many have attached eateries serving standard backpacker fare.

The following places are either on Ao Yai, a pleasant 3km-long sweep of sandy beach, or Ao Khao Kwai further north. Ao Yai has rolling surf and a low-key party backpacker vibe, while Ao Khao Kwai has a calm bay and is popular with couples and families. At low tide Ao Khao Kwai turns to mud and is no longer swimmable, and snorkelling isn't great on either beach.

Tang Tong Bungalows (☎ 0 8483 96836; Ao Khao Kwai; bungalows 200B) Basic but large and clean solar-powered bamboo huts are on a gorgeous stretch of beach in a hippy-style setting with an adjacent bar.

our pick **Vijit** (☎ 0 7783 4082; www.kohpayam-vijit.com; Ao Khao Kwai; bungalows 200-500B; 💻) You can choose from dozens of styles of basic bungalows around a sandy lot planted with shady trees. All are immaculate, huge, have indoor/outdoor bathrooms and little artistic touches. The restaurant here also comes highly recommended and the staff offer fishing and snorkelling trips. Contact in advance for transport from Ranong.

Contact Bungalows (☎ 0 8578 12006; bungalows 250B) Perched on a cliff with access to Ao Khao Kwai at low tide, these well-kept, albeit rustic, bamboo bungalows with tiled bathrooms have excellent, hammock-strewn terraces with sea breezes and luscious views.

Mountain Resort (☎ 0 7782 0098; Ao Khao Kwai; bungalows from 350B) Tucked into a shady palm grove at the far northern end of the bay, this is one of the most picturesque and serene spots on the island. White concrete bungalows sit on a grassy lawn while hornbills swoop overhead.

Mr Gao (☎ 0 7787 0222; www.mr-gao-phayam.com; Ao Khao Kwai; bungalows from 350B) The painted and varnished wood bungalows here are a step up in style and comfort from the classic bamboo crash pad and are very popular with couples. Management would be improved by a smile or two.

Bamboo Bungalows (☎ 0 7782 0012; Ao Yai; bungalows 350-500B) It does exactly what it says in the name, plus you can also opt for more expensive concrete and tile bungalows. It is run by an Israeli-Thai couple, offers oodles of atmosphere and attracts plenty of backpackers; however, the bungalows are quite small. There's a solid eatery, a leafy garden and you can hire bodyboards if you fancy a boogie in the surf.

Coconuts (☎ 0 7782 0011; Ao Yai; bungalows 350-500B) A skip and a jump from Bamboo, this is a decent overflow place, with a range of bungalows – you pay for space here.

Buffalo Bay Vacation Club (☎ 0 7787 0208; www.buffalobayclub.com; Ao Khao Kwai; bungalows 2500-3500B; ❄ 💻) Catering primarily to Russian package tourists, this spiffy new place has large concrete bungalows with hot water and more comforts than the rest of Phayam's bungalows combined. Don't miss the very reasonably priced restaurant, which serves ice cream, wine by the glass (only 50B) and other oddities such as tacos and jacket potatoes – along with seafood and Thai specialities.

Drinking

You'll find driftwood-constructed Reggae-style beach bars along both main beaches.

Oscar's (☎ 0 7782 4236; 🕐 10am-11pm) Located in the main village on Ko Phayam, this modern bar looks a little incongruous in its backwater setting. If you're after late (for a remote island) night shenanigans, however, it is *the* place to go to hobnob with the locals.

Getting There & Away

The turn-off for Laem Son National Park is about 58km from Ranong down Hwy 4 (Petchkasem Hwy), between the 657km and 658km markers. Buses heading south from Ranong can drop you off here (ask for Hat Bang Ben). Once you're off the highway, however, you'll have to flag down a pick-up truck going towards the park. If you can't get a ride all the way, it's a 10km walk from Hwy 4 to the park entrance. At the police box at the junction you may be able to hire a motorcycle taxi for 40B; the road is paved, so if you're driving it's a breeze.

From Ranong, take a sŏrng·tăa·ou from Th Ruangrat Market (15B) or one of the many shuttles that service most guesthouses (50B) to Saphan Plaa.

There are daily boats from Saphan Plaa to Ko Phayam's pier (150B, 1½ to two hours) at 9am and 2pm. A motorcycle taxi from the pier to the main beaches costs 70B per person each way. From Ko Phayam back to Ranong the boats run at 8am and 1pm. During the high season there may be three runs daily. Longtail boat charters to Ko Chang are 1200B.

Boats out to the other various islands can be chartered from the park's visitors centre; the general cost is 1500B per day.

Getting Around

Transport around Ko Phayam is provided by motorcycle taxis; there are no cars or trucks, and roads are pleasantly motorcycle-sized. A ride to your bungalow will cost 70B. Walking is possible but distances are long – it's about 45 minutes from the pier to Ao Khao Kwai, the nearest bay.

The shady low-lying island is perfect for biking and walking. Motorcycle rentals are available at **Oscar's** (☎ 0 7782 4236; per day approx 250B), the only bar in Ko Phayam's village, or you can rent **bicycles** (per day 70B) from Koy Shop behind Coconuts (opposite). Some of the bigger guesthouses might be able to arrange rentals, too.

KHURABURI
กุระบุรี/ตะกั่วป่า

This dusty, Wild West–feeling town is a one-road affair that is the jumping-off point for the Surin Islands (p274) and the home of some excellent community-based tourism opportunities through Andaman Discoveries (see the boxed text, p278) – ask at Cucina Andaburi (right) for directions. Along with Khao Lak (p276), this area was one of the places hardest hit by the 2004 Boxing Day tsunami, but up here, where tourism is a less important industry, recovery has been much slower.

For internet access and excellent coffee (from 25B), stop into **Friends de Sea Internet** (per hr 40B; ☺ 8am-8.30pm) just north of the southbound bus stop. For tourist information try Cucina Andaburi, or **Tom & Am Tour** (☎ 08 6272 0588) next to the bus stop on the northbound traffic side of the road.

Sleeping & Eating

Tararain River Hut Resort (☎ 0 7649 1789; bungalows 300-500B; ❄) Tumbledown but charming, this resort has tiny fan rooms and ever-so-slightly-less-tiny air-con rooms. The best are the fan rooms on the riverside.

Boon Piya Resort (☎ 08 1752 5457; bungalows 650B; ❄) Across the street from Tom & Am Tour, modern concrete bungalows here are spick-and-span and have hot showers.

Kuraburi Greenview Resort (☎ 0 7640 1400; www.kuraburigreenview.co.th; bungalows 1900-2400B; ❄ ▨) The rooms here have luxurious (for Khuraburi) amenities and breakfast is on the house, but it's actually about 12km south of Khuraburi, right off Hwy 4. The same company runs the main speedboat to the Surin Islands (see p275), so this is a convenient choice for diving (from 4500B per person) and nondiving (from 2700B per person) trips to the park.

Cucina Andaburi (☎ 0 7649 1590; ☺ 6.30am-midnight; mains 30-100B) Just in front of Tararain River Hut Resort, this is a breezy and charming spot that serves Western breakfasts and excellent Thai food. It's a great stop for tourist info as well.

Getting There & Away

Any Ranong- or Phuket-bound bus will stop in Khuraburi. Take a Phuket-bound bus to Takua Pa, about 50km south of Khuraburi, to

---

LOCAL VOICE: PUCHONG TIRAWANTA

As a Thai lawyer working from Phuket Town, Puchong Tirawanta has been working with private organisations and NGOs providing tsunami aid since shortly after the wave hit in 2004. His primary job has been to ensure that funds and donations are distributed properly.

What are aid organisations doing now, three years after the tsunami? Tourists won't see much of the recovery that's going on now, since most of it is within the Moken (sea gypsy) communities that were most affected. These people are still actively recovering. Aid is going towards social programs, such as skilled labour programs to help out those who have lost their trade.

As a whole do you think aid programs have been successful? There is a lot of corruption and everyone wants control of the money. The Moken are not Thai citizens so they can't own land. In one case, for example, a temple offered to buy the land for them – but then the temple leaders decided they would have the power to kick the Moken off the land if they didn't abide by their religious rules. Also there have been problems where home- or boat-building supplies have been dropped off in the villages; when we've gone back to check on the progress, the supplies have, on occasion, been sold and the money has gone towards alcohol. If the heads of Moken communities are given the money to distribute, they sometimes end up taking a cut for themselves. It's all very complicated, but there have been so many donations and so much good will that the results overall have been very good.

To find out how you can help, see the boxed text, p278.

As told to Celeste Brash

transfer to destinations such as Surat Thani (ordinary/air-con 75/100B, three hours), Krabi (ordinary 75B, four hours) and Khao Sok National Park (ordinary 30B, one hour, nine daily).

The pier for the Surin Islands is about 9km north of town – the only public transport is motorcycle taxi for around 60B, but if you've booked your boat to the islands with a tour company (see opposite) you'll be picked up for free.

SURIN ISLANDS MARINE NATIONAL PARK (MU KO SURIN NATIONAL PARK)
อุทยานแห่งชาติหมู่เกาะสุรินทร์

The five gorgeous islands that make up the **Surin Islands Marine National Park** (www.dnp.go.th; admission 400B; ☉ mid-Nov–mid-May) sit 60km offshore, just 5km from the Thai–Myanmar marine border. Healthy rainforest, pockets of white-sand beach in sheltered bays and rocky headlands that jut into the ocean characterise these granite-outcrop islands. The clearest of water makes for great marine life, with underwater visibility often up to 20m. The islands' sheltered waters also attract *chow lair,* who live in a village onshore during the May to November monsoon season. This group is known as Moken, from the local word *ôr gaang* meaning 'salt water'.

Ko Surin Neua (north) and Ko Surin Tai (south) are the two largest islands. Park headquarters and all visitor facilities are at Ao Chong Khad on Ko Surin Neua, near the jetty. The setting of flaxen sand and spar-

kling blue-green bays is jaw-droppingly spectacular.

Khuraburi is the jumping-off point for the park. The pier is about 9km north of town, as is the mainland **national park office** (☎ 0 7649 1378; ☉ 8am-5pm), with good information, maps and helpful staff.

Sights & Activities
DIVING & SNORKELLING

Dive sites in the park include **Ko Surin Tai** and **HQ Channel** between the two main islands. In the vicinity is **Richelieu Rock** (a seamount 14km southeast), where whale sharks are sometimes spotted during March and April. Sixty kilometres northwest of the Surins – but often combined with dive trips to the park – are the famed **Burma Banks**, a system of submerged seamounts. The three major banks, **Silvertip**, **Roe** and **Rainbow**, provide five-star diving experiences, with coral gardens laid over flat plateaus, and large oceanic and smaller reef marine species. There's presently no dive facility in the park itself, so dive trips (four-day live-aboards around 20,000B) must be booked from the mainland; see Getting There & Away, opposite, and the Khao Lak section, p277, for more information.

Snorkelling is excellent due to relatively shallow reef depths of 5m to 6m, and most coral survived the tsunami intact. Two-hour snorkelling trips (per person 80B, gear per day 150B) leave park headquarters at 9am and 2pm daily. If you are staying at headquarters expect to be in the company of mostly Thais who swim fully clothed – so you'll need some swimmable cover-ups (a big T-shirt is ideal) on these trips.

WILDLIFE & HIKING

Around park headquarters you can explore the forest fringes, looking out for crab-eating macaques and some of the 57 resident bird species, which include the fabulous Nicobar pigeon, endemic to the islands of the Andaman Sea. Along the coast you're likely to see the chestnut Brahminy kite soaring, and reef herons on the rocks. Twelve species of bat live here, most noticeably the tree-dwelling fruit bats, also known as flying foxes.

A rough-and-ready **walking trail** – not for the unsteady – winds 2km along the coast and through forest to the beach at **Ao Mai Ngam**, where there's good snorkelling. At

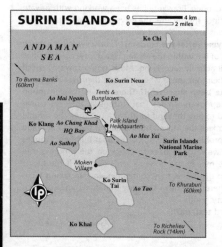

SURIN ISLANDS

0 — 4 km
0 — 2 miles

ANDAMAN SEA

Ko Chi

To Burma Banks (60km)

Ko Surin Neua

Tents & Bungalows

Ao Mai Ngam

Ao Sai En

Ko Klang   Ao Chang Khad   Park Island
            HQ Bay   Headquarters

Ao Suthep   Ao Mae Yai

Surin Islands National Marine Park

Moken Village

Ko Surin Tai   Ao Tao   To Khuraburi (60km)

Ko Khai   To Richelieu Rock (14km)

low tide it's easy to walk between the bays near headquarters.

OTHER ACTIVITIES

On Ko Surin Tai, the **Moken village** at Ao Bon welcomes visitors; take a long-tail boat from headquarters (100B). Post-tsunami, Moken have settled in this one sheltered bay where a major ancestral worship ceremony (Loi Reua) takes place in April. If you do visit the village, cover up and bring cash to buy handicrafts to help support their economy. There's also a clothing donation box at park headquarters for the Moken, so this is a good, responsible place to lighten your load.

Sleeping & Eating

Park accommodation is simple and fine, but because of the island's short, narrow beaches it's *very* close together and can feel seriously crowded when full (around 300 people). Book online at www.dnp.go.th or with the mainland **national park office** (☎ 0 7649 1378) in Khuraburi. The clientele is mostly Thai, giving the place a lively Asian holiday camp feel.

Bungalows (incl fan, bathroom & balcony 2000B) and good, new **tents** (1-/2-person 300/450B; bedding per person 60B) are available or you can pitch your own **tent** (per night 80B). There's generator power until about 10pm.

A park **restaurant** (dishes from 80B) serves authentic, delicious Thai food.

Getting There & Away

A 'big boat', which was docked for repairs when we passed through, theoretically leaves the Khuraburi pier at 9am daily when the park is open, returning at 1pm (return 1200B, 2½ hours one way). Tour operators use speedboats (return 1700B, one hour one way) that leave around 8am or 9am and will transfer independent travellers on their daily runs.

Several tour operators, all located near the pier, run day/overnight tours (around 2800/3700B including food and park lodging) to the park; the best in safety and service is **Greenview Tour** (☎ 0 7640 1400; www.kuraburigreen view.co.th), which is run by Kuraburi Greenview Resort (p273). Agencies in Khao Lak (p277) and Phuket (p288) are the most convenient booking options for boat travel and dive trips if you don't want to spend the night in Khuraburi – transfers from the place of purchase are always included in prices.

KO PHRA THONG

เกาะพระทอง

Legend has it that many centuries ago, pirates docked here and buried a golden Buddha beneath the sands. Translated as 'Golden Buddha Island', it is now unlikely that Ko Phra Thong will give up its secret, but tourists can still make good use of its pleasant sandy beaches.

The island is as quiet as a church mouse, and fishing (squid, shrimp and jellyfish) remains the island's key industry. The local delicacy is pungent *gà·bì* (fermented shrimp paste) – it stinks, but what a flavour.

ourpick **Golden Buddha Beach Resort** (☎ 0 1892 2208; www.goldenbuddharesort.com; bungalows 3200-6500B) is the island's number one resort, attracting a stream of yoga aficionados keen for a spiritual getaway. Accommodation is in naturalistic-chic wooden houses. All have open-air bathrooms with views of the sea and also the surrounding forest – the setting really fulfils dreams of a private beach getaway.

There are no regular boats to Ko Phra Thong, but if you're set on going to the island independently you can hop on a Surin-bound diving boat at the Khuraburi pier (see p273) and ask the boat driver to drop you off. It's better to contact Golden Buddha Beach Resort in advance to arrange transport. In any case, you'll have to negotiate a price with the boat driver, since there's no set price and it's only 15 to 20 minutes from the Khuraburi Pier.

On the north end of the island is **Mr Choi** (☎ 08 4855 9886; bungalows 500B) who has a few small bamboo huts and a bar that pumps out loud reggae music – the place has developed a bit of a traveller cult following. Call ahead for transport.

Locals of Tung Dap village on the southern tip of the island have requested that tourists not visit their area, so please be respectful and avoid this corner.

HAT BANG SAK

หาดบางสัก

A long, sleepy stretch of sand, the beach at Bang Sak had been attracting an ever-growing number of tourists striking north from the more heavily developed resorts of Phuket and nearby Khao Lak. Low-lying and flat, however, the area was badly hit by the 2004 tsunami and scores of businesses and hotels were washed away in an instant. While most areas had recovered from the tsunami by the end of 2007, Bang Sak was still looking rather sparse. The disheartening reason for this is that most of the local owners on this beach were killed in the tsunami and surviving locals are afraid to move back. The exceptions are the big resorts that are owned by multinationals or Bangkok big wigs – this is the main type of rebuilding that has happened along the waterfront and, thus, it's become a decidedly midrange to upscale area.

Sleeping & Eating

There are just a few hotels along this pretty stretch of beach, making it an ideal romantic hideaway.

Similana Resort (☎ 0 7648 7166; www.similana resort.com; r 2900-6500B; ⊗) Each bungalow here is a small work of art, with handcrafted furnishings, dark-wood floors, quilted bedcovers, bay windows and private decks with panoramic views. Try traveller-recommended tree houses nestled in the forest, which descends down to the sand. Similana is a romantic place that is rather secluded. The beach here is lovely, however, and there's a good on-site restaurant so there's little reason to leave.

Sarojin (☎ 0 7642 7900-4; www.sarojin.com; r 12,500-23,250B; ⊗ ⊡ ⊗) A quiet retreat with a Japanese-meets-modern-Thai style, service here is stellar and the whole setting (there are only 56 rooms) is elegant and intimate. The very private spa, which takes in views of coconut groves and mangroves, has a very good reputation. We especially love the pool with its stylish lounging huts that hover above the crystal blue water like little islands. The hotel is also a contributor to community tsunami recovery projects. The hotel has two ambient restaurants and a bar as well as the option to take your meal to your room or enjoy it as a picnic on the beach.

Getting There & Away

Buses running between Takua Pa and Phuket will get you here; just ask to be let off at Hat Bang Sak. From Khao Lak catch a frequent sǒrng·tǎa·ou (15B) between 8.30am and 5pm.

HAT KHAO LAK
หาดเขาหลัก

As the most practical base for exploring the Similan and Surin islands as well as the main-

land wonders of Khao Sok and Khao Lak/Lam Ru National Parks, it's no wonder that the beautiful, bronze beach of Khao Lak has been experiencing a tourist gold rush in recent years. After the area's near total devastation from the Boxing Day tsunami and subsequent rebuilding, resorts have been flinging open their doors, tourists (especially divers) have been flooding in and new infrastructure has been laid down at a terrific rate.

Nowadays Khao Lak has a bit of a package tour vibe, and there are shops, restaurants, bars and tour offices covering every square inch of space along the highway. Towards the beach it gets much quieter and you can almost forget that you're sharing the town with hundreds of others as you watch the lazy sun disappear into an orange hue on the horizon.

Internet is available at any of a slew of tour agents in the town centre, and banks and ATMs are seemingly everywhere to entice you to buy, buy, buy.

Sights & Activities
TREKKING & BOAT TRIPS

The area immediately south of Hat Khao Lak has been incorporated into the vast 125-sq-km **Khao Lak/Lam Ru National Park** (☎ 0 7642 0243; www.dnp.go.th; adult/child 200/100B; ⊗ 8am-4.30pm), a beautiful collection of sea cliffs, 1000m hills, beaches, estuaries, forested valleys and mangroves. Wildlife seen in the park includes hornbills, drongos, tapirs, gibbons, monkeys and Asiatic black bears. The visitors centre, just off Hwy 4 between the 56km and 57km markers, has little in the way of maps or printed information, but there's a very nice open-air restaurant perched on a shady slope overlooking the sea. From the restaurant you can take a fairly easy 3km round-trip nature trail that heads along the cape and ends at an often deserted sandy Hat Lek beach.

Guided treks along the coast or inland can be arranged through many tour agencies in town, as can long-tail boat trips up the scenic **Khlong Thap Liang** estuary. The latter affords opportunities to view mangrove communities of crab-eating macaques. Between Khao Lak and Bang Sak is a network of sandy **beach trails** – some of which lead to deserted beaches – which are fun to explore on foot or by rented motorcycle. Most of the hotels in town rent out motorbikes for 250B per day.

About 2.5km north of Hat Khao Lak, **Hat Bang Niang** was also flattened by the tsunami, but is well worth a trip if you are looking for a little more peace and quiet.

DIVING & SNORKELLING

Diving or snorkelling day-excursions to the Similan and Surin islands are immensely popular, but if you can, opt for a live-aboard. Since the islands are around 60km away from the mainland (about three hours by boat), you'll have a more relaxing trip as well as be able to experience the islands without day-tripper crowds if you stay the night or longer. All dive shops offer live-aboard trips for around 6500/10,000/13,500B for one-/two-/three-day packages and day trips for 4900B to 5900B.

Although geared towards divers, all dive shops cater to snorkellers who can hop on selected dive excursions or live-aboards for a discount of around 40%; otherwise, tour agencies all around town offer even cheaper snorkelling trips for around 2700B. PADI Open Water certification courses cost around 16,000B or you can do a first test dive in the Similans on a 'discover scuba' day trip for around 7400B.

Recommended dive shops (all along Th Petchkasem) include the following:

Sea Dragon Dive Center (☎ 0 7642 0420; www.sea dragondivecenter.com) Specialises in live-aboards and is one of the few centres to reliably offer trips year-round. It has an impeccable reputation.

Sub Aqua (☎ 0 7648 5165; www.subaqua-divecenter .com) Owns great big boats that herd divers and snorkellers out to the islands on day trips.

Wicked Diving (☎ 0 7648 5868; www.wickeddiving .com) A new, exceptionally well-run and environmentally conscious outfit that runs diving and snorkelling overnight trips, where you can sleep in national-park bungalows, as well as a range of live-aboards and open water certification options.

Sleeping

Backpacker accommodation predominates in the busy and congested centre of town, while grand resorts dominate the outskirts of town along the coast and now offer some of the swankiest beds this side of Phuket.

BUDGET

Fasai House (☎ 0 7648 5867; www.fasaihouse.com; r 500-700B; ❄ 🖳) Apartment block–style rooms are plain, but big, modern and super comfy for the price. The staff get our highest marks for service.

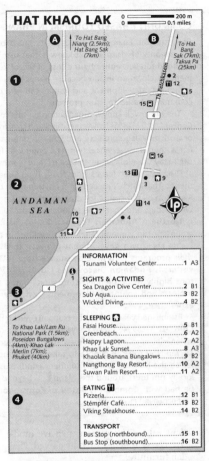

HAT KHAO LAK

INFORMATION	
Tsunami Volunteer Center..............	1 A3

SIGHTS & ACTIVITIES	
Sea Dragon Dive Center...............	2 B1
Sub Aqua.............................	3 B2
Wicked Diving.......................	4 B2

SLEEPING 🛏	
Fasai House...........................	5 B1
Greenbeach...........................	6 A2
Happy Lagoon........................	7 A2
Khao Lak Sunset.....................	8 A3
Khaolak Banana Bungalows........	9 B2
Nangthong Bay Resort...............	10 A2
Suwan Palm Resort..................	11 A2

EATING 🍴	
Pizzeria..............................	12 B1
Stémpfer Café.......................	13 B2
Viking Steakhouse...................	14 B2

TRANSPORT	
Bus Stop (northbound)...............	15 B1
Bus Stop (southbound)..............	16 B2

ourpick **Khaolak Banana Bungalows** (☎ 0 7648 5889; www.khaolakbanana.com; 4/147 Moo 7 Kukkak; bungalows 500-1200B; ❄ 🖳) The adorable little bungalows here have swirly painted cement floors, bright yellow exteriors and indoor/outdoor bathrooms with giant ceramic Thai-style pots to take a splash shower – as well as Western showerheads. All rooms have safety boxes and there's a cute pool surrounded by deck chairs.

Happy Lagoon (☎ 0 7642 3408; r 600-1200B; ❄) A short hop from the beach, this somewhat cheesy spot, complete with fake concrete karsts, has a popular open-air restaurant-bar that lends the whole place a lively air. Bungalows that extend back into a garden maze are clean, have hot water and are

COMMUNITY BASED TOURISM IN PHANG-NGA PROVINCE

Post tsunami, Phang-Nga looks pretty much back to normal if you stay in tourist areas. What the majority of visitors don't know is that many fishing communities have had their way of life changed forever, either by the loss of life of key family members, destruction of fishing equipment or relocation inland because of necessity or fear. Recovery nowadays is taking the form of community development and visitors can help out by taking part in one of the region's fabulous community based tourism projects.

The most well-known organisation on this coast is the excellent, Thai-run **Tsunami Volunteer Center** (☎ 0 7648 5541; www.tsunamivolunteer.net) in Khao Lak. Volunteers are needed to teach English or work on village projects, and you can simultaneously take Thai language and cooking courses. For a shorter experience, two-day, one-night homestay tours are available from 3000B. If you can't stay the night, at least take its very worthwhile **'Post Tsunami Experience' tour** (tour 100B; ⏲ 9am Tue), which leaves from Nang Tong Supermarket in central Khao Lak and includes an authentic Thai lunch. Proceeds and anything you buy along the way help support local economies. Also stop by the centre for drop-in Thai cooking (200B) or language (100B) classes at 3pm every Wednesday, and check the schedule for occasional craft and dancing classes.

Northern Andaman Tsunami Relief (NATR; www.northandamantsunamirelief.com) began as a volunteer-run tsunami relief organisation, but as needs changed it began to help communities create their own development projects; today the communities are self-sufficiently running their programs with little assistance from NATR. The NATR success story of most interest to visitors is **Andaman Discoveries** (☎ 08 7917 7165; www.andamandiscoveries.com; Khuraburi), which runs highly recommended community-based tours including homestays, community-service projects and volunteer placement – whatever you decide to do, it will be an unforgettable experience.

Established years before the tsunami even hit the Andaman Coast, the **Koh Yao Noi Eco-Tourism Club** (☎ 0 7659 7409; www.koh-yao-noi-eco-tourism-club.com) is the happy and successful fruit of island visionaries who were concerned about the effects of tourism on their tiny Muslim fishing isle of Ko Yao Noi. You can choose to take a simple homestay (150B per person per night plus a 100B fee to the Koh Yao Noi Environment Fund) plus three meals (150B per person per day), or add locally run tours around the island and beyond from 300B per person. A similar experience can be had with **Community Based of Kohyaohomestay** (☎ 0 7659 7428; www.kohyaohomestay.com; r per person incl meals 650B).

---

excellent value. The more expensive models have classy touches such as carved Thai wooden furniture.

MIDRANGE

Poseidon Bungalows (☎ 0 7644 3258; www.similantour.com; bungalows 900-1400B) On the other side of the headland from Khao Lak/Lam Ru National Park, about 4km south of Hat Khao Lak, this quiet spot has huts that are discreetly dispersed among huge boulders and coastal forest, affording plenty of privacy. The socially and environmentally conscious proprietors dispense information on the area and organise boat excursions and dive trips to the local reef and to the Similan Islands. The restaurant serves Thai and European food.

Greenbeach (☎ 0 7648 5845; greenbeach_th@yahoo.com; bungalows 1200-2000B; ⏲) On an excellent stretch of beach and extending back into a packed-mud garden, the nicest bungalows here are actually the fan-cooled ones, which are large and have louvred wooden doors. All bungalows have woven bamboo walls and tiny terraces.

Khao Lak/Lam Ru National Park Bungalows (☎ 0 2562 0760; reserve@dnp.go.th; bungalows 1200-2500B) There is a handful of four- and six-bed bungalows in the national park. Standards are basic, but the setting will suit those after an eco-experience. Perfect for ramblers.

our pick Nangthong Bay Resort (☎ 0 7648 5088; www.nangthongbayresort.de; r 1200-3000B; ⏲ 🖵 🖳) This is the best midranger on the beach and it's no secret, so it fills up fast. Rooms are designed with a sparse black-and-white chic décor and have bathrooms that open up to the bedrooms. The cheapest rooms are set back from the beach but are fantastic value with views of the sea. Grounds are lush and service is excellent.

Khao Lak Sunset (☎ 0 7642 0075; Th Petchkasem; r 2690-3490B; ✕ 🏊) What this last generation resort lacks in style, it makes up for with a prime beachfront location and good service. Prices are good and if you want a comfy sleep without blowing big bucks, you can't go wrong here. It's at the southern end of town.

TOP END

Suwan Palm Resort (☎ 0 7648 5830; www.suwan palm.com; Hat Nang Thong; r 2800-9500B; ✕ ⬛ 🏊) Rechristened after the tsunami (it used to be the Khaolak Orchid Resortel), this hotel has rooms with floor-to-ceiling glass doors opening onto a patio overlooking the water. Beautiful! The rooms are tastefully decorated with light teak furniture. Beds are firm and the air-con can be a tad noisy. The on-site restaurant and Irish pub add lively ambience come dark.

Khao Lak Merlin (☎ 0 7642 8300; www.khaolak-hotels .com/khaolakmerlin; Hwy 4; r 6800-35,000B; ✕ ⬛ 🏊) This majestic resort 7km south of town features a maze of swimming pools, colonial meets Zen–style rooms and creature comforts aplenty, all amongst 15 acres of lush gardens. The beach here is as quiet as it is lovely and all the privacy makes this a splurge-worthy romantic getaway.

Eating

All midrange to top-end resorts have their own atmospheric but expensive restaurants, but there are heaps of simple, very good restaurants – mostly specialising in seafood – along the main road.

Stémpfer Café (breakfast around 60B; sandwiches 90-120B; ⏰ 9am-10pm) An excellent German bakery serving the best coffee in town, as well as healthy and not-so-healthy breakfasts, sandwiches, fresh bread, light Thai meals, ice cream (20B a scoop) and cocktails.

Viking Steakhouse (☎ 0 7642 0815; Th Petchkasem; mains 140-600B; ⏰ breakfast, lunch & dinner) Offering a fine line in pizzas, pastas and Nordic meat feasts, this is a longstanding favourite. The cosy, open-fronted interior features all sorts of welcome trimmings.

our pick Pizzeria (☎ 0 7648 5271; mains 200-380B; ⏰ noon-11pm) The footpath setting here on the northern part of the main drag is pretty bleak, but by Georgio! – the authentic and rich Italian dishes are phenomenal. We loved the

gnocchi and lasagne, and just the look of the pizzas brought us back in for another go.

Getting There & Away

Any bus running along Hwy 4 between Takua Pa (50B, 45 minutes) and Phuket (80B, two hours) will stop at Hat Khao Lak if you ask the driver. Buses will also stop near the Merlin resort and the Khao Lak/Lam Ru National Park headquarters. By taxi it's only one hour to Phuket Airport (1500B).

SIMILAN ISLANDS MARINE NATIONAL PARK (MU KO SIMILAN NATIONAL PARK)
อุทยานแห่งชาติหมู่เกาะสิมิลัน

Known to divers the world over, beautiful **Similan Islands Marine National Park** (www.dnp.go.th; admission 400B; ⏰ Nov-May) is 70km offshore. Its smooth granite islands are as impressive above water as below, topped with rainforest, edged with white-sand beaches and fringed with coral reef.

Two of the nine islands here, Island 4 (Ko Miang) and Island 8 (Ko Similan), have ranger stations and accommodation; park headquarters and most visitor activity centres are on Island 4. 'Similan' comes from the Malay word *sembilan*, meaning 'nine', and while each island is named, they're more commonly known by their numbers.

Khao Lak is the jumping-off point for the park. The pier is at Thap Lamu, about 10km south of town, where you'll find a cluster of tour operators. The **mainland park office** (☎ 0 7659 5045; ⏰ 8am-4pm) is about 500m before the pier, but there's no information in English available.

Sights & Activities
DIVING & SNORKELLING

The Similans offer exceptional diving for all levels of experience, at depths from 2m to 30m. There are seamounts (at **Fantasy Rocks**), rock reefs (at **Ko Payu**) and dive-throughs (at **Hin Pousar** or 'Elephant-head'), with marine life ranging from tiny plume worms and soft corals to schooling fish and whale sharks. There are dive sites at each of the six islands north of Ko Miang; the southern part of the park (Islands 1, 2 and 3) is off-limits to divers and is a turtle nesting ground. No facilities for divers exist in the national park itself, so you'll need to take a dive tour. Agencies in Khao Lak and Phuket book dive trips (three-

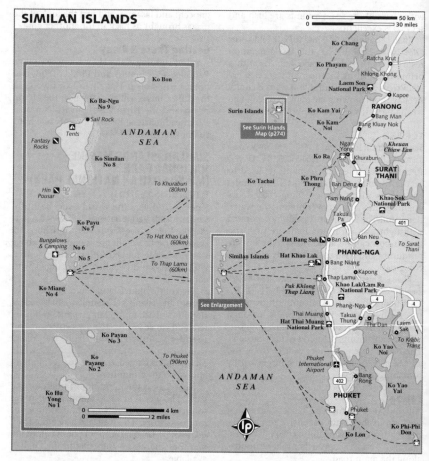

SIMILAN ISLANDS

day live-aboards from around 13,500B). The best Similan Islands for diving are Island 9, which has excellent coral slopes, and Islands 5 and 6.

If you're a snorkeller trying to decide between the Surin or Similan islands, opt for the Surin Islands where the majority of corals are relatively close to the surface. That said, snorkelling is good at several points around Island 4, especially in the main channel, and on Islands 7 and 8; you can hire snorkel gear from the park headquarters (per day 100B). Day-tour operators usually visit three or four different snorkelling sites. Plenty of tour agencies in Khao Lak offer snorkelling-only trips (day trips 2700B, three-day live-aboard trips around 8000B). See p277 for more details.

WILDLIFE & HIKING

The forest around park headquarters on Ko Miang has a couple of walking trails and some great wildlife. The fabulous Nicobar pigeon, with its wild mane of grey-green feathers, is common here. Endemic to the islands of the Andaman Sea, it's one of some 39 bird species in the park. Hairy-legged land crabs and flying foxes (or fruit bats) are relatively easily seen in the forest, as are flying squirrels.

Small Beach Track, with information panels, leads 400m to a tiny, pretty snorkelling bay. Detouring from it, the **Viewpoint Trail** – 500m or so of steep scrambling – has panoramic vistas from the top. A 500m walk to **Sunset Point** takes you through forest to a smooth granite platform facing – obviously – west.

On Ko Similan there's a 2.5km forest hike to a **viewpoint**, and a shorter, steep scramble off the main beach to the top of **Sail Rock**.

Sleeping & Eating

Accommodation in the park is available for all budgets. Book online at www.dnp.go.th or with the mainland **national park office** (☎ 0 7659 5045) at Khao Lak. Tour agents in Khao Lak also arrange overnight to multiday trips that include transport, food and lodging at the park – these cost little more than it would to go solo.

On Ko Miang there are sea-view **bungalows** (r 2000B; ❉) with balconies; two dark five-room wood-and-bamboo **longhouses** (r 1000B) with fans; and crowded on-site **tents** (2-person 570B). There's electricity from 6pm to 6am.

On-site tents are also available on Ko Similan. You can pitch your own **tent** (per night 80B) on either island.

A **restaurant** (dishes 100B) near park headquarters serves simple Thai food.

Getting There & Away

There's no public transport to the park, but independent travellers can book a speedboat transfer (return 1700B, 1½ hours one way) with a day-tour operator. They will collect you from Phuket or Khao Lak, but if you book through national parks (which uses the same tour-operators' boats anyway), be aware that you'll have to find your own way to their office, and then wait for a transfer to the pier.

Agencies in Khao Lak and Phuket book day/overnight tours (from around 2500/3500B) and dive trips (three-day live-aboards from around 11,000B), and generally these cost little more than what you'd pay trying to get to the islands independently.

AO PHANG-NGA & PHANG-NGA

อ่าวพังงา/อ.เมืองพังงา

pop 11,000

With turquoise bays, peppered with craggy limestone rock towers, soda white beaches and tumbledown fishing villages, Ao Phang-Nga is one of the region's most spectacular escapes. Little wonder then that it was here, among the towering cliffs and the swifts' nests, that James Bond's nemesis, the Man with the Golden Gun, chose to build his lair. Wanted assassins with goals of world domination would not be recommended to hide out here nowa-

days though, since the area is swarming with tourists in motorboats and sea kayaks nearly year-round. Much of the bay, and some of the coastline, has now been incorporated into the Ao Phang-Nga National Park (p283).

Information

Phang-Nga town doesn't have a tourist office, but the one in Phuket Town (p300) provides maps and good information on the region. **Immigration office** (☎ 0 7641 2011; ☽ 8.30am-4.30pm Mon-Fri) A few kilometres south of town; you'll probably never find it on your own, so take a motorcycle taxi. **Siam Commercial Bank** (Hwy 4; ☽ 9am-4pm Mon-Fri) On the main road through town; has an ATM and exchange facilities.

Sights & Activities

The old 'city of contrasts' cliché really does apply to the town of Phang-Nga: it is a scruffy, luckless town in a sublime location. It backs up against some beautiful limestone cliffs and, while the main street looks rather downtrodden, there is a handful of decent places to bed down for the night. There isn't a whole lot to see or do unless you happen to be here during the annual **Vegetarian Festival** in October (see p302).

About 8.5km south of the town centre is Tha Dan. From here, you can charter boats to see half-submerged **caves**, oddly shaped islands and **Ko Panyi**, a Muslim village on stilts. There are tours to **Ko Phing Kan** ('James Bond Island'; the island rock in *The Man with the Golden Gun*) and Ao Phang-Nga National Park (500B per person for a two- to three-hour tour). Takua Thung, another pier area about 10km further west of Tha Dan, also has private boats for hire for similar prices; ask at the restaurants. The park office, inside Ao Phang-Nga National Park (p283) also offers boat tours.

Unless you enjoy haggling with boatmen, it's much easier (and not that expensive) to go with an organised tour through an agency in town. **Sayan Tours** (☎ 0 7643 0348; www.sayantour .com) has been doing tours of Ao Phang-Nga for many years now, and continues to receive good reviews from travellers. Half-/full-day tours cost from 500/800B per person and include **Tham Lawt** (a large water cave), Ko Phing Kan and Ko Panyi, among other destinations. Meals and very rustic accommodation on Ko Panyi are part of the longer packages (750B to 1000B).

NORTHERN ANDAMAN COAST

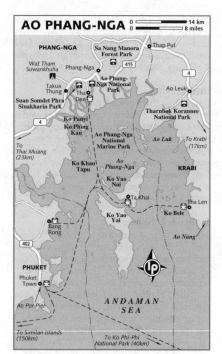

The overnight trip is a less rushed way to see the area, but Ko Panyi has seen so many visitors over the years that the warm welcome guests once experienced in homestays has become a rarity – while it was an interesting experience, we felt unwanted in this active fishing village that must relish its privacy after peak tourist hours. Sayan Tours also offers **kayaking trips** and tours to other nearby destinations, including Sa Nang Manora Forest Park and the various caves near town.

MR Kean Tours (☎ 0 7643 0619) is another option, and has offices at the bus terminal in the centre of town. There are also kayaking tours available from Phuket (see p297).

Sleeping

Phang-Nga Guest House (☎ 0 7641 1358; Th Petchkasem; r 250-380B; ☒) On the whole, this is a gloom-free zone that was getting a fresh coat of pastel paint in the rooms when we passed. Staff are helpful and the clean, basic rooms with TVs are a bargain.

ourpick **Phang-Nga Inn** (☎ 0 7641 1963; 2/2 Soi Lohakit; r 400-1600B; ☒) This converted residential villa is an absolute gem with its heavy wood staircases, louvred cabinets and peaceful gardens. It's well furnished (comfy beds year-round but hot water in the high season only), there's a little eatery and the staff are gracious. The most expensive room is the massive family suite.

Old Lukmuang Hotel (☎ 0 7641 2125; fax 0 7641 1512; 1/2 Muu 1, Th Petchkasem; r 450B) This place is awfully dingy, but Bond fanatics will be interested to know that it housed some of the crew from *The Man with the Golden Gun* when they based themselves here during filming.

Phang-Nga Bay Resort Hotel (☎ 0 7641 2067; fax 0 7641 2070; Th Petchkasem; r from 2000B; ☒) The views across the bay are great, but this flaky old-timer has certainly seen better days. The rooms still come with plenty of amenities (TV, fridge), but whether they work is something of a lottery. It's 8.5km south of town, in Tha Dan.

Eating

Several food stalls on the main street of Phang-Nga sell delicious *kà·nŏm jeen* (thin wheat noodles) with chicken curry, *nám yah* (spicy ground-fish curry) or *nám prík* (spicy sauce). *Roti gaang* (fried flatbread dipped in mild curry sauce, served with jam or fruit fillings) is available from the morning market, which is open from 5am to 10am daily. There's also a small night market on Tuesday, Wednesday and Thursday evenings, located just south of Soi Lohakit.

If you're coming in from Phuket, keep an eye out for Food Safety St – 1km past the New Lukmuang Hotel, next to the Caltex petrol station. At night, it's filled with excellent – and presumably hygiene-conscious – food stalls.

Cha-Leang (☎ 0 7641 3831; Th Petchkasem; dishes 40-90B; ☻ lunch & dinner) The best – and often busiest – eatery in town cooks up a smorgasbord of well-priced seafood dishes. Try the 'clams with basil leaf and chilli' or 'edible inflorescence of banana plant salad'. There's a pleasant veranda out the back.

Bismilla (☎ 0 1125 6440; Th Petchkasem; mains 60-120B; ☻ lunch & dinner) With dishes such as 'yum fish's spawn' on the menu, how can you resist an evening at this basic Thai-Muslim outfit? The food is good and the prices are excellent.

Getting There & Away

If you're arriving in the Ao Phang-Nga area from Krabi on Hwy 4, you can go two ways. After Thap Put, you can either continue straight on Hwy 4 or go left onto Hwy 415. Turning onto 415 will keep you on the shorter, straighter path, while staying on Hwy 4 will take you onto a narrow, very curvy and pretty stretch of highway, which is 5km longer than the direct route. It's your choice.

Phang-Nga's bus terminal is located just off the main street on Soi Bamrung Rat. Bangkok buses to/from Phang-Nga include VIP (685B, 12 hours, one daily), 1st class (441B to 459B, 12 to 13 hours, two daily) and 2nd class (357B, 12 hours, three to four daily). There are several other services available:

Destination	Price	Frequency	Duration
Hat Yai	250B	2 daily	6hr
Ko Pha-Ngan	580B	2 daily	6hr
Ko Samui	480B	2 daily	5hr
Krabi	100B	frequent	1½hr
Phuket	80B	frequent	1½hr
Ranong	160B	4 daily	5hr
Satun	292B	2 daily	6hr
Surat Thani	160B	9 daily	3hr
Trang	150B	frequent	3½hr

Getting Around

Most places in town are accessible on foot. Motorcycle taxis around town cost 20B.

Sayan Tours (p281), located at the bus terminal, can assist with motorcycle rental (200B per day). Sŏrng·tăa·ou/motorcycle taxis to Tha Dan cost 20/40B.

AROUND PHANG-NGA
Ao Phang-Nga National Park
อุทยานแห่งชาติอ่าวพังงา

Established in 1981 and covering an area of 400 sq km, **Ao Phang-Nga National Park** (☎ 07641 1136; www.dnp.go.th; admission 200B; ☒ 8am-4pm) is noted for its classic karst scenery created by fault movements on the mainland that pushed massive limestone blocks into geometric patterns. As these blocks extend southwards into Ao Phang-Nga, they form over 40 islands with huge vertical cliffs. The bay itself is composed of large and small tidal channels that originally connected with the mainland fluvial system. The main tidal channels – Khlong Ko Phanyi, Khlong Phang-Nga, Khlong Bang Toi and Khlong Bo Saen – run through vast mangroves in a north–south direction and today are used by fisherfolk and island inhabitants as aquatic highways. These mangroves are the largest remaining primary mangrove forests in Thailand. Over 80% of the area

within the park boundaries is covered by the Andaman Sea.

The biggest tourist drawcard in the park is the so-called James Bond Island, known to Thais as **Ko Phing Kan** (literally 'Leaning on Itself Island'). Once used as a location setting for *The Man with the Golden Gun*, the island is now full of vendors hawking coral and shells that should have stayed in the sea, along with butterflies, scorpions and spiders encased in plastic.

There are a couple of **caves** you can walk through and a couple of small sand **beaches**, often littered with rubbish from tourist boats. About the only positive development has been the addition of a concrete pier so that tourist boats don't have to moor directly on the island's beaches, but this still happens when the water level is high and the pier is crowded with other boats.

PLANTS & ANIMALS

Two types of forest predominate in the park: limestone scrub forest and true evergreen forest. The marine limestone environment favours a long list of reptiles, including Bengal monitor lizards, flying lizards, banded sea snakes, dogface water snakes, shore pit vipers and Malayan pit vipers. Keep an eye out for a two-banded (or water) monitor (*Varanus salvator*), which looks like a crocodile when seen swimming in the mangrove swamp and can measure up to 2.2m in length.

Amphibians in the Ao Phang-Nga region include marsh frogs, common bush frogs and crab-eating frogs. Avian residents of note are helmeted hornbills (the largest of Thailand's 12 hornbill species, with a body length of up to 127cm), the edible-nest swiftlets (*Aerodramus fuciphagus*), white-bellied sea eagles, ospreys and Pacific reef egrets.

In the mangrove forests and on some of the larger islands reside over 200 species of mammals, including white-handed gibbons, serows, dusky langurs and crab-eating macaques.

ROCK ART

Many of the limestone islands in Ao Phang-Nga feature prehistoric rock art painted or carved onto the walls and ceilings of caves, rock shelters, cliffs and rock massifs. In particular you can see rock art on Khao Khian, Ko Panyi, Ko Raya, Tham Nak and Ko Phra At Thao. Khao Khian (Inscription Mountain) is probably the most visited of the sites. The images contain scenes of human figures, fish, crabs, shrimp, bats, birds and elephants, as well as boats and fishing equipment – it's obvious this was some sort of communal effort tied to the all-important harvesting of sustenance from the sea. Some drawings also contain rows of lines thought to be some sort of cabbalistic writing. The rock paintings don't fall on any one plane of reference; they may be placed right-side up, upside-down or sideways. Most of the paintings are monochrome, while some have been traced several times over in orange-yellow, blue, grey and black.

SLEEPING & EATING
National Park Bungalows (☎ 0 2562 0760; reserve@dnp.go.th; bungalows 700-900B; ☒) These are on the mainland, near the park headquarters. The cheaper bungalows sleep four and are fan-cooled; the pricier air-con bungalows sleep two. Camping is permitted in certain areas within park boundaries but you should ask permission at the office first.

There's a small, clean restaurant in front of the office with views looking out over the mangroves.

GETTING THERE & AROUND
From the centre of town, drive about 6km south on Hwy 4, then turn left onto Rte 4144 (the road to Tha Dan) and travel 2.6km to the park headquarters. Without your own transport you'll need to take a sŏrng·tǎa·ou to Tha Dan (20B).

From the park office, you can hire a boat (1000B, maximum four passengers) for a 2½-hour tour of the surrounding islands.

Ko Yao
เกาะยาว
The pretty islands of **Ko Yao Yai** (Big Long Island) and **Ko Yao Noi** (Little Long Island) are part of the Ao Phang-Nga National Park (p283) and are about as photogenic as the park gets. Encompassing 137 sq km of knotted forest, pristine beach and unspoilt shoreline, they offer a great vantage point for kicking back and soaking up the bay's beautiful scenery.

Despite being the relative pipsqueak, Ko Yao Noi is the main population centre of the two, with fishing, coconut farming and tourism sustaining its small, year-round population. **Hat Pa Sai** and **Hat Tha Khao** are excellent beaches, but bring along a mountain bike

(pick one up from your resort in Phuket) if you want to explore the island's numerous dirt trails. **Ta Khai**, the largest settlement on Ko Yao Noi, is a subdistrict government seat and the source of minimal supplies. Boat trips to neighbouring islands are possible.

Ko Yao Yai is less developed than Ko Yao Noi. **Hat Lo Paa Raet** and **Hat Tiikut** are the island's best beaches – the former lined with coconut palms, the latter with casuarina trees. **Koh Yao Diving Centre** (☎ 0 9724 5134; www.kohyaodiving.com) on the west coast leads dives around Phang-Nga and beyond.

Ko Bele, a small island east of the twin Ko Yao, features a large tidal lagoon, three white-sand beaches, and easily accessible caves and coral reefs.

There's an ATM in the village on Ko Yao Noi but it tends to break down so make sure you have plenty of cash in-pocket.

Please remember to respect the beliefs of the local Muslim population and wear modest clothing when away from the beaches.

SLEEPING & EATING
Ko Yao Noi
Once known for its budget digs, Ko Yao Noi is seeing a lot of development these days, much of it upscale – there's not much here for midrangers. Another sleeping option is a homestay – see p278 for details.

Sabai Corner Bungalows (☎ 0 1892 7827; www.sabaicornerbungalows.com; bungalows 500-2000B) There's a great social ambience here led by Colin, a long-time British expat and rather special character. Bungalows are sturdy thatch-and-wood with small verandas; the cheapest ones have rudimentary shared bathrooms. The restaurant is quite good and you get the usual fabulous views.

Tha Khao Bungalow (☎ 0 1676 7726; www.kohyaobungalow.com; bungalows 550-1200B) Thatch-and-wood bungalows are the staple at these Hat Tha Khao digs. It's well set up for tourists, rents out bikes and kayaks, and features a restaurant serving tasty food.

Pasai Bungalows (☎ 0 7659 7064; bungalows 600-700B) Across the street from a little white beach, these tidy, wooden bungalows are great value. Management is super friendly and there's a social café-bar out front.

Island Nature Lodge (☎ 08 9868 8639; www.thailandbirdwatching.com/kohyao_nature_camp.html; bungalows incl breakfast 700-900B) Stay in one of these tidy bamboo-thatched numbers if you're into birding, mountain biking or just getting a taste of secluded beach and jungle.

ourpick Lom Lea (☎ 08 9868 8642; www.lomlae .com; bungalows 2100-5000B) The stylish, naturalist wooden bungalows here are fronted by a stunning and secluded beach with views of Phang-Nga's signature karst islands. There's a dive centre, a good restaurant and plenty of activities on offer. We found the bungalows a bit rustic for the price, but the setting and service do merit extra baht.

Koyao Island Resort (☎ 0 1606 1517; www.koyao .com; villas from 8060-11,200B; ✄ ▣ ▨) Open-plan, thatched bungalows offer serene views across a palm-shaded garden and infinity pool to a skinny white beach. We love the elegant, near safari-esque feel of the villas here, with their fan-cooled patios and indoor/outdoor bathrooms. There's a busy and posh restaurant-bar and service is stellar.

Six Senses Hideaway (☎ 0 7641 8500; www.sixsenses .com/hideaway-yaonoi; r 32,000-74,250B; ✄ ▣ ▨) This is an over-the-top luxury resort where all rooms – which are essentially ultra-chic house complexes – have their own pool and butler service. Of course there's the signature Six Senses Spa, which is one of the best in the region. If you can afford to stay here, you may as well take advantage of the resort's helicopter service from Phuket.

Ko Yao Yai

With fewer lodging choices, Ko Yao Yai offers a more remote and wild getaway.

Halavee Resort (☎ 0 7881 1238; halawee_r@yahoo .co.th; bungalows 500-1000B) Inland from the pier on Prunai Rd and perched on a hillside with panoramic views, this popular place doesn't have much charm but is well-run and well-priced.

YaoYai Island Resort (☎ 08 9471 9110; www.yao yairesort.com; bungalows 1200-2200B; ✄) Located on the gem of a beach at Loh Pared on the western side of the island and with sunset views, the bungalows here are comfy and there's plenty to do despite the remote setting. There's an on-site restaurant and a great laid-back vibe.

GETTING THERE & AROUND

Although both islands fall within the Phang-Nga Province boundaries, the easiest places to find boat transport to Ko Yao Noi and Ko Yao Yai are Phuket (Phuket Province) and Krabi. In Phuket Town, catch a sŏrng·tǎa·ou from the front of the day market to the public

pier at Bang Rong (on Ao Po) for 40B. From here, there are up to six boats daily between 8am and 5pm – the 12.30pm boat is the most reliable from May to November. Alternatively, there are boats at 10am and 4pm from Tha Ao Por near Phuket Town, at 11am and 1pm from Krabi's Tha Len and at 1pm from Tha Dan in Phang-Nga. All boats cost 100B each way and take between one and two hours. Once you arrive on Ko Yao Noi, it's 70B to 100B for transport to the resorts.

To get from Ko Yao Noi to Ko Yao Yai, catch a shuttle boat from Tha Manok (20B, 15 minutes). On the islands, you can travel by túk-túk (pronounced dúk dúk; motorised vehicle) for about 80B per ride.

Suan Somdet Phra Sinakharin Park
สวนสมเด็จพระศรีนครินทร์

This public **park** (admission free; ☼ dawn-dusk) has two entrances. The most dramatic is through a huge hole in a limestone cliff near the Phang-Nga Bay Resort Hotel (p282), in Tha Dan. The main – less scenic – entrance is at the southern end of Phang-Nga. The park is surrounded by limestone cliffs and bluffs, cut through with caves and tunnels. Wooden walkways link the water-filled caverns so that visitors can admire the ponds and amazing limestone formations. One of the larger caves, **Tham Reusi Sawan**, is marked by a gilded statue of a reu·sĕe (Hindu sage) – complete with tiger skins. The other main cavern is known locally as **Tham Luk Seua** (Tiger Cub Cave).

Sa Nang Manora Forest Park
สวนป่าสระนางมโนราห์

This beautiful and little-visited **park** (admission free; ☼ dawn-dusk) features an impressive fairyland setting, with lots of dense rainforest, rattan vines, moss-encrusted roots and rocks and multilevel waterfalls with several pools suitable for swimming. Primitive trails run along (and at times through) the falls, level after level and beyond – you could easily get a full day's hiking in without walking along the same path twice. Bring plenty of drinking water – although the shade and the falls moderate the temperature, the humidity in the park is quite high.

The park's name comes from a local folk belief that the mythical Princess Manora bathes in the pools of the park when no one else is around. Facilities include some picnic tables and a small restaurant.

To get here, head north out of Phang-Nga on Hwy 4. Go 3.2km past the Shell petrol station, then turn left and go down a curvy road for another 4km. Motorcycle taxis from Phang-Nga cost 60B.

Wat Tham Suwankhuha
วัดถ้ำสุวรรณคูหา

A cave wát (temple), **Wat Tham Suwankhuha** (Heaven Grotto Temple; admission 10B; ☼ dawn-dusk) is full of Buddha images. The shrine consists of two main caverns, the larger one containing a 15m reclining Buddha and tiled with *lai·krahm* and *benjarong* (two coloured patterns more common in pottery), and the smaller cavern displaying spirit flags and a *reu·sĕe* statue. Royal seals of several kings, including Rama V, Rama VII and Rama IX – as well as those of lesser royalty – have been inscribed on one wall of the latter cave. Many monkeys hang around the area, and if you don't lock your car doors they're likely to break in to get at your travel snacks.

The wát is 10km southwest of Phang-Nga. To get here without your own transport, hop on any sŏrng·tăa·ou running between Phang-Nga and Takua Thung (30B). The wát is down a side road.

PHUKET PROVINCE

Just the name Phuket (poo-*get*) gets folks daydreaming; it's the ultimate tropical resort getaway where the sand is white, the sea is blue and the booze is cheap. And this island really does live up to expectations: the beaches all around the island are simply dazzling and there's one to suit every taste. Bad boy Patong hoovers in throngs of package tourists, partiers and the region's less savoury characters with its water sports à gogo, electric nightlife and girlie bars. A few notches down on the sleazy and cheesy scale, Hat Karon and Hat Kata are twin-resort, busybody socialites attracting holidaymakers who like to mingle and shop in between tanning sessions. Hat Surin and Ao Bang Thao offer a more refined and exclusive version of paradise, with private beaches and the gated and meticulously mowed Laguna Complex. The rest of the island houses the areas that don't fit the mould: the relatively undeveloped beaches of Nai Hang and Mai Khao, the real-life Thailand of Phuket Town, lush inland vistas and a few remote swathes of rainforest. Go with the tourist flow or branch off on your own; this island is big enough for everybody. In fact, Phuket is Thailand's largest and most populous island.

The region has been prosperous since the 19th century thanks to tin mining, sea trade and rubber plantations, but today it's tourists who bring in the big bucks. Luxury resorts are becoming more numerous and radically more luxurious – you can now get a room with its own private 9m pool as well as 24-hour butler service – and as higher-end foreigners holiday here or move in, prices on everything from backpacker lodging to transport will continue to soar.

Information
INTERNET RESOURCES

Phuket.com (www.phuket.com) Offers a sophisticated compendium of many kinds of information, including accommodation on the island.

Phuket-Info.com (www.phuket-info.com) You'll find more info on Phuket Province here.

Phuket.Net (www.phuket.net) An internet service that provides forums for tourism and business-oriented exchange, and has limited listings.

MEDICAL SERVICES

Both hospitals listed are equipped with modern facilities, emergency rooms and outpatient-care clinics. For information on dive-related medicine, see p288.

Bangkok Phuket Hospital (Map p287; ☎ 0 7625 4425; Th Yongyok.Uthit) Reputedly the favourite with locals.

Phuket International Hospital (Map p287; ☎ 0 7624 9400, emergency 0 7621 0935; Airport Bypass Rd) International doctors rate this hospital as the best on the island.

TOURIST INFORMATION

The weekly English-language *Phuket Gazette* (20B) publishes lots of information on activities, events, dining and entertainment in Phuket Town, and around the island. It can be accessed online at www.phuketgazette .net. The same publisher issues *Gazette Guide* (140B), a sizeable tome listing businesses and services on the island.

Dangers & Annoyances

Drownings are quite common on Phuket's beaches, especially on the western coast (Surin, Laem Singh and Kamala). Red flags are posted on beaches to warn bathers of

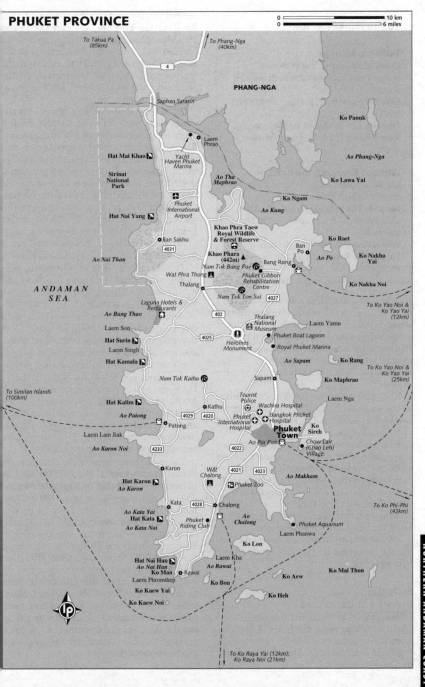

PHUKET PROVINCE

TOP 10 PHUKET RESORTS

Taking a Splurge

Chedi (p320) Location, location, location.

Indigo Pearl (p323) Hardware meets high-style Tropicana.

Layalina Hotel (p319) Boutique gem on a quiet beach.

Trisara (p323) The ultimate in Asian pampering.

Twin Palms (p320) A classic beauty in *haute couture*.

Without Breaking the Bank

Baipho & Baithong (p315) Serene spa-like design in the heart of the action.

Benyada Lodge (p320) Modern, chic comfort.

Casa Brazil (p312) Latin colours liven up a fun guesthouse.

Sino House (p303) Chinese-style luxury.

Sugar Palm Resort (p309) Young, fun and cosmopolitan.

---

riptides and other dangerous conditions. If a red flag is flying at a beach, don't go into the water. Especially during the May to October monsoon, the waves on the western coast of Phuket sometimes make it too dangerous to swim. Hat Rawai, on the southern edge of the island, is usually a safe bet at any time of year.

Keep an eye out for jet skis when you're in the water. Although the Phuket governor declared jet skis illegal in 1997, enforcement of the ban is cyclic.

Renting a motorcycle can be a high-risk proposition. Thousands of people are injured or killed every year on Phuket highways. Some have been travellers who weren't familiar with riding motorcycles and navigating the island's roads, highways and traffic patterns. If you must rent a motorcycle, make sure you at least know the basics and wear a helmet.

Recently there have been late-night motorbike muggings on the road leading from Patong to Hat Karon.

Activities

DIVING & SNORKELLING

Although there are scores of dive sites around Thailand, Phuket is at the heart of the Thai scuba diving industry and is one of the world's top 10 dive destinations. The island is ringed by good-to-excellent dive sites, including several small islands to the south (Ko Hae, Ko Raya Yai, Ko Raya Noi, Hin Daeng and Hin Muang) and to the east (Ko Yao Noi and Ko Yao Yai). Live-aboard excursions to the fantastic Surin and Similan islands, or to the Burma Banks/Mergui Archipelago off the southern coast of Myanmar, are also possible from Phuket.

Phuket has heaps of 'dive' shops – at last count there were over 100, though most of them are the equivalent of a booking agency. The more serious ones often operate their own boat(s) while others send you off with another operator, so ask if you're concerned. And it doesn't hurt if an operator is a five-star PADI dive centre, though this isn't always the best criterion for dive shops. Many of these operations are centred on Hat Patong, though the smaller beach towns certainly have their share. Some of the bigger (but not necessarily better) places have multiple branch offices all over Phuket.

Typical one-day dive trips to nearby sites cost around 3000B, including two dives and equipment. Nondivers (and snorkellers) are permitted to join such dive trips for a significant discount. PADI Open Water certification courses cost around 11,000B for four days of instruction and all equipment. Most places also rent out all the basic equipment.

It's very wise to obtain your own private diving insurance before travelling. PADI or DAN are best – regular insurance doesn't often cover diving accidents or decompression costs, but you could check with your insurance representative. Your dive shop will also have some insurance, but some shops have better insurance than others; ask.

There are three hyperbaric chambers on Phuket. **Wachira Hospital** (Map p287; ☎ 0 7621 1114; Th Taowarat) and **Phuket International Hospital** (Map p287; ☎ 0 7624 9400, emergency 0 7621 0935) are both just outside Phuket Town; a private **hyperbaric chamber** (Map p314; ☎ 0 7634 2518; 231-233 Th Rat Uthit) is in Patong. The chamber at Phuket International Hospital is considered the best of the three. Dive shop affiliation with the private hyperbaric chamber in Patong mostly means that clients who need to use that chamber will be charged US$200 rather than US$800 per hour of treatment (five-hour minimum), though if a dive shop has the right kind of insurance it will cover much of this cost. Again, ask for specifics if you're concerned.

(Continued on page 297)

Diving
& Other
Activities

Thailand's outstanding reef coral attracts eager divers from all over the world

Clownfish in familiar surrounds, Ko Phi-Phi (p343)
IMAGESTATE/ALAMY

top five

DIVE HUBS

Similan & Surin Islands (p279 and p274) A hushed tropical archipelago teeming with marine life that is mostly the domain of live-aboard divers. Check out Richelieu Rock – a stunning spot uncovered by Jacques Cousteau.

Ko Tao (p227) Fantastic frenetic dive energy and scores of world-class dive sites that are sometimes visited by plankton-chewing whale sharks. Sail Rock (closer to Ko Pha-Ngan) and Chumphon Pinnacle are the star sites.

Ko Phi-Phi (p343) A triumphant comeback after the tsunami with loads of shimmering reefs swaying under perfectly clear waters frequented by whale sharks. Hin Bida or Ko Bida Nok are the local faves as is the *King Cruiser* wreck.

Ko Lanta (p350) Another top spot for crystal-clear waters and loads of marine life, including recurrent visits by manta rays and whale sharks. Try the submerged pinnacles at Hin Daeng and Hin Muang.

Ko Chang Archipelago (p138) The diving is not quite as impressive as a number of the other hubs around the kingdom, but the reefs are more pristine.

A trip out to Thailand's delightful islands and beaches: days lounging under the shade of a coconut palm, evenings spent watching the fiery sunset – the true definition of paradise.

But after several extended sessions of muscle-shrivelling relaxation, it becomes increasingly difficult to avoid that little voice in your head encouraging you to go and explore. Good thing Thailand has some of the best scuba diving in the world, not to mention excellent hiking, rock climbing, caving and sea kayaking. There's so much to do that, at the end of your trip, you might find that you'll need a holiday from your holiday.

DIVING

Those who have explored the deep can undoubtedly agree with Jacques Cousteau: 'the sea, once it casts its spell, holds one in its net of wonder forever'. He also uttered 'the sea is the universal sewer', but he was definitely *not* referring to Thailand's mind-blowing dive sites. In fact, when Cousteau sang the sea's praises, he was probably talking about the Land of Smiles, since he himself discovered several of the sites explored by many today. Those who are willing to strap on some scuba gear can easily access this stunning realm, which rivals the beauty of the kingdom's idyllic on-land scenery.

For detailed information about the basic ins and outs of diving in Thailand, see p383. Recommended operators are listed in the destination chapters.

Andaman Coast vs Gulf Coast

The most popular dive sites throughout the kingdom are reef-encrusted limestone outcrops and submerged limestone pinnacles. These sights are often surrounded by deep water and act as feeding stations for large pelagic fish including manta rays, reef sharks and whale sharks. Underwater caverns, walls and seamounts are quickly gaining popularity as the 'established' sites become overrun with divers.

Thailand's unique coastal topography sits at the junction of two oceanic zones – the Andaman waters roll in from the west, while the gulf coast draws its waters from the islands of Indonesia and the South China Sea. The seas off both coasts benefit from their equatorial positioning and offer bathwater-warm temperatures of around 29°C throughout the year. Although the marine life is somewhat similar on both sides of the peninsula, each region has telltale differences. An ideal diving holiday in Thailand would involve stops along both bodies of water.

Sea floor, Surin Islands (p274)
MICHAEL AW

When the weather is right, the Andaman Sea has some of the finest diving in the world. Many would argue that the Andaman has better diving than the Gulf, but this is mostly attributed to excellent visibility during favourable sea conditions. Post-tsunami evaluations of the coral reefs in the Andaman have shown that the damage caused was surprisingly small. At least 210 hard corals and 108 species of reef fish have been recorded here, and encounters with large pelagic creatures are quite frequent along the southern provinces. Live-aboard dive trips regularly depart Phuket for the quiet archipelagos further west known as the Surin and Similan Islands. Further south, Ko Phi-Phi and Ko Lanta are great places to hang your rucksack and put on some fins.

The best part about diving the Gulf of Thailand is that sea conditions are generally favourable throughout the year. This C-shaped coastline is about twice as long as the Andaman side and changes drastically as it links the Malaysian border to Cambodia to the east. The southwestern gulf coast has the finest diving spots, located near the islands of Ko Tao (p227), Ko Pha-Ngan (p211) and Ko Samui (p191). Ko Tao currently certifies more divers than any other place in world.

On the far eastern side of the coast, the Ko Chang Archipelago (p138) is quickly gaining momentum as the second hub of the region, although choppy seas limit the season to November to May. Pattaya, just a quick two-hour hop from the Bangkok bustle, offers a few memorable dives as well, including a couple of wrecks.

Thailand's Marine Life

If speaking were possible underwater, almost every dive site in Thailand would be a noisy jumble of bubbly 'oohs' and 'aahs' as divers gleefully point at passing creatures. Thailand's aquatic food chain is as colourful as it is complicated. Hard and soft corals provide the foundation for schooling fish ranging from teeny 'Nemos', to large visitors such as giant trevally, tuna, grouper, barracuda, king-

HITTING THE UNDERWATER JACKPOT

Most divers come to Thailand with the hope of spotting an elusive whale shark – the largest fish in the sea with a giant mouth that can measure about 2m wide (so imagine how big their bodies are!) Don't worry; they are filter feeders, which means that they mostly feed on plankton, krill and other tiny organisms. In fact, divers often report that adult whale sharks are quite friendly and enjoy swimming through the streams of bubbles emitted by divers. Although whale-shark sightings are becoming increasingly rare with each passing year, it is still well within the realm of possibility to see one. In the past there were 'spotting seasons', but recent shifts in weather patterns means that they can be spotted at any time of the year. Most diving instructors we encountered said that they average around three to seven sightings per year.

Usually these gentle creatures gravitate towards submerged pinnacles and often hang out at a site for several days before moving on. So, if word is flying around about a recent sighting, then strap on your scuba gear and hit the high seas.

The awesome sight of a whale shark, Ko Tao (p227)
BRANDON PRESSER

fish, manta rays and reef sharks. The gigantic whale shark is the Big Kahuna. For more on whale sharks, see the boxed text, opposite.

SNORKELLING

Snorkelling is a popular choice with visitors. Orchestrating your own snorkelling trip is a cinch – there are loads of resorts and dive shops along all of the coasts that rent out gear for 100B to 200B per day. Many islands, including Ko Tao (p231), Ko Kut (p157), Ko Mak (p159), Ko Rang (p163), Ko Pha-Ngan (p216), Ko Tarutao (p376) and Ko Phi-Phi (p345) have phenomenal snorkelling spots right off shore, while in other destinations you will have to hire a boat taxi or join a tour. Check out the boxed text, p335, for an exciting day with the fishes near Krabi.

Expect to pay between 500B and 1000B for an organised snorkelling daytrip depending on how far you travel. High-end excursions usually use fancy speedboats and expensive equipment, while cheaper deals tend to focus more on the social aspect of the trip, taking customers to so-so reefs. Chartering your own speedboat or long-tail boat is an option. With a little research, it's not too difficult to scout out undisturbed reefs.

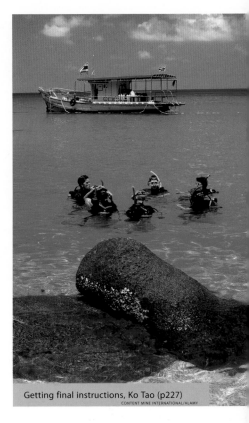

Getting final instructions, Ko Tao (p227)
CONTENT MINE INTERNATIONAL/ALAMY

In general you can see plenty of marine life while snorkelling, although at busy tourist destinations such as Ko Phi-Phi the numbers of visitors are starting to tell on the marine environment. The general rule is that the further you get from human habitation, the better the condition of the reefs. However, some developed islands have hidden corners where healthy coral still persists, usually around areas of rocky shoreline. See p384 for some hints for responsible snorkelling.

SEA KAYAKING

Although Thailand's coastal regions are famous for the action occurring below sea level, sea kayaking is a great way to check out some remote islands and hidden coves.

The thin chain of islands between Ko Samui and the mainland, known as Ang Thong Marine National Park (p240), is a must for any kayaking fanatic. This stunning collection of easily anthropomorphised islands stretches along the cerulean waters like an emerald necklace. All of the islands are uninhabited (save for five bungalows on one) and feature pristine terrain that can only be accessed by long-tail boat or kayak. Tours here depart from Ko Samui (p191) and Ko Pha-Ngan (p211), both about an hour's ride away by speedboat.

Drifting almost soundlessly through the mangroves and karst cliffs, Ao Phang-Nga (p281)

Sea-kayaking tours of remote islands and mangroves around the Andaman Sea are hugely popular at tourist centres such as Phuket (p297), Ko Phi-Phi (p345), Ao Nang (p333), Krabi (p328), Ko Libong (p367) and elsewhere along the coast.

In some cases equipment can be rented for solo expeditions, but more typically outings are organised tours, which include transfers, guides, gear, lunch and usually snorkelling equipment as a bonus.

CAVING

Spelunking is as much fun as it sounds and bounding through crevices and dangling stalactites has become popular. Millions of years of monsoons have etched elaborate systems of tunnels throughout Thailand. Join a cave tour in Ko Lanta (p352) or Khao Sok National Park (p244), or visit the undulating coastline of Trang Province (p359 and p365), which offers a fascinating mix of intense crawl spaces and hidden shrines.

'Millions of years of monsoons have etched elaborate systems of tunnels throughout Thailand'

Many caves throughout Thailand have been transformed into unusual religious sanctuaries. Although these caverns are by no means a heart-pumping expedition, they offer an insight into the kingdom's history and customs. The dramatic caves at Khao Sam Roi Yot (p181) are a cherished royal stomping ground and feature a dazzling golden pavilion that shimmers as the afternoon sunlight pours in from above. Temple caves in Phetchaburi (p166) are lit up by an ethereal light as the sun descends.

When visiting caves, wear sensible clothing and pay attention to local warnings as flash floods are known to occur after rains.

HIKING

Despite the region's focus on water sports, Thailand's coasts and islands have numerous hiking opportunities featuring unique biodiversity and photo opps fit for *National Geographic*.

A network of inland jungles stretches along the long, thin Isthmus of Kra from Krabi all the way up to Phetchaburi near Bangkok. Along the way, hikers will find the oldest rainforest in the world, over 500 species of birds, and wild elephants. Two virgin archipelagos bookend coastal Thailand – the Ko Chang Archipelago hugs the Cambodian border and features dozens of tiny islands primed for exploration, while the Ko Tarutao Marine National Park near Malaysia benefits from strict laws that prohibit development.

For information on responsible hiking see p384.

ROCK CLIMBING

Thailand's numerous jagged outcroppings of sky-reaching limestone make most tourists drool, but for rock-climbing enthusiasts they're a whole lot more. These swirling stone masses are a world-class playground of crags and crevices that lures adventurers from around the globe.

The Andaman Coast delivers all the goods with several fantastic spots along the sharp, twisting coast. With nearly 500 bolted routes and top-notch views from the summits, Railay (p338) can claim to be one of the best places in the world for climbing. Try your hand at One, Two, Three Wall, which boasts over 40 climbs of varying difficulty. Advanced climbers should test their muscles at Thaiwand Wall, a slippery, sky-scraping limestone mass at Hat Rai Leh West. 'Deep water soloing' is the latest craze – adventurers free-climb steep, limestone ledges and use the deep seas below as their

top five
TREKS

Khao Sok (p244) This majestic national park protects the world's oldest rainforest, which features shimmering limestone outcrops, gushing waterfalls, giant flowers, curious creatures and thickets of dripping jungle ferns.

Ko Tarutao Marine National Park (p374) One of the original marine parks in Thailand, this pristine archipelago is home to 51 jungle islands with loads of opportunities for nature enthusiasts to tread quietly among tumbling vegetation and scampering wildlife.

Ko Chang (p143) Endless hectacres of untouched terrain lie hidden deep within this gargantuan floating jungle. Elephant treks exist for those wanting a break from hiking.

Khao Sam Roi Yot (p180) A network of easily navigable paths criss-crosses through a steep jungle of dense flora and leaping dusky langur monkeys.

Khao Lak/Lam Ru National Park (p276) This quiet national park is a stunning expanse of dramatic hills, sea cliffs, estuaries and forested valleys. Scurrying fauna includes tapirs, monkeys and Asiatic black bears.

Rainforest, Khao Sok National Park (p244)
ZOE SOMERVILLE/ALAMY

safety net if they fall. The Trang Islands (p362) are another popular spot for some monkey action, as is Ko Phi-Phi (p345).

Bolts are replaced every few years and are generally solid, though some of the more-remote routes are re-bolted less frequently and may even be off-limits for safety reasons. Final anchors are usually fixed at two or three points and have opposing karabiners or double rings for lowering off. Climbing newbies should check out the boxed text, p340, for information about picking a climbing school. Schools generally charge from around 800/5000B for a half-/three-day course. For more details on the basics, see p339.

An adventurer foregoes the beach for some spectacular, world-class rock climbing, Railay (p338)
SCOTT STULBERG

(Continued from page 288)

Snorkelling is best along Phuket's western coast, particularly at the rocky headlands between beaches. Mask, snorkel and fins can be rented for around 250B a day. As with scuba diving, you'll find better snorkelling, with greater visibility and variety of marine life along the shores of small outlying islands such as Ko Raya Yai and Ko Raya Noi.

As elsewhere in the Andaman Sea, the best diving months are December to May, when the weather is good and the sea is at its clearest (and boat trips are much safer).

There are numerous dive shops with supplies, including the following:

All 4 Diving (Map p314; ☎ 0 7634 4611; 5/4 Th Sawatdirak, Hat Patong) Phuket's largest dive store.

Andaman Sea Sport (Map p301; ☎ 0 7621 1752; 69 Th Phuket, Phuket Town) Stocks diving and snorkelling supplies.

Dive Supply (Map p314; ☎ 0 7634 2513; www.divesupply.com; 189 Th Rat Uthit, Hat Patong) Has a great variety of diving equipment, and offers a good service in several languages.

HORSE RIDING

Phuket Riding Club (Map p287; ☎ 0 7628 8213; pemika2006@hotmail.com), near Ao Chalong, offers one-hour (per person 650B) and two-hour (1250B) rides in the jungle and along nearby beaches.

KAYAKING

Several companies based in Phuket offer canoe tours of scenic Ao Phang-Nga. The kayaks are able to enter semisubmerged caves (which Thai fishermen have called *hôrng* or 'room' for centuries) inaccessible to long-tail boats. A day paddle costs from 3000B per person including meals, equipment and transfer; many outfits also run all-inclusive, three-day (from 13,000B) or six-day (from 42,000B) kayak/camping trips. The following operators are based in Phuket Town:

John Gray's Seacanoe (off Map p301; ☎ 0 7625 4505-7; www.johngray-seacanoe.com; 124 Soi 1, Th Yaowarat) One of the oldest and most reputable companies on the island. Like any good brand in Thailand, his 'Seacanoe' name has been frequently copied. He's north of Phuket Town.

Paddle Asia (☎ 0 7624 0952; www.paddleasia.com; 19/3 Th Rasdanusorn) Caters to beginners and those who don't enjoy being surrounded by noisy tour groups.

Sea Canoe Thailand (Map p301; ☎ 0 7621 2172; www.seacanoe.net; 367/4 Th Yaowarat) Has a great reputation despite the unoriginal name. It's north of Phuket Town.

SURFING

Phuket's west coast beaches get a good pounding during the May to October monsoon. Kata and Nai Han are said to be the best for surfing, especially after a storm has blown through from the southwest. Hat Surin and Ao Bang Thao are also great spots to learn to surf, with the wave season sometimes extending through to October. There are a few surf shops with boards for rent in Kata and Patong, including the following:

Aloha Surf Sports Co (☎ 0 7634 4504; 124/14 Th Thawiwong, Hat Patong) Rents out surfboards and other surfing accessories.

WHICH DIVE SHOP?

Choosing the right dive shop can be an intimidating business. After all, there are so many flashy storefronts advertising the wonders of the diving world – over 100 in Phuket alone. How on earth can you be sure you're making the right choice?

When choosing a dive company on Phuket (or anywhere in Thailand, for that matter) there are a few key questions you should ask. For example, how long has the dive shop existed? How many divers will be on the boat? What is the dive instructor-to-client ratio? What kind of insurance do they have and what does it cover? Is it a licensed Tourism Authority of Thailand (TAT) operator? If it's a live-aboard trip, is there oxygen on board? Talk to the staff (if they're not out diving): how experienced are they and how much of this experience is local? Do they make you feel comfortable and confident? If you're taking a class, what kind of certification do the instructors have? And do they speak your language well enough that you understand each other? One last thing: look at the equipment – is it in good shape and well-maintained?

Perhaps the best way to choose an excellent dive operation, however, is to get a glowing recommendation from other divers who've already done the underwater deed. Word-of-mouth is often the best indicator of the quality of a company – and in the competitive diving world, a good reputation can really make or break a business.

TOP 5 PHUKET SPAS

There seems to be a massage shop on every corner in Phuket. Most are low-key family affairs where traditional Thai massage goes for about 250B per hour, and a basic pedi-mani costs around 100B – a real steal. The quality of service at these places varies, and changes rapidly as staff turnover is high. Go with your gut instinct or ask fellow travellers or your hotel staff for recommendations. No matter where you choose, it's hard to go wrong.

If you're looking for a more Westernised spa experience, head to one of Phuket's plentiful spa resorts. These places are often affiliated with a ritzy hotel (but nearly all are open to nonguests). They are *haute couture* affairs with sumptuous Zen designs and huge treatment menus. Prices vary depending on location, but treatments generally start at around 1000B and go up and up from there.

Our top five Phuket spa picks are:

- At the JW Marriott resort (p323), the **Mandara Spa** is perfect for couples. There are 10 couples' treatment suites that include indoor and outdoor space. The 'Healing Hot Stones' massage (US$175) is one of the signature treatments.
- The **Six Senses Spa** at the Evason Phuket Resort (p306) is sublimely back-to-nature in setting, yet cutting edge as far as treatments are concerned. Try the 'Sensory Spa Journey' (90 minutes, 8000B), which includes a four-hand massage (two therapists), luxurious footbath and goody bag of product samples used in your treatment.
- Try the signature three-hour 'Royal Banyan Treatment' (US$195) at the **Banyan Tree Spa** at Banyan Tree Phuket (p321). It includes a mint footbath, a cucumber and lemongrass rub, Thai herbal massage and a soak in a flower-filled tub.
- One of Phuket's first spas, **Hideaway Day Spa** (p321) still enjoys an excellent reputation. More reasonably priced than many hotel counterparts, the Hideaway offers treatments in a tranquil setting by a lagoon.
- As posh as it gets: the **Trisara Spa** at Trisara (p323) is very private, faces the ocean and opens onto breezy pavilions surrounded by ponds. Try one of the holistic oil massages (from 2000B). The oils used are made without chemicals or preservatives.

Blujelly (☎ 08 5880 7954; www.blujelly.com; Ao Bang Thao) Offers kids' lessons and is a good source of info about surfing around Ao Bang Thao.

Phuket Surf (Map p309; ☎ 08 1002 2496; www.phuketsurf.com) On Hat Kata Yai's southern cove; offers surf lessons starting at 1500B, as well as board rentals. Check its website for more info about the local surfing community.

YACHTING

Phuket is one of Southeast Asia's main yacht destinations, and you'll find all manner of craft anchored along its shores – from 80-year-old wooden sloops that look like they can barely stay afloat to the latest in hi-tech motor cruisers. Marina-style facilities with year-round anchorage are presently available at a few locations.

Phuket Boat Lagoon (Map p287; ☎ 0 7623 9055; fax 0 7623 9056) is located at Ao Sapam, about 10km north of Phuket Town on the eastern shore. It offers an enclosed marina with tidal channel access, serviced pontoon berths, 60- and 120-tonne travel lifts, a hard-stand area, plus a resort hotel, laundry, coffee shop, fuel, water, repairs and maintenance services.

The US$25 million **Royal Phuket Marina** (Map p287; ☎ 0 7623 9762; www.royalphuketmarina.com) is located just south of Phuket Boat Lagoon's luxury villas. Townhouses and a hotel join 190 berths and a spa here.

Yacht Haven Phuket Marina (Map p287; ☎ 0 7620 6705; www.yacht-haven-phuket.com) is at Laem Phrao on the northeastern tip. The Yacht Haven boasts 130 berths and a scenic restaurant, and also does yacht maintenance.

If you need sails, **Rolly Tasker Sailmakers** (☎ 0 7628 0347; www.rollytasker.com; 26/2 Th Chaofa, Ao Chalong) can outfit you with these; riggings, spars and hardware are also available.

Port clearance is rather complicated; the marinas will take care of the paperwork (for a fee, of course) if notified of your arrival in advance. For information on yacht charters (both bareboat and crewed), yacht sales and yacht deliveries, contact the following:

Faraway Sail & Dive Expeditions (☎ 0 7628 0701; www.far-away.net; 112/8 Muu 4, Th Taina, Hat Karon)

Sunsail Yacht Charters (☎ 0 7623 9057; www.sunsailthailand.com; Phuket Boat Lagoon)

Thai Marine Leisure (☎ 0 7623 9111; www.thaimarine.com; Phuket Boat Lagoon)

Yachtpro International (☎ 0 7623 2960; www.sailing-thailand.com; Yacht Haven Phuket Marina)

Expect to pay from 19,000B per day for a high-season, bareboat charter.

The TAT office (p300) in Phuket Town also has an extensive list of yacht charters and brokers. For insurance purposes, it's a good idea to see if the boat you want to charter is registered in Thailand.

Tours

Siam Safari (☎ 0 7628 0116; www.saiamsafari.com; 45 Th Chao Far, Chalong) and **Adventure Safaris** (☎ 0 7634 1988) combine 4WD tours of the island's interior with short elephant rides and short hikes for around 2500B per day. Half-day trips are also available, although the difference in price is not that great.

Courses

Pum Thai Cooking School (Map p314; ☎ 0 7634 6269, 0 1521 8904; www.pumthaifoodchain.com; 204/32 Tha Rat Uthit, Hat Patong) Runs excellent Thai restaurants in Phuket, Ko Phi-Phi and France. At the Phuket branch you can learn easy *haute cuisine* the Thai way for 450B for a one-dish class, 900B for a two-dish class, and up to 4650B for an over-six-hour, five-dish class.

The Boathouse (see p310) Offers a thrilling two-day Thai cooking class (per person one day/weekend 2000/3000B) each weekend with its chef, Tamanoon.

Phuket for Children

There's plenty for kids to do in Phuket and while the seedier face of the sex industry is on full show in Patong (we wouldn't bring our kids there, although many people do), the rest of the island is fairly G-rated.

In terms of activities, the usual array of water sports is offered at the bigger resorts up and down the coast. Many of the activities already mentioned will also appeal to children of all ages. Young animal lovers will enjoy **Phuket Zoo** (Map p287; ☎ 0 7638 1227; www.phuketzoo.com; 23/2 Muu 3 Soi, Th Phalai Chaofa; admission 200B; ☒ 8.30am-6pm), which has the usual monkey, elephant and crocodile shows, as well as a butterfly farm. The **Phuket Aquarium** (p306) and the **Phuket Gibbon Rehabilitation Centre** (p324) could also be interesting for older children.

The main family-flogged feature of Phuket, however, is **Phuket Fantasea** (p318), which is a pricey extravaganza of wild animals, costumes, song, dance, special effects, pyrotechnics, a lousy dinner and magic (marvel at the disappearing elephants) – but it's all very, very cheesy.

Volunteering

Soi Dog Foundation (☎ 08 7050 8688; www.soidog.org) is a well organised unit aimed at sterilizing, providing medical care for and feeding stray dogs. Volunteers are needed for feeding the dogs but it's just as helpful to donate funds towards the projects. Check the website for updates and details.

Getting There & Away

AIR

Thirty kilometres northwest of Phuket Town, **Phuket International Airport** (Map p287; ☎ 0 7632 7230) has a post office, bookshop, restaurants and cafés, **left-luggage facility** (per piece per day 40B; ☒ 6am-10pm) and very expensive **internet connection** (per 15min 100B) in the domestic departure area. There are plenty of foreign exchange booths in both sections and, in the arrivals area, you'll find ATMs and a tourist office. Note that it takes around 45 minutes to an hour to reach the southern beaches from here.

THAI (Map p301; ☎ 0 7621 1195; www.thaiairways.com; 78/1 Th Ranong, Phuket Town) operates about a dozen daily flights to Bangkok (from 1515B one way); it also has regular flights to/from 11 other cities in Thailand and international destinations including Penang, Langkawi, Kuala Lumpur, Singapore, Hong Kong, Taipei and Tokyo.

Bangkok Airways (Map p301; ☎ 0 7622 5033; www.bangkokair.com; 58/2-3 Th Yaowarat) has daily flights to Ko Samui (1975B one way), Bangkok (2725B one way) and Utapau for Pattaya (3100B one way).

Nok Air (☎ 1318; www.nokair.co.th; Phuket International Airport) links Phuket with Bangkok, as do **One-Two-Go** (☎ 1141, ext 1126; www.fly12go.com; Phuket International Airport) and web-based **Air Asia** (www.airasia.com), from 726B one way. Air Asia also flies to Kuala Lumpur (from 1089B one way) and Singapore (989B one way).

NORTHERN ANDAMAN COAST

There are several international airlines with offices in Phuket Town, including the following:

Dragonair (Map p301; ☎ 0 7621 5734; Th Phang-Nga)
Malaysia Airlines (Map p301; ☎ 0 7621 6675; 1/8-9 Th Thungkha)
Silk Air (Map p301; ☎ 0 7621 3891; www.silkair.com; 183/103 Th Phang-Nga)

FERRY
During the high season, several boats ply the waters between Ao Ton Sai on Ko Phi-Phi and ports on Phuket. **Chao Koh Group** (☎ 0 7624 6512) boats depart from Tha Rasada, near Phuket Town, for Phi-Phi at 8.30am, 1.30pm and 2.30pm and return at 9am, 2.30pm and 3pm (400B one way). Get the going price before you turn up at the port since many of the touts here will try to charge up to double the real fare.

MINIVAN
Some Phuket travel agencies sell tickets (including ferry fare) for air-con minivans down to Ko Samui and Ko Phang-Ngan. Air-con minivan services to Krabi, Ranong, Surat Thani and several other locations are also available. Departure locations vary: see the TAT office in Phuket Town. Prices are slightly more than the buses, which all stop in Phuket town (see p305).

PHUKET TOWN
อ.เมืองงภูเก็ต
pop 70,000
You've picked up this book titled *Thailand's Islands & Beaches*, so chances are you're looking for surf and sand. If this is the case, skip Phuket Town. If, on the other hand, you'd like to spend a day or more meandering through back streets in search of hole-in-the-wall art galleries, restaurants and bars, far from the hubbub of touristville, you will love this place.

Before Bermuda shorts and flip-flops, Phuket was an island of traders, rubber, tin and cash. Attracting entrepreneurs from as far afield as Arabia, China, India and Portugal, Phuket Town was a hotchpotch of cultural influences, cobbled together by tentative compromise and – sometimes grudgingly – cooperation. Today multiculturalism isn't the first word that comes to mind when describing the town, but there is still plenty of Sino-Portuguese architecture to lend it a nos-

talgic charm, and life moves forward in a Thai manner that is refreshingly real.

If you're on a budget, Phuket Town has some of the best lodging bargains on the island and is a good option for a base. From here you can hop on regular sŏrng·tǎa·ou to any of Phuket's beaches (which will take between half an hour and 1½ hours; see p305).

Information
There are numerous internet cafés and ATMs around Th Phuket, Th Ranong, Th Montri and Th Phang-Nga.

BOOKSHOPS
The Books (☎ 0 7621 1115; www.thebooksphuket.com; 53-55 Th Phuket; ☯ 8.30am-9.30pm) Offers English- language magazines, guidebooks and novels.

EMERGENCY
Police (☎ 191, 0 7622 3555; cnr Th Phang-Nga & Th Phuket)

MEDICAL SERVICES
Bangkok Phuket Hospital (☎ 0 7625 4425; www .phukethospital.com; Th Yongyok Uthit) This private hospital is the best bet within easy reach of Phuket Town.

POST
DHL World Wide Express (☎ 0 7625 8500; 61/4 Th Thepkasatri) Offers a swift and reliable courier service.
Main post office (Th Montri; ☯ 8.30am-4pm Mon-Fri, 9am-noon Sat)

TELEPHONE
Phuket CAT office (Th Phang-Nga; ☯ 8am-midnight) Offers Home Country Direct service.

TOURIST INFORMATION
TAT office (☎ 0 7621 2213; www.tat.or.th; 191 Th Thalang; ☯ 8.30am-4.30pm) Has maps, information brochures, a list of standard sŏrng·tǎa·ou fares out to the various beaches, and also the recommended charter costs for a vehicle.

TRAVEL AGENCIES
Phuket Centre Tour (☎ 0 7621 2892; centre@e-mail .in.th; Th Rasada; ☯ 8am-5pm Mon-Fri, to 4pm Sat) Offers car hire, airline ticketing and tour packages.

Sights & Activities
Phuket's historic **Sino-Portuguese architecture** is the town's most evocative sight: stroll along Thalang, Dibuk, Yaowarat, Ranong, Phang-Nga, Rasada and Krabi for a glimpse

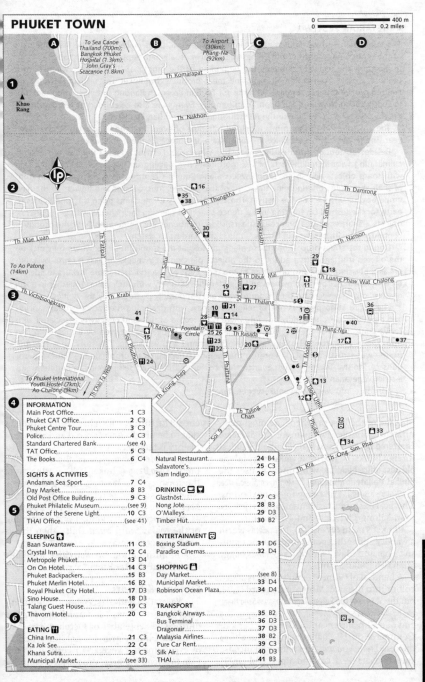

PHUKET TOWN

0	400 m
0	0.2 miles

To Sea Canoe Thailand (700m); Bangkok Phuket Hospital (1.3km); John Gray's Seacanoe (1.8km)

To Airport (30km); Phang-Na (92km)

Khao Rang

Th Komarapat

Th Nakhon

Th Chumphon

Th Damrong

Th Thungkha

Th Mae Luan

To Ao Patong (14km)

Th Dibuk

Th Narison

Th Krabi

Th Vichitsongkram

Th Dibuk Mai

Th Luang Phaw Wat Chalong

Th Thalang

Th Ranong

Fountain Circle

Th Rasada

Th Phang-Nga

To Phuket International Youth Hostel (7km); Ao Chalong (9km)

Th Krung Thep

Th Phattana

Th Taling Chan

Th Ong Sim Phai

Th Kra

VEGETARIAN FESTIVAL

The Vegetarian Festival, Phuket's most important festival, takes place during the first nine days of the ninth lunar month of the Chinese calendar – usually late September or October.

Basically, the festival celebrates the beginning of the month of 'Taoist Lent', when devout Chinese abstain from eating all meat and meat products. In Phuket, the festival activities are centred on five Chinese temples, with the Jui Tui temple on Th Ranong the most important, followed by Bang Niaw and Sui Boon Tong temples. Events are also celebrated at temples in the nearby towns of Kathu (where the festival originated) and Ban Tha Reua.

The TAT office in Phuket prints a helpful schedule of events for the Vegetarian Festival each year. The festival also takes place in Trang, Krabi and other southern Thai towns.

Besides abstention from eating meat, the Vegetarian Festival involves various processions culminating with incredible acts of self-mortification – walking on hot coals, piercing the skin with sharp objects and so on. Shop owners along Phuket's central streets set up altars in front of their shopfronts offering nine tiny cups of tea, incense, fruit, candles and flowers to the nine emperor gods invoked by the festival. Those participating as mediums bring the nine deities to earth for the festival by entering into a trance state and piercing their cheeks with all manner of objects – sharpened tree branches, spears, slide trombones etc. Some even hack their tongues continuously with saw or axe blades – this is the hardest to watch.

During the street processions these mediums stop at the shopfront altars, where they pick up the offered fruit and either add it to the objects piercing their cheeks or pass it on to bystanders as a blessing. They also drink one of the nine cups of tea and grab some flowers to stick in their waistbands. The shop owners and their families stand by with their palms together in a *wâi* gesture, out of respect for the mediums who are temporarily possessed by the deities.

The entire atmosphere is one of religious frenzy, with deafening firecrackers, ritual dancing and bloody shirt fronts. Oddly enough, there is no record of this kind of activity associated with Taoist Lent in China. The local Chinese claim that the festival was started by a theatre troupe from China that stopped off in nearby Kathu around 150 years ago. The story goes that the troupe was struck seriously ill because the members had failed to propitiate the nine emperor gods of Taoism. The nine-day penance they performed included self-piercing, meditation and a strict vegetarian diet.

For more info, visit www.phuketvegetarian.com.

of some of the best on offer. The most magnificent examples in town are the **Standard Chartered Bank** (Th Phang-Nga), Thailand's oldest foreign bank; the **THAI office** (Th Ranong); and the **old post office building**, which now houses the **Phuket Philatelic Museum** (Th Montri; admission free; 9.30am-5.30pm), a first-stop for stamp boffins. The best-restored residential properties are found along Th Dibuk and Th Thalang.

Phuket's main **day market** (Th Ranong) is worth a wander and is the spot to invest in the requisite Thai and Malay sarongs, as well as baggy Shan fisherman's pants.

A handful of Chinese temples injects added colour into the area. Most are standard issue, but the **Shrine of the Serene Light** (Saan Jao Sang Tham; 8.30am-noon & 1.30-5.30pm), tucked away at the end of a 50m alley near the Bangkok Bank of Commerce on Th Phang-Nga, is a cut above the rest. Here, you will find plumes of incense smoke, dazzling décor and a peaceful ambi-

ence. The shrine, which has been restored, is said to be nearly 200 years old and a sense of history is tangible.

For a bird's-eye view of the city, climb pretty **Khao Rang** (Phuket Hill), northwest of the town centre. It's best during the week, when the summit is relatively peaceful, but keep an eye out for mobs of snarling dogs. If, as many people say, Phuket is a corruption of the Malay word *bukit* (hill), then this is probably its namesake.

For information on activities available throughout Phuket Province, see p288.

Festivals & Events

The **Vegetarian Festival** (see above) is Phuket's most important event and usually takes place during late September or October. The TAT office in Phuket prints a helpful schedule of events for the Vegetarian Festival. If you plan to attend the street processions, consider bringing earplugs to make the noise of the firecrackers more tolerable.

Sleeping

Phuket Town is the cheapest place on the island to get some 'Z's and is a treasure trove of budget lodging. Head out to the beaches for more midrange and top end options.

BUDGET

On On Hotel (☎ 0 7621 1154; 19 Th Phang-Nga; r 180-400B; ✗) This bare-bones classic scooped a bit-part in *The Beach* (2000) – not necessarily a good thing – and despite its musty rooms and peeling paint, retains a whiff of Old Phuket. Expect sagging beds, squeaking fans, squat toilets and padlocked doors: budget authenticity in a nutshell. It is clean though and there's an old-school dingy café downstairs where you can sweat it out with other guests and a handful of old Chinese guys.

Phuket International Youth Hostel (☎ 0 7628 1325; www.phukethostel.com; 73/11 Th Chao Fa, Ao Chalong; dm 200B, r 360-440B; ✗) As a bona fide Hostelling International outfit, this contemporary spot offers comfortable sleeps in typically sterile surrounds. 'Reliable' is the buzzword here and while you won't be dazzled by its authentic charm, you will sleep safe in the knowledge that you're not being stalked by creeping cockroaches. It is 7km south of Phuket Town.

Phuket Backpackers (☎ 0 7625 6680; www.phuket backpackers.com; 167 Th Ranong; dm 250B, r 600-700B; ✗ ▯) It's only worth staying in this over-priced yet central backpackers if you stay in the super-flashy, urban-chic dorms. Rooms are big yet shabby, while common areas are pleasant, social and have touches such as modern art on the walls.

our pick Talang Guest House (☎ 0 7621 4225; ta langgh@phuket.ksc.co.th; 37 Th Thalang; r 250-450B; ✗) Taking a beeline back to the old school, this decrepit shophouse is something of an architectural classic. Creature comforts are at a premium, but it bags extra points for character and charm. If you really want to soak up the atmosphere, check in to the 3rd-floor room overlooking the street. It's a fan room with a large veranda and is ideal for nostalgia junkies.

Thavorn Hotel (☎ 0 7621 1333; fax 0 7621 5559; 74 Th Rasada; r 280-550B; ✗) Established in 1964 – hey, they think it's worth mentioning – this city centre giant looks like a monument to ar-chitectural Stalinism. On the inside, however, things take a turn for the better. The lobby houses the self-styled 'Phuket Museum' – a collection of intriguing local bric-a-brac – while the upper floors contain tatty rooms catering to a variety of budgets.

Crystal Inn (☎ 0 7625 6789; www.phuketcrystalinn.com; 2/1-10 Soi Surin, Th Phuket; r from 900B; ✗ ▯) Some thought obviously went into this place: there are Rothko-style murals and the décor is con-temporary, soothing and way above standard for this price range. It might not age well, but for now this is an excellent choice.

MIDRANGE & TOP END

Baan Suwantawe (☎ 0 7621 2879; www.baansuwantawe .co.th; 1/10 Th Dibuk; r from 1300B; ✗ ▯ ▨) With Zen art, hardwood floors, good-sized tile bath-rooms and comfy lounge areas, these studio-style rooms are a steal. Higher priced rooms have terraces overlooking the blue-tiled pool and lily pond and the whole place smells like lemongrass. It's geared towards long-term stays but will rent by the night.

Phuket Merlin Hotel (☎ 0 7621 2866; www.phuket merlinhotel.com; 158/1 Th Yaowarat; r 1500-5000B; ✗ ▯ ▨) This Merlin has seen better days. There is, however, a swimming pool and fitness cen-tre, as well as a nightclub and sauna.

Royal Phuket City Hotel (☎ 0 7623 3333; www .royalphuketcity.com; 154 Th Phang-Nga; r 1900-5500B; ✗ ▨) Phuket's swankiest business-style out-fit offers all the usual thrills and spills: pool, sauna, spa, zebra-print disco. Expect plentiful mod cons, smiling, attentive staff, CNN or the BBC on your telly and a great night's sleep.

our pick Sino House (☎ 0 7622 1398; www.sinohouse phuket.com; 1 Th Montri; r 2000-2500; ✗ ▯) Shanghai style meets old-world Phuket at this chic new hotel. Every one of the room types is mas-sive, albeit dark, and has a fantastic bathroom with a handmade ceramic basin and quarter-moon-shaped shower tub. Some rooms have big squishy couches and Thai-style kitchens. There's an on-site spa and long-term rates. In short, this is the most stylish and comfortable place to stay in Phuket Town. Staff are lovely and speak excellent English.

Metropole Phuket (☎ 0 7621 5050; www.metro polephuket.com; 1 Soi Surin, Th Montri; r 3000-24,000B; ✗ ▨) The Metropole fancies itself as a big-hitter. The seahorse fountain is a little kitsch, the rooms are frumpy (think shimmering polyester bedspreads) and the staff are a lit-tle inattentive, but this is a good bet for those looking for city-centre comforts. There are great views from the upper floors.

Eating

There's good food in Phuket Town, and meals here cost a lot less than those at the beach – as much as 50% less. Southeast of the centre, on Th Ong Sim Phai, is the town's municipal market where you can buy fresh fruit and vegetables. Around three sides of this market you'll find a night market that features Thai and Chinese food.

Natural Restaurant (☎ 0 7622 4287; 62/5 Soi Phuthon; dishes 50–200B; ⏰ lunch & dinner) Travel around the world in 80 plates at this dazzlingly green Phuket eatery. The décor – all pot plants and bamboo – is *Swiss Family Robinson* meets *The Beach*, and the picture menu promises everything from Wiener schnitzel to Singaporean noodles and green curry. Whatever you're craving, you won't go wrong going Natural.

Khana Sutra (☎ 0 7625 6192; 18–20 Th Takua Pa; dishes 80–250B; ⏰ lunch & dinner; ❄) The curries here, which are claimed to have aphrodisiac properties, are authentically Indian and are served among the decorative charms of an authentic Delhi diner. If the owner's around, be prepared for opinionated discussions about British football.

China Inn (Th Thalang; dishes 80–250B; ⏰ dinner Mon-Sat) Offers top-notch Chinese in old-world surrounds (check out the beautiful, old wooden doorway).

Siam Indigo (☎ 0 7625 6697; Th Phang-Nga; dishes 130–290B; ⏰ lunch & dinner Wed-Mon) One of Phuket Town's swankiest choices, this fusion cuisine restaurant serves everything from Asian tapas to New Zealand rack of lamb (490B). The setting in a historic building is minimalist and modern while remaining relaxed and subtly romantic.

Ka Jok See (☎ 0 7621 7903; kajoksee@hotmail.com; 26 Th Takua Pa; dishes 180–480B; ⏰ dinner Tue-Sun) Dining here is reason enough to come to town. Dripping old Phuket charm and creaking under the weight of the owner's fabulous trinket collection, this atmospheric little eatery offers great food, top-notch music and – if you're lucky – some sensationally camp cabaret. Enjoy your dinner, sip some wine and then dance the night away. Book ahead.

Salavatore's (☎ 0 9871 1184; 15 Th Rasada; dishes 200–680B; ⏰ lunch & dinner Tue-Sun; ❄) This authentic Italian restaurant (read checked tablecloths, giant pepper grinders, opera and a portly owner) cooks up all of mama's favourites, from a mean pizza to a sizzling fillet steak.

Drinking

Phuket Town is more a place to chat over a beer than to boogie the night away. That said, the major hotels have discos and/or karaoke clubs. If you really want to get down, try Zanzibar located in the Royal Phuket City Hotel (p303).

O'Malleys (☎ 0 7622 0170; 2/20-21 Th Montri; ⏰ 4pm-1am) Travelling thousands of miles to sink Guinness in an Irish pub always feels a little daft, but Phuket's homesick flock to this cosy Celtic watering hole for pool and assorted shenanigans. It has a generally welcoming atmosphere and the interior is almost authentic, if a little clean.

Timber Hut (☎ 0 7621 1839; 118/1 Th Yaowarat; ⏰ 6pm-2am) This red-brick spot has Wild West décor and live music from 10pm. The tunes can be deafeningly loud but it's popular with Thai 20-somethings and there's usually plenty of entertainment on offer.

our pick Glastnöst (☎ 08 4058 0288; 14 Soi Rommani) With the unusual moniker of 'Law & Notary Public Bar', this place doubles as a law office but don't let that intimidate you. It's about as laid-back and intimate a setting as you could find, and spontaneous jazz jam sessions are the norm.

Nong Jote (☎ 07 621 1139; 16 Th Yaowarat; ⏰ 5pm-midnight) Go and hop into this classic Chinese-shophouse–style bar for a beer (from 40B), a light meal (from 60B) and laid-back socialising with locals, expats and travellers – be prepared to discuss British football.

Entertainment

Paradise Cinemas (☎ 0 7622 0174; Th Tilok Uthit; tickets 80B) For addicts of celluloid, Paradise screens English-language blockbusters.

Boxing Stadium (tickets 500-1000B) Thai boxing can be witnessed Tuesday and Friday nights at 8pm. Ticket prices vary depending on where you sit and include one-way transport. The stadium is at the southern edge of town near the pier; túk-túk cost 70B. Get your tickets at the On On Hotel (p303).

Shopping

There's some reasonable shopping in the provincial capital.

Day Market (Th Ranong) This market near the town centre traces its history back to the days when pirates, Indians, Chinese, Malays and Europeans traded in Phuket. You might still find some fabrics from Southeast Asia, though for the most part it sells food now.

Municipal Market (Th Ong Sim Phai) Southeast of the centre, the focus of this market is on fresh produce and other things to eat.

Robinson Ocean Plaza (36 Th Tilok Uthit; 🕑 9am-10pm) You'll find this air-conditioned shopping mall near the municipal market.

Getting There & Around
TO/FROM THE AIRPORT
There is a minibus service at the airport that will take you into Phuket Town for 120B per person; Patong, Kata and Karon beaches cost 180B. If there aren't enough passengers to make the minibus run profitable, you may have to shell out for a taxi. Taxis between the airport and Phuket Town cost 500B; between the airport and beaches is 700B to 800B.

BUS
You'll find the **bus terminal** (☎ 0 7621 1977) just to the east of the centre, within walking distance of the many hotels. Services from here are in the table below:

Destination	Bus type	Fare	Duration
Bangkok	ordinary	501B	15hr
	air-con	626B	13-14hr
	VIP	970B	13hr
Chumphon	air-con	320B	6½hr
Hat Yai	ordinary	250B	8hr
	air-con	370B	6-7hr
Ko Samui	air-con	494B	8hr (bus/boat)
Krabi	ordinary	95B	4hr
	air-con	146B	3½hr
Nakhon Si Thammarat	ordinary	225B	8hr
	air-con	300B	7hr
Phang-Nga	ordinary	86B	2½hr
Ranong	ordinary	153B	6hr
	air-con	233B	5hr
Surat Thani	ordinary	124B	6hr
	air-con	195B	5hr
Takua Pa	ordinary	120B	3hr
Trang	ordinary	135B	6hr
	air-con	241B	5hr

CAR
There are cheap car rental agencies on Th Rasada near Pure Car Rent. Suzuki jeeps go for about 1400B per day (including insurance), though in the low season the rates can go down to 750B. And if you rent for a week or more, you should get a discount.

The rates are always better at local places than at the better-known internationals, though you may be able to get deals with the familiar companies if you reserve in advance.

Pure Car Rent (☎ 0 7621 1002; www.purecarrent.com; 75 Th Rasada) A good choice in the centre of town.

Via Rent-A-Car (☎ 0 7638 5718; www.via-phuket.com; 189/6 Th Rat Uthit, Patong) Offers similar rates to Pure, and can deliver to anywhere on the island.

MOTORCYCLE
You can rent motorcycles on Th Rasada near Pure Car Rent, or from various places at the beaches. Costs are anywhere from 200B to 300B per day, and can vary depending on the season. Bigger bikes (over 125cc) can be rented at a couple of shops in Patong and Karon.

SŎRNG·TĂA·OU & TÚK-TÚK
Large bus-sized sŏrng·tăa·ou run regularly from Th Ranong near the market to the various Phuket beaches for 40B to 70B per person – see the respective destination for details. These run from around 7am to 5pm; outside these times you have to charter a túk-túk to the beaches, which will set you back 250B to Patong, 280B to Karon and Kata, and 340B for Nai Han and Kamala. You'll probably have to bargain. Beware of tales about the tourist office being 5km away, or that the only way to reach the beaches is by taxi, or even that you'll need a taxi to get from the bus terminal to the town centre (it is more or less in the town centre). For a ride around town, túk-túk drivers should charge 30B.

Motorcycle taxis around town cost 20B.

KO SIREH
เกาะสิเหร่

This tiny island, 4km east of the district capital and connected to the main island by a bridge over a canal, is known for its *chow lair* village and a hilltop reclining Buddha.

This village, the largest settlement of Urak Lawoi *chow lair* in Thailand, is little more than a poverty-stricken cluster of tin shacks on stilts, plus one seafood restaurant called Gypsy World. The Urak Lawoi, the most sedentary of the three *chow lair* groups, are found only between the Mergui Archipelago and the Tarutao-Langkawi Archipelago, and speak a creolised mixture of Malay and Mon-Khmer.

NORTHERN ANDAMAN COAST

A loop road goes around the island, passing a few residences, shrimp farms, lots of rubber plantations and a bit of untouched forest. On the eastern side of the island is a public beach called **Hat Teum Suk** with a few chairs and thatched-roof shelters; it's nothing special, rather a local hang-out.

LAEM PHANWA
แหลมพันวา

Laem Phanwa is an elongated cape, jutting into the sea south of Phuket. At the tip of the cape, **Phuket Aquarium** (Map p287; ☎ 0 7639 1126; adult/child 100/50B; ⏱ 8.30am-4pm) displays a varied collection of tropical fish and other marine life. There are 32 tanks and you can experience underwater life with a stroll along the walk-through tunnel.

The seafood restaurants along the Laem Phanwa waterfront are a great place to hang out and watch the pleasure skiffs and painted fishing boats passing by.

To get to the cape, take Rte 4021 south and then turn down Rte 4023 just outside Phuket Town.

HAT RAWAI & HAT LAEM KA
หาดราไวย์และแหลมกา

On the up side, Rawai is relatively quiet and if you'd rather spend your time away from the jet skis, trinket sellers and boom boxes of the bigger resorts, it may just be your ticket to a little peace and quiet. But the beach is a little unimpressive, extremely narrow in places and not good for swimming, so committed beach lizards should head northeast to nearby Hat Laem Ka instead, which is an easy 1km walk away.

There's quite a lot to see and do in the surrounding area, including a **chow lair village**, boats to the nearby islands and good **snorkelling** off Laem Phromthep at the southern tip of Phuket Island. In fact, most of Rawai's visitors these days are divers who want to be near Phromthep and/or boat facilities for offshore diving trips.

Laem Phromthep is also a popular viewing point at sunset, when busloads of Thai tourists come to pose for photos and enjoy the view. On a hill next to the viewpoint is a **shrine to Phra Phrom** (Brahma).

Sleeping
Laemka Beach Inn (☎ 0 7638 1305; fax 0 7628 8547; Hat Laem Ka; bungalows 600-1500B; 🏊) Laemka features 30 thatched bungalows spread among coconut

groves above Laem Ka beach, which is much nicer than Rawai. Only the more expensive bungalows have air-con, but all have screen doors and windows (a rare bonus in these parts). The shoreline along the rounded cape is an interesting mix of clean sand and large boulders, with good swimming. Many speedboats depart from here for nearby islands, and it's a favourite local picnic spot.

Evason Phuket Resort (☎ 0 7638 1010; www.sixsenses.com; 100 Th Vised, Hat Rawai; r 7500-38,200B; 🏊 💻 🏊) This spa hotel extraordinaire offers copious amounts of luxury. Hip and heavily designed, it is the type of place that appeals to rock stars and moneyed media types. Expect beautiful people tapping away at their wireless gadgetry beside the infinity pool and immaculately turned-out staff. Room prices – opulent villas top the billing – stretch from reasonable to extraordinary.

Eating & Drinking
Besides the restaurants attached to the resorts in Rawai, there are oodles of seafood and noodle vendors along the roadside near Hat Rawai.

Flint's Bakery (☎ 0 7628 9210; Hat Rawai; ⏱ breakfast, lunch & dinner) Cakes, coffees and pizzas are on offer at this little bakery. It's right next door to Freedom Pub.

Freedom Pub (☎ 0 7628 7402; Hat Rawai; dishes 80-200B; ⏱ lunch & dinner) More watering hole than restaurant, this Rawai boozer features outdoor seating, a pool table, live music on the weekends, a free barbecue on Friday nights and – beware – an on-site tattoo parlour.

Nikita's (☎ 0 7628 8703; Hat Rawai; dishes 80-225B; ⏱ lunch & dinner) Diners and boozers attend Nikita's in equal numbers. The result is a lively atmosphere with plenty of fun and frolics when the town is busy. The menu is the usual melange of East meets West and the décor is bright and quirky.

Don's Mall (☎ 0 7638 3100; 48-5 Soi Sai Yuan; dishes 100-650B; ⏱ breakfast, lunch & dinner) This Texan-run food-and-entertainment complex showcases American meat feasts barbecued over a mesquite-wood fire. It also has an extensive wine list, fresh baked goods and much more. It's about 2km from downtown Rawai or to get here from Phuket Town (and many people make the trip just for the food), turn right onto Th Soi Sai Yuan, just south of the Chalong roundabout, and proceed for 3km; you can't miss it.

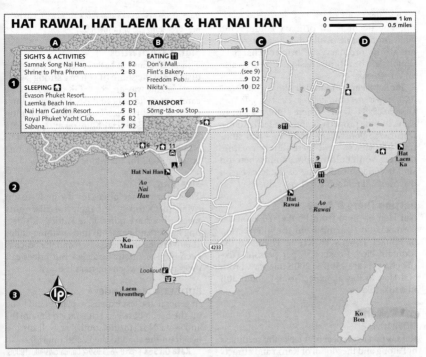

HAT RAWAI, HAT LAEM KA & HAT NAI HAN

	0	1 km
	0	0.5 miles

SIGHTS & ACTIVITIES
Samnak Song Nai Han.................1 B2
Shrine to Phra Phrom.................2 B3

SLEEPING
Evason Phuket Resort.................3 D1
Laemka Beach Inn......................4 D2
Nai Harn Garden Resort.............5 B1
Royal Phuket Yacht Club............6 B2
Sabana.......................................7 B2

EATING
Don's Mall.................................8 C1
Flint's Bakery.........................(see 9)
Freedom Pub.............................9 D2
Nikita's...................................10 D2

TRANSPORT
Sŏrng·tăa·ou Stop....................11 B2

Getting There & Away

Rawai is about 18km from Phuket Town and getting there costs 20B by sŏrng·tăa·ou from Phuket's fountain circle at Th Ranong. Túk-túk charters cost at least 150B from Phuket Town. The túk-túk trip from Rawai to Nai Han is a hefty 20B.

Long-tail boats are available for charter right along Hat Rawai – a charter to Ko Phi-Phi costs 3500B (maximum six passengers).

HAT NAI HAN
หาดในหาน

The tourist earthquake has yet to hit Hat Nai Han, 10km south of Kata. The colossal **Royal Phuket Yacht Club** dominates one hillside, but **Samnak Song Nai Han** (Map p307), a monastic centre, claims the lion's share of the beachfront land and has thus far managed to stave off the developers. Whatever the reasons, this beautiful little bay remains one of the quietest in Phuket and – from your balcony at the Yacht Club – you can just about catch a glimpse of the Phuket of three decades ago.

Hat Nai Han is a dangerous place to swim during the monsoon season (May to October),

when the sea becomes particularly rough – look out for the red flag, which means dangerous swimming conditions. Beach chairs and umbrellas can be rented for 60B from stalls along the beachfront.

Sleeping & Eating

Except for the Yacht Club, there's not much accommodation with views of the beach. Restaurants at the Yacht Club cater for expensive appetites, while a handful of no-frills beachside food stalls will fill you up for a pittance.

Nai Harn Garden Resort (Map p307; ☎ 0 7628 8319; www.naiharngardenresort.com; 15/12 Muu 1, Th Viset; r 2100-8300B; ❊ 🖳 🖳) Back from the beach, on the far side of the reservoir, this resort offers a range of bungalows and villas in a spacious garden setting. The atmosphere is a little suburban cul-de-sac, but standards are high, there are plenty of masseurs at hand – massage is something of a hotel speciality – and prices are reasonable.

Sabana (Map p307; ☎ 0 7628 9327; www.sabana-resort.com; 14/53 Muu 1, Th Viset; r 3500-8500B; ❊ 🖳 🖳) Right on The Royal Phuket's doorstep, this is an excellent and much less expensive back-up. The décor is all primary colours and Thai motifs and, while the cheaper rooms are a little ordinary, the pricier 'Thai Sala' options are beautifully designed. There's also an on-site spa.

The Royal Phuket Yacht Club (Map p307; ☎ 0 7638 0200; www.phuket.com/yacht-club; 23/3 Muu 1, Th Viset; r from 8000B; 🛇 🖳 🗷) There's not a yacht in sight, but the property is grand indeed. Rooms feature fabulously large terraces – and stunning bay views – and there's every creature comfort you could imagine somewhere on site. If you can cadge one of the low season discounts, it really is excellent value.

Getting There & Away

Nai Han is 18km from Phuket Town and a sŏrng·tăa·ou (leaving from the intersection of Phuket Town's Th Krung Thep and the fountain circle) costs 25B per person. Túk-túk charters are 150B to 200B one way. From Nai Han to Rawai, expect to pay about 20B in a túk-túk.

HAT KATA

หาดกะตะ

Kata is just a fun beach. It lacks the seediness of Patong and the gloom of Karon and attracts travellers of all ages with its shopping, surfing, lively beach and fine dining. While you might not find a secluded strip of sand, you will find plenty to do and plenty of easy-going folks to meet.

The beach here is actually divided into two distinct parts, separated by a rocky headland: Hat Kata Yai to the north and Hat Kata Noi to the south. Both offer plenty of soft, golden sand and attract a somewhat bohemian crowd compared with the rest of the island.

The main commercial street of Th Thai Na is perpendicular to the shore and has most of the restaurants and shops, along with some cheaper places to stay. Expats have moved into the area in large numbers, with Scandinavians appearing to hold most of the best cards; you won't get five paces without passing a 'Viking' this or a 'Horned Helmet' that.

Information

There are plenty of ATMs along Kata's main drag.

Kata Bookshop (☎ 0 7633 0109; 82 Th Kata; 🕑 10am-9pm) Great selection of new and used books and helpful service.

Post office (🕑 9am-4.30pm Mon-Fri, to noon Sat) On Rte 4028, at the end of Th Thai Na.

Sights & Activities

The small island of **Ko Pu** is within swimming distance of the shore (if you're a strong swimmer); on the way are some OK coral reefs. Be careful of riptides; heed the red flags and don't go past the breakers (ask about swimming conditions). Both Hat Kata Yai and Hat Kata Noi offer decent **surfing** waves from April to November. Board rental costs 150B for one hour or 600B for the whole day.

Sleeping

These are average prices for the high season (May to October) – haggle for discounts when things are quiet. Like Patong, it's getting harder and harder to find anything under 1000B during the high season and the beach is becoming distinctly upscale – but prices can drop radically when tourism is down.

BUDGET & MIDRANGE

In general, the less expensive places tend to be off the beach between Kata Yai (to the north) and Kata Noi (to the south) or well off the beach on the road to the island interior.

Kata On Sea (☎ 0 7633 0594; bungalows 400-1000B; 🛇) It's a steep 100m climb to this clutch of 29 modest bungalows dotting a quiet green hilltop, but for this price, it's well worth the effort. The bungalows are large and maximize the views with giant windows, and the minifridges are a score for keeping beer and water cold on hot days. Rooms with air-con start at 800B and there's a low-key family atmosphere.

Family Smile (☎ 0 7633 0594; www.familyinnphuket.com; 147-151 Th Thai Na; r 1000-1400B; 🛇) The good-sized standard rooms here have some quirky antiques that give the otherwise plain style more personality. It's a multistorey place on a busy street corner, but rooms are quiet.

Kata Country House (☎ 0 7633 3210; www.katacountryhouse.com; 7/23 Th Kata; r 1800-3000B; 🛇 🗷) We can't tell if the retro '60s/70s kitsch is done on purpose here or if it's just a lovely accident. Whatever the case, it's authentic. Expect wagon-wheel railings on the terraces, a tiki-style lounge that plays everything from swing to country and western, and sculptures everywhere ranging from elephants to Native American chiefs. The staff seem to get as big a hoot out of the place as the guests.

HAT KATA & HAT KARON

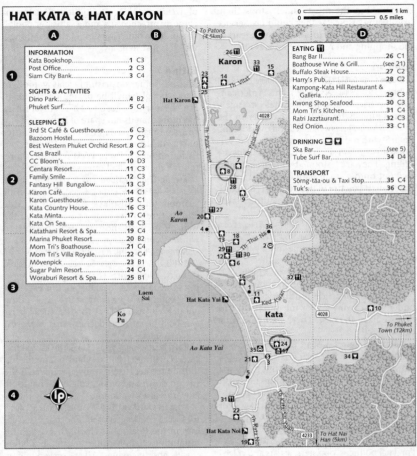

INFORMATION
Kata Bookshop 1 C3
Post Office 2 C3
Siam City Bank 3 C4

SIGHTS & ACTIVITIES
Dino Park 4 B2
Phuket Surf 5 C4

SLEEPING
3rd St Café & Guesthouse 6 C3
Bazoom Hostel 7 C2
Best Western Phuket Orchid Resort.8 C2
Casa Brazil 9 C2
CC Bloom's 10 D3
Centara Resort 11 C3
Family Smile 12 C3
Fantasy Hill Bungalow 13 C3
Karon Café 14 C1
Karon Guesthouse 15 C1
Kata Country House 16 C3
Kata Minta 17 C4
Kata On Sea 18 C3
Katathani Resort & Spa 19 C4
Marina Phuket Resort 20 B2
Mom Tri's Boathouse 21 C4
Mom Tri's Villa Royale 22 C4
Mövenpick 23 B1
Sugar Palm Resort 24 C4
Woraburi Resort & Spa 25 B1

EATING
Bang Bar II 26 C1
Boathouse Wine & Grill ....(see 21)
Buffalo Steak House 27 C2
Harry's Pub 28 C2
Kampong-Kata Hill Restaurant &
  Galleria 29 C3
Kwong Shop Seafood 30 C3
Mom Tri's Kitchen 31 C4
Ratri Jazztaurant 32 C3
Red Onion 33 C1

DRINKING
Ska Bar ....(see 5)
Tube Surf Bar 34 D4

TRANSPORT
Sŏrng·tǎa·ou & Taxi Stop 35 C4
Tuk's 36 C2

It's nothing luxurious but we give it five stars for character.

Sugar Palm Resort (☎ 0 7628 4404; www.sugarpalmphuket.com; 20/10 Th Kata; r incl breakfast 1800-6100B;) It's a 'chic chill-out world' at the Sugar Palm, as this Miami-meets-Thailand–style resort claims. Rooms, decorated in urban whites, blacks and lavender, are exceptional value and sublimely comfy, and all surround a black-bottomed, U-shaped pool. You feel a bit on stage going for a swim here, but the beach isn't far and you're in the heart of Kata's lively shopping and restaurant strip. Those who hang out in their room will find that the bath tubs are perfectly positioned for watching the plasma-screen TVs. High-end touches, such as the welcome fruit

juice, tip-top service, free tea and coffee, and bathrobes, are just the cherry on top of this already delicious cake.

3rd St Café & Guesthouse (☎ 0 7628 4510; www.3rdstreetcafe.com; 100 3/4 Th Patak West; r 2000-2500B;) The six rooms are each styled differently at this eclectic guesthouse with a knack for decorating. Walls are done up in muted earthy tones with lots of bright modern art. Furniture and fixings are classy, and make use of natural materials such as rich, red Thai silk. The guesthouse is just minutes from the beach. An American breakfast is included.

Kata Minta (☎ 0 7633 3283; www.kataminta.com; 6/56-58 Moo 2, Th Patak; r 2600-2800B;) Distinctly Thai-style rooms here have plenty of trimmings such as teak furniture and silk bed

NORTHERN ANDAMAN COAST

runners, but the musty smell stops them from being as nice as they could be. Service is lukewarm but the location, in the heart of the shopping and restaurant area, is OK.

TOP END

CC Bloom's (☎ 076333322; www.ccbloomshotel.com; 84/21 Th Patak; r 3400-3900B; ✗ 🖳 🖵) This American-run gay-friendly boutique hotel (strangely named after Bette Midler's character in the movie *Beaches*) has a fab location overlooking Kata. Stylish rooms are done up in creamy yellow with crimson silk panels draped from the ceiling. They are festooned with orchids and face out onto a small pool decorated with a waterfall. If you tire of the isolation (it's quite a hike from the beach), a free shuttle makes multiple runs to the waves.

Centara Resort (☎ 0 7637 0300; www.phuket.com /centralkata; 54 Th Ked Kwan; r from 5850B; ✗ 🖳 🖵) If you've got kids in tow, some money to burn and an aversion to the sleazy and cheesy, head straight here. Rooms are modern, simply stylish and filled with every comfort, but it's the pool, with a water slide, little bridges to swim under and a swim-up bar for mum and dad that we liked the best. There's a free shuttle to the beach.

Katathani Resort & Spa (☎ 0 7633 0124; www .katathani.com; 14 Th Kata Noi; r from 7000B; ✗ 🖵) Down on quieter Hat Kata Noi, this glitzy spa resort offers all the usual trimmings in stylish surrounds. It features a spa, a handful of pools, a beauty salon and heaps of space. Excellent low season deals are on offer if you haggle.

Mom Tri's Boathouse (☎ 0 7633 0015; www.boat housephuket.com; 2/2 Th Patak West; r 8000-25,000B; ✗ 🖵) For Thai politicos, pop stars, artists and celebrity authors, the intimate boutique Boathouse is still the only place to stay on Phuket. Rooms were remodelled after the tsunami and are spacious, gorgeous affairs, some sporting large breezy verandas. Critics complain that the Boathouse is a bit stiff-lipped old-fashioned for this century, but no-one can deny that the main reason to stay here is for the food. The three on-site restaurants are the best on the island.

ourpick Mom Tri's Villa Royale (☎ 0 7633 3568; www.villaroyalephuket.com; ste incl breakfast from 11,500B; ✗ 🖳 🖵) Tucked away in a secluded Kata Noi location with the grandest of views, Villa Royale opened in 2006 to nearly instant acclaim. The romantic place with fabulous food offers beautiful rooms straight out of the pages

of *Architectural Digest*. Guiltless pleasures include an attached spa and a saltwater pool, if you prefer a tamer version of the real thing – which is just steps away.

Eating

There's some surprisingly classy food in Kata, though you'll be paying dearly for it. For cheaper eats, head to Th Thai Na, which has more than its fair share of Italian and – of course – Scandinavian restaurants. A cluster of affordable, casual seafood restaurants can be found on Th Patak West near the shore, though they don't all offer sea views.

Kwong Shop Seafood (☎ 0 1273 3707; Th Thai Na; mains 40-130B; 🕑 lunch & dinner) This no-frills seafood joint displays fresh fish outside and pictures of its happy customers on the walls. It is cheap and very, very cheerful – a winning combination.

Kampong-Kata Hill Restaurant & Galleria (☎ 0 7633 0103; Th Patak West; dishes 80-260B; 🕑 lunch & dinner) Chock-a-block with Thai antiques and serving some fabulous local dishes, this excellent little eatery is up a long stairway. Finding good, well-priced Thai food in these parts can be a bit of a headache – this is a great place to start.

Ratri Jazztaurant (☎ 0 7633 3538; Th Chalong-Karon; dishes 145-345B; 🕑 11am-1am) Hang out on the hip hillside terrace, listen to live jazz, watch the sun go down and enjoy delicious Thai food. Now *this* is a vacation.

Mom Tri's Kitchen (☎ 0 7633 0015; Th Kata Noi; dishes 180-880B; 🕑 6.30am-midnight) The more casual link in the Boathouse chain, this delightful restaurant offers Mediterranean/Thai *haute cuisine* and fine wines. All are served in gorgeous grounds overlooking the beach and the atmosphere is intimate.

ourpick Boathouse Wine & Grill (☎ 0 7633 0015; www.boathousephuket.com; Th Patak West; mains 450-950B; 🕑 7am-midnight) The perfect place to wow a fussy date, the Boathouse is the pick of the bunch for most local foodies. The atmosphere can be a little stuffy – this is the closest Phuket gets to old-school dining – but the Mediterranean fusion food is fabulous, the wine list expansive and the sea views sublime.

Drinking

Kata's nightlife tends to be pretty mellow.

At Kata's southernmost cove, Ska Bar, tucked into the rocks and seemingly inter-

---

DETOUR: ISLANDS AROUND PHUKET

There are several islands off the coast of Phuket that make for quieter, more romantic getaways. **Ko Heh** (also known as Coral Island and sometimes spelled Ko Hae) is a few kilometres south of Ao Chalong. It's a good spot for diving and snorkelling, although jet skis and other pleasure craft can be an annoyance. The island gets lots of day trippers from Phuket, but at night it's pretty quiet. Most of the 64 concrete bungalows of **Coral Island Resort** (☎ 0 7628 1060; www .coralislandresort.com; bungalows 2800-3600B; 🔀 🛎) are arranged around the swimming pool, but the more expensive bungalows are seaside. There's also a karaoke lounge, and cable TV in the lobby just in case you can't live without your daily dose of the tube.

Southeast of Laem Phanwa is **Ko Mai Thon**, which is similar to, but smaller than, Ko Heh. Stay at **Maiton Resort** (☎ 0 7621 4954; www.maitonisland.com/room.html; bungalows 7500-12,750B; 🔀 🖳 🛎), which offers semiluxurious hillside or beachside bungalows, two pools (indoor and outdoor), a sauna, fitness centre, tennis court and five restaurants.

Ko Raya Yai and **Ko Raya Noi**, about 1½ hours by boat south of Phuket, are also known as Ko Racha Yai/Noi. They are highly favoured by divers and snorkellers for their hard coral reefs, which are found in both shallow and deep waters, making it a good area for both novices and pros. Accommodation is available on both islands.

Most people use travel agencies in Phuket Town to get to these islands. If you want to go it alone, boats leave Ao Chalong and Hat Rawai for Ko Heh; the trip takes 30 minutes and costs 100B. You can also charter a long-tail boat or speedboat from Rawai or Ao Chalong for 1500B.

Songserm Travel (☎ 0 7622 2570; 51-55 Th Satoon) runs passenger boats to Ko Raya Yai from Phuket Town port every morning. The trip takes 30 minutes and costs 400B each way. **Pal Travel Service** (☎ 0 7634 4920) runs a similar service. Both companies suspend service from May to October.

---

twined with the trunk of a sturdy tree, is our choice for oceanside sundowners. The Thai bartenders add to Ska's funky Rasta vibe. It stays open late.

Tube Surf Bar (☎ 0 7285 4718; dishes from 30B) This surf bar gets going on Tuesday and Friday nights (in particular), when surf videos are screened; if you're looking to find out more about local surfing culture, this is where to head. It's a bit difficult to find – if you get lost ask for directions (during the day) from Phuket Surf (which runs the Tube), next to the Ska Bar.

Getting There & Around

Sŏrng·tăa·ou and buses to both Kata and Karon (per person 50B) leave frequently from the Th Ranong market in Phuket from 7am to 5pm. The main sŏrng·tăa·ou stop is in front of Kata Beach Resort.

Taxis from Kata go to Phuket Town (300B), Patong (250B) and Karon (150B).

Motorcycle rentals are available at **Tuk's** (☎ 0 7628 4049) for 300B.

HAT KARON

หาดกะรน

A long sweep of gently curving beach, Hat Karon has a dash of package holiday ambience

mixed in with tranquil beach paradise and a smidgen of Patong sleaze. There's an element of hush about the place that can either make it seem wonderfully peaceful or depressingly backwater – it depends on your attitude. The northern section of town, around Th Vitat, is a little dowdy, but features a handful of decent budget hotels, while the southern beach section blends seamlessly into much livelier Hat Kata. **Siam City Bank** (Th Patak East; ☼ 9am-4pm Mon-Fri) has money exchange (until 6pm) and ATM facilities.

Things can get very quiet here during the low season and the resort suffers from the off-peak gloom that tends to afflict seaside towns when visitors are thin on the ground.

Dino Park (☎ 0 7633 0625; Th Patak West; adult/child 260/200B; ☼ 10am-midnight) is a bizarre, Flintstones-esque outdoorsy area with mini-golf, leafy gardens (with waterfall) and an eatery serving 'Bronto' burgers. It is at the southern edge of Hat Karon.

Sleeping

BUDGET & MIDRANGE

Hat Karon is lined with inns and deluxe bungalows, along with some cheaper places. Ask for discounts in the low season, and if you stay more than a few days. Less expensive

NORTHERN ANDAMAN COAST

places will naturally be found well off the beach, often on small hillocks to the east of the main road.

Bazoom Hostel (☎ 0 7639 6914; www.bazoom hostel.com; 64/76-77 Th Patak East; dm/r 250/590B; ❄ 🖳) One of Phuket's bona fide backpacker haunts, Bazoom offers the usual standard features: psychedelic décor, an internet café, plenty of banter and staff who are savvy with the intricacies of doing Phuket on the cheap. The dorm is basic (with 14 beds), or you can opt for one of the no-frills but comfy rooms. Air-con is available in the pricier doubles. Some sŏrng·tăa·ou drivers may pretend they've never heard of this place, as Bazoom doesn't pay them commissions – be adamant. Also, we've heard rumours that Bazoom may change its name. From Phuket Town, you can catch the Kata/Karon bus (40B). Alternatively, call for a pick-up (150B).

Karon Guesthouse (☎ 0 7639 6860; r 400-500B; ❄ 🔊) Furniture is of the scratched, mismatched variety and bathrooms are tiny, but this family-run hotel is very cheap, the staff are friendly and beds are firm. It offers free left-luggage service and safe deposit, plus satellite TV in the lobby. Guests have pool privileges at the nearby Golden Sands Hotel.

Fantasy Hill Bungalow (☎ 0 7633 0106; fantasyhill@ hotmail.com; bungalows 500-1500B; ❄) Sitting in a lush garden on a hill, the bungalows here are good value and of the type that's pretty much disappeared from this beach. Fantasy Hill isn't a fancy spot, but it's better than average for the price.

Karon Café (☎ 0 7639 6217; www.karon-phuket-hotels .com; 526/17 Soi Islandia Park Resort; r 800-900B, family ste 1100B; ❄) Way less 'sexy' than most places back on this bar-filled lane. Rooms here are clean and above a friendly little café.

ourpick Casa Brazil (☎ 0 7639 6317; www.phuket homestay.com; Soi 1, 9 Th Luang Pho Chuan; r 1100-1500B; ❄) Simple rooms have Brazilian colour and flair, which makes this friendly, clean spot stand out from the rest. There's a whimsically styled and very social café on the ground floor and the 21 rooms are spacious and tastefully decorated. There are also very small verandas in each room overlooking the neighbourhood, which is mostly residential. It is a short and pleasant walk to the beach, with both Hat Karon and Hat Kata being almost equidistant.

Best Western Phuket Orchid Resort (☎ 0 7639 6599; www.bestwestern.com; 562 Th Patak; r from 2500B; ❄ 🖳 🔊) This Best Western, with sleek architecture effortlessly blending into the hill upon which it sits, gives you more than your money's worth. The amenities, along with the spacious, posh rooms, feel as if they belong at a much pricier place. The hotel is family oriented, with babysitting services. The pool is the most popular hang-out for sunbathers.

TOP END

Many of the remaining places to stay in Karon are newer resort-type hotels with all the posh amenities.

Woraburi Resort & Spa (☎ 0 7639 6638; www .woraburiphuket.com; 198-200 Th Patak West; r incl breakfast 4100-8500B; ❄ 🖳 🔊) Rooms here, just across the street from the beach, have some very nice Thai touches, such as sandstone 'carved' art in the bathrooms. The morning buffet breakfast is immense, tasty and served in a giant open-air pavilion. When we passed there was a snooker table and a giant TV in the lobby, which detracted from an otherwise stylish setting.

Marina Phuket Resort (☎ 0 7633 0625; www.marina phuket.com; 47 Th Patak West; r from 5000B; ❄ 🖳 🔊) If you're after privacy, you could do a whole lot worse than a night here. Three types of villas are on offer: the most expensive 'sea' villas open up over the sea and you can fall asleep to the soporific sound of water lapping against the stilts. The gardens are an immense botanical explosion, and the setting is textbook romantic. It's also great for families.

ourpick Mövenpick (☎ 0 7639 6139; www.moeven pick-hotels.com; 509 Th Patak West; r from 8000B; ❄ 🔊) Grab a secluded villa and choose from a private plunge pool or outdoor rainforest shower; alternatively chill in the cubelike rooms with huge floor-to-ceiling glass windows (in some cases covering two entire walls) in the swank ultramodern white hotel. Besides a prime location across the street from a pretty stretch of the beach, the Mövenpick offers artistic décor, top-end linen, a big pool with swim-up bar, a spa, and an alfresco restaurant and bar with a giant selection of wood-fired pizzas.

Eating & Drinking

As usual, almost every place to stay has a restaurant. There are a few cheap Thai and seafood places off the roundabout (including beachside seafood stalls 100m north of it), but overall you'll find a better selection further south at Hat Kata Yai and Hat Kata Noi.

Red Onion (☎ 0 7639 6827; dishes 80-160B; ⓨ 4-11pm) This slap-up eatery in half of a garage with a tin roof is a bona fide faràng (foreigners of European descent) magnet. There is Thai food on the menu, along with Western titbits such as schnitzel and spaghetti. Cocktails and wine selections complement the meals, so try to forget the bad music. Dine at cheery red-clothed tables on chairs padded with silk pillows. It's about 300m east of the roundabout – look for the coloured lights.

Buffalo Steak House (☎ 0 7633 3013; Th Patak West; dishes 80-450B; ⓨ lunch & dinner) At the southern end of the town, this old-timer swears it serves the best steak in Phuket. It's not wildly off the mark and if you fancy large slabs of red meat, this is your place. The open front keeps the air fresh, and wood décor brings a taste of the Wild West to the table.

Harry's Pub (☎ 0 7635 7656; Th Patak East; dishes 100-300B; ⓨ lunch & dinner) Harry's is at its best in the high season, when it is one of the area's most popular watering holes. Whenever the doors are open though, you can count on big portions of anything that comes with fries. The beer's good, if a little expensive.

Bang Bar II (ⓨ noon-midnight) Built from flotsam and jetsam collected on the beach, this chilled-out bar is perfect for sundowners. It features your standard brand of Rastafarian décor and a collection of surfboards. A sun-bleached tarpaulin provides shelter during monsoon downpours.

Getting There & Away

For details on transport to Karon, see p311.

HAT PATONG
หาดป่าตอง

You'll either love Patong or you'll hate it. This beachside monument to hedonism is a place where many visitors get more sleep on the beach during the day than during the party-hard nights. From around 11am, sunburnt tourists wearing the latest Thai knockoff T-shirts, and often accompanied by small children wielding soft drinks, swarm the streets in search of bargains – as well as the curve of beach in search of a patch of sand to fry their skin some more. As the sun goes down, the families go in, the bar girls come out, the

booze starts to flow and the hips start gyrating. The rest is a blur, but judging by the aching of your head the next day you're pretty sure you had a great time. And is that a girl or a boy tucked in next to you?

But even if you're not the stay-out-all-night sort, Patong can entice the curious with its diving options, upscale dining, shopping, cabaret shows and Thai boxing. The beach is gorgeous but loud, and with all the jet skis, a dip in the water isn't all that peaceful. The swankiest resorts will offer more tranquility, but if that's what you're looking for, why are you in Patong? Plenty of parents bring their kids to this beach, but if you do, be prepared to answer questions such as as: 'Mummy, what's a hooker/ladyboy/junkie?'.

Information

There are banks with ATM and exchange facilities across town.

Bank of Ayudya (Th Rat Uthit; ⓨ 9am-4pm Mon-Fri, exchange booth 11am-9pm) Features an exchange booth.

Bookazine (☎ 0 7634 5834; 18 Th Bangla; ⓨ 10am-11pm) For English-language books and magazines.

Boots Pharmacy (☎ 0 7634 3713; Th Thawiwong; ⓨ 9am-6pm) A branch of the British pharmacy chain.

Immigration office (☎ 0 7634 0477; Th Kalim Beach; ⓨ 10am-noon & 1-3pm Mon-Fri) For visa extensions.

Post office (Th Thawiwong; ⓨ 9am-4.30pm Mon-Fri, to noon Sat)

TA Internet (☎ 0 7634 9014; Th Bangla; per min 2B; ⓨ 9am-3am)

Tourist Police (☎ 0 7634 0244; Th Thawiwong)

Activities

Patong is a centre for diving on the island; see p297 for a list of established dive shops. For excursions to the Similan and Surin islands, see p279 and p274, respectively.

Motor yachts, sailboats and catamarans can sometimes be chartered with or without crew; see p298.

Sleeping

It's getting pretty difficult to find anything in Patong under 1000B from approximately November to May (the period that corresponds to the prices listed in this book), but outside this time rates drop by 40% to 60%. This is a town known for prostitution so even most 'nice' places have a 'joiner fee' (anything from 500B upwards, depending on the hotel's rates) and condoms are a minibar standard.

NORTHERN ANDAMAN COAST

HAT PATONG

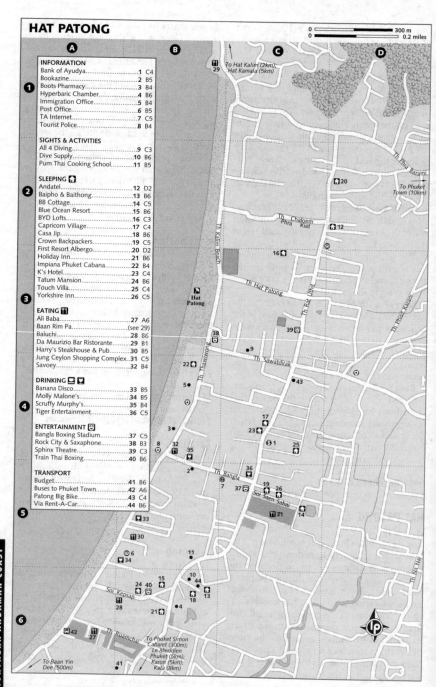

INFORMATION	
Bank of Ayudya	1 C4
Bookazine	2 B5
Boots Pharmacy	3 B4
Hyperbaric Chamber	4 B6
Immigration Office	5 B4
Post Office	6 B5
TA Internet	7 C5
Tourist Police	8 B4

SIGHTS & ACTIVITIES	
All 4 Diving	9 C3
Dive Supply	10 B6
Pum Thai Cooking School	11 B5

SLEEPING	
Andatel	12 D2
Baipho & Baithong	13 B6
BB Cottage	14 C5
Blue Ocean Resort	15 B6
BYD Lofts	16 C3
Capricorn Village	17 C4
Casa Jip	18 B6
Crown Backpackers	19 C5
First Resort Albergo	20 D2
Holiday Inn	21 B6
Impiana Phuket Cabana	22 B4
K's Hotel	23 C4
Tatum Mansion	24 B6
Touch Villa	25 C4
Yorkshire Inn	26 C5

EATING	
Ali Baba	27 A6
Baan Rim Pa	(see 29)
Baluchi	28 B6
Da Maurizio Bar Ristorante	29 B1
Harry's Steakhouse & Pub	30 B5
Jung Ceylon Shopping Complex	31 C5
Savoey	32 B4

DRINKING	
Banana Disco	33 B5
Molly Malone's	34 B5
Scruffy Murphy's	35 B4
Tiger Entertainment	36 C5

ENTERTAINMENT	
Bangla Boxing Stadium	37 C5
Rock City & Saxaphone	38 B3
Sphinx Theatre	39 C3
Train Thai Boxing	40 B6

TRANSPORT	
Budget	41 B6
Buses to Phuket Town	42 A6
Patong Big Bike	43 C4
Via Rent-A-Car	44 B6

0 — 300 m
0 — 0.2 miles

To Hat Kalim (2km);
Hat Kamala (5km)

To Phuket
Town (10km)

Th Phra Barami

Th Chaloem
Phra Kiat

Th Kalim Beach

Th Hat Patong

Th Hat Uthit

Th Phisit Karani

Th Thawiwong

Th Sawatdirak

Hat
Patong

Th Bangla

Soi Saen Sabai

Soi Kepsap

Th Ruamchai

Th Na Nai

To Phuket Simon
Cabaret (300m);
Le Meridien
Phuket (5km);
Karon (5km);
Kata (8km)

To Baan Yin
Dee (500m)

BUDGET

On the beach there is nothing in the budget range, but on and off Th Rat Uthit, especially in the Paradise Complex and along Soi Saen Sabai, there are several nondescript guesthouses with rooms that hover around 1000B in the high season but plummet to as low as 350B in the low season.

Crown Backpackers (☎ 0 7634 2297; crown_hostel@ yahoo.com; 169/3 Soi Sansabai; female only dm 250B, r from 400B) Expect bare-bones basics and late night rumblings in this hostel in the heart of the bar zone.

our pick **Capricorn Village** (☎ 0 7634 0390; 2/29 Th Rat Uthit; bungalows from 660B; 🔀 🖭) This is perhaps the best deal in Patong in the high season. Bright little bungalows with terraces wind back into a quiet garden and the service is lovely. Guests can use the pool at K's Hotel next door.

BB Cottage (☎ 0 7634 2948; 171/21 Soi Saen Sabai; bungalows 850-1450B; 🔀) Smacked right up against the massive Jungle Ceylon shopping mall, the scruffy bungalows here are uncommonly big and all except the smallest have kitchens. The garden is spacious and the whole place is quiet and central.

MIDRANGE

You won't get beachfront for midrange prices but you will get cleanliness and comfort.

Touch Villa (☎ 0 7634 4011; touchvilla@hotmail.com; 151/4 Th Rat Uthit; r 1000B; 🔀) Suspect name, reliable standards. This slightly crumbly spot has a twee garden setting and a holiday camp ambience. It's cheap and cheerful with just a 'touch' of Patong's seediness.

Casa Jip (☎ 0 7634 3019; www.casajip.com; 207/10 Th Rat Uthit; r 1000B; 🔀) Italian run and great value, this place has very big, relatively luxurious rooms with comfy beds and a taste of Thai style. You get cable TV and there's even a breakfast room service. It's popular with couples.

Tatum Mansion (☎ 0 7634 4332; tatummansion@ hotmail.com; 66/7-8 Soi Kepsap; r from 1400B; 🔀) On a street packed with budget offerings and massage parlours à gogo, this British-owned outfit comes up trumps. You get cable TV, hardwood furniture, a great bed and the low-down on town from the super-friendly management.

K's Hotel (☎ 0 7634 0832; www.k-hotel.com; 180 Th Rat Uthit; r from 1500; 🔀 🖭) While this place caters primarily to Germans, you'll feel plenty *willkommen* if you're not – and will feel especially comfortable after swilling quality beer at the on-site *biergarten*. Rooms are above standard with plasma TVs, big windows and stone-tile bathrooms. The surrounding gardens are lush and the pool feels like it's in a jungle. It's popular with families.

First Resort Albergo (☎ 0 7634 0980; firsthotel@ hotmail.com; 19/12 Th Rat Uthit; r from 1800B; 🔀 🖭) And so to Italy. This pleasant, Italian-run spot is as solid as mama's bust and offers stylish rooms around a pool. There's TV, a terrace restaurant (expect pizza and bolognese made with Thai basil) and plenty of warm Mediterranean hospitality.

Yorkshire Inn (☎ 0 7634 0904; www.yorkshireinn .com; 169/16 Soi Saen Sabai; r 1800-2100, apartments 4400B; 🔀 🖳) About as Thai as a plate of Yorkshire pud, this is one of a string of unabashedly British outfits, courting visitors who insist on putting the home in their comforts. This one offers a flicker of homey B&B charm and can at least put together a mean fry-up – the Yorkshire pudding is a little less successful. The rooms and apartments are spotless and come with cable TV.

our pick **Baipho & Baithong** (☎ 0 7629 2074; www .baipho.com; 205/12-13 & 205/14-15 Th Rat Uthit; r incl breakfast 1800-3300B; 🔀 🖳) This much style isn't usually found in this price range – particularly in Patong where chic is scarce. Buddha imagery and Zen-spa-type trimmings mingle with modern urban touches in the dimly lit, nest-like rooms of these twin hotels. 'The Lounge' downstairs serves upper-crust cocktails and very good Italian and Thai food, as well as gourmet snacks. Guests can use the pool at the unsightly Montana Grand Phuket next door.

Blue Ocean Resort (☎ 0 7634 5191; www.blueocean resort-phuket.com; 210/23 Soi Kepsap; r 1900-2100B; 🔀 🖭) The clean-cut rooms here are in a classy Thai-style house that's surrounded by plants, flowers and a pretty pool. It's great value and is regularly booked, so reserve ahead.

Andatel (☎ 0 7629 0489; www.andatelhotel.com; 419 Th Rat Uthit; r 2000-2800B; 🔀 🖭) Andatel offers fading Thai-meets-Andalusian styling and plentiful creature comforts in dark rooms with balconies. There's a decent restaurant out front.

TOP END

Holiday Inn (☎ 0 7634 0608; www.phuket.holiday-inn .com; Th Rat Uthit; r from 4560B; 🔀 🖳 🖭) This resort is a little glitzier than your run-of-the-mill Holiday Inn, and offers all the usual

GAY PRIDE IN PHUKET

Although there are big gay pride celebrations in Bangkok and Pattaya, the Phuket Gay Pride Festival is considered by many to be the best in Thailand, maybe even Southeast Asia.

The first Phuket Gay Festival started as a small community project in November 1999, in response to plans for similar events in the capital and in Pattaya. When the festival proved to be very successful, the planners realised that Phuket would be competing with the other cities' festivals so the festival was moved from November to February – a drier month in Phuket anyway. However, in 2007 it was held in August. Whenever it is on, the whole island – but the town of Patong specifically – is packed with (mostly male) revellers from all over the world.

Although Bangkok and Pattaya both have prominent gay scenes, Phuket's is possibly the most lovely, both because of the scenery and the light-hearted, open and friendly atmosphere. In recent years, the festival has also included social responsibility campaigns, such as HIV awareness, staying clean and sober, and the fight against child prostitution.

The main events of the four-day weekend party are a huge beach volleyball tournament and, of course, the Grand Parade, featuring floats, cheering crowds and beautiful costumes in the streets of Patong.

Prefestival parties start happening weeks before the event, and include things such as Gay Diving and Gay Sea Canoeing. Great package tours can be booked through many companies, including **Gay Guide Thailand** (www.gayguideinthailand.com) for men, and **Lesbian Adventures in Thailand** (www.lathailand.com) for women.

For updates on future festivals, or to sign up for the spectacular volleyball tournament, go to www.phuketpride.org.

amenities, plus one or two more. There's also a glossy spa featuring a smorgasbord of restorative treatments.

BYD Lofts (☎ 0 7634 3024; www.bydlofts.com; 5/28 Th Hat Patong; apt 5250-10,250B; ❄ 💻 ☎) If style and comfort are more important to you than beachfront (although it's only a minute's walk to the beach), look no further. Urban-style apartments with lots of white (floors, walls, blinds) and sharp lines feel angelic compared with the seedy world of Patong on the streets below. There's a day spa, a rooftop pool and an excellent *haute cuisine* restaurant on the premises.

our pick Baan Yin Dee (☎ 0 7629 4104; www.baanyin dee.com; 7/5 Th Muean Ngen; r from 5800B; ❄ ☎) On a hill overlooking town, this is Patong's premier boutique getaway. It's small but perfectly put together: spacious rooms with balconies, design magazine styling and a trickle of beautiful young things hanging out around the pool. If you're partying all night, this is the place to repair your soul and there's a fabulous restaurant for a fine culinary treat.

Le Meridien Phuket (☎ 0 7634 0480; www.le meridien.com; r from 8925B; ❄ 💻 ☎) Just outside town, this swanky resort has everything the international globetrotter could ask for, from tennis courts and swimming pools (both very much in the plural), to fabulous restaurants

and palatial rooms. There's even volleyball, minigolf and a climbing wall. It remains one of Phuket's great escapes.

Impiana Phuket Cabana (☎ 0 7634 0138; www .impiana.com; Th Thawiwong; r from 9200B; ❄ ☎) Cabana style and plumb on the best part of the beach, the rooms here are laden with chic and creature comforts and are close to all the action. We were surprised that we couldn't find English-speaking staff at such a high-end spot though.

Eating

Patong has stacks of restaurants, some of them quite good. Bargain seafood and noodle stalls pop up across town at night – try the lanes on and around Th Bangla.

Patong's most glamorous restaurants are in a little huddle above the cliffs on the northern edge of town. Back in town, expect the usual spread of expat diners, filled with topless (the men, that is) tourists.

Jung Ceylon Shopping Complex (Th Rat Uthit; dishes 60-150B; ☻ 11am-11pm) For excellent, cheap eats in sterile surrounds, head for the basement food court in this shopping complex, where you'll find stalls serving specialities from every corner of Thailand.

Ali Baba (☎ 0 7634 5024; 38 Th Ruamchai; dishes 100-300B; ☻ 11am-midnight) A favourite with Patong's resident Indians, Ali Baba serves delicious subcontinental specialities to diners swathed in hookah smoke.

Harry's Steakhouse & Pub (☎ 0 1787 3167; 110/2 Soi Big One; dishes 100-495B; breakfast, lunch & dinner) No surprises at Harry's: it's the usual, air-conditioned tourist boozer. If you fancy a slab of steak in fresh, clean surrounds, however, you could do a lot worse than a table here.

Savoey (☎ 0 7634 1171; 136 Th Thawiwong; dishes 120-350B; lunch & dinner) This perennially popular seafood haunt subscribes to the 'slay 'em and weigh 'em' fish restaurant philosophy. Cast an eye over the mountain of seafood piled up on ice outside, or the fish gulping away in tanks inside, point out your prey and then take a seat to enjoy your catch. Great food, good prices.

Baluchi (☎ 0 7629 2526; Horizon Beach Resort, Soi Kepsap; dishes 175-700B; lunch & dinner) Patong's showcase Indian restaurant features top-notch tandoori, air-conditioned comforts and a 'show' kitchen – go watch your food being made.

our pick **Baan Rim Pa** (☎ 0 7634 4079; Th Kalim Beach; dishes 215-475B; lunch & dinner) Stunning Thai food is served with a side order of spectacular views at this institution. Standards are high, with prices to match, but romance is in the air, with candlelight and piano music aplenty. The cooking is top-notch – book ahead and tuck in your shirt.

Da Maurizio Bar Ristorante (☎ 0 7634 4079; Th Kalim Beach; dishes 450-950B; lunch & dinner) This upmarket Italian joint is cut from similar cloth and serves pasta dishes so good you'll be composing arias on your napkin. Expect the requisite level of Roman romance and unctuous, mouth-watering cooking.

Drinking

Some visitors may find that Patong's bar scene is enough to put them off their *pàt tai*, but if you're in the mood for plenty of beer, winking neon and short skirts, it is certainly worth sampling.

Th Bangla is Patong's beer and bar-girl Mecca and features a number of spectacular, go-go extravaganzas, where you can expect the usual mix of gyrating Thai girls and often red-faced Western men. The music is loud (expect techno), the clothes are all but non-existent and the décor is typically slapstick with plenty of phallic imagery. That said, the atmosphere is more carnival than carnage and

you'll find plenty of Western women pushing their way through the throng to the bar.

Tiger Entertainment (☎ 0 7634 5112; Th Bangla; noon-2am) The strangest building in Phuket features concrete cave styling and a menagerie of unsettling – and extremely well-endowed – anthropomorphic tigers. More a congregation of go-go bars – topped with a nightclub – than a single entity, this is the first, and often last, stop on any odyssey through Patong's bar scene.

Banana Disco (☎ 0 1271 2469; 96 Th Thawiwong; admission 200B) If you're after a more sophisticated nightclub experience, this is your ticket. A corny Aztec theme prevails, but at least you can dance without skidding around in puddles of beer.

Molly Malone's (☎ 0 7629 2771; Th Thawiwong; noon-2am) Wildly popular with tourists, this pub rocks with Irish gigs every night at 9.45pm. There's a good atmosphere, lots of pub food and some great tables out the front from which to admire the ocean and legions of passers-by. Guinness is available for a mere 349B per pint.

Scruffy Murphy's (☎ 0 7629 2590; 5 Th Bangla; 11am-2am) Yep, it's another Irish bar. This is, however, one of Patong's more respectable bars – largely due to the price of the drinks – with cosy Celtic styling, live music, good beer and better *craic* (distinctly Irish brand of fun). If you're keen to escape the Thai bar girls, this is one of the better bets.

Entertainment

Once you've done the go-go, there's plenty more to see. Cabaret and Thai boxing, in particular, are something of a speciality here.

Phuket Simon Cabaret (☎ 0 7634 2011; www.phuket-simoncabaret.com; admission 550B) About 300m south of town on Th Sirirach, this cabaret offers entertaining transvestite shows. The 600-seat theatre is grand, the costumes are gorgeous and the ladyboys are convincing. The house is often full. Performances are given at 7.30pm and 9.30pm nightly – book ahead.

Rock City & Saxophone (Th Kalim Beach) These two new venues, next door to each other, have nightly live music. Rock City, well, rocks, with local and Western hard-rock bands. Saxophone focuses on jazz, funk and soul, and books acts from Bangkok on a regular basis.

Sphinx Theatre (☎ 0 7634 1500; 120 Th Rat Uthit; admission 350B) There's more cabaret on offer at the Sphinx, where shows kick off at 9pm and 10.30pm daily.

Bangla Boxing Stadium (☎ 0 7282 2348; Th Bangla; admission 1000B) This stadium stages bouts at 8pm every Sunday.

Train Thai Boxing (☎ 0 7629 2890; Soi Kepsap; ☻ 8am-9pm) You can learn a few moves of your own at Train Thai Boxing, where a 90-minute lesson costs 300B – but pack some Band-Aids.

Getting There & Around

Túk-túk circulate around Patong for 25B per ride. There are numerous places to rent 125cc motorcycles and jeeps. **Patong Big Bike** (☎ 0 7634 0380; Th Rat Uthit) rents proper motorcycles (500B to 1000B per day), not scooter/motorbikes, as well as off-road motorbikes (350B per day). Keep in mind that the helmet law is strictly enforced in Patong. **Via Rent-A-Car** (☎ 0 7638 5718; www.via-phuket.com), based in Kamala, has an unattended office in town (you call from the telephone there) and delivers rental cars to Patong. **Budget** (☎ 0 7629 2389; 44 Th Thaveewong; ☻ 9am-4pm) has an office in the Patong Merlin Hotel.

Sŏrng·tǎa·ou to Patong from Phuket Town leave from Th Ranong, near the day market and fountain circle; the fare is 50B. The after-hours charter fare is 250B. Buses from Patong to Phuket Town leave from the southern end of Th Thawiwong and cost 50B.

HAT KAMALA
หาดกมลา

Since its tsunami battering, Kamala has lost ground – in terms of tourist arrivals – to nearby Patong and Hat Surin. The upside of this is that the resorts are newer and the beaches are quieter than almost anywhere else on Phuket. This pretty beach is golden-white, the ambience is very mellow and everyone smiles and says hello to each other. This might not last for much longer though, as new resorts are popping up and several stray jet skis seem to have escaped from Patong to buzz around this otherwise quiet bay.

Sights & Activities

Local beach boffins will tell you that **Laem Singh**, just north of Kamala, is one of the best capes on the island. Walled in by cliffs, there is no road access so you have to park on the headland and clamber down a narrow path. You could camp here and eat at the rustic

roadside seafood places at the northern end of Singh or in **Ban Kamala**, a village further south. If you're renting a motorbike, this is a nice little trip down Rte 4025 and then over dirt roads from Surin to Kamala.

Phuket Fantasea (☎ 0 7638 5000; www.phuket -fantasea.com; admission with/without dinner 1900/1500B; ☻ 6-11.30pm Fri-Wed) is a US$60 million 'cultural theme park' located just east of Hat Kamala. Despite the billing, there aren't any rides, but there is a show that takes the colour and pageantry of traditional Thai dance and costumes and combines this with state-of-the-art light-and-sound techniques that rival anything found in Las Vegas (think 30 elephants). All of this takes place on a stage dominated by a full-scale replica of a Khmer temple reminiscent of Angkor Wat. Kids especially will be captivated by the spectacle but it is over-the-top cheesy. There is a good collection of souvenir shops in the park offering Thai handicrafts. The food on offer at Thai buffet dinner has a bad reputation among travellers, so consider taking in the show without the meal. Tickets can be booked through most hotels and tour agencies.

Don't bother bringing your camera to catch the splendour and spectacle on film – they are not allowed and if you do bring it, you'll have to deposit it for safekeeping before you enter.

Back in Kamala, you can organise diving through expat-run **Scuba Quest** (☎ 0 7627 9016; www.scuba-quest-phuket.de).

Sleeping & Eating

There's a string of mostly overpriced (from 1000B), dilapidated sleeping options along the north end of the beach clustered among some rickety beach bars and restaurants. All rates drop considerably in the low season. Pickings are slim for good food – if you have a car consider driving to Hat Surin (opposite) where there are lots of great choices.

Benjamin Resort (☎ 0 7638 5145; www.phuketdir .com/benjaminresort; r incl breakfast 1000-1500B; 🕸) With circa 1970 construction, but right on the beach, friendly Benjamin is looking a little crumbly, but was getting a fresh coat of paint when we passed through. Rooms all come with TVs and minifridges and the ones with views are the priciest. Rates drop 50% in the low season.

Orchid House (☎ 0 7638 5445; treepoppanat_kwan@ yahoo.com; r 1000-1500B; 🕸) This orchid is clean-cut and cutesy with patterned tiles and shim-

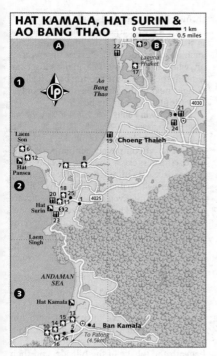

HAT KAMALA, HAT SURIN & AO BANG THAO

mering curtains. Blooming pot plants abound and there's a sweet downstairs bar-café. All in all, it's cleaner and better value than Benjamin and is only about 20m further away from the beach.

Kamala Dreams (☎ 0 7629 1131; www.kamala-beach .net; r 2520-3040B; ✷ ⚑) Two strides from the beach, expect sparkling surfaces and spotless (though slightly dowdy) rooms with tiled floors and blinding white paint. Grounds, though small, are lovely with more white walls, Buddha sculptures and an inviting oval-shaped pool.

Kamala Beach Hotel (☎ 0 7627 9580; www.kam alabeach.com; r 3100-3950B; bungalows 4350-5600B; ✷ ⌨ ⚑) There's not much flair to the design here, but the hotel is right on the beach and boasts two big pools. The spacious bungalows are nearly identical to the rooms and not worth the extra baht. A good choice for families.

our pick **Layalina Hotel** (☎ 0 7638 5942; www.lay alinahotel.com; r incl breakfast 5500-7700B; ✷ ⌨ ⚑) We loved this tiny beachfront boutique hotel, especially the split-level suites with very private rooftop terraces for romantic sunset views

over white sand and blue sea. Décor is simple, Thai and chic, with fluffy white duvets and honey-toned wood furniture. This is a place that is ideal for honeymooners, simply dripping in intimacy and sophistication. Room rates include a one-hour couple's massage at the on-site spa. The only downside is that the pool is ridiculously small – but that turquoise ocean *is* only steps away.

Getting There & Away

To catch a regular sŏrng·tăa·ou from Kamala to Patong costs 50B per person, while a sŏrng·tăa·ou charter (starting in the evenings) costs 250B. You can rent vehicles in Hat Kamala at **Via Rent-A-Car** (☎ 0 7638 5718; www.via-phuket.com).

HAT SURIN
หาดสุรินทร์

Surin is upscale but completely unpretentious. A distinctly Thai spirit lingers here along with the lazy, pampered vacationers – which is probably why expats love this area so much.

Development is fast and furious, but is mostly in the form of buy-in luxury condos and apartments. And we understand why: this golden beach with all the smiling faces makes us want to move here, too. Trees line the shore and dozens of cheap food shacks (offering some of the best value seafood on Phuket) shelter beneath them, while the grander resorts hide away on the hilltops.

The downside of all this, of course, is that the beach can get crowded. Hat Surin is extremely pretty, but stretches have already become a car crash of snack stalls and souvenir sellers. For celebrities, at least, the only way to do Surin today is from behind the guarded gates of the exclusive Amanpuri Resort (right).

Expect big, dangerous seas during the monsoon – swimmers beware, surfers rejoice.

Information

There is an ATM at Surin Plaza, just east of the beach on Rte 4025, and another outside the eternally closed Tourist Service Centre right at the turn-off towards Surin Beach. Internet access is available at **Andaman Car Rental** (☎ 0 7632 4422; per min 1B; ☒ 9am-9pm) and at most of the hotels.

Sleeping

Budget digs are at a real premium, but the midrange and luxury options are among the best on all of Phuket.

Capri Beach Resort (☎ 0 7627 0597; caprihotelsurin@yahoo.com; r 1500-2750B; ☒) This little yellow temple to Italian kitsch was getting a major makeover when we passed through. Even before the remodel, this welcoming spot offered great home cooking, snug rooms and more Italiana than you could stomach – so imagine what the new and improved version will be like. Expect opera, giant pepper grinders and high standards. It's a short hop from the beach.

Surin Bay Inn (☎ 0 7627 1601; www.surinbayinn.com; r 2000B; ☒ ☒) Right next door, this is another welcoming midranger. There's an eatery serving fabulous breakfasts below, clean, spacious, albeit plain, rooms above and a very useful book exchange.

our pick **Benyada Lodge** (☎ 0 7627 1261; www .benyadalodge-phuket.com; r 2500-5000B; ☒ ☒ ☒) Chic, modern rooms – with black louvred closets, terracotta tiled bathrooms that open up to the room, and silk, pastel-coloured

throw pillows scattered in the lounging corner – are a great bargain for this area. Service is stellar and we loved the high-end details, such as ice water service every time you sit anywhere in the lobby. Take in the sunset and a dip in the pool at the rooftop bar. The hotel is right next to the Surin Bay Inn and only a few minutes' walk to the beach.

our pick **Twin Palms** (☎ 0 7631 6500; www.twin palms-phuket.com; r 7800-50,000B; ☒ ☒ ☒) This is the Audrey Hepburn of Phuket's hotels – it's classic yet completely contemporary and oozes effortless class. There's a pervasive feeling of space with minimalist, artsy swimming pools everywhere that are fringed by delicate white frangipani. Even the simplest rooms are extra spacious and have oversized bathrooms, sublimely comfortable beds and a supreme sense of calm. It's a few minutes' walk to the beach. Expats from all over Phuket can be found eating the island's most popular brunch here on Sundays.

our pick **Chedi** (☎ 0 7632 4017; www.ghmhotels.com; r 17,000-41,000B; ☒ ☒) Almost any place that was located on a private beach this quiet and stunning would have to make it onto our top pick list. But Chedi's bungalows, with their naturalistic wooden exteriors that hide beneath the foliage of the hillside, and their earthy, luxurious interiors, make the site that much better. The restaurant has a dreamy, Crusoe feel and looks out over the water and an unexpectedly modern, six-sided pool. You'll have to be in decent shape for walking around the resort, since it can be quite a hoof up hills and over wooden walkways to get to many of the bungalows.

Amanpuri Resort (☎ 0 7632 4333; www.amanresorts .com; villas US$750-7900; ☒ ☒ ☒) Phuket's number one celebrity magnet, the Amanpuri offers lashings of glamour and palatial luxury – in fact, it was designed by the architect behind the former Shah of Iran's winter palace. With a staggering 3½ members of staff to every guest, this is exclusive service with bells on. Accommodation is in private villas and you can even book your own chef to cook for you.

Eating

There are plenty of excellent restaurants in and around Surin. For cheap seafood, your first stop should be the numerous, fun and delicious seafront snack stalls.

ourpick Taste (☎ 0 7886 6401; mains 160-225B; ☺ lunch & dinner Wed-Mon) The best of a new breed of urban-meets-surf eateries along the beach. Our Mandarin chicken salad was the best salad we had in Phuket and we found the house speciality (blue crab ravioli) small but impressively good. The Swedish–Nepali owners are great with service and smiles. This is also a great spot for a sundowner.

Silk (☎ 0 7627 1705; Rte 4025; mains 200-450B; ☺ lunch & dinner) This expansive stylish place is one of several upmarket restaurants in Surin Plaza, just east of the beach on Rte 4025. Silk is something of an expat magnet and draws locals from across the island. The décor is a hip cocktail of burgundy paint, wood and exotic flowers, while the menu focuses on beautifully executed Thai specialities.

ourpick The Catch (☎ 0 7631 6500; mains 250-450B; ☺ lunch & dinner) Slip on your breeziest dress or a pair of linen trousers to dine at this drapey, cabana-style eatery right on the beach. It's part of Twin Palms, even though it's not attached, and has all the same classy attributes as the hotel in both ambience and cuisine.

Getting There & Away

A regular sŏrng·tăa·ou from Phuket Town's Th Ranong to Hat Surin costs 50B per person, and túk-túk or sŏrng·tăa·ou charters cost 250B to 350B.

Rent cars from **Andaman Car Rental** (☎ 0 7632 4422; ☺ 9am-9pm), opposite the entrance to Twin Palms. A jeep costs from 1200B per day.

AO BANG THAO
อ่าวบางเทา

The 8km sweep of beautiful Ao Bang Thao is the stomping ground for many of Phuket's glitziest resorts. Buying up land, gating it off and practically establishing their own mini-state, these five-star super-hotels now operate out of a development named Laguna Phuket, which feels more like a ritzy California gated community than Thailand (but it's a great place to be an unabashed tourist and hobnob with big bucks). The pretty southern stretch of beach outside Laguna is the preserve of local fishers and some midrange tourist facilities, and is a lazy, favourite haunt for local expats. The beach down this end seems to go on forever and the colourful long-tail fishing boats in the far south lend it an old Thailand flavour.

The Hideaway Day Spa (Map p319) has an excellent reputation. It offers traditional Thai massage, sauna and mud body wraps in a tranquil wooded setting at the edge of a lagoon. Treatments start at 1500B. The Hideaway also has its own line of spa products.

Sleeping

Laguna Phuket is home to six luxury resorts, an 18-hole golf course and 30 restaurants (the gargantuan Sheraton Grande alone has eight restaurants). Guests at any one of the resorts can use the dining and recreation facilities at all of them. Frequent shuttle buses make the rounds of all the hotels, as do pontoon boats (via the linked lagoons).

Bangtao Lagoon Bungalows (Map p319; ☎ 0 7632 4260; info@phuket-bangtaolagoon.com; r 1350-5400B; ☒ ☐ ☒) The lowest-end rooms here are minuscule and fan cooled, while the top-end ones are beachfront but overpriced for how plain they are – but the beach location is so great it hardly matters. The staff are fabulously friendly.

Andaman Bangtao Bay Resort (Map p319; ☎ 0 7627 0246; www.andamanbangtaobayresort.com; bungalows incl breakfast 4970-7900B; ☒ ☒) Every bungalow has a sea view and there's a summer camp vibe at this pleasant little resort. The design is very Thai, with woodcarvings on the walls and coconuts hanging from the eaves of the roofs, but for this price we expected a little more luxury.

Sheraton Grande Laguna Phuket (Map p319; ☎ 0 7632 4101; www.starwoodhotels.com; r from 9000B; ☒ ☐ ☒) Gated away in Laguna Phuket, the Sheraton will appeal to a lively, active crowd. It features a gigantic 323m pool, water sports facilities galore, a kids' club and a whopping 423 rooms.

ourpick Banyan Tree Phuket (Map p319; ☎ 0 7632 4374; www.banyantree.com; villas from US$550; ☒ ☐ ☒) One of Asia's finest hotels, and the first on Phuket to introduce bungalows with their own private pool, the Banyan Tree Phuket (in Laguna Phuket) is an oasis of sedate, understated luxury. Accommodation is in villas – some take standards another indulgent step further with two private pools – and the on-site spa is one of the best on the continent. If you're after a rip-roaring time in Thailand, this is not the spot for you. If you really want to get away from it all, however, pick up the phone and book yourself a room now – it is very popular.

Eating

Despite what some local hoteliers would have you believe, there is good food to be had outside the confines of Bang Thao's luxury hotels. You will find much of it just outside Laguna's main gate.

Lotus Restaurant (Map p319; dishes 50-100B; ☿ lunch & dinner) An open-walled eatery 500m west of the entrance to Banyan Tree Phuket, this is the first in a row of beachside Thai and seafood restaurants that stretches to the south. It's clean, breezy and friendly, and has an amazing assortment of live crab, lobster, shrimp, fish and other visual and culinary delights in very well-tended tanks. Check out the crazy mantis shrimp!

English Pub (Map p319; ☎ 0 9872 1398; Th Srisoonthorn; dishes 100-300B; ☿ lunch & dinner) Aka 'The Whispering Cock', this timber and thatch watering hole is the most authentic English pub on the island – even the toilets smell. It has a sunny beer garden, a snug interior, a good range of beers and some decent pub grub. Shoot some darts or kick back with premiership footy.

Babylon Beach Club (Map p319; ☎ 08 1970 5302; Hat Bang Thao; dishes 120-250B; ☿ 10am-11pm) Grab a table right on the beach and enjoy anything from Thai to Italian seafood or cheeseburgers for the kids.

Tatonka (Map p319; ☎ 0 7632 4349; Th Srisoonthorn; dishes 250-300B; ☿ dinner Thu-Tue) This is the home of 'globetrotter cuisine', which owner-chef Harold Schwarz developed by taking fresh local products and combining them with cooking and presentation techniques learned in Europe, Colorado and Hawaii. The eclectic, tapas-style selection includes creative vegetarian and seafood dishes and such delights as Peking duck pizza (220B). There's also a tasting menu (750B per person, minimum two people), which lets you try a little of everything. Call ahead in the high season. Tatonka arranges free transport for guests of the resort complex.

Getting There & Away

A sŏrng·tǎa·ou between Bang Thao and Phuket Town's Th Ranong costs 50B per person. Túk-túk charters are 250B.

SIRINAT NATIONAL PARK
อุทยานแห่งชาติสิรินาถ

Comprising the beaches of Nai Thon, Nai Yang and Mai Khao, as well as the former Nai Yang National Park and Mai Khao wildlife reserve, **Sirinat National Park** (☎ 0 7632 8226; www.dnp.go.th; admission 200B; ☿ 8am-5pm) encompasses 22 sq km of coastal land, plus 68 sq km of sea. It runs from the western Phang-Nga provincial border south to the headland that separates Nai Yang from Nai Thon.

Improved roads to **Hat Nai Thon** have brought only a small amount of development to this otherwise pristine coast backed by casuarina and pandanus trees. On the beach, umbrellas and sling chairs are available from vendors. Swimming is quite good here except at the height of the monsoon, and there is some coral near the headlands at either end of the bay. The remains of a wrecked 50m-long tin dredger lie off the coast near tiny **Ko Waew** at a depth of 16m. Naithon Beach Resort (opposite) can arrange dive trips in the area.

Hat Nai Yang is good for snorkelling and is popular with Thai tourists. About a kilometre off Nai Yang is a large reef at a depth of 10m to 20m. Snorkelling equipment can be hired at many of the hotels. Judging from the lie of the reef, there could be a surfable reef break here during the southwest monsoon.

About 5km north of Nai Yang is **Hat Mai Khao**, Phuket's longest beach. Sea turtles lay their eggs on the beach between November and February each year. A visitors centre with toilets, showers and picnic tables is at Mai Khao, from where there are some short trails through the casuarinas to a steep beach. Take care when swimming at Mai Khao, as there's a strong year-round undertow. Except on weekends and holidays you'll have this place almost to yourself; even during peak periods, peace and solitude are usually only a few steps away, as there's so much space here.

The area between Nai Yang and Mai Khao is largely given over to **shrimp farming**. Fortunately shrimp farmers here don't dig artificial lagoons into the beach or mangroves (as at Ko Chang or Khao Sam Roi Yot), but rather they raise the spawn in self-contained concrete tanks, a practice significantly less harmful to the environment.

The whole area is only minutes from Phuket International Airport, which makes it particularly convenient for a first stop after a long trip.

Sleeping & Eating

HAT NAI THON

Naithon Beach Resort (☎ 0 7620 5379; fax 0 7620 5381; 22/2 Th Surin; cottages 1000-1500B; ❤ Nov-May; ❄) This resort has large, tastefully designed wooden cottages. A small restaurant serves sandwiches and Thai food. The resort closes in the rainy season. It is on the opposite side of the access road from the beach.

ourpick Trisara (☎ 0 7361 0100; www.trisara.com; villas from US$780; ❄ 🖳 🛋) If you can afford to stay here, do so. A tranquil oasis far removed from Patong's chaos, ultraexclusive Trisara's villas take in some of Phuket's most stunning views and are nestled in an idyllic location between jungle and sea. Minimalist yet soothing décor, private pools and steam rooms (for the spa review, see the boxed text, p298), and simply oodles of class make this one of the island's top choices. Honeymoon, anyone? Service is outstanding.

HAT NAI YANG & HAT MAI KHAO

Along the dirt road at the very southern end of Hat Nai Yang is a seemingly endless strip of seafood restaurants and, oddly enough, tailor shops. There is also a small minimart near the entrance to the Indigo Pearl resort. Camping is allowed on both Nai Yang and Mai Khao beaches without any permit.

Sirinat National Park (☎ 0 2562 0760; reserve@dnp .go.th; tents 50-100B, bungalows 800B) The park offers camp sites and large bungalows. Check in at the building opposite the visitors centre or book online. The restaurant serving basic Thai fare is open from 8am to 9pm.

Phuket Camp Ground (☎ 08 1676 4318; www .phuketcampground.com; tents per person 150B, r 600B; 🖳) Privately operated, this campground recently had to move off the beach but still rents out tents, now in a lovely area near a mangrove forest, each with rice mats, pillows, blankets and a torch. A small outdoor restaurant-bar provides sustenance and there are also two simple rooms. The owners will pick you up from the airport for 300B per trip.

Nai Yang Beach Resort (☎ 0 7632 8300; www.nai yangbeachresort.com; 65/23-24 Th Hat Nai Yang; bungalows 1000-8000B; ❄) This resort is clean, quiet and near the beach, and does a great barbecue at night. The lowest-end rooms are fan-cooled, while higher-end ones are modern Thai style and quite chic.

Golddigger Resort (☎ 08 1892 1178; www.airport -phuket.com; r 1200-3500B; ❄ 🖳 🛋) One of the better midrange options along this stretch of beach, Golddigger Resort is Swiss-run and has developed a loyal following. Something of a boutique arrangement, there are only 16 rooms in this one-storey hotel, all with a view of the pool area and thick tropical foliage that covers the grounds.

ourpick Indigo Pearl (☎ 0 7632 7006; www .indigo-pearl.com; r 5600-26,250B; ❄ 🖳 🛋) The most unique and hip of Phuket's high-end resorts takes its design cues from the island's tin mining history – although it sounds weird, this industrial theme melded with tropical luxe creates a spectacularly beautiful and soothing place to stay. Hardware, such as vices, scales and other mining tools, is used in the décor to the tiniest detail – even the toilet paper rolls are big bolts – and the common lounge areas are infused with indigo light. The gardens are modern and lush and surround a pool that looks like an oasis with a big waterfall. We especially love the décor of the Black Ginger restaurant, which is in a classical wooden Thai building painted entirely black, with black furniture and all, and perched over a bright lily pond. The more laid-back of the resort's two bars is called…wait for it…the Rebar.

JW Marriott Phuket Resort & Spa (☎ 0 7633 8000; www.marriott.com; 231 Moo 3; r from 8100B; ❄ 🖳 🛋) This big and uber-swanky Marriott has an enviable position on the beach. Among the most appreciated assets are mammoth rooms boasting superior sea views, raised *săh·ah* (often spelt *sala;* covered resting place) areas, triangular back cushions, massage mats and polished wood floors. A cooking school and pub with live music round out the deal. Don't miss the spa (see the boxed text, p298).

Getting There & Away

Sŏrng·tăa·ou from Phuket cost 50B per person and run between 7am and 5pm only. If you're coming from the airport, a taxi costs about 250B. There is no regular sŏrng·tăa·ou stop for Mai Khao, but a túk-túk charter from Phuket Town costs about 300B.

KHAO PHRA TAEW ROYAL WILDLIFE & FOREST RESERVE

อุทยานสัตว์ป่าเขาพระแทว

It's not all sand and sea. In the north of the island, this park protects 23 sq km of virgin island rainforest (evergreen monsoon forest). There are some pleasant hikes over the hills and a couple of photogenic waterfalls: **Ton Sai** and **Bang Pae**. The falls are best seen in the rainy season between June and November; in the dry months they slow to a trickle. The highest point in the park is the 442m **Khao Phara**. Because of its royal status, the reserve is better protected than the average national park in Thailand.

A German botanist discovered a rare and unique species of palm in Khao Phra Taew about 50 years ago. Called the white-backed palm or *langkow* palm, the fan-shaped plant stands 3m to 5m tall and is found only here and in Khao Sok National Park (p244).

Tigers, Malayan sun bears, rhinos and elephants once roamed the forest here, but nowadays resident mammals are limited to humans, pigs, monkeys, slow loris, langur, civets, flying foxes, squirrels, mousedeer and other smaller animals. Watch out for cobras and wild pigs.

The **Phuket Gibbon Rehabilitation Centre** (Map p287; ☎ 0 7626 0492; www.gibbonproject.org; donations encouraged; ☼ 9am-4pm), in the park near Nam Tok Bang Pae, is open to the public. Financed by donations (1500B will care for a gibbon for one year), the centre adopts gibbons that have been kept in captivity and reintroduces them to the wild.

Park rangers may act as guides for hikes in the park on request; payment for services is by donation.

To get to Khao Phra Taew from Phuket Town, take Th Thepkasatri north about 20km to Thalang District, and turn right at the intersection for Nam Tok Ton Sai, which is 3km down the road.

THALANG DISTRICT
อำเภอถลาง

A few hundred metres northeast of the famous **Heroines Monument** in Thalang District on Rte

4027, and about 11km northwest of Phuket Town, is **Thalang National Museum** (Map p287; ☎ 0 7631 1426; admission 30B; ☼ 8.30am-4pm). The museum contains five exhibition halls chronicling southern themes such as the history of Thalang-Phuket and the colonisation of the Andaman Coast, and describing the various ethnicities found in southern Thailand. The legend of the 'two heroines' (memorialised on the nearby monument), who supposedly drove off an 18th-century Burmese invasion force by convincing the island's women to dress as men, is also recounted in detail utilising backlit display panels and touch-screen electronic presentations. The focal point of one hall is the impressive 2.3m-tall statue of Vishnu, which dates to the 9th century and was found in Takua Pa early in the 20th century.

Also in Thalang District, just north of the crossroads near Thalang town, is **Wat Phra Thong** (Map p287; admission by donation; ☼ dawn-dusk), Phuket's 'Temple of the Gold Buddha'. The image is half buried so that only the head and shoulders are visible above ground. According to local legend, those who have tried to excavate the image have become very ill or encountered serious accidents soon after their failed attempts. The temple is particularly revered by Thai Chinese, many of whom believe the image hails from China. During Chinese New Year the temple is an important focus for pilgrims from Phang-Nga, Takua Pa and Krabi. In addition to Phra Thong there are several other Buddha images, including seven representing the different days of the week, plus a Phra Praket (an unusual pose in which the Buddha is touching his own head with his right hand) and a Phra Palelai (sitting in 'European pose').

Some parts of the movie *Good Morning Vietnam* were filmed on location in Thalang.

Southern Andaman Coast

Island hoppers, this is your dreamland. The south is the quieter half of the Andaman coast; even the tourist star of Ko Phi-Phi can't rival the glam and crowds of Phuket. Instead, this region is the ideal choice for serious relaxation, outdoor fun and chummy nights at beachside bars. Just slowly putter from white-sand isle to white-sand isle.

Social seekers will love the developed beauties such as Ko Phi-Phi and Ko Lanta where you can party into the wee hours and meet plenty of people on the beach, yet still find a peaceful strip of sand. And roads less travelled are just next door: head down through the lightly developed Trang islands to the even less visited Satun Province to find powder-white romantic beaches, outrageous snorkelling and plenty of spicy southern Thai culture. The entire region is made up of a spectacular undulating coastline pierced by sheer limestone formations, speckled with islands and cloaked in a carpet of verdant greenery.

Besides the phenomenal diving and snorkelling, some of the best rock climbing in the world can be found in Krabi and Trang Provinces. All that limestone also means there are plenty of caves to explore; some house shrines while others require that you shimmy on your stomach to get through. You can also kayak to islands or through coastal mangroves.

Much of this region shuts down in the April to November low season but even at that time you can still get to most places with determined effort.

HIGHLIGHTS

- Zipping around in long-tail boats and oohing and aahing at monolithic rock formations and perfect beaches throughout the **Trang islands** (p362) or **Ko Tarutao Marine National Park** (p374)

- Scaling a limestone cliff then recuperating on the sparkling beaches and in the blissful jade waters of **Railay** (p338)

- Trying to decide if **Ko Phi-Phi** (p343) is more beautiful above or below water and giving it up for a tie

- Forgetting what day it is and realising that electricity is really just a frivolous modern convenience on **Ko Jum** (p358)

- Snorkelling over healthy coral reefs by day and chilling at low-key reggae bars by night on **Ko Lipe** (p377)

Railay ★
★ Ko Jum
Ko Phi-Phi ★

Trang Islands ★

Ko Tarutao
Marine National Park
★

Ko Lipe ★

■ DRY SEASON: DECEMBER-MARCH   ■ WET SEASON: MAY-OCTOBER

Climate

The weather can be a big concern for travellers in this region. The Andaman coast receives more rain than the southern gulf provinces, with May to October being the months of heaviest rainfall. During this time passenger boats to some islands, such as Ko Tarutao, are suspended. If you find the weather on the Andaman coast unpleasant, you can easily travel to the southwestern gulf coast, where you're more likely to find the sun shining.

Top daytime temperatures average 32°C year-round (it's always hot!), with high humidity during the wet season.

National Parks

The most popular park along the Southern Andaman coast is the Ko Phi-Phi Marine National Park (p343), with its spectacular lagoons, beaches, impenetrable sea cliffs and rock climbing. Mu Ko Lanta Marine National Park (p352) is found in the south of the increasingly popular island of Ko Lanta and includes pristine islands, fine coral reefs and long sandy beaches. In the far south, bordering Malaysia is the momentarily tranquil (but becoming more popular) Ko Tarutao Marine National Park (p374), which preserves a group of jungle-covered islands, coral reefs and immaculate tropical beaches.

Lesser known parks include tiny Hat Chao Mai National Park (p363) near Trang, which contains coral-fringed islands; mountainous Khao Phanom Bencha National Park (see boxed text, p330) near Krabi town, whose jungles are full of exotic animals and rare birds; Satun Province's Mu Ko Phetra Marine National Park (see boxed text, p374) featuring islands and mangrove wildlife including dugongs and rare birds; and Tharnbok Korannee National Park (p332), near the town of Ao Luk, which preserves sprawling areas of mangroves full of limestone caves and cave paintings.

KRABI PROVINCE

With mind-bogglingly beautiful karsts (limestone rock formations) jutting up through tangled jungles, lining the crystalline beaches and forming knobby islands floating in the green sea, it's easy to understand why Krabi Province is the most popular region of the Southern Andaman coast. There are over 150 islands here and many are lined with the sorts of beaches you thought existed only on postcards. Not far from Krabi town, the province's small capital, the towering cliffs cast their shadows on mainland beaches; some feel as lost as a remote isle while others have every modern amenity right at hand. There's really something for everyone in this province whether it's partying and decadently lounging on magnificent Ko Phi-Phi, living out your lost-on-a-desert-island fantasies on quiet Ko Jum, or scrambling up some of the world's top climbing routes at Railay.

It's not all islands and beaches, however. The region's interior features tracts of primary rainforest that are home to a plethora of tropical birds and animals, waterfalls, swimming holes and caves.

The mainland has excellent links to the rest of Thailand year-round, and in high season, the islands do too.

KRABI

กระบี่

pop 29,300

When you arrive in Krabi you'll first notice that there are more guesthouses and travel agencies per square inch here than could possibly be practical. Western restaurants are ubiquitous, as are the gift shops that all sell the same 'ole woodcarvings, pashminas and trinkets. Yet if you hang out a while you'll see that there's a very local scene going on in between the cracks. The day market on Th Sukhon is filled with mysterious treats and few foreign faces as are several restaurants scattered, almost invisibly, throughout the tourist centre. It's a compact town that can win sceptics over with its quirks – and really, can anyone pass through town without doing a double take on the giant cavemen statues that hold up the traffic lights at the Th Maharat/Vogue crossroads?

Because a dozen island and beach destinations are serviced from this city, not many people linger here, although it's awfully cheap to do so. Boats can be organised to the islands of Ko Phi-Phi and Ko Lanta, and the beaches of Ao Nang and Railay. If you stay, travel agencies can help you arrange wildlife-spotting tours among the mangrove-dense riverside.

Orientation

Th Utarakit is the main road into and out of Krabi and most places of interest are on the

SOUTHERN ANDAMAN COAST

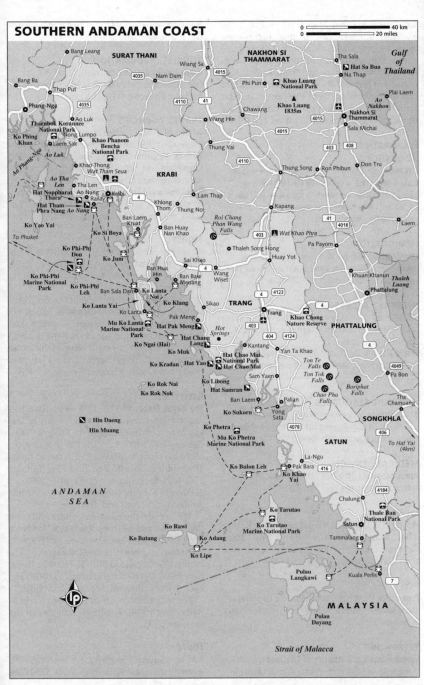

soi (laneways) that branch off it. Ferries to Ko Phi-Phi, Ko Lanta and other islands leave from Khlong Chilat (Krabi passenger pier) about 3km southwest of town, while long-tail boats to Railay depart from Khong Kha (Chao Fa) pier on Th Khong Kha. The Krabi bus terminal is north of the centre at Talat Kao, near the junction of Th Utarakit, while the airport is 17km northeast on Hwy 4.

Information

BOOKSHOPS
Pakaran (☎ 0 7561 1164; 151 Th Utarakit; ☽ 9am-8pm) A good place to stock up on second-hand books before you head for the islands. It has a large selection in English and many European languages as well as some quality handicrafts and antiques.

IMMIGRATION
Immigration Office (☎ 0 7561 1350; Th Chamai Anuson; ☽ 8.30am-4pm Mon-Fri) Just south of the post and telephone office; handles visa extensions.

INTERNET ACCESS
Almost all of Krabi's budget travel agencies and restaurants offer internet access for 40B to 60B per hour.
World Net (cnr Ths Utarakit & Issara; ☽ 8am-11pm) Has fast computers, switched-on staff and, sometimes, free bananas.

INTERNET RESOURCES
Krabi Directory (www.krabidir.com) Has lots of information on Krabi Province and links to most of the tourist-oriented businesses in the area.

MEDICAL SERVICES
Krabi Hospital (☎ 0 7561 1210; Th Utarakit) Located 1km north of the centre.

MONEY
Along Th Utarakit, Bangkok Bank, Krung Thai Bank, Siam City Bank and Siam Commercial Bank all exchange cash and travellers cheques and have ATMs.

POST
Post office (Th Utarakit) Just south of the turn-off to Khong Kha pier; there's a separate poste-restante entrance at the side.

TELEPHONE
Communications Authority of Thailand (CAT; Th Utarakit) About 500m north of Krabi Hospital, offering in-ternational calls. Travel agencies in town provide overseas calls at comparable rates.

TOURIST INFORMATION
Krabi Tourist Association (☎ 0 7562 2163/4; tatkrabi@tat.or.th; Th Utarakit) Provides a free map of Krabi with a smile, but no English is spoken.

TRAVEL AGENCIES
Many of Krabi's numerous travel agencies close monthly and reopen under different names. Recommended steadfast agencies:
Chen Phen Tour (☎ 0 7561 2004; Th Utarakit) Special-ises in mangrove tours (see below).
Krabi You and I Travel (☎ 0 7883 6399; www.krabi information.com; 181 Th Utarakit) Offers air, boat and bus tickets, tours and island accommodation booking.

Sights
There are not many must-see sights in Krabi itself. On the edge of town, **Wat Kaew** contains some interesting 19th- and early-20th-century buildings.

It's possible to climb one of the two lime-stone massifs of **Khao Khanap Nam**, just north of the town centre. A number of human skel-etons were found in the caves here, thought to be the remains of people trapped during an ancient flood. To get here, charter a long-tail boat from Khong Kha pier for about 300B.

Activities
Sea Kayak Krabi (☎ 0 7563 0270; www.seakayak-krabi .com; 40 Th Ruen Rudee) offers a wide variety of sea-kayaking tours, including to Ao Thalane (half-/full day 800/1400B), which has looming sea cliffs; Ko Hong (full day 1500B), famed for its emerald lagoon; and Ban Bho Tho (full day 1700B), which has sea caves with 2000- to 3000-year-old cave paintings. All rates include guides, lunch, fruit and drinking water.

While many diving agencies have offices on the islands and beaches, **Reefwatch Worldwide** (☎ 0 1979 0535; www.reefwatchworldwide.com; Th Utarakit) is in town and has two-dive packages to local islands (2900B) and to Phi-Phi (3500B). It also runs PADI Open-Water courses (13,000B) and live-aboards (three nights from 15,000B).

For rock climbing, boats go from Krabi to Railay (see p339). For more activities in the area, see p333.

Tours
Any travel agency in town can book tours with an environmental focus from Krabi. **Chen Phen**

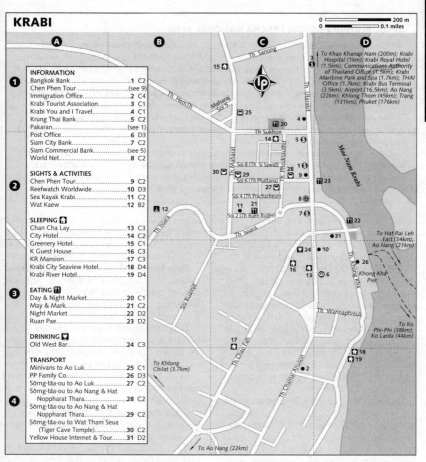

KRABI

0 ___ 200 m
0 ___ 0.1 miles

INFORMATION
Bangkok Bank...........................1 C2
Chen Phen Tour........................(see 9)
Immigration Office......................2 C4
Krabi Tourist Association...........3 C1
Krabi You and I Travel..............4 C1
Krung Thai Bank........................5 C2
Pakaran......................................(see 1)
Post Office................................6 D3
Siam City Bank..........................7 C2
Siam Commercial Bank.............(see 5)
World Net..................................8 C2

SIGHTS & ACTIVITIES
Chen Phen Tour........................9 C2
Reefwatch Worldwide..............10 D3
Sea Kayak Krabi.......................11 C2
Wat Kaew.................................12 B2

SLEEPING 🏠
Chan Cha Lay...........................13 C3
City Hotel..................................14 C2
Greenery Hotel.........................15 C1
K Guest House..........................16 C3
KR Mansion..............................17 C3
Krabi City Seaview Hotel..........18 D4
Krabi River Hotel......................19 D4

EATING 🍴
Day & Night Market..................20 C1
May & Mark..............................21 C2
Night Market............................22 D2
Ruan Pae.................................23 D2

DRINKING 🍸
Old West Bar............................24 C3

TRANSPORT
Minivans to Ao Luk...................25 C1
PP Family Co............................26 D3
Sŏrng·tǎa·ou to Ao Luk............27 C2
Sŏrng·tǎa·ou to Ao Nang & Hat
  Noppharat Thara....................28 C2
Sŏrng·tǎa·ou to Ao Nang & Hat
  Noppharat Thara....................29 C2
Sŏrng·tǎa·ou to Wat Tham Seua
  (Tiger Cave Temple)...............30 C2
Yellow House Internet & Tour....31 D2

To Khao Khanap Nam (200m); Krabi
Hospital (1km); Krabi Royal Hotel
(1.5km); Communications Authority
of Thailand Office (1.5km); Krabi
Maritime Park and Spa (1.7km); THAI
Office (1.7km); Krabi Bus Terminal
(3.5km); Airport (16.5km); Ao Nang
(22km); Khlong Thom (45km); Trang
(131km); Phuket (176km)

Mae Nam Krabi

To Hat Rai Leh
East (14km);
Ao Nang (21km)

Khong Kha
Pier

To Ko
Phi-Phi (38km);
Ko Lanta (44km)

To Khlong
Chilat (3.7km)

To Ao Nang (22km)

Th Sanong
Th Hemth
Maharaj Soi 5
Th Sukhon
Th Maharaj
Th Phrukchit
Th Utarakit
Th Issara
Soi Ruammit
Soi 8 (Th Si Sawat)
Soi 29
Soi 6 (Th Phattana)
Soi 4 (Th Prachacheun)
Soi 2 (Th Ruen Rudee)
Th Issara
Th Khong Kha
Th Wannaphreuk
Soi Ruammit
Th Chao Fai
Th Chamai Anuson

Tour (☎ 0 7561 2004; Th Utarakit) and others offer bird-watching tours in the mangroves around Krabi for about 650B per boat per hour (early morning is best); alternatively, you can hire a boat at Khong Kha pier for around 400B per hour. Keep an eye out for fiddler crabs and mudskippers on the exposed mud.

A number of companies offer day trips to **Khlong Thom**, about 45km southeast of Krabi on Hwy 4, taking in some nearby hot springs and freshwater pools. Expect to pay around 1050B, including transport, lunch and beverages; bring a swimsuit and good walking shoes. Various other 'jungle tour' itineraries are available.

Tours to surrounding islands (see boxed text, p335) are also deservedly popular.

Sleeping

New guesthouses (often named with a one or two letter initial) are appearing all over Krabi and most of them offer clean, tiled rooms with shared bathrooms. In low season, prices plummet to as low as 150B. Midrange quality options are available for under and around 1000B even during high season.

K Guest House (☎ 0 7562 3166; www.krabidir.com /kguesthouse; 15-25 Th Chao Fa; r 400-500B; 🖥️) This place has a Wild West feeling, with varnished wooden rooms, and all with verandas overlooking the street. Cow heads on the walls and easy socialising in the downstairs café add to the frontier appeal.

KR Mansion (☎ 0 7561 2761; krmansion@hotmail.com; 52/1 Th Chao Fa; r 300-600B; ❄️ 🖥️) Pink is the name

---

DETOUR: KHAO PHANOM BENCHA NATIONAL PARK

This 50-sq-km **park** (adult/child under 14 yr 200/100B) protects a dramatic area of virgin rainforest along the spine of 1350m-high Khao Phanom Bencha, just 20km north of Krabi. The park is full of scenic waterfalls, including the 11-tiered **Huay To Falls**, just 500m from the park headquarters. Nearby and almost as dramatic are Huay Sadeh Falls and Khlong Haeng Falls. On the way into the park you can visit **Tham Pheung**, a dramatic cave with shimmering mineral stalactites and stalagmites. Numerous trails wend through the area, providing excellent opportunities for hiking.

The park is home to abundant wildlife – but only the monkeys are commonly seen. Many bird-spotters come here to see white-crowned and helmeted hornbills, argus pheasants and the extremely rare Gurney's pitta.

There is no public transport to the park, but it's easy to get here from Krabi by hired motorcycle; follow the signposted turn-off from Hwy 4. Park your motorcycle by the park headquarters and remember to apply the steering lock and chain. Alternatively, you can hire a túk-túk (pronounced đúk đúk; motorised three-wheeled pedicab) for around 600B round-trip.

---

of the game in this place. The building has a funky rooftop beer garden with panoramic views over Krabi – great for a sundowner cocktail – and a variety of good rooms.

our pick Chan Cha Lay (☎ 0 7562 0952; www.geocities.com/chan_cha_lay; 55 Th Utarakit; r 300-650B;) More like a boutique hotel than a guesthouse, the en suite rooms at this exceptionally well-run place are decorated in Mediterranean blues and whites and have stylish, white pebble and polished concrete bathrooms. Shared-bathroom, fan-only rooms are plain, but are spotless and have good beds. The staff here are particularly helpful and honest with onward transport and information.

City Hotel (☎ 0 7562 1280-2; www.citykrabi.com; 15/2-3 Th Sukhon; r 400-750B;) Easily the best-value midranger (at a budget price) in the town centre, top-end rooms have details like louvred wooden bathroom doors and Thai silk bed runners on the beds. Lower-end rooms are fan only and are without fanfare although they are clean and well-kept. There's a great market just across the road.

Greenery Hotel (☎ 0 7562 3648; http://krabidir.com/thegreeneryhotel/index.htm; 167/2 Th Maharat; r 600-800B;) Rooms here are modern with bright-coloured bed boards, cable TV and mini-fridges in all the rooms. The semi-outdoor hallways look out over the namesake, lush little garden that lends a peaceful feel to the place. It's about a five- to 10-minute walk away from the town centre.

Krabi City Seaview Hotel (☎ 0 7562 2885-8; www.krabidir.com/krabicityseaview; 77/1 Th Khong Kha; r 700-1200B;) This slick establishment is right on the river and offers excellent views of green mangroves from the balconies of its better

rooms. There's a small, chilled lounge downstairs facing the river and surrounded by green lawn. The quiet, riverside location is only a few minutes' walk from the centre.

Krabi River Hotel (☎ 0 7561 2321; krabiriver@hotmail.com; 73/1 Th Khong Kha; r 700-1200B;) Just next door to the Krabi City Seaview, this place is the newer model with tidy, tiny rooms. You pay more for river views.

Krabi Maritime Park & Spa (☎ 0 7562 0028, Bangkok 0 2719 0034; www.maritimeparkandspa.com; r from 4500B;) On lovely riverside grounds, this swanky hotel is 2km from Krabi town proper. It sports a nightclub, stylish pool, fitness centre, spa and even a lake on which you can pedal swan-shaped boats. Rooms are classy and the balconies sport impressive views. Promotional rates of 1500B are often available. There are free shuttle buses to Krabi town and Ao Nang, and shuttle boats to Railay. It may actually be smart to stay here, instead of Railay or Ao Nang, in the high season as it's better value for money and you can easily make day trips to the other locations.

Eating & Drinking

Night markets (Th Khong Kha & Th Sukhon; meals 20-50B) The most popular and pleasant place for an evening meal is at the night market near the Khong Kha pier. The menus are in English but the food is authentic and excellent. Stalls here sell papaya salad, fried noodles, đôm yam gûng (prawn and lemon grass soup with mushrooms), fresh seafood and all manner of things on satay sticks, plus sweet milky Thai desserts. There's a similar market just north on Th Sukhon that's open day and night and caters to a more local crowd.

May & Mark (Maharat Soi 2; meals 40-80B; ☻ 6.30am-9pm) One of the first places in town to start serving Western food way back when, May & Mark still does it best thanks to recipes collected from helpful faràng (foreigners of European descent) over the years. Specialities range from excellent fresh bread to bangers and mash and cordon bleu meals.

Ruan Pae (☎ 0 7561 1956; Th Utarakit; dishes 60-150B; ☻ lunch & dinner) This old-fashioned floating restaurant is a fine place to watch the evening mist gather around the mangroves, though the atmosphere is sometimes better than the food. Mosquitoes can be a problem in the evening.

Old West Bar (Th Chao Fah; ☻ 1pm-2am) Bamboo and wood inside and out, this Wild West–themed bar booms music nightly and is one popular place for a tipple. There's a lively scene most nights and the cocktail list is long enough to keep you sampling for a while.

Getting There & Away
AIR
THAI Airways International (www.thaiairways.com), **Air Asia** (www.airasia.com), **Nok Air** (www.nokair.com), **Bangkok Air** (www.bangkokair.com) and **One 2 Go** (www.fly12go.com) all fly between Bangkok and Krabi (one-way around 3000B, 1¼ hours). Shop around – there are bargains to be had here.

Bangkok Air also has flights to Ko Samui (one-way 2110B) three to four times daily.

BOAT
Boats to Ko Lanta and Ko Phi-Phi leave from the passenger pier at Khlong Chilat, about 3km southwest of Krabi. Travel agencies will arrange free transfers when you buy a boat ticket with them.

The largest boat operator is **PP Family Co** (☎ 0 7562 0052; www.phiphifamily.com; Th Khong Kha), which has a ticket office right beside the pier in town. All year round there are boats to Ko Phi-Phi (350B, 1½ hours) at 10am and 2pm.

From November to May, there are boats to Ko Lanta (350B, two hours) leaving Krabi at 11am and 1.30pm. These can also stop at Ko Jum (one hour), where long-tails shuttle you to shore (though you'll pay the full 350B). During the off season, you can only get to Ko Lanta by frequent air-con vans (250B, 2½ hours) which also run throughout the high season.

If you want to get to Railay, long-tail boats leave from Krabi's Khong Kha pier to Hat Rai Leh East from 7.45am to 6pm (200B, 45 minutes). The boatmen will wait until they can

fill a boat with 10 people before they leave; if you're antsy to go before then you can charter the whole boat for 2000B.

BUS
Government Bus
With fewer touts and guaranteed departure times, taking a government bus from the **Krabi bus terminal** (☎ 0 7561 1804; cnr Th Utarakit & Hwy 4) in nearby Talat Kao, about 4km from Krabi, is an altogether more relaxing option than taking a private bus. Air-con government buses leave for Bangkok (700B, 12 hours) at 7am, 4pm and 5.30pm. There's a plush 24-seat VIP bus to Bangkok (1050B) departing at 5.30pm daily. From Bangkok's Southern Bus Terminal, buses leave at 7.30am and between 7pm and 8pm.

Other services for regular, air-con government buses are shown in the table below:

Destination	Price	Duration	Frequency
Hat Yai	169-203B	5hr	frequent
Nakhon Si Thammarat	89B	3hr	frequent
Phang-Nga	60-78B	2hr	hourly
Phuket	115B	3½hr	hourly
Ranong	190B	6hr	every 2hr
Surat Thani	130B	2½hr	frequent
Trang	90B	2hr	frequent

Private Bus
Travel agencies can book you onto private air-con buses to Bangkok (650B, 12 hours) departing 4pm, and to Surat Thani (280B, 3½ hours) departing 11am and 4pm. Most travel agencies also offer combined minibus and boat tickets direct to Ko Samui (450B, 5½ hours) and Ko Pha-Ngan (550B, 7½ hours).

MINIVAN
Dozens of travel agencies in Krabi run air-con minivans and VIP buses to popular tourist centres throughout southern Thailand, but staff tend to be very pushy and you may end up crammed cheek to jowl with other backpackers. Destinations from Krabi:

Destination	Price	Duration
Ao Luk	50B	1hr
Hat Yai	280B	3hr
Ko Lanta	250B	1½hr
Phuket	250B	2-3hr
Satun	400B	5hr
Trang	280B	2hr

SŎRNG·TĂA·OU

Sŏrng·tăa·ou (also spelt săwngthăew) run from the bus station to central Krabi and on to Hat Noppharat Thara (40B), Ao Nang (40B) and the Shell Cemetery at Ao Nam Mao (50B; see p338). There are services from 6am to 6.30pm. In the high season there are less-frequent services until 10pm for 70B. For Ao Luk (50B, one hour) there are frequent sŏrng·tăa·ou from the corner of Th Phattana and Th Phruksauthit; the last service leaves at around 3pm. Occasional sŏrng·tăa·ou to Wat Tham Seua leave from opposite the 7-Eleven (on Th Maharat) and cost 15B.

Getting Around

Central Krabi is easy to explore on foot, but the bus terminal and airport are both a long way from the centre. A taxi from the airport to town will cost 500B. In the reverse direction, taxis or túk-túk (motorised three-wheeled pedicabs) cost 300B, while motorcycle taxis cost 250B. Agencies in town can also arrange minivans to the airport for 250B. Sŏrng·tăa·ou between the bus terminal and central Krabi cost 30B.

Hiring a vehicle is an excellent way to explore the countryside around Krabi. Most of the travel agencies and guesthouses in town can rent you a Honda Dream motorcycle for around 150B per day. **Yellow House Internet & Tour** (☎ 0 7562 2809; 5 Th Chao Fah) hires out reliable bikes and provides helmets. A few of the travel agencies along Th Utarakit rent out small 4WDs for 1000B to 1600B per day.

AROUND KRABI

Wat Tham Seua

วัดถ้ำเสือ

Thailand has a lot of wát (temples), but **Wat Tham Seua** (Tiger Cave Temple), 8km northwest of Krabi, is unique. The main wí·hăhn (hall) is built into a long, shallow limestone cave. On either side of the cave, dozens of gù·dì (monastic cells) are built into various cliffs and caves. You may see a troop of monkeys roaming the grounds.

The most shocking thing about Wat Tham Seua is found in the large main cave. Alongside large portraits of Ajan Jamnien Silasettho, the wát's abbot, are close-up pictures of human entrails and internal organs, which are meant to remind guests of the impermanence of the body. Skulls and skele-tons scattered around the grounds are meant to serve the same educational purpose.

The best part of the temple grounds can be found in a little valley behind the ridge where the bòht (central sanctuary) is located. Walk beyond the main temple building, keeping the cliff on your left, and you'll come to a pair of steep stairways leading to a 600m karst peak. The fit and fearless will be rewarded with a Buddha statue, a gilded stupa and great views of the surrounding area; on a clear day you can see well out to sea.

The second stairway, next to a large statue of Kuan Yin (the Mahayana Buddhist Goddess of Mercy), leads over a gap in the ridge and into a valley of tall trees and limestone caves. Enter the caves on your left and look for light switches on the walls – walk chamber by chamber through the labyrinth until you rejoin the path on the other side.

If you go to the temple, please dress modestly: pants down to the ankles, shirts covering the shoulders and nothing too tight.

GETTING THERE & AWAY

A motorcycle taxi or túk-túk to Wat Tham Seua costs 200B while private taxis cost 250B. By sŏrng·tăa·ou, get on at Krabi's Th Maharat to the Talat Kao junction for 20B, then change to any bus or sŏrng·tăa·ou heading east on Hwy 4 towards Trang and tell the driver 'Wat Tham Seua' – these can be rather infrequent, though. Get off at the road on the left just past the small police station. Motorcycle taxis hang out here and drivers charge 25B to the wát, or you can walk the 2km straight up the road.

Tharnbok Korannee National Park

อุทยานแห่งชาติธารโบกขรณี

Close to the small town of Ao Luk, about 46km northwest of Krabi, **Tharnbok Korannee National Park** (Than Bok; adult/child under 14 yr 200/100B) protects a large area of islands, mangroves and limestone caves. The most important cave here is **Tham Pee Hua Toe** (Big-Headed Ghost Cave), reached by long-tail boat or sea kayak from the pier at Ban Bho Tho, 7km south of Ao Luk. Legend has it that a huge human skull was found in the cave, but the ghost story probably has more to do with the 2000- to 3000-year-old cave paintings that adorn the cave walls. Nearby **Tham Lot** (Tube Cave) can also be navigated by boat. Both caves are popular destinations for sea-kayaking tours from Krabi or Ao Nang, but you can also hire sea kayaks and guides at Bho Tho pier (900B); long-tails are available for 400B.

There are at least seven other caves in the park, including **Tham Sa Yuan Thong**, a few kilometres southeast of Ao Luk, which has a natural spring bubbling into a pool at its mouth. The national park also includes the uninhabited island of **Ko Hong**, with fine beaches, jungle-cloaked cliffs and a scenic hidden lagoon. Sea-kayak and long-tail tours come here from Ao Nang.

Just to the south of Ao Luk, the park headquarters is a popular picnic spot. It has a series of babbling brooks and emerald pools, shaded by small jungle trees and linked by little waterfalls. The usual vendors sell noodles, fried chicken, batter-fried squid and *sôm·dam* (spicy green papaya salad). There's also a small **visitors centre** (☼ 6am-6pm) that has displays in Thai and English.

Ao Luk has a few places to stay or you can camp (with permission from the park headquarters). Otherwise try the simple bamboo huts at **Ao Luk Bungalow** (☎ 0 7568 1369; bungalows 250-300B), just before the turn-off to the park headquarters.

GETTING THERE & AWAY

The park headquarters is about 1.5km south of Ao Luk town along Rte 4039. Buses and sŏrng·tǎa·ou from Krabi stop on Hwy 4. Catch a government bus to Pha-Ngan or Phuket and ask to be let off at Ao Luk (60B, one hour), from where you can walk down to the park headquarters or take a motorcycle taxi for 15B. The easiest way to get to Tham Pee Hua Toe and Tham Lot is on a sea-kayaking tour from Krabi or Ao Nang.

To get to Ban Bho Tho from Ao Luk under your own steam, take a motorcycle taxi (70B) or a Laem Sak sŏrng·tǎa·ou (20B) to the Tham Pee Hua Toe turn-off on Rte 4039. From the junction it's about 2km to Ban Bho Tho along the first signposted road on the left.

AO NANG
อ่าวนาง
pop 12,400

It's bland tourist land and a little cheesy, but if you've been out in the islands and are hankering for plentiful shopping, fast internet and maybe a fast-food burger, this is your stop. The beach here is nothing compared to those in Railay or on Ko Phi-Phi but it's white, clean and leads out to a gentle, emerald green sea. Accommodation standards are high, and although it's not cheap here compared with Krabi town or south towards Trang, this is a bargain basement in comparison to Phuket. With plenty to do (mangrove tours? snorkelling trips?) and only 40 minutes away from the Krabi airport, it's no wonder this beach is becoming increasingly popular.

This is the main jumping-off point for the nearby beaches of Railay, only a 20-minute long-tail boat ride away. If you're looking for a groovier beach scene, skip Ao Nang and get your pack to this next beach.

Information

All the information offices on the strip are private tour agencies, and most offer international calls and internet access for around 1B per minute. Several banks have ATMs and foreign exchange windows (open from 10am to 8pm) on the main drag.

Activities

Loads of activities are possible at Ao Nang and children under 12 years typically get a 50% discount.

KAYAKING

At least seven companies offer kayaking tours to mangroves and islands around Ao Nang. Popular destinations include the scenic sea lagoon at Ko Hong (1500B to 1800B), where you get to paddle inside the island and view collection points for sea swallow nests (used in the Chinese delicacy bird's-nest soup). There are also trips to the lofty sea cliffs and wildlife-filled mangroves at Ao Thalane (half-/full day 900/1300B) and to the sea caves and 2000- to 3000-year-old paintings at Ban Bho Tho (1400B; see opposite) – the caves are also filled with layers of archaeological shell formations. These rates include lunch, fruit, drinking water, sea kayaks and guides. The better companies are **Sea Canoe Thailand** (☎ 0 7569 5387) and **Ao Nang Group** (☎ 0 7563 7660/1).

DIVING & SNORKELLING

Ao Nang has numerous dive schools offering trips to dive sites at nearby Railay's Laem Phra Nang. It costs about 3000B for two dives. Ko Mae Urai is one of the more unique local

SOUTHERN ANDAMAN COAST

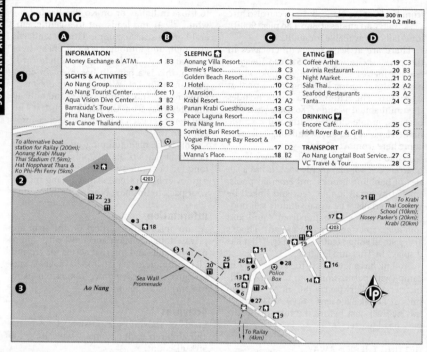

AO NANG

0 ____ 300 m
0 ____ 0.2 miles

INFORMATION		EATING	
Money Exchange & ATM............1 B3		Coffee Arthit...........................19 C3	
		Lavinia Restaurant.................20 B3	
SIGHTS & ACTIVITIES		Night Market........................21 D2	
Ao Nang Group.........................2 B2		Sala Thai................................22 A2	
Ao Nang Tourist Center............(see 1)		Seafood Restaurants 23 A2	
Aqua Vision Dive Center..........3 B2		Tanta.....................................24 C3	
Barracuda's Tour.......................4 B3			
Phra Nang Divers......................5 C3		DRINKING	
Sea Canoe Thailand..................6 C3		Encore Café...........................25 C3	
		Irish Rover Bar & Grill............26 C3	
SLEEPING			
Aonang Villa Resort..................7 C3		TRANSPORT	
Bernie's Place...........................8 C3		Ao Nang Longtail Boat Service..27 C3	
Golden Beach Resort................9 C3		VC Travel & Tour....................28 C3	
J Hotel.....................................10 C2			
J Mansion................................11 C3			
Krabi Resort.............................12 A2			
Panan Krabi Guesthouse.........13 C3			
Peace Laguna Resort...............14 C3			
Phra Nang Inn.........................15 C3			
Somkiet Buri Resort.................16 D3			
Vogue Phranang Bay Resort &			
Spa....................................17 D2			
Wanna's Place.........................18 B2			

To alternative boat station for Railay (200m); Aonang Krabi Muay Thai Stadium (1.5km); Hat Noppharat Thara & Ko Phi-Phi Ferry (5km)

To Krabi Thai Cookery School (10km); Nosey Parker's (20km); Krabi (20km)

To Krabi

Sea Wall Promenade

Ao Nang

Police Box

To Railay (4km)

---

dives, with two submarine tunnels lined with soft and hard corals. Other trips run further afield to sites around Ko Phi-Phi or Hin Daeng and Hin Muang, southwest of Ko Lanta (3600B for two dives). A PADI Open Water course will set you back 14,500B to 16,000B. Reliable dive schools include **Phra Nang Divers** (☎ 0 7563 7064; www.pndivers.com) and **Aqua Vision Dive Center** (☎ 0 7563 7415; www.aqua-vision.net). Most dive companies can also arrange snorkelling trips in the area. For snorkelling, also see boxed text, opposite.

ELEPHANT TREKKING

Several operators run elephant treks in the forest surrounding Ao Nang. **Nosey Parker's** (☎ 0 9291 0964; Rte 4202; adult/child 1hr trek 750/400B, half-day trek 1650/850B) is based about 7km from Ao Nang and offers treks along jungle streams where you have the chance to spot monkeys and exotic birds. You can also do elephant treks through the jungle to Tham Srakaew for 900B. This scenic cave with hanging stalactites was used as a location for the film *The Beach*.

ROCK CLIMBING

Most agencies can arrange rock-climbing courses in Railay, but these are just as easy to arrange yourself – just take a long-tail boat to Hat Rai Leh West (p337) first thing in the morning and approach any of the companies there.

CYCLING

Take a Tour de Krabi by hooking up with **Krabi Eco Cycle** (☎ 0 7563 7250; scubawut@yahoo.com; 41/2 Muu 5; half-/full day tour 700/1700B, half-day cycle & kayak tour 1000B). The recommended full-day 15.5km pedal takes you through rubber and oil plantations, small villages, hot springs and, finally, a cooler dip at the aptly named 'Emerald Pool'. Lunch is included on all tours except the half-day bike-only tour.

Courses

Krabi Thai Cookery School (☎ 0 7569 5133; www.thai cookeryschool.net; 269 Muu 2, Ao Nang, Rte 4204) is about 10km from Ao Nang between Wat Sai Thai and Ao Nam Mao and offers half-/one-day Thai-cooking courses for 1000/2200B; transfers are included in the price.

Tours

Any agency worth its salt can book you on one of the popular four-/five-island tours (see boxed text, below). Several tour agencies offer tours to Khlong Thom, including visits to freshwater pools, hot springs and the Wat Khlong Thom Museum; the price is 1200/900B per adult/child. So-called 'mystery tours' visit local snake farms, rural villages, crystal pools and rubber, pineapple, banana and papaya plantations and cost around 1300/600B. Tour agencies also offer trips to attractions around Ao Phang-Nga and to a number of dubious animal shows around Ao Nang.

You can also do day tours to Ko Phi-Phi on the **Ao Nang Princess** (per adult/child 1300/950B). The boat leaves from the Hat Noppharat Thara National Park headquarters at 9am and visits Bamboo Island, Phi-Phi Don and Phi-Phi Leh.

Reliable tour agencies include **Barracuda's Tour** (☎ 0 7563 7092) and the very helpful **Ao Nang Tourist Center** (☎ 0 7563 7551; www.aonangtouristcenter .com), both on the main beachfront strip.

Sleeping

Prices at all these places drop by 50% during the low season.

BUDGET

You'll find many guesthouses crammed together in a small alley. They are just up from the beach at the eastern end of the strip.

Bernie's Place (☎ 0 7563 7093; r 200-600B) Bernie's will excite the penniless in high season – rooms max out at just 600B. You'll have to share a bathroom and the mattresses are extremely soft, but rooms are big and bright with ceiling fans. The big bar and backpacker-priced buffets (all you can eat for 190B) mean it will likely have a travellers' vibe once word gets out.

Panan Krabi Guesthouse (☎ 0 7563 8105; r 600-800B; 🟦) The dinky rooms have a touch of style with their cream-coloured walls and arty fuzzy-paper light shades. Each room has its own TV and there's a chic café on the ground floor.

ourpick J Mansion (☎ 0 7569 5128/9; r 500-900B; 🟦 🟦) One of the best-value abodes in town – the rooms are spotless and come decked out with TVs, air-con and minifridges. As a result, it's eternally booked up – call well ahead if you want to stay here. The rooftop is the best asset. Head up here with a few beers at sunset and check out the fabulous views across to Railay. J Mansion also runs an honest, fairly priced travel agency.

J Hotel (☎ 0 7563 7878; j_hotelo@hotmail.com; r 350-1800B; 🟦 🟦) J Mansion's sister property (owned by the same friendly family), J Hotel is nearly as good as the original, is just up the street and might actually have a room available. Rooms are huge, bright and have satellite TV and terraces (angle for one with a sea/town view).

ISLAND HOP TILL YOU DROP

A must-do activity if you have the time is a half- or full-day island tour. You get to zoom around on a long-tail boat to several green isles that are fringed by luscious beaches, snorkel among vibrant coral and explore impressive caves and cliffs – it's the perfect day out.

Tours visit **Ko Hua Khwan** (Chicken Island), with excellent snorkelling reefs and a rock formation that looks surprisingly like poultry; **Ko Poda**, with a handsome stretch of white beach; and **Ko Taloo**, which is a tall rock formation that has an underwater swim-through. These trips also take in **Tham Phra Nang** (Princess Cave; p338), the location of a 'princess spirit house' that's revered by locals; **Ko Hong**, with a hidden lagoon surrounded by cliffs; **Ko Lading**, which is a major bird's-nest collection point and has sublime beaches; and **Ko Daeng**, where you'll find more great snorkelling. **Ko Rai** and **Ko Pakiba** are other island gems often tacked onto a tour.

From Ao Nang you can charter a long-tail from the **Ao Nang Longtail Boat Service** (☎ 0 7569 5474; www.aonanglongtailboatservice.com) to Ko Hong, Ko Lading and Ko Daeng (2500B) or to Ko Poda and Chicken Island with Tham Phra Nang (2000B). Prices are listed on the 'Boat Service' office window and are for a maximum of six people. You'll need your own gear. Otherwise pay more for a five-island all-inclusive tour at tour companies found all over Ao Nang, Railay and Krabi (around 850B per person). If you're willing to pay 200B to 400B extra you can even go by speedboat, which gives you more time to frolic at each destination.

SOUTHERN ANDAMAN COAST

MIDRANGE & TOP END

Most accommodation in Ao Nang falls into this bracket. The following places are recommended, but there are dozens of other options.

Somkiet Buri Resort (☎ 0 7563 7320; www.somkiet buri.com; r 2000-3000B; ✖ ✖) This place just might inspire you to slip into a yoga pose. The lush jungle grounds are filled with ferns and orchids, while lagoons, streams and meandering wooden walkways guide you to the 26 large and creatively designed rooms. A great swimming pool is set amid it all – balconies either face this pool or a peaceful pond. The service is first-rate.

Phra Nang Inn (☎ 0 7563 7130; phranang@sun.phuket .ksc.co.th; r incl breakfast 2300-5500B; ✖ ✖) An artistic explosion of rustic coconut wood, bright orange and purple paint and plenty of elaborate Thai tiles – Phra Nang is Boho and chic. There are two pools, and a second, similarly designed branch is across the road from the original.

Peace Laguna Resort (☎ 0 7563 7345; www.peace lagunaresort.com; r 1300-2200B; bungalows 2500-6000B; ✖ ✖) Sweet, modern cottages, some boasting polished ceramic floors, sit around a large lagoon on lush grounds while a limestone cliff basks in the background. The priciest rooms (deluxe and superior cottages) have open-air Balinese-style showers, in-room Jacuzzis and huge windows. You can score great deals in the off season.

Vogue Phranang Bay Resort & Spa (☎ 0 7563 7635; www.vogueresort.com; r 2100-6800B; ✖ ✖) Rooms have big windows – ask for one facing the sea – and mix tiles and wooden floors in a Zen architectural collage. Bathrooms have separate showers (complete with doors – rare here). The grounds are peaceful with lots of jungle foliage and there's a big round swimming pool, with sea and sunset views.

Krabi Resort (☎ 0 7563 7030, Bangkok 0 2208 9165; www.krabiresort.com; r & bungalows 4200-9000B; ✖ ✖) The original Ao Nang luxury resort is ageing gracefully, maintaining quality rooms and luxury bungalows on peaceful, 7-hectare grounds, some right near the beach. There is an on-site dive school, a restaurant and a bar.

Golden Beach Resort (☎ 0 7563 7870-74; www .krabigoldenbeach.com; r 4500-6000B, bungalows 6000-10,000B; ✖ ✖) This swanky modern resort is made up of large hotel blocks and stylish bungalows arranged in a tidy garden around a big pool. The outdoor restaurant is lit up like a Christmas tree at night and hosts slightly cheesy live music (think electric keyboards and '80s covers).

Also recommended:

Wanna's Place (☎ 0 7563 7322; www.wannasplace .com; r 1875-1975B, bungalows 2290-2390B; ✖) It's quite popular.

Aonang Villa Resort (☎ 0 7563 7270; www.aonangvilla resort.com; r 3400-7500B; ✖ ✖) A swank seaside joint.

Eating

At the western end of the beach is Soi Sunset, a narrow alley housing a number of seafood restaurants. They all have bamboo seating abutting the ocean, and model boats at the entrance showing off the day's catch. One of the best (and most popular) is **Sala Thai** (dishes 60-300B; ✖ lunch & dinner).

Coffee Arthit (☎ 0 7563 7847; breakfast from 80B; ✖ 8am-midnight) Serves excellent all-day Western-style breakfasts, espresso and cocktails and is one of the only places in town with wi-fi.

Lavinia Restaurant (pizza & pasta 80-200B; ✖ lunch & dinner) The best of several Italian places on the main drag, Lavinia does convincing pizza and pasta, served up at wooden bench tables.

Tanta (☎ 0 7563 7118; dishes 60-250B; ✖ lunch & dinner) Tanta offers a great selection of Thai and international dishes and the thin-crust pizza is delicious and not too doughy. It's a popular modern place with a raised covered terrace and wood accents.

For meals if on a tight budget, an informal night market is set up along the road to Krabi (near the McDonald's), serving *gài tôrt* (fried chicken), *pàt tai* (thin rice noodles fried with tofu, vegetables, egg and peanuts) and the like.

Drinking & Entertainment

Irish Rover Bar & Grill (☎ 0 7563 7607) Readers like this typical Irish pub specialising in draught Guinness and Kilkenny. Sports fans will appreciate the TV broadcasting English footy matches and South African cricket. The place also features live music, tropical cocktails and pool tables.

Encore Café (✖ 4pm-2am Dec-Mar; ✖) This modern air-con space has pool tables and live music five nights a week. It's mostly popular with holidaying Thais and has karaoke and sports on TV, depending on which night you go.

Aonang Krabi Muay Thai Stadium (☎ 0 7562 1042; admission 500B, ringside incl 1 beer 1000B) If you get tired of the beach-bars and video movies on the strip, this place has boisterous *moo·ay tai* (often spelt *muay thai*; Thai boxing) bouts every Friday from 8.45pm. A free sŏrng·tăa·ou runs along the strip at Ao Nang, collecting punters before the bouts.

Getting There & Around

Ao Nang is served by regular sŏrng·tăa·ou from Krabi (40B, 20 minutes). These start at the Krabi bus terminal (add 10B to the fare) and then pass by the 7-Eleven on Th Maharat and the Khong Kha pier in Krabi, continuing on to Hat Noppharat Thara, Ao Nang and finally the Shell Cemetery. From Ao Nang to Hat Noppharat Thara or the Shell Cemetery it's 20B.

Dozens of places along the strip rent out small motorcycles for 150B to 200B. **VC Travel & Tour** (☎ 0 1737 8450), right in front of the police box, has imported 400cc motorcycles for 500B per day. Budget Car Hire has desks at most of the big resort hotels and charges around 1600B per day for a dinky Suzuki micro-4WD.

Boats to Railay's Hat Rai Leh West are run by **Ao Nang Longtail Boat Service** (☎ 0 7569 5474; www.aonanglongtailboatservice.com) and rates are fixed at 100B per person for the 15-minute journey – boats leave when full. During hours when the 'Boat Service' office is closed you'll have to haggle with long-tail captains directly, although the price should still be 100B if the boat is full (seven to eight people). During rough seas, boats leave from a sheltered cove about 200m west of Ao Nang – you can get here from Ao Nang by motorcycle taxi (30B), sŏrng·tăa·ou (10B) or on foot.

There are also boats to Ko Phi-Phi from nearby Hat Noppharat Thara (see right).

AROUND AO NANG
Hat Noppharat Thara
หาดนพรัตน์ธารา

Ao Nang's growth spurt is quickly seeping over into once peaceful Hat Noppharat Thara and the effect is disheartening. The beach is currently in the phase of having too much in common with Ao Nang to have character, yet it's not developed enough to be much fun. Although technically 4km from Ao Nang, the two beaches have a commercial strip that links them together almost seamlessly. The further north you go along Hat Noppharat Thara (away from Ao Nang), the more peace you'll find.

This beach is the headquarters for Ko Phi-Phi Marine National Park and is a popular local picnic spot on weekends. There's a small visitors centre with displays on coral reefs and mangrove ecology, labelled in Thai and English.

SLEEPING & EATING

Midrange development dominates the main drag that runs along the beach from Ao Nang – budget digs are found inland towards the Ao Nang Krabi Muay Thai Boxing Stadium.

Government bungalows (☎ 0 7563 7200; 2-6-person tents 300B, 2-person bungalows 600B, 6-8-person bungalows 1200B or per person 200B) These bungalows at the park headquarters are well maintained with fans, bathrooms and mosquito nets on the windows. Tents are also available if you want the full primitive experience. A small canteen serves meals in the evenings.

Laughing Gecko (☎ 0 7569 5115; www.laughinggecko thailand.com; dm 150B, bungalows 300-700B) Island-style bamboo-basic huts are a welcome addition to this town. There's a great travellers' vibe and an artistically decorated restaurant with all-you-can-eat Thai buffets for around 150B.

Srisuksant Resort (☎ 0 7563 8002; www.srisuksant resort.com; r 1900-2100B; ✹ ✹) At the Ao Nang end of the beach, this new, vaguely stylish, roadside resort is great value for this standard. It's both a short walk to the attractions of Ao Nang or the quieter strip of Hat Noppharat Thara.

Emerald Bungalows (☎ 0 1956 2566; http://der-work shop.de/emerald/emeraldhomepage.html; bungalows 1700-2800B; ⚘ Oct-Apr; ✹) A comfy upmarket option with plain, clean bungalows in a large garden at the peaceful northern end of the beach.

Around the national park headquarters there are several restaurants serving the usual Thai snack meals such as fried chicken and papaya salad.

GETTING THERE & AWAY

Sŏrng·tăa·ou between Krabi and Ao Nang stop in Hat Noppharat Thara; the fare is 40B from Krabi or 10B from Ao Nang.

From November to May the *Ao Nang Princess* runs between Ko Phi-Phi Marine National Park headquarters and Ko Phi-Phi (350B, two hours). The boat leaves from the national park jetty at 9am, returning from Ko Phi-Phi at 3.30pm. It also stops at Railay's Hat Rai Leh West. This boat can also be used for day trips to Ko Phi-Phi (p343). During the same high-season months there's also a direct boat to Phuket, leaving from the same pier at 3.30pm (450B) and to Ko Lanta at 10.30am (450B).

Shell Cemetery
สุสานหอย

About 9km east of Ao Nang at the western end of Ao Nam Mao is the **Shell Cemetery**, also known as Gastropod Fossil or Su-San Hoi. Here you can see giant slabs formed from millions of tiny 75-million-year-old fossil shells. There's a small **visitors centre** (admission 50B; ☺ 8.30am-4.30pm) with geological displays and various stalls selling snacks. Sŏrng·tǎa·ou from Ao Nang cost 20B.

RAILAY
ไร่เลย์

With Krabi Province's signature vertical limestone karsts framing pearl-white beaches and luscious aquamarine sea, Railay (also spelled Rai Leh) is the kind of place you wish you had to yourself – but unfortunately this is no secret spot. It's just around the corner from Ao Nang and Krabi town but is protected by impenetrable cliffs, which completely cuts the peninsula off from the mainland hubbub. The only way to get here is by boat and there are no cars or motorbikes, so you'll have to keep reminding yourself you're not on an island.

Despite the fact that every beach out here has been filled in with bungalows, development is neatly tucked away in the coconut palms and lush gardens so it doesn't feel cramped. The beaches do get crowded in high season but there is so much more to do here than cook on the beach: for many adventure seekers Railay is best known for the hundreds of excellent rock-climbing routes afforded by the surrounding cliffs. Loads of climbing shops cater to visitors wishing to scramble up the karsts, providing equipment rental and instruction for beginners and advanced climbers alike. If rocks aren't your thing, check out the local caves, try diving, a snorkelling trip or rent out a kayak for the day.

Hat Rai Leh East is the most developed beach and is where boats from Krabi arrive. The shallow, muddy beach lined with mangroves is the heart of the action and only a five-minute walk over the peninsula to the lounge-worthy sands of **Hat Rai Leh West**. This near-flawless, white wonder is the best place to watch the sun go down. Tastefully designed midrange resorts line the beach and dozens of

long-tail boats make pick-ups and drop-offs from here to nearby Ao Nang. At the tip of the headland, **Hat Phra Nang** is quite possibly one of the world's most beautiful beaches with squeaky white sand, overhanging karst cliffs, frolicking monkeys and views of limestone islets peeking out of the cerulean sea. Rayavadee, the peninsula's most exclusive resort, is the only one on this beach but anyone can go and throw down their beach towel. Hat Ton Sai is the grittier climbers' and backpackers' retreat and is reached by long-tail (either directly from Ao Nang or from Hat Rai Leh West) or by a sweaty 20-minute scramble over limestone rocks from the northern end of Hat Rai Leh West.

Information

The website www.railay.com has lots of information about Railay. There are two ATMs along Hat Rai Leh East and another at the Flame Tree restaurant (p341) on Hat Rai Leh West. On Hat Ton Sai there is one ATM near the Ton Sai Bay Resort but it only operates from November through May. Several of the bigger resorts can change cash and travellers cheques. Internet access is available throughout all the beaches for 2B per minute. For minor climbing injuries there's a small clinic at Railay Bay Resort (p341).

Sights

At the eastern end of Hat Phra Nang is **Tham Phra Nang** (Princess Cave), an important shrine for local fishermen. Legend has it that a royal barge carrying an Indian princess foundered in a storm here during the 3rd century BC. The spirit of the drowned princess came to inhabit the cave, granting favours to all who came to pay respect. Local fishermen – Muslim and Buddhist – place carved wooden phalluses in the cave as offerings in the hope that the spirit will provide plenty of fish.

About halfway along the path from Hat Rai Leh East to Hat Phra Nang, a crude path leads up the jungle-cloaked cliff wall to a hidden lagoon known as **Sa Phra Nang** (Holy Princess Pool). There's a dramatic viewpoint over the peninsula from the nearby cliff top, but be warned that this is a strenuous hike with some serious vertigo-inducing parts.

Above Hat Rai Leh East is another large cave called **Tham Phra Nang Nai** (Inner Princess Cave; adult/child 40/20B; ☺ 5am-8pm), also known as Diamond Cave. A wooden boardwalk leads through a series of illuminated caverns full of beautiful limestone formations, including a splendid 'stone waterfall' of sparkling gold-coloured quartz.

Activities

ROCK CLIMBING

With nearly 500 bolted routes and unparalleled cliff-top vistas, it's no surprise that these dramatic rock faces lay claim to being among the top climbing spots in the world. There are so many climbing options, ranging from beginner routes to challenging advanced climbs, that you could spend months climbing and exploring – and many people do. The newest buzz is about deep water-soloing where climbers free-climb ledges over deep water – if you fall you will most likely just get wet so even daring beginners can give this a try.

Most climbers start off at **Muay Thai Wall** and **One, Two, Three Wall**, at the southern end of Hat Rai Leh East, which have at least 40 routes graded from 4b to 8b on the French system. The mighty **Thaiwand Wall** sits at the southern end of Hat Rai Leh West and offers a sheer limestone cliff with some of the most challenging climbing routes.

Other top climbs include: **Groove Tube** (good for beginners and intermediate climbers), **Humanility** (an exceedingly popular multi-pitch climb), **Lion King** (for a challenge), **Narsillon** (also challenging and only accessible at low tide) and **Ao Nang Tower** (a three-pitch climbing wall reached only by long-tail – many people only do the first two pitches as the last is so challenging).

The going rate for climbing courses is 800B to 1000B for a half-day and 1500B to 2000B for a full day. Three-day courses (5000B to 6000B) will involve lead-climbing, where you clip into bolts on the rock face as you ascend. Experienced climbers can hire gear sets from any of the climbing schools for 600/1000B for a half-/full day – the standard set consists of a 60m rope, two climbing harnesses and climbing shoes. If you're planning to climb independently, you're best off bringing your own gear from home; be sure to bring plenty of slings and quickdraws, chalk (sweaty palms

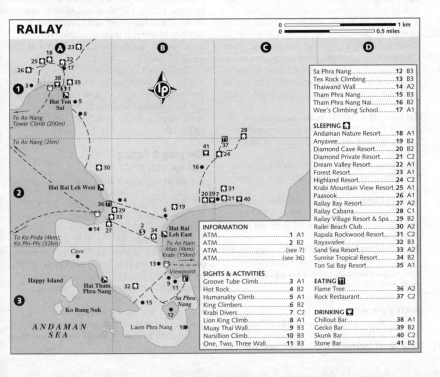

RAILAY

0 — 1 km
0 — 0.5 miles

To Ao Nang Tower Climb (200m)

To Ao Nang (2km)

Hat Ton Sai

Hat Rai Leh West

Hat Rai Leh East

To Ko Poda (4km); Ko Phi-Phi (32km)

To Ao Nam Mao (4km); Krabi (15km)

Cave

Happy Island

Hat Tham Phra Nang

Ko Rung Nok

ANDAMAN SEA

Laem Phra Nang

Viewpoint

Sa Phra Nang

SOUTHERN ANDAMAN COAST

LOCAL VOICE: ELKE SCHMITZ & WEE CHANGRUA

Elke Schmitz and Wee Changrua are the authors of *Rock Climbing in Thailand* and run Wee's Climbing School on Hat Ton Sai.

What are the most important things to look for when choosing a climbing school? Unlike diving, which has PADI, there is no independent organisation that certifies climbers and climbing schools so you'll have to judge a place on your own. For a half- or full-day introductory course everyone in Railay climbs in the same areas all together so it doesn't really matter which school you choose. If you want to take a longer course the quality will depend 100% on your instructor. Ask where the instructors were trained – also ask how long the instructor has been teaching. There should be a syllabus available that covers plenty of safety instruction and by the end of a three-day course you should know how to lead climb, belay another climber and be able to judge safety. For a five-day course there should be training in multi pitching. Make sure there are textbooks and theory, not just on-the-rock training. Your worst-case scenario is getting led around for three to five days with little instruction. Established shops should all have insurance – if you go climbing with some guy you meet on the beach, chances are you won't be insured or even get the best local support if you get hurt.

---

are inevitable in the tropics) and a small selection of nuts and cams as backup for thinly protected routes. If you forget anything, some climbing schools sell a small range of imported climbing gear but they might not have exactly what you need or the right size. A woven rattan mat (available locally for 100B to 150B) will help keep the sand out of your gear.

Several locally published books detail climbs in the area, but *Rock Climbing in Thailand* (1000B), by Elke Schmitz and Wee Changrua, is one of the more complete guides. There are climbing shops all over Railay – see boxed text, above, for details on how to pick the right one for you. Recommended shops include:

Hot Rock (☎ 0 7562 1771; www.railayadventure .com; Hat Rai Leh West) Has a very good reputation and is owned by Luang, one of the granddaddies of Railay climbing.

King Climbers (☎ 0 7563 7125; www.railay.com; Hat Rai Leh West) One of the biggest, oldest, most reputable and commercial schools.

Tex Rock Climbing (☎ 0 7563 1509; www.thaipro .com/z1032b/799_thailand.html; Hat Rai Leh East) A tiny, venerable school where the owner still climbs and runs the school direct from the shop.

Wee's Climbing School (www.geocities.com/wee _rocks/tonsai; Hat Ton Sai) The place to go if you're serious about learning to climb – this is arguably the most professional outfit in the area.

WATER SPORTS

Several **dive** operations in Railay run trips out to Ko Poda and other neighbouring dive sites. **Krabi Divers** (☎ 0 7562 1686/7; www.viewpoint resort66.com; Hat Rai Leh East), at Railay Viewpoint Resort, charges 6100B for two dives at outlying islands. A three- or four-day PADI Open Water dive course is 14,800B.

Snorkelling trips to Ko Poda and Ko Hua Khwan (Chicken Island) can be arranged through any of the resorts for about 850B by long-tail or 1100B by speedboat. Longer multi-island trips cost 1100/1900B per half-/full day. If you just want to snorkel off Railay, most resorts can rent you a mask set and fins for 150B each.

The Flame Tree restaurant (see opposite) at Hat Rai Leh West rents out **sea kayaks** for 200B per hour. Overnight trips to deserted islands can be arranged with local boat owners but you'll need to bring your own camping gear and food.

Sleeping & Eating

HAT RAI LEH WEST

It's all pretty much midrange and top-end options on this beach (where sunsets are fabulous), but rates often drop by 30% in the low season. All the resorts have decent restaurants.

Sand Sea Resort (☎ 0 7562 2170; www.krabisandsea .com; bungalows 1950-5950B; ✳ 🖳 ⚍) The lowest-priced resort on this beach offers everything from ageing fan-only bungalows to newly remodelled cottages with every amenity. The grounds aren't as swank as the neighbours, but rooms are comfy enough and there's a peaceful karst-view, foliage-enclosed pool – if you're able to tear yourself away from that sublime beach out front that is. The restaurant here does a full buffet breakfast, which is included in the room rate.

Railei Beach Club (☎ 0 7562 2582; www.raileibeach club.com; houses 3700-9000B) Hidden in forested grounds at the northern end of the beach, this is a collection of Thai-styled homes, each unique in size and design. The houses are rented out by their foreign owners while they are back home and come with patios, kitchens and amenities to make extended stays very comfortable. Some houses sleep up to eight people. Book well in advance for the high season.

Railay Village Resort & Spa (☎ 0 7562 2578-80; www.railayvillagekrabi.com; bungalows 5700-10,600B; 🌊 💻) Very posh bungalows with private hot tubs are spread throughout gardens of lily ponds, tall palms and gurgling fountains. The open-air restaurant serves excellent green curry and particularly convincing Western-style pastas that are a boon if you're travelling with children.

ourpick Railay Bay Resort (☎ 0 7562 2570-2; www .railaybayresort.com; bungalows 2900-11,500B; 🌊) The amoeba-shaped blue pool here faces onto the best bit of the beach so you can switch between salt and fresh water. Elegant bungalows with big windows, white walls and rustic-chic timber terraces run right across the peninsula to Hat Rai Leh East via gorgeously planted grounds and a second pool. Bungalows on the east side are older with dark-tinted windows and are the least expensive. The spa, which also overlooks the sea, offers a host of treatments at very reasonable prices. We found the restaurant here to be a notch up in style, service, cuisine and, of course price, from everywhere else on this beach and Hat Rai Leh East.

Flame Tree (dishes around 150B) A hopping joint packed all day and into the night. We found the food overpriced and mediocre and the service terrible but it does have an extensive menu and a lively atmosphere. The bar/restaurant now extends east into its own mini-mall with art galleries, clothing stores and a bookshop.

HAT RAI LEH EAST

Often referred to as Sunrise Beach, the beach along here tends towards mud flats during low tide. The resorts on the hillside above the beach get sea breezes, but down on the beach it can feel like a sauna in the evenings. The following rates drop by half in the low season.

Railay Cabana (☎ 0 8695 78096; bungalows 150-300B) Superbly located deep in the jungle and high in the hills in a bowl of karst cliffs, this uber-rustic, Rasta-run place is the cheapest in Railay.

Highland Resort (☎ 0 7562 1732; bungalows 500B) In the middle of a natural basin above Hat Rai Leh East, you'll find spacious, bamboo, stilted bungalows with stylish, elongated glass windows, mosquito net and fan.

Rapala Rockwood Resort (☎ 0 7562 2586; rapala@ loxinfo.co.th; bungalows 500-750B) Ramshackle bamboo bungalows have verandas, bathrooms, mosquito nets and fans. The delightful location atop a hill means breezes and views of the sea (as well as your neighbours). There's a cushion-lined restaurant that's perfect for chilling – it serves Thai as well as Indian food and is run by a charming Thai grandma.

Diamond Private Resort (☎ 0 7562 1729; www .diamondprivate-railay.com; r 1900-3500B; 🌊 💻) This resort has a pool high up on the hilltop with a deck sporting great views of the bay below. The rooms and bungalows come with TVs, hot showers and minibars and are set in well-landscaped gardens.

Diamond Cave Resort (☎ 0 7562 2589; www .diamondcave-railay.com; r 1500-4000B; 🌊 💻) It's pretty cheesy and the grounds are heavy on the concrete but these air-conditioned bungalows, up a hill and well off the beach, are OK if elsewhere is full. Fan-only rooms are flimsy but a good deal if you don't need air-con and don't like bamboo huts. There's a large restaurant right on the beach.

ourpick Sunrise Tropical Resort (☎ 0 7562 2599; www.sunrisetropical.com; bungalows 3500-4500B; 🌊 💻) Bungalows here rival the better ones on Hat Rai Leh West but are priced for Hat Rai Leh East – it's only a five-minute walk to the west beach and even easier access to Hat Tham Phra Nang (the best beach), so we think this is the best deal in Railay. Grand Thai-style villas smell like jasmine and have window nooks, satin settees and spa-like bathrooms with luminescent aqua green tiles. Everything is in a lush garden with an astounding variety of tropical plants; breakfast is included.

Anyavee (☎ 0 8153 75517; www.anyavee.com; bungalows 2500-7000B; 🌊 💻) An awkward resort but one with more style than most on this beach, bungalows here have lots of windows making them bright but not private. Interiors are country-chic with cream and beige plaid duvets and plenty of hardwoods.

our pick **Rock Restaurant** (meals 80–120B; ☺ breakfast, lunch & dinner) Up past Highland Resort, amid dense jungle and karst cliffs, it's actually best to dine here during the day to appreciate the view. The food (Thai and Western) is great anytime – try to get one of the intimate shaded booths at the jungle's edge.

There's a very social cluster of reasonably priced restaurants serving Westernised Thai food and fresh(ish) seafood from 50B to 200B at the far eastern end of this beach. Some show movies and later in the night the area turns into a fun, low-key bar scene.

HAT THAM PHRA NANG

There's only one place to stay on this magnificent beach and it's a doozy.

Rayavadee (☎ 0 7562 0740-3; www.rayavadee.com; pavilions 26,090–33,110B, villas 40,900–112,300B) This exclusive colonial-style resort has sprawling, immaculate grounds navigated by golf buggies and dotted with meandering ponds. The two-storey, mushroom-domed rooms are filled with antique furniture and every mod con you need in a home away from home. Classical music wafts throughout the lounge areas and there are a first-rate spa and yoga classes for guests. Two restaurants grace Hat Tham Phra Nang and nonguests can stop in for a pricey but divine meal of Thai or Mediterranean fare.

HAT TON SAI

The beach here isn't much to look at but with so many good climbs all around, most people don't mind. A huge Bangkok company (Deva; www.devaproperty.com) owns most of the beachfront and, at the time of writing, most bars and bungalows had been forced to move off-beach and back into the jungle. Deva had plans to build an assisted living community for the elderly on the beach until it realised that there is no road access. It's a little unclear what will happen in future but development plans could take years. For now, in the low season, rates for bungalows plummet as low as 100B.

Andaman Nature Resort (☎ 0 7562 1667; bungalows 300–500B) A very shabby outfit back in the jungle but this place also manages the old bamboo Mambo bungalows, and these are the closest budget offerings to the beach.

our pick **Paasook** (☎ 0 8964 53013; bungalows 500B) Definitely the most stylish budget establishment on Ton Sai, wooden bungalows here are huge, have elongated floor to ceiling windows and refreshingly nonsagging floors. This place is at the far western end of the beach, right beneath a karst cliff, so it can become very warm, but the gardens are lush, management is friendly and there's a rustic-chic outdoor restaurant, perfect for steamy evenings.

Forest Resort (☎ 0 8929 00262; bungalows 500–700B) A collection of large, basic thatched bungalows perched on a flowery hillside and run by a super smiley Thai family. A British-run, sari-clad Indian restaurant was just opening up when we passed.

Krabi Mountain View Resort (☎ 0 7562 2610-3; http://citykrabi.com/mountainview.html; bungalows 1200–1900B; ✿) Bright, cheery and immaculate with mint green walls, tiled floors and crisp sheets, this is where you'll find Ton Sai's best-value air-con rooms.

Ton Sai Bay Resort (☎ 0 7562 2584; www.tonsaibay resort.com; bungalows 1000–2800B; ✿ ▣) The poshest option on Ton Sai is also the busiest and the only one fully established on the beach (although only the restaurant is beachfront). Big concrete bungalows with terraces are comfy although a little dated. There's also a clutch of standard bamboo huts further back. With a diving centre, climbing school, minimart and a huge seafood restaurant, everything you need is here.

Dream Valley Resort (☎ 0 7562 2583; www.dream valleyresortkrabi.com; r 350–3000B; ✿) Bamboo bungalows are as rustic as the rest around here, while wooden ones with terracotta tiled bathrooms are a step up in comfort. A new block of rather pricey air-con rooms was under construction when we visited. There's a minimart and an OK seafood restaurant on-site.

There are a few other bamboo hut-style resorts along the jungle path that have bungalows with bathrooms for around 500B.

Drinking

There's a bunch of places on the beaches where you can unwind and get nicely inebriated.

Chillout Bar (Hat Ton Sai) This place boldly flies the Rasta colours and caters to the chilling needs of climbers after a hard day's scrambling. When we passed it still held its place on the beach.

Stone Bar (Hat Rai Leh East) Up the hill towards the Highland Resort, Stone Bar has an awesome setting under a massive climbing wall, is enveloped by jungle and has a drinking gazebo perched atop a boulder.

Gecko Bar (Hat Rai Leh East) One of several bars scattered around this beach, Gecko Bar keeps you out late then offers you yoga (in high season) on its front deck in the morning.

Skunk Bar (Hat Rai Leh East) Plays excellent, scratchy roots reggae on a turntable and has one of the liveliest vibes around.

Getting There & Around

The only way to get to Railay is by long-tail boat, either from Khong Kha pier in Krabi or from the seafronts of Ao Nang and Ao Nam Mao. Boats between Krabi and Hat Rai Leh East leave every 1½ hours from 7.45am to 6pm when they have 10 people (150B, 45 minutes). Chartering a special trip will set you back 1500B.

Boats to Hat Rai Leh West or Hat Ton Sai leave from the eastern end of the promenade at Ao Nang. The fare is 100B (15 minutes). If seas are rough, boats leave from a sheltered cove just west of Krabi Resort in Ao Nang. You can be dropped at Hat Phra Nang or Hat Ton Sai for the same fare.

During exceptionally high seas the boats from Ao Nang and Krabi stop running, but you may still be able to get from Hat Rai Leh East to Ao Nam Mao (90B, 15 minutes), where you can pick up a sŏrng·tǎa·ou to Krabi or Ao Nang.

From October to May the *Ao Nang Princess* runs from Hat Nopphorat Thara National Park headquarters to Ko Phi-Phi with a stop at Hat Rai Leh West. Long-tails run out to meet the boat at around 9.15am from in front of the Sand Sea Resort (p340). The fare to Ko Phi-Phi from Railay is 350B.

KO PHI-PHI DON
เกาะพีพีดอน

Oh, how beauty can be a burden. Like Marilyn Monroe, Phi-Phi Don's stunning looks have become its own demise. Everyone wants a piece of her. Though not exactly Hollywood, this is Thailand's Shangri-la: a hedonistic paradise where tourists cavort in radiant azure seas and snap pictures of long-tails puttering between craggy cliffs. With its flashy, curvy, blonde beaches, Technicolor corals and bodacious jungles it's no wonder that Phi-Phi has become the darling of the Andaman coast. And, like any good starlet, this island can party hard all night and still look like a million bucks the next morning. Unfortunately, nothing and nobody can withstand this glamorous

> **SHELL OUT**
>
> Numerous souvenir shops on Ko Phi-Phi Don sell seashells, but these are poached from the surrounding marine national parks. Shell species are becoming extinct here faster than you can say 'she sells seashells', so please don't buy souvenirs made from tropical shells.

pace and unless limits are set, Phi-Phi is in for an ecological crash.

The exceedingly tragic Boxing Day tsunami of 2004 turned back the eco-damage meter when it wiped out nearly every standing structure on the densely populated twin bays of Ao Ton Sai and Ao Lo Dalam. In terms of loss of life and property, Ko Phi-Phi Don was second only to Khao Lak and Bang Niang in Phang-Nga Province. Following the tsunami it was hoped that lessons could be learned from past mistakes, but Ao Ton Sai today looks almost exactly as it did before 24 December 2004. The only differences are a water-treatment plant, opened in 2006, that has suspended water-supply issues and that trash is starting to head into rubbish bins. Do your part in recycling – look for the new rubbish bins and deposit as much garbage as you can find. On the other bays as well, it's business as usual.

Strong tsunami feelings still linger on Phi-Phi through pictures of the volunteers that helped rebuild restaurants and guesthouses, memorials to those who died and a palpable air of thanks, both for being alive and to the tourist industry that helped bring this island back into business – this appreciation extends to all visitors, old and new, and you can't help but feel touched by it.

Although Ko Phi-Phi will seem expensive compared to the rest of Thailand (aside from Phuket and Ko Samui), if you compare it to other pin-up islands around the planet, we think you'll discover this paradise comes pretty damn cheap.

Orientation & Information

Ko Phi-Phi Don (usually just referred to as Ko Phi-Phi) is part of the Ko Phi-Phi Marine National Park, which also includes uninhabited Ko Phi-Phi Leh. Development is forbidden on Phi-Phi Don's little sister, but it can be visited on immensely popular day trips.

SOUTHERN ANDAMAN COAST

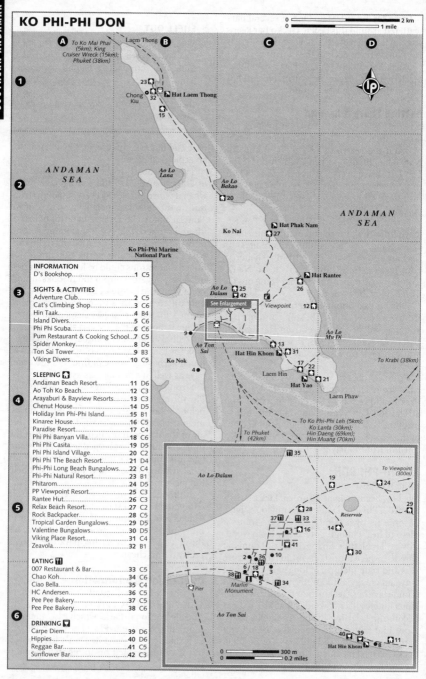

KO PHI-PHI DON

Phi-Phi Don is actually two islands joined by a narrow isthmus separating the two prized beaches of Ao Ton Sai and Ao Lo Dalam. Boats dock at the large concrete pier at Ao Ton Sai and a sandy path, crammed full of rickety shacks housing tour operators, bungalows, restaurants, bars and souvenir shops, stretches along the beach towards Hat Hin Khom. The maze of small streets in the middle of this sand bar is equally packed, more slumlike and is euphemistically called 'tourist village'. Hat Yao (Long Beach) faces south and has some of Phi-Phi Don's best coral reefs and one of its most impressive swimming beaches. The beautifully languid and long eastern bays of Hat Laem Thong and Ao Lo Bakao are reserved for several top-end resorts while the smaller bays of Hat Phak Nam, Hat Rantee and Ao Toh Ko play host to a few simple, low-key budget bungalow affairs.

ATMs and internet shops (2B per minute) are spread thickly throughout the tourist village but aren't available on the more remote eastern beaches. Wi-fi is available at **D's Bookshop** (10am-10pm) in the heart of the tourist village.

Activities

The strenuous climb to the **Phi Phi viewpoint** is a rewarding short hike. Follow the signs from the road heading east towards Ao Lo Dalam from the tourist village. The viewpoint is reached via a 300m vertical climb that includes hundreds of steep steps and narrow twisting paths. The views from the top are amazing – the marine park vistas stretch on forever in colours of aqua, emerald and jade. From here you can head over the hill through the jungle to the peaceful eastern beaches for a DIY snorkelling tour but don't walk there alone.

DIVING & SNORKELLING

The combination of perfectly clear Andaman waters and abundant coral means that Ko Phi-Phi is home to some world-class dive sites. Dozens upon dozens of dive shops compete for your business and tout dive trips and PADI Open Water courses.

The shipwrecked ferry *King Cruiser* lies only 12m below the surface and is visited by dive outfits from both Ko Phi-Phi and Phuket. Phi-Phi's dive shops all charge the same price – an Open Water certification course costs 12,500B, while the standard two-dive trips cost 3200B, or 3900B if you want to visit the

King Cruiser wreck. You can also dive out at **Hin Daeng** and **Hin Muang**, 60km off Ko Phi-Phi (5500B for two dives).

Phi Phi Scuba (0 7561 2665; www.ppscuba.com) and **Island Divers** (0 7560 1082; www.islanddiverspp .com) are the biggest operators. Both churn out dive certifications by the boatload, and some folks complain about the less-than-personalised service. On the plus side, Island Divers, in particular, pushes eco-friendly scuba – the company encourages wreck dives and doesn't allow clients to touch the coral. Both shops have access to a hyperbaric chamber. **Viking Divers** (0 1719 3375; www.vikingdiversthailand.com) is a much smaller outfit that helped with the post-tsunami clean-up of the reefs and comes with good recommendations.

One popular destination for snorkelling is **Ko Mai Phai** (Bamboo Island), north of Phi-Phi Don. There's a shallow area here where you may see small sharks. Snorkelling trips cost between 600B and 2400B, depending on whether you want a long-tail or motorboat. There is also good snorkelling along the eastern coast of **Ko Nok**, near Ao Ton Sai, and along the eastern coast of **Ko Nai**. Many snorkelling tours on bigger boats include short **kayaking** side trips, but some of these tours use minicruise ships that carry up to 100 people at a time – peace and quiet on these behemoths may not be an option. If you're going on your own, most bungalows and resorts rent out a snorkel, mask and fins for 150B to 200B per day.

ROCK CLIMBING

Yes, there are good limestone cliffs to climb on Ko Phi-Phi, and the views from the tops are spectacular. The main climbing areas are **Ton Sai Tower**, at the western edge of Ao Ton Sai, and **Hin Taak**, a short long-tail boat ride around the bay. There are at least six good climbing shops on the island and most places charge around 900B for a half-day of climbing or 1600B for a full day, including instruction and gear. **Spider Monkey** (0 9728 1608) is a tiny climbing shop run by Soley, one of the most impressive climbers on Phi-Phi. One of the bigger outfits around is the French-run **Cat's Climbing Shop** (0 1787 5101; www.catsclimbing shop.com) in the tourist village. Cat's gets good reports for safety and service. For tips on choosing a school, see boxed text, p340.

Travellers have complained of serious back injuries after cliff jumping into the sea while on tours. Take care.

KO PHI-PHI DIVE SITES

The dive sites around Ko Phi-Phi are some of the best in Thailand, and leopard sharks and hawksbill turtles are very common. Whale sharks sometimes make cameo appearances around Hin Bida (Phi-Phi Sub Shark Point) and Ko Bida Nok in February and March. The top five dives at Ko Phi-Phi:

Dive site	Depth	Features
Hin Bida (Phi-Phi Sub Shark Point)	15-30m	Submerged pinnacle with hard coral, turtles, leopard sharks and occasional whale sharks.
Ko Bida Nok	18-22m	Karst massif with gorgonians, leopard sharks, barracuda and occasional whale sharks.
Anemone Reef	17-26m	Hard coral reef with plentiful anemones and clownfish.
Hin Musang (Phuket Shark Point)	19-24m	Submerged pinnacle with a few leopard sharks, grouper, barracuda and moray eels.
Phi-Phi Leh	5-18m	The whole island rim is covered in coral and oysters where you can see moray eels and seahorses, and do lots of swim-throughs.

Courses

Thai-food fans can take cooking courses at the recommended **Pum Restaurant & Cooking School** (☎ 0 1521 8904; www.pumthaifoodchain.com; 4hr class 2500B) in the tourist village. You'll learn to make some of the excellent dishes that are served in its restaurant and go home with a great cookbook.

Tours

As well as the popular long-tail tours to Phi-Phi Leh and Ko Mai Phai (Bamboo Island), tour agencies can arrange sunset tours to Monkey Bay and the beach at Wang Long (600B). **Adventure Club** (☎ 0 1895 1334; www.phi-phi-adventures.com) is a green organisation that was instrumental in helping clean up Phi-Phi's underwater habitat after the tsunami. It runs educational, ecofocused tours and dive trips, including shark-watching snorkelling trips, reef restoration dive trips, cliff jumping (entirely at your own risk) and hiking.

Sleeping

Finding accommodation on this ever-popular island has never been easy and you can expect serious room shortages at peak holiday times. Masses of touts meet incoming boats and, while often annoying, can make your life easier.

Be sure you lock the door while you sleep and close all the windows when you go out as break-ins can be a problem.

AO TON SAI & AO LO DALAM

Accommodation in the centre of this area can be claustrophobic and noisy – the most peaceful options are found along Ao Lo Dalam beach and on the paths leading from the centre towards the viewpoint and other beaches.

Rock Backpacker (☎ 0 7561 2402; therockbackpacker@hotmail.com; dm 350B, r 800B) The funky restaurant, on a boat dry-docked on the hillside, is conducive to mingling and the 16-bed dorm room is a real rarity on Ko Phi-Phi. Digs are clean, if rather cramped and central.

Valentine Bungalows (☎ 0 1894 2842; r 500-700B) The cheaper wooden bungalows fill up fast here so book in advance. Otherwise pay a little more for more-comfy concrete and tile cottages. Everything is in a local-feeling part of the village near a mosque and the bungalows surround a big courtyard.

Tropical Garden Bungalows (☎ 0 9729 1436; r 800-1400B; ⚲) Backed against the mountainside, the best part of this laid-back lodge is the jungle pool complete with ancient Thai-style fountains and a sundeck. Large en suite cabins are frontier-style log affairs, while a two-storey complex has cheaper shared-bathroom units.

Chenut House (☎ 0 8189 41026; bungalows 1000-1200B) On a quiet path away from the bazaar of the tourist village, this place is refreshingly tranquil. Spacious wooden and bamboo bungalows are dripping with naturalistic mobiles, planters and crafty touches, plus have clean tiled bathrooms. It's family run and set in a shady garden that oozes friendly smiles and encouragements to chill.

Phi Phi Casita (☎ 0 7560 1214; bungalows 1000-2000B; ⚹ ⚲) A step back from Ao Lo Dalam beach, this place looks like a classy fishermen's village – tiny wooden bungalows hover on stilts over flower-planted mud flats. There's not much privacy but the stylish infinity pool and proximity to the beach are major draws.

Kinaree House (☎ 0 8185 45187; www.geoci ties.com/kinnaree_house; r 1500-2100B; 🕸) It's got more style than anywhere else in central Ton Sai (walls in shocking hues of orange, turquoise and purples, contemporary Thai art and so on) and its location can be great if tranquility is an afterthought to shopping and partying. Rooms are small but reception is friendly.

PP Viewpoint Resort (☎ 0 7562 2351; www.phi phiviewpoint.com; bungalows 1500-8000B; 🕸 🔁) At the far end of Ao Lo Dalam, this place rests on a rise with marvellous views of the bay. Wooden bungalows sit high on stilts and share the views. There is a small swimming pool that practically drops into the ocean below and a glass-walled tower with 360-degree views where you can pamper yourself with a Thai massage.

Phi Phi Banyan Villa (☎ 0 7561 1233; www.phiphi -hotel.com; r 2500-2800B; 🕸 🔁) There are lots of rooms snaking inland from the beach here. The comfy quarters have all the mod cons and some have a balcony overlooking a garden-lined path. There's a seaside restaurant and the hotel's namesake, a large gnarled banyan tree, sits out front.

Phitarom (☎ 0 7560 1121; www.phiphiresortphi tarom.com; bungalows 2400-3800B; 🕸 🔁) Designed to blend in with the hillside, these villas are connected by a series of steps and walkways and are fringed with bird-filled trees. Elegant rooms have polished wood floors, Zen-style furniture and good mattresses topped with neutral toned silk bed runners. Every room has its own terrace that looks out over sea or jungle but not all are that private – the higher up the hill you go the more serenity (and thigh workout) you'll get. Fresh flowers add a beautiful touch throughout and rates include breakfast.

HAT HIN KHOM

The beach here was never Phi-Phi's best, but there's a bunch of abodes and the area is a short walk from both the stunning Hat Yao and the Ao Ton Sai bustle.

Viking Place Resort (☎ 0 7581 9399; Tak_blonk@ hotmail.com; bungalows 800-1600B) Wood, thatch and bamboo bungalows here are exceptionally creative and stylish with lots of driftwood, shell mobiles and art all around. All bunga-lows have mosquito nets and balconies but unfortunately the cheaper rooms don't have their own bathrooms. That said, both shared and attached bathrooms are exquisite and are always stocked with plenty of soaps, shampoos and fresh flowers. At night candles add flickering light to the peace and quiet.

Andaman Beach Resort (☎ 0 7562 1427; www.anda manbeachresort.com; bungalows 1650-4350B; 🕸 🔁) A U-shape of neat, tiled huts sits around a large spartan lawn. The biggest attraction is the small pool at its epicentre – perfect for sleeping off nights spent at Hippies bar next door.

Arayaburi & Bayview Resorts (☎ 0 7628 1360; www .phiphibayview.com; bungalows 3400-5500B; 🕸 🔁) These twin resorts under common management offer a cornucopia of huts straddling the rocky headland of the coast. Most of the bungalows are modern in design, come stacked with amenities, have excellent ocean views from their front decks and breakfast is included.

HAT YAO

You can either walk here in about 20 minutes from Ton Sai via Hat Him Khom beach or take a long-tail (100B) from Ton Sai pier. This long, stunning stretch of pure-white beach is perfect for swimming and well worth the walk. A trail leads from here over to beautiful and secluded Ao Lo Mu Di.

Phi-Phi Long Beach Bungalows (☎ 0 6281 4349; bungalows 500-1000B) Basic cement-floor, wooden bungalows might not be luxe but they sure are cheap – plus the sheets are clean and the beach in front is simply sublime. In high season it's buzzing with backpackers.

Paradise Resort (☎ 0 7562 2100; www.paradiseresort .co.th; bungalows 1500-2500B; 🕸 🖳) Location is the

---

TOP FIVE PHI-PHI RESORTS

- ■ **Viking Place Resort** (left) No horned helmets but plenty of driftwood chic.

- ■ **Ao Toh Ko Beach** (p348) Groovy travellers scene on a near forgotten beach.

- ■ **Phitarom** (left) Hillside elegance and a free thigh workout.

- ■ **Phi-Phi Island Village (p348)** Vacation central for all, from families to romantic hipsters.

- ■ **Zeavola** (p349) Indulgent and sleek Thai style.

SOUTHERN ANDAMAN COAST

key and families are the clientele at this average but very well-managed and laid-back place. There's a swathe of jungle behind for young lizard hunters.

Phi Phi The Beach Resort (☎ 0 7561 8267; phiphithe beachresort@hotmail.com; bungalows 3200-3500B; ❄ ♨) An expanding class act with a good pool and chic bar, this place swarms with package tourists looking for (and finding) comfort. It's relatively new so good service can be off and on but management seems eager to iron out the kinks.

HAT RANTEE & AO TOH KO

Still fairly low-key, this series of small, remote bays is home to a few modest bungalow operations. The pretty beach here has rocky outcroppings and the snorkelling is excellent. You can either get here by long-tail from Ao Ton Sai pier (300B going but only 150B on the way back) or by making the strenuous 45-minute hike over the viewpoint.

Rantee Hut (☎ 0 8974 14846; bungalows 600B) You're in with a lovely Thai family when you stay at these basic bamboo huts (complete with in-room fans and on-deck hammocks) right on Hat Rantee. There's a tiny restaurant that serves inexpensive and relatively authentic Thai fare and you can play with the resident monkey while waiting for your food.

Ao Toh Ko Beach (☎ 0 8153 70528; tohkobeach@yahoo .com; bungalows 500-2000B) All alone on white, mellow Ao Toh Ko, there's a summer camp camaraderie here with several long-term guests and plenty of new guests who wish they were long-term. A surprising variety of rooms are perched on a hill but none are anything more than basic. The most interesting are the ones south beyond the cliff-side bar that have stone-work bathrooms. There are also family rooms and a big, friendly restaurant right on the beach. We didn't ever, ever want to leave.

HAT PHAK NAM

This beach consists of one bay separated by a rocky outcrop, with a small fishing hamlet on one beach and a lonely resort on the other. To get here, you can either charter a long-tail from Ao Ton Sai for around 400B, or make the sweaty one-hour trek over the viewpoint (not recommended with roller luggage).

Relax Beach Resort (☎ 0 1083 0194; bungalows 1200-1800B) There are only 18 unpretentious

but attractive Thai-styled bungalows here, so it pays to call ahead to make sure rooms are available. The bungalows are bright yellow with tall pointy roofs and are rimmed by lush jungle – there's a good restaurant, cruisy bar and an all-round old-school Phi-Phi vibe.

AO LO BAKAO

On the northeastern coast on Ko Nai, this fine stretch of palm-backed sand is ringed by dramatic hills and is home to a single upmarket resort. From Ao Ton Sai, you will have to charter a long-tail to get here (500B). Phi Phi Island Village also arranges transfers for guests.

Phi Phi Island Village (☎ Phuket 0 7621 5014; www.ppisland.com; bungalows 6500-25,000B; ❄ ♨) This place really is a village unto itself: its whopping 100 bungalows take up much of the beachfront with palms swaying between them. Facilities vary from the family-friendly and casual – there are lots of daily activities on offer – to romantic dining experiences and pampering spa treatments. The infinity pool blends seamlessly into the ocean, and fresh flowers are artfully arranged throughout the resort. It's popular with Japanese and Australian jet-setters.

HAT LAEM THONG

At the northern end of Ko Nai, the beach here is long and sandy, with several showy resorts. There's also a small *chow lair* (sea gypsy) settlement of corrugated metal shacks at the end of the beach. A long-tail charter from Ao Ton Sai costs 600B. Operators can also arrange transfers.

Holiday Inn Phi-Phi Island (☎ 0 7521 1334; www .phiphi-palmbeach.com; bungalows 7850-9000B; ❄ ♨) These handsome Thai-Malay-style stilt bungalows are set on lovely grounds awash with grass and palm tree action. Wandering the grounds you'll find tennis courts, beckoning hammocks, a spa and dive centre, as well as discreetly disguised receptacles that encourage recycling. The restaurant allows you to dine alfresco or inside, buffet or à la carte.

Phi-Phi Natural Resort (☎ 0 7561 3010; www.phiphi natural.com; bungalows 2950-11,150B; ❄ ♨) While this place is a bargain for this beach, it's starting to blend a little too well into its overgrown environs. The atmosphere is casual – which spills over into housekeeping. Yet the setting, with a powder-white beach and water in all directions, is worth suffering through some dust in the corners.

Zeavola (☎ 0 7562 7024; www.zeavola.com; bungalows 14,000-26,000B; ✖ 🖳 🖫) If you have money to burn, let this be your pyre. This is an outstanding top-end resort with gorgeous teak bungalows that incorporate a traditional Thai style with simple, sleek modern design. Each well-spaced bungalow comes with glass walls on three sides (with remote-controlled bamboo shutters for privacy), beautiful 1940s fixtures and antique furniture, a patio and impeccable service. Some villas come with a private pool and there's a fabulous couples-oriented spa.

Eating

Most of the resorts, hotels and bungalows around the island have their own restaurants. Ao Ton Sai is home to some reasonably priced restaurants that span the world's cuisines but don't expect *haute cuisine.*

Pee Pee Bakery (dishes 40-150B; ☷ breakfast, lunch & dinner) It's best at breakfast, when you'll be lucky to find an open table. Also on tap are pizza, steak and Thai food. The atmosphere is modern and movies are shown on the tube. The bakery has two branches; one is on the main walkway east of the piers, while the other is further inland near 007 Restaurant & Bar.

007 Restaurant & Bar (dishes 100-200B; ☷ breakfast, lunch & dinner) Owned by a talkative Scot named James, 007 features ultramodern chrome tables, red cushion booths and, of course, all the Bond paraphernalia you could want. There's a big selection of beer (including British favourites) on tap, and solid food cooked in a very clean kitchen. Sport is shown on the TV by day; the latest blockbusters are played at night.

HC Anderson (☎ 0 1894 5287; dishes 90-200B, steaks 320-280B; ☷ lunch & dinner) A very reliable Scandinavian restaurant serving delicious imported New Zealand steaks, among other creative dishes. It's on the most easterly path from Ao Ton Sai to Ao Lo Dalam.

Chao Koh (☎ 0 7560 1083; dishes 80-300B; ☷ lunch & dinner) Right on the beach, this is an open-air seafood place that displays its freshly caught critters on ice. It's popular and offers well-priced and tasty food. A self-service salad bar is included with most mains.

our pick **Ciao Bella** (dishes 150-300B; ☷ breakfast, lunch & dinner) At night, twinkling candles and stars provide the atmosphere for alfresco dining, while lapping waves provides the soundtrack. Dine on authentic Italian or Thai fare

and be prepared to feel romantic. Ciao Bella is in Ao Lo Dalam.

Drinking

The rowdy nightlife scene on Phi-Phi is returning with a vengeance, with several old-timers reopened for business.

Carpe Diem (☎ 0 4840 1219; Hat Hin Khom) Sit on pillows in the upstairs lounge and watch the sun go down then rock into the night with fire shows, dance parties and live music on the beach. It's an easy spot for mingling if you're travelling alone.

Hippies (☎ 0 1970 5483; Hat Hin Khom) Hippies is a good place to end the evening. There are candlelit tables on the beach and chill-out tunes on the sound system. Moon parties are thrown throughout the month.

Reggae Bar (tourist village) This classic has three floors of Rasta colours, drinking competitions, a *moo·ay tai* boxing ring with regular show bouts (where you can fight for free booze) and the occasional *gà·teu·i* (also spelt *kàthoey*; ladyboy) cabaret – you either love it or you hate it but it's the wildest place in town.

Sunflower Bar (Ao Lo Dalam) A great place for a sundowner with chilled-out reggae and Gilligan's Island-esque architecture.

Getting There & Away

Ko Phi-Phi can be reached from Krabi, Phuket, Ao Nang and Ko Lanta. Most boats moor at Ao Ton Sai, though a few from Phuket use the isolated northern pier at Laem Thong. The Phuket and Krabi boats operate year-round while the Ko Lanta and Ao Nang boats only run in the October to April high season.

Boats depart from Krabi for Ko Phi-Phi (350B, 1½ hours) at 10am and 2pm. From Phuket, boats leave at 8.30am, 1.30pm and 2.30pm, and return from Ko Phi-Phi at 9am, 2.30pm and 3pm (400B, 1¾ to two hours). To Ko Lanta, boats leave Phi-Phi at 11.30am and 2pm and return from Ko Lanta at 8am and 1pm (350B, 1½ hours). A boat departs from Ko Phi-Phi Marine National Park headquarters jetty at 9am, returning from Ko Phi-Phi (via Railay) at 3.30pm (350B, two hours).

Getting Around

There are no roads on Phi-Phi Don so transport on the island is mostly by foot, although long-tail boats can be chartered at Ao Ton Sai for short hops around Ko Phi-Phi Don and Ko Phi-Phi Leh.

Long-tails leave from the Ao Ton Sai pier to Hat Yao (100B), Laem Thong (600B), Hat Rantee (300B) and Viking Cave (400B). Chartering speedboats for six hours costs around 6500B, while chartering a long-tail boat costs 1200B for three hours or 2500B for the whole day.

KO PHI-PHI LEH
เกาะพีพีเล

The rugged Phi-Phi Leh is the smaller of the two islands and is protected on all sides by soaring cliffs. Coral reefs crawling with marine life lie beneath the crystal-clear waters and are hugely popular with day-tripping snorkellers. Two gorgeous lagoons await in the island's interior – **Pilah** on the eastern coast and **Ao Maya** on the western coast. In 1999 Ao Maya was controversially used as the setting for the filming of *The Beach*, based on the popular novel by Alex Garland, and visitor numbers soared.

At the northeastern tip of the island, **Viking Cave** (Tham Phaya Naak; admission 20B) is a big collection point for swifts' nests. Bamboo scaffolding reaches its way to the roof of the cave as nimble collectors scamper up to gather the nests built high up the cliffs. Before ascending the scaffolds, the collectors pray and make offerings of tobacco, incense and liquor to the cavern spirits. This cave gets its misleading moniker from the 400-year-old graffiti made by crews of passing Chinese fishing junks.

There are no places to stay on Phi-Phi Leh and most people come here on one of the ludicrously popular day trips out of Phi-Phi Don. Tours last about half a day and include snorkelling stops at various points around the island, with detours to Viking Cave and Ao Maya. Long-tail trips cost 800B; by motorboat you'll pay around 2400B.

KO LANTA
เกาะลันตา
pop 20,000

It's still grasping at its reputation as a kick-back island where tired travellers can get away from the tourist hullabaloo, but Ko Lanta has quickly grown up into a midrange and very popular destination. Ferries shuttling people to Ko Phi-Phi and onto Phuket in one direction and to Krabi town, the Trang islands and even as far as Ko Lipe in the other, have helped turn this low-lying, beach-fringed island into a transportation hub as well as a major stop

unto itself. You'll still find old-school, hippy-ish Lanta charm on the southwest beaches but in the north every spot of beach and murky little back road has bungalows popping up like pimples on an adolescent's chin. Even so, the lack of jet-skis and girly bars makes this a far cry from Phuket. The island doesn't have those stunning karst cliffs found all around Krabi Province, or even particularly good coral around the island proper; what it does promise is miles of sandy beaches and plenty to do – you can take cooking classes in the morning, ride elephants in the afternoon and party til the wee hours at happening beach-bars.

The island will always retain a good deal of its cultural identity thanks to its 20,000 local residents, who are mixed descendants of Muslim Malay and sea-faring *chow lair* (sea gypsies; see boxed text, p353). The eastern part of the island remains their stronghold and development has yet to touch it.

Orientation & Information

The Ko Lanta region is made up of 52 islands, but the term is most commonly used to refer to Ko Lanta Yai, the biggest and most popular of the lot. At the north of the island, Ban Sala Dan is the main port of entry to Ko Lanta with lots of restaurants, tour agencies and dive shops, in addition to passenger- and vehicle-ferry piers. Ko Lanta's western coast has the best beaches, particularly further south where things get much quieter. Hat Khlong Dao is the most occupied stretch of beach, while the main budget travellers centre is Hat Phra Ae (Long Beach). At the far southern tip of the island and surrounded by wonderful wild beaches is the headquarters of Mu Ko Lanta Marine National Park.

During the wet season, rain drenches Ko Lanta and the tide washes right up to the front of the resorts, bringing plenty of driftwood and rubbish with it. Only a few resorts remain open during this time and transport connections become thin on the ground.

There's no official tourist office but the websites www.ko-lanta.com and www.lanta info.com have useful information on the area. Siam City Bank has a **foreign-exchange booth** (8.30am-4pm Mon-Fri low season) and ATMs are found all over Ban Sala Dan. There are also ATMs on many of the more popular beaches, including Hat Phra Ae and Hat Klong Nin. The main **police station** (0 7569 7085) and the **Ko Lanta Hospital** (0 7569 7017) are near Ban Ko

KO LANTA & AROUND

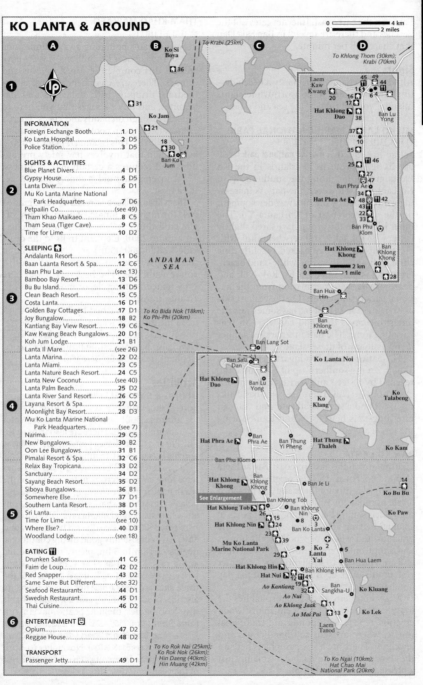

INFORMATION
Foreign Exchange Booth..............1 D1
Ko Lanta Hospital........................2 D5
Police Station...............................3 D5

SIGHTS & ACTIVITIES
Blue Planet Divers........................4 D1
Gypsy House.................................5 D5
Lanta Diver...................................6 D1
Mu Ko Lanta Marine National
  Park Headquarters.....................7 D6
Petpailin Co............................(see 49)
Tham Khao Maikaeo.....................8 C5
Tham Seua (Tiger Cave)................9 C5
Time for Lime.............................10 D2

SLEEPING
Andalanta Resort........................11 D6
Baan Laanta Resort & Spa............12 C6
Baan Phu Lae.........................(see 13)
Bamboo Bay Resort.....................13 D6
Bu Bu Island...............................14 D5
Clean Beach Resort.....................15 C5
Costa Lanta.................................16 D1
Golden Bay Cottages...................17 D1
Joy Bungalow..............................18 B2
Kantiang Bay View Resort............19 C6
Kaw Kwang Beach Bungalows......20 D1
Koh Jum Lodge............................21 B1
Lanta II Mare.........................(see 26)
Lanta Marina...............................22 D2
Lanta Miami................................23 C5
Lanta Nature Beach Resort...........24 C5
Lanta New Coconut................(see 40)
Lanta Palm Beach.......................25 D2
Lanta River Sand Resort...............26 C5
Layana Resort & Spa....................27 D2
Moonlight Bay Resort..................28 D3
Mu Ko Lanta Marine National
  Park Headquarters................(see 7)
Narima.......................................29 C5
New Bungalows..........................30 B2
Oon Lee Bungalows.....................31 B1
Pimalai Resort & Spa...................32 C6
Relax Bay Tropicana....................33 D2
Sanctuary....................................34 D2
Sayang Beach Resort...................35 D2
Siboya Bungalows.......................36 B1
Somewhere Else?.........................37 D1
Southern Lanta Resort..................38 D1
Sri Lanta.....................................39 C5
Time for Lime........................(see 10)
Where Else?................................40 D3
Woodland Lodge....................(see 18)

EATING
Drunken Sailors...........................41 C6
Faim de Loup...............................42 D2
Red Snapper................................43 D2
Same Same But Different........(see 32)
Seafood Restaurants....................44 D1
Swedish Restaurant......................45 D1
Thai Cuisine................................46 D2

ENTERTAINMENT
Opium..47 D2
Reggae House..............................48 D2

TRANSPORT
Passenger Jetty...........................49 D1

Lanta on the east coast. Internet cafés dot the beaches and there are several in Ban Sala Dan that charge 1B per minute.

Sights

Although Ko Lanta is primarily a beach destination, there are some worthwhile sights inland if you get tired of the sea and sand.

MU KO LANTA MARINE NATIONAL PARK
อุทยานแห่งชาติเกาะลันตา

Set up in 1990, this **marine national park** (adult/child 200/100B) protects 15 islands in the Ko Lanta group, including the southern tip of Ko Lanta Yai. However, the park is increasingly threatened by the runaway development on the western coast of Ko Lanta Yai. The other islands in the group have fared slightly better – **Ko Rok Nok** is still very beautiful, with a crescent-shaped bay backed by cliffs, fine coral reefs and a sparkling white-sand beach. Camping is permitted on Ko Rok Nok and nearby **Ko Ha**, with permission from the national park headquarters. On the eastern side of Ko Lanta Yai, **Ko Talabeng** has some dramatic limestone caves that you can visit on sea-kayaking tours. The national park fee applies if you visit any of these islands.

The national park headquarters is at Laem Tanod, on the southern tip of Ko Lanta Yai, reached by a steep and corrugated 7km dirt track from Ao Nui. There are some basic hiking trails and a **scenic lighthouse**, and you can hire long-tails here for island tours during the low season.

BAN KO LANTA

Halfway down the eastern coast, **Ban Ko Lanta** (Lanta Old Town) was the original port and commercial centre for the island and provided a safe harbour for Arabic and Chinese trading vessels sailing between the larger ports of Phuket, Penang and Singapore. Some of the gracious and well-kept wooden stilt houses and shopfronts here are over 100 years old and are a pleasure to stroll through. A few pier restaurants offer up fresh catches of the day and have prime views over the sea.

A few kilometres past the hospital lies the **Gypsy House** (Ban Ko Lanta), a bohemian driftwood creation replete with ponds and traditional music, where artisans sell handicrafts and jewellery. There are a few pamphlets here on the *chow lair* of Ko Lanta, but it's mainly just a pleasant waterside chill-out space.

THAM KHAO MAIKAEO
ถ้ำเขาไม้แก้ว

Monsoon rains pounding away at limestone cracks and crevices for millions of years have created this complex of forest caverns and tunnels. There are chambers as large as cathedrals, dripping with stalactites and stalagmites, and tiny passages that you have to squeeze through on hands and knees. There's even a subterranean pool you can take a chilly, creepy swim in. This is '*Raiders of the Lost Ark*' kind of fun that involves few safety precautions and requires a certain level of fitness. Total coverage in mud is almost guaranteed. It's a blast.

Tham Khao Maikaeo is reached via a guided trek through the jungle. A local family offers guided treks to the caves (with torches) for around 200B. Elephant treks to the caves (adult/child 900/450B) are also possible in the high season but are only really fun if you're with kids. The best way to get here is by rented motorcycle, or most resorts can arrange transport.

Close by, but reached by a separate track from the dirt road leading to the marine national park headquarters, **Tham Seua** (Tiger Cave) also has interesting tunnels to explore; elephant treks run up here from Hat Nui.

Activities
DIVING & SNORKELLING

Several shops run two-dive trips to local sights for around 2300B, while PADI Open Water courses are 12,500B. There are also trips to Ko Phi-Phi and the undersea pinnacles at **Hin Muang** and **Hin Daeng**, about 45 minutes from Ban Sala Dan by speedboat. These world-class dive sites have lone coral outcrops in the middle of the sea that are important feeding stations for large pelagic fish such as sharks, tuna and occasionally whale sharks and manta rays. Dive trips out here cost 3500B for two dives. The sites around **Ko Ha** have consistently good diving conditions, depths of 18m to 34m, plenty of marine life and a cave known as 'The Cathedral'. Your best chance of spotting leopard sharks is at the three sites around **Ko Bida Nok**, where there are also lots of scorpion fish and lionfish. Reliable dive companies include Scandinavian-run **Lanta Diver** (☎ 0 7568 4208; www.lantadiver.com; Ban Sala Dan) and **Blue Planet Divers** (☎ 0 7568 4165; www.blueplanetdivers.net; Ban Sala Dan). November to April is the best time for diving at Ko Lanta; the rest of the year most dive shops close.

THE DEMISE OF THE CHOW LAIR

Seminomadic seafarers have plied the coastal waters of the Malay Peninsula since time immemorial, largely untouched by the coming and going of the kingdoms and dynasties of Southeast Asia. Until the 19th century, the *chow lair* (also spelt *chao leh*) migrated freely along the coast, fishing for reef fish and squid and establishing temporary camps on uninhabited islands along the shore. Even the arrival of Islam had little effect on their way of life – most incorporated their animist beliefs into the new faith and continued much as before.

The real change for the *chow lair* came with the arrival of European powers. New ideas about borders and boundaries were adopted throughout the region and the landless wanderers became an inconvenience – citizens who could not be taxed and might set sail at any minute for an enemy state. The *chow lair* were actively encouraged to adopt a more sedentary lifestyle, by force if necessary, settling on the islands between Phuket and Singapore.

Once settled, the *chow lair* were neglected but mostly ignored until their islands became valuable for tourism. Entrepreneurs bought up large tracts of beachfront land and the *chow lair* moved on to smaller, less valuable islands. With these pressures, it was perhaps inevitable that the *chow lair* culture would slowly disappear. Many sea gypsies now make a living ferrying tourists around the islands or harvesting fish for seafood buffets at tourist resorts. One vestige of traditional *chow lair* life you may see is the biannual 'boat floating' ceremony in May and November, in which an elaborate model boat is set adrift, carrying away bad luck.

Numerous tour agencies along the strip can organise snorkelling trips out to Ko Rok Nok, Ko Phi-Phi and other nearby islands. **Petpailin Co** (☎ 0 7568 4428), near the passenger jetty at Ban Sala Dan, offers day trips to Ko Phi-Phi for 800B and four-island tours to Ko Muk, Ko Kradan, Ko Ngai and Ko Cheuk in Hat Chao Mai National Park for 900B.

ELEPHANT TREKKING

There are elephant-trekking camps at Hat Phra Ae (p354), Hat Nui (p355) – from where you can visit Tham Seua – and Ao Khlong Jaak (Waterfall Bay; p356). All charge 900/450B per adult/child for a two-hour trek. If you have your own transport, you can just show up at any of these elephant-trekking camps, otherwise most travel agencies or bungalow operators can arrange treks and transfers. All outings are slow, uneventful lumberings that are best suited for families with children.

OTHER ACTIVITIES

There are several other activities available: **horse riding** (per hr adult/child 700/350B) along the beach at Southern Lanta Resort; **sea kayaking** (adult/child 1000/500B) around the mangroves near Ban Hua Hin and Ko Pang; and **deep-sea fishing** (by long-tail/speedboat 2000/6000B). All of these can be arranged through resort tour desks or tour agencies in Ban Sala Dan.

Courses

Time for Lime (☎ 0 7568 4590; www.timeforlime.net), at Hat Khlong Dao, has a huge, professional kitchen with plenty of room to run amok. It offers excellent cooking courses with a slightly more exciting selection of dishes than most cookery schools in Thailand; half-day courses cost from 1500B to 1800B. There are also good bungalows here (see p354).

Sleeping

Ko Lanta is home to many long stretches of good-looking beach packed with accommodation. Many resorts close down for the May to October low season and rates drop by 50% or even more during these times. Resorts usually have their own restaurants and tour-booking facilities that can arrange island snorkelling, massages, tours and motorcycle rental.

LAEM KAW KWANG

This secluded beach sits on the spit of land at the northern end of Hat Khlong Dao.

Kaw Kwang Beach Bungalows (☎ 0 7562 1373; www.lanta-kawkwangresort.com; bungalows 400-3400B; 🔀) This is the oldest resort on Ko Lanta and is still owned by local people. There are roomy, recently remodelled, contemporary-style bungalows lined up neatly with plenty of shrubbery. There's also a satisfactory stretch of sand out the front and the feeling of seclusion so close to Ban Sala Dan earns Kaw Kwang brownie points. The low-end rooms here are some of the cheapest on the island.

HAT KHLONG DAO

With perfect white sand stretching for over 2km, it's no wonder this was one of the first beaches to attract the eyes of tourists and developers. There are numerous small lanes snaking from the main road towards the beach, all chock-a-block with bungalows with prices hovering around midrange. The beach here is great for swimming but there's little here for folks on a budget.

Somewhere Else (☎ 0 8153 60858; bungalows 500-800B) Big octagonal bamboo huts grace a shady lawn right on a very social and lounge-worthy stretch of beach. Bathrooms are big and clean, as is the beachfront restaurant that serves Indian, Thai and European food. It's not private but is a lot of fun and is run by the folks of Where Else? on Hat Khlong Khong.

Time For Lime (☎ 0 7568 4590; www.timeforlime.net; bungalows 1000-1500B; 🖳) An ideal spot if you're serious about Thai cooking (see p353). Plain but clean bungalows line up in a garden behind the beachfront cooking school and restaurant. The owner takes in stray dogs (with ideas to start a local animal centre) so you'll have plenty of friendly and furry company.

Golden Bay Cottages (☎ 0 7568 4161; www.golden baylanta.com; bungalows 1200-2800B; 🗙 🖳) With trim-and-proper little cottages surrounding a leafy courtyard, Golden Bay is one of the better operations here. There's a lot of variety in the rooms – the beachfront air-con deals are the nicest, while the fan rooms are probably not worth the money. Breakfast is included at the very good on-site restaurant.

Southern Lanta Resort (☎ 0 7568 4174/7; www .southernlanta.com; bungalows incl breakfast 1800-5000B; 🗙 🖳) There's loads of shade in the tropical garden and a good-sized beachfront. The pool has a water slide and the bungalows come kitted out with TVs, hot showers and minibars, and breakfast is included. The resort is family friendly and you can organise horseback riding from here for 650B per hour.

Costa Lanta (☎ 0 2662 3550; www.costalanta.com; r 6050-9460B; 🗙 🖳 🖳) With a pool in a black block, spartan grounds and near-militant security, all the concrete and sharp edges might seem out of place on such a mellow beach, but amazingly it comes off as intensely stylish. Guests rave about the airy, uncluttered rooms and stellar service. If minimalist city chic is your thing, don't miss this place.

HAT PHRA AE

A large travellers' village has grown up at Hat Phra Ae, with loads of faràng-oriented restaurants, beach-bars, internet cafés and tour offices.

Lanta Marina (☎ 0 1677 4522; www.lantamarina.com; bungalows 600-800B; 🌣 Oct-Apr) For something really cool, try out these giant bungalows, which almost look like towering hay bales. It has a tribal feel: breezy sleeping options have bamboo cross-bars for windows and are linked by an elevated boardwalk.

Sanctuary (☎ 0 1891 3055; sanctuary_93@yahoo.com; bungalows 700-1200B) This is a delightful place to stay. There are artistically designed wood and thatch bungalows with lots of grass and a hippyish atmosphere that's low-key and friendly. The restaurant is one of the island's best and offers Indian and vegetarian eats among the Thai usuals. It also holds yoga classes and has a small art gallery displaying local talent.

ourpick Relax Bay Tropicana (☎ 0 7568 4194; www .relaxbay.com; bungalows 700-3700B; 🌣 Oct-Apr; 🗙) This gorgeous French-run place is spread out over a tree-covered headland by a small beach. Its wooden bungalows sit on stilts with large decks overlooking the bay and stunning sunsets, and there's a huge bar and restaurant. You can get a pummelling here of either the Thai- or Swedish-massage variety.

Lanta Palm Beach (☎ 0 1606 5433; www.lantapalm beachresort.com; bungalows 1500-3500B; 🗙 🖳) This large place has good facilities and strikes a nice balance between social and private. There are large, modern, concrete air-con bungalows with hot showers and old-fashioned bamboo bungalows with fans. The beach in front is truly lounge-worthy.

Sayang Beach Resort (☎ 0 7568 4156; bungalows 950-4400B; 🗙) Here you'll find a relaxed atmosphere and neat wooden bungalows well spread out in plenty of scruffy greenery. There's a big restaurant and you're right at the rocky headland that marks the peaceful, northern end of this beach.

Layana Resort & Spa (☎ 0 7560 7100; www.layana resort.com; r 10,000-15,720B; 🅿 🖳 🖳) Not a hair is out of place at this very popular, Los Angeles-meets-Thailand condominium-style resort. Rooms are plush nests that completely remove you from the outside world and there's a luscious pool that extends languidly past the formal restaurant to the beach. The atmosphere feels like a posh Hollywood beach party. Rates drop if you reserve a month or more in advance.

HAT KHLONG KHONG

Only the resorts at the northern end of this rather rocky beach are worth looking at. There's a travellers vibe here with plenty of mellow little beach-bars.

Lanta New Coconut (☎ 0 1537 7590; bungalows 500B) The Coconut has a small farm of simple huts surrounded by swaying palms. It's not much, but it's darn cheap.

Where Else? (☎ 0 1536 4870; www.lanta-where-else .com; bungalows 500-1500B) Make your way here for Ko Lanta's little slice of bohemia. The bungalows may be a bit shaky but there is great mojo here and the place swarms with backpackers. The restaurant is a growing piece of art in itself, but the bamboo and coconut knick-knacks are threatening to take over. The pricier bungalows are all unique, multilevel abodes sleeping up to four people.

Moonlight Bay Resort (☎ 0 7568 4401; bungalows 1750-6000B; ✉ 🖳 🛋) A Scandinavian resort that plays up the ecoresort angle with natural materials, simple Nordic design and gorgeous bungalows either along a lush river, facing verdant greenery or right on the beach. It sits on a private rocky cove where most of the flora is labelled for your edification.

HAT KHLONG TOB

Just before the turn-off to Ban Khlong Nin, this beach is a bit rocky at low tide.

Lanta River Sand Resort (☎ 0 7566 2660; www .lantariversand.com; bungalows 1000B) It's all primitive bungalows here with environmentally sound construction and thatch and bamboo through and through. The basic lifestyle is all part of the attraction, and there's plenty of nature around with which to commune.

HAT KHLONG NIN

After Hat Khlong Tob, the main road heading south forks: head left for the inland road which runs to the east coast; go right and the country road hugs the coastline for 14km to the tip of Ko Lanta. The first beach here is lovely Hat Khlong Nin, which gets progressively nicer as you travel south.

Lanta Nature Beach Resort (☎ 0 1397 0785; bungalows 300-700B; ✉) The bungalows here look like neat little pink ducks all lined up in a row. There are wooden bungalows with fans and comfortable concrete bungalows with little verandas, furniture and tiled bathrooms with bath tubs. Some of the huts sit on the beachfront, while others are on the opposite side of the road.

Lanta II Mare (☎ 0 1540 7257; www.lantariversand .com; bungalows 1200-1900B, f 4500B; ✉ 🛋) The bungalows here are fairly deluxe deals, albeit not very stylish, with verandas, greenery and a small, intimate feel that's often missing from larger places. The beach is one of the best swimming beaches on Hat Khlong Nin.

Sri Lanta (☎ 0 7569 7288; www.srilanta.com; villas 5400-24,000B; ✉ 🖳 🛋) At the southern end of the beach, this sophisticated resort consists of minimalist, naturalistic wooden villas in lush and wild gardens set back from the shore. There's a very stylish beachside area with a restaurant, infinity pool and private drapery-swathed pavilions where you can get a traditional Thai massage or stretch like a cat at the daily yoga class. Breakfast is included.

You'll find good, clean bungalows similar in style and rates to Lanta Nature Beach Resort at **Clean Beach Resort** (☎ 0 7569 7112; ✉ 🛋) and **Lanta Miami** (☎ 0 7569 7081; ✉).

HAT NUI

There are several small beaches around here with upmarket places to stay.

our pick Narima (☎ 0 7560 7700; www.narima-lanta .com; bungalows 2000-3500B; ✉ 🖳 🛋) This resort calls itself 'eco-chic' and we have to agree. It's run by an exceptionally friendly Thai couple and the private, high-ceilinged huts are artistically created from natural materials – all have spotless indoor/outdoor bathrooms. Every bungalow has something of a sea view. The large, lantern-lit, all-wood restaurant has some massive gnarled wood furniture and the whole place is surrounded by near jungle.

AO KANTIANG

This bay's tip-top beach has a good sprinkling of sand, and several nearby tour offices provide internet access and rent out motorcycles.

Kantiang Bay View Resort (☎ 0 1787 5192; kan tiangbayview@hotmail.com; bungalows 1200-2200B; ✉) Sharing the bay's fantastic beach, this resort has tidy, modern, concrete air-con bungalows with tiled roofs and a stand of old-fashioned wooden bungalows with bathrooms and fans.

It's popular even in the low season and has a great social buzz.

Baan Laanta Resort & Spa (☎ 0 7566 5091; www .baanlaanta.com; bungalows 3500-4500B; ✂ ❑ ☞) Fragrant, green, landscaped grounds wind around stylish wooden bungalows and a pool that drops off to a stretch of white sandy beach. A futon-style bed on a raised wooden platform, under a gauzy veil of mosquito netting, is the room's centrepiece. White bed linen and cream-coloured curtains complement the natural woods in the rooms, while bamboo-lined bathrooms are clean and bright.

Pimalai Resort & Spa (☎ 0 7560 7999; www.pimalai .com; bungalows 12,000-85,000B; ✂ ☞) The sprawling, manicured gardens are interspersed with calming water features and luxurious villas all have slick, modern Thai furnishings and sultry views of the bay below. There are several pools and restaurants on the grounds, a spa and small library. For something special, this class act is worth every baht.

AO KHLONG JAAK

There's a splendid beach here at Ao Khlong Jaak and the namesake waterfall is inland along Khlong Jaak.

Andalanta Resort (☎ 0 1836 4877; www.andalanta .com; bungalows 2300-6900B; ✂) You'll find beach-stylish, modern air-con bungalows (some with loft) and simple fan-cooled ones, facing the sea. The garden is a delight, there's an ambient restaurant and the waterfall is just a 30- to 40-minute walk away. An excellent choice for families.

AO MAI PAI

Bamboo Bay Resort (☎ 0 7561 8240; www.bamboobay .net; bungalows 500-1700B) Clinging to the hillside above Ao Mai Pai beach, this place has a variety of brick and concrete bungalows, with bathrooms, on stilts and a fine restaurant down by the beach. The better bungalows have balconies with grand sea views.

ourpick Baan Phu Lae (☎ 0 1201 1704; www.baan phulae.com; bungalows 900-1300B; ✂) Awash in bamboo-chic, the easy vibe of this place keeps folks returning year after year. The restaurant and many of the bungalows sit right on a private beach and have perfect sunset views. Bungalows come with bamboo-framed beds and rustic, hammock-friendly porches. You can rent mountain bikes here or just loll around in the gazillion areas designed for chilling out.

LAEM TANOD

The road on to the marine national park headquarters fords the *klong* (canal), which can get quite deep in the wet season.

Mu Ko Lanta Marine National Park Headquarters (☎ Bangkok 0 2561 4292; camping with own tent per person 40B, camping with tent hire 300-400B) The secluded grounds of the national park headquarters are a wonderfully serene place to camp. The flat camping areas are covered in shade and sit in the wilds of the tropical jungle. Out the front lie craggy outcroppings, and the sounds of the ocean lapping up the rocks. There are toilets and running water, but you should bring your own food. You can also get permission for camping on Ko Rok Nok or Ko Ha here. National park entry fees apply (see p352).

Eating

The best places to grab a bite are the seafood restaurants along the lane at the northern end of Ban Sala Dan. With tables on verandas over the water, they offer fresh seafood sold by weight (which includes cooking costs). Expect to pay 700B per kilogram for prawns and 350B per kilogram for squid, fish and crabs. The best option is Rimnum Seafood, but come early if you want to get a table.

Swedish Restaurant (pizzas from 220B; ☯ lunch & dinner) At the western end of the alley, this friendly place has the best pizzas around and quirky knick-knacks on the walls, plus a bar and pool table.

Around the tourist villages of Hat Phra Ae and Hat Khlong Dao, and at beaches further south, you can find interesting places catering to faràng, but most close down in the low season.

Drunken Sailors (☎ 0 7011 0683; meals 40-90B; ☯ breakfast, lunch & dinner) This hip octagonal pad is decked out with beanbags and a laid-back attitude. It serves basic Thai and Western dishes and yummy, refreshing drinks like the banana-choc frappé – Starbucks, eat your heart out.

Thai Cuisine (mains 60-180B; ☯ lunch & dinner) Some of the most authentic Thai food in the area can be found at this raised, wooden Thai-style place in central Ao Phra Ae.

Same Same But Different (☎ 0 1787 8670; meals 50-120B; ☯ breakfast, lunch & dinner) In a perfect seaside setting on Ao Kantiang, with tables right on the beach, you can sample some of the tastiest Thai cuisine on the island. The ambience is hard to beat.

GETTING AWAY FROM IT ALL: KO BU BU

If you really want to live out your castaway dreams, this private island, a few kilometres off Ko Lanta's east coast, is the place. There are a couple of gorgeous white-sand beaches, mangrove forests, and an interior thick with vegetation. There's some decent snorkelling just offshore.

For accommodation, there are about a dozen basic but creatively decorated bungalows simply called **Bu Bu Island** (☎ 0 1228 4510; bungalows 400-700B; Oct-Apr) where you can swing in your hammock till the buffalos come home. You should call ahead to confirm availability and to see about arranging a pick-up from Ko Lanta. To get here on your own, you can charter a long-tail from the pier at Ban Ko Lanta (200B).

Faim de Loup (Hat Phra Ae; mains 60-120B; lunch & dinner) This little French bistro serves real filtered coffee and baguette sandwiches as well as Thai food.

Red Snapper (mains 90-200B; dinner) A Dutch-run restaurant on the roadside in Ao Phra Ae, the garden setting here is romantic and the European-fusion cuisine food comes highly recommended.

Drinking & Entertainment

During the high season Ko Lanta has a positively buzzing nightlife. Driftwood-style reggae bars are dotted all the way down the west coast so, during high season, there's always something going on; in low season the scene pretty much fizzles out.

Reggae House (Hat Phra Ae) A perennial favourite, Reggae House is the most renowned of dozens of beach-bars pumping out boisterous reggae and dance anthems, particularly around Hat Phra Ae.

Opium (☎ 0 8128 67182; Hat Phra Ae; from 6pm) This chic club has live music Thursday and Sunday nights, guest DJs other nights of the week and a big dance floor.

Getting There & Away

Most people come to Ko Lanta by boat or aircon minivan. If you're coming under your own steam, you'll need to use the frequent **vehicle ferries** (motorcycle 20B, car/4WD 75/150B; 7am-8pm) between Ban Hua Hin and Ban Khlong Mak (Ko Lanta Noi) and on to Ko Lanta Yai.

BOAT

There are two piers at Ban Sala Dan. The passenger jetty is about 300m from the main strip of shops; vehicle ferries leave from a second jetty that's several kilometres further east.

Passenger boats between Krabi's Khlong Chilat passenger pier and Ko Lanta run from November through May and take 1½ hours. Boats depart from Ko Lanta at 8am and 1pm (350B). In the reverse direction boats leave at 11am and 1.30pm. These boats will also stop at Ko Jum (for the full 350B fare) although in the fringe months of November and May only the morning boat will stop.

Boats between Ko Lanta and Ko Phi-Phi technically run year-round although service can peter out in the off season if there are too few passengers. Ferries usually leave Ko Lanta at 8am and 1pm (350B, 1½ hours); in the opposite direction boats leave Ko Phi-Phi at 11.30am and 2pm.

From around 21 October through to May, four-island snorkelling tour boats also act as ferries to Ko Ngai (300B, two hours), Ko Muk (350B, three hours) and Ko Kradan (400B, four hours) in Trang Province (p359). You'll get to snorkel on the way if you go to Ko Muk or Ko Kradan so bring your gear. These boats leave Ban Sala Dan at 8.30am and return from the islands at around at 3pm.

There's a new high-speed ferry that runs every other day from Ban Sala Dan to Ko Lipe (p377; 1900B, three hours) stopping at Ko Ngai (600B, 30 minutes), Ko Muk (1200B, one hour) and Ko Bulon Leh (1600B, 2½ hours). The service leaves at 1pm. The next day the same boat makes the return trip from Ko Lipe departing at 9am and arriving in Ban Sala Dan at noon.

MINIVAN

This is the main way of getting to and from Ko Lanta: vans run year-round. Daily minivans to Krabi leave between 7am and 8am (350B, 1½ hours) and there are sometimes afternoon services at 1pm and 3.30pm. From Krabi, vans depart frequently from 8am till 4pm. **KK Tour & Travel** (☎ Trang 0 7521 1198) has several daily aircon vans between Trang and Ko Lanta (250B, two hours). Note that all of these services tend to take much longer than the time they claim to take so give yourself a few extra hours if you have a flight to catch from Krabi or Trang.

Getting Around

Most resorts send vehicles to meet the ferries and you'll get a free ride *to* your resort. In the opposite direction expect to pay 80B to 150B. Alternatively, you can take a motorcycle taxi from opposite the 7-Eleven in Ban Sala Dan; fares vary from 50B to 200B depending on distance.

Motorcycles can be rented all over. Unfortunately, very few places provide helmets and none provide insurance, so take extra care on the bumpy roads. The going rate is 250B per day.

Several places rent out small 4WDs for around 1600B per day, including insurance.

KO JUM & KO SI BOYA

เกาะจำ(เกาะปู) /เกาะศรีบอยา

Just north of Ko Lanta, Ko Jum and its neighbour Ko Si Boya have surprisingly little development; what's there is neatly tucked away in the trees making the islands look and feel nearly deserted. There's little to do here but laze on the beach and amble through the friendly Muslim villages, but that's what makes coming here such a treat: this is near total removal from the modern world. Although technically one island, the locals consider only the flatter southern part of Ko Jum to be Ko Jum; the northern hilly bit is called Ko Pu.

Sleeping & Eating

Accommodation on Ko Jum is still mostly basic – though things are developing – and lies spread out along the beaches along the west coast of the island. Some places rent out sea kayaks and most have a restaurant on the grounds. Public transport to Ko Jum and Ko Si Boya is very limited in the low season so most resorts close down between May and October.

New Bungalows (☎ 0 7567 8116; chanchalay@hot mail.com; bungalows 150-600B) Roomy huts in varying degrees of comfort are found here at the southern end of the beach. The cheapie tree houses get brownie points for charisma.

Siboya Bungalows (☎ 0 7561 8026; www.siboyabun galows.com; bungalows 200-1200B) The well-designed huts sit on a lush lawn and are covered in heaps of shade by expansive palm and rubber trees. Verandas and hammocks come as standard and there are also a couple of self-contained houses that are ideal for long-term rentals. There's a restaurant here serving excellent Thai fare.

Woodland Lodge (☎ 0 1893 5330; www.woodland -koh-jum.tk; bungalows 300-1400B) Typical bamboo huts here come with shiny, polished wood verandas and mosquito netting as standard. The exceptionally friendly British-Thai owners can organise boat trips and fishing, have an excellent, sociable restaurant and run a cooking course in the high season. It also has larger family bungalows and stays open year-round.

Joy Bungalow (☎ 0 1464 6153; www.kohjum.com/joy; bungalows 600-3000B) On the southwestern coast of Ko Jum, Joy has thatch and wood stilt bungalows on grassy, palm-shaded grounds. The beach restaurant here has a good vibe but the popularity of this place has become a turn-off for some.

Oon Lee Bungalows (☎ 0 8720 0805; www.koh-jum -resort.com; bungalows 700-3800B) This Crusoe-chic Thai-French family-run resort is nestled on a deserted white beach on the Ko Pu part of Ko Jum. Wooden stilted bungalows are in a shady garden and plenty of activities, including some of the island's best trekking, are on offer. The fantastic fusion restaurant here is reason enough for a visit.

our pick **Koh Jum Lodge** (☎ 0 7561 8275; www.koh jumlodge.com; bungalows 4000-5000B; ✪ May-Mar; ⚥) An ecolodge with style: imagine lots of hard woods and bamboo, gauzy mosquito netting, manicured grounds and a hammock-strewn curve of white sand out front. Bliss.

Ko Si Boya has one place to stay on the western coast just south of the main village, Ban Lang Ko.

Getting There & Away

From November to May, boats between Krabi and Ko Lanta can drop you at Ko Jum, but you'll pay full fare (350B, one hour) – see p331. In the fringe months of November and May only the early boat will drop you. There are also small boats to Ko Jum and Ko Si Boya a few times a day from Ban Laem Kruat, a village about 30km from Krabi, at the end of Rte 4036, off Hwy 4. The cost is 80B to Ko Si Boya and 100B to Ban Ko Jum.

TRANG PROVINCE

Lining the Andaman Sea south of Krabi Province, Trang Province has an impressive limestone-covered coast with several sublime islands. For the adventurous, there are also plenty of natural sites to explore in the province's lush interior, including dozens of scenic waterfalls and limestone caves.

Though nowhere near as popular as Krabi and parts of the gulf coast, this region is starting to make a name for itself. It has dozens of mellow islands offering good-value accommodation and an escape from peak-season multitudes. You're more likely to see tall rubber plantations here than rows of vendors selling the same 'same same but different' T-shirts. Transport links are improving every year and during the high season it's now possible to island-hop all the way to Malaysia.

TRANG

อ.เมืองตรัง
pop 77,200

Most visitors to Trang are in transit to nearby islands, but if you're an aficionado of culture, Thai food or markets, you really should plan to stay a day or more. It's an easy-to-manage town where you can get lost in wet markets by day and hawker markets and late-night Chinese coffee shops by night; at nearly any time of the year, there's likely to be some minor festival that oozes with local colour. Although there aren't any must-see attractions, there are lots of travel agencies in town dedicated to helping you hop to your island of choice as fast as possible. Many of the Trang islands resorts maintain satellite offices here that can assist with bookings and transfers to their island. Trang is also a popular place for Thais to get married before they head off for honeymoons in nearby Hat Chao Mai National Park.

Most of the tourist facilities lie along the main drag, Th Praram VI, between the clock tower and the train station.

Information

You'll find several internet cafés on Th Praram. Various banks have ATMs and foreign exchange booths.

Ani's (☎ 0 1397 4574; 285 Th Ratchadamnoen; ⏰ 9am-10pm) For books in English and European languages as well as information on the area and motorcycle rental.

Bangkok Bank (Th Praram VI)

Post office (cnr Th Praram VI & Th Kantang) Also sells CAT cards for international phone calls.

Thai Farmers Bank (Th Praram VI)

Tosit (285 Th Visetkul; internet per hr 20B) Fast computers, knowledgeable staff and a real café serving real coffee from around the world.

Sights

Trang is more of a business and market centre than a tourist town. **Wat Tantayaphirom** (Th Tha Klang) has a huge *chedi* (stupa) enshrining a Buddha footprint, and the imposing Confucian **Kew Ong Yia Temple** is across the road. The Chinese **Meunram Temple**, between Soi 1 and Soi 3, sometimes sponsors performances of southern Thai shadow theatre. It's also recommended to stroll around the large **wet and dry markets** on Th Ratchadamnoen and Th Sathani.

Activities

Tour agencies around the train station and along Th Praram VI offer various tours around Trang. **Boat trips** to Hat Chao Mai National Park start at 850B per person and take in Ko Muk, Ko Cheuk and Ko Kradan, with lunch and drinks thrown in. National park fees are extra. There are also **sea-kayaking** tours to Tham Chao Mai (850B), where you can explore mangrove forests and canoe under commanding stalactites. **Snorkelling** trips to Ko Rok (1400B) and **minivan trips** to local caves and waterfalls (950B) can also be arranged by most agencies. For a cultural fix you can spend a day **trekking** in the Khao Banthat Mountains to visit villages of the mountain Sa Kai people (1300B). This includes a visit to waterfalls, lunch and a knowledgeable local guide. Most of these trips need at least two to three people, otherwise you may have to pay extra.

Festivals & Events

Sailboat Regatta Over on the coast, Hat Chao Mai has an annual regatta for traditional wooden sailboats on the first weekend of May, accompanied by performances, including *li-gair bàh* (folk dance-drama) and *nǎng đà-lung* (shadow theatre).

Vegetarian Festival Trang's Chinese population celebrates this wonderful festival every October, coinciding with the similar festival in Phuket; for more about the latter festival, see boxed text, p302.

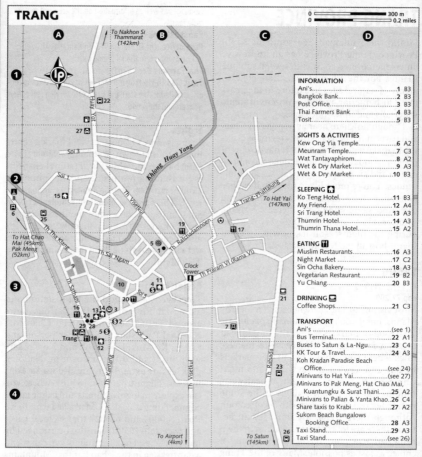

TRANG

Sleeping

Trang has good budget options but mid-range and top-end places leave much to be desired.

Ko Teng Hotel (☎ 0 7521 8148; 77-79 Th Praram VI; r 180-380B; ☒) The undisputed king of backpacker digs in Trang. If you're feeling optimistic, the huge, window-lit rooms here have an adventuresome kind of shabby charm to them; if not, the grunge factor might get you down. There's also a very good restaurant and helpful travel agent downstairs.

My Friend (☎ 0 7522 5447; 25/17-20 Th Sathani; r 450B; ☒ ▣) Very comfortable, modern rooms here have air-con and TV, but not all have windows – check first. There are some quirky decorative flourishes (Greek pillars,

hotel logos on everything, etc) and an on-site internet café.

Sri Trang Hotel (☎ 0 7521 8122; fax 0 7521 8451; 24 Th Praram VI; r 600-800B; ☒) This place was still under construction when we passed but it already looked like the hippest place in town with a large range of rooms. It's a renovated older hotel with some oversized teak windows, butter-coloured walls and a European flavour.

Thumrin Hotel (☎ 0 7521 1011-5; www.thumrin.co.th; 99 Th Sathani; r 450-3500B; ☒) This obvious white building near the train station has cheesy business-class rooms with TVs, ageing carpets and bathtubs.

Thumrin Thana Hotel (☎ 0 7521 1211; www.thumrin.co.th; 69/8 Th Huay Yot; r 1200-40,000B; ☒ ▨) The poshest option in town. The rooms are new and have plenty of conveniences, and there's a gleaming marbled lobby, three restaurants, a bakery, a pool and a spa. Some rooms have great views of the city.

Eating

Trang is famous for its *mŏo yâhng* (crispy barbecued pork) and *ráhn goh·ĥée* (coffee shops). *Ráhn goh·ĥée* serve real filtered coffee (look for the charcoal-fired aluminium coffee boilers with stubby smokestacks) and you can find *mŏo yâhng* in the mornings at some coffee shops or by weight at the wet market (Old Market) on Th Ratchadamnoen. To really get into the local scene stay out late at the coffee shops along Th Ratsada.

While you're waiting for a train or air-conditioned van, there are several Muslim restaurants on Th Sathani that serve cheap Malay dishes such as roti with curry. There are several OK Western bar-restaurants also opening up in this area.

Vegetarian Restaurant (Pong's; Th Ratchadamnoen; meals 20B; ☻ breakfast & lunch) Coffee and pork not your thing? The colourful Thai buffet here often has brown rice and also sells veggie snacks and supplies. It's across from the police station.

our pick **Night market** (meals around 20B) The best night market on the Andaman coast will have you salivating over an impressive selection of goodies from simple *pàt tai* and rice dishes to fried grubs and Thai desserts. Go with an empty stomach and a sense of adventure.

Sin Ocha Bakery (☎ 0 7521 1191; Th Sathani; meals from 50B; ☻ breakfast & lunch) Near the train station, this ambient, fan-cooled place has round marble tables and serves traditional Trang *goh·ĥée*, fresh cakes, light Thai meals and good Western breakfasts.

Yu Chiang (Th Praram VI; dishes from 50B; ☻ breakfast & dinner) This funky place on the corner of Soi 1 and Th Praram VI (there's no Roman script sign) is the classic stop for filtered coffee and *mŏo yâhng*.

Getting There & Away

AIR

Nok Air (www.nokair.com) operates daily flights from Bangkok (Don Muang) to Trang (around 1000B one-way), but there have been problems landing at this airport during rain. The airport is 4km south of Trang;

minivans meet flights and charge 60B to town. In the reverse direction a taxi or túk-túk will cost 80B to 100B.

BUS

Public buses leave from the well-organised Trang **bus terminal** (Th Huay Yot). Air-con buses from Trang to Bangkok cost 600B to 650B (12 hours, morning and afternoon). More comfortable are the VIP 24-seater buses at 5pm and 5.30pm (1050B). From Bangkok, VIP/air-con buses leave between 6.30pm and 7pm. Buses to Satun and La-Ngu depart from the **Southern bus terminal** (Th Ratsada).

Other services are shown in the table below:

Destination	Price	Frequency	Duration
Hat Yai	110B	frequent	3hr
Krabi	133B	frequent	2hr
Phang-Nga	175B	hourly	3½hr
Phuket	241B	hourly	4hr
Satun	126B	frequent	3hr

MINIVAN & SHARE TAXI

There are share taxis to Krabi (180B, two hours) and air-con minivans to Hat Yai (160B, two hours) from offices just west of the Trang bus terminal. Hourly vans heading to Surat Thani (210B, 2½ hours) leave from a **depot** (Th Tha Klang), just before Th Tha Klang crosses the railway tracks. There are also departures directly to Ko Samui (485B) and Ko Pha-Ngan (685B) every day at 12.30pm and 3pm from the same depot. **KK Tour & Travel** (☎ 0 7521 1198; 40 Th Sathani), near the train station, has several daily air-con vans to Ko Lanta (250B, two hours).

Local share taxis can be hired for custom trips from depots; sample fares include 500B to Pak Meng, and 700B to Hat Yao or Hat Chang Lang.

Local transport is mainly by air-con minivan rather than *sŏrng·tăa·ou*. Vans leave regularly from the depot on Th Tha Klang for Pak Meng (60B, 45 minutes), Hat Chao Mai (80B, one hour) and Kuantungku pier (100B, one hour). To get to Ko Sukorn, *sŏrng·tăa·ou* carrying market-going, Sukorn fishermen's wives leave the wet market on Th Ratchadamnoen at 11.30am to both the jetties at Palian (60B) and Ban Ta Seh (60B) – it's best to reserve this trip through **Sukorn Beach Bungalows booking office** (☎ 0 7521 1457; 22 Th Suthanee). See p368 for boat details.

SOUTHERN ANDAMAN COAST

TRAIN

Only two trains go all the way from Bangkok to Trang: the express 83, which leaves from Bangkok's Hualamphong station at 5.05pm and arrives in Trang at 7.35am the next day, and the rapid 167, which leaves from Hualamphong station at 6.20pm, arriving in Trang at 10.11am. From Trang, trains leave at 1.45pm and 5.30pm. Fares are 1280B/731B for a 1st-/2nd-class air-con sleeper and 521B for a 2nd-class (fan) sleeper.

Getting Around

Túk-túk hover around near the intersection of Th Praram VI and Th Kantang and charge 20B to 30B for local trips. Motorcycle taxis are around 15B around town. Motorcycles can be rented at travel agencies or at **Ani's** (285 Th Ratchadamnoen) for about 200B per day. Most agencies can also help you arrange car rental for around 1400B per day.

TRANG BEACHES & ISLANDS

The Trang islands and beaches are like smaller models of those found in Krabi Province, are easy to get to and, for now, are most often visited on day trips. If you stay longer than a snorkelling tour they can feel delightfully off-the-beaten-track with opportunities to climb some of the karst formations. All this is changing of course, particularly on Ko Muk and Ko Ngai, which are easy stopover islands between Ko Lanta (p350) and Ko Lipe (p377). Some islands in the chain are protected by the Hat

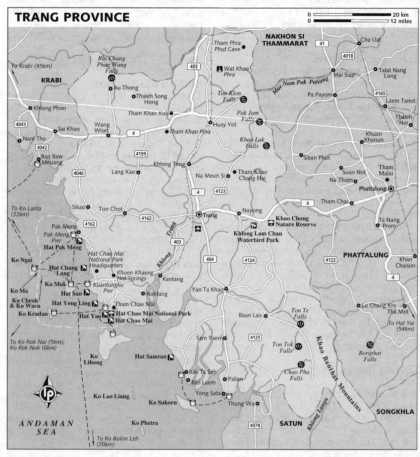

TRANG PROVINCE

Chao Mai National Park, including Ko Muk, Ko Kradan and Ko Cheuk. The beaches of Hat Pak Meng to Hat Chao Mai, which hosts an annual regatta in May for traditional wooden sailboats, also fall under its jurisdiction.

The Trang beaches are even more forgotten than the islands and are places to sample southern Thai village life. From north to south these are Hat Pak Meng, Hat Chang Lang, Hat San, Hat Yong Ling, Hat Yao, Hat Chao Mai and Hat Samran. The coast here gets some of Thailand's biggest surf, but it's really only worth investigating in March or after big storms during the rainy season.

Hat Pak Meng
หาดปากเม็ง

Thirty-nine kilometres from Trang in Sikao District, Hat Pak Meng has been developed as the main jumping-off point for the nearby island of Ko Ngai. There's a wild-looking stretch of coastline here, with a couple of so-so pockets of sand, but much of the beach is rather marred by a big concrete sea wall. The main pier is at the northern end of the beach and there are several fresh seafood restaurants with deck chairs under casuarinas where Rte 4162 meets the coast.

Tour agencies at the jetty and the Lay Trang Resort (below) organise one-day boat tours to Ko Muk, Tham Morakot (Emerald Cave, on Ko Muk), Ko Cheuk, Ko Ma and Ko Kradan for 950B per person (minimum three people), including lunch and beverages. There are also snorkelling day tours to Ko Ngai (750B) and Ko Rok (1200B to 1400B, plus national park fees). Mask and snorkel sets and fins can be rented by the pier for 50B each.

SLEEPING

Lay Trang Resort (☎ 0 7527 4027/8; www.laytrang .com; r 400-1500B, tents 200B; 🕸) There's a range of options here in smart bungalows, rooms or tents, all in a tidy garden. Staff can arrange all sorts of tours in the area and there's a very good beachfront restaurant.

Amari Trang Beach Resort & Spa (☎ 0 7520 5888; www.amari.com/trangbeach; r 5000-8000B; 🕸 🥤) All the rooms at this secluded resort have sea-facing terraces, polished wood floors and a soothing olive, cream and brick-red colour scheme. The beach goes on for miles and there are views of the islands, only a short speedboat ride away – the resort also has a

day area set up on Ko Kradan. Guests rave about the quality of service here.

GETTING THERE & AWAY

There are several daily boats from Pak Meng to Ko Ngai at 10am, returning from Ko Ngai between 8am and 9am. You have a choice of a 30-minute ride by speedboat (350B) or a slower ride by 'big boat' (150B, one hour). A long-tail charter is 900B.

There are regular air-con minivans from Th Kha Klang in Trang to Hat Pak Meng (60B, 45 minutes). You may have to take a motorcycle taxi from the Rte 4162 junction to the pier.

Ko Ngai
เกาะไหง(ไห)

The squeaky white beach along the developed eastern coast of Ko Ngai (Ko Hai) extends into blue water with a sandy bottom (perfect for children) that ends at a reef drop-off with excellent snorkelling. Coral and clear waters encircle the entire densely forested island; it's a stunning place. With no indigenous population living here, the several spiffy resorts have the whole island to themselves. Mask and snorkel sets and fins can be rented from resorts for 60B each, sea kayaks for around 150B per hour, or you can take half-day snorkelling tours of nearby islands (850B per person). Trips to Ko Rok Nok, 29km southwest of Ko Ngai, cost 1500B by speedboat (plus the marine national park fee). Internet at the big resorts is slow and 100B per hour.

Even though it's technically a part of Krabi Province, the island's main land link is with Pak Meng.

SLEEPING

There's little here for budgetarians and most places are decidedly midrange, with their own restaurants and 24-hour electricity. The boat pier is at Koh Ngai Resort, but if you book ahead resorts on the other beaches will arrange transfers. Only the top-end rooms at most places have air-con.

Koh Hai Villa (☎ 0 7520 3263; bungalows 300-800B; 🕸) Budget huts of all description dot a large garden but don't expect more than a basic room with a hard bed and a mosquito net. The owner here can be disagreeable but fortunately it's the charming staff who take care of clients. Food at the beachside restaurant is reasonably priced and tasty.

ourpick **Coco Cottages** (☎ 0 7521 2375/6; www.coco
-cottage.com; bungalows 1600-4500B; 🔀) The beach
here is pretty skinny, but the quality of the
coconut and bamboo ultra-stylish bungalows,
artistically designed grounds and happy service more than make up for it. There are no
manmade materials in sight, massage huts dot
the beach, a groovy restaurant/bar saddles a
river and it feels like heaven.

Thapwarin Resort (☎ 0 1894 3585; www.thapwarin
.com; bungalows 1900-4500B; 🔀) Small, intimate and
with a bona fide lost-on-a-desert-island feel,
thatched and polished wood bungalows here
have luxurious touches like Thai cushions,
luscious fabrics and oil lamp lighting at night.
All rooms have chic bathrooms filled with
rock and plant features.

Fantasy Resort & Spa (☎ Trang 0 7521 0317; www
.kohhai.com; r 2000-8500B; 🔀 🖳 🖭) Fantasy is a
massive Angkor-Wat-meets-cheesy-cruise-
ship–style place that extends from the beach
and up the hillside. The bungalows are comfy
but a little gaudy (floral wallpaper matched
with red Chinese art), with nice wooden
decks, all mod cons and breakfast included.
There are also plainer hotel-style rooms up
the hill. Service is tip-top and the restaurant
serves excellent seafood.

Koh Ngai Resort (☎ 0 7520 6924; www.kohngairesort
.com; bungalows 1500-15,000B; 🔀 🖳 🖭) In a separate cove at the southern end of the island,
this resort has its own private jetty and elegant
wooden bungalows with huge verandas. The
garden is immense and the resort has a small
beach all to itself.

GETTING THERE & AWAY
The resorts provide daily boats from Hat Pak
Meng to Ko Ngai at 10am, returning from
Ko Ngai between 8am and 9am. Speedboat
transfers cost 350B (30 minutes), while the
slower 'big boats' cost 150B (one hour).
Unless you're staying at Koh Ngai Resort
you'll have to take a long-tail for the ship-
to-shore ride (40B) or arrange for one of the
other resorts to provide transfers. You can
also privately charter a long-tail from Pak
Meng for 900B.

In the high season, high-speed boats running between Ban Sala Dan (600B, 30 minutes) on Ko Lanta and Ko Lipe (via Ko Muk
and Ko Bulon Leh; 1600B, 2½ hours) stop
at Koh Ngai Resort – see p379 and p357
for more details. Snorkelling tours from Ko
Lanta (300B, two hours) also pick up from

Ko Ngai Resort in the high season at 3pm,
returning from Ko Lanta at 8am.

Hat Chang Lang
หาดฉางหลาง
Hat Chang Lang is the next beach south from
Hat Pak Meng and it continues the casuarina-
backed sand motif. At the southern end of
Hat Chang Lang, where the beachfront road
turns inland, is the headquarters of **Hat Chao
Mai National Park** (☎ 0 7521 3260; adult/child under 14
yr 200/100B; 🕑 6am-6pm).

The 231-sq-km park covers the shoreline
from Hat Pak Meng to Laem Chao Mai and
encompasses the islands of Ko Muk, Ko
Kradan and Ko Cheuk plus a host of small
islets. In various parts of the park you may
see endangered dugong and rare black-necked
storks, as well as more common species such
as sea otters, macaques, langurs, wild pigs,
pangolins, little herons, Pacific reef-egrets,
white-bellied sea eagles and monitor lizards.

You usually only need to pay the national
park fees if you visit the park headquarters, Ko
Kradan or Hat San and Hat Yong Ling (the
next two beaches south of Hat Chang Lang).

National park headquarters (☎ 0 7521 3260;
Bangkok 0 2562 0760; www.dnp.go.th/index_eng.asp; camping with own tent free, camping with tent hire 150B, r 800B,
cabins 800-1500B) is the best place to stay. There
are simple cabins that can be rented by the
room – they sleep six to eight people and have
fans. You can also camp under the casuarinas
on the foreshore. There's a restaurant and a
small shop near the accommodation.

Frequent minivans run from Th Kha Klang
in Trang to Chao Mai (60B, one hour), or you
can charter a taxi from Trang for 650B. The
park headquarters is about 1km off this road,
down a clearly signposted track.

Ko Muk
เกาะมุก
The beach-laden, *chow-lair* (sea-gypsy) island of Ko Muk is on the brink of going upscale. While Charlie Beach resort has thus far
achieved near total domination of wide and
white **Hat Faràng** (Hat Sai Yao) on the west
coast, a Bangkok company has recently bought
up the other handful of resorts on this beach
with plans to go even bigger. A few lower-end
accommodation places remain back in the
bush. The interior of the island is filled with
soaring rubber plantations and you are likely
to see rubber collection going on all through-

REMARKABLE RUBBER TREES

If you ever wondered where the bounce in your rubber comes from, wonder no further: unlike money, it grows on trees. All over the Trang region, particularly on the islands floating off its coast, you are likely to come across tracts of these rubber-tree plantations.

Rubber trees produce the milky liquid known as latex in vessels that grow within the bark of the tree at a rakish 30-degree angle. It's a common misconception that latex is the actual sap of the tree. Once trees reach maturity after five to six years, collection begins. The trees are 'tapped' by making a thin incision into the bark at an angle parallel with the latex vessels. A small cup, usually made from a coconut shell, collects the latex as it drips down the tree. New scores are made every day – you can see these notched trees and collection cups throughout the region.

Latex from multiple trees is collected, poured into flat pans and mixed with formic acid, which serves as a coagulant. After a few hours the very wet sheets of rubber are wrung out by squishing them through a press. They're then hung out to dry. You'll see these large, yellowish pancakes drying on bamboo poles wherever rubber trees are grown. The gooey ovals are then shipped to processing plants where they are turned into rubber as we know it.

---

out the island (see boxed text, above). The east coast is home to the main village, a handful of quiet midrange options and the island's newest and most swanky resort. Note that much of Ko Muk shuts down in the low season.

Good snorkelling opportunities lie offshore and one of the island's star attractions, **Tham Morakot** (Emerald Cave), hides at the northern end of the island. This cave is a beautiful limestone tunnel that leads 80m to a sea lagoon. You have to swim through here at high tide, part of the way in pitch blackness, to a small concealed white-sand beach surrounded by lofty limestone, with a chimney that lets in a piercing shaft of light around midday. Boats can enter at low tide and the cave features on most tour itineraries so it can get pretty crowded in high season, and during the busiest months can reek of urine.

Between Ko Muk and Ko Ngai are the small karst islets of **Ko Cheuk** and **Ko Waen**, which have good snorkelling and small sandy beaches.

SLEEPING & EATING

The following places are a short walk from the pier on a shallow beach.

Ko Mook Resort (☎ Trang 0 7520 3303; 45 Th Praram VI; bungalows 500-1000B) These comfortable huts are excellent value and lie concealed in a thick garden covered with wild-looking ferns. The design here is unadorned and the tropical isolation is perfect for those searching for a romantic getaway. There's a free daily boat to Hat Faràng and snorkelling can be arranged for 350B.

Silavai (☎ 0 8945 95219; bungalows incl breakfast 5990-6880B; ⊠) Straddling an arrow-shaped penin-

sula of white sand and surrounded by views of karst islands and the mainland, you can't beat this new resort's location. The grounds have yet to grow in so it looks a little sparse between the coconut palms but bungalows are large, stylish and made from hardwoods. For this price though, they aren't that private.

To stay on Hat Faràng on the west coast, you'll need to take a 10-minute, 80B motorbike taxi from the pier. Don't let Charlie Beach Resort touts tell you they're the only place over here. A few little restaurants serving Thai and Western food are popping up inland behind Charlie Beach Resort.

Mookies (tents 200B) You'll find some scruffy tents backed into the rubber trees here, but it's comfy enough and there's a social atmosphere. The Australian owner Brian claims to sell the coldest beer in Thailand and checks his stock regularly to ensure he stays true to his claim. It's open year-round and is always a fun place to stop for a meal or a drink.

Rubber Tree Bungalow (☎ 0 7520 3284; bungalows 500-1000B) Inland from the beach, Rubber Tree Bungalow was remodelling when we passed and has spiffy pink concrete bungalows on stilts and a large wooden restaurant high up among rubber trees.

Charlie Beach Resort (☎ 0 7520 3281/3; www.kohmook.com; bungalows 1000-4000B; ⊠ ⊡) There's a bunch of different bungalow options, ranging from basic clean shacks to swish air-con deals at this sprawling resort, which is currently the only one right on this beach. It is starting to get a little crowded, but the beach is lovely. Skip the restaurant. Staff, although not always helpful, can organise snorkelling tours to

Tham Morakot and other islands for around 1000B. Charlie's is open year-round.

GETTING THERE & AWAY

Boats to Ko Muk leave from the pier at Kuantungku, a few kilometres south of the national park headquarters. There are several ferries to Ko Muk leave around noon and returning at 8am (50B, 30 minutes). A chartered long-tail from Kuantungku to Ko Muk costs 700B and to either Pak Meng or Hat Yao it's around 1200B. Air-con vans run frequently from Trang to Kuantungku for 100B (one hour).

From November to May, high-speed boats running between Ko Lanta (via Ko Ngai; 1200B, one hour) and Ko Lipe (via Ko Bulon Leh; 1400B, two hours) stop at the pier on Ko Muk – see p379 and p357 for more details. Snorkelling tours from Ko Lanta (350B, two hours) also pick up at the pier in the high season at around 3pm, returning from Ko Lanta at 8am.

Hat Yao
หาดยาว

A rickety, scruffy fishing hamlet just south of Hat Yong Ling, Hat Yao is sandwiched between the sea and imposing limestone cliffs. A rocky headland at the southern end of Hat Yao is pockmarked with caves and there's good snorkelling around the island immediately offshore. The best beach in the area is the tiny **Hat Apo**, hidden away among the cliffs; you can get here by long-tail or wade around from the sandy spit in front of Sinchai's Chaomai Resort.

Tham Chao Mai is a vast cave full of crystal cascades and impressive stalactites and stalagmites that can be explored by boat. To visit it, you can charter a long-tail for 400B per hour from Yao pier. Haad Yao Nature Resort offers sea-kayaking trips to the cave, including lunch, for around 900B per person, including guide. You can also rent a kayak and self-explore the cave for 600B (map included).

Just south of the headland in Ban Chao Mai is the Yao pier, the main departure point for Ko Kradan and Ko Libong.

SLEEPING & EATING

There are just two accommodation options at Hat Yao and both offer plenty of tours and activities.

Haad Yao Nature Resort (☎ 0 1894 6936; www .trangsea.com; r 300-600B, bungalows 800B; ✷ ⌨) Run by enthusiastic naturalists, this place offers a variety of environmental-focused tours in the Hat Yao area. Very orderly bungalows come with shared bathrooms, while the better self-contained bungalows have verandas. There's also a pier restaurant here where you can watch the fishermen ply their trade over tasty Thai victuals.

Sinchai's Chaomai Resort (☎ 0 7520 3034; bungalows 300-1500B; ✷) Self-sufficient, friendly Sinchai's has a handful of bungalows nestled under the rocky cliffs at the northern end of Hat Yao. The scenery here is reason enough to stay. The family can arrange kayaking tours (700B) and multi-day touring packages around Trang and the Andaman coast.

On the northern side of the headland is a collection of wooden seafood restaurants selling cheap Thai meals.

GETTING THERE & AROUND

From here, you can catch one of the regular long-tail boats to Ko Libong (50B, 20 minutes). You can also charter long-tail boats from here to Ko Libong for 300B or to Ko Muk for 1200B each way. Sŏrng·tǎa·ou to Trang (one hour, 100B) leave when full from the pier – your best bet is before 9am. To Kuantungku pier (10B, 15 minutes) for boats to Ko Kradan and Ko Ngai, sŏrng·tǎa·ou leave when full or it's 100B to charter a whole one.

You can rent motorcycles (250B per day) and mountain bikes (100B per day) at Sinchai's Chaomai Resort.

Ko Kradan
เกาะกระดาน

The main beach of Ko Kradan has sweeping views over aqua waters to the other islands scattered about the Andaman. There are great, untouched coral reefs just offshore, and rubber plantations fill large tracts of the island's core. Ko Kradan is part of Hat Chao Mai National Park and has so far been spared major developments. At the moment there are only two places to stay on the island, though the Hat Pak Meng–based Amari Trang Beach Resort (p363) has a day area here and plenty of day-trippers pour onto the shore during the high season. Camping is possible with permission from the national park staff.

Unfortunately, lodging options are not stellar. The new management will hopefully

save **Koh Kradan Paradise Beach** (☎ 0 7521 1391; www
.kradanisland.com; bungalows 2000B, tents 1600-4500B; ☒),
which when we passed was still less-than-
charming, with several attached and free-
standing wooden bungalows lined up behind
the main beach; 'resort tents' were planned
for the future. Inland and with easy access to
the island's other two, more remote beaches
is **Paradise Lost** (☎ 0 8958 72409; bungalows 500-1000B),
which has large but grungy bungalows, a good
vibe and an even better restaurant (meals
around 120B). It's open year-round.

The Koh Kradan Paradise Beach resort
provides transfers for guests from its **office**
(☎ 0 7521 1391) opposite the train station in
Trang – this is included in the room rate.
A chartered long-tail from Kuantungku will
cost around 800B one-way. Snorkelling tours
from Ko Lanta (400B, four hours from Ko
Lanta via Ko Ngai and Ko Muk, two hours to
Ko Lanta) pick up on the main beach in the
high season at around 2pm returning from
Ko Lanta at 8am.

Ko Libong
เกาะลิบง

Trang's largest island is just 15 minutes by
long-tail from Hat Yao. Less visited than
neighbouring isles, Ko Libong is known for
its flora and fauna as much as for its beaches.
The island is home to a small Muslim fishing
community and has a few resorts on the lovely
isolated beaches of the western coast.

On the eastern coast of Ko Libong at **Laem
Ju Hoi** is a large area of mangroves protected
by the Botanical Department as the **Libong
Archipelago Wildlife Reserve** (☎ 0 7525 1932). The
sea channels here are one of the last habitats
of the rare dugong, and around 40 of them
graze on the sea grass that flourishes in the
bay. The nature resorts in Hat Yao and Ko
Libong offer dugong-spotting tours by sea
kayak, led by trained naturalists, for 1000B.
Sea kayaks can also be rented at most resorts
for 150B per hour.

SLEEPING
Le Dugong Resort (☎ 0 7972 7228; www.libongresort
.com; bungalows 350-800B) This neat little budget
affair is positively dripping with thatch from
its many charming, beachfront bamboo huts –
each partly concealed by luxuriant greenery
and palms. Indoor-outdoor bathrooms en-
hance the naturalistic flair. Motorbikes can
be rented here for 300B per day.

NICE DAY FOR A WET WEDDING
Every Valentine's Day (14 February), Ko
Kradan is the setting for a rather unusual
wedding ceremony. Around 35 brides and
grooms don scuba gear and descend to
an altar among the coral reefs, exchanging
their vows in front of the Trang District
Officer. Quite how the couples manage to
say 'I do' underwater has never been fully
explained, but the ceremony has made it
into *Guinness World Records* for the Most
Couples Married Underwater. Before and
after the scuba ceremony, the couples are
paraded along the coast in a flotilla of motorboats. If you think this might be right
for your special day, visit www.trangonline
.com/underwaterwedding.

Libong Nature Beach Bungalow (☎ 0 1894 6936;
www.trangsea.com; bungalows 600-1000B; ☒) Set on
a grassy garden and surrounded by rubber
plantations, this place is run by the same
friendly, environmentally conscious people as
the nature resort in Hat Yao but it was looking
rather worn when we passed. There's a simple
restaurant with tasty food and the owners run
excellent sea-kayaking tours of the mangroves.
The resort is closed in the low season.

our pick **Libong Beach Resort** (☎ 0 7522 5205; www
.libongbeachresort.com; bungalows 700-2500B; ☒) Right
next door to Le Dugong Resort, this is the only
place on the island that's open year-round –
rates drop considerably in the low season.
There are several options from bland slap-
up shacks backed behind a murky stream to
beachfront and very comfortable wood and
thatch chalets. We had our best meal on the
Andaman coast here (fresh curry crab) and
there are guests who come back year after year
just for the food served at the basic-looking
restaurant. There's also a dive centre (two
dives 3500B) open during the high season.

GETTING THERE & AWAY
Long-tail boats to Ban Ma Phrao on the eastern coast of Ko Libong leave regularly from
Hat Yao (20 minutes) during daylight hours
for 50B per person; the long-tail jetty at Hat
Yao is just before the new Yao pier. On Ko
Libong, motorcycle taxis run across to the
resorts on the western coast for 80B. A chartered long-tail directly to the resorts will cost
600B each way.

Ko Lao Liang

Ko Lao Liang is actually two islands right next to each other: Ko Laoliang Nong, the smaller of the two where the only resort is found, and the larger Ko Laoliang Pi where there's a small fishermen's settlement. The islands are karst formations with small white sand beaches, clear water and plenty of coral close to shore.

The only place to stay is **Laoliang Island Resort** (☎ 0 8430 44077; www.laoliangresort.com; 3-day/2-night package per person 5000B) and, so far, this place is known better by Thais than Westerners. Lodging is in comfy luxury tents equipped with mattresses and fans, right on the beach, and there are plenty of activities on offer including diving, snorkelling, climbing the islands' karst cliffs and sea kayaking. At night there's a small bar and the restaurant sometimes puts together seafood barbecues. Only package rates including all meals, gear and a few activities are available. Transport to/from Krabi, Ao Nang, Trang or Ko Lipe is also included in the price.

Ko Sukorn

เกาะสุกร

With about 2800 Muslim fisherfolk, only four cars, three dogs (locals don't like 'em) and hundreds of water buffalo, Ko Sukorn is a place to soak in local culture as well as a few rays. The beaches here are a deep golden colour and, although less flashy than those on more popular islands, are more intimate and good for swimming. Clean and friendly little villages are strewn between rubber plantations and rice paddies in the interior and watermelon fields and coconut palms near the coast.

The best way to see the island is by renting a mountain bike for the day (about 50B) – with few hills, stunning panoramas, lots of shade and plenty of opportunities to meet locals, this will get you right into the slower pace of life here. Covering up is an absolute must when you go off the beach because this is a strongly Muslim island.

SLEEPING

There's limited electricity on Sukorn so expect power only in the evenings. For serious backpackers, ask around at the Sukorn boat pier for homestay opportunities. **Pawadee Guesthouse** (☎ 0 8988 74756; r 100B) is recommended.

Sukorn Island Resort (☎ 0 7521 1460; fax 0 7521 5648; bungalows 800-1500B; ☻ Nov-Apr) The 49 concrete bungalows packed among the rubber

trees lack style and are overpriced but the beach here is particularly good. Bikes can be rented here.

Sukorn Cabana (☎ 0 1079 3412; www.sukorncabana.com; bungalows 800-1600B; ☒) Sloping grounds dotted with large and clean bungalows meet interesting conglomerate rock formations on the shore. There are lots of places for lounging in the flower-filled garden and a good restaurant.

our pick **Sukorn Beach Bungalows** (☎ 0 7520 7707, booking office 0 7521 1457; www.sukorn-island-trang.com; bungalows 850-1950B) Easily the most professionally run place on this island, the concrete and wood bungalows all have comfy verandas and a long beach out front from which you can watch the sun set over outlying islands. The friendly Dutch owner is chock-full of information and can arrange excellent tailor-made island-hopping tours throughout the region. The resort is open year-round (rates drop by 60% in the low season), and the booking office near the train station in Trang can arrange transfers to Sukorn as well as other islands.

GETTING THERE & AWAY

The easiest way to get to Sukorn is by private transfers available with the resorts for 1850B per person. The more adventurous way is to catch one of the sŏrng·tǎa·ou carrying market-going Sukorn villagers that leave the wet market on Th Ratchadamnoen in Trang at 11.30am to the jetties at Palian (transfer in Yan Ta Khao; 60B, two hours) and Ban Ta Seh (60B, 1½ hours). These trucks meet long-tails at the piers that take you onto Sukorn (15 minutes from Ban Ta Seh, 45 minutes from Palian) for 60B per person – it's best to reserve this trip through the **Sukorn Beach Bungalows booking office** (☎ 0 7521 1457; 22 Th Suthanee), which will arrange for the sŏrng·tǎa·ou to pick you up.

Otherwise, air-con minivans run from Th Ratsada in Trang to Palian (transfer in Yan Ta Khao; 40B) or Ban Ta Seh (35B), where you can charter a long-tail to Ban Saimai (200B to 300B), the main village on Ko Sukorn. The resorts are a 20-minute walk or 40B motorcycle taxi ride from Ban Saimai.

From Ko Sukorn you can also charter long-tail boats to get to Ko Bulon Leh or Ko Libong (2500B) as well as to Ko Kradan, Ko Ngai or Ko Muk (3000B). Contact Sukorn Beach Bungalows (above) for more information.

AROUND TRANG PROVINCE

The eastern edge of Trang Province is lined with forested hills that are full of dramatic limestone caves and scenic waterfalls. Unfortunately, none of these can be reached by public transport, so you'll usually need to take a tour or rent a vehicle. If you want to explore the region under your own steam, travel agencies in Trang (see p359) can help you arrange either motorcycle rental (150B per day) or car rental (around 1400B per day). These agencies can also arrange tours around the province on your behalf.

Waterfalls

Trang Province is famous for its waterfalls, particularly in the southeast, where the Trang and Palian Rivers meet the Khao Banthat Mountains. A scenic paved road branches south from Hwy 4 near the Trang–Phattalung border, passing several cascades, including the towering **Ton Te Falls**. A hiking trail leads 1km from here to **Ton Tok Falls**, which offers grand views back over Ton Te Falls. In the Palian District near Laem Som, **Chao Pha Falls** has about 25 stepped falls of 5m to 10m each, with pools at every level.

There's another cluster of falls between Trang and Huay Yot off Rte 4123, including **Ton Klon**, **Pak Jam** and **Khao Lak**. Perhaps the most unusual waterfall in the province is **Roi Chang Phan Wang** (Hundred Levels, Thousand Palaces), about 70km northwest of Trang in Wang Wiset District, a little-explored corner of the region. Surrounded by rubber groves, dozens of thin cascades of water tumble down limestone rock formations into pools below.

You'll need your own transport to reach most of these falls, but Trang travel agencies (see p359) can arrange tours to Ton Te and surrounding falls for around 750/500B per adult/child.

Caves

Dramatic caves are another speciality of the Trang region. Close to the Trang River, near Wang Wiset in the north, **Tham Khao Kob** (Lay Cave) has scenic limestone formations and a 4km-long subterranean stream that you can explore by sea kayak. The local Tambon administration rents out boats for 50B per person. Nearby is **Tham Khao Pina**, off Hwy 4 at the 43km marker, which contains a large, multilevel Buddhist shrine that's popular with Thai tourists.

North of Huay Yot at the very top of the province is **Tham Phra Phut**, a cave temple with a large Ayuthaya-period reclining Buddha. Nearby **Wat Khao Phra** is housed in a cave-temple with mysterious red seals carved into the walls. About 15km northeast of Trang, near the weaving village of Na Meun Si on Rte 4123, is **Tham Khao Chang Hai**, another famous cavern with impressive limestone formations.

Travel agencies in Trang charge 800B per person for tours to Tham Khao Kob and 700B to Tham Khao Chang Hai, including a stop at Na Meun Si. You'll need private transport to visit the other caves.

SATUN PROVINCE

As the Andaman coast's southernmost region, Satun has never seen much tourist action. Yet nowadays, with the Malay border on the east coast off limits, more and more travellers are making their way to or from Malaysia via Ko Lipe in the otherwise undeveloped Ko Tarutao Marine National Park. This phenomenal park encompasses some of the most pristine untamed islands in the Andaman, all drenched in luxuriant greenery and edged by stereotypically splendid tropical beaches; fortunately much of it is well protected. Beyond Ko Lipe the province still hardly rates a blink of the eye as visitors rush north to Ko Lanta or south to Pulau Langkawi, Malaysia. Plucky explorers willing to go the extra distance to get here will not be disappointed.

Until 1813 Satun was a district of the Malay state of Kedah, but the region was ceded to Britain in 1909 under the Anglo-Siamese Treaty and became a province of Siam in 1925. Largely Muslim in make-up, Satun has seen little of the political turmoil that plagues the neighbouring regions of Yala, Pattani and Narathiwat (see boxed text, p252). Around 60% of people here speak Yawi or Malay as a first language, and the few wát in the region are small, impoverished and vastly outnumbered by mosques.

SATUN

อ.เมือง สตูล

pop 33,400

Lying in a steamy jungle valley surrounded by limestone cliffs, and framed by a murky river, isolated Satun is a relaxing coastal settlement that gets few tourists – so much so that it can be hard to convince minivan drivers that you actually want to stop here. Yachties passing through for cheap boat repairs are the only travellers who seem to frequent this town. Light on real attractions, the nearby Tammalang pier has boats to Kuala Perlis and Pulau Langkawi in Malaysia. There's some interesting religious architecture to see if you wander around, lots of friendly smiles and the riverside market has gritty charm.

Information

Bangkok Bank (Th Burivanich) Has a foreign exchange desk and ATM.

CAT office (Th Satun Thanee) Same location as the post office.

Immigration Office (☎ 0 7471 1080; Th Burivanich; ☷ 8.30am-4.30pm Mon-Fri) Handles visa issues and extensions. It's easier and cheaper to exit Thailand via the border check post at Tammalang pier and immediately re-enter to obtain a new tourist visa. You will need to catch the boat and enter Malaysia before you come back, however.

Post office (cnr Ths Satun Thanee & Samanta Prasit)

Rose Internet (Th Aphinuratsumuluk; per min 1B; ☷ 10am-10pm)

Siam Commercial Bank (Th Satun Thanee) Also has foreign exchange and an ATM.

Sights
KU DEN MUSEUM

Housed in a lovely old Sino-Portuguese mansion just off Th Satun Thanee is the excellent **Ku Den Museum** (Satun National Museum;

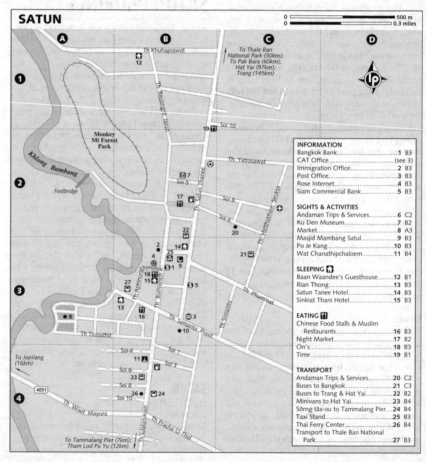

SATUN

| | 0 | | 500 m |
| 0 | | 0.3 miles | |

To Thale Ban National Park (30km);
To Pak Bara (60km);
Hat Yai (97km);
Trang (145km)

Th Khuhaprawat

Th Reungreo Thanoo

Soi 10

Th Yatrasawat

Monkey Mt Forest Park

Khlong Bambang

Footbridge

Th Satun Thanee

Soi 5

Soi 8

Soi 6

Th Hatthathani Seuksa

Th Aphinuratsumuluk

Th Burivanich

Th Phuminat

Th Simwith

Th Samanta Prasit

Th Tirasathit

To Jepilang (16km)

Soi 4

Soi 1

Soi 3

Soi 6

Soi 8

4051

Soi 10

Th Wiset Mayura

Th Sirasaynkoon

Th Pracha-U-Thid

To Tammalang Pier (7km);
Tham Lod Pu Yu (12km)

Soi 5, Th Satun Thanee; 8.30am-4.30pm Wed-Sun). The building was constructed to house King Rama V during a royal visit, but the governor of Satun took the house as his private residence when the king failed to show up. The building has been lovingly restored and now has exhibits and dioramas with soundtracks in Thai and English, covering every aspect of southern Muslim life.

OTHER SIGHTS

There aren't any must-see sights in Satun apart from the museum. If you're killing time here, there's some Sino-Portuguese shophouses along Th Buriwanit. Parachute-domed **Masjid Mambang Satul** is a modern Malay-style mosque (1979). Other religious buildings include peaceful **Wat Chanathipchaloem** (Th Sulakanukoon), south of the centre, and the small **Po Je Kang** (Th Samanta Prasit) joss house. The **market** by the river is worth a look in the morning.

If you head down to Tammalang pier, a 7km sŏrng·tăa·ou ride south of Satun, you can hire long-tail boats to visit **Tham Lod Pu Yu**, a picturesque limestone cave dripping with stalactites, right on the Malaysian border. Boat operators charge about 500B round-trip.

Tours

Travel agencies in town can arrange boat trips to the islands in Ko Tarutao Marine National Park and tours to surrounding caves and waterfalls. The friendly **Andaman Trips & Services** (0 7472 2988; www.andamantrip.com; 74 Soi 6) has English-speaking staff, can book boats and buses, arrange trips to Thale Ban National Park and moonlights as a day-care centre. Day trips to Thale Ban cost around 2200B per person including transport, a knowledgeable local guide, trekking to caves and waterfalls, and lunch.

Sleeping

Don't expect anything upscale in Satun.

Rian Thong (0 7471 1036; 4 Th Samanta Prasit; r from 140B) Clean and bright but uber-basic rooms with fan, hard beds, concrete floors and squat toilets are right near the river and market.

Satun Tanee Hotel (0 7471 1010; 90 Th Satun Thanee; r 170-380B;) A rather institutional-feeling place, but the rooms are clean, beds are springy and the non-English-speaking staff are friendly.

Baan Waandee's Guesthouse (0 7473 0469; baan-wandee@yahoo.com; 49 Th Khuhaprawat; r 300-600B) This

place, about 10 minutes' walk from central Satun, was just opening its doors when we passed and hopes to become the first groovy backpackers pad in Satun. It's owned by charming Waandee who understands travellers thanks to her day job at On's eatery.

Sinkiat Thani Hotel (0 7473 0255; 50 Th Burivanich; r 663B;) Satun's most comfortable choice is right in the centre of town. It's housed in a tall building and big rooms have plenty of mod cons – the best have fantastic views over the town and jungle.

Eating

Quick and cheap Chinese and Muslim restaurants can be found on Th Burivanich and Th Samanta Prasit. The Chinese food stalls specialise in *kôw mŏo daang* (red pork with rice), while the Muslim restaurants offer roti with southern-style chicken curry (around 50B each). For a predominantly Muslim town, there are a surprising number of bars around.

On's (48 Th Burivanich; meals from 50B) The only Western-oriented place in town, it has a good ambience and plenty of yachties. The food is good, there's a bar and some of the best travel information in town.

Time (0 7478 1176; 43 Th Satun Thanee; dishes 80-220B; breakfast, lunch & dinner;) This highly recommended air-conditioned place has chirpy staff and a fun atmosphere. It serves excellent Thai food.

Night market (Th Satun Thanee) This excellent market, just north of Satun Tanee Hotel, comes to life around 5pm and serves great Thai fast food, including southern-style curries – spicy!

Getting There & Away
BOAT

Boats to Malaysia leave from Tammalang pier, 7km south of Satun along Th Sulakanukoon. Large long-tail boats run regularly when full to Kuala Perlis in Malaysia (100B, one hour) between 8am and 2pm. From Malaysia the fare is M$20.

For Pulau Langkawi in Malaysia, boats leave from Tammalang pier daily at 9.30am, 1.30pm and 4pm (Monday to Friday 270B, Saturday and Sunday 280B, 1½ hours). In the reverse direction, boats leave from Pulau Langkawi at 8.30am, 12.30pm and 4pm and cost M$27. Keep in mind there is a one-hour time difference between Thailand and Malaysia. You

---

DETOUR: THALE BAN NATIONAL PARK

Very few foreigners make it out to this park, which lies on the Malaysian border about 30km northeast of Satun. Its main feature is a freshwater lake that sits in the middle of the 196-sq-km park, a scenic area of upland rainforest with captivating wildlife, waterfalls and caverns. Next to the lake are 13 national park cottages, which can be rented for 500B to 1000B per night. Contact the **Royal Forest Department** (Map pp70-1; ☎ 0 2561 4292/3) in Bangkok for bookings.

There's no public transport to the park, but you can get here by hired taxi from Satun or Hat Yai. See below for more details.

---

can buy boat tickets for these trips in Satun at the **Thai Ferry Centre** (☎ 0 7473 0511; Th Sulakanukoon), near Wat Chanathipchaloem.

The boat that used to make the Ko Tarutao and Ko Lipe run from Tammalang pier was being used to make the Ko Lipe to Ko Lanta (see p379) crossing in the 2007 to 2008 season. Hopes were that another boat would become available for the Satun to Ko Tarutao crossing in following years – check with the Thai Ferry Centre before you arrive.

BUS

Buses to Bangkok leave from a small depot on Th Hatthakham Seuksa, just east of the centre. Air-con services (800B, 14 hours) leave at 7am and at 2pm and 3pm. A single VIP bus leaves at 4.30pm (1030B). Ordinary and air-con buses to Hat Yai (70B, two hours) and Trang (90B, 1½ hours) leave regularly from in front of the 7-Eleven on Th Satun Thanee.

Your best bet for getting to Thale Ban National Park by public transport is to catch a sŏrng·tǎa·ou to the Malaysian border from near the market and walk the 1km or so to the park entrance. These cost 50B if the sŏrng·tǎa·ou is full, but you may have to charter the whole thing if you don't want to wait all day (450B). **Andaman Trips & Services** (☎ 0 7472 2988; www.andamantrip.com; 74 Soi 6) can organise day trips.

MINIVAN & SHARE TAXI

There are regular vans to the train station in Hat Yai (150B, one hour) from a depot south of Wat Chanathipchaloem on Th Sulakanukoon.

Occasional minivans run to Trang, but buses are much more frequent. If you're arriving by boat at Tammalang pier, there are direct air-con vans to Hat Yai (170B), Hat Yai airport (220B) and Trang (220B).

Share taxis can be hired from next to the Masjid Mambang Satul to Pak Bara (400B, 45 minutes), La-Ngu (260B, 30 minutes) or Hat Yai (400B, one hour).

Getting Around

Small orange sŏrng·tǎa·ou to Tammalang pier (for boats to Malaysia) cost 40B and leave every 20 minutes or so between 8am and 5pm from a depot opposite the Thai Ferry Center. A motorcycle taxi from the same area costs 60B.

AROUND SATUN
Pak Bara
ปากบารา

The coast northeast of Satun has a few little towns that serve as jumping-off points for the islands in the Mu Ko Phetra and Ko Tarutao Marine National Parks, but the small fishing community of Pak Bara is the main transit point. Tourist facilities are slowly improving as Pak Bara becomes increasingly busy with tourists discovering these dazzling isles in the south Andaman. The peaceful town has some decent sleeping options and great seafood and is even turning into a popular place to hang out for a while.

The main road from La-Ngu terminates at the pier where there are several travel agencies, internet cafés, cheap restaurants and shops selling beach gear. There's a **visitors centre** (☎ 0 7478 3485) for Ko Tarutao Marine National Park just back from the pier, where you can book accommodation and obtain permission for camping. Travel agencies here can arrange tours to the islands in the national park.

TOURS

There are several travel agencies near the pier that will vie for your transport custom. **Adang Sea Tours** (☎ 0 1276 1930; adang_sea_tour@hotmail.com) and **Andrew Tour** (☎ 08 1897 8482) are two of the more reliable agencies. Shop around for day trips by kayak through the impressive caves at **Tham Chet Khok** (1800B per person including lunch) and two-day island-hopping and snorkelling tours around the region (from 2600B per person). You can arrange car hire here for 1200B per day.

During the high season, the **Satun Pakbara Speedboat Club** (☎ 0 7478 3643-5; www.tarutaolipeisland .com) runs speedboat tours to Ko Tarutao, Ko Bulon Leh and Ko Lipe – visit the website for the latest details.

SLEEPING & EATING

The following guesthouses are all on the main road leading to the pier.

Diamond Beach Bungalows (☎ 0 7478 3138; r 300-400B; ☒) On a good beach, 350m up from the pier, the bungalows at Diamond Beach are clean, have real showers, and sit in a little garden. There's a very popular restaurant right on the beach from which you can watch fishing village life go by.

Best House Resort (☎ 0 7578 3058; bungalows 590B; ☒) This place is the closest to the pier and has tidy concrete bungalows around a pond. The owner is super-friendly and there's a café serving mediocre Western and Thai fare.

Elephant Joe Bar & Restaurant (meals 60-150B; ☒ 7am-10pm) Stop here while waiting for your ferry for Western breakfasts, espresso drinks, cocktails or the house speciality, soft shell crab (150B).

There are several elementary restaurants and vendors near the Pak Bara pier that serve good Malay Muslim food for 20B to 50B. There's also a market on the main beach on Mondays and Thursdays where you can buy amazingly cheap seafood by the kilogram as well as second-hand clothing and fruit.

GETTING THERE & AWAY

There are hourly buses from Hat Yai to the pier at Pak Bara (90B, 2½ hours) between 7am and 4pm. Coming from Satun, you can take an ordinary bus towards Trang and get off at La-Ngu (40B, 30 minutes), continuing by sŏrng·tǎa·ou to Pak Bara (20B, 15 minutes). You can also charter a taxi to Pak Bara from Satun for 450B.

Air-con minivans leave hourly for Hat Yai (150B, two hours) from travel agencies near Pak Bara pier. There are also vans to Trang (200B, 1½ hours) which connect to numerous destinations like Krabi (450B, four hours) and Phuket (650B, six hours). It's cheaper, although more complicated, to get a minibus to Trang and then organise your own transport from there.

From 21 October to the end of May there are boats to Ao Pante Malacca on Ko Tarutao and on to Ko Lipe at 11.30am and 1.30pm (550B to 650B, 1½ hours); in the reverse direction it's inexplicably cheaper (400B) and boats leave at 9am and 10am. From 16 November these boats also stop at Ko Adang for the same price. For Ko Bulon Leh, boats depart at 2pm, arriving in Ko Bulon Leh one hour later (300B round-trip). During the low season services to Ko Lipe and Ko Bulon Leh peter out to one per week (usually Friday with the return on Sunday) at best – it depends on the weather. Boats to Ko Tarutao and Ko Adang stop entirely.

Ko Bulon Leh
เกาะบุโหลนเล

This pretty island, 23km west of Pak Bara, is surrounded by the Andaman's signature clear waters and has its share of faultless white-sand beaches with swaying casuarinas. Gracious Ko Bulon Leh is in that perfect phase of being developed enough to offer comfortable facilities, yet not so popular that you have to book umbrella beach-time days in advance.

On the southern part of the island you'll find the alluring beaches of **Mango Bay**, while in the north sits a rocky bay that's home to small settlements of *chow lair*. The island is perfect for hiking – the interior is interlaced with tracks and trails. The tracks are lined with rubber plantations thick with birds, and you can reach most places on the island within half an hour. There are some bizarre rock formations along the coastline reminiscent of a Salvador Dali dream. A fine golden-sand beach runs along the eastern coast of the island with good coral reefs immediately offshore.

Resorts can arrange snorkelling trips to other islands in the Ko Bulon group for around 900B, and fishing trips for 300B per hour. You can also rent masks and snorkels (100B), fins (70B) and sea kayaks (150B per hour).

SLEEPING & EATING

Most places here shut down in the low season, though at this time caretakers at some of the resorts might rent out bungalows for discount rates.

Bulon Marina Resort (☎ 0 7568 4168; www .marina-kobulon.com; bungalows 600-1000B) Inland from Pansand Resort, this unique place is built from natural materials and has lovely thatched huts on stilts and a funky castaway-style restaurant with tables on a large bamboo veranda.

DETOUR: MU KO PHETRA MARINE NATIONAL PARK

A chain of smaller islands stretches north from Ko Tarutao, 22 of which are protected as **Mu Ko Phetra Marine National Park** (☎ 0 7478 1582; adult/child under 14 yr 200/100B). This little-visited park covers 495 sq km and includes the islands of the **Ko Bulon** group, as well as many uninhabited islands and islets. The largest island here is **Ko Khao Yai**, which has several pristine beaches suitable for swimming, snorkelling and camping and a rock formation resembling a Gothic castle.

Nearby **Ko Lidee** features a number of beautiful coves with some shallow beaches and a large cave to which you can climb up. The sea-grass beds around the island's Ao Jit support a small number of dugongs. Long-tail tours and sea-kayaking trips to Ko Lidee cost around 1200B per person and can be arranged at the national park headquarters on the mainland at Ao Nun, about 3km southeast of Pak Bara.

The park headquarters has a small visitors centre and a pleasing restaurant on stilts over the water, plus a nature trail through the forest. Bungalows here cost 1000B to 2000B and sleep four to nine people, or there are longhouse rooms with fans for 600B. With permission, camping is possible on many of the uninhabited islands in the park. Park fees only apply if you visit the islands offshore. To get to the park headquarters, turn off Rte 4052 between the 5km and 6km distance markers, near the gold-domed mosque.

Bulon Viewpoint (☎ 0 7472 8005/6; www.bulon -view-point.20m.com; bungalows 500-1550B) Around the rocky headland north of Bulone Resort, this place rolls down the hill into the ocean and has an exotic garden of cashew, mango and Malay apple trees. Some of the humble rooms share bathrooms while the larger deluxe rooms come with verandas and vistas. There's a beach-bar and restaurant down on the beach.

Bulone Resort (☎ 0 8189 7908; www.bulone-resort .com; bungalows 600-1200B) The pick of the bunch when it comes to budget options, Bulone has airy cottages in various sizes, with plenty of shade under tall casuarinas that line the northern part of the beach. It's a simple affair – not all rooms have attached bathroom – but the restaurant here is highly recommended.

Pansand Resort (☎ 0 7521 8035; www.pansand -resort.com; 82-84 Th Visetkul; cottages 1000-1700B; 🖳) The most upscale place to stay on Bulon Leh, Pansand sits on the island's best bit of beach. There are amiable colonial-style bungalows and cottages lined up along green grounds, a well-kept garden and breakfast is included. The restaurant here is great and staff can arrange snorkelling trips to White Rock Island (1500B for up to eight people). It's popular – call ahead.

There are a few local restaurants and a small shop in the Muslim village next to Bulon Viewpoint.

GETTING THERE & AWAY

The boat to Ko Bulon Leh leaves from Pak Bara at 2pm daily if there are enough takers; the fare is 300B. Ship-to-shore transfers to the beach by long-tail cost 30B. In the reverse direction, the boat moors in the bay in front of Bulone Resort at around 9am; you may have to wave your arms around to get the pilot's attention. In the low season these boats often stop altogether. You can charter a long-tail from Pak Bara for around 2000B.

From November to May there is also a high-speed ferry to Ko Bulon Leh from Ko Lipe in Ko Tarutao Marine National Park and from Ko Lanta in Krabi Province via Ko Muk and Ko Ngai in the Trang islands; these leave every other day from Ko Lipe at 9am (600B, 30 minutes), arriving in Ko Bulone around 9.30am and then continue on to Ko Muk (1200B, 1½ hours), Ko Ngai (1400B, two hours) and Ko Lanta (1700B, 2½ hours). Boats leave the following day in the opposite direction from Ko Lanta (departing at 1pm) and the Trang islands, arriving in Ko Bulon Leh at 3.30pm before departing to Ko Lipe.

KO TARUTAO MARINE NATIONAL PARK
อุทยานแห่งชาติหมู่เกาะตะรุเตา

Protected partly by its national-park status, and mostly by its relative inaccessibility, **Ko Tarutao Marine National Park** (☎ 0 7478 1285; www .dnp.go.th/parkreserve; adult/child under 14 yr 200/100B) is one of the most exquisite and unspoiled regions in all of Thailand. This massive park encompasses 51 islands covered with well-preserved virgin rainforest teeming with fauna, as well as sparkling coral reefs and radiant beaches.

KO TARUTAO MARINE NATIONAL PARK & AROUND

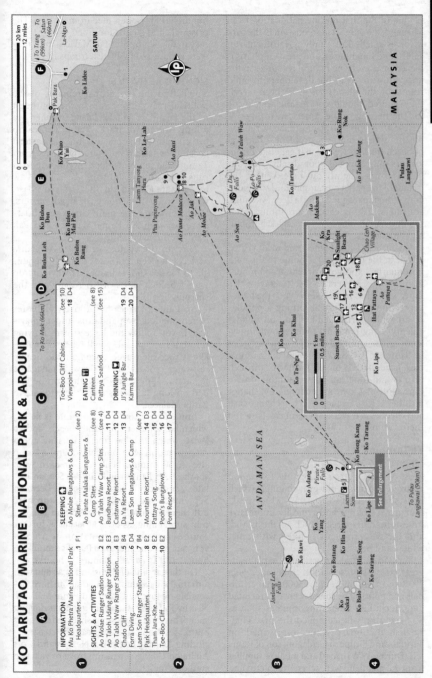

INFORMATION

Mu Ko Phetra Marine National Park Headquarters....................	**1** F1

SIGHTS & ACTIVITIES

Ao Molae Ranger Station............	**2** E2
Ao Taloh Udang Ranger Station...	**3** E3
Ao Taloh Waw Ranger Station......	**4** E3
Chado Cliff...............................	**5** B4
Forra Diving.............................	**6** D4
Laem Son Ranger Station............	**7** B4
Park Headquarters.....................	**8** E2
Tham Jara-Khe..........................	**9** E2
Toe-Boo Cliff............................	**10** E2

SLEEPING

Ao Molae Bungalows & Camp Sites......................	(see 2)
Ao Pante Malaka Bungalows & Camp Sites............	(see 8)
Ao Taloh Waw Camp Sites........	**11** D4
Bundhaya Resort.....................	**12** D4
Castaway Resort......................	**13** D4
Da Ya Resort...........................	**14** D3
Laem Son Bungalows & Camp Sites................	(see 7)
Mountain Resort......................	**15** D4
Pattaya Song..........................	**16** D4
Pooh's Bungalows....................	**17** D4
Toe-Boo Cliff Cabins................	(see 10)
Viewpoint...............................	**18** D4

EATING

Canteen................................	(see 8)
Pattaya Seafood.....................	(see 15)

DRINKING

JJ's Jungle Bar.......................	**19** D4
Karma Bar.............................	**20** D4

One of the first marine national parks in Thailand, the only accommodation in the park involves small, ecofriendly government-run cabins and longhouses, and great emphasis is placed on preserving natural resources in the area. Pressure from big developers to build resorts on the islands has so far been mercifully ignored, though concessions were made for the filming of the American reality-TV series *Survivor* in 2001. Unfortunately, rubbish on the islands can be a problem – removal of beach trash as well as that generated from visitors only happens sporadically. Do your part and tread lightly out here. Within the islands of the park you can spot dusky langurs, crab-eating macaques, mouse deer, wild pigs, sea otters, fishing cats, tree pythons, water monitors, Brahminy kites, sea eagles, hornbills and kingfishers.

Ko Tarutao is the biggest and most visited island in the group and is home to the park headquarters and government accommodation. Many travellers choose to stay on Ko Lipe, which has managed to evade the park's protection and is fast becoming a popular resort with tourist facilities and bungalows aplenty. Long-tail tours to other outlying islands can be arranged through travel agencies in Satun or Pak Bara, through the national park headquarters on Ko Tarutao or through resorts and long-tail boat operators on Ko Lipe. Note that there are no foreign-exchange facilities at Ko Tarutao – you can change cash and cheques at travel agencies in Pak Bara and there's an ATM at La-Ngu.

Ko Tarutao
เกาะตะรุเตา
Most of Ko Tarutao's whopping 152 sq km is covered in dense, old-growth jungle which rises sharply up to the park's 713m peak. Mangrove swamps and typically impressive limestone cliffs circle much of the island, and the western coast is lined with quiet white-sand beaches.

Tarutao's sordid history partly explains its great state of preservation today. Between 1938 and 1948, more than 3000 Thai criminals and political prisoners were incarcerated here, including interesting inmates such as So Setabutra, who compiled the first Thai-English dictionary while imprisoned on Tarutao, and Sittiporn Gridagon, son of Rama VII. During WWII, food and medical supplies from the mainland were severely depleted and

hundreds of prisoners died from malaria. The prisoners and guards mutinied, taking to piracy in the nearby Strait of Malacca until they were suppressed by British troops in 1944.

SIGHTS & ACTIVITIES
You'll find the overgrown remains of the political prisoners' camp in the southeast of the island at **Ao Taloh Udang**, reached via a long overgrown track. The prison camp for civilian prisoners was on the eastern coast at **Ao Taloh Waw** where the boats from Tammalang pier now dock. A concrete road runs across the island from Ao Taloh Waw to **Ao Pante Malacca** on the western coast, where you'll find the park headquarters, bungalows and the main camp site. Boats leave between Ao Pante Malacca and Pak Bara on the mainland.

Next to the visitors centre at Ao Pante Malacca, a steep trail leads through the jungle to **Toe-Boo Cliff**, a dramatic rocky outcrop with fabulous views of Ko Adang and the surrounding islands.

Ao Pante Malacca has a lovely alabaster beach shaded by pandanus and casuarinas. If you follow the large stream flowing through here inland, you'll reach **Tham Jara-Khe** (Crocodile Cave), once home to deadly saltwater crocodiles. The cave is navigable for about 1km at low tide and can be visited on long-tail tours from the jetty at Ao Pante Malacca.

Immediately south of Ao Pante is **Ao Jak**, which has another fine sandy beach, and **Ao Molae**, which also has fine white sand and a ranger station with bungalows and a camp site. A 30-minute boat ride or 8km walk south of Ao Pante you'll find **Ao Son**, an isolated sandy bay where turtles nest between September and April. You can camp here but there are no facilities. Ao Son has decent snorkelling, as does **Ao Makham**, further south. From the ranger station at Ao Son you can walk inland to **Lu Du Falls** (about 1½ hours) and **Lo Po Falls** (about 2½ hours).

On the far side of the island is **Ao Rusi** with a dramatic cave and good coral offshore, accessible by long-tail from Ao Pante Malacca. Nearby **Ko Le-Lah** is another good snorkelling spot. There are interesting sheer-sided rocky buttresses along the southeastern coast, including **Ko Rung Nok** (Bird-Nest Island), off Ao Taloh Udang, a treasure trove of valuable swallows' nests.

SLEEPING & EATING

All the formal park accommodation on Ko Tarutao is around the park headquarters at Ao Pante Malacca and at Ao Molae. The accommodation (open mid-November to mid-May) is far more sensitive to the environment than the average Thai resort. Water is rationed, rubbish is (sporadically) transported back to the mainland, lighting is provided by power-saving light bulbs and electricity is available between 6pm and 7am only.

There are large fan-cooled **cabins** (r 600-1200B) with two or three rooms at the foot of Toe-Boo Cliff, while at Ao Molae you'll find 10 recently constructed deluxe **bungalows** (up to 4 people 1000-5000B). There are also simple **longhouse rooms** (r 500B) at Ao Pante Malacca, with four mattresses on the floor (you must take a whole room). All rooms have mosquito nets, but bring some repellent as backup. Accommodation can be booked at the **park office** (☎ 0 7478 3485) in Pak Bara, or through the **Royal Forest Department** (☎ 0 2561 4292/3) in Bangkok. National park entry fees can be paid at Ao Pante Malacca or Ao Taloh Waw.

Camping is permitted under casuarinas at Ao Pante Malacca, Ao Molae and Ao Taloh Waw, where there are toilet and shower blocks, and on the wild beaches of Ao Son, Ao Makham and Ao Taloh Udang, where you will need to be absolutely self-sufficient. The cost is 50B per person with your own tent, or you can hire tents for 200B. Camping is also permitted on Ko Adang and other islands in the park, with permission.

The park authorities run an excellent **canteen** (dishes 40-120B) at Ao Pante Malacca. The food is satisfying and tasty and they even have cold beer. If you stay at Ao Taloh Waw you can eat at the small canteen by the jetty.

GETTING THERE & AROUND

From Pak Bara (p372), boats stop at Ao Pante Malacca at 11.30am and 1.30pm (400B, one hour) on their way to Ko Lipe (250B, one hour); in the reverse direction, boats arriving from Ko Lipe towards Pak Bara dock at 10am. The island officially closes from the end of May to 15 September. Regular boats run from 21 October to the end of May; when the boats aren't running, you'll have to charter a long-tail from Pak Bara for 1500B. During the high season you can also come here on speedboat day tours from Pak Bara for 2000B, including national park fees, lunch, drinks and snorkelling.

Long-tails can be hired from the jetty at Ao Pante Malacca for trips to Tham Jara-Khe or Ao Son for around 600B. To Ao Taloh Udang you'll pay about 1500B round-trip.

Ko Khai & Ko Klang
เกาะไข่/เกาะกลาง

Between Ko Tarutao and Ko Adang there's a small cluster of three islands collectively known as **Muu Ko Klang** (Middle Island Group). Most interesting is **Ko Khai**, which has a neat white-sand beach and a scenic rock arch. The coral here has suffered a bit due to boat anchors, but both Ko Khai and **Ko Klang** have crystal-clear water for swimming. You can get here by chartered long-tail from either Ao Pante Malacca on Ko Tarutao, or Ko Lipe; a round-trip will cost around 1500B from either end.

Ko Lipe
เกาะหลีเป๊ะ

With more than its share of white beaches, mountainous woodland and flashy blue water housing extraordinarily healthy coral, Ko Lipe is the home of a 700-strong community of *chow lair* villagers and a growing legion of private developers. Falling outside the protection of the national park, partly because of the entrenched local population, this little isle is rapidly emerging as the tourist centre for the far-southern Andaman. For the moment there's a chummy, eco-minded feel, but we shed tears just thinking about the potential for overdevelopment on this rising star.

The densest development is along the wide curving beach of **Hat Pattaya** on the southern coast – this is the prettiest bay and there's a party vibe here during high season. **Sunlight Beach** is near the *chow lair* village on the eastern coast – all the bungalows are spread out between locals' houses and at the northern end a sand bar carves out a tranquil, translucent cove of emerald water. On **Sunset Beach**, which has fabulous views to Ko Adang, there's just one friendly resort – a footpath leads here from behind the village school. Luckily, the rest of Ko Lipe is still very mellow, with peaceful jungle trails and some delightful secluded beaches that have a romantic *Gilligan's Island* feel.

There are no banks or ATMs on the island, though several of the bigger resorts can change travellers cheques, cash or give advances on credit cards – all for a hefty fee. It's also a good idea to stock up on necessities such as insect repellent before you arrive, as things can be quite pricey on the island. Internet is available mostly along the cross-island path for 3B per minute.

SIGHTS & ACTIVITIES
There's good coral all along the southern coast and around **Ko Kra**, the little island opposite the *chow lair* village. Most resorts rent out mask and snorkel sets and fins for 50B each and can arrange long-tail trips to Ko Adang and other coral-fringed islands for around 1500B. On Sunlight and Pattaya Beaches, French-run **Forra Diving** (☎ 0 4633 6274; www.forradiving.com) offers PADI Open Water dive courses for 1200B, and day trips with two dives for 3000B.

SLEEPING & EATING
Nearly all resorts on Ko Lipe close from May to October, when the boats stop running. Many resorts offer water refills to ease rubbish problems – please, please take advantage of these services. If you tire of Westernised Thai food, try some of the rustic food shacks in the village.

Fisheries Department Bungalows (☎ 0 8747 87958; Sunset Beach; bungalows 250-500B) One of the few places open year-round and often one of the last places on the island to have a room available during peak times, this place is a great bargain.

Viewpoint (Sunlight Beach; bungalows 350-500B) Perched on a hill overlooking Ko Kra, this is a remote spot with rudimentary but big bamboo bungalows all with breezy terraces and jaw-dropping views.

Porn Resort (☎ 0 7472 8032; Sunset Beach; bungalows 500-800B) This popular old-fashioned bamboo place is the only privately owned resort on comely Sunset Beach. The restaurant is highly recommended – handy since serious bush tracking is required to leave the area at night.

Pooh's Bungalows (☎ 0 7472 8019; www.poohlipe .com; r 600-1200B; 💻) Everything you could possibly want – good food, a bar, dive shop, big-screen movies, internet, excellent tourist services, immaculate rooms and more – can be found at Pooh's, except the beach. It's OK though because five minutes in one direction you find Hat Pattaya, in the other there's Sunlight Beach. This is the only resort on the island that's open year-round.

Mountain Resort (☎ 0 7472 8131; www.mountain resortkohlipe.com; Sunlight Beach; bungalows 600-2200B; 💥 💻) This big resort has views from its hillside location out over Ko Adang and winding wooden walkways lead down to the sublime beach on Sunrise Beach's northern sand bar. The huts are intricately designed from thatch and wood and come with verandas. The restaurant has a huge menu as well as gargantuan views of the sea.

Da Ya Resort (☎ 0 7472 8030; Hat Pattaya; bungalows 800-2000B) A family-run place, the bungalows here are your standard slap-up wooden affairs but the beach is fantastic and the back garden is charming. The restaurant here is known for its fresh seafood.

Pattaya Song (☎ 0 7472 8034; www.pattayasong resort.com; Hat Pattaya; bungalows 1000-1500B) Above the rocks at the western end of the beach, this Italian-run pad has decent wood and concrete huts strung out either along the ocean or a little way up the hill. The Pattaya Seafood restaurant here serves excellent food and the resort can organise fishing and island-hopping trips around the area.

our pick Castaway Resort (☎ 0 8313 87472; www .castaway-resorts.com; Sunlight Beach; bungalows 2000-3000B; 💻) While not on the best stretch of beach, the roomy wood bungalows with hammock-laden terraces, pillows everywhere, overhead fans and fabulous, modern-meets-naturalistic outdoor bathrooms are the most chic on Lipe. It's also one of the most environmentally friendly – with solar water heaters and lights, and the owners are trying to convert their diesel generators to use palm oil. The candlelit restaurant here is pricey, but the food is excellent and the ambience divinely romantic.

Bundhaya Resort (☎ 0 7475 0248-9; www.bundaya resort.com; Hat Pattaya; bungalows 1200-3700B; 💥 💻) Lipe's newest and most commercial resort doubles as the boat ticket and immigration office. Characterless wooden bungalows are overpriced but comfortable enough and rates include a decent buffet breakfast at the beachside restaurant.

DRINKING
There are lots of driftwood-clad Rasta bars along Hat Pattaya. A little bit inland, JJ's Jungle Bar is another good place for a tipple, as is **Karma Bar** (☎ 0 5199 3101), nestled against the base of a limestone cliff below Mountain Resort.

GETTING THERE & AWAY

From 21 October to the end of May there are boats from Pak Bara (see p372) to Ko Lipe via Ao Pante Malacca on Ko Tarutao, at 11.30am and 1.30pm (550B to 650B, 1½ hours); in the reverse direction it's inexplicably cheaper (400B) and boats leave at 9am and 10am. Low-season transport depends on the weather but there is usually one boat per week (usually Friday with the return on Sunday). You always have the option of chartering a boat to Ko Lipe from Pak Bara for a hefty 4000B each way.

There's a new high-speed ferry run by the **Satun-Pak Bara Speedboat Club** (www.tarutaolipeisland .com) every other day from Ko Lipe at 9am to Ban Saladan on Ko Lanta (p350; 1900B, three hours) stopping at Ko Bulon Leh (600B, 30 minutes), Ko Muk (1400B, two hours) and Ko Ngai (1600B, 2½ hours). The next day the same boat makes the return trip from Ko Lanta departing at 1pm and arriving on Ko Lipe at 4pm.

Another ferry goes daily to Pulau Langkawi (1200B, one hour) in Malaysia from November to May. Departure is at 4pm but you need to be at the immigration office at the Bundhaya Resort by 2.30pm to get stamped out. In reverse, boats leave from Pulau Langkawi for Ko Lipe at 9.30am Malay time.

Ko Adang & Ko Rawi
เกาะอาดัง/เกาะราวี

The island immediately north of Ko Lipe, **Ko Adang** has brooding, densely forested hills, white-sand beaches and healthy coral reefs.

Lots of snorkelling tours make a stop here but there are mooring buoys to prevent damage from anchors. Inland are jungle trails and tumbling waterfalls, including **Pirate's Falls**, which is rumoured to have been used as a freshwater source by pirates. There are great views from **Chado Cliff**, above the main beach, and green turtles lay their eggs here between September and December. The only accommodation is provided by the national park service, which maintains a ranger station at **Laem Son** in the southeast of the island.

Ko Rawi is 11km west of Ko Adang and has similar limestone hills and dense jungle, with first-rate beaches and large coral reefs offshore. Wild camping is allowed, with permission from the national park authorities. Excellent snorkelling spots include the northern side of **Ko Yang** and tiny **Ko Hin Ngam**, which is known for its unique stripy pebbles. Legend has it that the stones are cursed and anyone who takes any away will experience bad luck until the stones are returned to their source.

Park accommodation is provided near the ranger station at Laem Son. There are **bungalows** (3-9 people 800-1500B), **longhouses** (4-bed r 400B) and facilities for **camping** (with own tent per person 20B, with tent hire 200B). A small restaurant provides basic meals.

GETTING THERE & AWAY

You can get to Ko Adang on any of the boats that run to Ko Lipe, and for the same fare (left); just tell the driver that you want to go to Ko Adang. Long-tails from Ko Lipe are 50B.

Directory

CONTENTS

PRACTICALITIES

- Thailand uses an electrical current of 220V AC, 50Hz (cycles). Electrical plugs have two flat or two round pins; adapters and voltage converters are widely available.

- The main English-language daily newspapers are the reliable *Nation* (www.nationmultimedia.com) and *Bangkok Post* (www.bangkokpost.net), which usually become available in beach destinations mid-morning.

- Thailand has five VHF TV networks based in Bangkok and broadcasting in Thai, but not all are available in the south. Most midrange and top-end hotels have satellite or cable TV. The Thai video system is PAL and Thailand is in DVD Zone 3.

- Thailand has more than 400AM and FM radio stations, some with hourly newscasts in English.

- Thailand uses the metric system of measurements, with exceptions: Gold and silver are weighed in *bàht* (15g), and land area is often measured in *râi* (equivalent to 1600 sq m).

ACCOMMODATION

The accommodation on Thailand's islands and beaches is astonishing both for its range of quality and design. From bare-bones bamboo shacks under swaying palms to vast resort complexes where every whim is taken into consideration, you won't need to look too hard to find a place to suit your sensibility and your budget.

Beach Bungalows

Simple beach huts used to make up most of the accommodation on Thailand's islands and beaches. But these old-style A-frame huts are quickly being replaced by sturdier concrete huts (if not full blown resorts) that are universally known as bungalows, no matter what they look like.

The cheapest huts are made of palm thatch and woven bamboo, with or without simple tiled bathrooms attached. These bungalows may contain nothing more than a basic bed or mattress, a bare light bulb, and (if you're lucky) a mosquito net and fan. However, there is often a small balcony where you can dry your beach towel and swing in your hammock. Bungalows generally house two people. Increasingly, resort owners are demolishing their wooden bungalows and replacing them with less appealing but smarter-looking tin-roofed concrete huts. Predictably, rates are two or three times higher than for wooden bungalows and facilities may include air-con, TVs and tiled bathrooms with hot showers.

Nightly rates vary greatly according to the popularity of the beach, the quality of the bungalows and the season. In the high season, wooden bungalows on the cheapest beaches start from 150B per night with shared bathroom, and closer to 300B with private bathroom. Concrete bungalows usually have bathrooms and air-con, and cost from 400B in low season and 1000B in high season. Bungalows in upmarket resorts, such as Ko Samui's Hat Chaweng and Phuket's Hat Surin, can cost upwards of 2500B.

National Parks Accommodation

Some national parks provide accommodation in bungalows (sleeping up to 10 people) and *reu·an tǎa·ou* (longhouses), which consist of small rooms with mattresses on the floor for three or four people. Bungalows and longhouses usually have lights and fans, but electricity is often only available from 6pm to midnight or 6pm to 6am. Parks with bungalows often have a basic restaurant and many have a simple provisions shop. Rooms in longhouses cost between 400B and 600B, while bungalows vary from 1000B to 2000B, depending on their size and condition.

Advance booking is advisable at the more popular parks, especially on holidays and weekends when it's essential. The **National Park Office** (☎ 0 2562 0760; www.dnp.go.th/parkreserve; 61 Th Phahonyothin, Chatuchak, Bangkok 10900) has a very convenient, easy-to-use online booking facility.

While few people bother carrying camping equipment in Thailand (the guesthouses are just too cheap), camping is possible at many parks. Expect to pay between 20B and 50B per person if you bring your own tent, and 200B to 450B if you hire one, plus 60B for bedding.

Most camp sites will have toilets, running water, cold showers and sometimes a canteen serving authentic Thai meals. With permission from park authorities, you can camp in more remote locations, including some wonderful uninhabited islands and isolated beaches. However, you'll need to be totally self-sufficient, which includes bringing your own water and food.

Thai students get first preference for sites and equipment, so make reservations in advance or have a back-up plan.

Note that you'll usually be required to pay the national-park entry fee if you stay overnight – for foreigners this is usually 200B per adult or 100B for each child under 14, but in some parks it's double that. Hold on to your

---

ROOM RATES & SEASONS

In this book, accommodation is arranged by budget and listed from cheapest to most expensive. The categories, with high season rates, are:

Budget Up to 1000B.
Midrange 1000B to 3000B (4500B in Bangkok).
Top End More than 3000B (4500B in Bangkok).

Bangkok suffers from capital-city syndrome and while hotel quality is often higher, it comes at a significantly higher price; see the boxed text, p92 for details. Rates on the high-profile beaches on Ko Samui and Phuket are also much higher than elsewhere.

Be aware that, for some listings in this book, the cheapest price quoted for an establishment is often for a single cheap room, which is almost invariably booked out.

Thailand has a 7% value-added tax (VAT) on many goods and services. Many midrange lodgings and almost all top-end hotels (and restaurants) will add this and a 10% service tax to the bill. When the two are combined this becomes the 17% king hit known as 'plus plus', or '++'. Prices for listings in this book include the taxes.

Discounts of up to 50% can be found on the internet (see the boxed text, p382) and, in the case of guesthouses, by just turning up during the low season. In general, Thailand's tourist high season runs from November to April, with prices peaking between mid-December and mid-January, and around Songkran (mid-April). Low season runs from May to October, with the biggest discounts usually in May and early June, and mid-September until the beginning of November.

Let us reemphasise that these dates are fairly general, as local weather variations also impact on prices. See p12 and the destination chapters for more on the weather.

receipt as rangers randomly check visitors. Note also that securing a tent is obviously harder than locking a room.

Guesthouses

Apart from in some provincial capitals and island commercial centres, rooms in a converted family home are not common in southern Thailand, though Bangkok has plenty. By and large, most people will refer to modest collections of beach bungalows as guesthouses, as a matter of habit in referring to places where backpackers stay.

Traditionally Thai guesthouses have featured tiny box rooms with a bed or mattress on the floor, a fan, and not much else, but competition is forcing standards up. In general, rooms with shared bathroom range from 100B to all the way up to 900B per night for trendier places in Bangkok. With a private bathroom, expect to pay from about 300B to 1200B. Many guesthouses are in old wooden Thai houses so remove your shoes before entering and expect creaking floorboards at night.

Once ubiquitous, squat toilets are rare as rocking horse–shit these days. Showers are often cold. Many guesthouses will have an attached restaurant serving simple Thai meals.

Hotels

In provincial towns you can often find cheap hotels – often run by Thai–Chinese families – with basic box rooms, though in recent years many of these have been given a makeover. Expect to pay 300B for a room with a fan and shared bathroom, and 500B to 1000B for more privacy and cool air. The cheaper places can be grim, may be rented by the hour and are not great for women travelling alone. The midrange options are more wholesome and good value, with bathrooms, TVs, phones and air-con.

Larger towns and tourist resorts have bigger, tidier business- or tourist-class hotels, which offer air-con, satellite TV and bathrooms containing hot showers and Western-style toilets. Most also have attached restaurants or coffee shops. These hotels vary

BOOKING ONLINE: JUST DO IT

'You know,' said the woman as she glanced conspiratorially around the reception of one of Bangkok's top hotels, 'if you book online the rates are much cheaper…about 30% usually.' We were offered similar surprisingly honest advice several times while researching this guide, with the general message being that for many midrange and most top-end hotels booking ahead gets you discounts you can't even contemplate when you walk in.

During the low season (see the boxed text, p381) rates can fall to less than half the listed tariff as hotels and resorts compete to fill rooms. The number of budget places bookable online is also rising, but for these and a lot of relatively cheaper midrange places that don't have the same economies of scale, old-style bargaining at reception remains a good plan. Indeed, for budget places this is the best option except at the busiest times. And if you're arriving by plane there is often a desk at the airport offering last-minute discounts; Phuket is particularly good for this.

So where should you look online? There are dozens of hotel booking websites but most allow the hotels to write their own reviews. As fellow LP scribe Karla Zimmerman discovered after arriving in Bangkok, the room of 'luxurious comfort' with 'teakwood decorations and cable TV' that she'd booked online was actually located in a de facto brothel. The website had conveniently neglected to mention that 'easy access, 24 hours' meant more than just being near to the Skytrain. As Karla put it: 'Despite the distraction of drinking one's beer and eating one's pàt tai in venues where most of the patrons were getting hand jobs, we appreciated our unplanned bite of this classic slice of Bangkok.' Mind you, she also said that she'll be more careful when booking online next time. Quite.

Fortunately there are websites that offer independent reviews rather than endless superlatives. **Lonely Planet's Hotels & Hostels** (www.lonelyplanet.com) features thorough reviews of more places than listed in this book from authors, and traveller feedback. The website also has a booking facility. For a one-stop look at the sort of discounts available, the independent website **Travelfish** (www.travelfish.org) has a handy list of nothing more than the hotel name and current online price for the relevant island or beach.

dramatically – some are old, some are brand new, some have pools, some have business centres, some have views. Most are centrally located and room rates fall between 800B and 3000B per room.

At the top of the market are the genuine luxury hotels run by Thai and international chains. Rates start at around 3000B and climb to thousands of US dollars per night. These places typically have several restaurants and bars and at least one infinity pool, plus a spa and business centre. Bangkok, Ko Samui and Phuket have dozens of such hotels. There are also some very appealing independent 'boutique' hotels, particularly in Bangkok (see p96).

Resorts

In most countries, 'resort' refers to hotels that offer substantial recreational facilities (eg tennis, golf, swimming, sailing, dive school, water sports) in addition to accommodation and dining. In Thai hotel lingo, however, the term simply refers to any hotel that isn't in an urban area. Hence a few thatched beach huts or a cluster of bungalows in a forest may be called a 'resort'.

However, in recent years many a beach-shack 'resort' has been transformed into the sort of genuine resort you dream of on wet winter's days. Indeed, the islands and beaches of southern Thailand are the new Caribbean, boasting some of the most-luxurious resorts on earth, with plenty more on the way. While all resorts were not created equal many are simply stunning, with outlandish luxuries at rates that could go some way toward clearing the debts of small African nations. The better resorts have taken a refreshingly holistic approach to design, incorporating Thai themes to create a luxury experience that differs from international resorts elsewhere. Most of the major resorts are within striking distance of an airport, with Phuket, Ko Samui, Pattaya, Krabi and Ao Nang hosting the lion's share.

Along with the top-end places there are plenty of more modest midrange affairs. You'll find everything from the TVs to the single infinity pool – via the bar tabs – at these places is smaller, but when you're paying just a couple of thousand baht a night such privations are bearable. Or as one traveller we met put it: 'Is my $70-dollar bungalow really 10 times worse than that resort?'

While researching this guide the authors gave the resorts a good looking over and we've highlighted some of our favourites, both for people seeking value and those for whom money is no object. More reviews of these places, with more detail, can be found in the Hotels & Hostels section of www.lonelyplanet.com.

ACTIVITIES

Thailand is Asia's adventure capital and in the south, the focus is on the marine world. There are hundreds of places you can go snorkelling and scuba diving. Sea kayaking around islands and mangroves is becoming increasingly popular, and you can go sailboarding at many of the bigger resorts. Back on dry land, rock climbing is a major drawcard in the area around Krabi, while trekking is possible in some national parks and elephant trekking is widely available. Below are some of the details you'll need to know before disappearing below the surface. For a full rundown of the diving and other active options, see the Diving & Other Activities chapter (p289).

Diving Basics

COURSES & TOURS

Most dive centres offer first-timers Open Water certification with PADI or SSI for around 9500B to 18,500B. Courses are three-and-a-half days and include several classroom sessions and four guided dives testing various skills. Ko Tao is the dive-school capital of the universe. For detailed information about choosing dive schools, see p230.

For experienced divers, most centres offer all-inclusive day trips featuring two dives, lunch, guides and taxi transfers for around 2000B to 4000B. Live-aboard tours are popular on the Andaman side, particularly around the Surin and Similan Islands. Most operators are based in Phuket.

For more details on dive sites, see p289.

DIVE MEDICINE

For the amount of diving throughout Thailand, the kingdom has a surprisingly limited amount of medical facilities dedicated to diving accidents. Having said that, hyperbaric chambers can be found at most major hubs, including Ko Samui (p193), Ko Tao (p228), and Phuket (p288). Ask your dive centre about the best local facilities before hitting the waves.

DIRECTORY

DIVING PACKING LIST

If you're planning to dive, organising the following items in advance will greatly ease your ability to hop right in and explore the deep.

Diving insurance Check whether your travel-insurance provider offers extra insurance for divers. If not, check out www.daneurope.org for more information.

Doctor's note Divers with any medical problem (including mild asthma) must have a doctor sign off on their ability to dive safely. Skip the unnecessary (and sometimes costly) trip to a local clinic and take care of this before you leave.

Dive log & certification You must bring proof of your previous experience, especially for deep dives and night dives.

Non-drowsy motion sickness pills It is technically illegal for dive operators to give out medicine, and purchasing your own in your native country will better assure unwanted side effects.

DIVE SEASONS

Generally speaking, the Gulf of Thailand has a year-round dive season, although tropical storms sometimes temporarily blow out visibility. The southwestern monsoon seems to affect the Ko Chang archipelago more than other eastern gulf coast dive sites; hence, November to early May is the ideal season for these islands.

Off the Andaman coast the best diving conditions (calm surf and good visibility) fall between December and April; from May to November monsoon conditions prevail and visibility is often poor. Dive centres at Ko Lanta and the islands further south close down, but diving is still possible out of Phuket, Ao Nang and Ko Phi-Phi.

Whale sharks and manta rays can often be seen in the Andaman Sea and Gulf of Thailand (particularly on dives at submerged pinnacles) during the annual planktonic blooms from February to March. For more details on choosing between these waters, see p291.

RESPONSIBLE DIVING & SNORKELLING

'Over-diving' has become a common problem in Thailand. Many reefs see hundreds of divers per day, which puts a great strain on the environment. Corals wilt and die and marine life leaves to seek new feeding grounds. Many dive operators actively participate in reef rehabilitation programs; however every diver should do their part to keep the sites pristine. Before diving, make sure that you are properly weighted; buoyancy control is essential in ensuring that you don't bang against outcroppings and sea walls. Never stand on coral – if you must secure yourself to the reef, only hold fast to exposed rock or dead coral. Fin kicks often disturb reefs as well; heavy strokes can create tiny eddies and displace sand over delicate organisms. The rest is quite logical: don't bully the marine creatures and don't loot the sea. If you see unscrupulous activity underwater, report it when you get back to shore.

Hiking

For ideas of where to hike in southern Thailand, see p295.

When hiking in Thailand, take some basic precautions:

- Don't go hiking alone and let someone in the local community know where you are going and for how long
- Always take plenty of water and insect repellent
- Take your rubbish back with you
- Walk in sturdy shoes and long pants in case of leeches and snakes

Meditation & Thai Massage

The region offers many opportunities to relax with some meditation or a Thai massage. Places to try include Ko Chang (p144), Ko Tao (p232), Ko Samui (p197), Ko Pha-Ngan (p217) and Phuket (p298). Massages are also available in Bangkok (p87).

For information on courses, see p386.

BUSINESS HOURS

Most government offices are open from 8.30am to 4.30pm, Monday to Friday, though the wheels grind almost to a halt during the noon to 1pm lunch hour. Banks are generally open from 8.30am to 3.30pm Monday to Friday, sometimes until 4.30pm (usually on Friday). Many banks run foreign-exchange booths in Bangkok and at tourist resorts, and they are open from around 8am to 8pm daily. Note that government offices and banks are closed on public holidays (see p393).

Commercial businesses usually operate between 8.30am and 5pm on weekdays and sometimes Saturday morning as well. Larger shops usually open from 10am to 6.30pm or 7pm, but the big Bangkok malls are open later (until 9pm or 10pm) and smaller shops may open earlier and close later. Hours for restaurants and cafés vary greatly. Some local Thai places open as early as 7am, while bigger places usually open around 11am and still others are open in the evenings only. Some places close as early as 9pm, many open until 10pm or 11pm, while others stay open all night. Bars, by law, can't open before 4pm and must close by 1am. This law has been enforced with renewed vigour by the new government. Do note that shops operated by Muslims might close on Friday, the Islamic holy day.

CHILDREN

Thailand is a surprisingly easy place to travel with children and many former solo backpackers are returning to Thailand with their own families. Thais love children and in many instances will shower attention on your offspring, who will find ready playmates among their Thai counterparts.

Of course, travel with children in Thailand is still subject to the same obstacles that are faced by parents travelling with children anywhere, ie keeping the little 'uns healthy and entertained. Lonely Planet's *Travel with Children* contains advice on how to cope with kids on the road, with special attention to travel in the developing world.

Practicalities

Transport is an important consideration for parents, as children will get bored quickly on long bus or boat rides so if you're heading to the far south consider flying. There are cheap, direct flights from Bangkok to Ko Samui, Phuket, Krabi, Trang and Trat. Though not as fast, the train does offer sleeping compartments and room to explore and runs to Surat Thani (for boat transfer to Ko Samui), Trang and Hat Yai.

Bus companies charge full fare for children using a seat, but it's free for those who ride on their parent's lap. On the train children under 12 pay half, while under-threes travel free if they don't take up a seat.

Thailand is one of the few tropical countries that doesn't require specific jabs, and malaria prophylaxis usually isn't necessary. Having said that, the incidence of dengue fever is on the rise so protecting against mosquito bites (at any time of day) is very important – BYO good repellent. The biggest problem for children is keeping them hydrated and free of the bellyache. The Health chapter (p422) has details of good practices for keeping adults and children healthy.

A high-factor sunscreen is essential. Warn your children not to play with dogs and cats; pets in Thailand are typically more the guard dog or trash-eating variety than Mr Snuggles. Rabies is also a concern. Be particularly wary of aggressive monkeys.

Only in the best hotels will you find high chairs, and strollers are rarely seen outside top resort areas. Most Thais just carry their children in their arms and hold them at the dinner table. While strollers might be convenient on some of the more popular resort islands, Thai pavements are such that elsewhere it will feel more like off-roading than strolling. International-style beach resorts and upmarket hotels usually provide childcare facilities and crèches. Thai food is often a little too spicy for young palates, but fried rice, roti, pasta and especially fried noodles are widely available. Big supermarkets in large cities sell Western staples.

If you are travelling with very young children, public breast-feeding is far less frowned upon than in the West, but it's always done discreetly. However, breast-feeding is losing ground amongst Thais due to the relentless marketing of powdered milk formula, which is portrayed as a miracle tonic that will transform children into academically brilliant prodigies. It's widely available from shops and pharmacies.

Sights & Activities

Bangkok has plenty of attractions for kids, from shimmering gold and giant statues at Bangkok's wát (temples) to a world-class oceanarium (see p90). However, warn your children about touching religious objects such as shrines, offerings and spirit houses (which can look a lot like dolls' houses to a child). Hotels with swimming pools help work off city claustrophobia.

The vast majority of Thai beaches are well-suited to swimmers, sand-castle builders and fish spotters, though be aware of seasonal strong currents off Phuket. Pattaya (p121), Phuket (p299) and Ko Samui (p198) have plenty of non-beach diversions that don't involve prostitutes or vodka shots.

Many of the fantastic range of activities available in Krabi (p328), including rock-climbing and sea-kayaking tours, are open to children. For more on outdoor activities see the chapter, p289.

CLIMATE CHARTS

The climate charts below give you a reasonable idea of what are the hottest and wettest months in the region. For more information on the best times to visit Thailand's islands and beaches, see p12. And for even more detail on when it's likely to rain where, and for how long, see the excellent inter-active map on the website www.travelfish.org/weather_fish.php.

COURSES

If you'll be staying in Thailand for a while, there are some good courses on offer. You can learn to speak Thai or study meditation, learn Thai cooking or Thai massage, or train as a scuba-diver or Thai boxer. For cooking courses, see p51; for dive courses, see p291.

Language

Bangkok has the largest concentration of formal language schools and tuition rates, see p89. But there are plenty of informal language schools in most places where foreigners congregate. The best way to find them is on notice boards (often outside grocery stores) and by just asking around.

Meditation

Thailand has long been a popular place for Western students of Buddhism, particularly

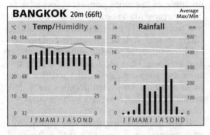

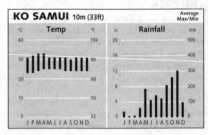

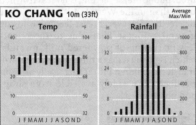

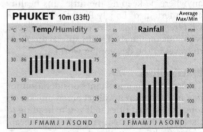

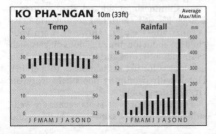

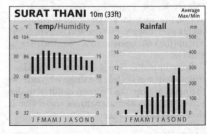

those interested in meditation. Two basic systems of meditation, *samatha* (calm) and *vipassana* (insight), are taught. Most places specialise in *vipassana*, which focuses on concentration to achieve personal insight – it's sometimes called 'mindfulness' meditation.

Foreigners who come to Thailand can choose from dozens of temples and meditation centres *(săm·nák wí·bàt·sà·nah)* and there is usually no charge, but you must attend daily prayers and make a daily contribution between 50B and 100B towards expenses. Most places teach in Thai, but there are a few English-speaking instructors. Contact the centres in advance before turning up on the doorstep. For even a brief visit, wear clean and neat clothing (ie long trousers or skirt, and sleeves that cover the shoulders).

A two-month tourist visa is ample for most courses. If you formally ordain as a Buddhist monk or nun, you will be allowed to stay in Thailand as long as you remain in robes.

English-language meditation instruction is available in Bangkok; see p90. Elsewhere, meditation courses are available in Ko Si Chang (p118); Ko Chang (p144); outside Surat Thani (see boxed text, p242); on Ko Pha-Ngan (p216); and at these places, among others, on Ko Samui (p195 and p205).

For a detailed if a little dated look at *vipassana* study in Thailand, read *A Guide to Buddhist Monasteries and Meditation Centres in Thailand,* by Bill Weir, distributed by the World Fellowship of Buddhists in Thailand.

Useful online resources include:

Dharma Thai (www.dhammathai.org)
House of Dhamma (www.houseofdhamma.com)
World Fellowship of Buddhists (www.wfb-hq.org)

Moo·ay Tai (Thai Boxing)

The martial art of *moo·ay tai* (often spelt as *muay thai*; Thai boxing) is legendary around the world, but you'll need to be tough to last long at a traditional Thai *moo·ay tai* camp. As well as a rigorous training regimen, you may also have to adopt a special (often rudimentary) diet and learn the Thai language. Unlike most East Asian martial arts, *moo·ay tai* training features full-contact sparring.

As the sport's popularity has exploded, however, several schools have adapted their programs to better suit Westerners. Bangkok has several of these, with English-speaking trainers and better equipment but which charge higher tuition fees; see p90.

Training periods can range from a one-day course to multiweek sessions. Do be aware that the potential for some camps to be interested only in tuition fees is a concern and it pays to do your research.

The website www.muaythai.com contains useful information including the addresses of training camps. For more on *moo·ay tai*, see boxed text, p178.

Thai Massage

Described as a 'brutally pleasant experience', this ancient form of healing has been practised in Thailand for over 1000 years and was modified from ancient Indian meditation techniques. Unlike Western massage techniques, Thai massage *(nôo·at păan boh·rahn)* uses the elbows, forearms, knees and feet as well as the fingers and palms to apply pressure to traditional pressure points along various *sên* (meridians – lines of energy in the human body) in order to distribute energies evenly through the nervous system.

If you want to study Thai massage, Wat Pho in Bangkok (see p83) is the national authority on traditional healing and offers massage training courses; see also p90.

CUSTOMS

The white-uniformed officers of Thai customs prohibit the import or export of the usual goods – porn, weapons and drugs. If you're caught with drugs, in particular, expect life never to be the same again. Otherwise, customs regulations are quite reasonable. The usual 200 cigarettes or 250g of tobacco are allowed in without duty, along with 1L of wine or spirits. Ditto for electronic goods as long as you don't look like you're planning to sell them – best to leave your third and fourth laptops at home.

There is no limit to the amount of Thai or foreign currency you can bring into the country, but you can only take out 50,000B per person without special authorisation. If you're going to one of Thailand's neighbouring countries, you can take as much as 500,000B per person. The exportation of foreign currencies is unrestricted.

Thailand has strict regulations on the export of antiques and some religious items (see p388). For hours of fun reading other customs details, check out www.customs .go.th/Customs-Eng/indexEng.jsp.

DIRECTORY

Claiming Back VAT

Visitors to Thailand who depart by air and who haven't spent more than 180 days in Thailand during the previous calendar year can apply for a VAT refund on purchases made at approved stores; look for the blue and white VAT Refund sticker in store windows. Minimum purchases must add up to 2000B per store in a single day, with a minimum total of 5000B. You must get a VAT Refund form and tax invoice from the shop. In Bangkok the major malls will probably direct you to a desk dealing with VAT refunds, but elsewhere you might need to ask.

At the airport, take the items (preferably in original packaging) to the customs desk, which will issue the paperwork. You can then check larger items in, but smaller items (such as watches and jewellery) must be carried by hand as they will need to be reinspected once past immigration. Either way, you actually get your money at a VAT Refund Tourist Office once you've passed through immigration. For all the details, see www.rd.go.th/vrt.

Exporting Antiques, Art & Buddha Images

After centuries of being plundered by foreign antique and art collectors, the Thais have introduced strict regulations governing the export of antiques, *objets d'art* and images of Buddha or other Buddhist deities. To carry any of these out of the country, you'll need a permit from the Fine Arts Department, which can take several days to arrange. The Thai definition of an antique is fairly broad. If in doubt, contact the Fine Arts Department at the **Office of Archaeology & National Museums** (Map pp72-3; ☎ 0 2226 1661) at the Fine Arts Department.

DANGERS & ANNOYANCES

Although Thailand is generally a pretty safe place to visit, it's easy to get taken for a ride. It's wise to be a little cautious, particularly if you're travelling alone. For information on diseases and environmental dangers such as jellyfish stings, see p423. The following might help you stay out of trouble.

Drugging

It doesn't happen as much as it used to, but beware of friendly strangers offering cigarettes, drinks or sweets, especially in hostess bars or other houses of dubious repute. In some cases the food is drugged and the victim wakes up hours later without a wallet or valuables.

Drugs

Despite Thailand's party reputation, it is illegal to buy, sell or possess all of the good-times drugs in any quantity and there are severe penalties – they don't get much more severe than death – if caught. Even more than in most countries, drugs are a huge political issue in Thailand. The government of Thaksin Shinawatra was notoriously hardline on drugs (see boxed text, opposite) and popular for it, and the successor Peoples Power Party is following a similar line.

This means police raids on tourist areas have returned and police themselves are under pressure to deliver convictions; attempting to bribe your way out of trouble will likely be futile. If you're lucky, you will be fined 50,000B (at least) and asked to leave the country; if you're not, you could end up in Bangkok's infamous Bang Khwang Prison (aka the Bangkok Hilton).

With such a hardline stance (we're talking raiding bars, saunas and nightclubs, particularly in Bangkok, and holding everyone until they've been photographed and submitted a urine sample), it makes you wonder how every mind-altering substance known to man can be available at the full-moon parties (see boxed text, p215) on Ko Pha-Ngan; and this is despite regular spot searches of people and vehicles heading to Hat Rin for the full moon.

As well as manufactured drugs, the ban extends to so-called 'natural' drugs, such as *grà·tôrm* (a leaf of the *Mitragyna speciosa* tree) and hallucinogenic 'magic mushrooms'. 'Special omelettes' containing magic mushrooms are a long-running tradition at Ko Pha-Ngan, but these have always been a risky proposition and hundreds of foreigners have ended up with severe mental-health problems over the years after taking hallucinogenic drugs in Thailand. A hallucinogenic plant called *đôn lam·pong,* which can cause permanent psychosis, has recently appeared on the scene at Ko Pha-Ngan.

Insurgent Activity

The far south of Thailand continues to be troubled by separatist violence, and travel in Yala, Pattani and Narathiwat Provinces can be dangerous. Many governments advise against nonessential travel to Thailand's deep south and it is worth checking your government's travel advisory before hitting the road. Having

ADDICTED TO THE WAR ON DRUGS

In January 2003, as the world's attention was focused on the impending advance of the 'War on Terror' into Iraq, the Thai police embarked on a crackdown on drug dealers and users with the stated aim of declaring Thailand 'drug-free' within months. In announcing the move, the words of former prime minister Thaksin Shinawatra were ominous: 'Because drug traders are ruthless to our children, so being ruthless back to them is not a bad thing… It may be necessary to have casualties… If there are deaths among traders, it's normal.'

Thailand's 'War on Drugs' was initially met with broad support from the public, which had become understandably frightened of the impact of growing methamphetamine use. But what followed was criticised by the UN Commission on Human Rights. In just three months more than 50,000 people were arrested and at least 2275 killed (the police figure). The government claimed most of the killings were carried out by rival drug gangs. But many of the dead had been summarily executed by the police themselves. The dead included many who had some involvement in the drug trade, but a government report states that over a thousand probably had nothing to do with drugs whatsoever. Three months after the campaign began Shinawatra hastily declared 'mission accomplished'. Five years later and the dead are still dead, most of the police are still police and the drugs trade shows no sign of having disappeared.

Not surprisingly, new kingpins rose up to meet the demand and the battle against methamphetamine (*yah bâh;* crazy-medicine) continues in a more conventional manner. The Thai government's attempts to coordinate with poorly funded and poorly motivated police in Myanmar, Laos and Cambodia have resulted in some high-profile busts, but no killer blow. Because of this, and despite the public-relations disaster of the 2003 War on Drugs, the government declared a second War on Drugs in early 2008. We can only hope it doesn't descend into the sort of festival of death seen in 2003.

said that, a steady trickle of travellers passes through these provinces en route to or from Malaysia and most report no trouble.

For more on the long history of trouble between Muslims and Buddhists in the south, see boxed text, p28. For details on travelling there, see boxed text, p252. If you are thinking of heading to this part of Thailand be sure to check online for fresh information; the Thorn Tree bulletin board at www.lonleyplanet.com is a good place to start.

Physical Safety

Violent crime is rare in Thailand, but not unheard of. During the last few years several women travellers have been raped – and some murdered – on remote beaches, and in early 2008 a man was stabbed to death while trying to break up a fight at a Hat Rin full moon party. For beach safety precautions for women, see p403.

Wherever you are in Thailand it makes sense to exercise the same street smarts you would anywhere else. These include the obvious, like ensuring your room is securely locked and bolted and avoiding quiet, dark places at night. Women should also inspect cheap, thin-walled rooms for strategic peepholes.

Motorbikes, however, pose the greatest risk. Tourist motorcyclists are killed fairly regularly, and many others end up with a 'Thai tattoo' – burned inner right calf – or worse. See boxed text, p414, for more on motorcycle safety.

Scams

Well, just where do we start? Thailand has its fair share of scams that have been consistently separating tourists from their cash for years. Bangkok is the centre of Thai scamming, but islands such as Ko Samui and Phuket are doing their best to claim the title. Of the various scams, the gem scam (see boxed text, p390) and the transit and lodging scams are those you're most likely to come across.

TRANSIT & LODGING SCAMS

In terms of infrastructure, it is a breeze getting from point A to point B in Thailand. But there are still the taxi and túk-túk drivers and bogus travel agents to dodge – nearly an Olympic event. Several well-established scams exist – see boxed text, p412 for details.

Don't believe anyone who tells you that a hotel or guesthouse is 'closed', 'full', 'dirty',

DIRECTORY

THE WORLD-FAMOUS BANGKOK GEM SCAM! *Andrew Burke*

'Hello sir, where are you going?' asked the well-dressed man in his early 50s, 'Where are you from?' When I told him 'Australia' I could almost see the memory whirring into action. 'Ah, Australia! Sydney or Melbourne? My daughter is studying at university in Melbourne.' My new friend, acquired as I walked along a touristy Bangkok street, went on to correctly answer questions about Melbourne universities (he knew all the main schools) and Australian university holidays. It was only when he asked 'How long have you been in Bangkok?', and I told him 'two years', that his interest suddenly and dramatically waned.

My 'friend' was a scammer, a con artist expert in inveigling unsuspecting new arrivals into his trust and then subtly bullying them into buying something for way more than its real worth – usually gems. Every question or statement was a leading question designed to push emotional buttons. My 'friend' told me how expensive Australian universities were and how hard it was to pay for his daughter's education, and rising inflation was making it so hard to keep paying for the school she needed so she could have a better life.

So what should you do? The truth is that Thais don't usually act this way so, as much as it pains us to say this, if you're in a touristy area (not just in Bangkok) treat anyone who approaches you from out of the blue with suspicion. And look for the signs. Assume the scam is in gear when your new friend asks if you have a map (a major clue since most Thais can't be bothered with maps) and/or a túk-túk magically arrives. Don't believe people who claim major tourist sites are closed for renovations or government holidays unless you see it for yourself.

'haunted' or 'burnt down' (we're not making this up) until you see if for yourself. Săhm·lór and túk-túk drivers often offer free or low-cost rides to the place they're touting but you'll be paying for the ride later on, either in terms of cash or discomfort; see boxed text, above, for one likely outcome.

Theft & Fraud

People seem so friendly in Thailand that a visitor can forget to follow the basic precautions of travelling abroad.

While violent crime is rare, there are plenty of stories of bags being snatched and pockets picked, particularly in Bangkok's crowded markets; Chatuchak is probably the worst. Use your common sense, however, and you should be fine; keep your bags in front of you and in sight at all times. On the islands, don't put your bag in the front basket of rented bicycles or motorbikes, as you might as well just put out a sign saying 'rob me'.

The best way to keep your money safe is to split the risk. Bring a mixture of cash and travellers cheques, and keep an emergency stash of money separate from your main finances. Credit cards are very useful in Thailand but keep them safe and have the emergency cancellation phone number

on hand. If you have two cards, keep them in separate places. Money belts or pouches worn under clothing are much safer than wallets or purses.

We'd say keep your valuables, including credit cards, cash or travellers cheques, with you at all times, but clearly that's going to be a problem when you're lounging around the beach all day. At these times it's best to store them in the safety box at your hotel or guesthouse. In cheaper places, this means a locked drawer or a mysterious place behind the counter.

It also pays to seal your valuables before you hand them over. A taped-up envelope with a signature over the top is the best way. If you can't do this, then at least make a show of counting and noting your money before you hand it over. This works for both parties as while most staff are trustworthy, there are exceptions and the same applies to foreigners. In the case of an alleged theft, the staff have as much reason to suspect you of fraud as you do them.

Never let vendors take your credit card out of sight to run it through the machine. Unscrupulous merchants have been known to run off multiple receipts with one credit-card purchase, forging your signature on the blanks after you have left the shop.

It's just a ploy to give them an excuse to take you somewhere else – somewhere you don't want to go.

If I'd allowed it, my 'friend' would probably have taken me to a local wát (temple) or some other mildly interesting attraction as a means of building trust. We'd end up taking a convenient túk-túk (everyone in the scam gets a cut) to a gem shop where the scammers might tell me about a 'government gem sale' that will soon end, or some other unlikely scheme. The government doesn't do 'gem sales', nor does it have schemes for students to sell gems to raise money for education. Eventually I'd be talked into buying large amounts of gems either for cash or on my credit card, with assurances that I can resell the stones for a huge profit at home. At home I'd find the gems were real, but worth a fraction of the price paid in Bangkok. In a worst-case scenario my credit card would also be billed for extra items using forged credit-card imprints.

If you find yourself in any of these scenarios, remember that you can stop it at any time. A good countermeasure is to ask for a photo with your 'friend' – and as many of the maybe-scammers as possible – if they refuse, it's a scam. Even better, don't allow yourself to be tempted. The scammer will often play on your greed – don't be greedy.

That scams like this have been going on for years, by the same operators, is a sad indictment on the Thai government's legislative ability and on the credit-card companies that continue to do business with dodgy dealers. The names of the culprits are all over the internet – why can't they be stopped? For more on the gem scam (including lists of known operators) or to seek solace from the scammed, check out www.bangkokscams.com, www.geocities.com/thaigemscamgroup and www.2bangkok.com, which has an anti-scam campaign.

Finally, remember that a padlock on a bag doesn't turn it into Fort Knox, particularly on long-distance bus trips. See p412 for bus theft horror stories.

DISCOUNT CARDS

Apart from airlines and travel agents, youth discounts are rarely offered in Thailand, and discounts for seniors are almost unheard of. The cost of living is so low that this isn't really an issue. **Hostelling International** (HI; www.tyha.org) issues a membership card that will allow you to stay at the country's handful of associated hostels without having to pay the additional surcharge for nonmembers; membership can be bought for 200B at the relevant hostels.

Student & Youth Cards

The International Student Identity Card (ISIC) can be used for the student discount offered at some museums in Thailand, but is most useful for getting discount airfares from travel agents and airlines. Some travel agents will give student discounts even if you don't have a student card. For a list of agents that issue ISIC cards, visit the International Student Travelling Confederation's website, www.istc.org. The phoney ISIC cards produced on Th Khao San may fool museum staff, but probably won't fool the airlines.

EMBASSIES & CONSULATES
Thai Embassies & Consulates

Most nationalities can obtain a free one-month tourist visa on arrival in Thailand, but if your country is exempt or you want more time in Thailand, contact the Thai embassy (or consulate) in your home country. For a full and regularly updated list of Thai embassies and consulates see the website of the **Thai Ministry of Foreign Affairs** (www.mfa.go.th/web/12.php) and click through to About the Ministry. Or look it up in the phone book.

Embassies & Consulates in Thailand

Bangkok is an excellent place to collect visas for onward travel. The visa sections of most embassies and consulates are open from 9am to noon Monday to Friday, but call first to be sure. Some Bangkok embassies are listed here. For a full and regularly updated list, go to www.mfa.go.th/web/12.php and click through to Foreign Missions in Thailand.

Australia (Map pp72-3; ☎ 0 2344 6300; www.aust embassy.or.th; 37 Th Sathon Tai)

Cambodia (Map pp70-1; ☎ 0 2957 5851; 518/4 Th Pracha Uthit, Soi Ramkamhaeng 39, Wangthonglang)

Canada (Map pp72-3; ☎ 0 2636 0540; geo.international .gc.ca/asia/bangkok; 15th fl, Abdulrahim Bldg, 990 Th Phra Ram IV, Lumphini)

China (Map pp70-1; ☎ 0 2245 0088; www.chinaembassy
.or.th; 57 Th Ratchadaphisek, Din Daeng)

European Union (Map pp80-1; ☎ 0 2305 2600; www
.deltha.ec.europa.eu; 19th fl, Kian Gwan House II, 1410/1
Th Withayu)

France Embassy (Map pp78-9; ☎ 0 2266 8250-6; www
.ambafrance-th.org; 35 Soi 36, Th Charoen Krung); Consulate (Map pp72-3; ☎ 0 2287 1592; 29 Th Sathon Tai)

Germany (Map pp72-3; ☎ 0 2287 9000; www.bangkok
.diplo.de; 9 Th Sathon Tai)

India Embassy (p82; ☎ 0 2258 0300-6; http://indian
embassy.gov.in/bangkok; 46 Soi 23, Th Sukhumvit);
Consulate (p82; ☎ 0 2665 2968; www.ivac-th.com; 15th
fl, Glas Haus Bldg, Soi 25, Th Sukhumvit)

Israel (Map p82; ☎ 0 2204 9200; http://bangkok.mfa
.gov.il; 25th fl, Ocean Tower II, 75 Soi 19, Th Sukhumvit)

Indonesia (Map pp80-1; ☎ 0 2252 3135; 600-602 Th
Phetburi, Ratchathewi)

Japan (Map pp72-3; ☎ 0 2207 8500; www.th.emb
-japan.go.jp; 177 Th Withayu, Lumphini)

Laos (Map pp70-1; ☎ 0 2539 6667; www.bkklaoembassy
.com; 520/1-3 Soi Sahakarnpramoon, Th Pracha Uthit,
Wangthonglong)

Malaysia (Map pp72-3; ☎ 0 2679 2190-9; 33-35 Th
Sathon Tai)

Myanmar (Map pp78-9; ☎ 0 2234 0278; 132 Th Sathon
Neua)

Netherlands (Map pp80-1; ☎ 0 2309 5200; www.nether
landsembassy.in.th; 15 Soi Tonson, Ploenchit)

New Zealand (Map pp80-1; ☎ 0 2254 2530-3; www.nz
embassy.com; 19th fl, M Thai Tower, All Seasons Place, 87
Th Withayu)

South Africa (Map pp80-1; ☎ 0 2659 2900; www.sa
embbangkok.com; 12h fl, M-Thai Tower, All Seasons Place,
Th Withayu)

Sweden (Map p82; ☎ 2263 7200; www.sweden
abroad.com; 20th fl, One Pacific Place, 140 Th Sukhumvit)

UK (Map pp80-1; ☎ 0 2305 8333; www.britishembassy
.gov.uk; 1031 Th Withayu, Ploenchit)

USA (Map pp80-1; ☎ 0 2205 4000; http://bangkok.us
embassy.gov; 120-122 Th Withayu, Lumphini)

Vietnam (Map pp80-1; ☎ 0 2251 5836-8; 83/1 Th
Withayu, Ploenchit)

FESTIVALS & EVENTS

Festivals that generally occur on set months
are shown on p19. Many festivals are organised around a fixed lunar year so, like
Easter, exact dates vary each year. For example, dates for the Chinese Lunar New Year
are: 26 January 2009, 14 February 2010 and
4 February 2011.

Thailand's Muslim community has its own
festivals, which are celebrated throughout the
south. These are all linked to a lunar calendar
in a way that the dates come forward usually
by 11 or 12 days every year. For example, the
fasting month of Ramadan starts on about (it
depends when the moon is sighted) 22 August
2009, 11 August 2010 and 1 August 2011.
During Ramadan, which lasts one month,
celebrants are barred from eating, drinking
or smoking between sunrise and sunset. The
end of Ramadan is Eid al-Fitr, probably the
biggest party of the Islamic year.

For details of holidays, see opposite.

FOOD

Thai food is legendary around the world for
its chilli heat and exotic spices. There is a
huge variety of food on offer, and you can pay
as much or as little as you like and still get a
fantastic meal. Places to eat in this book have
been arranged by location and then price.

The budget category includes street food,
food courts, night markets and cheap local
restaurants, with prices ranging up to 150B.
Midrange eateries are mainly sit-down restaurants – most restaurants in this book fall
into this bracket, except in Bangkok, which
is amply stocked with upmarket restaurants.
In midrange restaurants, you can expect to
pay 150B to 500B, while meals at top-end
restaurants start at about 500B and climb
far beyond.

Prices given in the regional chapters are
typically for meals or main courses. Side orders, such as rice, salads and vegetables, cost
extra, with prices reflecting the quality of the
establishment. For the low-down on food in
Thailand, see p44.

GAY & LESBIAN TRAVELLERS

While Thai culture may seem very tolerant of
homosexuality, both male and female, there
is a difference between tolerance and accept-
ance. Although there is little risk of being
verbally or physically abused, the Thais are
quite conservative and it wasn't until early
2003 that the Department of Mental Health
formally accepted that homosexuality was not
a psychiatric disease.

The reasons for this ambiguous stance are
rooted in the importance of the family in Thai
society. Gays are often seen as being immature

GÀ·TEU·I CULTURE

Thailand has a long-established transgender tradition. Transvestites appear in some of Thailand's earliest folk operas and gà·teu·i (also spelt kàthoey; transgender males) are a visible part of Thai society – far more so than in the West. Almost all gà·teu·i are male-to-female transsexuals and most adopt a feminine persona from a very early age. Many take female sex hormones later in life to reduce male characteristics or undergo sexual reassignment surgery. Although foreigners tend to see gà·teu·i as either cultural curiosities or sexual objects, in Thailand they are usually simply regarded as a third sex.

Many gà·teu·i have high-profile jobs as entertainers, actors, game-show hosts and business owners. Performers in gà·teu·i cabarets, such as Calypso in Bangkok (p105), Tiffany's in Pattaya (p127) and Phuket Simon Cabaret in Hat Patong (Phuket; p317), often become big stars. Most of the time, you may not even know you are meeting gà·teu·i. The female persona adopted by gà·teu·i can be very convincing to a Westerner, but a Thai knows that too much swish isn't the genuine dish. The Third Sex, by Richard Totman, is an interesting and sensitive exploration of this phenomenon.

and selfish for refusing to get married and have children. As a result, many gay men live a double life: raising a family by day and having clandestine meetings by night. As in the West, people with a high-profile public life rarely admit they are gay, while entertainers and comedians often make a living out of their sexuality.

Bangkok is the undisputed gay capital of Southeast Asia – probably the whole of Asia – with several streets dedicated to gay bars and clubs (see boxed text, p104). There is a well-established scene, but prostitution is endemic in bars where foreign gays hang out. On top of this, a Western boyfriend is perceived by many as an easy route to money or emigration, so it can be very hard to meet Thai gays on an even footing. As is the case with straight relationships, many Thais are openly offended by Western gays who come to Thailand to pick up Thai boyfriends.

After Bangkok, the other main gay areas are Phuket and Pattaya. The scene is relaxed and least commercial in Phuket, which has a huge and colourful **gay pride festival** (www.phuketgaypridefestival.com). Bangkok and Pattaya hold gay festivals every November or December (visit www.bangkokpride.org and www.pattayagayfestival.com).

For an idea of what's going on in the GLBT scene, see these sites:

Dreaded Ned (www.dreadedned.com) Listings, forums, personal ads.
Gay Guide in Thailand (www.gayguideinthailand.com) What it says on the (six)-pack.
Lesbian Adventures Thailand (www.lathailand.com) Travel company owned and operated by women, for women.

Lesbian Guide to Bangkok (www.bangkoklesbian.com) Active site run by a faràng lesbian, with helpful forums and news on venues. Mainly in English.
Lesla (www.lesla.com) The most-established group for Thai and faràng lesbians, particularly younger women.
Long Yang Club (www.longyangclub.org/thailand) A 'multicultural social group for male-oriented men who want to meet outside the gay scene', with branches all over the world. The Thailand chapter hosts events in Bangkok.
Utopia (www.utopia-asia.com/thaibang.htm) Long-running and well-respected gay and lesbian website with lots of Bangkok information and member reviews.

HOLIDAYS

Chinese New Year (held in February or early March) and Songkran (mid-April) are the two holiday periods that most affect Thailand. For up to a week before and after these holidays public transport is packed full of people heading for their home towns to celebrate with family. This means all transport from Bangkok is full before the date but seats are available afterwards, when people are heading back to Bangkok and work. See p19 for more on individual festivals and holidays.

Public Holidays

Government offices and banks close down on the following public holidays. For the exact dates of lunar holidays, see the website of TAT (www.tourismthailand.org/travel-information).

New Year's Day	1 January
Magha Puja Day (mah·ká boo·chah)	February/March (lunar)
Chakri Day	6 April
Songkran	13-15 April

DIRECTORY

Labour Day	1 May
Coronation Day	5 May
Visakha Puja Day (wí·săh·kà boo·chah)	May/June (lunar)
Khao Phansa	July/August (lunar)
Queen's Birthday	12 August
King Chulalongkorn Day	23 October
Ok Phansa	October/November (lunar)
King's Birthday	5 December
Constitution Day	10 December
New Year's Eve	31 December

School Holidays

As well as the main public holidays, children and staff get a day off every 16 January for Teachers' Day. The main school vacations fall during March and April and the end of May; exact dates vary from school to school.

INSURANCE

With travel anywhere, the golden rule about travel insurance is 'get some!'. While Thailand is generally a safe country to travel in, sickness, accidents and theft are not uncommon. A travel-insurance policy covering theft, loss and medical problems is an integral part of travel. If you can't afford to pay for travel insurance, you certainly can't afford to cover the costs of theft or medical expenses if the worst happens. There is a wide variety of policies, all with varying prices, inclusions, terms and conditions. Your travel agent will be able to advise you or you can shop around on the Web.

Always check the small print to see if the policy covers potentially dangerous sporting activities, such as diving, rock climbing, trekking and riding motorbikes (they often don't). Premiums tend to vary depending on the level of cover for theft (where most claims come from). But the most important factor is health cover. We know of travellers who have died or had limbs amputated because they weren't insured (though not in Thailand), so even if it's just a policy that covers emergency health (these are relatively cheap) be sure to have one. For more information, see p420.

Worldwide cover for travellers is available online at www.lonelyplanet.com/travel_services.

INTERNET ACCESS

Thailand is pretty well wired. In all but the most remote locales you'll find at least one internet café, and this includes many islands off the Thai coast. Connections are dependent on the local phone lines and how many computers are networked to the same connection.

Internet cafés usually charge 1B to 2B per minute in towns and 3B to 4B per minute on the islands and more remote beaches. There are also internet stations in shopping malls, at most airports and in an ever-growing number of hotels and guesthouses, where connections range from free to more than 700B an hour. Because internet cafés are so ubiquitous, in this book we've mainly provided directions to where they congregate rather than to individual businesses.

On any shared computer be sure to be careful with your personal information. If you're banking online, always delete the cache (or 'cookies') and history on the Web browser when you finish so no-one can access your account.

Laptops are becoming almost as common as backpacks on Thai islands and beaches, and the price you need to pay for a room that has internet is steadily falling. In Bangkok, almost all midrange and top-end lodgings have wi-fi and/or hard-wired connections, and several budget places have joined the party.

If you can't find a hot spot and need to plug in, Thailand uses RJ11 phone jacks; and prepaid dial-up accounts are available from 7-Elevens and internet cafés. They come with a list of dial-up numbers for towns around the country, a user name and password, plus a number of free hours – a 20-hour card costs about 200B.

LEGAL MATTERS

In general Thai police don't hassle foreigners, especially tourists. The one major exception involves drugs, which are public enemy number one. With the outbreak of the second War on Drugs (see boxed text, p389) the Thai police have begun sweeping bars and clubs

---

ARE YOU OLD ENOUGH?

Thailand has legal minimum ages for many activities:

- Drinking – 18 years to buy alcohol (hello 7-Eleven!), or 21 to enter a bar
- Driving – 21 years (for car hire)
- Sexual consent – 18 years for heterosexual and gay sex
- Voting – 18 years

FINDING ADDRESSES

The Thai word thanŏn means road, street or avenue (it's shortened to 'Th' in this book). Hence Ratchadamnoen Rd or Ave is called Thanon Ratchadamnoen in Thai.

A soi is a small street or lane that runs off a larger street. An address referred to as 48/3-5 Soi 1, Th Sukhumvit will be located off Th Sukhumvit on Soi 1. The same address may be written as 48/3-5 Th Sukhumvit Soi 1, or even just 48/3-5 Sukhumvit 1.

Smaller than a soi is a dròrk (often spelt tràwk or trok) or alley.

Many street addresses show a string of numbers divided by slashes and dashes; for example, 48/3-5 Soi 1, Th Sukhumvit. The number before the slash is the original lot number; the numbers after the slash indicate buildings (or entrances) within that lot. These lot numbers are often useless, as they usually don't run sequentially. But don't worry, if you can find the main number (in this case 3-5), then you'll be fine.

In rural areas, along beaches and on most islands, addresses sometimes consist of a house number followed by a village number. For example, 34 Mŏo 7 would be house 34 in village 7 (mŏo, also spelt as muu, is short for 'mŏo bâhn, Thai for 'village'). Villagers almost never display this address anywhere on their houses, as it is really only used by postal workers and other officials. Places such as guesthouses do sometimes display such an address, though you're more likely to spot a sign with the name of the guesthouse before you see the address. Further complicating matters, street and town names usually have variant spellings as there is no standard convention for transliterating Thai into English.

If it gets too confusing just ask a local, showing or telling them the address you're after. As most Thais have grown up in a world devoid of maps, asking for directions on a map will often lead to confusion.

---

in search of offenders. If the music suddenly stops and men in brown shirts begin filing into the room, expect to be there until you've been searched and tested (usually a urine test) for drugs. Resistance is futile – unless you know someone powerful.

If you are arrested for any offence, the police will allow you to make a phone call – if you don't know what powerful person then your embassy or consulate in Thailand is probably the best place to start. Once arrested, the time you can be held without charge depends on the police officers and how much respect you show the arresting officers. Thai law does not presume an indicted detainee to be either 'guilty' or 'innocent' but rather a 'suspect' whose guilt or innocence will be decided in court. Trials are usually speedy and Thailand has plenty of private attorneys (preferable to the state-appointed counsels).

Tourist Police Hotline

If you get into any kind of trouble, immediately contact the Tourist Police, who specialise in dealing with foreigners. The 24-hour Tourist Police hotline is ☎ 1155. The Tourist Police don't have all the powers of the regular police, but they can help with translation or with contacting your embassy.

MAPS

Periplus Travel Maps publishes a reliable map of *Thailand* (1:2,000,000), plus more detailed maps of Bangkok, Phuket and Ko Samui. The *Phuket Southern Thailand* and *Ko Samui Southern Thailand* maps have useful insets for places along the Andaman and gulf coasts respectively. **ThinkNet** (www.thinknet .co.th) produces a high-quality city and country series, including the large-scale *Bilingual Map of Southern Thailand* (1:500,000), which is widely available for 120B.

Popular resort destinations, including Ko Samui, Phuket and Pattaya, are well served by free maps and for most travellers these will be all you'll need; they're usually available at airports and tourist offices.

Anyone planning to drive should buy the Roads Association of Thailand's large-format, bilingual road atlas called *Thailand Highway Map*.

MONEY

Most travellers rely on credit or debit cards to access cash in Bangkok, where ATMs are everywhere. The basic unit of Thai currency is the baht. There are 100 satang in one baht – though almost the only place you'll be able to spend them is in the ubiquitous 7-Elevens. Coins come in denominations of 25 satang, 50 satang, 1B, 5B and 10B. Paper currency comes in denominations of 20B (green), 50B (blue), 100B (red), 500B (purple) and 1000B (brown).

Cash machines and currency exchanges typically dispense funds in 1000B notes, which can be difficult for the average vendor or taxi driver to change. It is not advisable to pull out a big note to pay a small bar tab; sometimes the change returned doesn't agree with both parties. Break big bills at 7-Elevens or when paying for a room, so you have small notes for everyday purchases. See the inside cover of this book for exchange rates, or check the web or the *Bangkok Post* or the *Nation* newspapers.

ATMs

In most towns in Thailand you won't need a map to find an ATM – they're everywhere. Most bank ATMs accept major international credit cards and many will also cough up cash (Thai baht only) if your savings/current account from home has a card affiliated with the Cirrus or Plus networks. You can withdraw up to 20,000B at a time from most ATMs; home banks will charge a fee for every international transaction.

Credit Cards

International credit cards such as Visa and MasterCard (and bank debit cards backed by these companies) can be used to withdraw local currency from ATMs. You can also use credit cards to purchase currency over the counter at many foreign exchange booths; however, the commission can be astronomical, so ask first.

Credit cards and debit cards can also be used almost anywhere you'll spend enough to need one. The most commonly accepted cards are Visa and MasterCard, followed by Amex and JCB. Credit-card fraud is widespread, particularly in shops that use the old-fashioned card imprint system. See p390 for more on avoiding scams.

If your card is lost or stolen, contact the Tourist Police for a police report. To report a lost or stolen card, call the following telephone hotlines:

Amex (☎ 0 2273 5544)
MasterCard (☎ 001 800 11 887 0663)
Visa (☎ 001 800 441 3485)

Moneychangers

There is no black market for baht. Banks or legal moneychangers offer the best exchange rates. US dollars and euros are the most readily accepted currencies, followed by British pounds and Australian dollars. Travellers cheques get better exchange rates than cash, and large banknotes are often worth more than small bills. There are exchange facilities at many branches of Bangkok Bank, Krung Thai Bank, Siam City Bank, Siam Commercial Bank and Kasikorn Bank; look for the 'Exchange' signs. Standard banking hours are 8.30am to 3.30pm Monday to Friday, though they will often stay open until 4.30pm Fridays. Some banks in popular tourist areas maintain foreign exchange booths, which are usually open daily from around 10am until 8pm.

Many Thai banks refuse to exchange Malaysian ringgit, Indonesian rupiah, Nepali rupees, Cambodian riel, Lao kip, Vietnamese dong or Myanmar kyat – in other words, it's best to change your money at the border and bargain hard when you do it. If you need to buy or sell any of these currencies in Thailand the moneychangers along Th Charoen Krung and Th Silom in Bangkok are your best bet, though rates won't be great.

Money Transfers

International money-transfer companies such as **Western Union** (www.westernunion.com) and **Moneygram** (www.moneygram.com) have operations in Thailand. Western Union has offices worldwide where friends or family can transfer money to you instantly. Within Thailand, you can receive Western Union transfers at the Bank of Ayuthaya, Siam City Bank and Thailand Post offices. Moneygram offers similar services through branches of Siam Commercial Bank. The downside of these services is the cost, which is typically 5% to 10% of the value transferred.

Tipping

Tipping is uncommon in Thailand, except in big hotels and posh restaurants. Having said that, in tourist areas such as Bangkok and the islands and beaches of the south Thais are becoming increasingly familiar with tipping. Taxi drivers will automatically round the price up to the nearest 10B. For most places, however, tips remain appreciated rather than expected.

Travellers Cheques

All banks with foreign exchange facilities and private foreign exchange desks accept travellers cheques backed by Visa, MasterCard, Thomas Cook and American Express. Commonly accepted currencies of cheque include the euro; British pound; Swedish, Danish and Norwegian Kroner; the Swiss franc; and the US, Canadian, New Zealand and Australian dollar. In practice, US dollars, UK pounds and euros are most useful. Banks charge a standard commission for each travellers cheque cashed, so you can save on commissions by using large denomination cheques. Some banks partner with certain providers of travellers cheques in commission-free exchanges. Remember to keep the receipts for your cheques separate from your main finances, so you can have the cheques replaced if they are stolen.

PHOTOGRAPHY & VIDEO

Thailand is a photographer's dream and there are myriad opportunities for still and video photography. The usual rules apply: ask permission before photographing or filming local people, particularly at religious sites. Thai Buddhists may be flattered to have their portraits taken, but this is less true with Thai Muslims. Either way, engaging your potential subject in even the briefest conversation before asking them, with a smile, will greatly improve your chances of an affirmative answer – it's also the polite thing to do. Never agree or promise to send a photo to your subject if you won't actually do that.

Thailand is humid (understatement alert!), so pack some silica gel with your lenses and camera to keep the mould away. A polarising filter is useful for cutting down tropical glare, particularly when taking photos around water and the shimmering gold at wát. In these conditions, bracketing (ie taking extra shots that are one stop overexposed and one stop underexposed) is also a good idea.

Thais have eagerly embraced digital photography and all but the common 100, 200 and 400ASA print film is hard to find outside of Bangkok. On the plus side, photo labs can print your digi shots fast and cheap, and most internet cafés can burn your memories onto CDs and/or DVDs. Camera batteries and Mini-DV tapes are widely available in Bangkok and tourist areas.

POST

Thailand Post (☎ call centre 1545; www.thailandpost.com) runs a reliable and highly efficient postal service and staff at Thai post offices almost always speak some English. Aside from Bangkok's main post office (p68), most post offices open from 8.30am to 4.30pm Monday to Friday and 9am to noon on Saturday; some open Sunday mornings, too. Some larger offices often have phone offices and offer poste restante, and most offer parcel services, with cardboard boxes for sale and tape and string provided free. Don't send valuables or money through the mail.

For courier packages, Thai Post EMS (available at post offices) is a good option and usually less than half the price of private courier companies. **DHL** (www.dhl.co.th) and **Fedex** (www.fedex.com/th) have offices in Bangkok and the major tourist centres.

Postal Rates

The rates for internal and international postage are very reasonable. Postcards to anywhere in the world cost 12B or 15B, depending on size. Airmail letters weighing 10g cost 12B to 20B to Western countries. Aerograms cost 15B regardless of the destination. Letters sent by registered mail cost 25B in addition to regular airmail postage.

By airmail, a parcel weighing one/two/five kilograms will cost about 880/1230/2280B to Europe and take about two weeks. Sea mail takes about three months to Europe or the US and is about 60% cheaper than airmail. Surface-air-lifted mail (by air and sea) takes about one month to most places and costs about double the sea mail rate. Rates vary slightly by country; ask to see the post office's magic folder for every variable you can imagine.

You can insure a package's contents for 7B per US$20 of the goods' value.

Receiving Mail

You can receive mail in Thailand through the poste-restante service at most post offices, including the main post office in Bangkok: Your Name (surname first), Poste Restante, General Post Office, Charoen Krung Rd, Bangrak, Bangkok, 10501.

SHOPPING

Thailand is a shopper's paradise and many travellers come home with their bags bulging with wooden carvings, sarongs, jewellery and clothes. Bangkok has the best selection of goods, from knock-offs to the real McCoy; see p106.

Surely you know a friend who had a fabulous outfit made in Thailand. While there are more tailors than public garbage cans in Thailand, you're better off having something made in Bangkok where some tailor shops rely on repeat business from the diplomatic corps and expat community instead of tourist shops who don't depend on satisfied customers. Do some research before you leave home about fabric quality and styles so that you're an educated shopper.

Genuine brand-name clothes are also a good buy for some. Bangkok has the most fashion-conscious stores and foreign sizes are available. Bangkok's high-end malls stock the real deal, while markets and the Mahboonkrong (MBK) shopping centre have the not-so-real deal.

Dive gear is super-cheap in southern Thailand (if they have your size), and most dive centres have shops where you can buy scuba gear and prescription masks.

Almost all visitors to Thailand bring home some handicrafts. Silver jewellery is extremely popular and portable, but unless you own a shop, do not get talked into buying bulk jewellery to sell back home. Gemstones are a particularly hazardous buy (see boxed text, p390). As a general rule, anything made from shells or endangered animals should be avoided. Lots of shops sell ivory, tortoiseshell and seashells poached from marine national parks.

Antiques and convincing reproductions of antiques are widely available, but note that genuine antiques and Buddha images may not be taken out of the kingdom without a permit – see p388.

Basketware is light to carry and is available all over the south, as is traditional Thai clothing, such as Thai fishermen's pants, sarongs and the like. Other popular handicrafts include hill tribe jewellery, wooden chopsticks (sold only to the tourists), Thai axe pillows, Thai and Lao silk, lacquerware, stainless steel Thai cutlery, wooden bowls and vases, and woodcarvings. The cheapest markets are those provincial markets off the tourist trail, such as in Trang. If you don't want to carry stuff around, most of these items can be obtained more cheaply in Bangkok before your flight home.

All over Thailand you'll find OTOP outlets. OTOP is the sanctioned local crafts centre.

SOLO TRAVELLERS

Thailand is one of the easiest countries in the world for solo travellers. Even the most timid traveller should be able to meet people in the guesthouses and beach-bars of southern Thailand, though resorts heavy with couples or sex workers can get lonely. In Bangkok, Th Khao San is the world's greatest concentration of travellers, though oddly it can be such a fashion show that it's not as easy to meet people here as elsewhere; hanging around your guesthouse is the best idea. Wherever you meet your fellow wanderers, there's a pretty good chance you'll meet them again on

---

WHAT A BARGAIN!

As a general rule, if you have to ask the price then you can bargain. As a general rule; markets are bargaining-friendly and shopping centres are bargaining-free. If you don't like to bargain, then shop at the shopping centres. On the other hand, for souvenir-type products, suits, jewellery and unmetered taxis, bargaining is essential.

Bargaining can be tough if you're not used to it, so here are a couple of pointers. First, when you find something you like be sure not to show too much interest. Vendors can smell desperation a mile away. Second, don't buy the first one you see; subtly check out a few alternatives to get an idea of the price and quality. With this knowledge, casually enquire as to the price and then make a counter-offer (usually half or less), thus beginning the bargaining process. The vendor will often beseech you to make a better offer: 'This is my first sale for the day' or 'I must feed my six children'. However, having looked at the competition you know the fair price so only edge up slowly. As you volley numbers back and forth remember to keep it good-natured; your smile is your best weapon and getting angry or upset while bargaining causes everyone to lose face.

Remember that bargaining is not a life and death battle. A good bargain is when *both* parties are happy and doesn't necessarily require you to screw every last baht from the vendor. If you paid more than your travelling companion, don't worry. As long as you're happy, it was a good deal. Remember too that no-one is forcing you to buy anything. Your money will stay in your pocket until you decide to take it out.

the well-defined tourist circuit of Thailand's islands and beaches.

Thais might be a little bewildered that you would want to go out and about without friends, a reflection of their social nature. But many are impressed by Westerners', especially solo women's, courage to venture into the unknown. For more on women travellers, see p403.

TELEPHONE

The Thai telephone system is efficient enough that you should be able to direct-dial most major centres without trouble. Thailand's country code is ☎ 66.

Inside Thailand you must dial the area code no matter where you are. In effect, that means all numbers are nine digits; in Bangkok they begin with 02 then a seven-digit number. The only time you drop the initial 0 is when you're calling from outside Thailand. Calling the provinces will usually involve a three-digit code beginning with 0, then a six-digit number. Mobile phone numbers all have 10 digits, beginning with 08.

To direct-dial an international number first dial ☎ 001 or, if available, ☎ 007, ☎ 008 or ☎ 009, which are significantly cheaper. For operator-assisted international calls, dial ☎ 100. For free local directory assistance in English call ☎ 1133. Tell the operator the name of the province you are trying to reach, before giving the name of the person or business. If the line goes quiet be patient, they're finding an English-speaker.

When calling long-distance or to mobile phones within Thailand from private phones or payphones (not mobiles), call ☎ 1234 before the number to reduce per-minute costs to less than 2B.

International Calls

The cheapest way to call internationally is via the internet, and many internet cafés and travel agents are set up for phone calls. Some have Skype loaded and (assuming there's a working headset) you can use that for just the regular per-hour internet fee. Others might have their own VoIP (Voice over Internet Protocol) service at cheap international rates. Usually such a call is made at a desk beside a clerk, so if you need privacy you might want to get a phone card and a room. Getting someone at home to call back (Skype to Thailand costs US6c a minute calling Bangkok land lines, and 11c for land lines outside Bangkok and mobiles) is often a good idea.

Two Home Country Direct services exist, providing an easy connection to international operators in countries around the world. The original is provided by the Communications Authority of Thailand (CAT) and is available from dedicated phones in CAT offices or other government phone offices, or by dialling ☎ 001 999 followed by the appropriate number from any private land line or mobile phone (most hotel phones won't work). Your home phone service operator should have the appropriate number, though note that this service is often more expensive than calling direct from a mobile. Another agency run by the government, Telecom of Thailand (TOT), runs a similar but cheaper service from TOT offices.

Mobile Phones

Travelling with a mobile (cell) phone has largely eclipsed older forms of telephone communication. Thailand's network is well developed and service plans are flexible. If you have a GSM 900MHz or GSM 1800MHz phone (or a dual-/tri-/quad-band phone) it should roam in Thailand, provided you have activated international roaming on your phone. If you have endless cash, or you only want to send text messages, you might be happy to do that. Otherwise, think about buying a local SIM card.

Buying a prepaid SIM is as easy as finding the nearest 7-Eleven store. The market is super-competitive and deals vary so check websites first, but expect to get a SIM, with 100 or 300 minutes talk time, for between 99B and 300B. Per-minute rates start at less than 50 satang. Recharge cards are sold at the same stores. Calling internationally, the network will have a promotional code (eg 009 instead of 001) that affords big discounts on the standard international rates, though you might have to go into a phone company office to get the full list of rates. The three main networks are:

AIS (www.one-2-call.com) Wide coverage across Thailand; One-2-Call is the prepaid option.

DTAC (www.dtac.co.th) Lots of options, including Happy (www.happy.co.th) for prepaid SIM.

True Move (www.truemove.com) Offers a Welcome SIM package for visitors, with domestic calls for 2B a minute and cheap international rates. Network not as good outside Bangkok.

DIRECTORY

If your phone is locked, head down to Mahboonkrong (MBK) shopping centre (p107) to get it unlocked, or to shop for a new or cheap used phone (they start at less than 2000B). If you are using your home account remember to carry the emergency number for your phone company, in case your phone is stolen.

Payphones & Phone Cards

There are three types of public payphone. For international calls, you have a choice of yellow (for international and domestic Lenso calling cards), blue (operated by CAT for local coin calls) and green (for TOT local calls or regional calls to Malaysia, Myanmar, Cambodia and Laos at semi-local rates). Don't rely on public payphones being in working order, even in Bangkok.

Local calls from coin-operated blue phones cost 1B for the first three minutes, then 1B per additional minute; calls to mobile phones cost more.

Yellow public phones use Lenso phone cards, which come in denominations of 250B and 500B and can be purchased in 7-Eleven stores. CAT offers the Thaicard, which involves dialling an access number and then a passcode. You can use this card from any CAT phone (including those at provincial post offices) and most private phones, and calls are priced at standard ISD rates. Cards come in 300B, 500B, 1000B and 3000B denominations. Various private companies also offer international calling cards, often undercutting CAT's rates.

CAT also offers the PhoneNet card in denominations of 300B, 500B and 1000B. It allows you to call overseas via VoIP for a 40% to 86% saving over regular rates. The difference with PhoneNet is that you can call from any phone; land line, your mobile, payphones etc. Quality is good and rates represent excellent value. Cards are available from any CAT office or online at www.thaitelephone.com, from which you get the necessary codes and numbers immediately. See http://thaitelephone.com/EN/RateTable/for rates.

Some green TOT payphones take dedicated phone cards in units of 50B, 100B, 200B and 500B, available from 7-Eleven stores.

TIME

Thailand is seven hours ahead of GMT/UTC. Thus, noon in Bangkok is 9pm the previous day in Los Angeles, midnight the same day in New York, 5am in London, 6am in Paris, 1pm in Perth, and 3pm in Sydney and Melbourne. Thailand does not use daylight saving time. See also the World Time Zones map, p462.

The official year in Thailand is reckoned from the Western calendar year 543 BC, the beginning of the Buddhist Era, so that AD 2009 is 2552 BE, AD 2010 is 2553 BE etc. All dates in this book refer to the Western calendar.

TOILETS

Public toilets can be found at bus and train stations, in shopping malls and in fast-food restaurants. There is often an entrance charge of between 1B and 3B, and sometimes there are machines dispensing tissue paper (don't flush the paper, put it in the bin). In tourist areas, Western-style thrones are ubiquitous, but at cheaper guesthouses and at bus and train stations you can expect to squat. In the vast majority of squat toilets you'll need to BYO paper (widely available in convenience stores) or embrace another option. The most obvious of these is to go local and use the hose or jug and tap in your stall, which will result in you getting wet until you've acquired the skills. If you must have paper and don't have a stash, you could always use this page – though we won't vouch for its softness.

TOURIST INFORMATION

Tourism contributes a huge amount to the Thai economy so it's little surprise that the government-run **Tourism Authority of Thailand** (TAT; ☎ tourist information line 1672, ☺ 8am-8pm; www .tourismthailand.org) is highly organised and has offices around the country and 20 offices overseas; for the full list see www.tourismthailand .org/tat-oversea-office. TAT is also the main regulatory body for tourism in Thailand, and issues licences to businesses that pass its exacting standards. It produces a huge range of pamphlets and booklets, which are available at the offices listed in the relevant chapters of this book. TAT also has handy information counters in the international and domestic terminals of Suvarnabhumi International Airport.

Bangkok Metropolitan Administration runs the excellent **Bangkok Tourist Bureau** (☎ 0 2225 7612-4; www.bangkoktourist.com), which covers Bangkok and its environs in detail. Other private information organisations can be found in many provincial centres – see the regional chapters for details.

TOURS

Even if you're short on time, most of southern Thailand can be visited independently. Once you have reached your destination, there are plenty of local tour operators who will shuttle you to secluded beaches, on snorkelling tours, to visit waterfalls, ride elephants and whatever else you can imagine, all for less than you'd pay for an organised tour.

Most travellers do sign up for a jungle tour of Khao Sok National Park (p244), though, as reaching it via public transport is very time-consuming and touring is enhanced with a guide. On-the-ground recommendations for Khao Sok tour guides will be more accurate than a print endorsement. Elsewhere, the following tour operators are worth an investigation:

Barefoot Traveller (www.barefoot-traveller.com) Beaches and diving trips, including live-aboards.

Intrepid Travel (www.intrepidtravel.com) Big adventure tour company offering small, down-to-earth trips.

JYSK Rejsebureau (www.jysk-rejsebureau.dk) Low-budget trips with strong backpacker clientele; Ko Chang Archipelago by boat a highlight.

Paddle Asia (www.paddleasia.com) Kayaking tours to various southern Thailand destinations. Good choice.

Spice Roads (www.spiceroads.com) Cycling trips to southern Thailand and elsewhere.

TRAVELLERS WITH DISABILITIES

Travelling in Thailand can be challenging for the disabled. The government makes few infrastructure provisions and footpaths are often cracked and uneven, making them difficult to manoeuvre if you're in a wheelchair. But Thais are used to doing things for themselves in these matters and most people will lend a hand without fear or embarrassment.

Large international hotel chains usually have handicapped access to their properties, and home-grown luxury hotels use their high employee-to-guest ratios to help accommodate the mobility impaired. Elsewhere, you are pretty much left to your own resources.

Consider hiring a private car and driver for transport. Disabled travellers have reported that túk-túk can carry two people and a wheelchair. Many activities in Thailand are open to the disabled, including snorkelling trips and elephant riding.

For a developing country without a sophisticated social safety net, Thailand is pretty creative at incorporating the disabled into society. The disabled in poor families typically rely on family members for mobility as wheelchairs and other aides are prohibitively expensive. The blind are considered auspicious lottery ticket sellers and regarded as adept at traditional massage because their sense of touch is more refined than the sighted. In Bangkok, an association of deaf vendors sells souvenirs in tourist areas.

However, it's not all positive. Many disabled people without family support migrate to Bangkok for marginal jobs as itinerant troubadours or beggars. Some of these beggars might be pocketing whatever meagre coinage comes their way, but many others – particularly Cambodian land-mine and burn victims – are little more than slaves to a callous begging mafia.

Organisations

Help & Care Travel Company Ltd (☎ 0 2720 5395; www.wheelchairtours.com) specialises in tours of Thailand for wheelchair users, the aged and deaf travellers using modified vehicles and trained guides. *Exotic Destinations for Wheelchair Travelers* by Ed Hansen and Bruce Gordon contains a useful chapter on Thailand. Other books of value include Rough Guides' *Able to Travel: True Stories by and for People with Disabilities*.

Other companies and resources worth checking out for travel to Thailand include:

Access-Able Travel Source (www.access-able.com)

Access Foundation (www.accessibility.com.au)

Accessible Journeys (www.disabilitytravel.com)

Asia Pacific Development Centre on Disability (www.apcdproject.org)

Routes International (www.routesinternational.com)

Society for Accessible Travel & Hospitality (www.sath.org)

Travelability Ltd (www.accessibletravel.co.uk)

Worldwide Dive & Sail (www.worldwidediveand sail.com)

VISAS

Thailand has been much stricter in enforcing its visa laws since the coup d'état of 2006, but the citizens of 42 countries, including most Western European countries, Australia, Canada, Hong Kong, Japan, New Zealand, Singapore and USA, can still enter Thailand without a visa and stay for up to 30 days. Citizens of Brazil, Republic of Korea and Peru may enter without a visa for 90 days. For a list of eligible countries and other visa matters, see the Royal Thai Ministry of Foreign Affairs website www.mfa.go.th/web/12.php.

The crackdown, apparently designed to get rid of illegal workers and 'bad influences' such as sex tourists, has seen the once-ignored requirement of an onward ticket being more strictly enforced, usually by airline staff in the departing city. We've heard of several people who have been forced to buy an onward ticket (which they have later refunded, for a fee). One possible way around this is to already have a visa to your next country. It should go without saying that the better you are dressed when you check in, the less likely you are to be hassled.

If you're planning to stay longer than 30 days it's best to get a 60-day tourist visa (about US$35, depending on the country) before you arrive. This can then be extended by 30 days at any visa office in the country; see right.

Other Visas

Thai embassies and consulates issue a variety of other visas for people on business, students or those with employment in Thailand. The non-immigrant visa comes in several classifications (eg non-immigrant B for people planning to do business or work) and is good for 90 days. If you plan to apply for a Thai work permit and stay in the kingdom longer-term, you'll need to possess a non-immigrant visa first before you can start the process of getting the permit. Getting a non-immigrant visa with the intention of working in Thailand can be difficult and involves a tedious amount of paperwork. If you get one, usually with the support of an employer, you'll likely end up at the **One-Stop Service Centre** (Map pp70-1; ☎ 0 2937 1155; 16th fl, Rasa Tower, 555 Th Phahonyothin, Bangkok) for several hours of paper pushing – get there early! For more information on all things visa see the **Ministry of Foreign Affairs** (www.mfa.go.th/web/12 .php) and **Bureau of Immigration** (www.immigration .go.th) websites; if you still have questions, seek help on www.thaivisa.com.

Citizens from a list of 14 nations, including the People's Republic of China, Taiwan and several countries in Central and South Asia, can obtain a 15-day transit visa (800B). You might be required to show you have 10,000B per person or 20,000B per family to obtain this visa.

Visa Extensions & Visa Runs

Without a long-term visa you cannot stay in Thailand for more than 90 days out of 180, and there must be a 90-day gap before you return. Assuming you're within these limits, extensions are pretty straightforward. All extensions cost 1900B and you'll need the usual mug shots and photocopies of face and visa pages from your passport. It pays to forgo the flip-flops and board shorts and dress up a little. In Bangkok, the **Immigration Bureau** (Map pp72-3; ☎ 0 2287 3101; Soi Suan Phlu, Th Sathon Tai) does the deed. Elsewhere any immigration office will do; all border provinces have at least one, usually in the provincial capital.

The 60-day tourist visa can be extended by up to 30 days at the discretion of Thai immigration authorities. The 30-day, no-visa stay (the stamp you get on arrival at the airport) can be extended for a maximum of seven days. The 15-day transit visa can be extended for seven days only if you hold a passport from a country that has no Thai embassy.

The 1900B fee is pretty steep, so it's well worth planning your itinerary so you can leave the country on a 'visa run' when your visa expires and return immediately on a fresh, free 30-day visa (if you are eligible). Handy borders are Hat Lek (see boxed text, p162) to Cambodia, Victoria Point (see boxed text, p268) to Myanmar, and via Satun (p371) to Malaysia. The visa run has been a well-used tool of travellers (and in the past, residents) for years, and several companies exist just to cater to this market. Of course, the 90 days within 180 rule means it's not the endless ticket to life in Thailand it used to be.

If you overstay your visa the usual penalty is a fine of 500B for each extra day, with a 20,000B limit (after that, more trouble awaits). Fines can be paid at international airports and border crossings, or at an Immigration Bureau office in advance. Children under 14 travelling with a parent do not have to pay the penalty.

VOLUNTEERING

Volunteering seems to be all the rage at the moment and Thailand is a favourite destination. Working in some capacity with disadvantaged people can make a difference and be rewarding both to you and them. But it's not all sweetness and light, and it's important to understand what you're getting yourself into. Unless you know the country, speak the language and have the skills needed in a particular field (computing, health and teaching, for example), what you can offer in a short period will largely be limited to manual labour – a commodity not in short supply in Thailand. Having said that, if you can match your skills to a project that needs them, this can be a great way to spend time in Thailand.

There are two main forms of volunteering. For those interested in a long-term commitment, typically two or three years, there are a few long-established organisations that will help you learn the language, place you in a position that will, hopefully, be appropriate to your skills, and pay you (just barely). Such organisations include:

Australian Volunteers International (www.australian volunteers.com)

US Peace Corps (www.peacecorps.gov)

Voluntary Service Overseas (VSO Canada; www.vso canada.org)

VSO UK (www.vso.org.uk)

Volunteer Service Abroad (VSO NZ; www.vsa.org.nz)

The more popular form of volunteering, sometimes called 'voluntourism', is something you actually pay to do. This is a fast-growing market, and a quick web search for 'Thailand volunteering' will turn up pages of companies offering to place you in a project in return for your hard-earned. With these companies you can be a volunteer for as little as a single week up to six months or longer. Fees vary, but start at about €500 for four weeks. The projects can be very good, ongoing affairs with a solid chance of success. But some are not. The list below is a starting point and should not be read as a recommendation. Do your own research and check out all the options before making a decision.

For details on volunteering for environmental groups, see p64.

Locally focused organisations include **Volunthai** (www.volunthai.com) and **Thai Experience** (www.thai-experience.org). Other general volunteering sites worth looking at are **Global Volunteer Network** (www.volunteer.org.nz), **Idealist** (www.idealist .org) and **Volunteer Abroad** (www.volunteerabroad.com), which lists available positions with a variety of companies.

Multicountry organisations that sell volunteering trips include:

Cross Cultural Solutions (www.crossculturalsolutions.org)

Cultural Embrace (www.culturalembrace.com)

Global Crossroad (www.globalcrossroad.com)

Global Service Corps (www.globalservicecorps.org)

Institute for Field Research Expeditions (www .ifrevolunteers.org)

Open Mind Projects (www.openmindprojects.org)

Starfish Ventures (www.starfishventures.co.uk)

Transitions Abroad (www.transitionsabroad.com)

Travel to Teach (www.travel-to-teach.org)

Youth International (www.youthinternational.org)

WOMEN TRAVELLERS

Women travellers generally face few problems in Thailand, a fact that has made Thailand Asia's most popular destination for women independent travellers. But like anywhere, there are cultural differences that need to be respected, both to keep you safe and because it's the right thing to do.

In the provincial towns, it is advisable to dress conservatively, covering shoulders, knees and belly buttons. Outside Bangkok, most Thai women cover up in the sun to avoid unnecessary exposure since white skin is considered more beautiful. That Westerners believe the opposite is an endless source of amusement and confusion.

This isn't as much of an issue in Bangkok or in beach resorts where dress codes are looser. However, topless sunbathing is frowned upon by Thais (except the men who stare hungrily). In recent years such men have attacked and killed more than one foreign woman who has been sunbathing topless on a remote beach. Going topless is actually banned under the government guidelines for many national parks.

Codes of conduct are more conservative in the Muslim south, where local women cover their heads and bodies. You should also refrain from public displays of affection with the opposite sex.

Attacks and rapes are less common in Thailand than in many Western countries, but incidents do occur, especially when an attacker observes a vulnerable target, a drunk or solo woman. Perhaps you went to the bar to find someone, but if you do return alone, be sure to have your wits about you. Full moon parties at Ko Pha-Ngan are another trouble hot spot and we have heard from several women who were sexually assaulted during these parties. Avoid taking dodgy gypsy cabs or accepting rides from strangers late at night – common sense stuff that might escape your notice in a new environment filled with hospitable people. And remember there is safety in numbers – if you're going to collapse, do it near some friends. In cases of rape or other assault, the Thai police will investigate and prosecute the crime, but offer little in the way of counselling. If you need to talk with someone, try **Community Services of Bangkok** (Map p82; ☎ 0 2258 4998; 15 Soi 33, Th Sukhumvit), which offers a range of counselling services to foreign residents and newcomers to Thailand.

While Bangkok might be a men's paradise, foreign women are finding their own Romeos on Thai beaches. Women who aren't interested in romantic encounters should not presume that Thai men have equally platonic motives. Often, Thai men ignore their own culture's strictures when it comes to dealing with a foreign woman. There's usually no threat, rather misconceptions – the same sort of stuff that happens back home.

There aren't a lot of places in Thailand that foreign women will feel threatened. But if your gut tells you no, then heed it and move on. The hotels around the lower end of Th Sukhumvit in Bangkok, or on Patong Beach in Phuket, are the centres of Bangkok's sex tourism and are filled with what can be construed as demeaning attitudes towards women. Sex tourists can act nervously when a reminder from home encroaches on their naughty playground.

Sanitary napkins (pâh à·nah·mai) are widely available at minimarts and supermarkets throughout Thailand. Thai women generally don't use tampons (taam·porn) but minimarts and pharmacies in tourist areas usually stock a few local and imported brands. Bring your own supplies if you're heading to any of the more remote islands.

WORK

Thailand's steady economic growth has provided a variety of work opportunities for foreigners, but obtaining permission to work in Thailand is harder than you might expect. Thailand is increasingly refusing to issue work permits if a Thai citizen can be found for the job (as is the norm in most Western nations). One prominent exception is English teaching.

All work, whether paid or voluntary, officially requires a Thai work permit. Work permits must be obtained through an employer, who can apply before you enter Thailand, but the permit itself is not issued until you physically enter Thailand on a valid non-immigrant visa. For information about work permits, contact any Thai embassy abroad or check the **Ministry of Foreign Affairs** (www.mfa.go.th/web/12.php) website. No joy? Seek solace and advice on the message boards of www.thaivisa.com.

For information on doing business in Thailand, see the Thai Board of Investment website www.boi.go.th/english/.

Scuba Diving

PADI instructors and qualified dive masters often find work at major dive resorts, such as Ko Tao, Phuket, Ko Phi-Phi, Hat Khao Lak, Ao Nang and, increasingly, Ko Chang. A second language apart from English is an advantage. Some schools offer subsidised training to dive-master level, if you'll work for them when you complete your training. Technically, you must have a work permit for all these jobs.

Teaching English

Many foreigners come to Thailand to teach English, but generally you need academic credentials, such as a TEFL (Teachers of English as a Foreign Language) certificate, to get the decent jobs. There may also be opportunities for private tutoring in the larger cities. Private language academies across Thailand sometimes hire nonqualified teachers by the hour. A work permit is almost always required.

A website maintained by a Bangkok-based English teacher, www.ajarn.com, has tips on finding jobs and pretty much everything else you need to know about getting into the teaching game in Thailand. If you're more dedicated (or desperate) the **Yellow Pages** (www.yellow.co.th/Bangkok) has contact details for hundreds of schools, universities and also language schools.

Transport

CONTENTS

GETTING THERE & AWAY

ENTERING THE COUNTRY

Entry procedures for Thailand, by air or by land, are straightforward. You'll have to show your passport, with at least six months validity remaining, and any visa you may have obtained beforehand. You'll also need to present completed arrival and departure cards. These are usually distributed on the incoming flight or, if arriving by land, can be picked up at the immigration counter. You do not have to fill in a customs form on arrival unless you have imported goods to declare. In that case you can get the proper form from Thai customs officials at the point of entry (look for the white suits).

An immigration crackdown has seen some airlines refuse to allow passengers to board flights to Thailand unless they have an onward ticket; see p401 for details on this and other visa requirements.

AIR

Bangkok is a major regional air hub and Thailand is well served by airlines from Europe, Australia, North America, the Middle East and pretty much every major airport in Asia. There is a 700B departure tax on all international flights, which is now included in the ticket price.

Airports & Airlines

Most international flights arrive in Bangkok and have connecting domestic services to Phuket, Krabi, Ko Samui, Hat Yai and other southern towns. Phuket and Ko Samui both receive some international flights from elsewhere in Asia and, in Phuket, charter flights from Europe. For details on Suvarnabhumi International Airport in Bangkok and transport into the city, see p109.

Thailand's national carrier is **Thai Airways International** (THAI; www.thaiair.com), which also operates a number of domestic air routes. Some of the other airlines flying to Bangkok at the time of writing are listed below, and the four airlines that fly Thai domestic routes, including those linking Bangkok to the south, are listed with their destinations on p409. Speak to a travel agent or search online for the latest information or take a look at the Suvarnabhumi airport Wikipedia page, which has a fairly up-to-date and complete list. Details here include Bangkok phone numbers.

Air Asia (code AK; ☎ 0 2515 9999; www.airasia.com; hub Kuala Lumpur)

Air Canada (code AC; ☎ 0 2670 0400; www.aircanada.ca; hub Toronto)

Air France (code AF; ☎ 0 2635 1191; www.airfrance .com; hub Charles de Gaulle airport, Paris)

Air India (code AI; ☎ 0 2653 2288; www.airindia.com; hub New Delhi/Mumbai)

Air New Zealand (code NZ; ☎ 0 2235 8280; www.air newzealand.com; hub Auckland)

Bangkok Airways (code PG; ☎ 1771 or 0 2265 5555; www.bangkokair.com, www.bangkokair.com; hub Bangkok)

Bangladesh Biman Airlines (code BG; ☎ 0 2233 3640; www.bimanair.com; hub Dhaka)

British Airways (code BA; ☎ 0 2236 2800; www.ba .com; hub Heathrow Airport, London)

Cathay Pacific Airways (code CX; ☎ 0 2263 0606; www.cathaypacific.com; hub Hong Kong)

China Airlines (code CI; ☎ 0 2250 9898; www.china -airlines.com; hub Taipei)

China Southern Airlines (code CZ; ☎ 0 2677 7388; www.flychinasouthern.com; hub Guangzhou)

Dragonair (code KA; ☎ 0 2263 0606, in Phuket 1 800 700 707; www.dragonair.com; hub Hong Kong)

Emirates (code EK; ☎ 0 2664 1040; www.emirates.com; hub Dubai)

EVA Airways (code BR; ☎ 0 2269 6300; www.evaair .com; hub Taipei)

Finnair (code AY; ☎ 0 2634 0238; www.finnair.com; hub Helsinki)

Garuda Indonesia (code GA; ☎ 0 2679 7371-2; www.garuda-indonesia.com; hub Jakarta)

Indian Airlines (code IC; ☎ 0 2231 0555; www.indianairlines.in; hub New Delhi/Mumbai)

Japan Airlines (code JL; ☎ 0 2649 9500; www .jal.co.jp/en/; hub Narita Airport, Tokyo)

Jetstar (code 3K; ☎ 0 2267 5125; www.jetstar.com; hub Singapore)

KLM Royal Dutch Airlines (code KL; ☎ 0 2635 2400; www.klm.com; hub Amsterdam)

Korean Airlines (code KE; ☎ 0 2635 0465; www.korean air.com; hub Seoul)

Lao Airlines (code QV; ☎ 0 2664 0661; www.laoairlines .com; hub Vientiane)

Lufthansa Airlines (code LH; ☎ 0 2264 2400; www.lufthansa.com; hub Frankfurt)

Philippine Airlines (code PR; ☎ 0 2633 5713/4; www.philippineairlines.com; hub Manila)

Malaysia Airlines (code MH; ☎ 0 2263 0565; www.malaysiaairlines.com; hub Kuala Lumpur)

Qantas (code QF; ☎ 0 2627 1701; www.qantas.com.au; hub Sydney)

Scandinavian Airlines System (SAS; code SK; ☎ 0 2645 8200; www.scandinavianairlines.net; hub Copenhagen)

Siem Reap Airways International (code FT; ☎ 1771 or 0 2265 5555; www.siemreapairways.com; hub Siem Reap)

Singapore Airlines (code SQ; ☎ 0 2353 6000; www.singaporeair.com; hub Singapore)

Sri Lankan Airlines (code UL; ☎ 0 2236 8450; www.srilankan.lk; hub Colombo)

Swiss (code LX; ☎ 0 2204 7744; www.swiss.com; hub Geneva)

Thai Airways International (THAI; code TG; ☎ 0 2232 8000; www.thaiair.com; hub Bangkok)

Tiger Airways (code TR; ☎ 0 2351 8333; www.tigerair ways.com; hub Singapore)

United Airlines (code UA; ☎ 0 2253 0558; www.united airlines.co.th; hubs San Francisco/Washington-Dulles)

Vietnam Airlines (code VN; ☎ 0 2655 4137/40; www.vietnamairlines.com; hub Ho Chi Minh City)

Tickets

Tickets can be purchased cheaply on the internet through booking and airline websites. Online ticket sales work well if you are doing a simple one-way or return trip on specified dates. However, online fare generators are no substitute for a travel agent who knows the special deals, has strategies for avoiding layovers, and can offer advice on everything from picking the airline with great vegetarian food to the best travel insurance to bundle with your ticket.

When you're looking for tickets, it's worth remembering that the more circuitous the route, the cheaper it will probably be. For example, if you spend 24 hours flying from Europe to Bangkok via Dhaka in Bangladesh, you'll almost certainly pay less than a direct flight with THAI or your national carrier. However, it's also worth remembering that your carbon footprint becomes bigger every time you take off and land; see opposite for more on climate change.

In Thailand, domestic routes are increasingly booked online, with budget airlines including Air Asia and Nok Air (p409) dealing almost exclusively with online and phone bookings. Travel agents can book these flights for you, but they will just make an online booking and charge you 50B for it. Most international flights are booked through an agent. Most firms are honest and solvent, but there are some fly-by-night outfits around, particularly in the Th Khao San area. Paying by credit card generally offers protection, as most card issuers provide refunds if you can prove you didn't get what you paid for. Agents who accept only cash should hand over the tickets straight away and not tell you to 'come back tomorrow'. After you've made a booking or paid your deposit, call the airline and confirm that the booking was made.

Booking flights in and out of Bangkok during the high season (December to March) can be difficult and expensive. For air travel during these months you should make your bookings as far in advance as possible. Some airlines require you to reconfirm return or ongoing tickets.

TRANSPORT

TRANSPORT

CLIMATE CHANGE & TRAVEL

Climate change is a serious threat to the ecosystems that humans rely upon, and air travel is the fastest-growing contributor to the problem. Lonely Planet regards travel, overall, as a global benefit, but believes we all have a responsibility to limit our personal impact on global warming.

Flying & Climate Change

Pretty much every form of motorised travel generates CO_2 (the main cause of human-induced climate change) but planes are far and away the worst offenders, not just because of the sheer distances they allow us to travel, but because they release greenhouse gases high into the atmosphere. The statistics are frightening: two people taking a return flight between Europe and the US will contribute as much to climate change as an average household's gas and electricity consumption over a whole year.

Carbon Offset Schemes

Climatecare.org and other websites use 'carbon calculators' that allow travellers to offset the level of greenhouse gases they are responsible for with financial contributions to sustainable travel schemes that reduce global warming, including projects in India, Honduras, Kazakhstan and Uganda.

Lonely Planet, together with Rough Guides and other concerned partners in the travel industry, supports the carbon offset scheme run by climatecare.org. Lonely Planet offsets all of its staff and author travel. For more information, check out our website: www.lonelyplanet.com.

Flights, tours and rail tickets can all be booked online at www.lonelyplanet.com/travel_services.

ROUND-THE-WORLD (RTW) TICKETS

If you're travelling to multiple countries, then a round-the-world (RTW) ticket – where you pay a single discounted price for several connections – may be the most economical way to go.

Here are a few online companies to try:

Airstop & Go (www.airstop.be)
Airtreks (www.airtreks.com)
Air Brokers International (www.airbrokers.com)
Around the Worlds (www.aroundtheworlds.com)

Asia

There are regular flights to Suvarnabhumi International Airport from almost every major city in Asia. With the emergence of budget airlines, quick hops from, say, Bangkok to Kuala Lumpur, Singapore or Hong Kong are part of the Asian yuppie's weekend budget. Air Asia, Tiger Air and Jetstar are discount carriers that run frequent promotions. It's also worth asking your agent about cheap seats on airlines you might not expect, such as Emirates, Ethiopian or China Airlines between Bangkok and Hong Kong. Bangkok Airways flies direct to Ko Samui from Hong Kong and Singapore, and Air Asia links Phuket directly to Kuala Lumpur and Singapore.

Recommended booking agencies for reserving flights from Asia include **STA Travel** (www.statravel.com), which has offices in Bangkok, Hong Kong, Japan and Singapore. Another resource in Japan is **No1 Travel** (www.no1-travel.com); in Hong Kong try **Four Seas Tours** (www.fourseastravel.com). For India, try **STIC Travels** (www.stictravel.com), which has offices in dozens of Indian cities.

Australia

THAI, Qantas, British Airways, Jetstar and Emirates, among others, have direct flights to Bangkok, and Jetstar flies directly between Phuket and Melbourne. Garuda Indonesia, Singapore Airlines, Philippine Airlines, Malaysia Airlines and Royal Brunei Airlines also have frequent flights with stopovers to Bangkok.

Shop for cheap tickets from **STA Travel** (☎ 134 782; www.statravel.com.au) and **Flight Centre** (☎ 133 133; www.flightcentre.com.au), both of which have offices throughout Australia.

Canada

Air Canada, THAI, Cathay Pacific and several US-based airlines fly from different Canadian cities to Bangkok. **Travel Cuts** (☎ 800-667-2887; www.travelcuts.com) is Canada's national student travel agency. For online bookings try www.expedia.ca and www.travelocity.ca.

TRANSPORT

Continental Europe
Following are some recommended agencies across Europe.

France
Anyway (☎ 08 92 3023 01; www.anyway.fr)
Lastminute (☎ 08 99 78 50 00; www.lastminute.fr)
Nouvelles Frontières (☎ 08 25 00 07 47; www.nouvelles-frontieres.fr)
OTU Voyages (www.otu.fr) Specialising in student and youth travellers.
Voyageurs du Monde (www.vdm.com)

Germany
Expedia (www.expedia.de)
Just Travel (☎ 089 747 3330; www.justtravel.de)
Lastminute (☎ 0 180 528 4366; www.lastminute.de)
STA Travel (☎ 0 697 430 3292; www.statravel.de) Good choice for travellers under the age of 26.

Italy
CTS Viaggi (☎ 06 462 0431; www.cts.it) Specialises in student and youth travel.

Netherlands
Airfair (☎ 0 900 7717 717; www.airfair.nl)

Spain
Barcelo Viajes (☎ 902 116 226; www.barceloviajes.com)

Middle East
Some recommended agencies include the following:
Egypt Panorama Tours (☎ 2-359 0200; www.eptours.com) In Cairo.
Orion-Tour (www.oriontour.com) In Istanbul.

New Zealand
Air New Zealand, British Airways, THAI and Australian-based airlines have direct flights to Bangkok. Malaysian Airlines, Qantas and Garuda International also have flights to Bangkok, with stopovers.

Both **Flight Centre** (☎ 0800 243 544; www.flight centre.co.nz) and **STA Travel** (☎ 0800 474 400; www.statravel.co.nz) have branches throughout the country. The site www.goholidays.co.nz is recommended for online bookings.

South America
Some recommended agencies include the following:
Asatej (www.asatej.com) In Argentina, Mexico and Uruguay.
Student Travel Bureau (☎ 3038 1555; www.stb.com.br) In Brazil.

UK
At least two dozen airlines fly between London and Bangkok, although only three of them – British Airways, Qantas and THAI – fly nonstop. Discount air-travel ads appear in *Time Out*, the *Evening Standard* and in the free magazine *TNT*.

Recommended travel agencies include the following:
Bridge the World (☎ 0800 082 5000; www.b-t-w.co.uk)
Flight Centre (☎ 0870 499 0040; flightcentre.co.uk)
Flightbookers (☎ 0800 082 3000; www.ebookers.com)
North South Travel (www.northsouthtravel.com) Part of this company's profit is donated to projects in the developing world.
Quest Travel (☎ 0871 423 0135; www.questtravel.com)
STA Travel (☎ 0871 230 0040; www.statravel.co.uk) Popular with travellers under 26, sells tickets to all. Has branches throughout the UK.
Trailfinders (☎ 0845 058 5858; www.trailfinders.co.uk)
Travel Bag (☎ 0800 082 5000; www.travelbag.co.uk)

USA
It's cheaper to fly to Bangkok from West Coast cities than from the East Coast.

The airlines that generally offer the lowest fares include China Airlines, EVA Airways and Korean Air. EVA Airways (Taiwan) offers the 'Evergreen Deluxe' class between the USA and Bangkok, via Taipei, which has business-class–sized seats and personal movie screens for about the same cost as regular economy fares on most other airlines.

One of the most reliable discounters is **Avia Travel** (☎ 800 950 2842, 510 558 2150; www.aviatravel.com), which specialises in custom-designed RTW fares.

The following agencies are recommended for online bookings:
- www.cheaptickets.com
- www.expedia.com
- www.itn.net
- www.lowestfare.com
- www.orbitz.com
- www.sta.com (for travellers under the age of 26)
- www.travelocity.com.

BORDER CROSSINGS
Thailand has borders with Myanmar, Laos, Cambodia and Malaysia and you can enter all these countries by land, or by crossing a river. The borders listed here assume you are coming from Bangkok or the south. Border details are prone to unexpected change so ask around be-

fore you set off, or check Lonely Planet's Thorn Tree bulletin board at www.lonelyplanet.com, or the dedicated border pages on **Travelfish** (www.travelfish.org/board/topic/visabordercrossings).

Cambodia

There is a land border crossing between Thailand and Cambodia at Poipet, the seedy frontier town 6km from the Thai town of Aranya Prathet. It is a long haul, but if you're going to Siem Reap and Angkor this is the route most people take.

Catch an air-con bus from Bangkok's Northern and Northeastern (Mo Chit) station to Aranya Prathet (220B), then take a túk-túk (pronounced đúk đúk; motorised, open-sided cab) to the border. You can purchase a Cambodian visa on arrival. You can also reach Aranya Prathet from Bangkok's Hualamphong station (54B, 3rd class). A tourist shuttle bus outside the Cambodian immigration office delivers passengers free of charge to Poipet's shark-tank-cum-taxi stand, where onward transport can be arranged to Siem Reap. The most important advice on this route is to steer clear of the agents on Th Khao San offering dirt-cheap trips; they're dodgy. And do some research on the Thorn Tree to be aware of the host of other scams. See Lonely Planet's *Cambodia* guidebook for details of less direct border crossings, and for a rundown of the scams.

More useful if you're coming from the coast is the crossing at Hat Lek, on the coast southeast of Trat. From here you can take direct buses to Sihanoukville or Phnom Penh – a trip you'll remember until you lose your mind or die. Taking the fast ferry from Ko Kong to Sihanoukville is more comfortable. For the details, see boxed text, p162.

Malaysia

It is possible to cross by land from Thailand to Malaysia at several points but by far the most popular route is from Hat Yai to Alor Setar. Hat Yai can be reached from Bangkok by train or bus. Alternatively, you can book all the way from Bangkok to Butterworth (Malaysia) with a stop-off for border formalities. Entry permits for Thailand and Malaysia for most nationalities are available at the border crossings. See Hat Yai (p253) for more transport details.

South of Hat Yai, the train separates into two spurs: one headed to the west coast of the Malay Peninsula and the other to the east coast. The border crossing in the east is at Sungai Kolok (p262). The border is 1km from the train station and most travellers walk across to the Malaysian side where they catch a train or share a taxi to Kota Bharu. This is also the most common route to Pulau Perhentian. Note that the Sungai Kolok train station has been targeted by bomb attacks in the past. Note too that Israeli passport-holders are prohibited from crossing from Thailand to Malaysia.

There are several ways of travelling between southern Thailand and Malaysia by sea. The easiest border crossing is from Satun to Kuala Perlis (Malaysia) or Pulau Langkawi (Malaysia); see p371 for details. Most nationalities can obtain an entry permit for either Thailand or Malaysia at the border.

Myanmar

The land crossings into Myanmar have peculiar restrictions that often don't allow full access to the country. For information on the current status of border crossings into Myanmar, contact the Myanmar embassy in Bangkok (p391).

The only crossing open to foreigners in the south is a crossing by boat from Ranong to Kawthoung (aka Victoria Point) via the Gulf of Martaban and Pakchan estuary. Many people cross on a day trip to renew their Thai visas; for day passes, no Myanmar visa is required. See boxed text, p268, for details. If you plan to stay longer, or travel further, you'll need to arrange your visa in advance.

GETTING AROUND

AIR

Flying around Thailand is more affordable than ever and it's not unusual to find seats to cities in the south for less than 2000B, including extras (like, umm, fuel) that usually double the advertised fare. The exceptions are Ko Samui and Trat, where competition is less intense.

Bangkok is the primary hub for domestic flights, but you can also fly to some other Thai cities from Phuket and Ko Samui. If you are heading to northern Thailand from anywhere in the south, you'll usually have to connect through Bangkok. Remember that Bangkok has two airports and if you don't want to

TRANSPORT

AIRFARES & RAIL TICKETS

Airfares
One-way fares, including tax and other charges.
These are mid-priced, mid-season fares,
cheaper seats are usually available.
Rail
2nd-class air-con sleeper,
lower-berth fares from Bangkok.
All fares in baht.

transfer then be sure to book your domestic connection through Suvarnabhumi; see p109 for more details.

Thailand has several airlines flying domestic routes. THAI is the full-service carrier with the most-expensive tickets; Bangkok Airways is a good mid-market option with airport lounges open to everyone and prices higher than the budget airlines, Air Asia and Nok Air, which are the cheapest. The Airfares & Rail Tickets map (p410) offers an idea of average fares, but they can vary enormously even on the same day. Most airlines deal only in e-tickets, so there's no reason to schlep out to their distant offices to book a fare; use a travel agent, the internet or the phone. For last-minute fares, shop at the departures level

in the relevant airport. If you have the choice, avoid flying out of Bangkok on a Friday or Sunday, when seats can cost double the weekday fares. Reliable airlines flying to destinations in the south include:

Air Asia (code AK; ☎ 0 2515 9999; www.airasia.com) From Bangkok (Suvarnabhumi) to Hat Yai, Krabi, Phuket, Ranong, Surat Thani and Narathiwat. It also flies from Phuket to Kuala Lumpur and Singapore.

Bangkok Airways (code PG; ☎ 1771 or 0 2265 5555; www.bangkokair.com) From Bangkok (Suvarnabhumi) to Ko Samui, Krabi, Phuket and Trat; from Ko Samui to Chiang Mai, Krabi, Pattaya, Phuket, Hong Kong and Singapore; and from Phuket to Pattaya.

Nok Air (code OX; ☎ 1318; www.nokair.com) From Bangkok (Don Muang) to Hat Yai, Krabi, Nakhon Si Thammarat, Phuket and Trang. From Suvarnabhumi to Hua Hin.

Thai Airways International (☎ 0 2232 8000; www
.thaiair.com) From Bangkok (Suvarnabhumi) to Ko Samui,
Krabi, Phuket and from Bangkok (Don Muang) to those
plus Hat Yai and Surat Thani. From Phuket to Hat Yai. Most
domestic services from Don Muang.

If you don't fancy taking the ferry around the
Andaman islands, Phuket-based **Destination Air**
(☎ 0 7632 8638; www.destinationair.com) has scheduled seaplane services to Ko Phi-Phi (3000B
from Patong) and charter flights to Ko Lanta,
Ao Nang, Ko Yao (Noi and Yai), the Similan
Islands and Khao Lak.

Air Passes

Most air passes available aren't particularly
valuable if you are just visiting southern
Thailand as most flights have to go through
Bangkok. THAI offers a three-city package
for US$199; three budget airline flights will
probably cost less.

BICYCLE

The quiet back roads in the low-lying south
of Thailand are perfect for bicycle touring.
Most roads are sealed and the hard shoulder is kept deliberately wide to accommodate two-wheeled vehicles. The road surface
is generally pretty good but punctures are
common. There is also plenty of opportunity
for off-road pedalling.

You can take bicycles on the train for
about what you'd pay for a 3rd-class ticket.
Buses charge a nominal fee for bikes (if they
charge at all). On ordinary buses, your bike
will probably be put on the roof; on air-con
buses it will go in the cargo hold. Locals routinely carry their bikes on long-tail boats,
so getting between islands shouldn't be a
problem.

Thais tend to use their bikes for short
journeys, so long-distance cyclists are still
something of a novelty – expect to see plenty
of smiles and surprised stares. Established in
1959, the **Thailand Cycling Club** (☎ 081 555 2901;
www.thaicycling.com; 849/53 Chulalongkorn 6, Th Bantadtong,
Bangkok) serves as an information clearing
house on bicycling tours and cycling clubs
throughout the country; see also p401 for
recommended companies.

Hire

Bicycles can be hired in many locations, including guesthouses in the south, for about
50B to 100B per day. Take the bike for a quick

spin before you hire – there are some real
boneshakers out there. Some historical sites
also offer rental bikes.

Purchase

Bangkok has a number of shops selling imported bicycles and their components. A
good choice is **Velo Thailand** (Map pp74-5; ☎ 089
201 7782; www.velothailand.com; 88 Soi 2, Th Samsen,
Banglamphu), which also rents and repairs bikes
and runs cycling tours. Prices are comparable
to Europe or the USA. Resale is possible, but
you'll need to stick around long enough to
find an interested traveller or expat. Bangkok
and Phuket are the best places to sell your
wheels; try putting up fliers in hostels and
backpacker hotels.

BOAT

Private boat operators link the various islands
and ports of the Andaman Sea and the Gulf
of Thailand. Your floating conveyance could
be anything from a simple wooden fishing
boat with open deck to an air-conditioned
jetfoil with hot food and video entertainment.
Life jackets are usually provided but many
boats have inadequate emergency exits, so
open-decked boats are often safer than super-
ferries. See the regional chapters for information on specific ferry routes to and between
the Thai islands.

The waters off many Thai islands are too
shallow for large boats, so long-tail boats are
used to transfer passengers to the shore. There
is usually a per person charge for this service.

BUS

The bus network in Thailand is prolific and
reliable and is a great way to see the countryside and sit among the locals. The Thai
government subsidises the **Transport Company**
(bò·rí·sàt kŏn sòng; ☎ 0 2936 2841; www.transport.co.th
/Eng/HomeEnglish.htm), usually abbreviated to Baw
Khaw Saw (BKS), and every city and town
in Thailand linked by bus has a BKS station,
even if it's just a patch of dirt by the side of
the road. BKS buses are generally the safest
and most reliable.

Government (BKS) Bus

The cheapest and slowest of the BKS buses
are the orange 'ordinary' or 2nd-class buses
(rót tam·má·dah). These tend to run regularly but they have no air-con and stop in
every little town and hamlet along the way –

THERE'S A MAN IN MY LUGGAGE

Buying a bus ticket south through a travel agent on Th Khao San might seem convenient, but too often it ends in tears. Buses are often late, or they depart as scheduled only to drive around town for three hours picking up other passengers. Other common woes include buying a VIP ticket and then being picked up in a jalopy or buying a boat and ferry combination that no one will honour during the second leg of the trip.

But perhaps the worst scam is one that has been operating for years and which the Thai police seem totally incapable of stopping (ask yourself how hard it should be?). It's a crude but very effective scheme – while you are (hopefully) sleeping your way south on the overnight bus, a man is hiding in the luggage hold and slowly working his way through all the bags, stealing whatever takes his fancy. Locks are no great deterrent as such cat burglars can pick one faster than you can tie your shoes. By the time you realise you've been robbed, you're far away and the thieves (and evidence) are long gone. If you do take these buses, pack anything valuable in your hand luggage and keep those bags with you at all times.

Of course, the best way to avoid these scams is to skip the tourist buses and deal with the official government bus stations. These buses are much safer, cheaper and you get to hang out with Thais instead of fuming foreigners.

---

indeed, you can flag these buses down wherever you see them. The faster, blue-and-white air-conditioned buses are called *rót air, rót ʼbràp ah·gàht* (air-conditioned bus) or *rót too·a* (tour bus) and typically run throughout the day. On the bottom rung of the air-con class is 2nd class, without a toilet, and 1st class with a toilet. VIP buses have 34 seats while 'Super VIP' buses have only 24 seats and all sorts of trimmings: plush reclining seats, Arctic air-con (bring something warm) and onboard entertainment. VIP buses are good options for long-haul routes, but there are typically only a few departures a day, usually in the evenings.

There are ticket windows for the various bus companies at most bus stations. At popular tourist destinations, the schedule is often listed in English by the ticket window. If you're headed further south than Hua Hin, call the bus station (p109 in Bangkok) as it can be worth buying your ticket the day before to confirm departure times. See the regional chapters for detailed information on fares and trip duration.

Tourist Bus & Minivan

As well as government-run buses, numerous tourist bus companies ply between the various tourist centres in the south. These companies use large air-con buses typically painted with chintzy tropical scenes and have onboard toilets, reclining seats and some form of video entertainment. Unlike the BKS buses, private buses tend to leave from offices in the

middle of town and tickets are sold through travel agents and hotel and guesthouse desks. Fares are usually more expensive than on BKS buses.

While tourist buses save you a trip to the bus station, there are countless tales of woe; see boxed text, above.

Minivans typically hang around the bus stations and pick up passengers who have missed their bus or tourists who don't know better. Typically the agent will tell you that the bus is leaving in five minutes, which really means you'll have to wait until more people show up to make it profitable enough to leave.

In general, private bus companies that deal mostly with Thais are good, while those that deal predominantly with *faràng* (foreigners) – especially those connected with Th Khao San in Bangkok – are the worst. To minimise the chance of trouble, book bus tickets directly at the bus station rather than with an agency.

CAR & MOTORCYCLE

One look at the traffic in Bangkok may be enough to put you off driving in Thailand, but things are a little calmer in the countryside. Nonetheless, driving in Asia will definitely take a little getting used to. If you keep your speed down and drive *very* defensively, you should be able to get by. However, driving a car in Thailand is never going to be a relaxing experience. If you feel up to the challenge, there are car-hire companies in Bangkok and most other tourist centres – see p414.

Motorcycles are a great way to explore the Thai countryside but you must adapt to local riding rules. Most importantly, motorcyclists are 2nd-class citizens on Thai roads and are expected to give way to all larger vehicles.

Bringing Your Own Vehicle

Few people bother with their own vehicles if they're coming to see Thailand's islands and beaches. However, passenger vehicles (eg car, van, truck or motorcycle) can be brought into Thailand for tourist purposes for up to six months. Documents needed for the crossing are a valid International Driving Permit, passport, vehicle registration papers (in the case of a borrowed or hired vehicle you will need authorisation from the owner) and a cash or bank guarantee equal to the value of the vehicle plus 20%. For entry through Khlong Toey Port or Suvarnabhumi Airport, this means a letter of bank credit; for overland crossings via Malaysia, Cambodia or Laos a 'self-guarantee' filled in at the border should be sufficient. For more information, see the website of the **Customs Department** (www.customs .go.th) and click through the Personal Vehicles

link; for news from others try the **Horizons Unlimited** (www.horizonsunlimited.com) bulletin board (the HUBB) or **GT Rider** (www.gt-rider.com).

Driving Licence

Foreigners who want to drive motor vehicles (including motorcycles) in Thailand need either a Thai licence or a valid International Drivers Permit (with a motorcycle entitlement if applicable), though such bothersome details are often overlooked by small island operators. International Drivers Permits are available from driving associations in your home country.

If the police catch you driving without a licence, they may well request an arbitrary cash bribe to let you go. If you find yourself in this situation, it's best to do as the locals do and pay up. If you have an accident and you don't have the appropriate licence, the penalties can be much more severe.

Long-term visitors can apply for a Thai driver's licence through the provincial office of the Department of Land Transport. In Bangkok, there are five district offices. To determine the location of your assigned office

ROAD DISTANCES (KM)

	Aranya Prathet	Ayuthaya	Bangkok	Chumphon	Hat Yai	Hua Hin	Krabi	Nakhon Si Thammarat	Narathiwat	Pattani	Phuket	Prachinburi	Ranong	Rayong	Sungai Kolok	Surat Thani	Trang
Ayuthaya	246																
Bangkok	275	79															
Chumphon	727	531	452														
Hat Yai	1268	1072	993	555													
Hua Hin	458	262	183	269	810												
Krabi	1278	1082	1003	551	287	820											
Nakhon Si Thammarat	971	775	696	244	192	513	209										
Narathiwat	1495	1299	1220	782	227	1037	514	580									
Pattani	1402	1206	1127	689	134	944	421	487	93								
Phuket	1125	929	862	412	474	667	185	394	701	608							
Prachinburi	161	124	155	607	1148	338	1158	851	1375	1282	1017						
Ranong	855	659	580	128	368	397	368	372	882	789	287	735					
Rayong	321	279	200	652	1193	383	1203	1008	1420	1327	1062	248	780				
Sungai Kolok	1555	1359	1280	842	287	1097	576	640	60	153	761	1435	944	1480			
Surat Thani	927	731	652	214	469	318	151	731	638	286	807	315	852	791			
Trang	1417	1221	1142	690	147	959	139	142	374	281	324	1297	507	1342	437	234	
Trat	285	392	313	765	1306	496	1316	1009	1533	1440	1175	334	893	180	1593	965	1455

TRANSPORT

TRANSPORT

based on residence, contact the **Department of Land Transport** (☎ 0 2272 5322).

Fuel & Spare Parts

As well as modern petrol (gasoline) stations with electric pumps, Thailand has roadside stands selling petrol (*ben·sin* or *nám·man rót yon*) from petrol drums and even smaller stalls selling petrol in recycled Coke bottles. All fuel is lead-free in Thailand.

Spare parts for the kinds of vehicles commonly hired out in Thailand are easy to come by in larger towns but can be hard to find in rural areas. If you get into mechanical trouble, it's best to let the hire company sort out the repairs. Be warned that many of the spare parts in motorcycle shops are pirate copies made from inferior materials. For news updates about fuel options and other car talk, see **BKK Auto** (www.bkkautos.com).

Hire

CAR

Big international car-hire companies, such as Avis and Budget, have offices in Bangkok and at large hotels and resorts around the country. All offer Japanese-made sedans, 12-seater minivans, miniature jeeps and luxury 4WD vehicles, usually with manual transmission. There are local car-hire companies in tourist centres such as Ko Lanta and Ko Samui that rent out small Suzuki jeeps for about 1000B a day. If you're heading south, fly or take a train or bus to your destination and hire a car on arrival. See regional chapters for details.

International company rates start at about 1500B per day and include unlimited mileage and tax with an extra 100B a day for insurance. Check the small print carefully to make sure you are fully insured. Drivers can usually be hired with a rental for an additional 500B to 800B per day. Several companies offer

---

STAYING SAFE ON TWO WHEELS

While motorcycle touring is undoubtedly one of the most liberating and exciting ways to see Thailand, dozens of travellers are injured or killed on Thai roads every year. Inexperience is the main cause, so if you don't have much experience, think twice before renting. If you go ahead, take heed of the following to maximise your chances of getting home in one piece. Check your rental bike thoroughly before you hire it – pay particular attention to the brakes and tyre tread, look for oil leaks and make sure the lights and horn work and the engine starts cleanly from the kick-starter.

■ Get insurance with your rental if at all possible, and be extra careful if you can't. If you crash or the bike is stolen you will be responsible for the full cost. Make sure that your travel health insurance covers you for motorcycles before you ride (many do not).

■ Always wear a helmet, even if you're riding a small scooter on an empty dirt road.

■ Cover your arms and legs. As well as protecting yourself from sunburn, you'll save some skin if you come off.

■ If you have an open-fronted helmet (pretty likely), wear sunglasses, glasses or goggles to keep the bugs and dust out of your eyes.

■ When you get onto a bike, always do it from the left side to keep clear of the hot exhaust. Likewise, if you come off and are not already dead then make sure you get away from the bike as quickly as possible, lest you end up with the 'Thai tattoo' – a burned inner right calf – seen festering on beaches across the country.

■ Keep your speed down. Thai roads are often full of potholes and there are loads of unfamiliar obstacles to watch out for.

■ Try to avoid riding alone in remote areas at night. A number of faràng bikers have been attacked while riding alone in rural areas.

■ Motorcycles are always expected to give way to bigger vehicles. Do as local riders do and keep to the hard shoulder with your speed way down.

■ Keep an eye on oil levels during long rides. For two-stroke bikes, add two-stroke engine oil in with the gasoline.

cheap one-way rental between Bangkok and Phuket or Krabi.

MOTORCYCLE

Touring around the countryside on a rented motorcycle has become almost a rite of passage for travellers in Thailand and at most of the beaches and islands you'll find someone (or many people) renting bikes. It's different in Bangkok, where renting is not a good idea unless you are an adrenaline junkie or just enjoy the taste of smog.

The standard rental bike in Thailand is the Honda Dream or something very similar no-frills 100cc to 150cc machines with automatic clutches and 'four down' gear configurations. The keys have a tendency to pop out of the ignition on bumpy roads so remember to use the string provided to secure them. In general, the 100cc and 110cc bikes are more comfortable than the 125cc wannabe racing bikes, as the rear pegs are much lower.

The going rate for a 100cc to 150cc bike is 150B to 300B for 24 hours. You'll be expected to leave your passport or driver's licence (no shit!) as a deposit and you should return with as much fuel as it had to start with. Insurance usually isn't provided, so drive with extra care. According to Thai law, all riders and passengers must wear a helmet, but not all hire companies provide them. This is a pain as traffic police routinely stop foreigners who aren't wearing helmets and extract bribes. Traffic cops may also ask to see your passport and charge a 'fine' if you can't provide it.

In some tourist centres, you can pick up larger imported bikes such as Harley Davidsons, Japanese road-bikes and 250cc dirt-bikes, though there's limited scope for touring on an island. Rates for these vary from 500B to 1500B and they are usually rented on a standard hire agreement, with insurance and a substantial credit-card deposit.

Insurance

If it's available, ensure you are fully insured before signing a rental contract. With the exception of a few companies that rent out large, imported road-bikes, motorcycles are almost always rented without insurance. As most travel insurance policies do not cover motorcycling (some will if you have a dedicated motorcyclist's licence), that means you can have all the fun you like but you must also take all the responsibility, both to yourself and

anyone or anything you damage. Regardless of who actually caused the accident, foreigners are often forced to pay up for everything – if you do have an accident, get in contact with the **tourist police** (☏ 1155) immediately.

Road Rules & Conditions

Thailand has some of the best-maintained roads in the region and the traffic isn't too bad once you get away from the main highways. Main roads are well signed, often in Thai and English, but on small country roads most signs are in Thai script only. Large four-lane highways carry most of the long-distance traffic between major towns, but accidents are horribly common. Back roads are quieter and safer, but carry a map as it's easy to get lost.

Size matters in the Darwinian world of Thai driving. And if you only remember two road rules, remember to give way to anyone bigger and to forget about lanes and drive with 180-degree vision. Cars share the road with buses, trucks, motorcycles, bicycles, bullock-carts and wandering buffalo and wildlife, and you never know when a young buffalo (or child!) is going to leap out in front of you. Expect the unexpected, especially at dusk when animals are heading home. Overtaking on hills or blind corners is common and the largest vehicle has the right of way in any situation.

Motorcycles are relegated to the hard shoulder, so watch out for them when you turn off any highways. Don't be too surprised if you see another vehicle coming towards you on the hard shoulder on your side of the road – it's the only way to get to some turn-offs.

Turn signals are often used to warn passing drivers about oncoming traffic. A left-turn signal means it's OK to pass, while a right-turn signal means someone is approaching from the other direction. However, do not rely entirely on these signals when making the decision to overtake.

The official maximum speed limits are 50km/h within city limits and 100km/h on most highways, though these are widely flouted. Military and police checkpoints are common and you should always slow down and behave courteously – the sentries will usually wave you through without any hassles.

HITCHHIKING

Hitching is never entirely safe in any country in the world and we don't recommend it. Travellers who decide to hitch should

TRANSPORT

understand that they are taking a small but serious risk. On top of this, Thailand isn't a particularly easy place to hitch. Locals find it hard to comprehend why wealthy foreigners aren't willing to pay for public transport. Most of the vehicles that stop will be public buses or *sŏrng·tăa·ou* (small pick-up trucks), which you could have caught from the bus station anyway and which will ask for a fare.

If you do decide to hitch, never hitch alone, let someone know where you are planning to go, don't hitch at night and don't get into a car if you can smell alcohol on the driver. Be doubly cautious in the deep south, where foreigners may be perceived as a target for Islamic militants.

LOCAL TRANSPORT
Boat
Boats are used for public transport between the various islands and coastal villages of southern Thailand. The workhorse of inter-island transport is the charismatic, deafeningly noisy long-tail boat *(reu·a hăhng yow)*, which has a propeller mounted at the end of a 3m-long drive shaft. Passengers can get a drenching in rough seas (or heavy rain) so consider putting valuable items in plastic bags inside your rucksack. Long-tails either operate like sŏrng·tăa·ou, leaving whenever there are enough passengers, or offer custom charters. The relevant destination chapters have more information.

Bangkok has its own network of urban boat transport, following the network of canals that radiate out from the Chao Phraya; see p111 for details.

Local Bus
Most larger cities have a local bus system. Bangkok has a comprehensive service with several classes; in smaller towns local transport is usually provided by sŏrng·tăa·ou rather than buses. Provincial airports often provide a bus service into town whenever a flight arrives; however, you usually have to take a taxi in the other direction.

Motorcycle Taxi
Thais rely on motorcycle taxis for short journeys around town. Drivers wear coloured vests and hang around at bus stands and street corners waiting for passengers.

Within Bangkok, motorcycle taxis serve two purposes. Most commonly and popu-

larly they run from the corner of a main thoroughfare, such as Th Sukhumvit, to the far ends of soi (lanes) that run off that thoroughfare, usually charging about 20B for the trip. Their other purpose is as a means of beating the traffic. You tell your rider where you want to go, negotiate a price (from 20B for a short trip up to about 100B going across town), strap on the helmet (they will insist for longer trips) and say a prayer to whichever god you're into. Drivers range from responsible to kamikaze, but the average trip involves some time on the wrong side of the road and several near-death experiences. It's the sort of white-knuckle ride you'd pay good money for at Disneyland, but is all in a day's work for these riders. Comfort yourself with the knowledge that there are good hospitals nearby.

Women wearing skirts are expected to ride side-saddle; be sure to gather up loose material so that it doesn't get caught in the vehicle's drive chain.

Sähm·lór & Túk-Túk
Sähm·lór means 'three wheels', and that's just what they are – three-wheeled vehicles, usually without a motor. The motorised version is known as túk-túk (pronounced đúk đúk) from the noise they make. Most are powered by noisy two-stroke engines, usually running on LPG (liquid petroleum gas), and have open-sided cabs that let in all the noise, dust and traffic fumes.

Both provide taxi services in provincial towns and villages. You can flag them down anywhere but the fare must be established before you start the journey. In Bangkok, túk-túk are no cheaper than metered taxis and are roving scam artists. Away from the capital, túk-túk are the taxis.

Nonmotorised sähm·lór are basically bicycle rickshaws, of the kind seen all over Asia. The Thai version has the seat at the back, behind the driver, as in India. There are no bicycle sähm·lór in Bangkok but they are fairly common elsewhere in the country. Bicycle sähm·lór are cheaper than túk-túk, but far slower and can't go the same distances.

Sŏrng·tăa·ou
A *sŏrng·tăa·ou* (literally two rows) is a usually small truck with a row of bench seats down each side, similar to an Indonesian *bemo* or a Filipino *jeepney*. Sŏrng·tăa·ou

sometimes operate fixed routes, like buses, but can also be booked for special trips like a regular taxi. In rural towns, you can usually pick up *sŏrng·tăa·ou* from the bus stand or main market to outlying villages and beaches. If you are the first passenger on an empty *sŏrng·tăa·ou,* the driver may try and talk you into chartering the whole vehicle; stand firm if you want to wait for other passengers. *Sŏrng·tăa·ou* are also used on the islands and on Phuket and Ko Samui, where they make a refreshingly cheap and local way to get between beaches and avoid the taxi mafia rip-off merchants. Fares are charged per person, with foreigners often charged a few baht more than Thais.

Taxi

Western-style taxis are only really common in Bangkok, Pattaya and touristy islands like Phuket and Ko Samui. In most places, you have to rely on túk-túk and motorcycle taxis. Where you do find taxis in provincial towns, you'll have to establish the fare before you start your journey as the meter is rarely used.

Taxis operate between some towns on a share basis, with the fare split between passengers. Elsewhere pretty much any taxi can be persuaded to take a long-distance trip with enough notes. Taxis regularly run for fixed fares between Bangkok and centres such as Pattaya (1500B), Hua Hin (2300B), Ban Phe (for Ko Samet, 2300B) and Phetchaburi (1700B); see www.taxiradio.co.th for other fares. Fares back to Bangkok are often significantly cheaper – bargain.

Train

The train system in Thailand is only used for inter-city travel. Bangkok has the Skytrain (see p113) and the underground Metro (see p112).

TRAIN

The railway network in Thailand is run by the government-subsidised **State Railway of Thailand** (SRT; ☎ 1690; www.railway.co.th). The standard of service is very good and this is certainly one of the most pleasant ways to get around the kingdom. Apart from being smoother, more social and spacious than buses, trains are also safer, both in terms of accidents and thefts from baggage. Some trains have dining cars and snack vendors

so you don't have to wait for meal stops, and the scenery is usually better than that beside the highway.

The rail network covers 4500km and there are four main rail lines within the country – the northern, southern, northeastern and eastern lines. The line most island-bound travellers use is the southern route with stops at Hua Hin, Chumphon (for transfers to Ko Tao), Surat Thani (for transfers to Ko Samui), Hat Yai and the border with Malaysia. There are also a handful of branch lines, including the useful side route between Tung Song (on the main southern line) and Trang, terminating at Kantang. The southern line splits at Hat Yai; one branch follows the east coast to Sungai Kolok on the Malaysian border and the other heads west to Padang Besar, then over the Malaysian border to Butterworth. Almost all the long-distance trains originate from Bangkok's Hualamphong train station.

Trains are slightly slower than buses. There are plans to upgrade the line so high-speed trains can run from Bangkok to Padang Besar on the Malaysian border, but completion remains a way off. A branch from Surat Thani to Phang-Nga (Tha Nun) is also planned, and will provide easy access to Phuket.

All train stations within Thailand offer baggage-storage services. Meals are available in dining cars on most trains, or at your seat if you travel 1st or 2nd class; quality varies widely, but is rarely great. Roving vendors also wander up and down some trains selling bottled water, soft drink and beer for significantly more than you'll pay in a 7-Eleven.

Classes

There are three classes on SRT trains – 1st, 2nd and 3rd – but the standard of facilities in each varies considerably depending on whether you're on an ordinary, rapid or express train. Third-class seats are cheaper than ordinary buses, while 2nd class costs about the same as the equivalent journey by VIP or private bus. First class costs quite a lot more, but the extra luxury may be worth it on long journeys.

FIRST CLASS

First-class cars have private double cabins with individually controlled air-con, an electric fan, a washbasin and mirror, a small table and a long bench seat that converts

TRANSPORT

into two beds. Drinking water and towels are provided free of charge. First-class cars are available only on express and special express trains.

SECOND CLASS

There are two types of 2nd-class cars – seat cars and sleepers. Seat cars have two rows of padded seats, facing towards the front of the train, which recline back but aren't really comfortable enough for overnight trips. In a 2nd-class sleeper car a central aisle is flanked by a series of open compartments, each containing two facing padded seats that convert into berths. The lower berths cost a little more as they are roomier and cooler. When the berths are folded away, a table can be set up between the two seats for meals. Fresh linen is provided and each car has a toilet and basin. Second-class cars are found only on rapid and express trains and can either be fan-cooled, which gets hot once you've closed the curtains, or air-conditioned, which is usually so cold you'll be wondering if you're on the Trans-Siberian.

THIRD CLASS

A typical 3rd-class carriage consists of two rows of bench seats divided into facing pairs. Each bench seat is designed to seat two or three passengers, but you can expect four or more. On ordinary trains, 3rd-class seats may have hard wooden benches, but on rapid trains there is usually some padding to keep your bottom from going numb. Express trains do not carry 3rd-class carriages at all.

Costs

Ticket prices are very reasonable and you can check the latest on www.thairailways.co.th or www.thailandbytrain.com. Fares are calculated first by a base price then surcharges are added depending on the train type (special express, express, rapid, ordinary), class and distance. There is an 80B surcharge above the basic fare for *rót dòo·an* (express trains) and 60B for *rót re·hou* (rapid trains). These trains are somewhat faster than the ordinary trains, as they make fewer stops. For the *rót dòo·an pí·sèht* (special-express trains) that run between Bangkok and Padang Besar and between Bangkok and Chiang Mai there is a 100B to 120B surcharge. For distances under

500km, the base rate is 50B; over 500km, 70B to 80B.

Some 2nd- and 3rd-class services have air-con cars, in which case there is a 120B to 140B surcharge. Sleeping berths in 2nd class accrue another 100B to 240B surcharge. Upper berths are cheaper than lower – the difference being that there is a window next to the lower berth and more head room. No sleepers are available in 3rd class.

All 1st-class cabins come with individually controlled air-con. For a two-bed cabin the surcharge is 400B per person. Single 1st-class cabins are not available, so if you're travelling alone you may be paired with another passenger, although the SRT takes great care not to mix genders.

If all this surcharge stuff sounds confusing, the good news is that at most stations someone will be able to tell you in English when the train leaves, how long it takes and how much it costs – which is all you really need to know.

Reservations

Advance bookings may be made one to 60 days before your intended date of departure. For holiday-period travel – especially the middle of April approaching the Songkran Festival, during Chinese New Year and during the peak tourist-season months of December and January – it is advised to book tickets as far in advance as possible, especially for popular routes such as Surat Thani and Hat Yai.

You can make bookings from any train station, where ticket offices are generally open 8.30am to 6pm on weekdays, and 8.30am to noon on weekends and public holidays. Tickets can also be purchased by telephone at ☎ 1690, or at travel agencies in Bangkok, which charge a 50B processing fee but save you the trip to the station.

Midweek departures are always easier to book than weekends; during some months you can easily book a sleeper even one day before departure, as long as it's on a Tuesday, Wednesday or Thursday. With the exception of those departing Surat Thani or Chiang Mai, booking trains back to Bangkok is generally not as difficult as booking trains out of Bangkok.

If you change your plans you can get an 80% refund up to three days before travel and a 50% refund up to one hour after the train departs.

Train Passes

If you plan on doing a lot of rail travel, the SRT offers a rail pass that allows unlimited 2nd- and 3rd-class travel on Thai trains for 20 days. They cost 1500B, or 3000B including all supplemental charges (air-con, rapid and express charges). Passes are only available in Thailand and may be purchased at the advance booking office at Hualamphong train station in Bangkok. If you're just travelling in southern Thailand, the rail pass probably won't save you much money, but it can be a good deal if you are also planning to visit the north.

Passes must be validated at a local station before boarding the first train and reservations are recommended for later journeys. The pass is valid for all trains leaving before midnight on the last day of the pass.

Health Dr Trish Batchelor

CONTENTS

Health issues and the quality of medical facilities vary enormously depending on where and how you travel in Thailand. Bangkok has excellent hospitals (p68) and major cities have well-developed healthcare facilities. However, travel to rural areas can expose you to a variety of health risks and inadequate medical care.

Travellers may worry about contracting infectious diseases, but these rarely cause serious illness or death in travellers. Pre-existing medical conditions and accidental injury, especially traffic accidents, account for most life-threatening problems. Becoming ill, however, is relatively common. Most common illnesses can be prevented with common-sense behaviour or be treated easily with a well-stocked medical kit.

The following advice is a general guide only and does not replace the advice of a doctor trained in travel medicine.

BEFORE YOU GO

Pack medications in their original, clearly labelled containers. A signed and dated letter from your physician describing your medical conditions and medications, including generic names, is also a good idea. If carrying syringes or needles be sure to have a physician's letter documenting their medical necessity. If you have a heart condition, bring a copy of your ECG taken just prior to travelling.

If you happen to take any regular medication, bring double your needs in case of loss or theft. In most of Thailand, you can buy many medications over the counter without a doctor's prescription, but it can be difficult to find some newer drugs, particularly the latest antidepressant drugs, blood pressure medications and contraceptive pills, outside of Bangkok.

INSURANCE

Even if you are fit and healthy, don't travel without health insurance – accidents and illnesses do happen. If you are uninsured, emergency evacuation can be expensive; bills of over US$100,000 are not uncommon. Declare any existing medical conditions you have – the insurance company *will* check whether your problem is pre-existing and will not cover you if it is undeclared. You may require extra cover for adventure activities such as rock climbing and inquire if the insurance covers accidents on a motorbike. If your health insurance doesn't cover you for medical expenses abroad, consider getting additional insurance.

Find out in advance if your insurance plan pays providers directly or reimburses you later for expenditures. Some providers offer various medical-expense options; the higher ones are generally for countries with extremely high medical costs, such as the USA. You may prefer a plan that pays hospitals directly rather than having you pay on the spot and claim later. If you have to claim later, keep all documentation. Some policies might ask you to call (reverse charges) a centre in your home country where an immediate assessment of your problem is made.

VACCINATIONS

Specialised travel-medicine clinics are your best source of information; they stock all available vaccines and will be able to make recommendations tailored specifically for you and your trip. The doctors there will take into account factors such as your vaccination history, the length of your trip, activities you may be undertaking while away and underlying medical conditions, such as pregnancy.

POSSIBLE VACCINATIONS

There are no required vaccines for entering Thailand. Proof of vaccination against yellow fever is required only if you have visited a country in a yellow-fever zone within the six days prior to entering the region. If you are travelling to Southeast Asia from Africa or South America you should check to see if you require proof of vaccination.

Recommended Vaccinations

The World Health Organization recommends the following vaccinations for travellers heading to Thailand.

Adult diphtheria & tetanus Single booster recommended if not had in the previous 10 years. Side effects include sore arm and fever.

Hepatitis A Provides almost 100% protection for up to a year; a booster after 12 months provides at least another 20 years protection. Mild side effects such as headache and sore arm occur in 5% to 10% of people.

Hepatitis B Now considered routine for most travellers, it is given as three injections over six months. A rapid schedule is also available, as is a combined vaccination with Hepatitis A. Side effects are mild and uncommon, usually headache and sore arm. Lifetime protection occurs in 95% of people.

Measles, mumps & rubella Two doses of MMR required unless you have had the diseases. Occasionally a rash and flulike illness can develop a week after receiving the vaccine. Many young adults require a booster.

Polio In 2005 Thailand had no reported cases of polio. Only one booster required as an adult for lifetime protection. Inactivated polio vaccine is safe during pregnancy.

Typhoid Recommended unless your trip is less than a week and only to developed cities. The vaccine offers around 70% protection, lasts for two to three years and comes as a single injection. Tablets are also available, however the injection is usually recommended as it has fewer side effects. Sore arm and fever may occur.

Varicella If you haven't had chickenpox, discuss this vaccination with your doctor.

The following immunisations are recommended for long-term travellers (more than one month) or those at special risk.

Japanese B Encephalitis Three injections in all. Booster recommended after two years. Sore arm and headache are the most common side effects. Rarely will an allergic reaction comprising hives and swelling occur up to 10 days after any of the three doses.

Meningitis Single injection. There are two types of vaccination: the quadrivalent vaccine gives two to three years protection; meningitis group C vaccine gives around 10 years protection. Recommended for long-term backpackers aged under 25.

Rabies Three injections in all. A booster after one year will provide 10 years protection. Side effects are rare – occasionally headache and sore arm.

Tuberculosis Adult long-term travellers are usually recommended to have a TB skin test before and after travel, rather than a vaccination. Only one vaccine given in a lifetime.

Most vaccines don't produce immunity until at least two weeks after they're given, so visit a doctor four to eight weeks before departure. Ask your doctor for an International Certificate of Vaccination (otherwise known as the yellow booklet), which will list all the vaccinations you've received.

MEDICAL CHECKLIST

Recommended items for a personal medical kit:

- Antibacterial cream, eg Muciprocin
- Antibiotic for skin infections, eg Amoxicillin (Clavulanate) or Cephalexin
- Antibiotics for diarrhoea, eg Norfloxacin or Ciprofloxacin; for bacterial diarrhoea Azithromycin; for giardiasis or amoebic dysentery Tinidazole
- Antifungal cream, eg Clotrimazole
- Antihistamine – there are many options, eg Cetrizine for daytime and Promethazine for night
- Antiseptic, eg Betadine
- Antispasmodic for stomach cramps, eg Buscopa
- Contraceptives
- Decongestant, eg Pseudoephedrine
- DEET-based insect repellent

- Diarrhoea relief – consider a diarrhoea 'stopper' (eg Loperamide), an antinausea medication (eg Prochlorperazine) and an oral rehydration solution (eg Gastrolyte)
- First-aid items such as scissors, Elastoplasts, bandages, gauze, safety pins and tweezers, thermometer (but not mercury), and sterile needles and syringes.
- Ibuprofen or another anti-inflammatory
- Indigestion medication, eg Quick Eze or Mylanta
- Iodine tablets (unless you are pregnant or have a thyroid problem) to purify water
- Laxative, eg Coloxyl
- Migraine medicine if prone to migraines
- Paracetamol
- Permethrin to impregnate clothing and mosquito nets
- Steroid cream for allergic/itchy rashes, eg 1% to 2% hydrocortisone
- Sunscreen and hat
- Throat lozenges
- Thrush (vaginal yeast infection) treatment, eg Clotrimazole pessaries or Diflucan tablet
- Ural or equivalent if you're prone to urine infections

INTERNET RESOURCES

There is a wealth of travel health advice on the internet. For further information, **Lonely Planet** (www.lonelyplanet.com) is a good place to start. The **World Health Organization** (WHO; www.who.int/ith/) publishes a superb book, *International Travel & Health,* which is revised annually and is available free online. Another website of general interest is **MD Travel Health** (www.mdtravelhealth.com), which provides complete travel health recommendations for every country and is updated daily. The **Centers for Disease Control and Prevention** (CDC; www.cdc.gov) website also has good general information.

FURTHER READING

Lonely Planet's *Healthy Travel – Asia & India* is a handy pocket-size book that is packed with useful information including pretrip planning, emergency first aid, immunisation and disease information, and what to do if you get sick on the road. Other recommended references include *Traveller's Health,* by Dr Richard Dawood, and *Travelling Well,* by Dr Deborah Mills – check out the website www.travellingwell.com.au.

IN TRANSIT

DEEP VEIN THROMBOSIS (DVT)

Deep vein thrombosis (DVT) occurs when blood clots form in the legs during plane flights, chiefly due to prolonged immobility. The longer the flight, the greater the risk of developing deep vein thrombosis. While most clots are reabsorbed uneventfully, occasionally some clots break off and travel through blood vessels to the lungs, where they may result in life-threatening complications.

The chief symptom of DVT is swelling of or pain in the foot, ankle or calf, usually, but not always, on just one side. If a blood clot travels to the lungs it may cause chest pain and/or you could experience difficulty breathing. Travellers with any of these symptoms should immediately seek medical attention.

To prevent the development of DVT on long flights you should walk about the cabin, perform isometric compressions of the leg muscles (ie contract the leg muscles while sitting), drink plenty of fluids and avoid alcohol.

JET LAG & MOTION SICKNESS

Jet lag is common when crossing more than five time zones; it results in insomnia, fatigue, malaise or nausea. To avoid jet lag, drink plenty of nonalcoholic fluids and eat light meals during the flight. Upon arrival, expose yourself to natural sunlight and readjust your schedule (for meals, sleep etc) to that of the country you have arrived in as soon as possible.

Antihistamines such as dimenhydrinate (Dramamine) and meclizine (Antivert, Bonine) are usually the first choice for treating motion sickness. Their main side effect is drowsiness. A herbal alternative to antihistamines is ginger, which works like a charm for some people.

IN THAILAND

AVAILABILITY OF HEALTH CARE

Bangkok has become a medical centre for foreigners seeking cosmetic, elective and primary care. Hospitals geared towards these clients have internationally trained doctors, English-speaking staff and top-notch service, though, as in the whole of the country, over-prescription can be a problem. Other tourist areas, such as Phuket and Ko Samui, will have equally accessible hospital facilities. On the smaller islands, there will be rudimentary clinics for bumps, scrapes and minor infections. It is difficult to find reliable medical care in rural areas. Recommended hospitals in Bangkok are listed on p68. Your embassy and insurance company are also good contacts. Many pharmacies in Thailand are equipped to deal with minor health problems such as traveller's diarrhoea. If you think you may have a serious disease, especially malaria or dengue fever, do not waste time – travel to the nearest quality facility to receive attention. It is always better to be assessed by a doctor than to rely on self-treatment.

Do be aware that some medications in Thailand are either fake, poorly stored or out-of-date.

INFECTIOUS DISEASES
Cutaneous Larva Migrans
Cutaneous Larva Migrans, caused by dog hookworm, is particularly common on the beaches of Thailand. The rash starts as a small lump, then slowly spreads in a linear fashion. It is intensely itchy, especially at night. It is easily treated with medications and should not be cut out or frozen.

Dengue Fever
This mosquito-borne disease is becoming increasingly problematic throughout Southeast Asia, especially in the cities. As there is no vaccine available it can only be prevented by avoiding mosquito bites. The mosquito that carries dengue will bite day and night, so implement insect avoidance measures at all times. Symptoms include high fever, severe headache and body ache (dengue was previously known as 'breakbone fever'). Some people develop a rash and experience diarrhoea. The southern islands of Thailand are a particularly high risk. There is no specific treatment, just rest and paracetamol – do not take aspirin as it increases the likelihood of haemorrhaging. See a doctor to be diagnosed and monitored.

Filariasis
This is a mosquito-borne disease that is very common in the local population, yet very rare in travellers. Mosquito-avoidance measures are the best way to prevent this disease.

Hepatitis A
Hepatitis A is a problem throughout the region. This food- and water-borne virus infects the liver, causing jaundice (yellow skin and eyes), nausea and lethargy. There is no specific treatment for hepatitis A; you just need to allow the liver time to heal. All travellers to Southeast Asia should be vaccinated against hepatitis A.

Hepatitis B
The only sexually transmitted disease that can be prevented by vaccination, hepatitis B is spread by body fluids, including sexual contact. In some parts of Southeast Asia up to 20% of the population are carriers of hepatitis B, and usually are unaware of this. The long-term consequences can include liver cancer and cirrhosis.

Hepatitis E
Hepatitis E is transmitted through contaminated food and water and has symptoms similar to hepatitis A, but is far less common. It is a severe problem in pregnant women potentially resulting in the death of both mother and baby. There is currently no vaccine, and prevention is by following safe eating and drinking guidelines.

HIV
HIV is one of the most common causes of death in people under the age of 50 in Thailand. Heterosexual sex is the primary method of transmission both in Thailand and neighbouring countries, several of which have rising numbers of people living with HIV, and dying from AIDS. However, while more than 1% of Thais are infected with HIV, aggressive safe-sex campaigns in the 1990s have seen the incidence of new infections drop sharply, and made Thailand a global pin-up for effectively dealing with the disease.

Influenza
Present year-round in Thailand, influenza (flu) symptoms include a high fever, muscle aches, runny nose, cough and sore throat. It can be very severe in people over the age of 65 or in those with underlying medical conditions such as heart disease or diabetes; vaccination is recommended for these indi-

HEALTH

viduals. There is no specific treatment, just rest and paracetamol.

Japanese B Encephalitis

This viral disease is transmitted by mosquitoes. While rare in travellers, at least 50,000 locals are infected each year. Most cases occur in rural areas; travellers spending more than one month outside of cities should be vaccinated. There is no treatment, and one-third of infected people will die while another third will suffer permanent brain damage.

Leptospirosis

This is most commonly contracted after river rafting or canyoning. Early symptoms are very similar to the flu and include headache and fever. Severity can vary from very mild to a being fatal. Diagnosis is achieved through blood tests and it is easily treated with Doxycycline.

Malaria

For such a serious and potentially deadly disease, there is an enormous amount of misinformation concerning malaria. You must get expert advice as to whether your trip actually puts you at risk, particularly if you are pregnant. Many parts of Southeast Asia, particularly city and resort areas, have minimal to no risk of malaria, and the risk of side effects from taking prophylactics may outweigh the risk of getting the disease. For most rural areas, however, the risk of contracting the disease outweighs the risk of tablet side effects. Remember that malaria can be fatal. Before you travel, seek medical advice on the right medication and dosage for you.

Malaria is caused by a parasite transmitted by the bite of an infected mosquito. The most important symptom of malaria is fever, but general symptoms such as headache, diarrhoea, cough or chills may also occur. Diagnosis can only be made by taking a blood sample.

Two strategies should be combined to prevent malaria – mosquito avoidance and antimalarial medications. Most people who catch malaria are taking inadequate or no antimalarial medication.

Travellers are advised to prevent mosquito bites by taking these steps:

- Use insect repellent containing DEET on exposed skin. Wash this off at night, only if you are sleeping under a mosquito net. Natural repellents such as Citronella can

be effective, but must be applied more frequently than products containing DEET.
- Sleep under a mosquito net impregnated with Permethrin.
- Choose accommodation with fans (if not air-conditioning) and screens.
- Impregnate clothing with Permethrin in high-risk areas.
- Wear long sleeves and trousers in light colours.
- Use mosquito coils.
- Spray your room with insect repellent before going out for your evening meal.

There are a variety of malaria medications available:

Artesunate Derivatives of Artesunate are not suitable as a preventive medication. They are useful treatments under medical supervision.

Chloroquine & Paludrine The effectiveness of this combination is now limited in most of Southeast Asia. Common side effects include nausea (40% of people) and mouth ulcers. Not recommended.

Doxycycline This daily tablet is a broad-spectrum antibiotic that has the added benefit of helping to prevent a variety of tropical diseases, including leptospirosis, tick-borne disease, typhus and melioidosis. The potential side effects include photosensitivity (a tendency to sunburn), thrush in women, indigestion, heartburn, nausea and interference with the contraceptive pill. More serious side effects include ulceration of the oesophagus – you can help prevent this by taking your tablet with a meal and a large glass of water, and never lying down within half an hour of taking it. Must be taken for an additional four weeks after leaving the risk area.

Lariam (Mefloquine) Lariam has received a lot of bad press, some of it justified, some not. This weekly tablet suits many people. Serious side effects are rare but include depression, anxiety, psychosis and having fits. Anyone with a history of depression, anxiety, other psychological disorders or epilepsy should not take Lariam. It is considered safe in the second and third trimesters of pregnancy. It is around 90% effective in most parts of Southeast Asia, but there is significant resistance in parts of northern Thailand, Laos and Cambodia. Tablets must be taken for four weeks after leaving the risk area.

Malarone This newer drug is a combination of Atovaquone and Proguanil. Side effects are uncommon and mild, most commonly nausea and headache. It is the best tablet for scuba divers and for those on short trips to high-risk areas. It must be taken for one week after leaving the risk area.

A final option is to take no preventive medication but to have a supply of emergency medication should you develop the symptoms of malaria. This is not ideal and you will need to get to a good medical facility within 24 hours of developing a fever. If you choose this option the most effective and safest treatment is Malarone (four tablets once daily for three days). Other options include Artesunate, Mefloquine and Quinine but the side effects of the latter two drugs at treatment doses make them less desirable. Fansidar is no longer recommended.

Measles

Measles remains a problem in some parts of Southeast Asia. This highly contagious bacterial infection is spread via coughing and sneezing. Most people born before 1966 are immune as they had measles in childhood. Measles starts with a high fever and rash and can be complicated by pneumonia and brain disease. There is no specific treatment.

Melioidosis

This infection is contracted by skin contact with soil. It is rare in travellers, but in some parts of northeast Thailand up to 30% of the local population are infected. The symptoms are very similar to those experienced by tuberculosis sufferers. There is no vaccine but it can be treated with medication.

Rabies

Rabies is still a common problem in most parts of Southeast Asia. This uniformly fatal disease is spread by the bite or lick of an infected animal – most commonly a dog or monkey. Seek medical advice immediately after any animal bite and commence post-exposure treatment. Having a pre-travel vaccination means the post-bite treatment is simplified. If an animal bites you, gently wash the wound with soap and water, and apply iodine-based antiseptic. If you are not pre-vaccinated you will need to receive rabies immunoglobulin as soon as possible.

STDs

Sexually transmitted diseases most common in Southeast Asia include herpes, warts, syphilis, gonorrhoea and chlamydia. People carrying these diseases often have no signs of infection. Condoms will prevent gonorrhoea and chlamydia but not warts or herpes. If after a sexual encounter you develop any rash, lumps, discharge or pain when passing urine

seek immediate medical attention. If you have been sexually active during your travels have an STD check on your return home.

Strongyloides

This parasite, transmitted by skin contact with soil, is common in Thailand but rarely affects travellers. It is characterised by an unusual skin rash called *larva currens* – a linear rash on the trunk which comes and goes. Most people don't have other symptoms until their immune system becomes severely suppressed, when the parasite can cause an overwhelming infection. It can be treated with medications.

Tuberculosis

While rare in short-term travellers, medical and aid workers, and long-term travellers who have significant contact with the local population should take precautions. Vaccination is usually only given to children under the age of five, but adults at risk are recommended to take pre- and post-travel tuberculosis testing. The main symptoms are fever, cough, weight loss, night sweats and tiredness.

Typhoid

This serious bacterial infection is spread via food and water. Symptoms include a high, slowly progressive fever and headache, and may be accompanied by a dry cough and stomach pain. It is diagnosed by blood tests and treated with antibiotics. Vaccination is recommended for all travellers spending more than a week in Southeast Asia, or travelling outside the major cities. Be aware that vaccination is not 100% effective so you must still be careful with what you eat and drink.

Typhus

Murine typhus is spread by the bite of a flea, whereas scrub typhus is spread via a mite. These diseases are rare in travellers. Symptoms include fever, muscle pains and a rash. You can avoid these diseases by following general insect-avoidance measures. Doxycycline will also prevent them.

TRAVELLER'S DIARRHOEA

Traveller's diarrhoea is by far the most common problem affecting travellers – between 30% and 50% will suffer from it within two weeks of starting their trip. For the vast majority it won't be a huge problem. A change of diet can often loosen stools and when you

HEALTH

add copious amounts of chilli to unfamiliar cuisine there's a good chance you'll end up scampering to the throne sooner or later. Recovery is usually swift. So if the symptoms are not major (ie there's no blood in your stool) then the usual advice is to...errr...sit on it for a day or two before you reach for the antibiotics.

Having said that, genuine traveller's diarrhoea is usually caused by bacteria and therefore can be treated with antibiotics. Traveller's diarrhoea is defined as the passage of more than three watery bowel-actions within 24 hours, plus at least one other symptom such as fever, cramps, nausea, vomiting or feeling generally unwell.

Treatment includes staying hydrated; rehydration solutions such as Gastrolyte are the best for this. Antibiotics such as Norfloxacin, Ciprofloxacin or Azithromycin will kill the bacteria quickly.

Loperamide is just a 'stopper' and doesn't get to the cause of the problem. It can be helpful, for example if you have to go on a long bus ride. Don't take Loperamide if you have blood in your stools or a fever. Seek medical attention quickly if you don't respond to an appropriate antibiotic.

Amoebic Dysentery

Amoebic dysentery is very rare in travellers but is often misdiagnosed by poor quality labs in Southeast Asia. Symptoms are similar to bacterial diarrhoea (ie fever, bloody diarrhoea and generally feeling unwell). You should always seek reliable medical care if you have blood in your diarrhoea. Treatment involves two drugs: Tinidazole or Metronidazole will kill the parasite in your gut and a second drug will kill the cysts. If left untreated, complications such as liver or gut abscesses can occur.

Giardiasis

Giardia lamblia is a parasite that is relatively common in travellers. Symptoms include nausea, bloating, excess gas, fatigue and intermittent diarrhoea. 'Eggy' burps are often attributed solely to giardiasis, but work in Nepal has shown that they are not specific to this infection. The parasite will eventually go away if left untreated but this can take months. The treatment of choice is Tinidazole, with Metronidazole being a second line option.

ENVIRONMENTAL HAZARDS
Air Pollution

Air pollution, particularly from vehicles, is an increasing problem in most of Southeast Asia's major cities. If you have severe respiratory problems speak with your doctor before travelling to any heavily polluted urban centres. This pollution also causes minor respiratory problems such as sinusitis, dry throat and irritated eyes. If troubled by the pollution, leave the city for a few days and get some fresh air.

Diving

Divers and surfers should seek specialised advice before they travel to ensure their medical kit contains treatment for coral cuts and tropical ear infections, as well as the standard problems. Divers should ensure their insurance covers them for decompression illness – get specialised dive insurance through an organisation such as **Divers Alert Network** (DAN; www .danseap.org). Have a dive medical before you leave your home country – there are medical conditions that are incompatible with diving, and economic considerations may override health considerations for some Thai dive operators.

Food

Eating in restaurants is the biggest risk factor for contracting traveller's diarrhoea. Ways to avoid it include eating only freshly cooked food, and avoiding shellfish and food that has been sitting around in buffets. Peel all fruit, cook vegetables and soak salads in iodine water for at least 20 minutes. Eat in busy restaurants with a high turnover of customers.

Heat

Many parts of Thailand are hot and humid throughout the year. For most people it takes at least two weeks to adapt to the hot climate. Swelling of the feet and ankles is common, as are muscle cramps caused by excessive sweating. Prevent these by avoiding dehydration and excessive activity in the heat. Take it easy when you first arrive. Don't eat salt tablets (they aggravate the gut) but drinking rehydration solution or eating salty food helps. Treat cramps by stopping activity, resting, rehydrating with double-strength rehydration solution and gently stretching.

Dehydration is the main contributor to heat exhaustion. Symptoms include feeling weak, headache, irritability, nausea or vomiting, sweaty skin, a fast, weak pulse and normal or slightly elevated body temperature. Treatment involves getting out of the heat and/or sun, fanning the victim and applying cool wet cloths to the skin, laying the victim flat with their legs raised and rehydrating with water containing ¼ teaspoon of salt per litre. Recovery is usually rapid and it is common to feel weak for some days afterwards.

Heatstroke is a serious medical emergency. Symptoms come on suddenly and include weakness, nausea, a hot dry body, a body temperature of over 41°C, dizziness, confusion, loss of coordination, fits and eventually collapse and loss of consciousness. Seek medical help and commence cooling by getting the person out of the heat, removing their clothes, fanning them and applying cool wet cloths or ice to their body, especially the groin and armpits.

Prickly heat is a common skin rash in the tropics, caused by sweat being trapped under the skin. The result is an itchy rash of tiny lumps. Treat by moving out of the heat and into an air-conditioned area for a few hours and by having cool showers. Creams and ointments clog the skin so they should be avoided. Locally bought prickly-heat powder can be helpful.

Tropical fatigue is common in long-term expats based in the tropics. It's rarely due to disease and is caused by the climate, inadequate mental rest, excessive alcohol intake and the demands of daily work.

Insect Bites & Stings

Bedbugs don't carry disease but their bites are very itchy. They live in the cracks of furniture and walls and then migrate to the bed at night to feed on you. You can treat the itch with an antihistamine. Lice inhabit various parts of your body but most commonly your head and pubic area. Transmission is via close contact with an infected person. They can be difficult to treat and you may need numerous applications of an anti-lice shampoo such as Permethrin.

Ticks are contracted after walking in rural areas. Ticks are commonly found behind the ears, on the belly and in armpits. If you have had a tick bite and experience symptoms such as a rash at the site of the bite or elsewhere, fever or muscle aches, you should see a doctor. Doxycycline prevents tick-borne diseases.

Leeches are found in humid rainforest areas. They do not transmit any disease but their bites are often intensely itchy for weeks afterwards and can become infected. Apply an iodine-based antiseptic to any leech bite to help prevent infection.

Bee and wasp stings mainly cause problems for people who are allergic to them. Anyone with a major bee or wasp allergy should carry an injection of adrenaline (eg an Epipen) for emergency treatment. For others, to ease the pain, apply ice to the sting and take painkillers.

Jellyfish

Most jellyfish in Southeast Asian waters are not dangerous, just irritating, however there have been incidents of serious (and in rare cases, fatal) stings by box jellyfish on both the Andaman and Gulf coasts. First-aid for jellyfish stings involves pouring vinegar onto the affected area to neutralise the poison. Do not rub sand or water onto the stings. Take painkillers if necessary, and for box jellyfish stings in particular seek immediate medical attention. Heed advice from local authorities, dive shops and your hotel about seasonal water conditions, and if there are dangerous jellyfish around keep out of the water.

Parasites

Numerous parasites are common in local populations in Southeast Asia; however, most of these are rare in travellers. The two rules to follow if you wish to avoid parasitic infections are to wear shoes and to avoid eating raw food, especially fish, pork and vegetables. A number of parasites, including strongyloides, hookworm and *cutaneous larva migrans*, are transmitted via the skin by walking barefoot.

Skin Problems

Fungal rashes are common in humid climates. There are two fungal rashes that commonly affect travellers. The first occurs in moist areas that get less air such as the groin, armpits and between the toes. It starts as a red patch that slowly spreads and is usually itchy. Treatment involves keeping the skin dry, avoiding chafing and using an antifungal cream such as Clotrimazole or Lamisil. *Tinea versicolor* is also common. This fungus causes small, light-coloured patches, most commonly on the back, chest and shoulders. Consult a doctor.

Cuts and scratches can become easily infected in humid climates. Take meticulous care of any cuts and scratches to prevent complications such as abscesses. Immediately wash all wounds in clean water and apply antiseptic. If you develop signs of infection (increasing pain

HEALTH

TRADITIONAL MEDICINE

Throughout Thailand traditional medical systems are widely practised. There is a big difference between traditional healing systems and 'folk' medicine. Folk remedies should be avoided, as they often involve rather dubious procedures with potential medical complications. On the other hand, healing systems, such as traditional Chinese medicine, are well respected and aspects of them are being increasingly utilised by medical practitioners throughout the West.

All traditional Asian medical systems identify a vital life force, and see blockage or imbalance as the cause of disease. Techniques such as herbal medicines, massage and acupuncture are utilised to bring the vital force back into balance, or to maintain balance. These therapies are best used for treating chronic disease such as chronic fatigue, arthritis and some chronic skin conditions. Traditional medicines should be avoided for treating acute infections such as malaria.

Be aware that 'natural' doesn't always mean 'safe', and there can be drug interactions between herbal medicines and Western medicines. If you are utilising both systems, ensure you inform both practitioners what the other has prescribed.

---

and redness) see a doctor. Divers and surfers should be particularly careful with coral cuts as they become easily infected.

Snakes

Thailand is home to many species of both poisonous and harmless snakes. Assume all snakes are poisonous and never try to catch one. Always wear boots and long pants if walking in an area that may have snakes. First-aid in the event of a snakebite involves pressure immobilisation via an elastic bandage firmly wrapped around the affected limb, starting at the bite site and working up towards the chest. The bandage should not be so tight that the circulation is cut off, and the fingers or toes should be kept free so the circulation can be checked. Immobilise the limb with a splint and carry the victim to medical attention. Do not use tourniquets or try to suck the venom out. Antivenom is available for most species.

Sunburn

Even on a cloudy day sunburn occurs rapidly. Use a strong sunscreen (factor 30), reapply after a swim, and always wear a wide-brimmed hat and sunglasses outdoors. Avoid lying in the sun during the hottest part of the day (10am to 2pm). If you become sunburnt, stay out of the sun until you have recovered, apply cool compresses and take painkillers for the discomfort and apply a 1% hydrocortisone cream.

WOMEN'S HEALTH

In the urban areas of Thailand, supplies of sanitary products are readily available. Birth control is cheap but not all options are widely available so it's safest to bring adequate sup-

plies of your own form of contraception. Heat, humidity and taking antibiotics can all contribute to thrush. Treatment is with antifungal creams and pessaries such as Clotrimazole. A practical alternative is a single tablet of Fluconazole (Diflucan). Urinary tract infections can be precipitated by dehydration or long bus journeys without toilet stops; bring suitable antibiotics.

Pregnant women should receive specialised advice before travelling. The ideal time to travel is in the second trimester (between 16 and 28 weeks), when the risk of pregnancy-related problems is lowest and pregnant women generally feel at their best. During the first trimester there is a risk of miscarriage and in the third trimester complications such as premature labour and high blood pressure are possible. It's wise to travel with a companion. Always carry a list of quality medical facilities at your destination and ensure you continue your standard antenatal care at these facilities. Avoid rural travel in areas with poor transport and medical facilities. Most of all, ensure travel insurance covers all pregnancy-related possibilities, including premature labour.

Malaria is a high-risk disease during pregnancy. WHO recommends that pregnant women do *not* travel to areas with Chloroquine-resistant malaria. None of the more effective antimalarial drugs are completely safe during pregnancy.

Traveller's diarrhoea can quickly lead to dehydration and result in inadequate blood flow to the placenta. Many of the drugs used to treat various diarrhoea bugs are not recommended during pregnancy. Azithromycin is considered safe.

Language

CONTENTS

Learning some Thai is indispensable for travel in the kingdom; naturally, the more you pick up, the closer you get to Thailand's culture and people. Your first attempts to speak Thai will probably meet with mixed success, but keep trying. Listen closely to the way the Thais themselves use the various tones – you'll catch on quickly. Don't let laughter at your linguistic forays discourage you; this apparent amusement is really an expression of appreciation. Travellers are particularly urged to make the effort to meet Thai college and university students. Thai students are, by and large, eager to meet visitors from other countries. They will often know some English, so communication isn't as difficult as it may be with shop owners, civil servants etc, and they're generally willing to teach you useful Thai words and phrases.

DIALECTS

Thailand's official language is effectively the dialect spoken and written in central Thailand, which has successfully become the lingua franca of all Thai and non-Thai ethnic groups in the kingdom.

All Thai dialects are members of the Thai half of the Thai-Kadai family of languages. As such, they're closely related to languages spoken in Laos (Lao, northern Thai, Thai Lü), northern Myanmar (Shan, northern Thai), northwestern Vietnam (Nung, Tho), Assam (Ahom) and pockets of south China (Zhuang, Thai Lü).

Modern Thai linguists recognise four basic dialects within Thailand: Central Thai (spoken as a first dialect through central Thailand and throughout the country as a second dialect); Northern Thai (spoken from Tak Province north to the Myanmar border); Northeastern Thai (northeastern provinces towards the Lao and Cambodian borders); and Southern Thai (from Chumphon Province south to the Malaysian border). There are also a number of Thai minority dialects such as those spoken by the Phu Thai, Thai Dam, Thai Daeng, Phu Noi, Phuan and other tribal Thai groups, most of whom reside in the north and northeast.

VOCABULARY DIFFERENCES

Like most languages, Thai distinguishes between 'polite' and 'informal' vocabulary, so that *tahn*, for example, is a more polite everyday word for 'eat' than *gin*, and *sěe-sà* for 'head' is more polite than *hŏo·a*. When given a choice, it's better to use the polite terms, since these are less likely to lead to unintentional offence.

SCRIPT

The Thai script, a fairly recent development in comparison with the spoken language, consists of 44 consonants (but only 21 separate sounds) and 48 vowel and diphthong possibilities (32 separate signs). Though learning the alphabet is not difficult, the writing system itself is fairly complex, so unless you're planning a lengthy stay in Thailand it should perhaps be foregone in favour of actually learning to speak the language. The names of major places and food items included in this book are given in both Thai and Roman script, so that you can at least 'read' the names of destinations or dishes, or point to them if necessary.

TONES

In Thai the meaning of a single syllable may be altered by means of different tones – in standard Central Thai there are five: low tone, mid tone, falling tone, high tone and rising tone. For example, depending on the tone, the syllable *mai* can mean 'new', 'burn', 'wood', 'not?' or 'not'; ponder the phrase *mái mài mâi mâi mǎi* (New wood doesn't burn, does it?) and you begin to appreciate the importance of tones in spoken Thai. This makes it a rather tricky language to learn at first, especially for those of us unaccustomed to the concept of tones.

Even when we 'know' what the correct tone in Thai should be, our tendency to denote emotion, verbal stress, the interrogative etc through tone modulation often interferes with producing the correct tone. Therefore the first rule in learning to speak Thai is to divorce emotions from your speech, at least until you've learned the Thai way to express them without changing essential tone value.

The following is visual representation in chart form to show relative tone values:

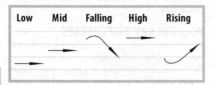

Low	Mid	Falling	High	Rising

The list below is a brief attempt to explain the tones. The only way to really understand the differences is by listening to a native or fluent non-native speaker. The range of all five tones is relative to each speaker's vocal range so there is no fixed 'pitch' intrinsic to the language.

low tone – 'flat' like the mid tone, but pronounced at the relative bottom of one's vocal range. It is low, level and has no inflection, eg *bàht* (baht – the Thai currency).

mid tone – pronounced 'flat', at the relative middle of the speaker's vocal range, eg *dee* (good); no tone mark is used.

falling tone – starting high and falling sharply, this tone is similar to the change in pitch in English when you are emphasising a word, or calling someone's name from afar, eg *mâi* (no/not).

high tone – usually the most difficult for Westerners. It's pronounced near the relative top of the vocal range, as level as possible, eg *máh* (horse).

rising tone – starting low and gradually rising, sounds like the inflection used by English speakers to imply a question – 'Yes?', eg *sǎhm* (three).

PRONUNCIATION

The following is a guide to the phonetic system that's been used for the words and phrases in this chapter (and throughout the rest of the book when transcribing directly from Thai). The dots indicate syllable breaks within words, including compound vowels..

Consonants

The majority of consonants correspond closely to their English counterparts. Here are a few exceptions:

g	similar to the 'g' in 'good'
b	a hard 'p' sound, almost like a 'b'; sounds something like the sound made when you say 'hi**p**-**b**ag'
đ	a hard 't' sound, like a sharp 'd'; sounds something like the sound made when you say 'mi**d**-**t**one'
k	as the 'k' in 'kite'
p	as the 'p' in 'pie'
t	as the 't' in 'tip'
ng	as the 'nging' in 'singing'; can occur as an initial consonant (practise by saying 'singing' without the 'si')
r	similar to the 'r' in 'run' but flapped (ie the tongue touches palate); in everyday speech it's often pronounced like 'l'

Vowels

i	as in 'bit'
ee	as the 'ee' in 'feet'
ai	as in 'aisle'
ah	as the 'a' in 'father'
a	as in 'about'; half as long as '**ah**'
aa	as the 'a' in 'bat' or 'tab'
e	as in 'hen'
air	as in English but with no final 'r' sound (for American speakers)
eu	as the 'er' in 'fern' (without the 'r' sound)
u	as the 'u' in 'put'
oo	as the 'oo' in 'food'
ow	as the 'ow' in 'now'
or	as the 'or' in 'torn' (without the 'r' sound)
o	as the 'o' in 'hot'
oh	as the 'o' in 'toe'
eu·a	a combination of 'eu' and 'a'

ee·a   as 'ee-ya', or as the 'ie' in French
       rien
oo·a   as the 'our' in 'tour'
oo·ay sounds like 'oo-way'
ew   as the 'ew' in 'new'
ee·o   as the 'io' in 'Rio'
aa·ou like the 'a' in 'cat' followed by a short
       'u' as in 'put'
eh·ou like the 'e' in bed, followed by a short
       'u' as in 'put'
oy   as the 'oi' in 'coin'

TRANSLITERATION

Writing Thai in Roman script is a perennial problem – no wholly satisfactory system has yet been devised to assure both consistency and readability. The Thai government uses the RTGS of transcription for official government documents in English and for most highway signs. However, local variations crop up on hotel signs, city street signs, menus and so on in such a way that visitors often become confused. Added to this is the fact that even the government system has its flaws.

Generally, names in this book follow the most common practice or simply copy their Roman script name, no matter what devious process was used in its transliteration. When this transliteration is markedly different from actual pronunciation, the pronunciation is included (according to the system outlined in this chapter) in parentheses after the transliteration. Where no Roman model was available, names have been transliterated phonetically, directly from Thai.

ACCOMMODATION

I'm looking for a ...
ผม/ดิฉันกำลังหา...
pŏm/dì·chăn gam·lang hăh ...

guesthouse
บ้านพัก/   *bâhn pák/*
เกสต์เฮาส์   *gèt hów ('guest house')*
hotel
โรงแรม   *rohng raam*
youth hostel
บ้านเยาวชน   *bâhn yow·wá·chon*

Where is a cheap hotel?
โรงแรมที่ราคาถูกอยู่ที่ไหน
rohng raam têe rah·kah tòok yòo têe năi?

What is the address?
ที่อยู่คืออะไร
têe yòo keu à·rai?
Could you write the address, please?
เขียนที่อยู่ให้ได้ไหม
kĕe·an têe yòo hâi dâi măi?
Do you have any rooms available?
มีห้องว่างไหม
mee hôrng wâhng măi?

I'd like (a) ...
ต้องการ...
dôrng gahn ...

bed
เตียงนอน   *đee·ang norn*
single room
ห้องเดี่ยว   *hôrng dèe·o*
double room
ห้องคู่   *hôrng kôo*
room with two beds
ห้องที่มีเตียง   *hôrng têe mee đee·ang*
  สองตัว   *sŏrng đoo·a*
room with a bathroom
ห้องที่มีห้องน้ำ   *hôrng têe mee hôrng nám*
ordinary room (with fan)
ห้องธรรมดา   *hôrng tam·má·*
  (มีพัดลม)   *dah (mee pát lom)*
to share a dorm
พักในหอพัก   *pák nai hŏr pák*

How much is it ...? ...เท่าไร? *... tôw rai?*

per night	คืนละ	*keun lá*
per person	คนละ	*kon lá*

May I see the room?
ดูห้องได้ไหม
doo hôrng dâi măi?
Where is the bathroom?
ห้องน้ำอยู่ที่ไหน
hôrng nám yòo têe năi?
I'm/We're leaving today.
ฉัน/พวกเราจะออกวันนี้
chăn/pôo·ak row jà òrk wan née

toilet	ห้องส้วม	*hôrng sôo·am*
room	ห้อง	*hôrng*
hot	ร้อน	*rórn*

cold	เย็น	*yen*
bath/shower	อาบน้ำ	*àhp nám*
towel	ผ้าเช็ดตัว	*pâh chét đoo·a*

CONVERSATION & ESSENTIALS

When being polite, the speaker ends his or her sentence with *kráp* (for men) or *kâ* (for women). It is the gender of the speaker that is being expressed here; it is also the common way to answer 'yes' to a question or show agreement.

Hello.
สวัสดี(ครับ/ค่ะ)   *sà·wàt·dee (kráp/kâ)*

Goodbye.
ลาก่อน   *lah gòrn*

Yes.
ใช่   *châi*

No.
ไม่ใช่   *mâi châi*

Please.
กรุณา   *gà·rú·nah*

Thank you.
ขอบคุณ   *kòrp kun*

That's fine. (You're welcome)
ไม่เป็นไร/ยินดี   *mâi ben rai/yin·dee*

Excuse me.
ขออภัย   *kŏr à·pai*

Sorry. (Forgive me)
ขอโทษ   *kŏr tôht*

How are you?
สบายดีหรือ?   *sà·bai dee rĕu?*

I'm fine, thanks.
สบายดี   *sà·bai dee*

What's your name?
คุณชื่ออะไร?   *kun chêu à·rai?*

My name is ...
ผมชื่อ...   *pŏm chêu ...* (men)
ดิฉันชื่อ...   *dì·chăn chêu ...* (women)

Where are you from?
มาจากที่ไหน   *mah jàhk têe năi?*

I'm from ...
มาจาก...   *mah jàhk ...*

See you soon.
เดี๋ยวเจอกันนะ   *dĕe·o jeu gan ná*

I like ...
ชอบ...   *chôrp ...*

I don't like ...
ไม่ชอบ...   *mâi chôrp ...*

Just a minute.
รอเดี๋ยว   *ror dĕe·o*

I/me (for men)
ผม   *pŏm*

I/me (for women)
ดิฉัน   *dì·chăn*

I/me (informal, men and women)
ฉัน   *chăn*

You (for peers)
คุณ   *kun*

Do you have ...?
มี... ไหม/...มีไหม?   *mee ... măi?/... mee măi?*

(I) would like ... (+ verb)
อยากจะ...   *yàhk jà ...*

(I) would like ... (+ noun)
อยากได้...   *yàhk dâi ...*

DIRECTIONS

Where is (the) ...?
...อยู่ที่ไหน?   *... yòo têe năi?*

(Go) Straight ahead.
ตรงไป   *đrong bai*

Turn left.
เลี้ยวซ้าย   *lée·o sái*

Turn right.
เลี้ยวขวา   *lée·o kwăh*

At the corner
ตรงมุม   *đrong mum*

At the traffic lights
ตรงไฟแดง   *đrong fai daang*

behind	ข้างหลัง	*kâhng lăng*
in front of	ตรงหน้า	*đrong nâh*
far	ไกล	*glai*
near	ใกล้	*glâi*
not far	ไม่ไกล	*mâi glai*
opposite	ตรงข้าม	*đrong kâhm*
left	ซ้าย	*sái*
right	ขวา	*kwăh*
beach	ชายหาด	*chai hàht*
bridge	สะพาน	*sà·pahn*
canal	คลอง	*klorng*
countryside	ชนบท	*chon·ná·bòt*

SIGNS

ทางเข้า	Entrance
ทางออก	Exit
ที่ติดต่อสอบถาม	Information
เปิด	Open
ปิด	Closed
ห้าม	Prohibited
สถานีตำรวจ	Police Station
ห้องน้ำ	Toilets
ชาย	Men
หญิง	Women

hill	เขา	kŏw
island	เกาะ	gò
lake	ทะเลสาบ	tá·leh sàhp
mountain	ภูเขา	poo kŏw
paddy (field)	(ทุ่ง)นา	(tûng) nah
palace	วัง	wang
pond	หนอง/บึง	nŏrng/beung
river	แม่น้ำ	mâa nám
sea	ทะเล	tá·leh
temple	วัด	wát
town	เมือง	meu·ang
track	ทาง	tahng
village	(หมู่)บ้าน	(mòo) bâhn
waterfall	น้ำตก	nám dòk

HEALTH

I need a (doctor).

| ต้องการ(หมอ) | đôrng gahn (mŏr) |

dentist

| หมอฟัน | mŏr fan |

hospital

| โรงพยาบาล | rohng pá·yah·bahn |

chemist/pharmacy

| ร้านขายยา | ráhn kăi yah |

I'm ill.

| ฉันป่วย | chăn bòo·ay |

It hurts here.

| เจ็บตรงนี้ | jèp đrong née |

I'm pregnant.

| ตั้งครรภ์แล้ว | đâng kan láa·ou |

I feel nauseous.

| รู้สึกคลื่นไส้ | róo·sèuk klêun sâi |

EMERGENCIES

Help!

| ช่วยด้วย | chôo·ay dôo·ay! |

There's been an accident.

| มีอุบัติเหตุ | mee ù·bàt·đì·hèt |

I'm lost.

| ฉันหลงทาง | chăn lŏng tahng |

Go away!

| ไปซิ | bai sí! |

Stop!

| หยุด | yùt! |

Call ...!

| เรียก...หน่อย | rêe·ak ... nòy! |

a doctor

| หมอ | mŏr |

the police

| ตำรวจ | đam·ròo·at |

I have a fever.

| เป็นไข้ | ben kâi |

I have diarrhoea.

| ท้องเสีย | tórng sĕe·a |

I'm allergic to ...

| ผม/ดิฉันแพ้... | pŏm/dì·chăn páa ... |

antibiotics

| ยาปฏิชีวนะ | yah bà·đì·chee·wá·ná |

aspirin

| ยาแอสไพริน | yah àt·sà·pai·rin |

penicillin

| ยาเพนิซิลลิน | yah pair·ní·sin·lin |

bees

| ตัวผึ้ง | đoo·a pêung |

peanuts

| ถั่วลิสง | tòo·a lí·sŏng |

I'm ...

| ผม/ดิฉัน... | pŏm/dì·chăn ... |

asthmatic

| เป็นโรคหืด | ben rôhk hèut |

diabetic

| เป็นโรคเบาหวาน | ben rôhk bow wăhn |

epileptic

| เป็นโรคลมบ้าหมู | ben rôhk lom bâh mŏo |

antiseptic
ยาฆ่าเชื้อ   *yah kâh chéu·a*
aspirin
ยาแอสไพริน   *yah àat·sà·pai·rin*
condoms
ถุงยางอนามัย   *tŭng yahng a·nah·mai*
contraceptive
การคุมกำเนิด   *gahn kum gam·nèut*
medicine
ยา   *yah*
mosquito coil
ยากันยุงแบบจุด   *yah gan yung bàap jùt*
mosquito repellent
ยากันยุง   *yaa gan yung*
painkiller
ยาแก้ปวด   *yaa gâe bòo·at*
sunblock cream
ครีมกันแดด   *kreem gan dàat*
tampons
แทมพอน   *taam·porn*

LANGUAGE DIFFICULTIES
Do you speak English?
คุณพูดภาษาอังกฤษได้ไหม
kun pôot pah·săh ang·grìt dâi măi?
Does anyone here speak English?
ที่นี่มีใครพูดภาษาอังกฤษได้ไหม
têe née mee krai pôot pah·săh ang·grìt dâi măi
How do you say ... in Thai?
...ว่าอย่างไรภาษาไทย
... wâh yàhng rai pah·săh tai
What do you call this in Thai?
นี่ภาษาไทยเรียกว่าอะไร
nêe pah·săh tai rêe·ak wâh à·rai?
What does ... mean?
...แปลว่าอะไร
... plaa wâh à·rai?
Do you understand?
เข้าใจไหม
kôw jai măi?
A little.
นิดหน่อย
nít nòy
I understand.
เข้าใจ
kôw jai
I don't understand.
ไม่เข้าใจ
mâi kôw jai

Please write it down.
กรุณาเขียนให้หน่อย
gà·rú·nah kĕe·an hâi nòy
Can you show me (on the map)?
ให้ดู(ในแผนที่) ได้ไหม
hâi doo (nai păen têe) dâi măi?

NUMBERS
0	ศูนย์	*sŏon*
1	หนึ่ง	*nèung*
2	สอง	*sŏrng*
3	สาม	*săhm*
4	สี่	*sèe*
5	ห้า	*hâh*
6	หก	*hòk*
7	เจ็ด	*jèt*
8	แปด	*bàat*
9	เก้า	*gôw*
10	สิบ	*sìp*
11	สิบเอ็ด	*sìp·èt*
12	สิบสอง	*sìp·sŏrng*
13	สิบสาม	*sìp·săhm*
14	สิบสี่	*sìp·sèe*
15	สิบห้า	*sìp·hâh*
16	สิบหก	*sìp·hòk*
17	สิบเจ็ด	*sìp·jèt*
18	สิบแปด	*sìp·bàat*
19	สิบเก้า	*sìp·gôw*
20	ยี่สิบ	*yêe·sìp*
21	ยี่สิบเอ็ด	*yêe·sìp·èt*
22	ยี่สิบสอง	*yêe·sìp·sŏrng*
30	สามสิบ	*săhm·sìp*
40	สี่สิบ	*sèe·sìp*
50	ห้าสิบ	*hâh·sìp*
60	หกสิบ	*hòk·sìp*
70	เจ็ดสิบ	*jèt·sìp*
80	แปดสิบ	*bàat·sìp*
90	เก้าสิบ	*gôw·sìp*
100	หนึ่งร้อย	*nèung róy*
200	สองร้อย	*sŏrng róy*
300	สามร้อย	*săhm róy*
1000	หนึ่งพัน	*nèung pan*

2000	สองพัน	sŏrng pan
10,000	หนึ่งหมื่น	nèung mèun
100,000	หนึ่งแสน	nèung sǎen
one million	หนึ่งล้าน	nèung láhn
one billion	พันล้าน	pan láhn

PAPERWORK

name	ชื่อ	chêu
nationality	สัญชาติ	sǎn-châht
date of birth	เกิดวันที่	gèut wan têe
place of birth	เกิดที่	gèut têe
sex (gender)	เพศ	pêt
passport	หนังสือเดิน ทาง	nǎng-sĕu deun tahng
visa	วีซ่า	wee-sâh

SHOPPING & SERVICES

I'd like to buy ...
อยากจะซื้อ...   yàhk jà séu ...
How much?
เท่าไร   tôw raí?
How much is this?
นี่เท่าไร/กี่บาท   nêe tôw rai?/gèe bàht?
I don't like it.
ไม่ชอบ   mâi chôrp
May I look at it?
ดูได้ไหม   doo dâi mǎi?
I'm just looking.
ดูเฉยๆ   doo chěr·i chěr·i
It's cheap.
ราคาถูก   rah·kah tòok
It's too expensive.
แพงเกินไป   paang geun bai
I'll take it.
เอา   ow

Can you reduce the price a little?
ลดราคาหน่อยได้ไหม
lót rah·kah nòy dâi mǎi?
Can you come down just a little more?
ลดราคาอีกนิดหนึ่งได้ไหม
lót rah·kah èek nít·nèung dâi mǎi?
Do you have something cheaper?
มีถูกว่านี้ไหม
mee tòok gwàh née mǎi?
Can you lower it more?
ลดอีกได้ไหม
lót èek dâi mǎi?

How about ... baht?
...บาทได้ไหม
... bàht dâi mǎi?
I won't give more than ... baht.
จะให้ไม่เกิน...บาท
jà hâi mâi geun ... bàht

Do you accept ...?
รับ...ไหม   ráp ... mǎi?
  credit cards
  บัตรเครดิต   bàt krair·dìt
  travellers cheques
  เช็คเดินทาง   chék deun tahng

more	อีก	èek
less	น้อยลง	nóy long
smaller	เล็กกว่า	lék gwàh
bigger	ใหญ่กว่า	yài gwàh
too expensive	แพงไป	paang bai
inexpensive	ราคา ประหยัด	rah·kah brà·yàt

I'm looking for ...
ผม/ดิฉันกำลังหา...   pŏm/dì·chăn gam·lang hǎh ...
  a bank
  ธนาคาร   tá·nah·kahn
  the city centre
  ใจกลางเมือง   jai glahng meu·ang
  the ... embassy
  สถานทูต...   sà·tǎhn tôot ...
  the market
  ตลาด   đà·làht
  the museum
  พิพิธภัณฑ์   pí·pít·tá·pan
  the post office
  ไปรษณีย์   brai·sà·nee
  a public toilet
  ห้องน้ำสาธารณะ   hôrng nám sǎh·tah·rá·ná
  a restaurant
  ร้านอาหาร   ráhn ah·hǎhn
  a temple
  วัด   wát
  the telephone centre
  ศูนย์โทรศัพท์   sŏon toh·rá·sàp
  the tourist office
  สำนักงานท่อง เที่ยว   sǎm·nák ngahn tôrng têe·o

I want to change ...

ต้องการแลก...   *đôrng gahn lâak ...*

  money

  เงิน   *ngeun*

  travellers cheques

  เช็คเดินทาง   *chék deun tahng*

Can I/we change money here?

แลกเงินที่นี่ได้ไหม

lâak ngeun têe née dâi măi?

What time does it open?

เปิดกี่โมง

bèut gèe mohng?

What time does it close?

ปิดกี่โมง

bìt gèe mohng?

TIME & DATES

Telling the time in Thai can be very challenging for an outsider to master. While the Western twelve-hour clock divides the day between two time periods, am and pm, the Thai system has four periods. The 24-hour clock is also commonly used by government and media. The list below shows each hour of the twelve-hour clock translated into the Thai system.

What time is it?

กี่โมงแล้ว   *gèe mohng láa·ou*

12 midnight	หกทุ่ม/	*hòk tûm/*
	เที่ยงคืน	*têe·ang keun*
1am	ตีหนึ่ง	*đee nèung*
2am	ตีสอง	*đee sŏrng*
3am	ตีสาม	*đee săhm*
4am	ตีสี่	*đee sèe*
5am	ตีห้า	*đee hâh*
6am	หกโมงเช้า	*hòk mohng chów*
7am	หนึ่งโมงเช้า	*nèung mohng chów*
11am	ห้าโมงเช้า	*hâh mohng chów*
12 noon	เที่ยง	*têe·ang*
1pm	บ่ายโมง	*bài mohng*
2pm	บ่ายสองโมง	*bài sŏrng mohng*
3pm	บ่ายสามโมง	*bài săhm mohng*

4pm	บ่ายสี่โมง/	*bài sèe mohng*
	(lit: afternoon four hours)	
	สี่โมงเย็น	*sèe mohng yen*
	(lit: four hours evening)	
5pm	ห้าโมงเย็น	*hâh mohng yen*
6pm	หกโมงเย็น	*hòk mohng yen*
7pm	หนึ่งทุ่ม	*nèung tûm*
8pm	สองทุ่ม	*sŏrng tûm*
9pm	สามทุ่ม	*săhm tûm*
10pm	สี่ทุ่ม	*sèe tûm*
11pm	ห้าทุ่ม	*hâh tûm*

For times after the hour, just add the number of minutes following the hour.

4.30pm

บ่ายสี่โมงครึ่ง

bài sèe mohng krêung (lit: four afternoon hours half)

4.15pm

บ่ายสี่โมงสิบห้านาที

bài sèe mohng sìp·hâh nah·tee (lit: four afternoon hours 15)

To give times before the hour, add the number of minutes beforehand.

3.45pm

อีกสิบห้านาทีบ่ายสี่โมง

èek sìp·hâh nah·tee bài sèe mohng (lit: another 15 minutes four afternoon hours)

When?	เมื่อไร	*mêu·a·rai?*
today	วันนี้	*wan née*
tomorrow	พรุ่งนี้	*prûng née*
yesterday	เมื่อวาน	*mêu·a wahn*

Monday	วันจันทร์	*wan jan*
Tuesday	วันอังคาร	*wan ang·kahn*
Wednesday	วันพุธ	*wan pút*
Thursday	วันพฤหัสฯ	*wan pá·réu·hàt*
Friday	วันศุกร์	*wan sùk*
Saturday	วันเสาร์	*wan sŏw*
Sunday	วันอาทิตย์	*wan ah·tít*

January	มกราคม	má·ga·rah·kom
February	กุมภาพันธ์	gum·pah·pan
March	มีนาคม	mee·naa·kom
April	เมษายน	mair·săh·yon
May	พฤษภาคม	préut·sà·pah·kom
June	มิถุนายน	mí·tù·nah·yon
July	กรกฎาคม	ga·rák·gà·đah·kom
August	สิงหาคม	sĭng·hăh·kom
September	กันยายน	gan·yah·yon
October	ตุลาคม	đù·lah·kom
November	พฤศจิกายน	préut·sà·ji·gah·yon
December	ธันวาคม	tan·wah·kom

TRANSPORT
Public Transport
What time does the ... leave?
...จะออกกี่โมง
... jà òrk gèe mohng?
What time does the ... arrive?
...จะถึงกี่โมง
... jà tĕung gèe mohng?

boat	เรือ	reu·a
bus	รถเมล์/	rót mair/
	รถบัส	rót bát
bus (city)	รถเมล์	rót mair
bus (intercity)	รถทัวร์	rót too·a
plane	เครื่องบิน	krêu·ang bin
train	รถไฟ	rót fai

I'd like ...
ผม/ดิฉันอยากได้...
pŏm/dì·chăn yàhk dâi ...

a one-way ticket
ตั๋วเที่ยวเดียว   đŏo·a têe·o dee·o
a return ticket
ตั๋วไปกลับ   đŏo·a bai glàp
two tickets
ตั๋วสองใบ   đŏo·a sŏrng bai
1st class
ชั้นหนึ่ง   chán nèung
2nd class
ชั้นสอง   chán sŏrng

I'd like a ticket.
อยากได้ตั๋ว   yàhk dâi đŏo·a

I want to go to ...
อยากจะไป...   yàhk jà bai ...
The train has been cancelled.
รถไฟถูกยกเลิกแล้ว   rót fai tùk yók lêuk láa·ou
The train has been delayed.
รถไฟช้าเวลา   rót fai cháh wair·lah
airport
สนามบิน   sa·năhm bin
bus station
สถานีขนส่ง   sa·tăh·nee kŏn sòng
bus stop
ป้ายรถเมล์   bâi rót mair
taxi stand
ที่จอดรถแท็กซี่   têe jòrt rót táak·sêe
train station
สถานีรถไฟ   sa·tăh·nee rót fai
platform number ...
ชานชาลาที่...   chahn·chah·lah têe ...
ticket office
ตู้ขายตั๋ว   đóo kăi đŏo·a
timetable
ตารางเวลา   đah·rahng wair·lah
the first
ที่แรก   têe râak
the last
สุดท้าย   sùt tái

Private Transport
I'd like to hire a/an ...
ผม/ดิฉันอยากเช่า...
pŏm/dì·chăn yàhk chôw ...
car
รถยนต์   rót yon
4WD
รถโฟร์วีล   rót foh ween
motorbike
รถมอเตอร์ไซค์   rót mor·đeu·sai
bicycle
รถจักรยาน   rót jàk·gà·yahn

Is this the road to ...?
ทางนี้ไป...ไหม   tahng née bai ... măi?
Where's a service station?
ปั้มน้ำมันอยู่ที่ไหน   bâm nám man yòo têe năi?
Please fill it up.
ขอเติมให้เต็ม   kŏr đeum hâi đem

LANGUAGE

I'd like (30) litres.

เอา(สามสิบ) ลิตร · *ow (sǎhm sìp) lít*

diesel

น้ำมันโซล่า · *nám man soh·lâh*

unleaded petrol

น้ำมันไร้สารตะกั่ว · *nám man rái sǎan đà·gòo·a*

Can I park here?

จอดที่นี่ได้ไหม · *jòrt têe née dâi mǎi?*

ROAD SIGNS

ให้ทาง	Give Way
ทางเบี่ยง	Detour
ห้ามเข้า	No Entry
ห้ามแซง	No Overtaking
ห้ามจอด	No Parking
ทางเข้า	Entrance
ห้ามขวางทาง	Keep Clear
เก็บเงินทางด่วน	Toll
อันตราย	Danger
ขับช้าลง	Slow Down
ทางเดียว	One Way
ทางออก	Exit

How long can I park here?

จอดที่นี่ได้นานเท่าไร · *jòrt têe née dâi nahn tôw·rai?*

Where do I pay?

จ่ายเงินที่ไหน · *jài ngeun têe nǎi?*

I need a mechanic.

ต้องการช่าง · *đôrng gahn châhng*

I have a flat tyre.

ยางแบน · *yahng baan*

I've run out of petrol.

หมดน้ำมัน · *mòt nám man*

I've had an accident.

มีอุบัติเหตุ · *mee ù·bàt·đi·hèt*

The car/motorbike has broken down (at ...)

รถ/มอเตอร์ไซค์เสียที่... · *rót/mor·đeu·sai sěe·a têe ...*

The car/motorbike won't start.

รถ/มอเตอร์ไซค์สตาร์ดไม่ติด · *rót/mor·đeu·sai sa·đáht mâi đìt*

TRAVEL WITH CHILDREN

Is there a/an ...

มี...ไหม · *mee ... mǎi*

baby change room

ห้องเปลี่ยนผ้าเด็ก · *hôrng blèe·an pâh dèk*

car baby seat

เบาะนั่งในรถสำหรับเด็ก · *bò nâng nai rót sǎm·ràp dèk*

child-minding service

บริการเลี้ยงเด็ก · *bor·rí·gahn lée·ang dèk*

children's menu

รายการอาหารสำหรับเด็ก · *rai gahn ah·hǎhn sǎm·ràp dèk*

(disposable) nappies/diapers

ผ้าอ้อม(แบบใช้แล้วทิ้ง) · *pâh ôrm (bàap chái láa·ou tíng)*

formula (milk)

นมผงสำหรับเด็ก · *nom pǒng sǎm·ràp dèk*

(English-speaking) babysitter

พี่เลี้ยงเด็ก(ที่พูดภาษาอังกฤษได้) · *pêe lée·ang dèk (têe pôot pah·sǎh ang·grìt dâi)*

highchair

เก้าอี้สูง · *gôw·êe sǒong*

potty

กระโถน · *grà·tǒhn*

stroller

รถเข็นเด็ก · *rót kěn dèk*

Are children allowed?

เด็กอนุญาตให้เข้าไหม · *dèk à·nú·yâht hâi kôw mǎi?*

Also available from Lonely Planet:
Thai Phrasebook

Glossary

See the Food Glossary, p52, for culinary terms and Thai dishes. See the Language chapter, p429, for some other useful words and phrases.

ah·hǎhn – food
ah·hǎhn jeh – vegetarian food
ah·hǎhn ù'làh – 'jungle food'; usually refers to dishes made with wild game
ah·hǎhn bàk ðâi – also spelt *ah·hǎhn pàk tâi;* southern Thai food
amphoe – also *amphur;* district, the next subdivision down from province
amphoe meu·ang – provincial capital
ao – also *ow;* bay or gulf

bâhn – also *ban;* house or village
bàht – traditional measure for gold and silver, equivalent to 15g
BMA – Bangkok Metropolitan Authority
bòht – central sanctuary or chapel in a Thai temple

CAT – Communications Authority of Thailand
chao leh – also *chow lair* or *chow nám;* sea gypsies
chedi – stupa; monument erected to house a Buddha relic
chow samǔi – 'Samui folk'; rural people on Ko Samui
chow lair – also *chao leh* or *chow nám;* sea gypsies

ða·làht – also *tàlàat;* market
ða·làht nám – also *tàlàat náam;* floating market
dhamma – right behaviour and truth according to Buddhist doctrine
ðròrk – also *trok* or *tràwk;* alley, smaller than a soi
ðrùð jeen – also *trùt jiin;* Chinese New Year

Eid al-Fitr – feasting at the end of the Muslim festival of Ramadan

faràng – foreigner of European descent

gâa·ou – also *kâew;* crystal, jewel, glass or gem
ga·teu·i – also *kàthoey;* 'ladyboy'; transvestites and transsexuals
gò – also *ko* or *koh;* island
gow·low – also *kaw-lae;* traditional fishing boats of southern Thailand
grà·tôrm – also *kràthâwm;* 'natural' drug, from the leaf of the Mitragyna speciosa tree
gù·ði – also *kùtì;* monk's hut or living quarters

hàht – also *hat;* beach
hǒrng – also *hâwng* or *hong;* room or chamber; island caves semisubmerged in the sea

ìsǎhn – also *ìsan;* general term for northeastern Thailand

jang·wàt – province
jataka – stories of the Buddha's previous lives
jeen – also *jiin;* Chinese

kâew – also *gâa·ou;* crystal, jewel, glass or gem
kàthoey – also *ga·teu·i;* 'ladyboy'; transvestites and transsexuals
kaw-lae – also *gow·low;* traditional fishing boats of southern Thailand
klong – also *khlong* or *khlawng;* canal
ko – also *gò* or *koh;* island
kǒw – also *khao;* hill or mountain
krêu·ang tom – nielloware; a silver-and-black alloy/enamel jewellery technique borrowed from China many centuries ago
krút – mythical creature, half-man and half-bird (known as Garuda in Pali), a symbol of Thai Brahminism and royal patronage
Kun – also *Khun;* honorific used before first name
kràthâwm – also *grà·tôrm;* 'natural' drug, from the leaf of the Mitragyna speciosa tree
kùtì – also *gù·ði;* monk's hut or living quarters

lǎam – also *laem;* geographical cape
lá·kon – classical Thai dance-drama
lí·gair bàh – also *lí·keh pàa* or *lí·gair bòk;* Thai folk dance-drama
longyi – Burmese sarong

mâa nám – river
masjid – also *mátsàyít;* mosque
meu·ang – also *muang;* city
moo·ay tai – also *muay thai;* Thai boxing
muay thai – also *moo·ay tai;* Thai boxing
mòo – also *mùu;* short for *mòo bâhn;* village

nám – water or juice
nám ðòk – also *náam tòk;* waterfall
ná·kon – also *nakhorn;* city
nǎng ðà·lung – Thai shadow theatre; movies
nibbana – nirvana; the 'blowing out' or extinction of all desire and thus of all suffering
nóy – also *noi;* small

nôo·at pǎan boh·rahn – also *nûat paen boh-raan;* Thai massage

ow – also *ao;* bay or gulf

pàk tâi – also *bàk ðâi;* southern Thailand
Pali – language derived from Sanskrit, in which the Buddhist scriptures are written
pěe – also *phǐi;* spirits
prá – also *phrà;* monk or Buddha image
pìi-phâat – also *bèe-pâht;* classical Thai orchestra
pôo nóy – also *phûu náwy;* 'little people'; those yet to attain social standing in the Thai system of deference and respect
pôo yài – also *phûu yài;* 'big people'; those who have higher social standing, expected to sponsor and provide for *pôo nóy*
prang – also *brang;* Khmer-style tower on temples

ráhn goh·bêe – also *ráhn ko-píi;* coffee shops (southern Thailand)
râi – an area of land measurement equal to 1600 sq m
Ramakian – Thai version of India's epic literary piece, the Ramayana
reu·a gow·low – also *reua kaw-lae;* large painted fishing boats, peculiar to Narathiwat and Pattani
reu·a hǎhng yow – also *reua hǎang yao;* long-tail taxi boat
reu·an tǎa·ou – a longhouse
reu·sěe – also *reusǐi;* Hindu rishi or sage
rót aa – blue-and-white air-conditioned buses
rót dòo·an – express trains
rót tam·má·dah – ordinary bus (no air-con) or ordinary train (not rapid or express)

sǎamláw – also *sǎhm-lór;* three-wheeled pedicab
sǎhm·lór – also *sǎamláw;* three-wheeled pedicab
sǎh·lah – also *sala* or *saalaa;* open-sided, covered meeting hall or resting place
sǎhn jôw – also *sǎan jâo;* Chinese shrine or joss house
sà·lěung – old system of Thai currency (one sà·lěung equals 25 satang)
samatha – meditation practice aimed at developing refined states of concentration
sǎm·nák wí·bàt·sà·nah – meditation centre
sangha – brotherhood of Buddhist monks; temple inhabitants (monks, nuns and lay residents)

sà·nùk – fun
sapahn – bridge
sǎwngthǎew – also *sǒrng·tǎa·ou;* small pickup truck with two benches in the back, used as bus/taxi
soi – lane or small street
Songkhran – Thai New Year, held in mid-April
sǒrng·tǎa·ou – also *sǎwngthǎew;* small pickup truck with two benches in the back, used as bus/taxi
SRT – State Railway of Thailand
stupa – domed edifice housing Buddhist relics
suttas – discourses of the Buddha

tâh – also *tha* or *thâa;* pier, landing
tàlàat – also *ða·làht;* market
tàlàat náam – also *ða·làht nám;* floating market
TAT – Tourism Authority of Thailand
tha – also *tâh* or *thâa;* pier, landing
Thai bàk ðâi – also *Thai pàk tâi;* southern Thais
tâm – also *thâm;* cave
thànǒn – street, road, avenue (we use the abbreviation 'Th' in this book)
trok – also *ðròrk* or *tràwk;* alley, smaller than a soi
Tripitaka – Theravada Buddhist scriptures
Trùt Jeen – also *ðrùð jeen;* Chinese New Year
túk·túk – motorised *sǎhm·lór*

Ummah – the Muslim community

vipassana – Buddhist insight meditation

wâi – palms-together Thai greeting
wan prá – Buddhist holy days, falling on the days of the main phases of the moon (full, new and half) each month
wang – palace
wát – temple, monastery
wí·hǎhn – also *wihan* or *viharn;* counterpart to *bòht* in Thai temple, containing Buddha images but not circumscribed by sema stones
WFT – Wildlife Fund Thailand

yah bâh – 'crazy-medicine'; methamphetamine
yài – big

bàk ðâi – also *pàk tâi;* southern Thailand
bèe·pâht – also *pìi-phâat;* classical Thai orchestra
brang – also *prang;* Khmer-style tower on temples

The Authors

ANDREW BURKE   Coordinating Author, Destination, Getting Started,
Itineraries, Events Calendar, Bangkok, Directory, Transport

Andrew has been coming to Thailand for long enough that he can remember when there was only one full moon party a month on Ko Pha-Ngan and there being very little neon on the Khao San Rd. Since then he's spent 15 years travelling through, photographing and writing about Asia, the Middle East and Africa, and the last eight living in Hong Kong, Phnom Penh and now the manic megalopolis that is Bangkok. Andrew has written or contributed to more than 15 books for Lonely Planet, including a guide to *Bangkok*.

CELESTE BRASH   Northern Andaman Coast, Southern Andaman Coast

Celeste first arrived in Thailand as a student of Thai language, history and culture at Chiang Mai University. She's come back several times since and has done the gamut from wild nights on Ko Pha-Ngan to weeks of silence at Wat Suan Mokkhaphalaram. This trip's stand-out moments included feeling like she'd stumbled into a war zone at the Phuket Vegetarian Festival and being barred from her bungalow for several hours by two intertwined tree vipers on Ko Lipe. More relaxing was floating around with sea turtles and psychedelic cuttlefish in the Surin and Similan Islands. When not dragging her husband and two children to exotic locales, she and her family live in Tahiti.

AUSTIN BUSH   History, The Culture, Food & Drink,
parts of Bangkok & Southwestern Gulf Coast

After graduating from the University of Oregon with a degree in linguistics, Austin received a scholarship to study Thai at Chiang Mai University, and has remained in Thailand ever since. After working for several years at a stable job, he made the questionable decision to pursue a career as a freelance photographer/writer. This choice has since taken him as far as northern Pakistan, and as near as a Bangkok market. He enjoys writing and taking photos about food most of all because it's a great way to connect with people.

BRANDON PRESSER
Diving & Other Activities, Eastern Gulf Coast, Northwestern Gulf Coast, Southwestern Gulf Coast

This thick-blooded Canadian refused to frown in the Land of Smiles even though he was there during what he thought was a record-breaking heat wave (turns out it was just business as usual). Brandon's first trip to Thailand was in 2002 as a member of a jazz group performing throughout Asia. He has since returned several times, swapping doo-wop for diving. A self-proclaimed 'scubaholic', Brandon has explored the oceans off the coasts of six continents, yet the past tense of 'dive' will forever remain a mystery (dived?, dove?, diven?)!

CONTRIBUTING AUTHORS

David Lukas wrote the Environment chapter. David is a professional naturalist who lives on the border of Yosemite National Park, where he conducts research and writes about the natural world. His many travels include spending a year in western Borneo studying the ecology of Southeast Asian rainforests. He is the author of environment chapters for about 20 Lonely Planet guides ranging from *Nova Scotia* to *Costa Rica*.

Dr Trish Bachelor wrote the Health chapter. She is a general practitioner and travel-medicine specialist who works at the Ciwec Clinic in Kathmandu, Nepal, as well as being a Medical Advisor to the Travel Doctor New Zealand clinics. Trish teaches travel medicine through the University of Otago, and is interested in underwater and high-altitude medicine, and in the impact of tourism on host countries. She has travelled extensively through Southeast and East Asia and particularly loves high-altitude trekking in the Himalayas.

Behind the Scenes

THIS BOOK

This 6th edition of *Thailand's Islands & Beaches* was researched and updated by Andrew Burke, Celeste Brash, Austin Bush and Brandon Presser, with contributions by David Lukas and Dr Trish Bachelor. This guidebook was commissioned in Lonely Planet's Melbourne office and produced by the following:

Commissioning Editor Carolyn Boicos
Coordinating Editor Evan Jones
Coordinating Cartographer Diana Duggan
Coordinating Layout Designer Katherine Marsh
Managing Editor Brigitte Ellemor
Managing Cartographer David Connolly
Managing Layout Designers Adam McCrow, Celia Wood
Assisting Editors Michelle Bennett, Anne Mulvaney, Susannah Farfor, Paul Harding, David Carroll
Assisting Cartographers Tadhgh Knaggs, Jacqueline Nguyen, Jolyon Philcox, Corey Hutchison
Cover Designer Pepi Bluck
Project Managers Fabrice Rocher, Rachel Imeson
Language Content Coordinator Quentin Frayne

Thanks to Bruce Evans, Mark Germanchis, John Mazzochi, Sin Choo, Lisa Knights, James Hardy, Errol Hunt, Glenn Beanland, Wayne Murphy

THANKS
ANDREW BURKE

I'd like to offer a heartfelt *kòrp kun kráp* to the many people in Bangkok who helped make this book possible. First and foremost it was great to have my wife Anne around for an entire LP job and get her feminine feedback on things Bangkok. Mason Florence and Stuart McDonald were generous with their tips, and May Nekkham, Whan Kullamas, Gun Aramwit and Tui (enjoy the monastery) at MeMay Café helped keep me sane during months of writing. Thanks to my co-authors Celeste, Brandon and Austin for total commitment to this project, and at LP HQ a big thank you to my wonderfully patient and good-natured commissioning editor Carolyn Boicos and her able assistants David Connolly, Evan Jones and Diana Duggan (among others).

CELESTE BRASH

Thanks to my husband Josh and kids Jasmine and Tevai for making the trip through Krabi more lizard-oriented and for not complaining about those weeks at home without mom. Brandon Presser provided hours of phone support while Andrew Burke and his wife Anne graciously put me up in Bangkok and were great company at the Vegetarian Festival. Thanks to Austin Bush for Trang tips and Carolyn Boicos for getting us all

---

THE LONELY PLANET STORY

Fresh from an epic journey across Europe, Asia and Australia in 1972, Tony and Maureen Wheeler sat at their kitchen table stapling together notes. The first Lonely Planet guidebook, *Across Asia on the Cheap,* was born.

Travellers snapped up the guides. Inspired by their success, the Wheelers began publishing books to Southeast Asia, India and beyond. Demand was prodigious, and the Wheelers expanded the business rapidly to keep up. Over the years, Lonely Planet extended its coverage to every country and into the virtual world via lonelyplanet.com and the Thorn Tree message board.

As Lonely Planet became a globally loved brand, Tony and Maureen received several offers for the company. But it wasn't until 2007 that they found a partner whom they trusted to remain true to the company's principles of travelling widely, treading lightly and giving sustainably. In October of that year, BBC Worldwide acquired a 75% share in the company, pledging to uphold Lonely Planet's commitment to independent travel, trustworthy advice and editorial independence.

Today, Lonely Planet has offices in Melbourne, London and Oakland, with over 500 staff members and 300 authors. Tony and Maureen are still actively involved with Lonely Planet. They're travelling more often than ever, and they're devoting their spare time to charitable projects. And the company is still driven by the philosophy of *Across Asia on the Cheap*: 'All you've got to do is decide to go and the hardest part is over. So go!'

BEHIND THE SCENES

together and then keeping us together. Special thanks to Bodhi Garrett and his phenomenal work with NATR, and to my local voice victims, Elke Schmitz and Puchong Tirawanta.

AUSTIN BUSH

I'd like to thank the following helpful people: Andrew Burke, Yuthika Charoenrungruang, Mason Florence, Nicholas Grossman, Wesley Hsu, Steven Pettifor, Kong Rithdee, Suthon Sukphisit, Daniel Ten Kate, China Williams, and the great editorial crew at LP Melbourne.

BRANDON PRESSER

So many acknowledgements, so little space! A big thank you to everyone I met along the way especially: John Romero, Neal Bambridge, Wayne Lunt, Eric Hallin, Suthinee Nuansawad, Jacob Bojsen, Andrew Khoo, Thawatchai Kuasakul, Charlie McGlynn, Louis Thompson, Soodjai Boonsook, Jim Donaldson, Vic Pass, Heather & Andy on Ko Tao, Chris Clark, Jesper Hansen, Dee in Nakhon, Brian in Khanom, Stephen Berger, Onanong Tepyoo-amnuay, Spaz on Ko Pha-Ngan, Jeremie in Bang Saphan, Wiyada Phetcharat, and Suzi Stein. Also, a special thanks to Carolyn Boicos, the production team at LP, Andrew Burke for his generosity, and Celeste Brash – phone buddy extraordinaire.

OUR READERS

Many thanks to the travellers who used the last edition and wrote to us with helpful hints, useful advice and interesting anecdotes:
Lale Ak, Veronika Amundsen, Tine Andersen, Rob Beach, Dafna Becker, Charles Bedard, Lisa Berggren, Natalie Bitunjac, John Bonner, Sarah Bowles, Aoife Brown, Camila Burda, Claire Cagney, Alex Cheong, Michael Christ, Mark & Debbie Copple, Jim Cunningham, Alastair Curry, Tanya Czmorova, Sarah Danckert, Ziemowit Debinski, Ann Delien, Thomas Dellschau, Lori Doyle, Winfried Draeger, Harmen Eikelboom, Anna Mikaela Ekstrand, Juri Estam, Paul Faherty, Liza Ferrari, Jennifer Fisher, Florian Franke, Carolyn Giles, Patrice Gordon, Simon Gormley, Joanna Groves, Judy Harcourt, Liza Hassum, Allan Healy, Scott Heidecke, Johanna Hellgren, Iris Henne, Alan Hoare, Lauren Hollyoak, Gunter Hormann, Andreas Jacobsen, Caron James, Mark Johaanson, Keith Johnson, Maxim Jurgens, Marco Kaelin, Niklas Kaellman, Linzi Kan, Bradley Kendal, James Kerslake, Melanie Kirol, Steven Kissoon, Simon Knuckey, Job Kuijpers Kuijpers, Kanthad Kulvanit, Maud De Lannurien, Kirsti Lervoll, Cathy Lewis, Garry Lloyd, Anish Malpani, Didier Martin, Anne De Mesmaeker, Kirsty Miller, Lucy Morris, Chloe Munts, Matthew Newland, Nikolaj Nielsen, Mario Niesser, Dave Pike, Victoria Port, Jackie Randall, Søren Rasmussen, Martin Rees, Anna Reeves, Hanna Reidmar, Dale Rossin, Yoav Rothschild, Chris Rowley, Jeff Saltzman, Michael Shilling, Bonnie Sjöblom, Rene Steinke, Felicity Stevens, Freddy Storheil, George Strueber, Chris Sutton, Gregory T'Kint, Chantelle Thomson, Martin Tolsgaard, Essa van Van Miltenburg, Essa van Oguchi, Marlynn Wolkoff, Christine Wright

ACKNOWLEDGMENTS
Many thanks to the following for the use of their content:
Globe on title page ©Mountain High Maps 1993 Digital Wisdom, Inc.

Internal photographs p150 (#5) Brandon Presser, author; p145 (#1) paul-hill.co.uk/Alamy; p151 (#2) Michele Falzone/Alamy. All other photographs by Lonely Planet Images, and by Austin Bush, author p145, p148 (#2, #3, #7); p149 (#1, #6); Richard Nebesky p146 (#3); Kristin Piljay p145 (#7); Bill Wassman p152; Andrew Bain p150 (#4).

All images are the copyright of the photographers unless otherwise indicated. Many images in this guide are available for licensing from Lonely Planet Images: www.lonelyplanetimages.com.

SEND US YOUR FEEDBACK
We love to hear from travellers – your comments keep us on our toes and help make our books better. Our well-travelled team reads every word on what you loved or loathed about this book. Although we cannot reply individually to postal submissions, we always guarantee that your feedback goes straight to the appropriate authors, in time for the next edition. Each person who sends us information is thanked in the next edition – and the most useful submissions are rewarded with a free book.

To send us your updates – and find out about Lonely Planet events, newsletters and travel news – visit our award-winning website: **www.lonelyplanet.com/contact**.

Note: we may edit, reproduce and incorporate your comments in Lonely Planet's guidebooks, websites and digital products, so let us know if you don't want your comments reproduced or your name acknowledged. For a copy of our privacy policy visit www.lonelyplanet.com/privacy.

Index

INDEX

INDEX

INDEX

000 Map pages
000 Photograph pages

GreenDex

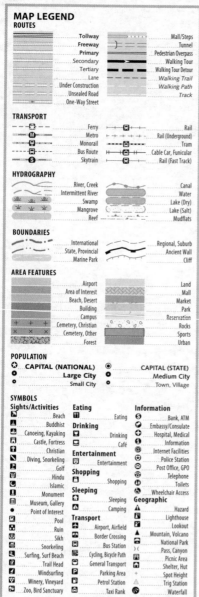

MAP LEGEND

ROUTES

Tollway · Freeway · Primary · Secondary · Tertiary · Lane · Under Construction · Unsealed Road · One-Way Street · Mall/Steps · Tunnel · Pedestrian Overpass · Walking Tour · Walking Tour Detour · Walking Trail · Walking Path · Track

TRANSPORT

Ferry · Metro · Monorail · Bus Route · Skytrain · Rail · Rail (Underground) · Tram · Cable Car, Funicular · Rail (Fast Track)

HYDROGRAPHY

River, Creek · Intermittent River · Swamp · Mangrove · Reef · Canal · Water · Lake (Dry) · Lake (Salt) · Mudflats

BOUNDARIES

International · State, Provincial · Marine Park · Regional, Suburb · Ancient Wall · Cliff

AREA FEATURES

Airport · Area of Interest · Beach, Desert · Building · Campus · Cemetery, Christian · Cemetery, Other · Forest · Land · Mall · Market · Park · Reservation · Rocks · Sports · Urban

POPULATION

○ CAPITAL (NATIONAL) · ◉ CAPITAL (STATE) · ● Large City · ◉ Medium City · ○ Small City · ○ Town, Village

SYMBOLS

Sights/Activities
Beach · Buddhist · Canoeing, Kayaking · Castle, Fortress · Christian · Diving, Snorkeling · Golf · Hindu · Islamic · Monument · Museum, Gallery · Point of Interest · Pool · Ruin · Sikh · Snorkeling · Surfing, Surf Beach · Trail Head · Windsurfing · Winery, Vineyard · Zoo, Bird Sanctuary

Eating
Eating

Drinking
Drinking · Café

Entertainment
Entertainment

Shopping
Shopping

Sleeping
Sleeping · Camping

Transport
Airport, Airfield · Border Crossing · Bus Station · Cycling, Bicycle Path · General Transport · Parking Area · Petrol Station · Taxi Rank

Information
Bank, ATM · Embassy/Consulate · Hospital, Medical · Information · Internet Facilities · Police Station · Post Office, GPO · Telephone · Toilets · Wheelchair Access

Geographic
Hazard · Lighthouse · Lookout · Mountain, Volcano · National Park · Pass, Canyon · Picnic Area · Shelter, Hut · Spot Height · Trig Station · Waterfall

LONELY PLANET OFFICES

Australia
Head Office
Locked Bag 1, Footscray, Victoria 3011
☎ 03-8379 8000, fax 03-8379 8111
talk2us@lonelyplanet.com.au

USA
150 Linden St, Oakland, CA 94607
☎ 510-250 6400, toll free 800 275 8555
fax 510-893 8572
info@lonelyplanet.com

UK
2nd fl, 186 City Rd,
London EC1V 2NT
☎ 020-7106 2100, fax 020-7106 2101
go@lonelyplanet.co.uk

Published by Lonely Planet Publications Pty Ltd
ABN 36 005 607 983

© Lonely Planet Publications Pty Ltd 2008

© photographers as indicated 2008

Cover photograph by Lonely Planet Images: Fisherman casts his drift net off Hat Patong, Tom Cockrem. Many of the images in this guide are available for licensing from Lonely Planet Images: www .lonelyplanetimages.com.

Although the authors and Lonely Planet have taken all reasonable care in preparing this book, we make no warranty about the accuracy or completeness of its content and, to the maximum extent permitted, disclaim all liability arising from its use.